Southern Italy

DISCARDED

Naples & Campania
p56

Puglia, Basilicata & Calabria
p123

Sicily
p185

Cristian Bonetto, Gregor Clark, Hugh McNaughtan

PLAN YOUR TRIP

ON THE ROAD

STROMBOLI P211

OSTUNI P145

Contents

SORRENTO P102

SPECIAL FEATURES

Welcome to Southern Italy

Italy's north may have the euros, but the south has the soul. Sun-bleached and weathered, this is Italy at its most ancient, complex and contradictory.

A Warm Benvenuto

You'll rarely be short of a conversation south of Rome. Family and friends are sacred, and time spent laughing, arguing or gossiping is as integral to southern life as lavish Sunday lunches and long, sizzling summers. One minute you're picking produce at a street market, the next you're in the middle of a feverish discussion about who grows Italy's sweetest *pomodori* (tomatoes) – Sicily or Campania? No one is a stranger for long, and a casual *chiacchiera* (chat) could easily land you at the dining table of your new best friend.

Culinary Prowess

Italy's fertile south is a mouth-watering, belt-busting feast: bubbling, wood-fired pizza and potent espresso in Naples; long, lazy lunches at vine-framed Pugliese farmhouses; just-caught sardines on a Tyrrhenian island; luscious *cannoli* (pastry shells with a sweet filling) at a Taormina *pasticceria* (pastry shop). Should you go mushroom hunting in the wilds of Calabria? Feast on fresh sea urchin on an Adriatic beach? Or just kick back with a glass of crisp local Falanghina as you debate who has the creamiest buffalo mozzarella: Caserta, Paestum or Foggia?

Gripping History

Southern Italy is littered with the detritus of diverse and gilded ages, from Greek and Roman to Saracen, Norman and Spanish. Every carved stone and painted fresco tells a story, from fiery Carthaginian invasions to the humble hopes of Roman slaves and gladiators. Here, ancient Greek temples are older than Rome, Byzantine mosaics attest to cosmopolitan encounters and royal palaces outsize Versailles. The south is home to 13 Unesco World Heritage cultural sites, each laced with tales of victory, failure and timeless humanity.

Natural Highs

Rugged mountains, fiery volcanoes and electric-blue grottoes – southern Italy feels like one giant adventure playground. Raft down Calabria's river Lao, scale Europe's most active volcano, Stromboli, or dive into prehistoric sea caves on Puglia's Promontorio del Gargano. If you need to bring it down a notch, consider slow pedalling across Puglia's gentle countryside, sailing along the Amalfi Coast or simply soaking in Vulcano's healing geothermal mud. The options may be many, but there is one constant: a landscape that is beautiful, diverse and just a little ethereal.

Why I Love Southern Italy

By Cristian Bonetto, Writer

Southern Italy is like the Slow Food of travel. While much of Europe marches to an increasingly homogenised beat, this raffish corner of the continent dances to its own hypnotic tune. Melancholy folk songs still fill the air, eyeshadow is applied thick and bright, and hearts are proudly worn on sleeves. Many of my fondest travel memories have been formed here: epic Sunday lunches to the sound of Pino Daniele; hot winds whistling through ancient temples; quiet swims in milky blue Tyrrhenian waters. I might hail from the north, but my heart belongs to the Mezzogiorno.

For more about our writers, see p320

Above: Atrani (p106), Amalfi Coast

Southern Italy

Naples
Glorious art, architecture and street life (p57)

Pompeii
A town frozen in time (p95)

Matera
An eerie and ancient townscape (p161)

Alberobello
Italy's kookiest-looking town (p141)

Lecce
The Florence of the south (p147)

ELEVATION
2500m
2000m
1500m
1000m
500m
300m
100m
0

Adriatic Sea

ROME

LAZIO

ABRUZZO

Pescara
Chieti

Vasto

Isole Tremiti

Termoli

Campobasso

Isernia

Caserta

Mt Vesuvius (1281m)
Naples
Ercolano
Pompeii
Procida
Ischia
Ponza

Gofo di Gaeta

Sorrento
Amalfi
Amalfi Coast
Capri

Salerno

CAMPANIA

Volturno

Paestum

Agropoli

Parco Nazionale del Cilento e Vallo di Diano

Maratea

Potenza

BASILICATA

Sele

Agri

Sinni

Brindisi

Lecce
Otranto
Galatina

PUGLIA

Oria

Taranto

Gofo di Taranto

Bisento

Bradano

Matera

Brudano

Peschici
Vieste

Trani

Polignano a Mare
Ostuni
Martina Franca
Locorotondo
Valle d'Itria
Alberobello

PUGLIA

100 km
50 miles

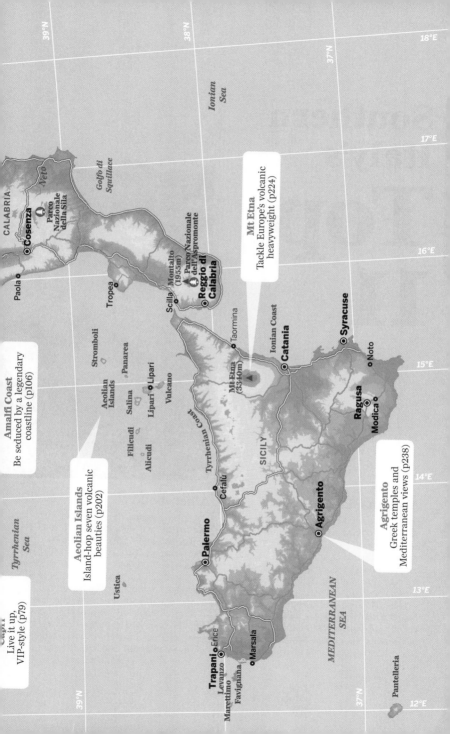

Amalfi Coast
Be seduced by a legendary coastline (p106)

Mt Etna
Tackle Europe's volcanic heavyweight (p224)

Aeolian Islands
Island-hop seven volcanic beauties (p202)

Agrigento
Greek temples and Mediterranean views (p238)

Live it up, VIP-style (p79)

39°N
38°N
37°N

18°E
17°E
16°E
15°E
14°E
13°E
12°E

Tyrrhenian Sea

Ionian Sea

MEDITERRANEAN SEA

CALABRIA

Cosenza
Parco Nazionale della Sila
Neto
Golfo di Squillace

Paola

Tropea

Scilla
Montalto (1955m)
Parco Nazionale dell'Aspromonte
Reggio di Calabria

Taormina
Ionian Coast
Catania
Mt Etna (3340m)
Syracuse
Noto

Stromboli
Panarea
Aeolian Islands
Salina
Lipari
Lipari
Vulcano

Filicudi
Alicudi

Tyrrhenian Coast

SICILY

Ragusa
Modica

Cefalù

Palermo

Ustica

Agrigento

Trapani
Erice
Levanzo
Marettimo
Favignana
Marsala

Pantelleria

Southern Italy's
Top 11

Aeolian Island-Hopping

1 The Greeks don't have a monopoly on Mediterranean island-hopping. Sicily's Aeolian Islands (p202) might be a little less famous than their Aegean Sea rivals, but they are no less stunning. Mix and match from seven volcanic outcrops, among them thermal hot-spot Vulcano (pictured above), vine-laced Salina, and lava-oozing Stromboli. But don't just take our word for it. The islands are one of only five Italian natural landscapes on Unesco's World Heritage list (the others include Sicily's fiery Mt Etna).

Alberobello

2 Imagination runs riot in Alberobello (p141), famed for its kooky, one-of-a-kind architecture. We're talking *trulli* – white-washed circular dwellings with cone-shaped roofs. Looking like they're straight out of a Disney cartoon, these sun-baked dwellings tumble down the slopes like armies of hatted dwarves. You can dine in some of them and sleep in others. Just don't be surprised if you feel the need to pinch yourself... Was that Snow White? Are you even on Earth? Unesco seems to thinks so; they're World Heritage treasures.

ALFIYA SAFIUANOVA/SHUTTERSTOCK ©

JOSEF SKACELJ/SHUTTERSTOCK ©

Amalfi Coast

3 Italy's most celebrated coastline (p106) is a gripping strip: coastal mountains plunge into creamy blue sea in a prime-time vertical scene of precipitous crags, sun-bleached villages and lush woodland. Between sea and sky, mountain-top hiking trails deliver Tyrrhenian panoramas fit for a god. While some may argue that the peninsula's most beautiful coast is Liguria's Cinque Terre or Calabria's Costa Viola, it is the Amalfi Coast that has seduced and inspired countless greats, from Wagner and DH Lawrence to Tennessee Williams, Rudolph Nureyev and Gore Vidal. Amalfi (p106)

Baroque Lecce

4 The extravagant architectural character of many Puglian towns exemplifies the region's homegrown *barocco leccese* (Lecce baroque). It's a style perfectly suited to the local stone, so soft it practically begs to be carved. Local craftsmen vied for ever-greater heights of creativity, crowding facades with swirling vegetal designs, gargoyles and strange zoomorphic figures. Lecce's Basilica di Santa Croce (p148; pictured right) is the high point of the style, so outrageously busy the Marchese Grimaldi said it made him think a lunatic was having a nightmare.

Capri

5 Rising from the Bay of Naples, Capri (p79) is Italy's most fabled island. Indeed, the place has been seducing mortals for millennia and even the summer hordes can't quite dilute its ethereal magic. Emperor Tiberius reputedly threw his lovers off its dizzying cliffs, travellers on the Grand Tour waxed lyrical about its electric-blue grotto and celebrities continue to moor their yachts in its turquoise waters. For a view you won't forget, head to the summit of Monte Solaro (think bath-time boats and sugar-cube houses).

6

7

8

Ghostly Pompeii

6 Frozen in its death throes, the sprawling, time-warped ruins of Pompeii (p96) hurtle you 2000 years into the past. Wander through chariot-grooved Roman streets and elegantly frescoed villas and bathhouses, food stores, markets, theatres and even an ancient brothel. Then, your eye on ominous Mt Vesuvius, ponder Pliny the Younger's terrifying account of the town's final hours: 'Darkness came on again, again ashes, thick and heavy. We got up repeatedly to shake these off; otherwise we would have been buried and crushed by the weight'.

Naples

7 Refined and rough, tough and tender, Naples (p57) is a contradictory, complex beast. Gritty alleyways hit palm-fringed boulevards; crumbling facades mask baroque naves and ballrooms; and cultish shrines flank street-art murals and a wave of hip new bars. This is a metropolis that thrives on intensity, from the muscular strength of Neapolitan espresso to the high-octane rush of the city's markets and cacophonous streets. It's also one of Italy's current tourist hot spots, its wealth of history, architecture, art and culinary riches finally winning the fans it deserves.
Bottom Left: Via San Gregorio Armeno (p61)

Matera

8 The best time to explore Matera (p161) is before it gets up. The town is tinged gold by the morning sun and the scent of the day's first coffee lingers in the air. Matera is an extraordinary place: its Unesco World Heritage–listed *sassi* (former cave dwellings) developed from caves that pock a dizzying ravine. In no other place do you come face to face with such powerful images of Italy's lost peasant culture; these cavernous dwellings echo a level of poverty difficult to fathom in an affluent, modern G8 country. Top right: Chiesa San Pietro Barisano (p162)

Scaling Mt Etna

9 Known to the Greeks as the 'column that holds up the sky', Mt Etna (p224) is one of the world's most active volcanoes. The ancients believed the giant Tifone (Typhoon) lived in its crater and lit up the sky with regular pyrotechnics. Towering above Sicily's Ionian Coast, its slopes are part of the Parco dell'Etna, an area that encompasses vineyards, alpine forests and the forbiddingly black summit. Whether scaled on foot or on wheels, the magnitude of its power, presence and otherworldly vistas are unforgettable.

Southern Flavours

10 Southern Italy's food obsession (p44) is utterly forgivable. After all, this is the country's gastronomic showcase, a sun-drenched platter of succulent produce and flavours. Should you devour perfectly charred pizza on an ancient Neapolitan street or luscious *burrata* (cream-filled buffalo mozzarella) by azure-tinged Puglian seas? Perhaps you're hankering for chilli-fuelled *salsiccie* (sausages) in the wilds of Basilicata and Calabria? Or fragrant couscous in the shadow of a sun-bleached Sicilian *palazzo*? Whatever you choose, we know you'll beg for seconds. Top right: Plate of *spaghetti alla puttanesca*

Temples in Agrigento

11 Few archaeological sites evoke the past like Agrigento's Valley of the Temples (p238). Located on a ridge overlooking the Mediterranean, its stoic temples belonged to Akragas, a once-great city settled by the Greeks. The scars of ancient battle endure in the 5th-century-BC Tempio di Hera, while the Tempio della Concordia's remarkable state of preservation inspired Unesco's own logo. To conjure the ghosts of the past, roam the ruins late in the afternoon, when the crowds have thinned and the wind whistles hauntingly between the columns.

Need to Know

For more information, see Survival Guide (p289)

Currency
Euro (€)

Language
Italian

Visas
Generally not required for stays of up to 90 days (or at all for EU nationals); some nationalities need a Schengen visa.

Money
ATMs are widespread in southern Italy. Major credit cards are widely accepted but some smaller shops, trattorias and hotels might not take them.

Mobile Phones
Local SIM cards can be used in European, Australian and some unlocked US phones. Other phones must be set to roaming.

Time
Central European Time (GMT/UTC plus one hour)

When to Go

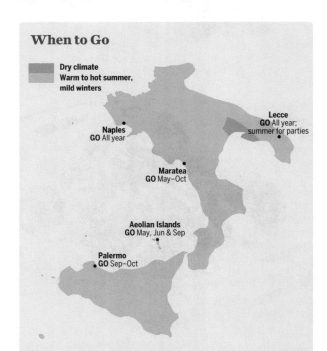

Dry climate
Warm to hot summer, mild winters

Lecce
GO All year; summer for parties

Naples
GO All year

Maratea
GO May–Oct

Aeolian Islands
GO May, Jun & Sep

Palermo
GO Sep–Oct

High Season (Jul–Aug)

➡ Queues and crowds at big sights and beaches, especially in August.

➡ High levels of traffic congestion in tourist areas, including the Amalfi Coast.

➡ A good period for cultural events and festivals in tourist areas.

Shoulder Season (Apr–Jun & Sep–Oct)

➡ Good deals on accommodation.

➡ Spring is best for wildflowers and local produce, with numerous festivals too.

➡ Autumn offers the grape harvest and warm weather without the crowds.

Low Season (Nov–Mar)

➡ Prices can be 30% lower than high season (except major holidays).

➡ Many sights, hotels and restaurants close in coastal and mountainous areas.

➡ Christmas feasting and colourful Carnevale.

Useful Websites

Lonely Planet (www.lonely planet.com/italy) Destination information, hotel bookings, traveller forum and more.

Trenitalia (www.trenitalia.com) Italian railways website.

Agriturismi (www.agriturismi.it) Guide to farm accommodation.

Enit Italia (www.italiantourism. com) Italy's official tourism website.

The Local (www.thelocal.it) English-language news from Italy, including travel-related stories.

Important Numbers

From outside Italy, dial your international access code, Italy's country code (⏀39) then the number (including the '⏀0').

Italy country code	⏀39
International access code	⏀00
Ambulance	⏀118
Police	⏀112, ⏀113
Fire	⏀115

Exchange Rates

Australia	A$1	€0.66
Canada	C$1	€0.68
Japan	¥100	€0.75
New Zealand	NZ$1	€0.61
Switzerland	Sfr1	€0.87
UK	UK£1	€1.12
US	US$1	€0.85

For current exchange rates see www.xe.com

Daily Costs

Budget: Less than €100

➡ Dorm bed: €15–30

➡ Double room in a budget hotel: €60–110

➡ Pizza or pasta: €6–12

Midrange: €100–250

➡ Double room in a hotel: €100–220

➡ Local restaurant dinner: €25–50

➡ Admission to museum: €4–15

Top end: More than €250

➡ Double room in a four- or five-star hotel: €200–450

➡ Top restaurant dinner: €50–150

➡ Opera ticket: €40–200

Opening Hours

Banks 8.30am–1pm or 1.30pm and 2.30–4.45pm Monday to Friday

Restaurants noon–3pm & 7.30–11pm or midnight

Cafes 7.30am–8pm, sometimes until 1am or 2am

Bars and clubs 10pm–4am or 5am

Shops 9am–1pm & 4–8pm Monday to Saturday; some also open Sunday, some close Monday morning and some in large cities and tourist areas open Sunday

Arriving in Southern Italy

Capodichino airport (Naples) A shuttle bus to the centre of Naples will cost €4; they run every 15 to 20 minutes from 6.30am to 11.40pm. Taxis have set fares ranging from €16 to €23 depending on your destination and take around 30 minutes.

Karol Wojtyła airport (Palese airport; Bari) A shuttle bus to the centre of Bari will cost €4; they run roughly hourly from 5.35am to 12.10am. A taxi will cost about €24 and will take 15 minutes.

Falcone-Borsellino airport (Palermo) A shuttle bus to the centre of Palermo will cost €6.30; they run half-hourly from 5am to 12.30am. A taxi will cost €35 to €45 and take 30 minutes.

Getting Around

Transport in southern Italy is reasonably priced and usually efficient.

Train Affordable, with extensive coverage and frequent departures.

Car Handy for travelling at your own pace or for visiting areas with minimal public transport. Not a good idea for travelling within major urban areas.

Bus Cheaper and slower than trains. Useful for more remote villages not serviced by trains.

Ferries & Hydrofoils Large ferries (navi) service Campania and Sicily. Smaller ferries (traghetti) and hydrofoils (aliscafi) service the Bay of Naples islands, the Amalfi Coast, Puglia's Isole Tremiti and Sicily's Aeolian Islands. Most services are pared back in winter.

For much more on **getting around**, see p303

Accommodation

Accommodation Types

Accommodation in southern Italy is ever-improving and increasingly varied. Hotels, B&Bs and *pensioni* (guesthouses) make up the bulk of the offerings, covering everything from cheap sleeps near the train station to trendy art hotels and five-star legends with ocean views. Youth hostels and camping grounds are available in most tourist areas, while *agriturismi* (farm stays) and *masserie* (southern Italian farms or estates) will indulge your bucolic Italian fantasies.

Booking Your Accommodation

When considering where (and when) to slumber, note the following:

➡ Book ahead if travelling in the high season, especially if visiting popular coastal areas. Also consider booking ahead if visiting cities or towns during major events.

➡ Some hotels, in particular the lower-end places, barely alter their prices throughout the year. In low season there's no harm in bargaining for a discount, especially if you intend to stay for several days.

➡ Hotels usually require that reservations be confirmed with a credit-card number. No-shows will be docked a night's accommodation.

➡ The high season is during July and August, though prices peak again around Easter and Christmas. It's essential to book in advance during these periods.

➡ Rates drop between 30% and 50% in low season. In the winter months (November to Easter) many places, particularly on the coast, completely shut down. In the cities and larger towns accommodation tends to remain open all year. The relative lack of visitors in these down periods means you should have little trouble getting a room in those places that do stay open.

➡ Most hotels offer breakfast, though this can vary from bountiful buffets to more modest offerings of pastries, packaged yoghurt and fruit. The same is true of B&Bs, where morning food options can sometimes be little more than pre-packaged *cornetti* (Italian croissants), biscuits, jam, coffee and tea.

➡ Where applicable, our accommodation reviews list minimum to maximum high-season rates. Where indicated, half-board means breakfast and either lunch or dinner; full board is breakfast, lunch and dinner.

Top Choices

Best B&Bs

Casa Turchetti, Taormina, Sicily (p216) A tastefully restored former music school turned luxe hideaway, with spectacular rooftop views.

B&B Al Salvatore di Lipari, Lipari, Sicily (p205) Gorgeous breakfasts, a panoramic terrace and warm hospitality from an artist and a physicist.

Atelier Ines, Naples, Campania (p74) A three-suite ode to the late Neapolitan sculptor and designer Annibale Oste.

Nòtia Rooms, Noto, Sicily (p234) A beautifully curated oasis with notable art and Modernist design.

Best for Honeymooners

Capri Palace, Capri, Campania (p83) A five-star legend high up on Capri, with private plunge pools and coveted spa treatments.

IZZARD/SHUTTERSTOCK ©

Trulli, Alberobello (p141)

OFFBEAT ACCOMMODATION

Looking for something out of the ordinary? Southern Italy offers a number of sleeping options that you won't find anywhere else in the world.

➡ Down near Italy's heel, rent a *trullo*, one of the characteristic whitewashed conical houses of southern Puglia.

➡ Ancient *sassi* (cave dwellings) have found new life as boutique hotels in otherworldly Matera, a Unesco World Heritage–listed town in the southern region of Basilicata.

➡ In Naples, spend a night or two slumbering in the aristocratic *palazzo* of a powerful Bourbon bishop. Now the Decumani Hotel de Charme (p74), the property comes complete with a sumptuous baroque salon.

Hotel Palazzo Murat, Positano, Campania
(p111) Enchanted gardens, precious art and luxurious slumber in a former king's summer *palazzo*.

Masseria Torre Maizza, Locorotondo, Puglia
(p144) A whitewashed, beachfront *masseria* complete with spa, golf course and horse riding.

Best for Families

Il Frantoio, Ostuni, Puglia (p144) A higher-end working farmhouse with fabulous food and hands-on activities.

Hotel La Vigna, Procida, Campania (p90) An 18th-century villa with lush gardens, vines and a swimming pool.

Casale Giancesare, Paestum, Campania (p120)
A stylish yet homely farmhouse complete with pool and homemade treats.

Hotel Villa Eva, Capri, Campania (p83) A bucolic retreat with space, a pool and bright rooms and apartments.

Best on a Budget

Palazzu Stidda, Catania, Sicily (p221) Unique apartments pimped with the owners' artworks and handmade furniture.

Palazzo Rollo, Lecce, Puglia (p150) Stylish studios and suites in a 17th-century family *palazzo*.

Casale Giancesare, Paestum, Campania (p120)
Gracious family hospitality at a 19th-century farmhouse with olive groves and a pool.

First Time Southern Italy

For more information, see Survival Guide (p289)

Checklist

➡ Ensure your passport is valid for at least six months past your departure date from Italy

➡ Check airline baggage restrictions

➡ Organise travel insurance

➡ Make bookings (for accommodation and entertainment)

➡ Inform your credit/debit card company of your travels

➡ Check if you can use your mobile (cell) phone in Italy

➡ Check requirements for hiring a car

What to Pack

➡ Hat, sunglasses, sunscreen and comfortable walking shoes

➡ Electrical adapter and phone charger

➡ A detailed driving map for southern Italy's rural backroads

➡ Smart threads and shoes for higher-end restaurants

➡ Patience: for coping with inefficiency

➡ Phrasebook: for ordering and charming

Top Tips for Your Trip

➡ Visit in the shoulder season (spring and autumn) – good weather and thinner crowds.

➡ If driving, get off the main roads where possible: some of the most stunning scenery is on secondary or tertiary roads.

➡ Avoid restaurants with touts and the mediocre *menu turistico* (tourist menu).

➡ Avoid keeping money, credit cards and other valuables in easy-to-reach pockets as pickpockets do operate on crowded metro trains, buses and at markets.

➡ Queue-jumping is common: be polite but assertive.

What to Wear

Appearances matter in Italy. In the cities, suitable wear for men is generally trousers (including stylish jeans) and shirts or polo shirts, and for women skirts, trousers or dresses. Shorts, T-shirts and sandals are fine in summer and at the beach, but long sleeves are required for dining out. For evening wear, smart casual is the norm. A light sweater or waterproof jacket is useful in spring and autumn, and sturdy, comfortable shoes are good when visiting archaeological sites.

Sleeping

➡ **Hotels** All prices and levels of quality, from cheap-and-charmless to sleek-and-exclusive boutique.

➡ **Agriturismi (Farm Stays)** Perfect for families and for relaxation, *agriturismi* range from rustic farmhouses to luxe country estates.

➡ **B&Bs** Often great value, options span rooms in family houses to self-catering studio apartments.

➡ **Pensions** Similar to hotels, though *pensioni* are generally of one-to three-star quality and family-run.

➡ **Hostels** You'll find both official HI-affiliated and privately run *ostelli* (hostels), many also offering private rooms with bathroom.

Money

➡ Do not rely on credit cards at museums or galleries.

➡ Note that using your credit card in ATMs can be costly. On every transaction there's a fee, which can reach US$10 with some credit-card issuers, as well as interest per withdrawal. Check with your issuer before leaving home.

➡ Always inform your bank of your travel plans to avoid your card being blocked for payments made in unusual locations.

Bargaining

Gentle haggling is common in markets. Haggling in stores is generally unacceptable, though good-humoured bargaining at smaller artisan or craft shops is not unusual if making multiple purchases.

Tipping

Italians are not big tippers. Use the following as a rough guide:

➡ **Taxis** Optional, but most people round up to the nearest euro.

➡ **Hotels** Tip porters about €5 at high-end hotels.

➡ **Restaurants** Service (*servizio*) is generally included in restaurants – if it's not, a euro or two is fine in pizzerias, 10% in restaurants.

➡ **Bars** Optional, though many Italians leave small change on the bar when ordering coffee (usually €0.10 per coffee). If drinks are brought to your table, a small tip is generally appreciated.

Language

Unlike many other European countries, English is not widely spoken in Italy. Of course, you can get by in the main tourist centres, but in the countryside and off the tourist track you'll need to master a few basic phrases. This will improve your experience no end, especially when ordering in restaurants, some of which have no written menu. It's also a good way of connecting with the locals, leading to a richer, more personable experience of the region and its people. For more on language, see p307.

1 **What's the local speciality?**
Qual'è la specialità di questa regione?
kwa·le la spe·cha·lee·ta dee kwes·ta re·jo·ne

A bit like the rivalry between medieval Italian city-states, these days the country's regions compete in speciality foods and wines.

2 **Which combined tickets do you have?**
Quali biglietti cumulativi avete?
kwa·lee bee·lye·tee koo·moo·la·tee·vee a·ve·te

Make the most of your euro by getting combined tickets to various sights; they are available in all major Italian cities.

3 **I'm here with my husband/boyfriend.**
Sono qui con il mio marito/ragazzo.
so·no kwee kon eel mee·o ma·ree·to/ra·ga·tso

Solo women travellers may receive unwanted attention in some parts of Italy; if ignoring fails have a polite rejection ready.

4 **Let's meet at 6pm for pre-dinner drinks.**
Ci vediamo alle sei per un aperitivo.
chee ve·dya·mo a·le say per oon a·pe·ree·tee·vo

At dusk, watch the main piazza get crowded with people sipping colourful cocktails and snacking the evening away: join your new friends for this authentic Italian ritual!

Etiquette

Italy is a surprisingly formal society; the following tips will help avoid awkward moments.

➡ **Greetings** Greet people in shops, restaurants and bars with a *buongiorno* (good morning) or *buonasera* (good evening); kiss both cheeks and say *come stai* (how are you) to friends. With older people, only use first names if invited.

➡ **Asking for help** Say *mi scusi* (excuse me) to attract attention; use *permesso* (permission) to pass someone in a crowded space.

➡ **Dress** Cover shoulders, torso and thighs when visiting churches and dress smartly when eating out at restaurants.

➡ **At the table** Eat pasta with a fork, not a spoon; it's OK to eat pizza with your hands. Summon the waiter by saying *mi scusi* (excuse me).

➡ **Gifts** If invited to someone's home, traditional gifts are a tray of *dolci* (sweets) from a *pasticceria* (pastry shop), a bottle of wine or flowers.

If You Like...

Baroque Architecture

Southern Italy found its soulmate in the baroque architecture of the 17th and 18th centuries. Plunge into a world of outrageous palaces, sweeping squares and bling-tastic details.

Noto The most impressive Sicilian-baroque town in the World Heritage–listed Val di Noto. (p233)

Lecce Puglia's hallucinogenic city is to the baroque what Florence is to the Renaissance. (p147)

Reggia di Caserta Caserta's gargantuan royal pad puts Versailles in its place. (p101)

Catania Sicily's second-biggest city comes with a Unesco-lauded baroque piazza. (p218)

Naples Once a magnet for baroque architects, packed with exuberant churches, chapels and staircases. (p57)

Extraordinary Churches

Astounding frescoes, sparkling mosaics and action-packed facades: in southern Italy's churches and chapels, divinity and human vanity conspire to soul-lifting effect.

Cattedrale di Monreale Lavish 12th-century mosaics bring the Old Testament to life in this Arab-Norman wonder. (p200)

Cappella Palatina A jaw-dropping Palermo chapel famed for its spectacular Byzantine-era mosaics. (p193)

Duomo Home to Giovanni Lanfranco's breathtaking cupola fresco and Western Europe's oldest baptistry. (p63)

Cattedrale di Palermo A breathtaking behemoth celebrated for its cross-cultural Arab-Norman beauty. (p193)

Basilica di Santa Croce An over-the-top facade that epitomises Lecce's indulgent take on baroque. (p148)

Certosa e Museo di San Martino Home to an exuberant church designed by some of Italy's greatest 17th-century artists and artisans. (p68)

Ancient Sites

Its backstory spanning thousands of years, southern Italy lays claim to some of Europe's oldest, most precious archaeological sites, from commanding Greek temples to early Christian catacombs.

Ruins of Pompeii One of the world's most extraordinary windows into ancient urban life, between Naples and Sorrento. (p96)

Villa Romana del Casale Sicily's top Roman site is home to the finest Roman floor mosaics in existence. (p237)

Valley of the Temples Sicily's top archaeological site, with temples dating back as far as the 6th century BC. (p238)

Museo Archeologico Nazionale Showstopping sculptures, frescoes and mosaics from Pompeii, Herculaneum and beyond at Naples' top museum. (p64)

Ruins of Herculaneum Pompeii's smaller, better-preserved alternative offers intimate glimpses of daily Roman life. (p91)

Paestum Home to World Heritage-listed temples dating back to the south's Hellenic era. (p119)

Oplontis Vivid wall paintings and a giant swimming pool hint at extravagant ancient living on the Bay of Naples. (p79)

Catacombe di San Gennaro Naples' most famous subterranean catacombs harbour some of the world's oldest Christian frescoes. (p65)

Top: Sentiero degli Dei (p113), Amalfi Coast
Bottom: *Pecorino* (sheep's milk cheese)

Food, Glorious Food

The Mezzogiorno's rich soils, produce-packed hillsides and turquoise seas are a giant natural larder. Traditions are fiercely protected and eating well is a given. Tuck in!

Palermo Mouth-watering markets, *panelle* (chickpea-flour fritters), *sfincione* (Sicilian-style pizza), *arancini* and stuffed sardines. (p189)

Naples Hometown of pizza and famous for fried street food, ricotta-filled *sfogliatella* pastries and rum-soaked *babà*. (p57)

Catania Legendary *arancini* and home to one of Italy's most famous fish markets. (p218)

Ischia A Campanian island famous for its succulent, slow-cooked rabbit with wild herbs. (p86)

Paestum Where water buffaloes produce Campania's most coveted *mozzarella di bufala*. (p119)

Peschici Feast on *crudo* (raw seafood) the Puglian way at superlative Al Trabucco da Mimì. (p137)

Modica A baroque Sicilian town famed across Italy for its artisan chocolate. (p235)

Islands & Beaches

Northern Italy would secretly sell its soul for a coastline this alluring. From bijou islands to crystal-clear grottoes, the south's offerings are as varied as they are beautiful.

Puglia The region's superlative beaches include Baia dei Turchi and the cliff-backed beaches of the Gargano. (p123)

Aeolian Islands Island-hop Sicily's seven volcanic gems. (p202)

Capri Golden light and a mesmerising grotto lure A-list jet-setters and wannabes. (p79)

Maratea Basilicata's Tyrrhenian beauty gives the Amalfi Coast a serious run for its money. (p171)

Procida The Bay of Naples' sleepiest island has featured in several famous films. (p89)

Medieval Towns

Cobbled streets snake up hillsides to sculpted fountains, the scent of *ragù* (meat and tomato sauce) wafts from shuttered windows and washing hangs like holiday bunting.

Ravello Romantic gardens, dreamy Tyrrhenian views and a world-class arts festival above the Amalfi Coast. (p114)

Taormina A chic summertime favourite, with secret gardens and a panoramic ancient amphitheatre. (p213)

Cefalù Lapping waves, mazelike narrow streets and an imposing Arab-Norman cathedral. (p200)

Maratea A 13th-century *borgo* (medieval town) with pint-sized piazzas and startling views across the Gulf of Policastro. (p171)

Erice Splendid coastal views from the hilltop Norman castle make this western Sicily's most photogenic village. (p249)

The Great Outdoors

Saunter between sea and sky in Campania, slip into silent forests in Basilicata and Calabria, or come face to face with Mother Nature's wrath in lava-spewing Sicily.

Sentiero degli Dei Hit the 'Path of the Gods' for a different take on the stunning Amalfi Coast. (p113)

Mt Etna Hike the picturesque slopes of Europe's tallest active volcano. (p224)

Parco Nazionale del Gargano Explore an enchanted world of Aleppo pines, springtime orchids and sacred pilgrimage sites. (p132)

Pollino National Park Go whitewater rafting, paragliding, diving or canyoning in the rugged wilds of Basilicata and Calabria. (p172)

Riserva Naturale dello Zingaro Dip in and out of picturesque coves along the wild coastline of Sicily's oldest nature reserve. (p245)

Ravello Lose yourself in heavenly panoramas from the romantic, sky-high gardens of Villa Rufolo and Villa Cimbrone. (p114)

La Mortella A tropical and Mediterranean paradise inspired by the gardens of Granada's Alhambra (p86)

Mt Vesuvius Peer into the ashen mouth of Naples' giant ticking time bomb. (p95)

Markets

The market is an integral part of southern Italian

life and a great place to pick up picnic provisions like crunchy bread, local cheeses, salami, antipasti, fruit and vegetables.

Mercato di Ballarò Spices, watermelons and giant swordfish under striped awnings down cobbled alleys: Palermo's market recalls an African bazaar. (p193)

Mercato del Capo Another mouthwatering street market in Palermo, peddling everything from fresh local seafood, vegetables and cheese, to spices and household goods. (p193)

La Pescheria A loud, wet, action-packed citadel of fresh fish, seafood and more in central Catania. (p218)

Mercato di Porta Nolana Elbow your way past bellowing fishing folk, fragrant bakeries and bootleg CD stalls for a slice of Neapolitan street theatre. (p68)

Diving

For divers ready to take the plunge, southern Italy delivers on all fronts, from abundant marine life to ethereal sea caves and submerged ancient ruins.

Aeolian Islands A Unesco-listed volcanic archipelago where grottoes surround the remains of old volcanoes. (p202)

Ustica Italy's first marine reserve, this volcanic island is also rich with underwater flora and fauna. (p200)

Isole Tremiti Wind-eroded islands off Puglia's Gargano Promontory, pock-marked with imposing sea caves. (p138)

Month by Month

February

Short and accursed is how Italians describe February. It might still be chilly down south, but almond trees start to blossom and Carnevale season brightens things up with confetti, costumes and sugar-dusted treats.

Carnevale

In the period leading up to Ash Wednesday, many southern towns stage pre-Lenten carnivals. One of the most flamboyant is the Carnevale di Acireale (www.carnevaleacireale. com), the elaborate and whimsical floats of which are famous throughout the country.

March

The weather in March is capricious: sunny, rainy and windy all at once. Understandably, the Italians call it *Marzo pazzo* (Crazy March). The official start of spring is 21 March, but the main holiday season starts with Easter week.

Settimana Santa

Processions and passion plays mark Easter Holy Week across the south. On Good Friday and the Thursday preceding it, hooded penitents walk through the streets of Sorrento (p104). On Procida, Good Friday sees wooden statues and life-size tableaux carted across the island for the Procession of the Misteri (p90).

May

The month of roses and early summer produce makes May a perfect time to travel, especially for walkers. The weather is warm but not too hot and prices throughout the south are good value. It's also patron-saint season.

Festa di San Gennaro

On the first Saturday in May, the faithful in Naples pour into the city's Duomo to witness the liquefaction of San Gennaro's blood. If this miracle occurs, the city is deemed safe from disaster. The event is repeated on 19 September and 16 December.

☆ Maggio dei Monumenti

As the weather warms up, Naples rolls out a mammoth, month-long program of art exhibitions, concerts, performances and tours around the city. Many historical and architectural treasures usually off-limits to the public are open and free to visit.

Wine & The City

A three-week celebration of regional vino in Naples, with free wine degustations, *aperitivo* sessions and cultural events in venues as diverse as museums and castles, art galleries, boutiques and restaurants. (www.wineandthecity.it)

June

The summer season kicks off in June. The temperature cranks up quickly, beach *lidi* start to open in earnest and some of the big summer festivals commence. There's a national holiday on 2 June, the Anniversary of the Republic.

☆ Ciclo di Rappresentazioni Classiche

Ancient intrigue in an evocative Sicilian setting, the Festival of Greek Theatre (www.indafondazione. org) brings Syracuse's 5th-century-BC amphitheatre to life with performances from Italy's acting greats. The season runs from mid-June to early July.

☆ Napoli Teatro Festival Italia

Naples celebrates all things performative with one month of theatre, dance and literary events (www. napoliteatrofestival.it). Using both conventional and unconventional venues, the program ranges from classic works to specially commissioned pieces from both local and international talent. Held from early June to early July.

July

School is out and Italians everywhere are heading out of the cities and to the mountains or beaches for their summer holidays. Prices and temperatures rise. The beach is in full swing, but many cities host summer art festivals.

☆ Festa di Sant'Anna

The Campanian island of Ischia celebrates the feast day of Sant'Anna to spectacular effect on July 26. Local municipalities build competing floats to sail in a flotilla, with spectacular fireworks and a symbolic 'burning' of Ischia Ponte's medieval Castello Aragonese.

Top: Carnevale di Acireale (p25)
Bottom: Dance of the Devils during Settimana Santa (p25)

⭐ Festival della Valle d'Itria

From mid-July to early August, the town of Martina Franca sets toes a-tapping with its esteemed music festival (www.festivaldella valleditria.it). The focus is on musical theatre, especially opera, though concertos and other recitals also abound.

⭐ Giffoni Film Festival

Europe's biggest children's film festival (www.giffoni filmfestival.it) livens up the town of Giffoni Valle Piana, east of Salerno, Campania. The nine-day event includes screenings, workshops, seminars and big-name guests such as Oscar-winning director Gabriele Salvatores and award-winning actor Bryan Cranston.

✨ Ravello Festival

Perched high above the Amalfi Coast, Ravello draws world-renowned artists during its eponymous festival (www.ravellofestival. com), which runs from early July to September. Covering everything from music and dance to film and art exhibitions, several events take place in the beautiful gardens of Villa Rufolo.

✨ Sagra della Madonna della Bruna

A week-long celebration of Matera's patron saint that culminates on 2 July with a colourful procession that sees the Madonna della Bruna escorted around town in a papier-mâché-adorned chariot. The chariot is ultimately torn to pieces by the crowd, who take home the scraps as souvenirs.

⭐ Taormina Arte

Ancient ruins and languid summer nights set a seductive scene for Taormina Arte (www.taoarte.it), a major arts festival held through July to September. Events include film screenings, theatre, opera and concerts.

August

August in southern Italy is hot, expensive and crowded. Everyone is on holiday and while it may no longer be true that everything is shut, many businesses and restaurants do close for part of the month.

✨ Ferragosto

After Christmas and Easter, Ferragosto is Italy's biggest holiday. While it now marks the Feast of the Assumption, even the ancient Romans honoured their pagan gods on Feriae Augusti. Naples lets loose with particular fervour.

⭐ La Notte della Taranta

Puglia celebrates its hypnotic *pizzica* dance with the Night of the Taranta (www. lanottedellataranta.it), a festival held in and around the Puglian town of Melpignano. Dancing aside, the event also showcases Salento's folk-music traditions.

September

This is a glorious month in the south. As summer wanes into autumn, the grape harvest begins. Adding to the culinary excitement are the many local *sagre* (food festivals),

celebrating regional produce and traditions.

🍴 Couscous Fest

The Sicilian town of St Vito celebrates multiculturalism and its famous fish couscous at this 10-day event in mid to late September (www. couscousfest.it). Highlights include an international couscous cook-off, tastings and live world-music gigs.

November

The advent of winter creeps down the peninsula in November, but there's plenty going on. This is the time for the chestnut harvest, mushroom picking and All Saints' Day.

✨ Ognissanti

Celebrated all over Italy as a national holiday, All Saints' Day on 1 November commemorates the Saint Martyrs, while All Souls' Day, on 2 November, is set aside to honour the deceased.

December

The days of alfresco living are at an end. Yet, despite the cooler days and longer nights, looming Christmas festivities warm things up with festive street lights, nativity scenes and Yuletide specialities.

✨ Natale

The weeks preceding Christmas are studded with religious events. Many churches set up nativity scenes known as *presepe*. While Naples is especially famous for these, you'll find impressive tableaux in many southern towns, including Erice in Sicily.

Plan Your Trip
Itineraries

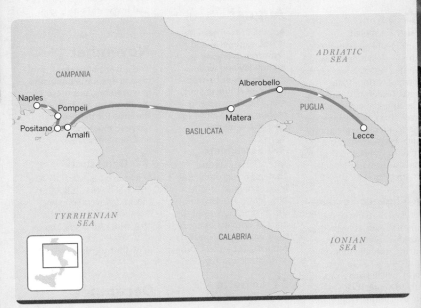

Southern Highlights

An easy introduction to some of southern Italy's must-see wonders, this 10-day overview covers everything from cosmopolitan city culture to ancient ruins, breathtaking coastal scenery and World Heritage–listed architecture.

Pique your appetite with two heady days in **Naples**, an urban wild child bursting with glorious art, architecture, street life and flavours. You'll be kept busy exploring its bounty of cultural treasures, which include Caravaggio masterpieces at Pio Monte della Misericordia, Palazzo Reale di Capo-

dimonte and the Galleria di Palazzo Zevallos Stigliano, as well as stirring baroque frescoes in churches such as the Duomo and Chiesa del Gesù Nuovo. The city's Cappella Sanseverio is home to the *Cristo velato* (Veiled Christ), widely considered one of Italy's finest sculptures.

Spend day three roaming the time-warped ruins of **Pompeii**, among them communal baths, private residences, shops and even a brothel etched with ancient graffiti. Leap back into the present and continue to **Positano**, the Amalfi Coast's undisputed pin-up town. Lap up two days

Positano (p109)

here, hiring a boat for a spot of coastal cruising or hiking the breathtaking Sentiero degli Dei (Path of the Gods). On day six, continue east along the Amalfi Coast, stopping briefly in atmospheric **Amalfi** to view its iconic Sicilian Arabic-Norman cathedral, the oldest part dating from the early 10th century. Continue on your way to the city of **Matera** in time for dinner, then spend the following day exploring its one-of-a-kind, Unesco-lauded *sassi* (former cave dwellings). Swap *sassi* for World Heritage-listed *trulli* (conical-roofed abodes) in **Alberobello** the following day. Late evening is the best time to experience the town's historic Rione Monti quarter, home to more than 1000 *trulli*. Spend the night, then hit the road one last time to the university city of **Lecce**. Dubbed the 'Florence of the South', its quixotic baroque buildings make for an extravagant epilogue to your southern overview.

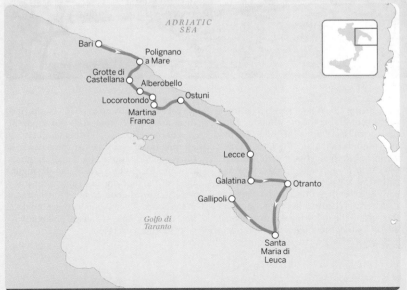

MITI/SHUTTERSTOCK ©

Perfect Puglia

PLAN YOUR TRIP ITINERARIES

Puglia is one of Italy's most underrated regions, its abundance of history and one-of-a-kind architecture melded with an enviable coastline and one of Italy's simplest, healthiest cuisines.

Start your explorations in dynamic **Bari**, roaming its ancient historic centre and huge Romanesque basilica; the latter is a pilgrimage site for both Catholic and Orthodox Christians. Strike out south, via **Polignano a Mare**, to the jaw-dropping limestone **Grotte di Castellana**. Italy's longest network of subterranean caves, its most famous feature is the Grotta Bianca (White Grotto), Mother Nature's alabaster take on Gothic architecture. From here, a two- to three-day drive south will take you through some of the finest towns in the celebrated Valle d'Itria. Among these is **Alberobello**, with its hobbit-like, Unesco World Heritage-listed *trulli* houses, wine-producing **Locorotondo**, beautiful baroque **Martina Franca** and chic, whitewashed **Ostuni**, the latter home to some particularly outstanding restaurants. Next up is inimitable **Lecce**, dubbed the 'Florence of the South' for its operatic architectural ensembles and scholarly bent. Hire a bike and spend at least three or four days exploring its wealth of cultural assets. Among these is the obsessively detailed Basilica di Santa Croce and the Museo Faggiano, the latter a veritable layer-cake of archaeology stretching back to the 5th century BC. From Lecce, move on to **Galatina**, its 14th-century basilica awash with astounding frescoes. Head east to the fortified port of **Otranto**, whose own 11th-century cathedral stands out for its extraordinary 12th-century floor mosaic. If the weather is warm, enjoy a little downtime on the inviting beaches of the Baia dei Turchi, then push south along the wild, vertiginous coastline to **Santa Maria di Leuca**, the very tip of the Italian stiletto. Finally, conclude your adventure in the walled island city of **Gallipoli**, feasting on raw sea urchin and octopus in its elegant town centre.

SABINO PARENTE/SHUTTERSTOCK ©

Top: Polignano a Mare (p131)
Bottom: Sea urchin

15 DAYS Sicily to Calabria

Ancient cultures and natural beauty collide in this two-week adventure. From Greek temples and Norman cathedrals to rugged mountains and coveted coastal resorts, strike out on a gripping journey through Italy's southern extremes.

Fly into **Palermo** and take two days to savour the city's cross-cultural food, markets and architecture. Soak up its glittering, 12th-century Cappella Palatina, snoop around the city's revamped archaeological museum, and detour to nearby **Monreale** to marvel at its mosaic-encrusted Norman cathedral, considered Sicily's finest. On day three, day-trip west to the 5th-century BC ruins of **Segesta**, one of Italy's most remarkable ancient sites.

From Palermo, head east to eye-candy **Cefalù** on day four. Spend a night – just enough time to admire its commanding Arab-Norman cathedral and crystalline sea. Come day five, shoot through to VIP-favourite **Taormina**, a long-time haunt of poets, painters and hopeless romantics. The town was once Sicily's Byzantine capital and its sweeping ancient Greek theatre is the island's second largest. Allow two nights of elegant slumming and consider hiking up nearby **Mt Etna** on one of your days.

Day seven sees you catching a ferry from Messina to **Reggio di Calabria** in time to see the *Bronzi di Riace* at the Museo Nazionale di Reggio Calabria. The finest examples of ancient Greek sculpture in existence, the bronze sculptures are southern Italy's answer to Florence's *David*. Rest your head in tiny Gambarie, using the town as your base as you explore the wild beauty of the **Parco Nazionale dell'Aspromonte** over the next two days.

Come day 10, head back down to the Tyrrhenian coast. Lunch on fresh swordfish in castle-capped **Scilla**, continuing through to dazzling **Tropea**, Calabria's coastal darling. Spend two nights recharging your weary bones, lazily ambling its labyrinthine streets and catching some of the south's finest sunsets. Restored, continue north to the gritty yet erudite city of **Cosenza** on day 12. After taking in its impressively preserved medieval core on day 13, hit Camigliatello Silano for two nights, concluding your adventure with soul-lifting hikes through the alpine beauty of the **Parco Nazionale della Sila**.

Top: Santa Maria dell'Isola (p183), Tropea
Bottom: Cattedrale di Monreale (p200), Monreale

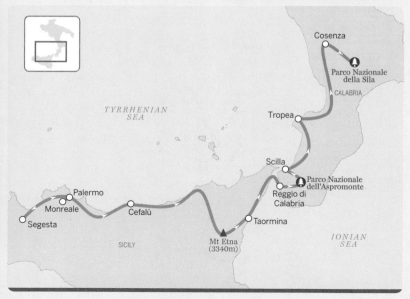

9 DAYS The Deep South

This itinerary touches some of the deepest, rawest, most surreal corners of the south, from a cave-studded city to rare Albanian mountain villages. Add a dose of sparkling Tyrrhenian blue and you have a journey guaranteed to get under your skin.

Start this soulful journey in the cave city of **Matera**, one of Europe's most unusual settlements. Spend a couple of days exploring its famous *sassi*, as well as the *chiese rupestri* (cave churches) on a hike along the Gravina. The dynamic Casa Noha museum offers valuable insight into both the *sassi* and the city's poverty-stricken past.

From Matera, escape south to the **Parco Nazionale del Pollino** for an invigorating fix of nature. Base yourself in **Terranova di Pollino** for four days, hiking through pine woods and beech forest to Basilicata's highest peak, Monte Pollino. Spanning alpine meadows and deep river canyons, the national park harbours rare stocks of roe deer, wild cats, wolves and birds of prey, among them the Egyptian vulture. It's also home to the curious Albanian villages of **San Paolo Albanese** and **San Costantino Albanese**, where you may just find yourself dancing to the *zampogne* (double-chantered pipes). Both towns were founded in the 16th century by ethnic Albanian refugees (*Arbëreshë*), who left Koroni in Greece during its Ottoman occupation. Another of the park's unexpected treasures is the rare Bosnian pine tree, *pino loricato*.

Lungs filled with mountain air, it's time to head west to the gorgeous coastal jewel of **Maratea**. Pass a couple of days relaxing in the town's crystalline Tyrrhenian waters and sailing to nearby grottoes and coves. Back in town, kick back at local bars and feast on fresh seafood. Recharged, it's time to head south to Calabria on the SS18 coastal road. If it's September, you might catch a chilli-eating competition in **Diamante**. Otherwise, keep moving until you reach Calabria's most arresting coastal town, **Tropea**. An ancient settlement whose past rulers have included the Arabs, Normans, Swabians and Anjous, its piercing views and sunsets make for a beautiful, soul-soothing wrap up.

Top: *Sasso*, Matera (p161)
Bottom: Fiumicello (p171), Maratea

3 WEEKS

The Grand Tour

Covering Campania, Basilicata, Calabria and Sicily, this three-week trip is rich in both blockbuster sights and off-the-beaten-track treasures.

Commence with a trio of days in **Naples**, roaming its secret catacombs, baroque churches and world-renowned Museo Archeologico Nazionale. Take an easy day trip to the formidable royal palace of **Caserta** or to the ill-fated ancient towns of **Pompeii** or **Herculaneum**. Whichever you choose, treat yourself to two romantic days on **Capri**, making time for quiet hikes, the spectacular Grotta Azzurra and the unforgettable views from atop Monte Solaro. Sail across to **Sorrento** for a night then hit the fabled Amalfi Coast on day six, allowing two days in see-and-be-seen **Positano** and a further night in **Amalfi** or hilltop **Ravello**. Travel back in time roaming millennia-old Greek temples in **Paestum** on day nine before continuing to fellow World Heritage marvel **Matera** and its otherworldly abodes.

Come day 12, drop into ancient **Metaponto**. The hometown of number-crunching Pythagoras, it's also where you'll find the so-called Palatine Tables, a reputed pit stop for Crusade-bound knights. Then it's time to escape to the wilds of the **Parco Nazionale del Pollino**. With Terranova di Pollino as your base, spend three days hiking through invigorating woods and exploring the curious Albanian villages of San Paolo Albanese and San Costantino Albanese.

Slide down to Calabria's Tyrrhenian coastline on day 16, home to seaside show-off **Tropea**. Allow two nights of waterside *dolce vita* (sweet life) before catching a ferry from Villa San Giovanni to Sicily on day 18. Allow yourself another two days of coastal slumming in chi-chi **Taormina**, home to a 3rd-century BC theatre and a world-class summertime arts festival. If you can pull yourself away on day 20, wrap things up with a couple of days exploring **Syracuse**, described by Roman philosopher Cicero as the 'greatest Greek city and the most beautiful of them all'. Its Hellenic past lives on at the Parco Archeologico della Neapolis, considered one of Sicily's most important archaeological sites.

Top: Teatro Greco (p215), Taormina

Bottom: Monti di Orsomarso (p172), Parco Nazionale Del Pollino

Isola Bella (p215), Taorn

Outdoor Activities

Southern Italy lays claim to some of the country's most dramatic, breathtaking terrain. For active types, this means endless possibilities for high-octane adventure and blissful relaxation. Whatever you're itching for – be it a dive off the Amalfi Coast, a hike in the wilds of Calabria's Pollino National Park or a muscle-soothing soak on a volcanic Aeolian beach – the Mezzogiorno delivers.

Best Activities

Diving & Snorkelling

Explore the underwater wonders of Lipari, Filicudi, Ustica or Isola Bella in Sicily.

Sailing Trips

Explore the coves and grottoes of Campania's Amalfi Coast and Bay of Naples' islands, Puglia's Promontorio del Gargano in Puglia or Sicily's Riserva Naturale dello Zingaro in Sicily.

Hiking

Climb into the Madonie Mountains above Cefalù, lose yourself in the rugged mountains of Calabria, or view the fabled Amalfi Coast from sky-high mountain paths.

Rafting & Kayaking

Ride wild river rapids in Calabria's Pollino National Park or soften the pace with an urban kayaking trip along the eclectic coastline of Naples.

Thermal Therapy

De-stress in natural hot springs on the Campanian island of Ischia or wallow in therapeutic mud on the Aeolian island of Vulcano.

Volcano Viewing

Watch Stromboli's nocturnal fireworks from the summit or a boat, or teeter on the edges of Etna or Vesuvius, two volcanoes on the rim of urban areas.

Hiking

The south's attention-grabbing scenery makes for some unforgettable hikes. For spectacular sea views in Campania, hit the Amalfi Coast (p106) and Sorrento Peninsula, where age-old paths such as the *Sentiero degli Dei* (Path of the Gods) disappear into wooded mountains and ancient lemon groves.

To the surprise of many, both Capri (p79) and Ischia (p86) offer some spectacular walks that will see you enjoying the islands away from the beach crowds. Enjoyable though precipitous trails lead you out of Capri Town to a Roman villa and a natural rock arch, or for a more arduous route you can follow a chain of forts and take in the western coast.

Southeast of the Amalfi Coast, the Parco Nazionale del Cilento e Vallo di Diano (p120) serves up relaxing walks and more challenging hikes, reliable guides and excellent maps. This remarkable wilderness area is home to around 3000 registered botanical species, as well as a number of rare birds, including the golden eagle and seacrow.

The park's most famous feature, however, is an incredible series of caves. Among these are the Grotte di Castelcivita (p120) and Grotte di Pertosa (p121), their Gothic-like stalagmites and stalactites yours to explore on regular speleological tours.

Crossing the border between Calabria and Basilicata is the Parco Nazionale del Pollino (p172), Italy's largest national park. Claiming the richest repository of flora and fauna in the south, its varied landscapes range from deep river canyons to alpine meadows. Calabria's other national parks – the Sila (p175) and Aspromonte (p178) – offer similarly dramatic hiking, particularly the area around Sersale in the Sila, studded with waterfalls and the possibility of trekking through the Valli Cupe canyon.

Close to the heel of the stiletto in the sun-baked region of Puglia, the Parco della Murgia Materana, part of the Matera (p161) Unesco World Heritage site, is full of fascinating cave churches and is great for birdwatching.

With their unique topographies, Sicily and Sardinia provide unforgettable walking opportunities. Take your pick of volcano hikes in Sicily: the mother of them all is Mt Etna (p224), but there's a whole host of lesser volcanoes on the Aeolian Islands, from the slumbering Vulcano (p207), where you can descend to the crater floor, to a three-hour climb to the summit of Stromboli (p211) to see it exploding against the night sky. On Salina, you can clamber up extinct volcano Monte Fossa delle Felci (p210) for staggering views of symmetrically aligned volcanic peaks. From Etna you can also trek across into the Madonie (p202) park, or on Sicily's northwest coast you can track the shoreline in the Riserva Naturale dello Zingaro (p245).

Online, www.parks.it offers useful information on southern Italy's national parks.

Diving & Snorkelling

Sparkling waters make diving and snorkelling popular activities on southern coasts, especially from May to October. Just off Campania's Sorrentine Peninsula, Punta Campanella is an 11-sq-km marine reserve well known for its underwater grottoes and abundant sea life.

Across the Tyrrhenian Sea, divers from around the world head to the offshore Sicilian island of Ustica (p200) to explore its magnificent underwater sites. The island's western shores are home to a protected marine reserve, which is divided into three zones. Highlights include the underwater archaeological trail off Punta Cavazzi, where artefacts including anchors and Roman amphorae can be admired. Other popular dive sites are the Scoglio del Medico, an outcrop of basalt riddled with caves and gorges that plunge to great depths; and Secca di Colombara, a magnificent rainbow-coloured display of sponges and gorgonias.

There are good dives off most of the Aeolians, with some of the best surrounding the main island of Lipari (p203). Seasonal diving operators can be found across the Aeolian islands.

West of Palermo, the Riserva Naturale dello Zingaro (p245) is also great for diving. **Cetaria Diving Centre** (www.cetaria.it) in Scopello organises guided dives in the waters off the nature reserve between April and October, visiting underwater caves and shipwrecks; it also offers boat excursions with snorkelling.

Near Taormina, the WWF-protected reserve of Isola Bella (p215) also has some good diving. Nike Diving Centre (p216) offers diving equipment and lessons, along with snorkelling excursions and stand-up paddleboarding.

Sailing

Southern Italy has a proud maritime tradition and you can hire a paddle boat or sleek sailing yacht across its coasts. Sailors

Parco Nazionale della Sila (p17

of all levels are catered for: experienced skippers can island-hop around Sicily or along the Amalfi on chartered yachts, while weekend boaters can explore hidden coves in rented dinghies, for which you need no experience – though be sure you understand the instructions before you set off!

On the Amalfi Coast (p106), prime swimming spots are often only accessible by boat. It's a similar story on the islands of Capri (p79), Ischia (p86) and Procida (p89).

In Puglia, the Promontorio del Gargano (p132) is studded with beautiful coastal grottoes. The promontory's seaside town of Vieste is home to numerous boat operators offering seasonal tours of the coast's caves and striking rock formations.

Boat trips of all kinds can be organised along Sicily's coast and in the outer islands. San Vito Lo Capo–based Buena Vida (www.buenavida.it) runs sailing and other boat excursions to the Riserva Naturale dello Zingaro and the Egadi Islands. Off Sicily's northeastern coast, the cobalt waters of the Aeolian Islands (p202) are perfect for idle island-hopping.

Kayaking near Capri (p79)

Reputable yacht charter companies which cover southern Italy include Bareboat Sailing Holidays (www.bareboat sailingholidays.com).

Rafting & Kayaking

One of the best spots for whitewater sports in the south is Calabria's Parco Nazionale del Pollino (p172). Here, the Lao river rapids provide exhilarating rafting, as well as canoeing and canyoning. Trips can be arranged in Scalea.

Across the sea, Sicily in Kayak (p207) offers kayaking tours around Vulcano and the other Aeolian islands, ranging from half a day to an entire week. It also offers sailing and stand-up paddleboarding excursions.

A number of other operators on the Aeolians organise round-the-island and inter-island boat trips exploring the islands' sea grottoes and secluded swimming spots.

Back on the Italian mainland, **Kayak Napoli** (www.kayaknapoli.com) offers a refreshingly different take on Naples, with great kayaking tours of the Neapolitan coastline for all levels. The tours tick off usually inaccessible ruins, neoclassical villas, gardens and grottoes from the water. It also offers stand-up paddleboarding tours.

Rockclimbing

Arrampicata (climbing) is increasingly popular in Sicliy. San Vito Lo Capo is the island's rock-climbing capital, luring climbers with its variety of challenging crags and the **San Vito Climbing Festival** (www.sanvitoclimbingfestival. it), a four-day event held annually in mid-October.

Other leading climbing destinations include Mt Etna, the limestone pinnacles of Rocche di Crasto in the Nebrodi Mountains, and multiple sites in the Madonie Mountains including Monte D'Oro outside Collesano, La Rocca di Sciara near Caltavuturo, Rocca di Sant'Otiero near Petralia Sottana and Passo Scuro outside Castelbuono.

TONY BRINDLEY/SHUTTERSTOCK ©

Top: Scala dei Turchi (p242)

Bottom: Bonelli's Eagle

Birdwatching

Given its prime position on the migratory flight path between Africa and Europe, Sicily is a great place for birdwatching. April and September are the best months. Hot spots include the following:

Riserva Naturale Oasi Faunistica di Vendicari (p226) The wetlands are home to flamingos, herons, spoonbills, cranes, ducks, cormorants and collared pratincoles.

Riserva Naturale dello Zingaro (p245) A nature reserve with over 40 species, including the rare Bonelli eagle, hawks, buzzards, kestrels, swifts and Imperial crows, as well as the 'Greek Partridge of Sicily'.

Mozia (San Pantaleo) A tiny island haven for many species, including flamingos, herons, storks and cranes, as well as grey herons.

Lingua Salina's lagoon attracts huge numbers of birds in April; scores of Eleonora's falcons (*Falco eleonorae*) return to nest here.

Companies offering birdwatching tours in Sicily include UK-based **Nature Trek** (www.naturetrek.co.uk) and **Limosa Holidays** (www.limosaholidays.co.uk).

Spas

The upside of southern Italy's volcanic activity is a string of natural spa experiences. The sulphurous mud at Vulcano's Laghetto di Fanghi (p207) is an excellent treatment for skin disorders and arthritis. Slip on your oldest swim suit (the smell of sulphur will *never* leave the fabric) and relax for a while – apply a mud face mask while you're at it. Finish off with a natural spa bath (hot bubbling springs in a natural seawater pool).

BEST BEACHES

Scala dei Turchi (p242) A dazzling white outcropping shaped like a staircase, with beaches on either side, perfect for wading or diving off the rocks.

Torre Salsa (p242) Perfect for fans of wild, unspoiled coastline, this off-the-beaten-track gem is part of a WWF-administered nature reserve.

Spiaggia di Cefalù (p201) A lovely, family-friendly expanse of sand backed by a dramatic promontory and one of Sicily's prettiest medieval towns.

Spiaggia Valle i Muria (p204) Fabulously far from civilisation, save for its cavelike beachside bar, this cliff-backed beach is one of the Aeolians' finest.

Spiaggia dei Faraglioni (p245) Scopello's rough-pebbled beach has shimmering turquoise waters backed by towering rock formations.

Isola Bella (p215) Facing the island preserve of the same name, this pebbly beach below Taormina is tucked into a supremely picturesque cove.

Baia di Sorgeto (p87) Catch a water taxi to this toasty thermal beach on Ischia.

In Campania, Ischia (p86) is considered one of the world's richest hydrothermal areas. The island's spas include Negombo (p86), which combines lush gardens with mineral pools and a private beach.

Parmigiana melanzane (batter-fried eggplant layered with parmesan, mozzarella, ham and tomato sau

Eat & Drink Like a Local

Italy is a gastronomic powerhouse and the country's south claims many of its most venerated exports, from Gragnano pasta and San Marzano tomatoes, to buffalo mozzarella and cannoli (pastry shells with a sweet filling of ricotta or custard). Here, businesses still close for lunch and Sunday *pranzo* (lunch) remains a long, sacred family affair. Famished? You've come to the right place.

The Year in Food

While *sagre* (local food festivals) go into overdrive in autumn, there's never a bad time to raise your fork in southern Italy.

Spring (Mar–May)

Come for asparagus, artichokes and Easter specialities like Naples' *casatiello:* rustic-style bread stuffed with Neapolitan salami, pancetta and hard cheeses.

Summer (Jun–Aug)

Eggplants, peppers, berries and fresh seafood by the sea. Beat the heat with Sicilian *granite* (ices made with coffee, fresh fruit, pistachios or almonds).

Autumn (Sep–Nov)

Hearty chestnuts, mushrooms and game. In September, celebrate fish couscous at San Vito's famous Couscous Fest.

Winter (Dec–Feb)

Time for festive treats like Campania's *raffioli* (sponge and marzipan biscuits) and Sicily's *cobaita* (hard, sesame-seed confectionery).

Food Experiences

So much produce, so many specialities, so little time! Fine-tune your culinary radar with the following edible musts.

Meals of a Lifetime

Il Frantoio, Ostuni (p144) Legendary 10-course lunches at an olive grove–fringed *masseria* (working farm).

Il Focolare, Ischia (p87) A carnivorous, Slow Food stalwart, especially famous for its *coniglio all'ischitana* (Ischian-style rabbit).

President, Pompeii (p101) A rising Michelin star, serving whimsical re-interpretations of Campanian cuisine.

Pizzeria Starita, Naples (p75) Over 60 types of perfectly wood-fired pizza in a historic Neapolitan pizzeria.

Soul Kitchen, Matera (p166) Bold, contemporary takes on Basilicatan flavours and traditions.

Osteria Nero d'Avola, Taormina (p217) Owner Turi Siligato regales guests with tales of personally fishing and foraging for his soul-lifting, ever-changing menu.

Osteria La Bettolaccia, Trapani (p248) Savour Trapani's famous fish couscous and other Slow Food seafood classics.

Cheap Treats

Arancini Deep-fried rice balls stuffed with *ragù* (meat sauce), tomato and vegetables.

Crocchè Deep-fried, mozzarella-filled potato croquettes.

Pizza fritta Neapolitan fried pizza dough stuffed with salami, dried lard cubes, smoked *provola* (provolone) cheese, ricotta and tomato.

Sgagliozze Deep-fried polenta cubes served streetside in Bari.

Pane e panelle Palermo chickpea fritters on a sesame roll.

Mozzarella di bufala Silky, snow-white mozzarella made with local buffalo milk.

Gelato The best Italian gelato uses seasonal ingredients and natural colours.

Dare to Try

Pani ca meusa A Palermo sandwich of beef spleen and lungs dipped in boiling lard.

Sanguinaccio Hearty pig's blood sausage, particularly popular in Calabria and Basilicata.

Cavallo Puglia's Salento region is famous for its horse meat. Taste it in dishes like *pezzetti di cavallo* (horse meat casserole with tomato, celery, carrot and bay leaf).

Stigghiola A classic Sicilian dish of grilled sheep's or goat's intestines stuffed with onions and parsley, and seasoned with salt or lemon.

'Mpanatigghiu A traditional Sicilian pastry from Modica, filled with minced meat, almonds and the town's famous chocolate.

Local Specialities

The Italian term for civic pride is *campanilismo*, but a more accurate word would be *formaggismo:* loyalty to the local cheese. Clashes among medieval duchies and principalities involving castle sieges and boiling oil have been replaced by competition in speciality foods and wine. Keep reading for a gut-rumbling overview of the Mezzogiono's culinary nuances.

Campania

Explosions of flavour come with the territory in Campania, where intensely sweet tomatoes and superlative citrus thrive in volcanic soil. In Naples, tuck into Italy's best pizza, a wood-fired masterpiece of thin charred crust and slightly chewy dough. Its on-the-go sibling is the surprisingly light *pizza fritta:* fried pizza dough stuffed with salami, dried lard cubes, smoked *provola* cheese, ricotta and tomato.

Vegetarian decadence comes in the form of *parmigiana di melanzana* (fried eggplants layered with hard-boiled eggs, mozzarella, onion, tomato sauce and basil), while the city's signature *spaghetti alla puttanesca* (whore's spaghetti) blends tomatoes and black olives with capers, anchovies and (in some cases) a dash of red chilli. Altogether more virtuous is Campania's unique *friarielli,* a bitter vegetable similar to broccoli rabe, *saltata in padella* (pan-fried), spiked with *peperoncino* (red

Ice cream in Naples

chilli) and often served with rustic *salsiccia di maiale* (pork sausage).

At the sweeter end of the spectrum are the *sfogliatella* (sweetened ricotta-filled pastry), *babà* (rum-soaked sponge cake) and *pastiera* (latticed tart filled with ricotta, cream, candied fruits and cereals flavoured with orange-blossom water).

Both Caserta and the Cilento region produce Italy's finest *mozzarella di bufala* (buffalo mozzarella), a star ingredient in Capri's refreshing *insalata caprese* (mozzarella, tomato and basil salad). The neighbouring island of Ischia is famed for its succulent *coniglio all'ischitana,* claypot-cooked local rabbit with garlic, chilli, tomato, basil, thyme and white wine.

Back on the mainland, Sorrento peddles sizzling *gnocchi alla sorrentina* (oven-baked gnocchi drizzled with mozzarella and *parmigiano reggiano* cheese) and ricotta-stuffed cannelloni, while the Amalfi Coast has no shortage of fish and seafood-based dishes. This star-studded coast is also famous for two larder essentials: Cetara's *colatura di alici* (an intense anchovy essence) and Salerno's Colline Salernitane DOP olive oil.

WHAT TO BOOK

Avoid disappointment with the following simple tips:

➡ Book high-end and popular restaurants, especially for Friday and Saturday evenings and Sunday lunch.

➡ In major tourist centres, always book restaurants in the summer high season and during Easter and Christmas.

➡ Book culinary and wine courses, such as Lecce's popular Awaiting Table (p150) cooking course, at least two months in advance.

Shops in Naples (p57)

Puglia, Basilicata & Calabria

Head southeast to Puglia for peppery olive oil, crunchy *pane* (bread), and honest *cucina povera*. Carbolicious snacks include *puccia* (bread with olives) and ring-shaped *taralli* (pretzel-like biscuits), while breadcrumbs lace everything from *strascinati con la mollica* (pasta with breadcrumbs and anchovies) to *tiella di verdure* (baked vegetable casserole). Vegetables play a leading role in Puglian cuisine, with herbivorous classics including *maritata,* a dish of boiled chicory, escarole, celery and fennel layered alternatively with *pecorino* (sheep's milk cheese) and pepper and covered in broth.

Puglia's coastline delivers spiky *ricci di mare* (sea urchins), caught south of Bari in spring and autumn. They might be a challenge to crack open, but once you've dipped your bread into the delicate, dark-red roe, chances are you'll be glad that you persisted. Easier to slurp is *zuppa di pesce* (fish soup), *riso cozze e patate* (baked rice, mussels and potatoes) and *polpo in umido* or *alla pignata* (steamed octopus teamed with garlic, onion, tomatoes, parsley, olive oil, black pepper, bay leaves and cinnamon).

Basilicata and Calabria have a knack for salami and sausages – pigs here are prized and fed on natural foods such as acorns. Basilicata's *lucanica* or *lucanega* sausage is seasoned with fennel, pepper, *peperoncino* and salt, and eaten fresh – roasted on a coal fire – or dried, or preserved in olive oil. The drooling continues with *soppressata,* the pork sausage from Rivello made from finely chopped pork grazed in pastures, dried and pressed and kept in extra-virgin olive oil, and *pezzenta* ('beggars' – probably a reference to their peasant origins) made from pork scraps and spicy Senise peppers. Across the border, the Calabrians turn pig's fat, organ meats and hot *peperoncino* into spicy, cured *'nduja* sausage.

In August, look out for red eggplants (aubergines), unique to Rotonda and Basilicata, but originally from Africa. Spicy and bitter, they're often dried, pickled or preserved in oil and served as antipasti. When autumn comes, the mountains yield delicious *funghi* (mushrooms) of all shapes and sizes. A favourite of the ancient Romans was the small, wild umbel oyster mushroom, eaten fried with garlic

Gelato

and parsley or accompanying lamb or vegetables. One of the best spots for a little mushroom hunting is Calabria's Parco Nazionale della Sila, which even hosts a *fungo*-focussed *sagra* (local festival).

For a year-round treat, nibble on provolone, a semi-hard, wax-rind cheese. Though now commonly produced in the northern Italian regions of Lombardy and the Veneto, its roots lie firmly in Basilicata. Like mozzarella, the cheese is made using the *pasta filata* method, which sees the curd heated until it becomes stringy (*filata*). Aged two to three months, *provolone dolce* is milder and sweeter than the more piquant *provolone piccante*, which is aged for more than four months.

Sicily

Sicily's history as a cultural crossroad shines through in its sweet and sour flavours. The Saracens brought the eggplant and spiced up dishes with saffron and sultanas. These ancient Arab and North African influences live on in western Sicily's fragrant fish couscous, as well as the island's spectacular sweets. Sink your teeth

into *cannoli, cuccia* (grain, honey and ricotta cake) and the queen of Sicilian desserts, the *cassata* (made with ricotta, sugar, vanilla, diced chocolate and candied fruits). Almonds are put to heavenly use in *pasta di mandorle* (almond cookies) and *frutti della Martorana,* marzipan sweets shaped to resemble fruits or vegetables. Both Arab and New World influences flavour Modica's lauded chocolate, spiked with anything from cinnamon to fiery red chilli.

Sicily's Norman invaders live on in *pasta alla Norma* (pasta with basil, eggplant, ricotta and tomato), while the island's bountiful seafood shines in staples like *pasta con le sarde* (pasta with sardines, pine nuts, raisins and wild fennel), Palermo's *sarde a beccafico alla Palermitana* (sardines stuffed with anchovies, pine nuts, currants and parsley) and Messina's *agghiotta di pesce spada* (swordfish flavoured with pine nuts, sultanas, garlic, basil and tomatoes). Swordfish also gets top billing in *involtini di pesce spada* (thinly sliced swordfish fillets rolled up and filled with breadcrumbs, capers, tomatoes and olives).

Then there are Sicily's finger-licking *buffitieri* (hot street snacks), among them *sfincione* (spongy, oily pizza made with *caciocavallo* cheese, tomatoes, onions and occasionally anchovies) and Palermo's *pane e panelle* (fried chickpea-flour fritters, often served in a roll). Other doughy morsels include *calzone* (a pocket of pizza-like dough baked with ham, cheese or other stuffings), *impanata* (bread-dough snacks stuffed with meat, vegetables or cheese) and *scaccie* (discs of bread dough spread with a filling and rolled up into a crêpe). Queen of the street scene, however, is the ubiquitous *arancino* (rice ball stuffed with meat or cheese, coated with breadcrumbs and fried).

How to Eat & Drink Like a Local

Now that your appetite is piqued, it's time for the technicalities of eating *all'italiana*.

When to Eat

Colazione (breakfast) A continental affair, often little more than a pre-work espresso, accompanied

Top: Fish market, Naples (p57)

Bottom: Pastries in Palermo (p189)

SERGIOBOCCARDO/SHUTTERSTOCK ©

by a *cornetto* (Italian croissant) or *brioche* (breakfast pastry). In Sicily, your brioche might be filled with gelato or *granita* (flavoured crushed ice).

Pranzo (lunch) A sacred time, with most businesses closing for *la pausa* (afternoon break). Traditionally the main meal of the day, lunch usually consists of a *primo* (first course), *secondo* (second course) and *dolce* (dessert). Standard restaurant times are noon to 3pm, though most locals don't lunch before 1pm.

Aperitivo Especially popular in larger cities like Naples, Palermo and Catania, post-work drinks usually take place between 7pm and 9pm, when the price of your drink includes a buffet of tasty morsels.

Cena (dinner) Traditionally a little lighter than lunch, though still a main meal. Standard restaurant times are 7.30pm to around 11pm, though many southern Italians don't sit down to dinner until 9pm or even later.

Where to Eat

Ristorante (restaurant) Formal service and refined dishes.

Trattoria Cheaper than a restaurant, with more-relaxed service and home-style classics.

Osteria Historically a tavern focused on wine, the modern version is often an intimate trattoria or wine bar offering a handful of dishes.

Enoteca Wine bars often serve snacks or meals to accompany your tipple.

Agriturismo A working farmhouse offering food made with farm-grown produce.

Pizzeria Cheap grub, cold beer and a convivial vibe. The best pizzerias are often crowded: be patient.

Tavola calda Cafeteria-style spots serving cheap pre-made food like pasta and roast meats.

Friggitoria Simple, take-away businesses specialising in deep-fried street snacks like *arancini*, *crocchè* and tempura-style vegetables.

Menu Decoder

Menù alla carta Choose whatever you like from the menu.

Menù di degustazione Degustation menu, usually consisting of six to eight 'tasting size' courses.

Menù turistico The 'tourist menu' usually signals mediocre fare – steer clear!

TABLE MANNERS

➡ Cardinal sins: skipping or being late for lunch.

➡ *Buon appetito* is what you say before eating. *Salute!* (cheers!) is the toast used for alcoholic drinks – always make eye contact when toasting.

➡ Never order a coffee *with* your lunch or dinner.

➡ Eat spaghetti with a fork, not a spoon.

➡ Don't eat bread with your pasta; using it to wipe any remaining sauce from your plate (called *fare la scarpetta*) is fine.

➡ Unless you have hollow legs, don't accept a second helping of that delicious *primo* – you might not have room for the *secondo*, *dolce*, *sopratavola* and fruit.

➡ Whoever invites usually pays. Splitting *il conto* (the bill) is common enough, itemising it is not.

➡ If invited to someone's house, bring flowers, wine or a tray of *dolcetti* from a local *pasticceria* (pastry shop).

Piatto del giorno Dish of the day.

Antipasto A hot or cold appetiser. For a tasting plate of different appetisers, request an *antipasto misto* (mixed antipasto).

Primo First course, usually a substantial pasta, rice or *zuppa* (soup) dish.

Secondo Second course, often *carne* (meat) or *pesce* (fish).

Contorno Side dish, usually *verdura* (vegetable).

Dolce Dessert, including *torta* (cake).

Sopratavola Raw vegetables such as fennel or chicory eaten after a meal.

Frutta Fruit, usually the epilogue to a meal.

Nostra produzione Made in-house.

Surgelato Frozen, usually used to denote fish or seafood that's not freshly caught.

Travel with Children

Southern Italians adore bambini (children) and acts of face pinching are as common as Vespas, espresso and olive groves. On the flipside, Italy's southern regions offer few special amenities for little ones, which makes a little planning go a long way.

Southern Italy for Kids

Southern Italy bursts with extraordinary archaeological sites and museums. But while Pompeian frescoes might thrill mum or dad, a youngster unversed in the wonders of history and art might not be quite as keen. Kids' books or films about the places you visit can help bring these sights to life.

If you're travelling with young children, punctuate museum visits with plenty of rest stops – *gelaterie* (ice-cream shops), parks and beaches are always a good backup – and always ask tourist offices about any special family activities or festivals, especially in the high-season.

For more information, see Lonely Planet's *Travel with Children* book.

Children's Highlights

Brushes with History

Galleria Borbonica (p71) Escape routes, hideouts and vintage smugglers' cars bring wartime Naples to life.

Herculaneum (p91) Smaller and better-preserved than Pompeii, Herculaneum is easier to visit in a shorter time.

Best Regions for Kids

Naples & Campania

Subterranean ruins and secret passageways in Naples will intrigue those over five. Kids under 10 may need a piggyback for part of the walk up Mt Vesuvius, though most kids and teens will enjoy exploring ancient Pompeii and Herculaneum. Ischia's bubbling beach and thermal pools have wide appeal.

Puglia, Basilicata & Calabria

Valle d'Itria in Puglia and Matera in Basilicata intrigue with otherworldly abodes. Puglia's countless soft, sandy beaches suit all ages, while its relatively flat terrain makes for easy cycling adventures. The national parks of Basilicata and Calabria offer hikes, skiing and white-water rafting for active teens.

Sicily

Fire up the imagination of primary (elementary) and high-school students with ancient temples and glittering Byzantine mosaics. Younger kids will love Sicilian puppet shows, while teens will get a kick from climbing a volcano. Young and old will appreciate Sicily's superlative sweet treats.

Valley of the Temples (p238) Agrigento's astounding Greek temples come with picnic-friendly grounds and space to move.

Castel del Monte (p131) Puglia's octagonal 13th-century castle boasts Europe's very first flush toilet.

Outdoor Thrills

Aeolian Islands (p202) Seven tiny volcanic islands off Sicily with everything from spewing lava to black-sand beaches.

Mt Vesuvius (p95) Play 'spot the landmark' from the summit of Naples' formidable, slumbering volcano.

Ischia (p86) Catch a water taxi to a bubbling thermal beach or pool-hop at a verdant spa resort.

Pollino National Park (p172) Kids over 10 can join the grown-ups for white-water-rafting adventures in Calabria's wilds.

Maratea (p171) Shallow, sandy beaches and a very walkable town centre.

Kooky Kicks

Cimitero delle Fontanelle (p72) Tour Naples' bizarre Fontanelle Cemetery, stacked with skulls, shrines and fantastical tales.

Alberobello (p141) Was that Snow White? Imagination runs riot in this World Heritage–listed town in Puglia, famous for its cone-roofed *trulli* abodes.

Matera (p161) Relive the *Flintstones* exploring Matera's Unesco-protected *sassi* (stone houses carved out of caves and cliffs).

Piccolo Teatro dei Pupi (p232) Syracuse's little Sicilian puppet theatre brings old Sicilian tales to vivid life.

Planning

Where to Stay

Southern Italy's *agriturismi* (farmstays) are especially wonderful for families: think self-catering facilities, fresh air and outdoor activities that might include any number of options, from horse-riding, cycling and swimming, to animal feeding, olive picking and cooking. Kids will love slumbering in conical-roofed *trulli* and atmospheric *masserie* (fortified farmhouses), among them family-friendly Masseria Torre Coccaro (p144) near Alberobello in Puglia.

Self-contained apartments are also sound options for families, offering multibed rooms, guest kitchens, lounge facilities and, often, washing machines. In high season (July and August), many camping grounds offer activities for kids.

Book accommodation in advance whenever possible. In hotels, some double rooms can't accommodate an extra bed for kids, so always check. If your toddler is small enough to share your bed, some hotels will let you do so for free. The website www.booking.com specifies the 'kid policy' for each hotel listed and any extra charges incurred.

Dining

Kids are more than welcome at most eateries. Highchairs are often available and though kids' menus are rare, it's perfectly acceptable to order a *mezzo piatto* (half portion).

Arancini (rice balls), *crocchè* (potato croquettes) and *pizza al taglio* (pizza by the slice) are great on-the-run snacks, as are *panini* from little grocery stores.

You can buy baby formula in powder or liquid form, as well as sterilising solutions such as Milton, at pharmacies. Fresh cow's milk is sold in cartons in supermarkets and in bars with a 'Latteria' sign. UHT milk is popular and in many out-of-the-way areas the only kind available.

Transportation

Arrange car rental before leaving home. Car seats for infants and children are available from most car-rental agencies, but should be booked in advance.

Public transport discounts are available for children. In some cases, young children travel free if accompanied by a paying adult. Check details in specific destination coverage or ask at the tourist office. Intercity trains and buses are safe, convenient and relatively inexpensive.

Cobbled stones and potholes can make stroller use challenging. Consider purchasing an ergonomic baby carrier before leaving home.

Regions at a Glance

Home to A-list coastal destinations like Capri and the Amalfi Coast, not to mention the cultural riches of Naples, it's not surprising that Campania has traditionally played southern Italy's leading role.

Puglia and Basilicata have become the darlings of in-the-know travellers, both regions famed for their gorgeous beaches, fantastic food, architectural quirks and authentic festivals. While off-the-radar Calabria may lack big-hitter sights and cosmopolitan cities, it's well compensated by its rugged natural beauty, adventure sports and spicy, earthy cuisine.

Like Campania, Sicily offers an enviable repertoire of landscapes, from volcanic peaks and vine-laced slopes to irresistible beaches. It's also home to some of Italy's greatest Graeco-Roman temples and amphitheatres, baroque architecture, food and wine.

Naples & Campania

History
Food & Wine
Scenery

Ancient Ruins

Sitting beneath Mt Vesuvius, Neapolitans abide by the motto *carpe diem* (seize the day). And why not? All around them – at Pompeii, Herculaneum and the Campi Flegrei – they have reminders that life is short. Further afield, Paestum's stoic Greek temples defy the test of time.

Standout Specialities

Campania claims some of Italy's most iconic bites: pizza, pasta, San Marzano tomatoes, *sfogliatelle* (sweet ricotta pastries) and vibrant Falanghina wine. Head to the Cilento for buffalo mozzarella and up Ischia's hills for pit-reared *coniglio* (rabbit), slow-cooked with wild herbs.

Stunning Coastline

From the Amalfi Coast's citrus-fringed panoramas to Ischia's subtropical gardens and Capri's dramatic cliffs, the views from this coastline are as famous as its holidaying celebrities. Add thermal beaches and enchanted grottoes, and the appeal is as crystal clear as the sea itself.

p56

Puglia, Basilicata & Calabria

Beaches
Outdoor Activities
Food & Wine

Sand & Sun

Italy's northern shores may have all the drama, but the south has much of the sand. Lounge beneath white cliffs on the Gargano Peninsula, gaze at the violet sunsets in Tropea and spend summer on the golden beaches of Otranto and Gallipoli.

Pure Adrenalin

With its crush of spiky mountains, Basilicata and Calabria are top spots to go wild. Burst through the clouds in mountaintop Pietrapertosa, white-water raft down the Lao river, pick bergamot in the Aspromonte and keep an eye out for Apennine wolves.

Vibrant Flavours

Puglia has turned its poverty into a culinary art: sample vibrant, vegetable-based pasta dishes like *orecchiette con le cime di rape* ('little ears' pasta with turnip greens), taste-test creamy *burrata* (cheese made from mozzarella and cream) and toast with a rustic Salento red.

p123

Sicily

Food & Wine
History
Outdoor Activities

A Bountiful Larder

Sicilian cuisine seduces seafood lovers and sets sweet tooths on edge. Tuna, sardines, swordfish and shellfish come grilled, fried or seasoned with mint or wild fennel. Desserts, laden with citrus fruits, ricotta and nuts, include Arab-Italian dishes such as *cannoli* (pastry shells filled with sweetened ricotta), while libations span luscious Nero d'Avola to silky Marsala.

Temples & Tesserae

A Mediterranean crossroads for centuries, Sicily keeps history buffs busy with its cachet of Greek temples, Roman and Byzantine mosaics, Phoenician statues, Norman-Romanesque castles and art nouveau villas.

Volcanic Highs

Sicily's restless geology gives outdoor activities a thrilling edge. Pamper weary muscles in warm volcanic waters, hike the Aeolian Islands' dramatic coastlines or take in the natural firework displays of volcanic Stromboli and Etna.

p185

On the Road

Naples & Campania
p56

Puglia, Basilicata & Calabria
p123

Sicily
p185

Naples & Campania

Best Places to Eat

→ Casa Mele (p111)

→ Da Salvatore (p115)

→ La Cantina del Feudo (p118)

→ Salumeria (p74)

→ Soul & Fish (p105)

Best Places to Sleep

→ Atelier Ines (p74)

→ Casa Mariantonia (p83)

→ Albergo il Monastero (p87)

→ Hotel Piazza Bellini (p74)

→ Palazzo Marziale (p104)

Why Go?

Campania is the Italy of your wildest dreams; a rich, intense, hypnotic *ragù* of Arabesque street life, decadent palaces, pastel-hued villages and aria-inspiring vistas.

Few corners of Europe can match the cultural conundrums here. Should you spend the morning waltzing through chandeliered Bourbon bedrooms or the frescoed villa of a Roman emperor's wife? And which of Caravaggio's canvases shouldn't you miss: the multi-scene masterpiece inside Naples' Pio Monte della Misericordia, or the artist's brooding swansong inside the city's belle époque Palazzo Zevallos?

Mother Nature let loose in Italy's south, creating a thrilling playground of rugged mountains, steaming fumaroles, and ethereal coastal grottoes. Horse ride the slopes of Mt Vesuvius, sail the Amalfi Coast or simply soak at a thermal beach on Ischia. Afterwards, local feasts await; bubbling, wood-fired pizza in Naples, long lunches at Cilento *agriturismi* (farm stays), and lavish pastries at celebrity-status Amalfi Coast *pasticcerie* (pastry shops).

When to Go
Naples

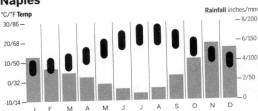

May Best month to visit the region. Warm days, with many special events on.

Jun & Sep Generally deliver summer heat without the August crowds and traffic.

Aug Hottest month; many shops and restaurants close while locals go on holiday.

NAPLES

📱 081 / POP 970,200

Italy's third-largest city is one of its oldest, most artistic and most appetising. Naples' *centro storico* (historic centre) is a Unesco World Heritage Site, its archaeological treasures are among the world's most important, and its palaces, castles and churches make Rome look positively provincial.

Then there's the food. Blessed with rich volcanic soils, a bountiful sea, and centuries of culinary know-how, the Naples region is one of Italy's epicurean heavyweights, serving up the country's best pizza, pasta and coffee, and many of its most celebrated seafood dishes, street snacks and sweet treats.

Certainly, Naples' urban sprawl can feel anarchic, tattered and unloved. But look beyond the grime, graffiti and occasional gruffness and you'll uncover a city of breathtaking frescoes, sculptures and panoramas, of unexpected elegance, of spontaneous conversations and profound humanity. Welcome to Italy's most unlikely masterpiece.

History

After founding nearby Cuma in the 8th century BC, the ancient Greeks settled the city in around 680 BC, calling it Parthenope. Under the Romans, the area became an ancient Miami of sorts: a sun-soaked spa region that drew the likes of Virgil. Dampening the bonhomie was Mt Vesuvius' eruption in AD 79.

Naples fell into Norman hands in 1139 before the French Angevins took control a century later, boosting the city's cred with the mighty Castel Nuovo. By the 16th century, Naples was under Spanish rule and riding high on Spain's colonial riches. By 1600, it was Europe's largest city and a burgeoning baroque beauty adorned by artists like Luca Giordano, Giuseppe de Ribera and Caravaggio.

Despite a devastating plague in 1656, Naples' ego soared under the Bourbons (1734–1860), with epic constructions such as the Teatro San Carlo and the Reggia di Caserta sealing the city's showcase reputation.

An ill-fated attempt at republican rule in 1799 was followed by a short stint under the French and a final period of Bourbon governance before nationalist rebel Giuseppe Garibaldi inspired the city to snip off the puppet strings and join a united Italy in 1860.

Although the Nazis took Naples in 1943, they were quickly forced out by a series of popular uprisings between 26 and 30 September, famously known as the *Quattro giornate di Napoli* (Four Days of Naples). Led by locals, especially by young *scugnizzi* (Neapolitan for 'street urchins') and ex-soldiers, the street battles paved the way for the Allies to enter the city on 1 October.

Despite setting up a provisional government in Naples, the Allies were confronted with an anarchic mass of troops, German prisoners of war and bands of Italian fascists all competing with the city's starving population for food. Overwhelmed, Allied authorities turned to the underworld for assistance. As long as the Allies agreed to turn a blind eye to their black-market activities, the Mafia was willing to help. And so the Camorra (Neapolitan Mafia) was given a boost.

On 23 November 1980, a devastating earthquake struck the mountainous area of Irpinia, 100km east of Naples. The quake, which left more than 2700 people dead and thousands more homeless, caused extensive damage in Naples. It is believed that US$6.4 billion of the funds poured into the region to assist the victims and rebuilding ended up in the pockets of the Camorra.

In 2011, Neapolitan voters elected the city's current mayor, Luigi de Magistris, a youthful former public prosecutor and vocal critic of both the mafia and government corruption. Determined to improve the city's liveability, de Magistris has pushed through a number of initiatives, including the transformation of the Lungomare from a traffic-clogged thoroughfare into a pedestrian and bike-friendly waterfront strip.

◎ Sights

◎ Centro Storico

★Complesso Monumentale
di Santa Chiara   BASILICA

(Map p62; 📱 081 551 66 73; www.monastero disantachiara.com; Via Santa Chiara 49c; basilica free, Complesso Monumentale adult/reduced €6/4.50; ⊙basilica 7.30am-1pm & 4.30-8pm, Complesso Monumentale 9.30am-5.30pm Mon-Sat, 10am-2.30pm Sun; Ⓜ Dante) Vast, Gothic and cleverly deceptive, the mighty **Basilica di Santa Chiara** stands at the heart of this tranquil monastery complex. The church was severely damaged in WWII: what you see today is a 20th-century recreation of Gagliardo Primario's 14th-century original. Adjoining it are the basilica's **cloisters**, adorned with brightly coloured 17th-century majolica tiles and frescoes.

Naples & Campania Highlights

1 Pompeii (p95) Channelling the ancients on the ill-fated streets of this erstwhile Roman city.

2 Grotta Azzurra (p82) Being bewitched by Capri's ethereal blue cave.

3 Sentieri degli Dei (p113) Walking with the gods on the Amalfi Coast.

4 Cappella Sansevero (p60) Re-evaluating artistic ingenuity in Naples.

5 Procida (p89) Lunching by lapping waves on the Bay of Naples' pastel-hued smallest island

6 Negombo (p86) Indulging in a little thermal therapy on Ischia.

7 Villa Rufolo (p114) Attending a concert at this dreamy Ravello villa and its cascading gardens.

8 Reggia di Caserta (p101) Pretending you're royalty at this monumental Unesco-listed palace complex.

9 Paestum (p119) Admiring ancient Hellenic ingenuity in the colossal ruins of Magna Graecia.

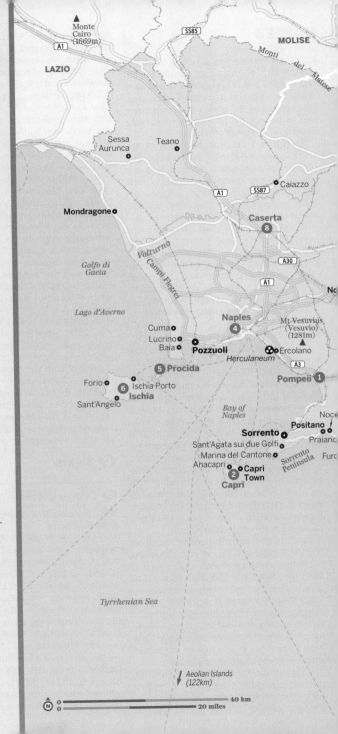

Naples

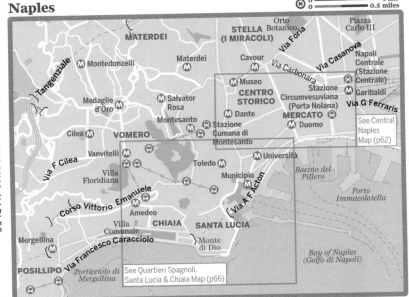

While the Angevin porticoes date back to the 14th century, the cloisters took on their current look in the 18th century thanks to the landscaping work of Domenico Antonio Vaccaro. The walkways that divide the central garden of lavender and citrus trees are lined with 72 ceramic-tiled octagonal columns connected by benches. Painted by Donato Giuseppe Massa, the tiles depict various rural scenes, from hunting sessions to vignettes of peasant life. The four internal walls are covered with soft, whimsical 17th-century frescoes of Franciscan tales.

Adjacent to the cloisters, a small and elegant museum of mostly ecclesiastical props also features the excavated ruins of a 1st-century spa complex, including a remarkably well-preserved *laconicum* (sauna).

Commissioned by Robert of Anjou for his wife Sancia di Maiorca, the monastic complex was built to house 200 monks and the tombs of the Angevin royal family. Dissed as a 'stable' by Robert's ungrateful son Charles of Anjou, the basilica received a luscious baroque makeover by Domenico Antonio Vaccaro, Gaetano Buonocore and Giovanni Del Gaizo in the 18th century before taking a direct hit during an Allied air raid on 4 August 1943. Its reconstruction was completed in 1953. Features that did survive the fire include part of a 14th-century fresco to the left of the main door and a chapel containing the tombs of the Bourbon kings from Ferdinand I to Francesco II.

The church forecourt makes a cameo in Pier Paolo Pasolini's film *Il Decameron* (The Decameron), itself based on Giovanni Boccaccio's 14th-century novel.

★ **Cappella Sansevero**   CHAPEL
(Map p62; ☏ 081 551 84 70; www.museosansevero.it; Via Francesco de Sanctis 19; adult/reduced €7/5; ☉ 9.30am-6.30pm Wed-Mon; M Dante) It's in this Masonic-inspired baroque chapel that you'll find Giuseppe Sanmartino's incredible sculpture, *Cristo velato* (Veiled Christ), its marble veil so realistic that it's tempting to try to lift it and view Christ underneath. It's one of several artistic wonders that include Francesco Queirolo's sculpture *Disinganno* (Disillusion), Antonio Corradini's *Pudicizia* (Modesty) and riotously colourful frescoes by Francesco Maria Russo, the latter untouched since their creation in 1749.

Originally built around the end of the 16th century to house the tombs of the di Sangro family, the chapel was given its current baroque fit-out by Prince Raimondo di Sangro, who, between 1749 and 1766, commissioned the finest artists to adorn the interior. In Queirolo's *Disinganno,* the man trying to untangle himself from a net represents Raimondo's father, Antonio, Duke of Torremaggiore. After the premature death of his wife, Antonio abandoned the young Raimondo, choosing instead a life of travel and hedonistic pleasures. Repentant in his later years, he returned to Naples and joined the priesthood, his attempt to free himself from sin represented in Queirolo's masterpiece.

Even more poignant is Antonio Corradini's *Pudicizia,* whose veiled female figure pays tribute to Raimondo's mother, Cecilia Gaetani d'Aquila d'Aragona. Raimondo was only 11 months old when she died, and the statue's lost gaze and broken plaque represent a life cruelly cut short.

The chapel's original polychrome marble flooring was badly damaged in a major collapse involving the chapel and the neighbouring Palazzo dei di Sangro in 1889. Designed by Francesco Celebrano, the flooring survives in fragmentary form in the passageway leading off from the chapel's right side. The passageway leads to a staircase, at the bottom of which you'll find two meticulously preserved human arterial systems – one of a man, the other of a woman. Debate still circles the models: are the arterial systems real or reproductions? And if they are real, just how was such an incredible state of preservation achieved? More than two centuries on, the mystery surrounding the alchemist prince lives on.

Queues here can be notoriously long so consider purchasing your ticket online in advance for fast-track entry into the chapel; it's worth the extra €2 booking fee, especially during peak holiday periods.

Chiesa del Gesù Nuovo CHURCH

(Map p62; ☑ 081 551 86 13; Piazza del Gesù Nuovo; ⏱ 7.30am-1pm & 4-8pm Mon-Sat, 7.30am-2pm & 4-9pm Sun; Ⓜ Dante) The extraordinary Chiesa del Gesù Nuovo is an architectural Kinder Surprise. Its shell is the 15th-century, Giuseppe Valeriani–designed facade of Palazzo Sanseverino, converted to create the 16th-century church. Inside, piperno-stone sobriety gives way to a gob-smacking blast of baroque that could make the Vatican blush: a vainglorious showcase for the work of toptier artists such as Francesco Solimena, Luca Giordano and Cosimo Fanzago.

The church is the final resting place of much-loved local saint Giuseppe Moscati (1880–1927), a doctor who served the city's poor. Adjacent to the right transept, the Sale

di San Giuseppe Moscati (Rooms of St Joseph Moscati) include a recreation of the great man's study, complete with the armchair in which he died. Scan the walls for *ex-votos,* gifts offered by the faithful for miracles purportedly received. The church itself received a miracle of sorts on 4 August 1943, when a bomb dropped on the site failed to explode. Its shell is aptly displayed beside the *ex-votos.*

The church flanks the northern side of beautiful **Piazza del Gesù Nuovo,** a favourite late-night hang-out for students and lefties. At its centre soars Giuseppe Genuino's lavish **Guglia dell'Immacolata** (Map p62; Ⓜ Dante), an obelisk built between 1747 and 1750. On 8 December, the Feast of the Immacolata, firemen scramble up to the top to place a wreath of flowers at the Virgin Mary's feet.

Via San Gregorio Armeno STREET

(Map p62; ☒ E1, E2 to Via Duomo) Dismissed by serious collectors, this narrow street remains famous across Italy for its *pastori* (Christmas crib figurines) nonetheless. Connecting Spaccanapoli with Via dei Tribunali, the *decumanus maior* (main road) of ancient Neapolis, its clutter of shops and workshops peddle everything from doting donkeys to kitsch celebrity caricatures. At No 8 you'll find the workshop of **Giuseppe Ferrigno,** whose terracotta figurines are the most famous and esteemed on the strip.

★ Complesso Monumentale di San Lorenzo Maggiore ARCHAEOLOGICAL SITE

(Map p62; ☑ 081 211 08 60; www.sanlorenzo maggiorenapoli.it; Via dei Tribunali 316; church admission free, excavations & museum adult/reduced €9/7; ⏱ church 8am-7pm, excavations & museum 9.30am-5.30pm; ☒ E1, E2 to Via Duomo) The **basilica** at this richly layered religious complex is deemed one of Naples' finest medieval buildings. Aside from Ferdinando Sanfelice's facade, the Cappella al Rosario and the Cappellone di Sant'Antonio, its baroque makeover was stripped away last century to reveal its austere, Gothic elegance. Beneath the basilica is a sprawl of extraordinary Graeco-Roman **ruins,** best explored on one of the regular one-hour guided tours (€1).

To better understand the ruins, start your explorations in the **Museo dell'Opera di San Lorenzo Maggiore,** which includes a model of the area as it appeared in ancient times. The museum also includes an intriguing collection of local archaeological finds, including Graeco-Roman sarcophagi, ceramics

Central Naples

400 m
0.2 miles

Catacombe di San Gennaro (1km)
Palazzo Reale di Capodimonte (2km)
Piazza Museo
Museo Nazionale
Museo Archeologico Nazionale
Via Tommasi
Via Brogia
Via Santa Maria di Costantinopoli
Via Bellini
Via Enrico Pessina
Via Port'Alba
Piazza Dante
M Dante
Via Toledo
Piazza Carità
Via Pignasecca
Via G Brombeis

Via S Gaudioso
Vico Giganti
Vico d'Afflitto
Via d'Anticaglia
Via Duomo
Cerasiello B&B (350m)
MADRE (50m)
Via Santissimi Apostoli
Duomo
Pio Monte della Misericordia
Vicolo Sedil Capuano
Via S Nicola dei Caserti
Via del Tribunali
Via S Nicola dei Caserti
Via Vico della Pace

Via S Pisanelli
Via San Paolo
Complesso Monumentale di San Lorenzo Maggiore
Via San Gregorio Armeno
Vico Zuroli
CENTRO STORICO
Via Vicaria Vecchia
Via del'Annunziata
Via C Muzii

Via Atri
Via F del Giudice
Via del Sole
Piazza Luigi Miraglia
Piazza Bellini
Cappella Sansevero
Via San Sebastiano
Via San Biagio dei Librai
Via dei Cimbri

Via S Benedetto Croce
Complesso Monumentale di Santa Chiara
Via San Chiara
Piazza San Domenico Maggiore
Vico San Domenico Maggiore
Piazza del Gesù Nuovo
Via S Anna dei Lombardi
Via D'Lioy
Piazza Carità

Vico San Severino
Vico S Nicola al Nilo
Via Donnaromita
Via Mezzocannone
Vico San Geronimo
Largo Giusso
Via G Paladino
Via B Capasso
Corso Umberto I
Piazza San Domenico Maggiore
Via Toledo
Via Donnalbina

Piazza Nicola Amore
Via Duomo
Duomo M
Via Scialoia
Corso Umberto I
Piazzetta Orefici
See Quartieri Spagnoli, Santa Lucia & Chiala Map (p66)

Piazza Principe Umberto
Via Carbonara
Via Duchesca
Via PS Mancini
Via Ranieri
Via del'Annunziata
Via S Nicola dei Caserti

Corso Novara
Via Firenze
Alibus Bus (Stazione Centrale stop)
Napoli Museo M
Stazione Centrale
Garibaldi M
Napoli (Stazione Centrale)
Piazza Garibaldi
Garibaldi M
Stazione Circumvesuviana (Piazza Garibaldi)
Terminal Bus
Metropark
Eccellenze Campane (1km)
Via S Cosmo Fuori Porta Nolana
Stazione Circumvesuviana (Porta Nolana)

Via G Pica
Via Nolana
Via Lavinaio
Corso G Garibaldi
Via C Carmignano
Via Sopramuro
Via A de Pace
Vico Barre
Via G Savarese
MERCATO
Piazza del Mercato
Piazza Masaniello
Via Sant'Eligio
Via Duca di San Donato
Via D Carmine
Via Nuova Marina
Calata Villa del Popolo

Via E Cosenz
Via S Giovanni
Via Amerigo Vespucci
Calata della Marinella
Piazza G Pepe

Central Naples

NAPLES & CAMPANIA NAPLES

and crockery from the digs below. Other treasures include vivacious 9th-century ceramics, Angevin frescoes, paintings by Giuseppe Marullo and Luigi Velpi, and fine examples of 17th- and 18th-century ecclesiastical vestments.

The ruins themselves will see you walking past ancient bakeries, wineries, laundries and barrel-vaulted rooms that once formed part of the city's two-storey *macellum* (market).

Above them, the basilica itself was commenced in 1270 by French architects, who built the apse. Local architects took over the following century, recycling ancient columns in the nave. Catherine of Austria, who died in 1323, is buried here in a beautiful mosaiced tomb. Legend has it that this was where Boccaccio first fell for Mary of Anjou, the inspiration for his character Fiammetta, while the poet Petrarch called the adjoining convent home in 1345.

★ Pio Monte
della Misericordia   CHURCH, MUSEUM
(Map p62; ☑081 44 69 44; www.piomontedella miscricordia.it; Via dei Tribunali 253; adult/reduced €7/5; ☉9am-6pm Mon-Sat, to 2.30pm Sun; ◘E1, E2 to Via Duomo) The 1st floor gallery of this octagonal, 17th-century church delivers a small, satisfying collection of Renaissance and baroque art, including works by Francesco de Mura, Giuseppe de Ribera, Andrea Vaccaro and Paul van Somer. It's also home to contemporary artworks by Italian and foreign artists, each inspired by Caravaggio's masterpiece *Le sette opere di Misericordia*

(The Seven Acts of Mercy). Considered by many to be the most important painting in Naples, you'll find it above the main altar in the ground-floor chapel.

Magnificently demonstrating the artist's chiaroscuro style, which had a revolutionary impact in Naples, *Le sette opere di Misericordia* was considered unique in its ability to illustrate the various acts in one seamlessly choreographed scene. On display in the 1st-floor gallery is the *Declaratoria del 14 Ottobre 1607*, an original church document acknowledging payment of 400 ducats to Caravaggio for the masterpiece. The painting itself is best viewed from the 1st-floor gallery's Sala del Coretto (Coretto Room), where the lighting used to illuminate the canvas is less glary.

On the opposite side of the street stands the **Guglia di San Gennaro** (Map p62; Piazza Riario Sforza; ◘C55 to Via Duomo). Dating back to 1636, with stonework by Cosimo Fanzago and a bronze statue by Tommaso Montani, the obelisk is a soaring *grazie* (thank you) to the city's patron saint for protecting Naples from the 1631 eruption of Mt Vesuvius.

★ Duomo   CATHEDRAL
(Map p62; ☑081 44 90 97; Via Duomo 149; cathedral/baptistry free/€2; ☉cathedral 8.30am-1.30pm & 2.30-7.30pm Mon-Sat, 8am-1pm & 4.30-7.30pm Sun, baptistry 8.30am-12.30pm & 4-6.30pm Mon-Sat, 8.30am-1pm Sun; ◘E1, E2 to Via Duomo) Whether you go for Giovanni Lanfranco's fresco in the **Cappella di San Gennaro** (Chapel of St Janarius), the 4th-century mosaics

in the baptistry, or the thrice-annual miracle of San Gennaro, do not miss Naples' cathedral. Kick-started by Charles I of Anjou in 1272 and consecrated in 1315, it was largely destroyed in a 1456 earthquake, with copious nips and tucks over the subsequent centuries.

Among these is the gleaming neo-Gothic facade, only added in the late 19th century. Step inside and you'll immediately notice the central nave's gilded coffered ceiling, studded with late-mannerist art. The high sections of the nave and the transept are the work of baroque overachiever Luca Giordano.

Off the right aisle, the 17th-century Cappella di San Gennaro (also known as the Chapel of the Treasury) was designed by Giovanni Cola di Franco and completed in 1637. The most sought-after artists of the period worked on the chapel, creating one of Naples' greatest baroque legacies. Highlights here include Giuseppe de Ribera's gripping canvas *St Gennaro Escaping the Furnace Unscathed* and Giovanni Lanfranco's dizzying dome fresco. Hidden away in a strongbox behind the altar is a 14th-century silver bust in which sit the skull of San Gennaro and the two phials that hold his miraculously liquefying blood.

The next chapel eastwards contains an urn with the saint's bones and a cupboard full of femurs, tibias and fibulas. Below the high altar is the Cappella Carafa, a Renaissance chapel built to house yet more of the saint's remains.

Off the left aisle lies the 4th-century Basilica di Santa Restituta, subject to an almost complete makeover after the earthquake of 1688. From it you can access the Battistero di San Giovanni in Fonte. Western Europe's oldest baptistry, it's encrusted with fragments of glittering 4th-century mosaics. The Duomo's subterranean archaeological zone, which includes fascinating remains of Greek and Roman buildings and roads, remains closed indefinitely.

MADRE GALLERY
(Museo d'Arte Contemporanea Donnaregina; ☑ 081 1931 3016; www.madrenapoli.it; Via Settembrini 79; adult/reduced €7/3.50, Mon free; ◷ 10am-7.30pm Mon & Wed-Sat, to 8pm Sun; ◻ E1, E2 to Via Duomo; Ⓜ Piazza Cavour) When *Madonna and Child* overload hits, reboot at Naples' museum of modern and contemporary art. Start on level three – the setting for temporary exhibitions – before hitting level two's permanent collection of painting, sculpture, photography and installations from prolific 20th- and 21st-century artists. Among these are Andy Warhol, Gilbert & George and Cindy Sherman, as well as Italian heavyweights Mario Merz and Michelangelo Pistoletto. Specially commissioned installations from the likes of Anish Kapoor and Rebecca Horn round things off on level one.

★ **Museo Archeologico Nazionale** MUSEUM
(Map p62; ☑ 848 80 02 88, from mobile 06 3996 7050; www.museoarcheologiconapoli.it; Piazza Museo Nazionale 19; adult/reduced €12/6; ◷ 9am-7.30pm Wed-Mon; Ⓜ Museo, Piazza Cavour) Naples' National Archaeological Museum serves up one of the world's finest collections of Graeco-Roman artefacts. Originally a cavalry barracks and later seat of the city's university, the museum was established by the Bourbon king Charles VII in the late 18th century to house the antiquities he inherited from his mother, Elisabetta Farnese, as well as treasures looted from Pompeii and Herculaneum. Star exhibits include the celebrated *Toro Farnese* (Farnese Bull) sculpture and a series of awe-inspiring mosaics from Pompeii's Casa del Fauno.

Before tackling the collection, consider investing in the *National Archaeological Museum of Naples* (€12), published by Electa; if you want to concentrate on the highlights, audio guides (€5) are available in English. It's also worth calling ahead to ensure that the galleries you want to see are open, as staff shortages often mean that sections of the museum close for part of the day.

Downstairs is the impressive, recently revamped Borgia collection of Egyptian epigraphs and relics, organised around themes including Tombs and Grave Goods, Mummification and Magic. The ground-floor Farnese collection of colossal Greek and Roman sculptures features the *Toro Farnese* and a muscle-bound *Ercole* (Hercules). Sculpted in the early 3rd century AD and noted in the writings of Pliny, the *Toro Farnese,* probably a Roman copy of a Greek original, depicts the humiliating death of Dirce, Queen of Thebes. Carved from a single colossal block of marble, the sculpture was discovered in 1545 near the Baths of Caracalla in Rome and was restored by Michelangelo, before eventually being shipped to Naples in 1787. *Ercole* was discovered in the same Roman excavations, albeit without his legs. When they turned up at a later dig, the Bourbons had them fitted.

If you're short on time, take in both these masterpieces before heading straight to the

CATACOMBA DI SAN GENNARO

Naples' oldest and most sacred catacombs, Catacombe di San Gennaro (☎081 744 37 14; www.catacombedinapoli.it; Via Capodimonte 13; adult/reduced €9/5; ⊙1hr tours every hour 10am-5pm Mon-Sat, to 2pm Sun; ☐R4, 178 to Via Capodimonte), became a Christian pilgrimage site when San Gennaro's body was interred here in the 5th century. The carefully restored site allows visitors to experience an evocative other world of tombs, corridors and broad vestibules, its treasures including 2nd-century Christian frescoes, 5th-century mosaics and the oldest known portrait of San Gennaro.

The catacombs are home to three types of tomb, each corresponding to a specific social class. The wealthy opted for the open-room *cubiculum,* originally guarded by gates and adorned with colourful wall frescoes. One *cubiculum* to the left of the entrance features an especially beautiful funerary fresco of a mother, father and child: it's made up of three layers of fresco, one commissioned for each death. The smaller, rectangular wall niches, known as *loculum,* were the domain of the middle classes, while the *forme* (floor tombs) were reserved for the poor.

Further ahead you'll stumble upon the *basilica minore* (minor basilica), home to the tombs of San Gennaro and 5th-century archbishop of Naples Giovanni I. Sometime between 413 and 431, Giovanni I accompanied the martyr's remains from Pozzuoli to Naples, burying them here before Lombard prince Sico I of Benevento snatched them in the 9th century. The *basilica minore* also harbours fragments of a fresco depicting Naples' first bishop, Sant'Aspreno. The city's bishops were buried here until the 11th century.

Close to the *basilica minore* is a 3rd-century tomb whose Pompeiian-hued artwork employs both Christian and pagan elements. In the image of three women building a castle, the figures represent the three virtues, while the castle symbolises the Church.

The lower level is even older, dating back to the 2nd century and speckled with typically pagan motifs like fruit and animals. The painting on the side of San Gennaro's tomb – depicting the saint with Mt Vesuvius and Mt Somma in the background – is the first known image of San Gennaro as the protector of Naples. Also on the lower level is the Basilica di Agrippino, named in honour of Sant'Agrippino. The sixth bishop of Naples, Agrippino was also the first Christian to be buried in the catacombs, back in the 3rd century.

Tours of the catacombs are run by the Cooperativa Sociale Onlus 'La Paranza' (p72), whose ticket office is to the left of the Chiesa di Madre di Buon Consiglio (☎081 741 00 06; Via Capodimonte 13; ⊙8am-noon & 5-7pm Mon-Sat, 9am-1pm & 5-7pm Sun; ☐R4, 178 to Via Capodimonte), a snack-sized replica of St Peter's in Rome completed in 1960. The co-operative also runs a fascinating Sunday morning walking tour called Il Miglio Sacro (The Holy Mile; adult/reduced €15/13), which explores the neighbouring Sanità district. It must be pre-booked; see its website for details.

The catacombs themselves also host occasional theatrical and live-music performances; see the website for upcoming events.

---

mezzanine floor, home to an exquisite collection of mosaics, mostly from Pompeii. Of the series taken from the Casa del Fauno, it is *La battaglia di Alessandro contro Dario* (The Battle of Alexander against Darius) that really stands out. The best-known depiction of Alexander the Great, the 20-sq-metre mosaic was probably made by Alexandrian craftsmen working in Italy around the end of the 2nd century BC.

Beyond the mosaics, the Gabinetto Segreto (Secret Chamber) contains a small but much-studied collection of ancient erotica. Pan is caught in the act with a nanny goat in the most famous piece – a small and surprisingly sophisticated statue taken from the Villa dei Papiri in Herculaneum. You'll also find a series of nine paintings depicting erotic positions – a menu for brothel patrons.

Originally the royal library, the Sala Meridiana (Great Hall of the Sundial) on the 1st floor is home to the *Farnese Atlante,* a statue of Atlas carrying a globe on his shoulders, as well as various paintings from the Farnese collection. Look up to find Pietro Bardellino's colourful 1781 fresco depicting the (short-lived) triumph of Ferdinand IV of Bourbon and Marie Caroline of Austria in Rome.

The rest of the 1st floor is largely devoted to fascinating discoveries from Pompeii,

Quartieri Spagnoli, Santa Lucia & Chiaia

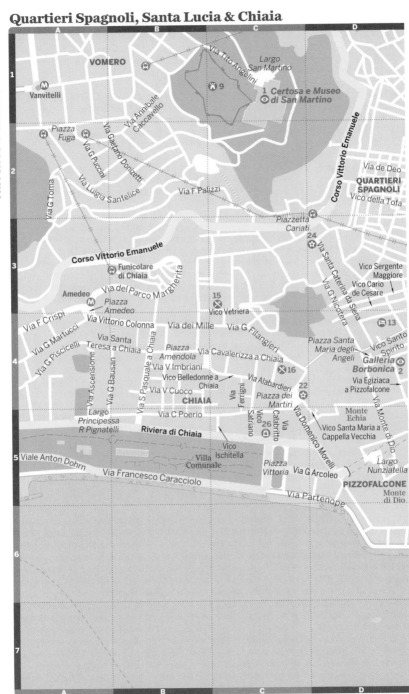

VOMERO

Via Tito Angelini

Largo San Martino

9

1 Certosa e Museo di San Martino

M Vanvitelli

Via Annibale Caccavello

Piazza Fuga

Via Gaetano Donizetti

Via G Puccini

Via Luigia Sanfelice

Via F Palizzi

Via G Toma

Corso Vittorio Emanuele

QUARTIERI SPAGNOLI

Via de Deo

Vico della Tofa

Piazzetta Cariati

24

Corso Vittorio Emanuele

Funicolare di Chiaia

Via del Parco Margherita

Amedeo M

Piazza Amedeo

15

Vico Vetriera

Via Santa Caterina da Siena

Via G Nicotera

Vico Sergente Maggiore

Vico Cario de Cesare

13

Via F Crispi

Via Vittorio Colonna

Via dei Mille

Via G Filangieri

Piazza Santa Maria degli Angeli

Vico Santo Spirito

Galleria Borbonica 2

Via G Martucci

Via G Piscicelli

Via Santa Teresa a Chiaia

Piazza Amendola

Via Cavalerizza a Chiaia

16

Via Egiziaca a Pizzofalcone

Via Ascensione

Via G Bausan

Via V Imbriani

Via S Pasquale a Chiaia

Vico Belledonne a Chiaia

Via Alabardieri

22

Via V Cuoco

CHIAIA

Via Ferrigni

Piazza dei Martiri

Monte Echia

Via Domenico Morelli

Vico Santa Maria a Cappella Vecchia

Largo Principessa R Pignatelli

Via C Poerio

Riviera di Chiaia

Vico Satriano

Via Calabritto

26

Largo Nunziatella

Viale Anton Dohrn

Villa Comunale

Vico Ischitella

Via Monte di Dio

PIZZOFALCONE

Piazza Vittoria

Via G Arcoleo

Monte di Dio

Via Francesco Caracciolo

Via Partenope

N
0 ——————————— 500 m
0 ——————————— 0.25 miles

Via Formale

See Central Naples Map (p62)

Via G Simonelli

Vico P Galluppi

Via Montecalvario

Via A Diaz

Via C Battisti

Via D Cerriglio

Corso Umberto I

Via G C Cortese

Piazza Bovio

Università

Toledo

Piazza Matteotti

Via D Fiorentini

14

Via S Tommaso d'Aquino

Teatro Nuovo

Vico Giardinetto

Via S Giacomo

Via Graziella

Via A Depretis

Via S Bartolomeo

Via G Melisurgo

Via Alside De Gasperi

Via Cristoforo Colombo

Calata Porta di Massa

Calata Porta di Massa

Galleria di Palazzo Zevallos Stigliano

Via Medina

Piazza del Municipio

17   3

Vico d'Aflitto

12

Via P E Imbriani

Piazza Francese

Municipio

Bacino del Piliero

Via Santa Brigida

Funicolare Centrale

23

Parco Castello

8

Alibus For Airport

Molo Angioino

Via Toledo

19

25

Via Nardones

Via Chiaia

Via San Carlo

21

10

5

Molo Beverello

Palazzo 4 Reale

Via A F Acton

Piazza del Plebiscito

Galleria della Vittoria

Via C Console

Porto Immacolatella

SANTA LUCIA

Via Pallonetto Santa Lucia

Via Santa Lucia

Via Cuma

Via Petronio

Via Nazario Sauro

Via Marino Turchi

Via Palepoli

18

Via Chiatamone   Via Lucilio

11   20

Via Partenope

Bay of Naples
(Golfo di Napoli)

Porto di Santa Lucia

Via Eldorado

7

6

BORGO MARINARO

Quartieri Spagnoli, Santa Lucia & Chiaia

Herculaneum, Boscoreale, Stabiae and Cuma. Among them are whimsical wall **frescoes** from the Villa di Agrippa Postumus and the Casa di Meleagro, extraordinary bronzes from the Villa dei Papiri, as well as ceramics, glassware, engraved coppers and Greek funerary vases.

Mercato di Porta Nolana MARKET
(Porta Nolana; ⊙ 8am-6pm Mon-Sat, to 2pm Sun; M Garibaldi) Naples at its most vociferous and intense, the Mercato di Porta Nolana is a heady, gritty street market where bellowing fishmongers and greengrocers collide with fragrant delis and bakeries, industrious Chinese traders and contraband cigarette stalls. Dive in for anything from buxom tomatoes and mozzarella to golden-fried street snacks, cheap luggage and bootleg CDs.

The market's namesake is medieval city gate **Porta Nolana**, which stands at the head of Via Sopramuro. Its two cylindrical towers, optimistically named Faith and Hope, support an arch decorated with a bas-relief of Ferdinand I of Aragon on horseback.

◉ Vomero

★ Certosa e Museo di San Martino MONASTERY, MUSEUM
(Map p66; ☎ 081 229 45 03; www.polomu sealenapoli.beniculturali.it; Largo San Martino 5; adult/reduced €6/3; ⊙ 8.30am-7.30pm Thu-Tue; M Vanvitelli, ⬚ Montesanto to Morghen) The high point (quite literally) of the Neapolitan baroque, this charterhouse-turned-museum was founded as a Carthusian monastery in the 14th century. Centred on one of the most beautiful cloisters in Italy, it has been decorated, adorned and altered over the centuries by some of Italy's finest talent, most importantly Giovanni Antonio Dosio in the 16th century and baroque master Cosimo Fanzago a century later. Nowadays, it's a superb repository of Neapolitan artistry.

The monastery's **church** and the rooms that flank it contain a feast of frescoes and paintings by some of Naples' greatest 17th-century artists, among them Francesco Solimena, Massimo Stanzione, Giuseppe de Ribera and Battista Caracciolo. In the nave, Cosimo Fanzago's inlaid marble work is simply extraordinary.

Adjacent to the church, the **Chiostro dei Procuratori** is the smaller of the monastery's two cloisters. A grand corridor on the left leads to the larger **Chiostro Grande** (Great Cloister). Originally designed by Dosio in the late 16th century and added to by Fanzago, it's a sublime composition of Tuscan-Doric porticoes, marble statues and vibrant camellias. The skulls mounted on the balustrade were a lighthearted reminder to the monks of their own mortality.

Just off the Chiostro dei Procuratori, the small **Sezione Navale** documents the history of the Bourbon navy from 1734 to 1860, and features a small collection of beautiful royal barges. The **Sezione Presepiale** houses a whimsical collection of rare Neapolitan *presepi* (nativity scenes) from the 18th and 19th centuries, including the colossal

18th-century Cuciniello creation, which covers one wall of what used to be the monastery's kitchen. The **Quarto del Priore** in the southern wing houses the bulk of the picture collection, as well as one of the museum's most famous pieces, Pietro Bernini's tender *Madonna col Bambino e San Giovannino* (Madonna and Child with the Infant John the Baptist).

A pictorial history of Naples is told in **Immagini e Memorie di Napoli** (Images and Memories of Naples). Here you'll find portraits of historic characters; antique maps, including a 35-panel copper map of 18th-century Naples in Room 45; and rooms dedicated to major historical events such as the Revolt of the Masaniello (Room 36) and the plague (Room 37). Room 32 boasts the beautiful *Tavola Strozzi* (Strozzi Table); its fabled depiction of 15th-century maritime Naples is one of the city's most celebrated historical records.

It's worth noting that some sections of the museum are only open at various times of the day; see the website for specific times.

Below the Certosa is the imposing **Sotterranei Gotici** (Gothic basement). The austere vaulted space harbours circa 150 marble sculptures and epigraphs, including a statue of St Francis of Assisi by 18th-century master sculptor Giuseppe Sanmartino. Guided tours (in Italian) of the Sotterranei Gotici usually take place at 11.30am on Saturday and Sunday and must be reserved about two weeks in advance by emailing accoglienza. sanmartino@beniculturali.it. Unfortunately, tours were suspended indefinitely in 2017; contact the museum for updates.

Castel Sant'Elmo   CASTLE
(Map p66; ☏ 081 558 77 08; www.coopculture.it; Via Tito Angelini 22; adult/reduced €5/2.50 Wed-Mon, €2.50/1.25 Tue; ⏱ castle 8.30am-7.30pm daily, museum 9.30am-5pm Wed-Mon; Ⓜ Vanvitelli, 🚋 Montesanto to Morghen) Star-shaped Castel Sant'Elmo was originally a church dedicated to St Erasmus. Some 400 years later, in 1349, Robert of Anjou turned it into a castle before Spanish viceroy Don Pedro de Toledo had it further fortified in 1538. Used as a military prison until the 1970s, it's now famed for its jaw-dropping panorama, and for its **Museo del Novecento**, dedicated to 20th-century Neapolitan art.

The museum's collection of paintings, sculpture and installations documents major influences in the local art scene, including Futurism and the Nuclear Art movement. Standout works include Eugenio Viti's sensual *La schiena* (The Back) in Room 7, Raffaele Lippi's unnerving *Le quattro giornate di Napoli* (The Four Days of Naples) in Room 9, and Giuseppe Desiato's magnetic photograph *Monumento* in Room 18. In Room 17, Salvatore Cotugno's untitled sculpture of a bound, wrapped, muted figure strangely recalls Giuseppe Sanmartino's *Cristo velato* (Veiled Christ) in the Cappella Sansevero (p60).

◉ Via Toledo & Quartieri Spagnoli

★ **Galleria di Palazzo Zevallos Stigliano**   GALLERY
(Map p66; ☏ 081 42 50 11; www.palazzozevallos. com; Via Toledo 185; adult/reduced €5/3; ⏱ 10am-6pm Tue-Fri, to 8pm Sat & Sun; Ⓜ Municipio) Built for a Spanish merchant in the 17th century and reconfigured in belle époque style by architect Luigi Platania in the early 20th century, Palazzo Zevallos Stigliano houses a compact yet stunning collection of Neapolitan and Italian art spanning the 17th to early-20th centuries. Star attraction is Caravaggio's mesmerising swansong, *The Martyrdom of St Ursula* (1610). Completed weeks before the artist's lonely death, the painting depicts a vengeful king of the Huns piercing the heart of his unwilling virgin bride-to-be, Ursula.

Positioned behind the dying martyr is a haunted Caravaggio, an eerie premonition of his own impending fate. The tumultuous history of both the artist and the painting is documented in the free and highly informative tablet audio guide.

Caravaggio's masterpiece is one of around 120 works on display in the *palazzo*'s sumptuous rooms. Among the numerous standouts are Luca Giordano's robust *The Rape of Helen,* a graphic *Judith Beheads Holophernes* attributed to Louis Finson, Francesco Solimena's *Hagar and Ishmael in the Desert Confronted by the Angel* and a series of bronze and terracotta sculptures by Vincenzo Gemito. A fine collection of landscape paintings includes Gasper van Wittel's *View of Naples with Largo di Palazzo,* which offers a fascinating early-18th-century depiction of what is now Piazza del Plebiscito. The triple-arched fountain in the bottom right corner of the painting is the Fontana dell'Immacolatella. Designed by Michelangelo Naccherini and Pietro Bernini in 1601, the fountain is now located at the corner of Via Partenope and Via Nazario Sauro, beside Borgo Marinaro.

Gaspar van Wittel was the father of celebrated Neapolitan architect Luigi Vanvitelli.

◉ Santa Lucia & Chiaia

★ Palazzo Reale   PALACE

(Royal Palace; Map p66; ☑ 081 40 05 47; Piazza del Plebiscito 1; adult/reduced €4/3; ⊙ 9am-8pm Thu-Tue; ▣ R2 to Via San Carlo, Ⓜ Municipio) Envisaged as a 16th-century monument to Spanish glory (Naples was under Spanish rule at the time), the magnificent Palazzo Reale is home to the **Museo del Palazzo Reale**, a rich and eclectic collection of baroque and neoclassical furnishings, porcelain, tapestries, sculpture and paintings, spread across the palace's royal apartments.

Among the many highlights is the Teatrino di Corte, a lavish private theatre created by Ferdinando Fuga in 1768 to celebrate the marriage of Ferdinand IV and Marie Caroline of Austria. Incredibly, Angelo Viva's statues of Apollo and the Muses set along the walls are made of papier mâché.

Sala (Room) VIII is home to a pair of vivid, allegorical 18th-century French tapestries representing earth and water respectively. Further along, Sala XII will leave you sniggering at the 16th-century canvas *Gli esattori delle imposte* (The Tax Collectors). Painted by Dutch artist Marinus Claesz Van Reymerswaele, it confirms that attitudes to tax collectors have changed little in 500 years. Sala XIII used to be Joachim Murat's study in the 19th century but was used as a snack bar by Allied troops in WWII. Meanwhile, what looks like a waterwheel in Sala XXIII is actually a nifty rotating reading desk made for Marie Caroline by Giovanni Uldrich in the 18th century.

The Cappella Reale (Royal Chapel) houses an 18th-century *presepe napoletano* (Neapolitan nativity crib). Fastidiously detailed, its cast of *pastori* (crib figurines) were crafted by a series of celebrated Neapolitan artists, including Giuseppe Sanmartino, creator of the *Cristo velato* (Veiled Christ) sculpture in the Cappella Sansevero.

The palace is also home to the **Biblioteca Nazionale** (National Library; Map p66; ☑ 081 781 91 11; www.bnnonline.it; ⊙ 8.30am-7pm Mon-Fri, to 2pm Sat, papyri exhibition 8.30am-2pm Mon-Fri, Sezione Lucchesi Palli 8.30am-6.45pm Mon-Thu, to 3.30pm Fri; ▣ R2 to Via San Carlo, Ⓜ Municipio) **FREE**, its own priceless treasures including at least 2000 papyri discovered at Herculaneum and fragments of a 5th-century Coptic Bible. The National Library's beautiful **Biblioteca Lucchesi Palli** (Lucchesi Palli Library) – designed by some of Naples' most celebrated 19th-century craftspeople – is home to fascinating artistic artefacts, including letters by composer Giuseppe Verdi. Bring photo ID to enter the Biblioteca Nazionale.

SUBTERRANEAN NAPLES

Mysterious shrines, secret passageways, forgotten burial crypts: it might sound like the set of an Indiana Jones film, but it's actually what lurks beneath Naples' loud and greasy streets. Subterranean Naples is one of the world's most thrilling urban wonderlands; a silent, mostly undiscovered sprawl of cathedral-like cisterns, pin-thin conduits, catacombs and ancient ruins.

Speleologists (cave specialists) estimate that about 60% of Neapolitans live and work above this network, known in Italian as the *sottosuolo* (underground). Since the end of WWII, some 700 cavities have been discovered, from original Greek-era grottoes to palaeo-Christian burial chambers and royal Bourbon escape routes. According to the experts, this is simply a prelude, with another 2 million sq metres of troglodytic treats to unfurl.

Naples' dedicated caving geeks are quick to tell you that their underworld is one of the largest and oldest on earth. Sure, Paris might claim a catacomb or two, but its subterranean offerings don't come close to this giant's 2500-year history.

And what a history it is. Naples' most famous saint, San Gennaro, was interred in the Catacombe di San Gennaro in the 5th century. A century later, in 536, Belisario and his troops caught Naples by surprise by storming the city through the city's ancient tunnels. According to legend, Alfonso of Aragon used the same trick in 1442, undermining the city walls by using an underground passageway leading into a tailor's shop and straight into town. Even the city's dreaded Camorra has got in on the act. In 1992 the notorious Stolder clan was busted for running a subterranean drug lab, with escape routes heading straight to the clan boss's pad.

★ **Galleria Borbonica**   HISTORIC SITE
(Map p66; ☏081 764 58 08, 366 2484151; www.
galleriaborbonica.com; Vico del Grottone 4; 75min
standard tour adult/reduced €10/5; ⊙standard tour
10am, noon, 3.30pm & 5.30pm Fri-Sun; 🚌R2 to Via
San Carlo) Traverse five centuries along Naples' engrossing Bourbon Tunnel. Conceived
by Ferdinand II in 1853 to link the Palazzo
Reale to the barracks and the sea, the never-
completed escape route is part of the
17th-century Carmignano Aqueduct system,
itself incorporating 16th-century cisterns.
An air-raid shelter and military hospital
during WWII, this underground labyrinth
rekindles the past with evocative wartime
artefacts. The standard tour doesn't require
pre-booking, though the Adventure Tour
(80 minutes; adult/reduced €15/10) and
adults-only Speleo Tour (2½ hours; €30) do.

Tours also depart from Galleria Borbonica's second entrance, reached through the
Parcheggio Morelli (Via Domenico Morelli
40) parking complex in Chiaia.

MeMus   MUSEUM
(Museum & Historical Archive of the Teatro San
Carlo; Map p66; http://memus.squarespace.com;
Palazzo Reale, Piazza del Plebiscito; adult/reduced
€6/5; ⊙9am-7pm Mon, Tue & Thu-Sat, to 3pm
Sun; 🚌R2 to Via San Carlo, Ⓜ Municipio) Located
inside the Palazzo Reale (purchase tickets at
the palace ticket booth), MeMus documents
the history of Europe's oldest working opera house, the Teatro San Carlo (p77). The
collection includes costumes, sketches, in-
struments and memorabilia, displayed in
annually changing themed exhibitions. One
interactive, immersive exhibit allows visitors
to enjoy the music of numerous celebrated
composers with accompanying visuals by
artists who have collaborated with the opera
house, among them William Kentridge.

Castel Nuovo   CASTLE
(Map p66; ☏081 795 77 22; Piazza Municipio;
adult/reduced €6/3, free Sun; ⊙9am-7pm Mon-
Sat, to 1.30pm Sun; Ⓜ Municipio) Locals know
this 13th-century castle as the Maschio
Angioino (Angevin Keep) and its Cappella
Palatina is home to fragments of frescoes
by Giotto; they're on the splays of the Gothic windows. You'll also find Roman ruins
under the glass-floored Sala dell'Armeria
(Armoury Hall). The castle's upper floors
(closed on Sunday) house a collection of
mostly 17th- to early-20th-century Neapolitan paintings. The top floor houses the more
interesting works, including landscape

paintings by Luigi Crisconio and a watercol-
our by architect Carlo Vanvitelli.

The history of the castle stretches back
to Charles I of Anjou, who upon taking over
Naples and the Swabians' Sicilian kingdom
found himself in control not only of his new
southern Italian acquisitions but also of
possessions in Tuscany, northern Italy and
Provence (France). It made sense to base the
new dynasty in Naples, rather than Palermo
in Sicily, and Charles launched an ambitious
construction program to expand the port
and city walls. His plans included convert-
ing a Franciscan convent into the castle that
still stands in Piazza Municipio.

Christened the Castrum Novum (New
Castle) to distinguish it from the older Castel
dell'Ovo and Castel Capuano, it was completed in 1282, becoming a popular hang-out for
the leading intellectuals and artists of the day
– Giotto repaid his royal hosts by painting
much of the interior. Of the original structure, however, only the Cappella Palatina
remains; the rest is the result of Aragonese
renovations two centuries later, as well as a
meticulous restoration effort prior to WWII.

The two-storey Renaissance triumphal
arch at the entrance – the **Torre della
Guardia** – commemorates the victorious
entry of Alfonso I of Aragon into Naples in
1443, while the stark stone **Sala dei Baro-
ni** (Hall of the Barons) is named after the
barons slaughtered here in 1486 for plot-
ting against King Ferdinand I of Aragon. Its
striking ribbed vault fuses ancient Roman
and Spanish late-Gothic influences.

Castel dell'Ovo   CASTLE
(Map p66; ☏081 795 45 93; Borgo Marinaro; ⊙8am-
7pm Mon-Sat, to 1.45pm Sun; 🚌128 to Via Santa
Lucia) **FREE** Built by the Normans in the 12th
century, Naples' oldest castle owes its name
(Castle of the Egg) to Virgil. The Roman scribe
reputedly buried an egg on the site where the
castle now stands, warning that when the
egg breaks, the castle (and Naples) will fall.
Thankfully, both are still standing, and walking up to the castle's ramparts will reward you
with a breathtaking panorama.

Used by the Swabians, Angevins and Alfonso of Aragon, who modified it to suit his
military needs, the castle sits on the rocky,
restaurant-lined 'island' of **Borgo Marinaro**
(Map p66). According to legend, the heart-
broken siren Partenope washed ashore here
after failing to seduce Ulysses with her song.
It's also where the Greeks first settled the
city in the 7th century BC, calling the island

Megaris. Its commanding position wasn't wasted on the Roman general Lucullus, either, who had his villa here long before the castle hit the skyline. Views aside, the castle is also the setting for temporary art exhibitions, special events, and no shortage of posing brides and grooms.

◉ Capodimonte & La Sanità

★**Palazzo Reale di Capodimonte**　MUSEUM
(☑081 749 91 11; www.museocapodimonte. beniculturali.it; Via Miano 2; adult/reduced €8/4; ◷8.30am-7.30pm Thu-Tue; ☒R4, 178 to Via Capodimonte, shuttle bus　Shuttle Capodimonte) Originally designed as a hunting lodge for Charles VII of Bourbon, this monumental palace was begun in 1738 and took more than a century to complete. It's now home to the **Museo Nazionale di Capodimonte**, southern Italy's largest and richest art gallery. Its vast collection – much of which Charles inherited from his mother, Elisabetta Farnese – was moved here in 1759 and ranges from exquisite 12th-century altarpieces to works by Botticelli, Caravaggio, Titian and Andy Warhol.

The gallery is spread over three floors and 160 rooms; for most people, a full morning or afternoon is enough for an abridged best-of tour. The 1st floor includes works by greats such as Michelangelo, Raphael and Titian, with highlights including Masaccio's *Crocifissione* (Crucifixion; Room 3), Botticelli's *Madonna col Bambino e due angeli* (Madonna with Child and Angels; Room 6), Bellini's *Trasfigurazione* (Transfiguration; Room 8) and Parmigianino's *Antea* (Room 12). The floor is also home to the royal apartments, a study in regal excess. The **Salottino di Porcellana** (Room 52) is an outrageous example of 18th-century chinoiserie, its walls and ceiling dense with whimsically themed porcelain 'stucco'. Originally created between 1757 and 1759 for the Palazzo Reale in Portici, it was transferred to Capodimonte in 1867.

Upstairs, the 2nd-floor galleries display work by Neapolitan artists from the 13th to the 19th centuries, including de Ribera, Giordano, Solimena and Stanzione. It's also home to some spectacular 16th-century Belgian tapestries. The piece that many come to see, however, is Caravaggio's *Flagellazione* (Flagellation; 1607–10), which hangs in reverential solitude in Room 78.

If you have any energy left, the small gallery of modern art on the 3rd floor is worth a quick look, if for nothing else than Andy Warhol's poptastic *Mt Vesuvius*.

Once you've finished in the museum, the **Parco di Capodimonte** – the palace's 130-hectare estate – provides a much-needed breath of fresh air.

In 2017, the museum launched a convenient, hourly shuttle bus service that runs between central Naples and the museum. Buses depart from Piazza Trieste e Trento (opposite Teatro San Carlo) and stop outside the Museo Archeologico Nazionale and Catacombe di San Gennaro en route. Return tickets (adult/reduced €12/6) include museum entry and can be purchased directly on the bus.

★**Cimitero delle Fontanelle**　CEMETERY
(☑081 1970 3197; www.cimiterofontanelle.com; Via Fontanelle 80; ◷10am-5pm; ☒C51 to Via Fontanelle) **FREE** Holding about eight million human bones, the ghoulish Fontanelle Cemetery was first used during the 1656 plague, before becoming Naples' main burial site during the 1837 cholera epidemic. At the end of the 19th century it became a hotspot for the *anime pezzentelle* (poor souls) cult, in which locals adopted skulls and prayed for their souls. Lack of information at the site makes joining a tour much more rewarding; reputable outfits include Cooperativa Sociale Onlus 'La Paranza'. Avoid guides offering tours at the entrance.

⌲ Tours

★**Cooperativa Sociale
Onlus 'La Paranza'**　TOURS
(☑081 744 37 14; www.catacombedinapoli.it; Via Capodimonte 13; ◷information point 10am-5pm Mon-Sat, to 2pm Sun; ☒R4, 178 to Via Capodimonte) Runs tours of the Catacombe di San Gennaro and a fascinating walking tour called Il Miglio Sacro (The Holy Mile), which explores the earthy Sanità district. The walking tour must be pre-booked; see website for details. The ticket office is to the left of the Chiesa di Madre di Buon Consiglio (Via Capodimonte 13).

Napoli Sotterranea　ARCHAEOLOGICAL SITE
(Underground Naples; Map p62; ☑081 29 69 44; www.napolisotterranea.org; Piazza San Gaetano 68; adult/reduced €10/8; ◷English tours 10am, noon, 2pm, 4pm & 6pm; ☒E1, E2 to Via Duomo) This evocative guided tour leads you 40m below street level to explore Naples' ancient labyrinth of aqueducts, passages and cisterns.

The passages were originally hewn by the Greeks to extract tufa stone used in construction and to channel water from Mt Vesuvius. Extended by the Romans, the network of conduits and cisterns was more recently used as an air-raid shelter in WWII. Part of the tour takes place by candlelight via extremely narrow passages – not suitable for expanded girths!

⭐ Festivals & Events

Maggio dei Monumenti CULTURAL
(☺ May) A month-long cultural feast, with a bounty of concerts, performances, exhibitions, guided tours and other events across Naples.

Napoli Teatro Festival THEATRE
(www.napoliteatrofestival.it; ☺ Jun/Jul) One month of local and international theatre and performance art, staged in conventional and unconventional venues.

Wine & The City WINE
(www.wineandthecity.it; ☺ May) A three-week celebration of regional *vino*, with free wine tastings and cultural events in palaces, museums, boutiques and eateries throughout the city.

Festa di San Gennaro RELIGIOUS
The faithful flock to the Duomo to witness the miraculous liquefaction of San Gennaro's blood on the Saturday before the first Sunday in May. Repeat performances take place on 19 September and 16 December.

🛏 Sleeping

Where to slumber? The *centro storico* is studded with important churches and sights, artisan studios and student-packed bars. Seafront Santa Lucia delivers grand hotels, while sceney Chiaia is best for fashionable shops and *aperitivo* bars. The lively, laundry-strung Quartieri Spagnoli is within walking distance of all three neighbourhoods.

B&B Arte e Musei B&B €
(Map p62; ☑ 333 6962469; www.facebook.com/bnbarteemusei; Via Salvator Rosa 345; s €40-50, d €60-100, tr €90-120; ❋ 🛜; Ⓜ Museo, Cavour) Close to the Museo Archeolgico Nazionale, this quiet, artful B&B is adorned with Neapolitan-themed paintings and ceramics by gracious owner and artist Federica. Both the double and triple room include a small balcony and spotless en suite bathroom, while the smaller single room (with double bed) has its private bathroom in the hallway.

All three simple, tasteful rooms are whitewashed and clean, with high ceilings and upbeat accents in pistachio and blue. Breakfast is served at a communal table in the dining room, set with colourful crockery made by Federica herself.

Nardones 48 APARTMENT €
(Map p66; ☑ 338 8818998; www.nardones48.it; Via Nardones 48; small apt €65-74, large apt €85-140; ❋ 🛜; 🚌 R2 to Via San Carlo) White-on-white Nardones 48 serves up seven smart mini-apartments in a historic Quartieri Spagnoli building. The five largest apartments, each with mezzanine bedroom, accommodate up to four; the two smallest, each with sofa bed, accommodate up to two. Three apartments boast a panoramic terrace, and all have modern kitchenette, flat-screen TV and contemporary bathroom with spacious shower.

Stays of one week or longer enjoy discounted rates and complimentary laundry service, and the apartment offers nearby parking (€20 per 24 hours).

Casa Latina B&B €
(Map p62; ☑ 338 9264453; www.casalatina.it; Vico Cinquesanti 47; s €40-55, d €55-75, tr €70-90, q €85-100; ❋ 🛜; Ⓜ Piazza Cavour, Museo) Creativity and style flow through this crisp new B&B, accented with eclectic lighting, boho photography, a fully equipped kitchen and a tranquil terrace. All four rooms are soothing and contemporary, with original architectural detailing and fetching bathrooms with recycled terracotta basins. One upper-level room features a tatami-style bed and banquettes, the latter transforming into extra bed space (ideal for young families).

Cerasiello B&B B&B €
(☑ 081 033 09 77, 338 9264453; www.cerasiello.it; Via Supportico Lopez 20; s €40-85, d €60-100, tr €75-110, q €90-125; ❋ 🛜; Ⓜ Piazza Cavour, Museo) This gorgeous B&B consists of four rooms with private bathrooms, an enchanting communal terrace and an ethno-chic look melding Neapolitan art with North African furnishings. The stylish kitchen offers a fabulous view of the Certosa di San Martino, a view shared by all rooms (or their bathroom) except Fuoco (Fire), which looks out at a beautiful church cupola.

Although technically in the Sanità district, the B&B is a short walk from Naples' *centro storico* (historic centre). Bring €0.20 for the lift.

Sui Tetti di Napoli B&B €
(Map p66; ✆338 9264453, 081 033 09 77; www.
suitettidinapoli.net; Vico Figuerelle a Montecalvario
6; s €35-60, d €45-80, tr €60-95, q €80-105; ✳✿;
Ⓜ Toledo) A block away from Via Toledo, this
well-priced B&B is more like four apartments atop a thigh-toning stairwell. While
two apartments share a small terrace, the
rooftop option boasts its own, complete
with mesmerising views. Recently refurbished, all apartments include a kitchenette
(the cheapest two share a kitchen), simple,
crisp, modern furnishings and comfy, new,
memory-foam mattresses.

⭐**Atelier Ines** B&B €
(✆349 4433422; www.atelierinesgallery.com; Via
Cristallini 138; d €125-150; ✳✿) A stylish, eclectic oasis in the heart of the earthy Sanità district, this three-suite B&B is a homage to the
late Neapolitan sculptor and designer Annibale Oste, whose workshop shares a leafy
courtyard. Everything from the lamps and
spiral towel racks to the one-of-a-kind sculptural bedheads are Oste's whimsical designs,
complimented by heavenly mattresses, a
choice of pillows, and Vietri-ceramic bathrooms with satisfying hot water.

Multilingual host Ines and her partner
Vincenzo (Annibale's son) are gracious and
passionate about their city, while breakfast
is a mostly made-from-scratch affair, with
house-made jams, yoghurt and cakes, as
well as farm-fresh scrambled eggs and organic fruit. Guests are welcome to explore
Oste's workshop and archive.

⭐**La Ciliegina**
Lifestyle Hotel BOUTIQUE HOTEL €€
(Map p66; ✆081 1971 8800; www.cilieginahotel.
it; Via PE Imbriani 30; d €160-300, junior ste €200-
400; ✳@✿; Ⓜ Municipio) An easy walk from
the hydrofoil terminal, this chic, contemporary slumber spot is a hit with fashion-
conscious urbanites. Spacious white rooms
are splashed with blue and red accents, each
with top-of-the-range Hästens beds, flat-
screen TVs and marble-clad bathrooms with
a water-jet Jacuzzi shower (one junior suite
has a Jacuzzi tub).

Breakfast in bed, or on the rooftop terrace, which comes with sunbeds, hot tub
and a view of Vesuvius. Complimentary iPad
use is a nice touch.

⭐**Hotel Piazza Bellini** BOUTIQUE HOTEL €€
(Map p62; ✆081 45 17 32; www.hotelpiazza
bellini.com; Via Santa Maria di Costantinopoli 101;

d €58-170; ✳@✿; Ⓜ Dante) Only steps from
buzzing Piazza Bellini, this sharp, contemporary hotel occupies a 16th-century *palazzo* (mansion), its mint white spaces spiked
with original majolica tiles and the work of
emerging artists. Rooms offer pared-back
cool, with designer fittings, chic bathrooms
and mirror frames drawn straight onto the
wall. Rooms on the 5th and 6th floors feature panoramic terraces. Check the hotel
website for decent discounts.

Decumani Hotel
de Charme BOUTIQUE HOTEL €€
(Map p62; ✆081 551 81 88; www.decumani.it; Via
San Giovanni Maggiore Pignatelli 15; s €99-124, d
€99-164; ✳@✿; Ⓜ Università) This classic
boutique hotel occupies the former *palazzo* of Cardinal Sisto Riario Sforza, the last
bishop of the Bourbon kingdom. Its simple, stylish 42 rooms feature high ceilings,
parquet floors, 19th-century furniture, and
modern bathrooms with spacious showers.
Deluxe rooms crank up the *dolce vita* with
personal hot tubs. The *pièce de résistance*,
however, is the property's breathtaking
baroque salon.

Grand Hotel Vesuvio HOTEL €€€
(Map p66; ✆081 764 00 44; www.vesuvio.it; Via
Partenope 45; s/d €280/310; ✳@✿; 🚌128 to Via
Santa Lucia) Known for hosting legends – past
guests include Rita Hayworth and Hum-
phrey Bogart – this five-star heavyweight is
a decadent melange of dripping chandeliers,
period antiques and opulent rooms. Count
your lucky stars while drinking a martini at
the rooftop restaurant.

🍴 **Eating**

Naples is one of Italy's gastronomic darlings, and the bonus of a bayside setting
makes for some seriously memorable meals.
While white linen, candlelight and €50 bills
are readily available, some of the best bites
await in the city's spit-and-sawdust trattorias, where two courses and house wine can
cost under €20. Even cheaper is Naples'
plethora of top-notch pizzerias and *friggi-
torie* (fried-food kiosks). On the downside,
many eateries close for two weeks in August,
so call ahead if visiting then.

⭐**Salumeria** BISTRO €
(Map p62; ✆081 1936 4649; www.salumeria
upnea.it; Via San Giovanni Maggiore Pignatelli 34/35;
sandwiches from €4.90, charcuterie platters from €8,
meals around €22; ⊙noon-5.30pm & 7pm-midnight

Mon, Tue & Thu, 7pm-midnight Wed, 7pm-12.30am Fri, 10am-12.30am Sat, 10am-midnight Sun; ☎; Ⓜ Dante) Small producers, local ingredients and contemporary takes on provincial Campanian recipes drive bistro-inspired Salumeria. Nibble on quality charcuterie and cheeses or fill up on artisanal *panini*, hamburgers and daily specials that might include pasta with a rich *ragù napoletano* sauce slow-cooked over two days. Even the ketchup here is made in-house, using DOP Piennolo tomatoes from Vesuvius.

On weekend mornings, don't miss the *polacca*, a cornetto-like pastry filled with custard and cherries. Libations include Campanian craft beers and the venue hosts rotating exhibitions of contemporary, Neapolitan-themed art.

★ Pizzeria Starita   PIZZA €

(☑ 081 557 36 82; Via Materdei 28; pizzas from €3.50; ⊙ noon-3.30pm & 7pm-midnight Tue-Sun; Ⓜ Materdei) The giant fork and ladle hanging on the wall at this historic pizzeria were used by Sophia Loren in *L'Oro di Napoli,* and the kitchen made the *pizze fritte* sold by the actress in the film. While the 60-plus pizza varieties include a tasty *fiorilli e zucchine* (zucchini, zucchini flowers and *provola*), our allegiance remains to its classic *marinara.*

★ Muu Muuzzarella Lounge   NEAPOLITAN €

(Map p66; ☑ 081 40 53 70; www.muumuuzzarella lounge.it; Vico II Alabardieri 7; dishes €7-16; ⊙ 12.30pm-midnight Tue-Sun; ☎; 🚌 C24 to Riviera di Chiaia) Pimped with milking-bucket lights and cow-hide patterned cushions, playful Muu is all about super-fresh Campanian mozzarella, from cheese and charcuterie platters to creative dishes like buffalo bocconcini with creamy pesto and crunchy apple. Leave room for the chef's secret recipe white-chocolate cheesecake, best paired with a glass of Guappa (buffalo-milk liqueur).

Serafino   SICILIAN €

(Map p62; ☑ 081 557 14 33; Via dei Tribunali 44; arancini €2.50, cannoli €2.50; ⊙ 11.30am-10pm) A veritable porthole to Sicily, this take-away stand peddles authentic island street food. Savoury bites include various types of *arancini* (deep-fried rice balls), among them *al ragù* (with meat sauce) and *alla Norma* (with fried eggplant and ricotta). The real reason to head here, however, is for the crisp, flawless cannoli, filled fresh with silky Sicilian ricotta and sprinkled with pistachio crumbs. Bliss.

Pizzeria Gino Sorbillo   PIZZA €

(Map p62; ☑ 081 44 66 43; www.sorbillo.it; Via dei Tribunali 32; pizzas from €3; ⊙ noon-3.30pm & 7-11.30pm Mon-Thu, to midnight Fri & Sat; ☎; Ⓜ Dante) Day in, day out, this cult-status pizzeria is besieged by hungry hordes. While debate may rage over whether Gino Sorbillo's pizzas are the best in town, there's no doubt that his giant, wood-fired discs – made using organic flour and tomatoes – will have you licking fingertips and whiskers. Head in super early or prepare to wait.

Pintauro   PASTRIES €

(Map p66; ☑ 081 41 73 39; Via Toledo 275; sfogliatelle €2; ⊙ 9am-8pm, closed mid-Jul–early Sep; 🚌 R2 to Via San Carlo, Ⓜ Municipio) Of Neapolitan *dolci* (sweets), the cream of the crop is the *sfogliatella,* a shell of flaky pastry stuffed with creamy, scented ricotta. This local institution has been selling *sfogliatelle* since the early 1800s, when its founder supposedly brought them to Naples from their culinary birthplace on the Amalfi Coast. The pastry comes in two versions: *frolla* (short-crust pastry) and *riccia* (filo-style pastry).

★ Benvenuti al Sud   NEAPOLITAN €€

(☑ 081 1934 9334; Corso Vittorio Emanuele 9; pizzas from €4.50, meals around €25; ⊙ noon-3.30pm & 6.30pm-midnight Tue-Sat, noon-3.30pm Sun; Ⓜ Mergellina) Its walls splashed with technicolour murals of market produce and Neapolitan vistas, this friendly, upbeat pizzeria-cum-trattoria flips great Neapolitan pie, from simple *marinara* (tomato, oregano, garlic and olive oil) to lesser-known classic *montanara*, which sees the base lightly fried before being topped and baked in the oven for a lovely sheen and crackle. Beyond the pizzas are some fantastic seafood pasta dishes.

★ Eccellenze Campane   NEAPOLITAN €€

(☑ 081 20 36 57; www.eccellenzecampane.it; Via Benedetto Brin 49; pizza from €6, meals around €30; ⊙ complex 7am-11pm Sun-Fri, to 12.30am Sat, restaurants 12.30-3.30pm & 7.30-11pm Sun-Fri, to 12.30am Sat; ☎; 🚌 192, 460, 472, 475) This is Naples' answer to Turin-based food emporium Eataly, an impressive, contemporary showcase for top-notch Campanian comestibles. The sprawling space is divided into various dining and shopping sections, offering everything from beautifully charred pizzas and light *fritture* (fried snacks) to finer-dining seafood, lust-inducing pastries, craft beers and no shortage of take-home pantry treats. A must for gastronomes.

★ **L'Ebbrezza di Noè** NEAPOLITAN €€
(Map p66; ☑ 081 40 01 04; www.lebbrezza dinoe.com; Vico Vetriera 9; meals around €37; ⊙ 6pm-midnight Tue-Thu, to 1am Fri & Sat, noon-3pm Sun; 🛜; Ⓜ Piazza Amedeo) A wine shop by day, 'Noah's Drunkenness' transforms into an intimate culinary hotspot by night. Slip inside for *vino* and conversation at the bar, or settle into one of the bottle-lined dining rooms for seductive, market-driven dishes such as house special *paccheri fritti* (fried pasta stuffed with eggplant and served with fresh basil and a rich tomato sauce).

Topping it off are circa 2800 wines, artfully selected by sommelier owner Luca Di Leva. Book ahead.

★ **Ristorantino dell'Avvocato** NEAPOLITAN €€
(Map p66; ☑ 081 032 00 47; www.ilristorantino dellavvocato.it; Via Santa Lucia 115-117; meals €40-45; ⊙ noon-3pm daily, also 7-11pm Tue-Sat; 🛜; 🚌 128 to Via Santa Lucia) This elegant yet welcoming restaurant is a favourite of Neapolitan gastronomes. Apple of their eye is affable lawyer turned head chef Raffaele Cardillo, whose passion for Campania's culinary heritage merges with a knack for subtle, refreshing twists – think coffee papardelle served with mullet ragù.

The degustation menus (€45 to €60) are good value, as is the weekday 'three courses on a plate' lunch special. Book ahead Thursday to Saturday.

La Taverna di Santa Chiara NEAPOLITAN €€
(Map p62; ☑ 081 048 49 08; Via Santa Chiara 6; meals €25; ⊙ 1-2.30pm & 8-10.30pm Mon, Wed & Thu, to 3pm Fri-Sun, 8-10.30pm Mon-Sat; 🛜; Ⓜ Dante) Gragnano pasta, Agerola pork, *con-cato romano*: this modest, two-level eatery is healthily obsessed with small, local producers and Slow Food ingredients. The result is a beautiful, seasonal journey across Campania.

For an inspiring overview, order the rustic *antipasto di terra* (an antipasto of cheese and cured meats), then tuck into lesser-known dishes like *genovese di polipo* (a rich onion and octopus pasta dish) with wine from a lesser-known regional wine-maker or a Campanian craft brew.

Trattoria San Ferdinando NEAPOLITAN €€
(Map p66; ☑ 081 42 19 64; Via Nardones 117; meals €25-32; ⊙ 12.30-3.30pm Mon-Sat, 7.30-11pm Tue-Fri; 🚌 R2 to Via San Carlo, Ⓜ Municipio) Hung with theatre posters, cosy San Ferdinando pulls in well-spoken theatre types and intellectuals. For a Neapolitan taste trip, ask

for a rundown of the day's antipasti and choose your favourites for an *antipasto misto* (mixed antipasto). Seafood standouts include a delicate *seppia ripieno* (stuffed squid), while the homemade desserts make for a satisfying dénouement.

🍷 **Drinking & Nightlife**

Neapolitans aren't big drinkers, and in the *centro storico* many people simply buy a bottle of beer from the nearest bar and hang out on the streets. Here, drinking hotspots include Piazza Bellini and Calata Trinità Maggiore off Piazza del Gesù Nuovo, where a high concentration of students, artists and bohemians lend an energetic, live-and-let-live vibe. Those after fashion-conscious *prosecco* sessions should aim for Chiaia's sleek bars, famed for their *aperitivo* spreads (gourmet nibbles for the price of a drink, nightly from around 6.30pm to 9.30pm). Popular strips include Via Ferrigni, Via Bisignano and Vico Belledonne a Chiaia.

★ **Ba-Bar** BAR
(Map p66; ☑ 081 764 35 25; www.ba-bar.it; Via Santa Lucia 169; 🚌 128 to Via Santa Lucia) Don't be fooled by the faux British-pub exterior. With its muted colour palette, soft lighting and subtle nautical motif, Ba-Bar sets a sophisticated scene for well-crafted cocktails made using fresh ingredients. A short, detail-orientated food menu includes the likes of sesame baguette stuffed with Campanian *provola* cheese, *culatello* (air-cured ham) and hazelnuts, not to mention regional staple *parmigiana di melanzane* (eggplant parmigiana).

★ **Donna Romita** BAR
(Map p62; ☑ 081 1851 5074; www.donnaromi ta.it; Vico Donnaromita 14; ⊙ 6pm-2am Mon-Sat, from 11am Sun; 🛜) Part of Napoli's new guard of genuinely hip, on-point drinking holes, Donna Romita eschews video screens, unflattering lighting and tacky decor for an architecturally designed combo of minimalist concrete, industrial lighting, sculptural furniture and well-crafted drinks. Not surprisingly, it's a hit with arty, cosmopolitan *centro storico* (historic centre) types.

Food options include artisan cheeses and *salumi* (charcuterie), and there's a sleek dining room downstairs serving gorgeous, locavore fare with competent modern tweaks.

Caffè Gambrinus CAFE
(Map p66; ☑ 081 41 75 82; www.grancaffegambrinus. com; Via Chiaia 1-2; ⊙ 7am-1am Sun-Thu, to 2am Fri

& Sat; R2 to Via San Carlo, Municipio) Grand, chandeliered Gambrinus is Naples' oldest and most venerable cafe. Oscar Wilde knocked back a few here and Mussolini had some of the rooms shut to keep out left-wing intellectuals. The prices may be steep, but the *aperitivo* nibbles are decent and sipping a *spritz* or a *cioccolata calda* (hot chocolate) in its belle époque rooms is something worth savouring.

Spazio Nea CAFE
(Map p62; 081 45 13 58; www.spazionea.it; Via Constantinopoli 53; 9am-2am, to 3am Fri & Sat; ; Dante) Aptly skirting bohemian Piazza Bellini, this whitewashed gallery features its own cafe-bar speckled with books, flowers, cultured crowds and alfresco seating at the bottom of a baroque staircase. Eye up exhibitions of contemporary Italian and foreign art, then kick back with a *caffè* or a *spritz*. Check Nea's Facebook page for upcoming readings, live music gigs or DJ sets. Bites include bountiful salads.

⭐ Entertainment

Although Naples is no London, Milan or Melbourne on the entertainment front, it does offer some top after-dark options, from opera and ballet to thought-provoking theatre and cultured classical ensembles. To see what's on, scan daily papers like *Corriere del Mezzogiorno* or *La Repubblica* (Naples edition), click onto www.napoliunplugged. com, or ask at the tourist office. In smaller venues you can usually buy your ticket at the door; for bigger events try the box office inside **Feltrinelli** (Map p66; 081 032 23 62; www.azzurroservice.net; Piazza dei Martiri 23; 11am-2pm & 3-8pm Mon-Sat; C24 to Piazza dei Martiri), or **Box Office** (Map p66; 081 551 91 88; www.boxofficenapoli.it; Galleria Umberto I 17; 9.30am-8pm Mon-Fri, 10am-1.30pm & 4.30-8pm Sat; R2 to Piazza Trieste e Trento, Municipio).

⭐ Teatro San Carlo OPERA, BALLET
(Map p66; 081 797 23 31; www.teatrosancarlo.it; Via San Carlo 98; box office 10am-5.30pm Mon-Sat, to 2pm Sun; R2 to Via San Carlo, Municipio) San Carlo's opera season usually runs from November or December to June, with occasional summer performances. Reckon on €50 for a place in the sixth tier, €100 for a seat in the stalls or – if you're under 30 (with ID) – €30 for a place in a side box. The ballet season generally runs from late October to April or early May. Ballet tickets range from €35 to €80, with €20 tickets for those under 30.

⭐ Lanificio 25 LIVE MUSIC
(Map p62; www.lanificio25.it; Piazza Enrico De Nicola 46; free-€10; varies; Garibaldi) This Bourbon-era wool factory and 15th-century cloister is now a burgeoning party and culture hub, strung with coloured lights and awash with video projections. Live music and performances are the mainstay, ranging from cabaret acts to mostly Italian outfits playing indie, rock, world music and electronica to an easy, arty, cosmopolitan crowd. Check the website or Facebook page for upcoming events.

⭐ Stadio San Paolo FOOTBALL
(Piazzale Vincenzo Tecchio; Napoli Campi Flegrei) Naples' football team, Napoli, is the third most supported in Italy after Juventus and Milan, and watching it play in the country's third-largest stadium is a rush. The season runs from late August to late May; seats cost from around €20 to €100. Tickets are available from selected tobacconists, the agency inside Feltrinelli, or Box Office; bring photo ID. On match days, tickets are also available at the stadium itself.

Centro di Musica Antica Pietà de' Turchini CLASSICAL MUSIC
(Map p66; 081 40 23 95; www.turchini.it; Via Santa Caterina da Siena 38; Centrale to Corso Vittorio Emanuele) Classical-music buffs are in for a treat at this beautiful deconsecrated church, an evocative setting for concerts of mostly 17th- to 19th-century Neapolitan works. Tickets usually cost €10 (reduced €7), and upcoming concerts are listed on the venue's website. Note that some concerts are held at the elegant Palazzo Zevallos Stigliano (p69) on Via Toledo.

🛍 Shopping

Bottega 21 FASHION & ACCESSORIES
(Map p62; 081 033 55 42; www.bottegaventuno. it; Vico San Domenico Maggiore 21; 9.30am-8pm Mon-Sat) Top-notch Tuscan leather and traditional, handcrafted methods translate into coveted, contemporary leather goods for sale at Bottega 21. Block colours and clean, simple designs underline the range, which includes stylish totes, handbags, backpacks and duffel bags, as well as wallets and coin purses, unisex belts, notebook covers and tobacco pouches. A solid choice for those who prefer to shop local and independent.

8

La Scarabattola
ARTS & CRAFTS

(Map p62; ☑ 081 29 17 35; www.lascarabattola.it; Via dei Tribunali 50; ⊗10.30am-2pm & 3.30-7.30pm Mon-Fri, 10am-6pm Sat; ☐E1, E2 to Via Duomo) Not only do La Scarabattola's handmade sculptures of *magi* (wise men), devils and Neapolitan folk figures constitute Jerusalem's official Christmas crèche, the artisan studio's fans include fashion designer Stefano Gabbana and Spanish royalty. Figurines aside, sleek ceramic creations (think Pulcinella-inspired place-card holders) inject Neapolitan folklore with refreshing contemporary style.

E. Marinella
FASHION & ACCESSORIES

(Map p66; ☑ 081 764 32 65; www.marinella napoli.it; Via Riviera di Chiaia 287; ⊗7am-8pm Mon-Sat, 9am-1pm Sun; ☐C25 to Riviera di Chiaia, C24 to Piazza dei Martiri) One-time favourite of Luchino Visconti and Aristotle Onassis, this pocket-sized, vintage boutique is *the* place for prêt-à-porter and made-to-measure silk ties in striking patterns and hues. Match them with an irresistible selection of luxury accessories, including shoes, vintage colognes, and scarves for female style queens.

ℹ️ Information

MEDICAL
Loreto Mare Hospital (Ospedale Maria di Loreto Nuovo; ☑ 081 254 21 11; www.asl napoli1centro.it/818; Via Vespucci 26; ☐154) Central-city hospital with an emergency department.

Pharmacy (Stazione Centrale; ⊗7am-9.30pm Mon-Sat, 8am-9pm Sun) Pharmacy inside the main train station.

POST
Main Post Office (Map p66; ☑ 081 552 44 10; www.posteitaliane.it; Piazza Matteotti 2) Naples' curvaceous main post office is famous for its Fascist-era architecture.

TOURIST INFORMATION
Tourist Information Office (Map p62; ☑ 081 26 87 79; Stazione Centrale; ⊗9am-8pm; Ⓜ Garibaldi) Tourist office inside Stazione Centrale (Central Station).
Tourist Information Office (Map p62; ☑ 081 551 27 01; www.inaples.it; Piazza del Gesù Nuovo 7; ⊗9am-5pm Mon-Sat, to 1pm Sun; Ⓜ Dante) Tourist office in the *centro storico*.
Tourist Information Office (Map p66; ☑ 081 40 23 94; www.inaples.it; Via San Carlo 9; ⊗9am-5pm Mon-Sat, to 1pm Sun; ☐R2 to Via San Carlo, Ⓜ Municipio) Tourist office at Galleria Umberto I, directly opposite Teatro San Carlo.

ℹ️ Getting There & Away

AIR
Naples International Airport (Capodichino; ☑ 081 789 62 59; www.aeroportodinapoli.it), 7km northeast of the city centre, is southern Italy's main airport, linking Naples with most Italian and several other European cities, as well as New York. Budget carrier easyJet operates several routes to/from Capodichino, including London, Paris, Brussels and Berlin.

BOAT
Fast ferries and hydrofoils for Capri, Ischia, Procida and Sorrento depart from **Molo Beverello** (Map p66) in front of Castel Nuovo; hydrofoils for Capri, Ischia and Procida also sail from Mergellina.

Ferries for Sicily, the Aeolian Islands and Sardinia sail from **Molo Angioino** (Map p66) (right beside Molo Beverello) and neighbouring **Calata Porta di Massa** (Map p66).

BUS
Most national and international buses leave from **Terminal Bus Metropark** (Map p62; ☑ 800 65 00 06; Corso Arnaldo Lucci; Ⓜ Garibaldi), located on the southern side of Stazione Centrale. The bus station is home to **Biglietteria Vecchione** (☑ 331 88969217, 081 563 03 20; www.biglietteriavecchione.it; ⊗6.30am-9.30pm Mon-Fri, to 7.30pm Sat & Sun), a ticket agency selling national and international bus tickets.

Terminal Bus Metropark serves numerous bus companies offering regional and inter-regional services, among them **FlixBus** (www.flixbus.com). The bus stop for **SITA Sud** (☑ 344 1031070; www.sitasudtrasporti.it) services to the Amalfi Coast is just around the corner on Via Galileo Ferraris (in front of the hulking Istituto Nazionale della Previdenza Sociale office building).

CAR & MOTORCYCLE
Naples is on the north–south Autostrada del Sole, the A1 (north to Rome and Milan) and the A3 (south to Salerno and Reggio di Calabria).

TRAIN
Naples is southern Italy's rail hub and on the main Milan–Palermo line, with good connections to other Italian cities and towns.

National rail company **Trenitalia** (☑ 892 021; www.trenitalia.com) runs regular services to Rome (2nd class €12 to €45, 70 minutes to three hours, up to 69 daily). High-speed private rail company **Italo** (☑ 892 020; www.italotreno.it) also runs daily services to Rome (2nd class €15 to €39, 70 minutes, up to 17 daily). Most Italo services stop at Roma Termini and Roma Tiburtina stations.

OPLONTIS

Buried beneath the unappealing streets of Torre Annunziata, **Oplontis** (☑ 081 857 53 47; www.pompeiisites.org; Via dei Sepolcri, Torre Annunziata; adult/reduced incl Boscoreale & Stabiae €5.50/2.75, incl Pompeii & Herculaneum €22/12; ◷ 9am-7.30pm, last entry 6pm Apr-Oct, to 5pm, last entry 3.30pm Nov-Mar; ☒ Circumvesuviana to Torre Annunziata) was once a blue-ribbon seafront suburb under the administrative control of Pompeii. First discovered in the 18th century, only two of its houses have been unearthed, and only one, Villa Poppaea, is open to the public. This villa is a magnificent example of an *otium* villa (a residential building used for rest and recreation), thought to have belonged to Sabina Poppaea, Nero's second wife.

Particularly outstanding are the richly coloured 1st-century wall paintings in the *triclinium* (dining room) and *calidarium* (hot bathroom) in the west wing. Marking the villa's eastern border is a garden with an envy-inducing swimming pool (17m by 61m). The villa is a straightforward 300m walk from Torre Annunziata Circumvesuviana train station.

NAPLES & CAMPANIA CAPRI

ⓘ Getting Around

BUS

A much cheaper alternative to a taxi, airport shuttle **Alibus** (☑ 800 639525; www.anm.it) connects the airport to **Via Novara** (Map p62; Corso Novara) (in front of the Deutsche Bank branch opposite Stazione Centrale) and the ferry port **Molo Angioino** (Map p66) (€4, 45 minutes, every 15 to 20 minutes). Buy tickets on board or from selected tobacconists.

ANM (☑ 800 639525; www.anm.it) buses serve the city and its periphery. Many routes pass through Piazza Garibaldi.

FUNICULAR

Three services connect central Naples to Vomero, while a fourth connects Mergellina to Posillipo.

Funiculare Centrale (www.anm.it; ◷ 6.30am-10pm Mon & Tue, to 12.30am Wed-Sun & holidays) Travels from Piazzetta Augusteo to Piazza Fuga. Expected to reopen in early 2018.

Funiculare di Chiaia (www.anm.it; ◷ 7am-10pm Wed & Thu, to 12.30am Sun-Tue, to 2am Fri & Sat) Travels from Via del Parco Margherita to Via Domenico Cimarosa.

Funiculare di Montesanto (◷ 7am-10pm) Travels from Piazza Montesanto to Via Raffaele Morghen.

Funiculare di Mergellina (◷ 7am-10pm) Connects the waterfront at Via Mergellina with Via Manzoni.

METRO

Metro Line 1 (Linea 1; www.anm.it) runs from Garibaldi (Stazione Centrale) to Vomero and the northern suburbs via the city centre. Useful stops include Duomo and Università (southern edge of the *centro storico*), Municipio (hydrofoil and ferry terminals), Toledo (Via Toledo and Quartieri Spagnoli), Dante (western edge of the *centro storico*) and Museo (National Archaeological Museum).

Metro Line 2 (Linea 2; www.trenitalia.com) runs from Gianturco to Garibaldi (Stazione Centrale) and on to Pozzuoli. Useful stops include Piazza Cavour (La Sanità and northern edge of *centro storico*), Piazza Amedeo (Chiaia) and Mergellina (Mergellina ferry terminal). Change between lines 1 and 2 at Garibaldi or Piazza Cavour (known as Museo on Line 1).

Metro Line 6 (Linea 6; www.anm.it) is a light-rail service running between Mergellina and Mostra.

TAXI

Official fares from the airport are as follows: €23 to a seafront hotel or to Mergellina hydrofoil terminal; €19 to Piazza del Municipio or Molo Beverello ferry terminal; and €16 to Stazione Centrale and the *centro storico* (historic centre).

Book a taxi by calling any of the following companies:

Consortaxi (☑ 081 22 22; www.consortaxi.com)

Taxi Napoli (☑ 081 88 88; www.taxinapoli.it)

Radio Taxi La Partenope (☑ 081 01 01; www.radiotaxilapartenope.it)

BAY OF NAPLES

Capri

☑ 081 / POP 14,200

Capri's fabled beauty and refined hedonism has charmed them all, from Roman rulers and Russian revolutionaries to Hollywood legends. It's a perfect microcosm of Mediterranean appeal, a fusion of glittering grottoes and coves, Roman ruins and chi-chi piazzas.

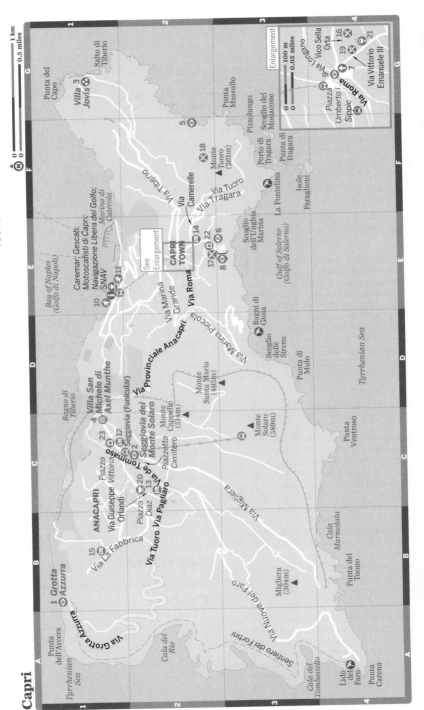

Capri

Capri

Already inhabited in the Palaeolithic period, the island was briefly occupied by the Greeks before Emperor Augustus made it his private playground and Tiberius retired here in AD 27. Its modern incarnation as a tourist centre dates from the early 20th century.

It's also a favourite day-trip destination and a summer favourite of holidaying VIPs. Inevitably, the two main centres, Capri Town and its uphill rival Anacapri, are almost entirely given over to tourism, with the high prices that follow. But explore beyond the designer boutiques and cafes and you'll find that Capri retains an unspoilt charm, with grand villas, overgrown vegetable plots, sun-bleached, peeling stucco and banks of brilliantly coloured bougainvillea.

◎ Sights

◎ Capri Town & Around

With its whitewashed stone buildings and tiny, car-free streets, Capri Town exudes a cinematic air. A diminutive model of upmarket Mediterranean chic, it's a well-tended playground of luxury hotels, expensive bars, smart restaurants and high-end boutiques. In summer the centre swells with crowds of camera-wielding day trippers and yacht-owning playboys (and girls), but don't be put off from exploring the atmospheric and ancient side streets, where the crowds quickly thin. The walk west out of town to Villa Jovis is especially wonderful.

★ **Villa Jovis**   RUINS
(Jupiter's Villa; Via A Maiuri; adult/reduced €4/2; ⊙10am-6pm Wed-Mon Jun, to 7pm Jul & Aug, reduced hours rest of year, closed Jan–mid-Mar) A 45-minute walk east of Capri along Via Tiberio, Villa Jovis was the largest and most sumptuous of the island's 12 Roman villas and Tiberius' main Capri residence. A vast pleasure complex, now reduced to ruins, it famously pandered to the emperor's supposedly debauched tastes, and included imperial quarters and extensive bathing areas set in dense gardens and woodland.

The villa's spectacular location posed major headaches for Tiberius' architects. The main problem was how to collect and store enough water to supply the villa's baths and 3000-sq-metre gardens. The solution they eventually hit upon was to build a complex canal system to transport rainwater to four giant storage tanks, whose remains you can still see today.

Beside the ticket office is the 330m-high **Salto di Tiberio** (Tiberius' Leap), a sheer cliff from where, as the story goes, Tiberius had out-of-favour subjects hurled into the sea. True or not, the stunning views are real enough; if you suffer from vertigo, tread carefully.

A shortish but steep walk from the villa, down Via Tiberio and Via Matermània, is the **Arco Naturale** – an imposing, Palaeolithic-era rock arch formed by the pounding sea; you can time this walk to take in lunch at nearby Le Grotelle (p84).

DON'T MISS

GROTTA AZZURRA

Capri's single most famous attraction is the **Grotta Azzurra** (Blue Grotto; €14; ⊘9am-5pm), a stunning sea cave illuminated by an other-worldly blue light. The easiest way to visit is to take a **tour** (☑081 837 56 46; www.motoscafisticapri.com; Private Pier 0, Marina Grande; €15) from Marina Grande; tickets include the return boat trip but the rowing boat into the cave and admission are paid separately. Allow a good hour.

The grotto had long been known to local fishermen when it was rediscovered by two Germans – writer Augustus Kopisch and painter Ernst Fries – in 1826. Subsequent research, however, revealed that Emperor Tiberius had built a quay in the cave around AD 30, complete with a *nymphaeum* (shrine to the water nymph). Remarkably, you can still see the carved Roman landing stage towards the rear of the cave.

Measuring 54m by 30m and rising to a height of 15m, the grotto is said to have sunk by up to 20m in prehistoric times, blocking every opening except the 1.3m-high entrance. And this is the key to the magical blue light. Sunlight enters through a small underwater aperture and is refracted through the water; this, combined with the reflection of the light off the white sandy seafloor, produces the vivid blue effect to which the cave owes its name.

The grotto is closed if the sea is too choppy and swimming in it is forbidden, although you can swim outside the entrance – get a bus to Grotta Azzurra, take the stairs down to the right and dive off the small concrete platform. When visiting, keep in mind that the singing 'captains' are included in the price, so don't feel any obligation if they push for a tip.

Giardini di Augusto　　　　　GARDENS
(Gardens of Augustus; €1; ⊘9am-7.30pm Apr-Oct, 9.30am-5.30pm Nov-Mar) As their name suggests, these gardens near the Certosa di San Giacomo were founded by Emperor Augustus. Rising in a series of flowered terraces, they lead to a lookout point offering breathtaking views over to the **Isole Faraglioni**, a group of three limestone stacks rising out of the sea.

Measuring 109m, 81m and 104m respectively, the *isole* are home to a rare blue lizard that was once thought to be unique to the Faraglioni but has since been found on the Sicilian coast.

From the gardens, pretty, hairpin **Via Krupp** winds down to Marina Piccola and past a bust of Lenin overlooking the road from a nearby platform. The Russian revolutionary visited Capri in 1908, during which time he was famously snapped engaged in a game of chess with fellow revolutionary Alexander Bogdanov. Looking on in the photograph is Russian writer Maxim Gorki, who called the island home between 1906 and 1909.

Certosa di San Giacomo　　MONASTERY
(☑081 837 62 18; Viale Certosa 40; adult/reduced €4/2; ⊘10am-7pm Tue-Sun Apr-Aug, to 5pm Sep-Dec, to 2pm Jan-Mar) Founded in 1363, this picturesque monastery is generally considered to be the finest remaining example of Caprese architecture and today houses a school, a library, a temporary exhibition space and a museum with some evocative 17th-century paintings. Be sure to look at the two cloisters, which have a real sense of faded glory (the smaller is 14th century, the larger 16th century).

To get here take Via Vittorio Emanuele III, east of Piazza Umberto I, which meanders down to the monastery.

The monastery's history is a harrowing one: it became the stronghold of the island's powerful Carthusian fraternity and was viciously attacked during Saracen pirate raids in the 16th century. A century later, monks retreated here to avoid the plague and were rewarded by an irate public (whom they should have been tending), who tossed corpses over the walls. There are some soothing 17th-century frescoes in the church, which will hopefully serve as an antidote as you contemplate the monastery's dark past.

Piazza Umberto I　　　　　PIAZZA
Located beneath the 17th-century clock tower and framed by see-and-be-seen cafes, this showy, open-air salon is central to your Capri experience, especially in the evening when the main activity in these parts is dressing up and hanging out. Be prepared for the cost of these front-row seats – the moment you sit down for a drink, you're going to pay handsomely for the grandstand views (around €6 for a cappuccino and €16 for a couple of glasses of white wine).

Chiesa di Santo Stefano CHURCH
(☑ 081 837 23 96; Piazza Umberto I; ⊙ 9am-7pm Apr-Oct, 10am-2pm rest of year) Overlooking Piazza Umberto I, this baroque 17th-century church boasts a well-preserved marble floor (taken from Villa Jovis) and a statue of San Costanzo, Capri's patron saint. Note the pair of languidly reclining patricians in the chapel to the south of the main altar, who seem to mirror some of the mildly debauched folk in the cafes outside. Beside the northern chapel is a reliquary with a saintly bone that reputedly saved Capri from the plague in the 19th century.

⊙ Anacapri & Around

Traditionally Capri Town's more subdued neighbour, Anacapri is no stranger to tourism. The focus is largely limited to Villa San Michele di Axel Munthe and the souvenir stores on the main streets. Delve further, though, and you'll discover that Anacapri is still, at heart, the laid-back, rural village that it's always been.

★ Seggiovia del Monte Solaro CABLE CAR
(☑ 081 837 14 38; www.capriseggiovia.it; single/return €8/11; ⊙ 9.30am-5pm May-Oct, to 4pm Mar & Apr, to 3.30pm Nov-Feb) A fast and painless way to reach Capri's highest peak, Anacapri's Seggiovia del Monte Solaro chairlift whisks you to the top of the mountain in a tranquil, beautiful ride of just 13 minutes. The views from the top are outstanding – on a clear day, you can see the entire Bay of Naples, the Amalfi Coast and the islands of Ischia and Procida.

**★ Villa San Michele
di Axel Munthe** MUSEUM, GARDENS
(☑ 081 837 14 01; www.villasanmichele.eu; Via Axel Munthe 34; €8; ⊙ 9am-6pm May-Sep, reduced hours rest of year) The former home of Swedish doctor, psychiatrist and animal-rights advocate Axel Munthe, San Michele di Axel Munthe should be included on every visitor's itinerary. Built on the site of the ruins of a Roman villa, the gardens make a beautiful setting for a tranquil stroll, with pathways flanked by immaculate flowerbeds. There are also superb views from here, plus some fine photo props in the form of Roman sculptures.

☀ Activities

★ Banana Sport BOATING
(☑ 348 5949665; Marina Grande; 2hr/day rental €90/220; ⊙ May-mid-Oct) Located on the eastern edge of the waterfront, Banana Sport hires out five-person motorised dinghies, allowing you to explore secluded coves and grottoes. You can also visit the popular swimming spot **Bagno di Tiberio** (€10), a small inlet west of Marina Grande; it's said that Tiberius once swam here.

★ Capri Whales BOATING
(☑ 081 837 58 33; www.capriwhales.it; Marina Grande 17; 2hr rental €90, 3hr tour €200; ⊙ May-Oct; ⊛) These dinghies are well equipped for families, with coolers, snorkelling gear, floats and water toys. The outfit also run tours around the island and to the mainland.

🛏 Sleeping

This island is all about lemon trees, pavement cafes, sultry summer evenings and wearing the largest pair of shades you can get your hands on. In other words, accommodation is strictly seasonal, which means bed space is tight and, in general, costly. Always book well ahead in the summer.

★ Casa Mariantonia BOUTIQUE HOTEL €€
(☑ 081 837 29 23; www.casamariantonia.com; Via Guiseppe Orlandi 80; d €120-280; ⊙ Apr-Oct; P ⊛ @ ⊛ ⊛) This fabulous boutique retreat counts Jean-Paul Sartre and Alberto Moravia among its past guests, which may well give you something to muse over while you are enjoying the tranquil beauty of the surroundings. Rooms deliver restrained elegance in soothing tones and there are private terraces with garden views. The in-house restaurant is set in a lemon grove, *naturally*.

★ Hotel Villa Eva HOTEL €€
(☑ 081 837 15 49; www.villaeva.com; Via La Fabbrica 8; d €120-200, tr €150-220, apt per person €60-90; ⊙ Apr-Oct; ⊛ @ ⊛ ⊛) Nestled amid fruit and olive trees in the countryside near Anacapri, Villa Eva is an idyllic retreat, complete with swimming pool, lush gardens and sunny rooms and apartments. Whitewashed domes, terracotta floors, stained-glass windows and vintage fireplaces add character, while the location ensures peace and quiet.

Capri Palace HOTEL €€€
(☑ 081 978 01 11; www.capripalace.com; Via Capodimonte 2b; d/ste from €500/1000; ⊙ Apr-Oct; ⊛ ⊛ ⊛) A VIP favourite (Gwyneth Paltrow, Liz Hurley and Naomi Campbell have all relaxed here), the super-chic Capri Palace takes *dolce vita* to dizzying levels. Its stylish

Mediterranean interior is enlivened with eye-catching contemporary art and its guest rooms are never less than lavish – some even have their own terraced garden and private plunge pool.

Grand Hotel Quisisana   HOTEL €€€
(☑ 081 837 07 88; www.quisi.com; Via Camerelle 2; r/ste from €330/850; ⊙ Easter-Oct; ❄ 🛜 🏊) Boasting a five-star luxury rating, the Quisisana is Capri's most prestigious address and is just few espadrille-clad steps from La Piazzetta (Piazza Umberto I). A slumber palace since the 19th century, it's a bastion of unashamed opulence, with two swimming pools, a fitness centre and spa, restaurants, bars and subtropical gardens. Rooms are suitably palatial, with cool colour schemes and mostly classic, conservative furniture.

 ## Eating

Traditional Campanian food served in traditional trattorias is what you'll mainly find on Capri. Prices are high but drop noticeably the further you get from Capri Town.

The island's culinary gift to the world is *insalata caprese,* a salad of fresh tomatoes, basil and silky mozzarella drizzled with olive oil. Look out for *caprese* cheese, a cross between mozzarella and ricotta, and *ravioli caprese,* ravioli stuffed with *cacciota* cheese and herbs. For a local sugar high, sink your teeth into *torta caprese,* a dense, flourless cake made with chocolate and almonds and best paired with a glass of Strega liqueur.

Many restaurants, like the hotels, close over winter and only reopen at Easter.

⭐**Raffaele Buonacore**   FAST FOOD €
(☑ 081 837 78 26; Via Vittorio Emanuele III 35; snacks €2-10, gelato from €2.50; ⊙ 8am-9pm, closed Tue Oct-Jun; 🍴) Ideal for a quick fill-up, this popular, down-to-earth snack bar does a roaring trade in savoury and sweet treats. Hit the spot with *frittate, panini* (sandwiches), *focaccie,* stuffed peppers, waffles and legendary ice cream. Hard to beat, though, are the delicious *sfogliatelle* (cinnamon-infused ricotta in a puff-pastry shell, €2.50) and the feather-light speciality *caprilu al limone* (lemon and almond cakes).

⭐**È Divino**   ITALIAN €€
(☑ 081 837 83 64; www.edivinocapri.com/divino; Vico Sella Orta 10a; meals €30-35; ⊙ 8pm-1am daily Jun-Aug, 12.30-2.30pm & 7.30pm-midnight Tue-Sun rest of the year; 🛜) Look hard for the sign: this Slow-Food restaurant is a well-kept

secret. Whether dining among lemon trees in the garden or among antiques, chandeliers, contemporary art (and a bed) inside, expect a thoughtful, regularly changing menu dictated by what's fresh from the garden or market. Favourites include a sultry pasta dish of *paccheri* with tuna, olives, capers and *datterini* tomatoes.

Le Grottelle   ITALIAN €€
(☑ 081 837 57 19; Via Arco Naturale 13; meals €27-40; ⊙ noon-3pm & 7-11pm Jul & Aug, noon-2.30pm & 7-11pm Fri-Wed Jun & Sep, noon-3pm Fri-Wed Apr, May & Oct; 🛜) This is a great place to impress someone – not so much for the food, which is decent enough, but for the dramatic setting. Close to the Arco Naturale, its two dining areas are set in a cave and on a hillside terrace with sea views. Dishes are rustic and honest, from homemade *fusilli* pasta with shrimps and zucchini to rabbit with onions, garlic and rosemary.

⭐**Il Geranio**   SEAFOOD €€€
(☑ 081 837 06 16; www.geraniocapri.com; Via Matteotti 8; meals €45-50; ⊙ noon-3pm & 7-11pm mid-Apr–mid-Oct) Time to pop the question or quell those pre-departure blues? The terrace at this sophisticated spot offers heart-stealing views over the pine trees to the Isole Faraglioni rocks. Seafood is the house speciality, particularly the salt-baked fish. Other fine choices include the octopus salad and linguine with saffron and mussels. Book at least three days ahead for a terrace table in high season.

🍷 Drinking & Nightlife

Capri's nightlife is a showy business. The main activity is styling up and hanging out, ideally at one of the cafes on La Piazzetta (Piazza Umberto I). Aside from the cafes, the nightlife here is fairly staid, with surprisingly few clubs. The most famous late-night party spot remains Taverna Anema e Core.

Taverna Anema e Core   CLUB
(☑ 329 4742508; www.anemaecore.com; Vico Sella Orta 39E, Capri Town; ⊙ 11pm-late Tue-Sun) Lying beyond a humble exterior is one of the island's most famous nightspots, run by the charismatic Guido Lembo. This smooth and sophisticated bar-club attracts an appealing mix of super-chic and casually dressed punters, here for the relaxed atmosphere and regular live music, including unwaveringly authentic Neapolitan guitar strumming and singing.

Caffè Michelangelo
CAFE

(Via Giuseppe Orlandi 138, Anacapri; ☺8am-2am Jul & Aug, to 1am Sep-Jun, closed Thu Nov & Dec; ☎) On a street flanked by tasteful shops and near two lovely piazzas, this modest, friendly corner cafe is a sound spot for a fix of people watching. Rate the passing parade over a *spritz con Cynar*, a less-sweet take on the classic Aperol *spritz*, made using a herbacious Italian bitter liqueur.

Shopping

Limoncello di Capri
DRINKS

(☑081 837 29 27; www.limoncello.com; Via Capodimonte 27, Anacapri; ☺9am-7.30pm) Don't be put off by the gaudy yellow display; this historic shop stocks some of the island's best *limoncello*. In fact, it was here that the drink was first concocted (or at least that is the claim…). Apparently, the grandmother of current owner Massimo made the tot as an after-dinner treat for the guests in her small guesthouse.

Carthusia I
Profumi di Capri
COSMETICS

(☑081 837 53 93; www.carthusia.it; Viale Matteotti 2d, Capri Town; ☺9am-8pm Apr-Sep, to 5pm rest of year) Allegedly, Capri's famous floral perfume was established in 1380 by the prior of the Certosa di San Giacomo. Caught unawares by a royal visit, he displayed the island's most beautiful flowers for the queen. Changing the water in the vase, he discovered a floral scent. This became the base of the classic perfume now sold at this smart laboratory outlet.

❶ Information

Post Office (www.poste.it; Via Roma 50; ☺8.20am-7pm Mon-Fri, to 12.30pm Sat) Located just west of the bus terminal in Capri Town.

Tourist Office (☑081 837 06 34; www.capritourism.com; Banchina del Porto, Marina Grande; ☺8.30am-4.15pm daily Jun–mid-Sep, 8.30am-2.30pm Mon-Sat rest of year) Can provide a map of the island, plus accommodation listings, ferry timetables and other useful information.

❶ Getting There & Away

The two major ferry routes to Capri are from Naples and Sorrento, although there are also seasonal connections with Ischia and the Amalfi Coast (Amalfi, Positano and Salerno).

Caremar (☑081 837 07 00; www.caremar.it) operates hydrofoils and ferries to/from Naples (€12.10 to €20, 40 minutes to 1¼ hours, up to seven daily) and hydrofoils to/from Sorrento €13.50 to €16, 25 minutes, four daily).

Gescab (☑081 428 55 55; www.gescab.it) runs hydrofoils to/from Naples (€20 to €22.50, 40 minutes, up to 17 daily) and to/from Sorrento (€17.70 to €20.20, 20 minutes, up to 19 daily).

Navigazione Libera del Golfo (NLG; ☑081 552 07 63; www.navlib.it) operates hydrofoils to/from Naples (from €18.70 to €22.50, 45 minutes, eight daily).

SNAV (☑081 428 55 55; www.snav.it) also operates hydrofoils to/from Naples (€22.20 to €23.50, 45 minutes, seven daily).

❶ Getting Around

BUS

Sippic (☑081 837 04 20; Bus Station, Via Roma, Capri Town; tickets €1.80, day tickets €8.60) Runs regular buses between Marina Grande and Anacapri, as well as between Anacapri and Capri Town.

Staiano Autotrasporti (☑081 837 24 22; www.staianotourcapri.com; Bus Station, Via Tommaso, Anacapri; tickets €2) These buses serve the Grotta Azzurra and Punta Carena *faro* (lighthouse).

FUNICULAR

Funicular (tickets €1.80; ☺6.30am-9.30pm) The first challenge facing visitors is how to get from Marina Grande to Capri Town. The most enjoyable option is the funicular, if only for the evocative en-route views over the lemon groves and surrounding countryside. The ticket booth in Marina Grande is not at the funicular station itself; it's behind the tourist office (turn right onto Via Marina Grande from the ferry port). Note that the funicular usually closes from January through March for maintenance; a substitute bus service is in place during this period.

SCOOTER

Ciro dei Motorini (☑338 3606918, 081 362 00 83; www.capriscooter.com; Via Marina Grande 55, Marina Grande; per 2/24hr €30/65) If you're looking to hire a scooter at Marina Grande, stop here.

TAXI

Taxi (☑in Anacapri 081 837 11 75, in Capri Town 081 837 66 57) From Marina Grande, a taxi costs from €17 to Capri and from €22 to Anacapri; from Capri to Anacapri costs from €18. These rates include one bag per vehicle. Each additional bag (with dimensions exceeding 40cm x 20cm x 50cm) costs an extra €2.

Ischia

081 / POP 64,000

The volcanic outcrop of Ischia is the most developed and largest of the islands in the Bay of Naples. It's an intriguing concoction of sprawling spa towns, abundant gardens, buried necropolises and spectacular scenery, with forests, vineyards and picturesque small towns.

Most visitors head straight for the north-coast towns of Ischia Porto, Ischia Ponte, Casamicciola Terme, Forio and Lacco Ameno. Of these, Ischia Porto boasts the best bars, Casamicciola the worst traffic and Ischia Ponte and Lacco Ameno the most appeal. On the calmer south coast, the car-free perfection of Sant'Angelo offers a languid blend of a cosy harbour and nearby bubbling beaches. In between the coasts lies a less-trodden landscape of dense chestnut forests, loomed over by Monte Epomeo, Ischia's highest peak.

Sights

★ **Castello Aragonese** CASTLE

(Aragon Castle; 081 99 28 34, 081 99 19 59; www.castelloaragoneseischia.com; Rocca del Castello, Ischia Ponte; adult/reduced €10/6; 9am-sunset) The elegant 15th-century Ponte Aragonese connects Ischia Ponte to Castello Aragonese, a magnificent, sprawling castle perched high and mighty on a rocky islet. While Syracusan tyrant Gerone I built the site's first fortress in 474 BC, the bulk of the current structure dates from the 1400s, when King Alfonso of Aragon gave the older Angevin fortress a thorough makeover, building the fortified bastions, current causeway and access ramp cut into the rock.

★ **La Mortella** GARDENS

(Place of the Myrtles; 081 98 62 20; www.lamortella.it; Via F Calese 39, Forio; adult/reduced €12/10; 9am-7pm Tue, Thu, Sat & Sun Apr-Oct) Designed by Russell Page and inspired by the Moorish gardens of Spain's Alhambra, La Mortella is recognised as one of Italy's finest botanical gardens and is well worth a couple of hours of your time. Stroll among terraces, pools, palms, fountains and more than 1000 rare and exotic plants from all over the world. The lower section of the garden is humid and tropical, while the upper level features Mediterranean plants and beautiful views over Forio and the coast.

Ischia's veritable Eden was established by the late British composer Sir William Walton and his Argentine wife, Susana (who died in March 2010, aged 83), who made it their home in 1949, entertaining such venerable house guests as Sir Laurence Olivier, Maria Callas and Charlie Chaplin. Walton's life is commemorated in a small museum and his music wafts over the loudspeakers at the elegant cafe. The gardens host chamber-music recitals in the spring and autumn, as well as symphonic concerts in the summer.

Activities

★ **Negombo** SPA

(081 98 61 52; www.negombo.it; Baia di San Montano, Lacco Ameno; admission all day €33, from 1.30pm/3.30pm/5.30pm €26/22/8; 8.30am-7pm mid-Apr–Oct) This is the place to come for a dose of pampering. Part spa resort, part botanical wonderland, with more than 500 exotic plant species, Negombo's combination of Zen-like thermal pools, hammam, contemporary sculpture and private beach on the Baia di San Montano tends to draw a younger crowd than many other Ischian spa spots.

There's a Japanese labyrinth pool for weary feet, a decent *tavola calda* (snack bar), and a full range of massage and beauty treatments. Those arriving by car or scooter can park all day on site (car €5, scooter €3). For a free dip in the bay, follow the signs to the *spiaggia* (beach) out the front of Negombo.

Monte Epomeo WALKING

Lace up those hiking boots and set out on a roughly 2.5km (50-minute) uphill walk from the village of Fontana, which will bring you to the top of Monte Epomeo (788m). Formed by an underwater eruption, it boasts superlative views of the Bay of Naples.

The little church near the top is the 15th-century **Cappella di San Nicola di Bari**, where you can check out the pretty majolica floor. The adjoining hermitage was built in the 18th century by an island governor who, after narrowly escaping death, swapped politics for poverty and spent the rest of his days here in saintly solitude. Have a peek inside, then head back down the hill, thankful that your saintliness doesn't exclude good wining and dining, Capri style.

Ischia Diving DIVING

(081 98 18 52; www.ischiadiving.net; Via Iasolino 106, Ischia Porto; single dive €40) This well-established diving outfit offers some

ISCHIA'S BEST BEACHES

Baia di Sorgeto (Via Sorgeto; ☉ Apr-Oct) Catch a water taxi from Sant'Angelo (€5 one way) or reach the beach on foot from the town of Panza. Waiting at the bottom is an intimate cove complete with bubbling thermal spring. Perfect for a winter dip.

Spiaggia dei Maronti Long, sandy and very popular; the sand here is warmed by natural steam geysers. Reach the beach by bus from Barano, by water taxi from Sant'Angelo (€3 one way) or on foot along the path leading east from Sant'Angelo.

Spiaggia dei Pescatori (Fishermen's Beach) Wedged between Ischia Porto and Ischia Ponte is the island's most down to earth and popular seaside strip; it's perfect for families.

Baia di San Montano Due west of Lacco Ameno, this gorgeous bay is the place for warm, shallow, crystal-clear waters. You'll also find the Negombo spa park here.

Punta Caruso Located on Ischia's northwestern tip, this secluded rocky spot is perfect for a swim in clear, deep water. To get here, follow the walking path that leads off Via Guardiola down to the beach. Not suitable for children or when seas are rough.

---

attractively priced dive packages, such as five dives including equipment for €180.

🛏 Sleeping

Camping Mirage　　　　　　CAMPGROUND €
(☎081 99 05 51; www.campingmirage.it; Via Maronti 37, Spiagga dei Maronti, Barano d'Ischia; camping per 2 people, car & tent €34-46; ☉ Easter-Oct; ℗) Located on Spiagga dei Maronti, one of Ischia's best beaches, and within walking distance of Sant'Angelo, this shady campground offers 50 places, showers, laundry facilities, a bar and a restaurant dishing up local special *tubettoni, cozze e pecorino* (pasta with mussels and sheep cheese).

Hotel Noris　　　　　　　　HOTEL €
(☎081 99 13 87; www.norishotel.it; Via A Sogliuzzo 2, Ischia Ponte; d €50-90; ☉ Easter-mid-Oct; ❋ 📶) This place has a great price and a great position within easy strolling distance of the Ponte sights. Some of the comfy, decent-sized rooms have small balconies. Breakfast is the standard, albeit slightly more expansive, continental buffet. Bonus points are due for the special parking deal (€10 per night) with the public car park across the way.

★Semiramis Hotel de Charme　　HOTEL €€
(☎081 90 75 11; www.hotelsemiramisischia.it; Spiaggia di Citara, Forio; d €140-185; ☉ mid-Apr-Oct; ℗ ❋ 📶 ▧) A few minutes' walk from the Poseidon spa complex, this bright hotel has a tropical-oasis feel with its outdoor thermal pool surrounded by lofty palms. Rooms are large and beautifully tiled in the traditional yellow-and-turquoise pattern, and the garden is glorious, with fig trees, vineyards and sea views.

**★Albergo
Il Monastero**　　　　　　　　HOTEL €€
(☎081 99 24 35; www.albergoilmonastero.it; Castello Aragonese, Rocca del Castello, Ischia Ponte; s €80-90, d €140-200; ☉ Easter-mid-Oct; ❋ 📶) The former monks' cells still have a certain appealing sobriety about them, with their dark-wood furniture, white walls, vintage terracotta tiles and no TV (the views are sufficiently prime time). Elsewhere, the hotel exudes a pleasing sense of space and style, with vaulted ceilings, plush sofas, antiques and contemporary art by the late owner and artist Gabriele Mattera. The hotel restaurant has an excellent reputation.

🍴 Eating

★Il Focolare　　　　　　　ITALIAN €€
(☎081 90 29 44; www.trattoriailfocolare.it; Via Creajo al Crocefisso 3, Barano d'Ischia; meals €30; ☉12.30-2.45pm Thu-Sun & 7.30-11.30pm daily Jun-Oct, closed Wed Nov-Jan & Mar-May, closed Feb) A good choice for those seeking a little turf instead of surf, this is one of the island's best-loved restaurants. Family run, homey and rustic, it has a solidly traditional meat-based menu with steaks, lamb cutlets and specialities including *coniglio all'Ischitana* (typical local rabbit dish with tomatoes, garlic and herbs). On the sweet front, the desserts are homemade and exquisite.

Owner Riccardo D'Ambra (who runs the restaurant together with his son, Agostino) is a leading local advocate of the Slow Food movement. If you want seafood, coffee or soft drinks, you'll have to go elsewhere; they're not on the menu here.

ISCHIA ON A FORK

Ischian restaurateur Carlo Buono of **Da Ciccio** (☎ 081 199 13 14; www.bardaciccio.it; Via Porto 1, Ischia Porto; snacks from €1; ⊗ 8am-midnight) gives the low-down on his cherished classic island cuisine:

'Fresh, seasonal ingredients are the cornerstone of Ischian cooking, from silky olive oil to plump *pomodorini* (cherry tomatoes). Like Neapolitan cooking, the emphasis is on simple, uncomplicated home cooking. Traditionally, there are two types of Ischian cuisine: coastal and mountain. For centuries, fishermen would barter with farmers, who'd offer wine, vegetables, pork and rabbit in exchange for the catch.

'Rabbit is a typical Ischian meat and we're seeing a revival of the traditional *fossa* (pit) breeding method, where rabbits are bred naturally in deep *fosse* instead of in cages. The result is a more tender, flavoursome meat. Leading this renaissance is local Slow Food advocate Riccardo D'Ambra, whose famous trattoria Il Focolare (p87) is well known for its rabbit and rustic mountain dishes. Definitely worth eating on the island is a popular Sunday dish called *coniglio all'ischitana* (Ischia-style rabbit), prepared with olive oil, unpeeled garlic, chilli, tomato, basil, thyme and white wine.

'Typical local fish include *pesce bandiera* (sailfish), the flat *castagna*, *lampuga* and *palamide* (a small tuna). A popular way of cooking it is in *acqua pazza* (crazy water). Traditionally prepared on the fishing boats, it's a delicate sauce made with *pomodorini*, garlic and parsley. Fried fish is also very typical; a fresh serve of *frittura di mare* (mixed fried seafood) drizzled with lemon juice is just superb. May to September is *totano* (squid) season and a great time to try *totani imbotti* (squid stuffed with olives, capers and breadcrumbs, and stewed in wine).

'Equally wonderful is fresh, wood-fired *casareccio* bread – it's perfect for doing the *scarpetta* (wiping your plate clean) or for filling with salami or *parmigiano* cheese. If you have any room left, track down a slice of *torta caprese*, a moist chocolate and almond cake. *Buon appetito*.'

★ **Ristorante Pietratorcia**   ITALIAN €€

(☎ 081 90 72 32; www.ristorantepietratorcia.it; Via Provinciale Panza 401, Forio; meals around €30; ⊗ 11am-2pm & 5.30pm-midnight Easter-Oct; 🛜) Enjoying a bucolic setting among tumbling vines, wild fig trees and rosemary bushes, this A-list winery is a foodie's nirvana. Tour the old stone cellars, sip a local drop (wine degustations from €20) and eye up a competent, seasonal turf-and-surf menu that might include artichoke parmigiana or *baccalà* (salted cod) with *scarole* (escarole) and toasted pine nuts. Consider booking ahead in high season. The CD and CS buses stop within metres of the winery's entrance; ask the driver to advise you when to alight.

Montecorvo   ITALIAN €€

(☎ 081 99 80 29; www.montecorvo.it; Via Montecorvo 33, Forio; meals €30; ⊗ 7.30pm-midnight daily, also 12.30-3pm Sun, closed Wed Dec-Mar; 🛜) Part of the dining room at hillside Montecorvo is tunnelled into a cave, while the verdant terrace offers spectacular sunset views. Hidden amid lush foliage outside Forio, the place is owned by Giovanni, who prides himself on the special dishes he makes daily.

There's an emphasis on grilled meat and fish, and an especially popular dish of local rabbit, cooked in a woodfired oven.

Despite its sneaky location, Montecorvo is well signposted along the side street that leads to it.

ℹ Information

Tourist Office (☎ 081 507 42 31; www.info ischiaprocida.it; Corso Sogliuzzo 72, Ischia Porto; ⊗ 9am-2pm & 3-8pm Mon-Sat) A slim selection of maps and brochures.

ℹ Getting There & Away

Caremar (☎ 081 98 48 18; www.caremar.it) operates up to six hydrofoils daily each way between Naples and Ischia Porto (€17.60, 45 minutes).

Alilauro (☎ 081 497 22 42; www.alilauro.it) operates up to 12 hydrofoils daily each way between Naples and Ischia Porto (€18.90 to €19.80, 50 minutes). It also runs up to six hydrofoils daily between Forio and Naples (€20.10 to €21.10).

SNAV (☎ 081 428 55 55; www.snav.it) operates hydrofoils between Naples and Casamicciola (€19.90 to €20.90, one hour), up to eight times daily.

ⓘ Getting Around

Ischia's main circular highway can get clogged with traffic in the height of summer. This, combined with the penchant the local youth have for overtaking on blind corners and the environmental impact of just too many cars, means that you may want to consider riding the excellent network of buses (cheap!) or hopping in a taxi (not cheap!) to get around. The distance between attractions and the lack of pavements on the busy roads makes walking unappealing.

The island's main **bus station** is a one-minute walk west of the **pier**, at Ischia Porto, with buses servicing all other parts of the island.

Procida

📕 081 / POP 10,500

The Bay of Naples' smallest island is also its best-kept secret. Mercifully off the mass-tourist radar, Procida is like the Portofino prototype and is refreshingly real. August aside – when beach-bound mainlanders flock to its shores – its narrow, sun-bleached streets are the domain of the locals: young boys clutch fishing rods, mothers push prams and old seamen swap yarns. Here, the hotels are smaller, fewer waiters speak broken German and the island's welcome is untainted by too much tourism.

If you have the time, Procida is an ideal place to explore on foot. The most compelling areas (and where you will also find most of the hotels, bars and restaurants) are Marina Grande, Marina Corricella and Marina di Chiaiolella. Beaches are not plentiful here, apart from the Lido di Procida, where, aside from August, you shouldn't have any trouble finding some towel space.

◉ Sights

Isola di Vivara NATURE RESERVE
(www.visitprocida.it; adult/reduced €10/5; ⏰ guided tours 10am & 3pm Fri-Sun) Linked to Procida by pedestrian bridge, pocket-sized Vivara is what remains of a volcanic crater dating back some 55,000 years. The island is home to unique flora and abundant bird life, while archaeological digs have uncovered traces of a Bronze-Age Mycenaean settlement as well as pottery fragments dating back to early Greek colonisation. Guided tours (including in English) of Vivara are run Friday to Sunday and must be booked two to three days in advance via the Visit Procida website.

Abbazia di San Michele Arcangelo CHURCH, MUSEUM
(📕 334 8514028, 334 8514252; www.abbaziasan micheleprocida.it; Via Terra Murata 89, Terra Murata; ⏰ 10am-12.45pm & 3-5pm) FREE Soak in the dizzying bay views at the belvedere before exploring the adjoining Abbazia di San Michele Arcangelo. Built in the 11th century and remodelled between the 17th and 19th centuries, this one-time Benedictine abbey houses a small museum with some arresting pictures created in gratitude by shipwrecked sailors, plus a church with a spectacular coffered ceiling and an ancient Greek alabaster basin converted into a font. On our last visit, the museum was closed indefinitely for maintenance.

The church apse features four paintings by Neapolitan artist Nicola Russo. Dating back to 1690, these works include a depiction of St Michael the Archangel protecting Procida from Saracen attack on 8 May 1535. The painting is especially fascinating for its depiction of Marina Grande in the 16th century.

Activities

Blue Dream Yacht Charter BOATING
(📕 339 5720874, 081 896 05 79; www.bluedream charter.com; Via Vittorio Emanuele 14, Marina Grande; 4/8-person yacht per week from €1300/2200) If you have 'champagne on the deck' aspirations, you can always charter your very own yacht or catamaran from here.

Procida Rent a Bike CYCLING
(📕 081 896 00 60, 338 1329102; Via Roma, Marina Grande; 1/4hr €10/15; 🚲) The bicycles for hire here are one of the best ways to explore the island. Small, open micro-taxis can also be hired for two to three hours for around €35, depending on your bargaining prowess.

Tours

Cesare Boat Trips BOATING
(📕 333 4603877; 2½hr tour per person €25; ⏰ Mar-Oct) On the harbour at Marina Corricella, ask for friendly Cesare in your best Italian. Check at one of the beach bars or by La Gorgonia restaurant – he won't be far away. Cesare runs some great boat trips as well as half-day trips in a traditional galleon for €100 (minimum 25 people).

Festivals & Events

Procession
of the Misteri
RELIGIOUS

Good Friday sees a colourful procession when a wooden statue of Christ and the Madonna Addolorata, along with life-size plaster and papier-mâché tableaux illustrating events leading to Christ's crucifixion, are carted across the island. Men dress in blue tunics with white hoods, while many of the young girls dress as the Madonna.

Sleeping

Bed & Breakfast La Terrazza
B&B €

(☎081 896 00 62; Via Faro 26, Marina Grande; s €50-70, d €75-90; �l Easter-Oct; ☎) An extremely attractive budget option, where the rooms are decked out with paintings, metal lamps, tiles and antiques. Take time out on the terracotta-floored terrace – thus the B&B's name – where you can lie back on a lounger and enjoy the sunset. Homemade breakfasts are served up here.

★ Hotel La Vigna
BOUTIQUE HOTEL €€

(☎081 896 04 69; www.albergolavigna.it; Via Principessa Margherita 46, Terra Murata; d €150-180, ste €180-230; �l Easter-Oct; ⓟ❄@☎☀) Enjoying a discreet cliff-side location, this 18th-century villa is a gorgeous retreat, complete with rambling garden, vines and a brand-new swimming pool. Five of the spacious, simply furnished rooms offer direct access to the garden. Superior rooms (€180 to €200) feature family-friendly mezzanines, while the main perk of the suite is the bedside hot tub: perfect for romancing couples.

The small in-house spa has wine-therapy treatments.

★ Casa Sul Mare
HOTEL €€

(☎081 896 87 99; www.lacasasulmare.it; Salita Castello 13, Marina Corricella; r €125-170; �l Mar-Oct; ❄☎) A crisp, white-washed place with the kind of evocative views that helped make *The Talented Mr Ripley* such a memorable film. Overlooking the pastel-hued fishing village of Marina Corricella, near the ruined Castello d'Avalos, its rooms are simple yet elegant, with fetching tiled floors, wrought-iron bedsteads and the odd piece of antique furniture.

The hotel treats its guests well: during summer there's a boat service to the nearby Spiaggia della Chiaia (Chiaia Beach), and the morning cappuccino, courtesy of Franco, may be the best you've ever had.

Eating

Da Giorgio
TRATTORIA €

(☎081 896 79 10; Via Roma 36, Marina Grande; meals €24; �l noon-3pm & 7-11.30pm Mar-Oct, closed Tue Nov-Feb) A retro, no-frills neighbourhood eatery close to the port. The menu holds few surprises, but the ingredients are fresh; try the *spaghetti con frutti di mare* (seafood spaghetti) or the *soutè di cozze e lupini* (sauté of mussels and small clams), the latter a perfect match for Da Giorgio's wonderfully spongy *casareccio* (homestyle) bread.

Fammivento
SEAFOOD €€

(☎081 896 90 20; Via Roma 39, Marina Grande; meals €25; �l noon-3.30pm & 8-11pm Tue-Sat, noon-3.30pm Sun, closed Dec-Feb) Get things going with the *frittura di calamari* (fried squid), then try the *fusilli carciofi e calamari* (pasta with artichokes and calamari). For a splurge, go for the house speciality of *zuppa di crostaci e moluschi* (crustacean and mollusc soup).

ⓘ Information

Pro Loco (☎344 1162932; www.facebook.com/proloco.procida.3; Via Roma, Stazione Marittima, Marina Grande; �l 10am-1pm daily, also 3-5pm Sat & Sun) Located at the Ferry & Hydrofoil Ticket Office, this modest office has sparse printed information but should be able to advise on activities, accommodation and the like.

ⓘ Getting There & Away

The **Ferry & Hydrofoil Terminal** is in Marina Grande.

Caremar (☎081 896 72 80; www.caremar.it) operates up to eight daily hydrofoils to/from Naples (€16.70, 25 minutes).

SNAV (☎081 428 55 55; www.snav.it) operates up to four hydrofoils daily to/from Naples (€17.30 to €18.80, 25 minutes).

SOUTH OF NAPLES

Herculaneum (Ercolano)

Ercolano is an uninspiring Neapolitan suburb that's home to one of Italy's best-preserved ancient sites: Herculaneum. A superbly conserved fishing town, the site is smaller and less daunting than Pompeii, allowing you to visit without the nagging feeling that you're bound to miss something.

⊙ Sights

★ Ruins of Herculaneum
ARCHAEOLOGICAL SITE

(🖉 081 857 53 47; www.pompeiisites.org; Corso Resina 187, Ercolano; adult/reduced €11/5.50, incl Pompeii €22/12; ⊗ 8.30am-7.30pm Apr-Oct, to 5pm Nov-Mar; 🚃 Circumvesuviana to Ercolano-Scavi) Upstaged by its larger rival, Pompeii, Herculaneum harbours a wealth of archaeological finds, from ancient advertisements and stylish mosaics to carbonised furniture and terror-struck skeletons. Indeed, this superbly conserved Roman fishing town of 4000 inhabitants is easier to navigate than Pompeii, and can be explored with a map and audio guide (€8).

To reach the ruins from Ercolano-Scavi train station, walk downhill to the very end of Via IV Novembre and through the archway across the street. The path leads down to the ticket office, which lies on your left. Ticket purchased, follow the walkway around to the actual entrance to the ruins, where you can also hire audio guides.

Herculaneum's fate runs parallel to that of Pompeii. Destroyed by an earthquake in AD 62, the AD 79 eruption of Mt Vesuvius saw it submerged in a 16m-thick sea of mud that essentially fossilised the city. This meant that even delicate items, such as furniture and clothing, were discovered remarkably well preserved. Tragically, the inhabitants didn't fare so well; thousands of people tried to escape by boat but were suffocated by the volcano's poisonous gases. Indeed, what appears to be a moat around the town is in fact the ancient shoreline. It was here in 1980 that archaeologists discovered some 300 skeletons, the remains of a crowd that had fled to the beach only to be overcome by the terrible heat of clouds surging down from Vesuvius.

The town itself was rediscovered in 1709 and amateur excavations were carried out intermittently until 1874, with many finds carted off to Naples to decorate the houses of the well-to-do or ending up in museums. Serious archaeological work began again in 1927 and continues to this day, although with much of the ancient site buried beneath modern Ercolano it's slow going. Indeed, note that at any given time some houses will invariably be shut for restoration.

➡ Casa d'Argo

(Argus House) This noble house would originally have opened onto Cardo II (as yet unearthed). Its porticoed garden opens onto a *triclinium* (dining room) and other residential rooms.

➡ Casa dello Scheletro

(House of the Skeleton) The modest Casa dello Scheletro features five styles of mosaic flooring, including a design of white arrows at the entrance to guide the most disorientated of guests. In the internal courtyard, don't miss the skylight, complete with the remnants of an ancient security grill. Of the house's mythically themed wall mosaics, only the faded ones are originals; the others now reside in Naples' Museo Archeologico Nazionale (p64).

➡ Terme Maschili

(Men's Baths) The Terme Maschili were the men's section of the **Terme del Foro** (Forum Baths). Note the ancient latrine to the left of the entrance before you step into the *apodyterium* (changing room), complete with bench for waiting patrons and a nifty wall shelf for sandal and toga storage.

While those after a bracing soak would pop into the *frigidarium* (cold bath) to the left, the less stoic headed straight into the *tepadarium* (tepid bath) to the right. The sunken mosaic floor here is testament to the seismic activity preceding Mt Vesuvius' catastrophic eruption. Beyond this room lies the *caldarium* (hot bath), as well as an exercise area.

➡ Decumano Massimo

Herculaneum's ancient high street is lined with shops, and fragments of advertisements – listing everything from the weight of goods to their price – still adorn the walls. Note the one to the right of the Casa del Salone Nero. Further east along the street, a crucifix found in an upstairs room of the Casa del Bicentenario (Bicentenary House) provides possible evidence of a Christian presence in pre-Vesuvius Herculaneum.

➡ Casa del Bel Cortile

(House of the Beautiful Courtyard) Closed on our last visit, the Casa del Bel Cortile is home to three of the 300 skeletons discovered on the ancient shore by archaeologists in 1980. Almost two millennia later, it's still poignant to see the forms of what are understood to be a mother, father and young child huddled together in the last, terrifying moments of their lives.

➡ Casa di Nettuno e Anfitrite

(House of Neptune and Amphitrite) This aristocratic pad takes its name from the extraordinary mosaic in the *nymphaeum* (fountain and bath). The warm colours in which the

DIEGO FIORE/SHUTTERSTOCK ©

1. Tempio di Cerere (p119), Paestum 2. Villa dei Misteri (p100), Pompeii 3. Herculaneum (p90) 4. Complesso Monumentale di San Lorenzo Maggiore (p61), Naples

DE AGOSTINI/ ARCHIVIO J. LANGE/GETTY IMAGES ©

Historical Riches

Few Italian regions can match Campania's historical legacy. Colonised by the ancient Greeks and loved by the Romans, it's a sun-drenched repository of A-list antiquities, from World Heritage wonders to lesser-known archaeological gems.

Paestum

Great Greek temples never go out of vogue and those at Paestum (p119) are among the greatest outside Greece itself. With the oldest structures stretching back to the 6th century BC, this place makes Rome's Colosseum feel positively modern.

Herculaneum

A bite-sized Pompeii, Herculaneum (p90) is even better preserved than its nearby rival. This is the place to delve into the details, from once-upon-a-time shop advertisements and furniture, to vivid mosaics, even an ancient security grille.

Pompeii

Short of stepping into the Tardis, Pompeii (p95) is your best bet for a little time travel. Locked in ash for centuries, its excavated streetscapes offer a tangible encounter with the ancients and their daily lives, from luxury homes to a racy brothel.

Subterranean Naples

Eerie aqueducts, mysterious burial crypts and ancient streetscapes: beneath Naples' hyperactive streets lies a wonderland of Graeco-Roman ruins. For a taste, head below the Complesso Monumentale di San Lorenzo Maggiore (p61) or follow the leader on a tour of the evocative Catacombe di San Gennaro (p65).

sea god and his nymph bride are depicted hint at how lavish the original interior must have been.

➡ Casa del Tramezzo di Legno

(House of the Wooden Partition) Unusually, this house features two atria, which very likely belonged to two separate dwellings that were merged in the 1st century AD. The most famous relic here is a wonderfully well-preserved wooden screen, which separates the atrium from the *tablinum*, where the owner talked business with his clients. The second room off on the left side of the atrium features the remains of an ancient bed.

➡ Casa dell'Atrio a Mosaico

(House of the Mosaic Atrium) An ancient mansion, the House of the Mosaic Atrium harbours extensive floor tile-work, although time and nature have left the floor buckled and uneven. Particularly noteworthy is the black-and-white chessboard mosaic in the atrium. Closed for restoration at the time of research.

➡ Casa del Gran Portale

(House of the Large Portal) Named after the elegant brick Corinthian columns that flank its main entrance, the House of the Large Portal is home to some well-preserved wall paintings.

➡ Casa dei Cervi

(House of the Stags) Closed indefinitely on our last visit, the Casa dei Cervi is an imposing example of a Roman noble family's house that, before the volcanic mud slide, boasted a seafront address. Constructed around a central courtyard, the two-storey villa contains murals and some beautiful still-life paintings. Waiting for you in the courtyard is a diminutive pair of marble deer assailed by dogs, and an engaging statue of a drunken, peeing Hercules.

➡ Villa dei Papiri

(Villa of the Papyri) The Villa dei Papiri was the most luxurious villa in Herculaneum. Owned by Lucius Calpurnius Piso Caesoninus, Julius Caesar's father-in-law, it was a vast four-storey, 245m-long complex stretching down to the sea; there were swimming pools, fountains and a collection of up to 80 sculptures. There was also an important library, whose 1800 papyrus scrolls lend the villa its name. Most of the carbonised scrolls are now in Naples' Museo Archeologico Nazionale.

➡ Terme Suburbane

(Suburban Baths) Marking Herculaneum's southernmost tip is the 1st-century-AD Terme Suburbane, one of the best-preserved Roman bath complexes in existence, with deep pools, stucco friezes and bas-reliefs looking down upon marble seats and floors. This is also one of the best places to observe the soaring volcanic deposits that smothered the ancient coastline.

MAV   MUSEUM

(Museo Archeologico Virtuale; ☑ 081 1777 6843; www.museomav.com; Via IV Novembre 44; adult/ reduced €7.50/6, with 3D documentary €11.50/10; ⊙ 9am-5.30pm daily Mar-May, 10am-6.30pm daily Jun-Sep, 10am-4pm Tue-Sun Oct-Feb; 🖪; 🚊 Circumvesuviana to Ercolano-Scavi) Using computer-generated recreations, this 'virtual archaeological museum' brings ruins such as the forum at Pompeii and Capri's Villa Jovis back to virtual life. Unfortunately, several of the panels are out of order and some of the displays are in Italian only. The short, optional documentary gives an overview of the history of Mt Vesuvius and its infamous eruption in AD 79…in rather lacklustre 3D. The museum is on the main street linking Ercolano-Scavi train station to the ruins of Herculaneum.

✗ Eating

Viva Lo Re   NEAPOLITAN €€
(☑ 081 739 02 07; www.vivalore.it; Corso Resina 261; meals €32; ⊙ noon-4pm & 7-11pm Tue-Sat, noon-4pm Sun) Located 500m southeast of the Herculaneum ruins on Corso Resina – dubbed the Miglio d'Oro (Golden Mile) for its once glorious stretch of 18th-century villas – Viva Lo Re is a stylish *osteria* (casual tavern), where vintage prints and bookshelves meet a superb wine list and competent regional cooking made using quality ingredients. On the downside, service can be a little patchy and portions somewhat small (ask before ordering).

❶ Information

Tourist Office (Via IV Novembre 44; ⊙ 9am-5.30pm Mon-Fri; 🚊 Circumvesuviana to Ercolano-Scavi) Ercolano's tourist office is located in the same building as MAV, between the Circumvesuviana Ercolano-Scavi train station and the Herculaneum *scavi* (ruins).

❶ Getting There & Away

If travelling by Circumvesuviana train (€2.20 from Naples or €2.90 from Sorrento), get off at Ercolano-Scavi station and walk 500m downhill to the ruins – follow the signs for the *scavi* down the main street, Via IV Novembre.

If driving from Naples, the A3 runs southeast along the Bay of Naples. To reach Herculaneum, exit at Ercolano Portico and follow the signs to car parks near the site. From Sorrento, head north along the SS145, which spills onto the A3.

From mid-April to mid-October, tourist train Campania Express runs four times daily between Naples (Porta Nolana and Piazza Garibaldi Circumvesuviana stations) and Sorrento, stopping at Ercolano-Scavi and Pompei-Scavi-Villa dei Misteri en route. One-day return tickets from Naples to Ercolano (€7) or from Sorrento to Ercolano (€11) can be purchased at the stations or online at www.eavsrl.it.

Mt Vesuvius

Rising formidably beside the Bay of Naples, Mt Vesuvius forms part of the Campanian volcanic arch, a string of active, dormant and extinct volcanoes that include the Campi Flegrei's Solfatara and Monte Nuovo, and Ischia's Monte Epomeo. Infamous for its explosive Plinian eruptions and surrounding urban sprawl, it's also one of the world's most carefully monitored volcanoes. Another full-scale eruption would be catastrophic. More than half a million people live in the so-called 'red zone', the area most vulnerable to pyroclastic flows and crushing pyroclastic deposits in a major eruption. Yet, despite government incentives to relocate, few residents are willing to leave.

◉ Sights

Mt Vesuvius   VOLCANO

(crater adult/reduced €10/8; ⊙ crater 9am-6pm Jul & Aug, to 5pm Apr-Jun & Sep, to 4pm Mar & Oct, to 3pm Nov-Feb, ticket office closes 1hr before crater) Since exploding into history in AD 79, Vesuvius has blown its top more than 30 times. What redeems this slumbering menace is the spectacular panorama from its crater, which takes in Naples, its world-famous bay, and part of the Apennine mountains. Vesuvius is the focal point of the Parco Nazionale del Vesuvio, with nine nature walks around the volcano – download a simple map from the park's website. **Horse Riding Tour Naples** (☑ 345 8560306; www.horseriding naples.com; guided tour €60) also runs three daily horse-riding tours (€60).

The mountain is widely believed to have been higher than it currently stands, claiming a single summit rising to about 3000m rather than the 1281m of today. Its violent outburst in AD 79 not only drowned Pompeii in pumice and pushed the coastline back several kilometres but also destroyed much of the mountain top, creating a huge caldera and two new peaks. The most destructive explosion after that of AD 79 was in 1631, while the most recent was in 1944.

❶ Getting There & Away

Vesuvius can be reached by bus from Pompeii and Ercolano.

The cheapest option is to catch the public **EAV bus** (☑ 800 211388; www.eavsrl.it) service from Piazza Anfiteatro in Pompeii. Buses depart every 50 minutes from 8am to 3.30pm and take around 50 minutes to reach the summit car park. Once here, purchase your entry ticket to the summit area (€10) and follow the 860m path (best tackled in trainers and with sweater in tow) up to the crater (roughly a 25-minute climb). In Pompeii, ignore any touts telling you that the public bus only runs in summer; they are merely trying to push private tours. Bus tickets cost €2.70 one-way and can be purchased on board.

If you do want to use a private company, **Busvia del Vesuvio** (☑ 081 878 21 03; www.busvia delvesuvio.com; Via Villa dei Misteri, Pompeii; return incl entry to summit adult/reduced €22/7; ⊙ hourly from 9am-4pm) runs hourly shuttle buses from outside Pompei-Scavi-Villa dei Misteri Circumvesuviana train station, travelling to Boscoreale Terminal Interchange. From here, it's a 25-minute journey up the national park in a 4WD-style bus. Bookings are not required.

In Ercolano, private company **Vesuvio Express** (☑ 081 739 36 66; www.vesuvioexpress. it; Piazzale Stazione Circumvesuviana, Ercolano; return incl admission to summit €20; ⊙ every 40min, 9.30am-4pm) runs buses to the summit car park from Piazzale Stazione Circumvesuviana, outside Ercolano-Scavi train station. A word of warning: this company has received very mixed reviews, with numerous claims of unreliability from travellers.

When the weather is bad the summit path is shut and bus departures are suspended.

If travelling by car, exit the A3 at Ercolano Portico and follow signs for the Parco Nazionale del Vesuvio.

Pompeii

Modern-day Pompeii (Pompei in Italian) may feel like a nondescript satellite of Naples, but it's here that you'll find Europe's most compelling archaeological site: the ruins of Pompeii. Sprawling and haunting, the site is a stark reminder of the malign forces that lie deep inside Vesuvius.

◎ Sights

★ **Ruins of Pompeii**   ARCHAEOLOGICAL SITE
(☏ 081 857 53 47; www.pompeiisites.org; entrances at Porta Marina, Piazza Esedra & Piazza Anfiteatro; adult/reduced €13/7.50, incl Herculaneum €22/12; ⊙ 9am-7.30pm, last entry 6pm Apr-Oct, to 5pm, last entry 3.30pm Nov-Mar) The ghostly ruins of ancient Pompeii make for one of the world's most engrossing archaeological experiences. Much of the site's value lies in the fact that the town wasn't simply blown away by Vesuvius in AD 79 but buried under a layer of *lapilli* (burning fragments of pumice stone). The result is a remarkably well-preserved slice of ancient life, where visitors can walk down Roman streets and snoop around millennia-old houses, temples, shops, cafes, amphitheatres, and even a brothel.

The origins of Pompeii are uncertain, but it seems likely that it was founded in the 7th century BC by the Campanian Oscans. Over the next seven centuries, the city fell to the Greeks and the Samnites before becoming a Roman colony in 80 BC.

In AD 62, a mere 17 years before Vesuvius erupted, the city was struck by a major earthquake. Damage was widespread and much of the city's 20,000-strong population was evacuated. Fortunately, many had not returned by the time Vesuvius blew, but 2000 men, women and children perished nevertheless.

After its catastrophic demise, Pompeii receded from the public eye until 1594, when the architect Domenico Fontana stumbled across the ruins while digging a canal. Exploration proper, however, didn't begin until 1748. Of Pompeii's original 66 hectares, 44 have now been excavated. Of course that doesn't mean you'll have unhindered access to every inch of the Unesco-listed site – expect to come across areas cordoned off for no apparent reason, a noticeable lack of clear signs, and the odd stray dog. Audio guides are a sensible investment (€8, cash only) and a good guidebook will also help – try *Pompeii*, published by Electa Napoli.

Maintenance work is ongoing, but progress is beset by political, financial and bureaucratic problems.

➡ **Terme Suburbane**
Just outside ancient Pompeii's city walls, this 1st-century-BC bathhouse is famous for several erotic frescoes that scandalised the Vatican when they were revealed in 2001.

The panels decorate what was once the *apodyterium* (changing room). The room leading to the colourfully frescoed *frigidarium* (cold bath) features fragments of stuccowork, as well as one of the few original roofs to survive at Pompeii. Beyond the *tepadarium* (tepid bath) and *caldarium* (hot bath) rooms are the remains of a heated outdoor swimming pool.

➡ **Porta Marina**
The ruin of Pompeii's main entrance is at Porta Marina, the most impressive of the seven gates that punctuated the ancient town walls. A busy passageway now, as it was then, it originally connected the town with the nearby harbour, hence the gateway's name. Immediately on the right as you enter the gate is the **Antiquarium** and the 1st-century-BC **Tempio di Venere** (Temple of Venus), formerly one of the town's most opulent temples.

➡ **Foro**
(Forum) A huge rectangle flanked by limestone columns, the *foro* was ancient Pompeii's main piazza, as well as the site of gladiatoral battles before the Anfiteatro was constructed. The buildings surrounding the forum are testament to its role as the city's hub of civic, commercial, political and religious activity.

➡ **Basilica**
The basilica was the 2nd-century-BC seat of Pompeii's law courts and exchange. Their semicircular apses would later influence the design of early Christian churches.

➡ **Tempio di Apollo**
(Temple of Apollo) The oldest and most important of Pompeii's religious buildings, the Tempio di Apollo largely dates to the 2nd century BC, including the striking columned portico. Fragments remain of an earlier version dating to the 6th century BC.

➡ **Tempio di Giove**
(Temple of Jupiter) One of the two flanking triumphal arches of the Tempio di Giove still remains.

➡ **Granai del Foro**
(Forum Granary) The Granai del Foro is now used to store hundreds of amphorae and a number of body casts that were made in the late 19th century by pouring plaster into the hollows left by disintegrated bodies. Among these casts is a pregnant slave; the belt

Old Pompeii

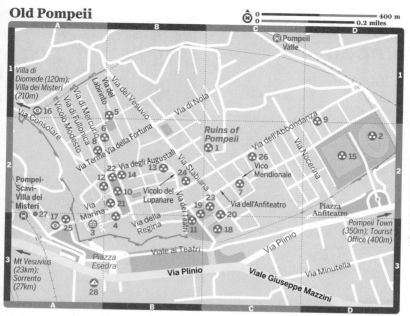

Old Pompeii

around her waist would have displayed the name of her owner.

➡ Macellum

The *macellum* was the city's main produce market. The circular area in the centre was the *tholos*, a covered space in which fish and seafood were sold. Surviving market frescoes reveal some of the goods for sale, including prawns.

➡ Lupanare

Ancient Pompeii's only dedicated brothel, Lupanare is a tiny two-storey building with five rooms on each floor. Its collection of raunchy frescoes was a menu of sorts for clients. The walls in the rooms are carved with graffiti – including declarations of love and hope written by the brothel workers – in various languages.

Tragedy in Pompeii

24 AUGUST AD 79

8am Buildings including the **① Terme Suburbane** and the **② Foro** are still undergoing repair after an earthquake in AD 63 caused significant damage to the city. Despite violent earth tremors overnight, residents have little idea of the catastrophe that lies ahead.

Midday Peckish locals pour into the **③ Thermopolium di Vetutius Placidus**. The lustful slip into the **④ Lupanare**, and gladiators practise for the evening's planned games at the **⑤ Anfiteatro**. A massive boom heralds the eruption. Shocked onlookers witness a dark cloud of volcanic matter shoot some 14km above the crater.

3pm–5pm Lapilli (burning pumice stone) rains down on Pompeii. Terrified locals begin to flee; others take shelter. Within two hours, the plume is 25km high and the sky has darkened. Roofs collapse under the weight of the debris, burying those inside.

25 AUGUST AD 79

Midnight Mudflows bury the town of Herculaneum. Lapilli and ash continue to rain down on Pompeii, bursting through buildings and suffocating those taking refuge within.

4am–8am Ash and gas avalanches hit Herculaneum. Subsequent surges smother Pompeii, killing all remaining residents, including those in the **⑥ Orto dei Fuggiaschi**. The volcanic 'blanket' will safeguard frescoed treasures like the **⑦ Casa del Menandro** and **⑧ Villa dei Misteri** for almost two millennia.

TOP TIPS

→ Visit in the afternoon.
→ Allow three hours.
→ Wear comfortable shoes and a hat.
→ Bring drinking water.
→ Don't use flash photography.

Terme Suburbane
The *laconicum* (sauna), *caldarium* (hot bath) and large, heated swimming pool weren't the only sources of heat here; scan the walls of this suburban bathhouse for some of the city's raunchiest frescoes.

VIACHESLAV LOPATIN / SHUTTERSTOCK ©

Villa di Diomede

Casa del Poeta Tragico

Porta Ercolano

Casa Faur

Tempio di Apollo

Basilica

Porta Marina

Terme del Foro

Macellum

Teatro Grande

Quadriportico dei Teatri

Porta di Stabia

Teatro Piccolo

Foro
An ancient Times Square of sorts, the forum sits at the intersection of Pompeii's main streets and was closed to traffic in the 1st century AD. The plinths on the southern edge featured statues of the imperial family.

PHODEY / GETTY IMAGES ©

Villa dei Misteri
Home to the world-famous *Dionysiac Frieze* fresco. Other highlights at this villa include *trompe l'oeil* wall decorations in the *cubiculum* (bedroom) and Egyptian-themed artwork in the *tablinum* (reception).

Lupanare
The prostitutes at this brothel were often slaves of Greek or Asian origin. Mattresses once covered the stone beds and the names engraved in the walls are possibly those of the workers and their clients.

Thermopolium di Vetutius Placidus
The counter at this ancient snack bar once held urns filled with hot food. The *lararium* (household shrine) on the back wall depicts Dionysus (the god of wine) and Mercury (the god of profit and commerce).

asa dei Vettii

Porta del Vesuvio

EYEWITNESS ACCOUNT

Pliny the Younger (AD 61–c 112) gives a gripping, first-hand account of the catastrophe in his letters to Tacitus (AD 56–117).

Porta di Nola

Casa della Venere in Conchiglia

Porta di Sarno

③

⑦

Grande Palestra

⑤

Tempio di Iside

Orto dei Fuggiaschi
The Garden of the Fugitives showcases the plaster moulds of 13 locals seeking refuge during Vesuvius' eruption – the largest number of victims found in any one area. The huddled bodies make for a moving scene.

⑥

Anfiteatro
Magistrates, local senators and the games' sponsors and organisers enjoyed front-row seating at this veteran amphitheatre, home to gladiatorial battles and the odd riot. The parapet circling the stadium featured paintings of combat, victory celebrations and hunting scenes.

Casa del Menandro
his dwelling most kely belonged to the amily of Poppaea abina, Nero's second ife. A room to the left the atrium features rojan War paintings nd a polychrome osaic of pygmies wing down the Nile.

➡ Foro Triangolare

The Foro Triangolare would originally have overlooked the sea.

➡ Teatro Grande

The 2nd-century-BC Teatro Grande was a huge 5000-seat theatre carved into the lava mass on which Pompeii was originally built.

➡ Quadriportico dei Teatri

Behind the Teatro Grande's stage, the porticoed Quadriportico dei Teatri was initially used for the audience to stroll between acts and later as a barracks for gladiators.

➡ Teatro Piccolo

Also known as the Odeion, the Teatro Piccolo was once an indoor theatre renowned for its acoustics.

➡ Tempio di Iside

(Temple of Isis) The pre-Roman Tempio di Iside was a popular place of cult worship.

➡ Casa del Menandro

Better preserved than the larger Casa del Fauno, luxurious Casa del Menandro has an outstanding, elegant peristyle (a colonnade-framed courtyard) beyond its beautifully frescoed atrium. On the peristyle's far right side a doorway leads to a private bathhouse, lavished with exquisite frescoes and mosaics. The central room off the far end of the peristyle features a striking fresco of the ancient Greek dramatist Menander, after which the rediscovered villa was named.

➡ Via dell'Abbondanza

(Street of Abundance) The Via dell'Abbondanza was ancient Pompeii's main street. The elevated stepping stones allowed people to cross the street without stepping into the waste that washed down the thoroughfare.

➡ Terme Stabiane

At this typical 2nd-century-BC bath complex, bathers would enter from the vestibule, stop off in the vaulted *apodyterium* (changing room), and then pass through to the *tepidarium* (warm baths) and *caldarium* (hot baths). Particularly impressive is the stuccoed vault in the men's changing room, complete with whimsical images of *putti* (winged babies) and nymphs.

➡ Casa della Venere in Conchiglia

(House of the Venus Marina) Casa della Venere in Conchiglia harbours a lovely peristyle looking onto a small, manicured garden. It's here in the garden that you'll find the large, striking Venus fresco after which the house is named.

➡ Anfiteatro

(Amphitheatre) Gladiatorial battles thrilled up to 20,000 spectators at the grassy *anfiteatro*. Built in 70 BC, it's the oldest known Roman amphitheatre in existence.

➡ Palestra Grande

Lithe ancients kept fit at the Palestra Grande, an athletics field with an impressive portico dating to the Augustan period. At its centre lie the grassy remains of a swimming pool. The site is now occasionally used to host temporary exhibitions.

➡ Casa del Fauno

(House of the Faun) Covering an entire *insula* (city block) and boasting two atria at its front end (humbler homes had one), Pompeii's largest private house is named after the delicate bronze statue in the *impluvium* (rain tank). It was here that early excavators found Pompeii's greatest mosaics, most of which are now in Naples' Museo Archeologico Nazionale (p64). Valuable on-site originals include a beautiful, geometrically patterned marble floor.

➡ Casa del Poeta Tragico

(House of the Tragic Poet) The Casa del Poeta Tragico features the world's first known 'beware of the dog' – *cave canem* – warnings, visible through a protective glass panel.

➡ Casa dei Vettii

The Casa dei Vettii is home to a famous depiction of Priapus with his gigantic phallus balanced on a pair of scales...much to the anxiety of many a male observer.

➡ Villa dei Misteri

(Villa of the Mysteries) This restored, 90-room villa is one of the most complete structures left standing in Pompeii. The **dionysiac frieze**, the most important fresco still on site, spans the walls of the large dining room. One of the biggest and most arresting paintings from the ancient world, it depicts the initiation of a bride-to-be into the cult of Dionysus, the Greek god of wine.

A farm for much of its life, the villa's *vino*-making area is still visible at the northern end.

Follow Via Consolare out of the town through **Porta Ercolano**. Continue past **Villa di Diomede**, turn right, and you'll come to Villa dei Misteri.

REGGIA DI CASERTA

The one compelling reason to visit the town of Caserta, 30km north of Naples, is to gasp at the colossal, World Heritage–listed **Reggia di Caserta** (Palazzo Reale; ☑ 0823 27 71 11; www.reggiadicaserta.beniculturali.it; Viale Douhet 22, Caserta; adult/reduced €12/6; ☺ palace 8.30am-7.30pm Wed-Mon, park & Giardino Inglese 8.30am-1hr before sunset Wed-Mon; ☒ Caserta). Italy's swansong to the baroque, the complex began life in 1752 after Charles VII ordered a palace to rival Versailles. Not one to disappoint, Neapolitan architect Luigi Vanvitelli delivered a palace bigger than its French rival. With its 1200 rooms, 1790 windows, 34 staircases and 250m-long facade, it was reputedly the largest building in 18th-century Europe.

Vanvitelli's immense staircase leads up to the royal apartments, lavishly decorated with frescoes, art, tapestries, period furniture and crystal.

The restored back rooms off the Sala di Astrea (Room of Astraea) house an extraordinary collection of historic wooden models of the Reggia, along with architectural drawings and early sketches of the building by Luigi Vanvitelli and his son, Carlo. The apartments are also home to the Mostra Terrea Motus, an underrated collection of international modern art commissioned after the region's devastating earthquake in 1980. Among the contributors are US heavyweights Cy Twombly, Robert Mapplethorpe and Keith Haring, as well as local luminaries like Mimmo Paladino and Jannis Kounellis.

The complex has appeared in numerous films, including *Mission: Impossible 3*, *Star Wars Episode 1: The Phantom Menace* and *Star Wars Episode 2: Attack of the Clones*, moonlighting as Queen Amidala's palace in the latter two.

To clear your head afterwards, explore the elegant landscaped park, which stretches for some 3km to a waterfall and a fountain of Diana. Within the park is the famous Giardino Inglese (English Garden), a romantic oasis of intricate pathways, exotic flora, pools and cascades. Bicycle hire (from €4) is available at the back of the palace building, as are pony-and-trap rides (€50 for 30 minutes, up to five people). Ignore the illegal souvenir hawkers roaming the grounds.

If you're feeling peckish, consider skipping the touristy palace cafeteria for local cafe Martucci, located 250m east of the complex. Great coffee aside, the counters here heave with freshly made *panini* (sandwiches), salads, vegetable dishes, pastries and substantial cooked-to-order meals.

Regular trains connect Naples to Caserta (€3.10, 30 to 50 minutes); always plan ahead and check times online before hitting the station. Caserta train station is located directly opposite the palace grounds. If you're driving, follow signs for the Reggia.

☞ Tours

Walks of Italy   TOURS
(www.walksofitaly.com; 3hr Pompeii guided tour per person €59) This American-based tour company specialises in tours of Italy, including walking tours of Pompeii.

◻ Sleeping & Eating

Although the town of Pompeii has a number of nondescript hotels, you're better off basing yourself in Sorrento or Naples and exploring the ruins as an easy day trip.

★ **President**   CAMPANIAN €€€
(☑ 081 850 72 45; www.ristorantepresident.it; Piazza Schettini 12; meals from €40, tasting menus €65-90; ☺ noon-3.30pm & 7pm-late Tue-Sun; ☒ FS to Pompei, ☒ Circumvesuviana to Pompei-Scavi-

Villa dei Misteri) At the helm of this Michelin-starred standout is charming owner-chef Paolo Gramaglia, whose passion for local produce, history and culinary creativity translates into bread made to ancient Roman recipes, slow-cooked snapper paired with tomato purée and sweet-onion gelato, and deconstructed *pastiera* (sweet Neapolitan tart).

The menu's creative and visual brilliance is matched by sommelier Eulalia Buondonno's swoon-inducing wine list, which features around 600 drops from esteemed and lesser-known Italian winemakers; best of all, the staff are happy to serve any bottle to the value of €100 by the glass.

A word of warning: if you plan on catching a *treno regionale* (regional train) back to Naples from nearby Pompei station (a closer, more convenient option than the Pompei-Scavi-Villa dei Misteri station on the Circumvesuviana train line), check train times first as the last service from Pompei can depart as early as 9.40pm.

ℹ Information

Tourist Office (📞 081 1951 7589; Via Sacra 16; ⊗ 8.30am-6pm) Located in the centre of the modern town.

ℹ Getting There & Away

To reach the *scavi* (ruins) by Circumvesuviana train (€2.80 from Naples, €2.40 from Sorrento), alight at Pompei-Scavi-Villa dei Misteri station, located beside the main entrance at Porta Marina. Regional trains (www.trenitalia.com) stop at Pompei station in the centre of the modern town.

From mid-April to mid-October, tourist train Campania Express runs four times daily between Naples (Porta Nolana and Piazza Garibaldi Circumvesuviana stations) and Sorrento, stopping at Ercolano-Scavi and Pompei-Scavi-Villa dei Misteri en route. One-day return tickets from Naples to Pompeii (€11) or from Sorrento to Pompeii (€7) can be purchased at the stations or online at www.eavsrl.it.

If driving from Naples, head southeast on the A3, using the Pompei exit and following the signs to Pompei Scavi. Car parks (about €5 all day) are clearly marked and vigorously touted. Among them is **Camping Spartacus** (📞 081 862 40 78; Via Plinio 127), conveniently located opposite the ruins. From Sorrento, head north along the SS145, which connects to the A3 and Pompeii.

Sorrento

📞 081 / POP 16,700

An unashamed resort, Sorrento is nonetheless a civilised and beautiful town. Even the souvenirs are a cut above the norm, with plenty of fine old shops selling the ceramics, lacework and *intarsio* (marquetry items) that are famously produced here. The main drawback is the lack of a proper beach: the town straddles the cliffs overlooking the water to Naples and Mt Vesuvius.

Sorrento makes a good base for exploring the region's highlights: to the south is the best of the peninsula's unspoilt countryside, to the east is the Amalfi Coast, to the north lie Pompeii and other archaeological sites, and offshore lies the fabled island of Capri.

◉ Sights

★ Museo Correale di Terranova   MUSEUM

(📞 081 878 18 46; www.museocorreale.it; Via Correale 50; €8; ⊗ 9.30am-6.30pm Tue-Sat, to 1.30pm Sun Apr-Oct, 9.30am-1.30pm Tue-Sun Nov-Mar) East of the city centre, this engaging museum is well worth a visit whether you're a clock collector, an archaeological egghead or into delicate ceramics. In addition to the rich assortment of 16th- to 19th-century Neapolitan art and crafts (including extraordinary examples of marquetry), you'll discover Japanese, Chinese and European ceramics, clocks, fans and, on the ground floor, ancient and medieval artefacts. Among these is a fragment of an ancient Egyptian carving uncovered in the vicinity of Sorrento's Sedile Dominova.

Chiostro di San Francesco   COURTYARD

To the left of the Chiesa di San Francesco are its beautiful cloisters, featuring an Arabic portico and interlaced arches supported by octagonal pillars. Surrounded by bougainvillea and birdsong, the cloisters are built on the ruins of a 7th-century monastery. Upstairs lies the **Sorrento International Photo School** (📞 344 0838503; www.raffaelecelentano.com; adult/reduced €2.50/free; ⊗ 10am-8pm Mar-Dec), a gallery space showcasing evocative black-and-white photographs of Italian life and landscapes by contemporary local photographer Raffaele Celentano.

Museo Bottega della Tarsia Lignea   MUSEUM

(📞 081 877 19 42; www.museomuta.it; Via San Nicola 28; adult/reduced €8/5; ⊗ 10am-6.30pm Apr-Oct, to 5.30pm Nov-Mar) Since the 18th century, Sorrento has been famous for its *intarsio* (marquetry) furniture, made with elaborately designed inlaid wood. Some wonderful examples can be found in this museum, housed in an 18th-century palace, complete with beautiful frescoes. There's also an interesting collection of paintings, prints and photographs that depict the town and surrounding area in the 19th century.

If you're interested in purchasing a new *intarsio* piece, visit **Gargiulo & Jannuzzi** (📞 081 878 10 41; www.gargiulo-jannuzzi.it; Viale Enrico Caruso 1; ⊗ 8am-8pm May-Oct, 9am-7pm Nov, Dec & Mar-Apr), one of the longest-established specialist shops in town; they are happy to ship.

Sorrento

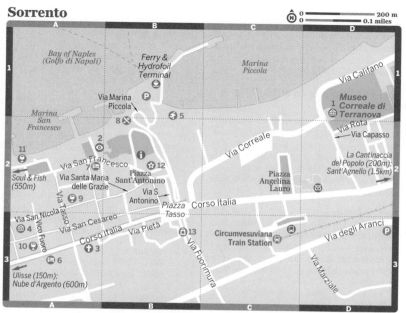

Sorrento

Duomo   CATHEDRAL
(☑ 081 878 22 48; Corso Italia; ⊙ 8am-12.30pm & 4.30-9pm) Sorrento's cathedral features a striking exterior fresco, triple-tiered bell tower, four classical columns and an elegant majolica clock. Inside, take note of the marble bishop's throne (1573), as well as both the wooden choir stalls and stations of the cross, decorated in the local *intarsio* (marquetry) style. Although the cathedral's original structure dates from the 15th century, the building has been altered several times, most recently in the early 20th century when the current facade was added.

🏃 Activities

★ **Sic Sic**   BOATING
(☑ 081 807 22 83; www.nauticasicsic.com; Marina Piccola; ⊙ May-Oct) Seek out the best beaches by rented boat, with or without a skipper. This outfit rents a variety of motor boats, starting at around €50 per hour or from €150 per day. It also organises boat excursions, wedding shoots and similar.

Bagni Regina Giovanna   SWIMMING
Sorrento lacks a decent beach, so consider heading to Bagni Regina Giovanna, a rocky

beach with clear, clean water about 2km west of town, set among the ruins of the Roman Villa Pollio Felix. It's possible to walk here (follow Via Capo), although you'll save your strength if you get the SITA Sud bus headed for Massa Lubrense.

🎊 Festivals & Events

Settimana Santa RELIGIOUS

(Holy Week) Famed throughout Italy; the first procession takes place at midnight on the Thursday preceding Good Friday, with robed and hooded penitents in white; the second occurs on Good Friday, when participants wear black robes and hoods to commemorate the death of Christ.

Sant'Antonino RELIGIOUS

(⊙14 Feb) The city's patron saint, Sant' Antonino, is remembered annually with processions and huge markets. The saint is credited with having saved Sorrento during WWII when Salerno and Naples were heavily bombed.

🛏 Sleeping

Accommodation is thick on the ground in this town, although if you're arriving in high summer (July and August), you'll need to book ahead. Most of the big city-centre hotels are geared towards package tourism and prices are correspondingly high. There are, however, some excellent choices, particularly on Via Capo, the coastal road west of the centre. This area is within walking distance of the city centre, but if you're carrying luggage it's easier to catch a SITA Sud bus for Sant'Agata or Massa Lubrense.

★**Ulisse** HOTEL €

(☑081 877 47 53; www.ulissedeluxe.com; Via del Mare 22; dm €20-35, d €60-150; P🅿❄🛰🏊) Although it calls itself a hostel, the Ulisse is about as far from a backpackers' pad as a hiking boot from a stiletto. Most rooms are plush, spacious affairs with swish if rather bland fabrics, gleaming floors and large ensuite bathrooms. There are two single-sex dorms, and quads for sharers. Breakfast is included in some rates but costs €10 with others.

Nube d'Argento CAMPGROUND €

(☑081 878 13 44; www.nubedargento.com; Via Capo 21; camping per 2 people, car & tent €27-43, 2-person bungalows €65-90, 4-person bungalows €95-125; ⊙Mar-Dec; @🏊) This inviting campground is an easy 1km drive west of the Sorrento city centre. Pitches and wooden chalet-style bungalows are spread out beneath a canopy of olive trees – a source of much-needed summer shade – and the facilities are excellent. Kids in particular will enjoy the open-air swimming pool, table-tennis table, slides and swings.

★**Hotel Cristina** HOTEL €€

(☑081 878 35 62; www.hotelcristinasorrento.it; Via Privata Rubinacci 6, Sant'Agnello; s €130, d €150-200, tr €220, q €240; ⊙Mar-Oct; P🅿❄🛰🏊) Located high above Sant'Agnello, this hotel has superb views, particularly from the swimming pool. The spacious rooms have sea-view balconies and combine inlaid wooden furniture with contemporary flourishes like Philippe Starck chairs. There's an in-house restaurant and a free shuttle bus to/from Sorrento's Circumvesuviana train station.

La Tonnarella HOTEL €€

(☑081 878 11 53; www.latonnarella.com; Via Capo 31; d €120-140, ste €240-350; ⊙Apr-Oct & Christmas; P🅿❄@🛰) A splendid choice – but not for minimalists – La Tonnarella is a dazzling canvas of majolica tiles, antiques, chandeliers and statues. Rooms, most with their own balcony or small terrace, continue the sumptuous classical theme with traditional furniture and discreet mod cons. The hotel also has its own private beach, accessible by lift, and a highly regarded terrace restaurant.

Casa Astarita B&B €€

(☑081 877 49 06; www.casastarita.com; Corso Italia 67; d €70-140, tr €95-165; ❄🛰) Housed in an 18th-century *palazzo* (mansion) on Sorrento's main strip, this charming B&B has a colourful, eclectic look with original vaulted ceilings, brightly painted doors and majolica-tiled floors. Its six simple but well-equipped rooms surround a central parlour, where breakfast is served on a large rustic table.

★**Palazzo Marziale** BOUTIQUE HOTEL €€€

(☑081 807 44 06; www.palazzomarziale.com; Largo San Francesco 2; d/ste from €199/459; ❄🛰) From cascading vines, Chinese porcelain urns and Persian rugs in the lobby lounge, to antique furniture, *objets* and artworks in the hallways and inlaid wood in the lift, this sophisticated, eleven-room hideaway is big on details. The family's elegant tastes extend to the rooms, resplendent with high ceilings, chaise longues and high-end mattresses and linens.

Eating

The centre of town heaves with bars, cafes, trattorias, restaurants and even the odd kebab takeaway shop. Many places, particularly those with waistcoated waiters stationed outside (or the ones displaying sun-bleached photos of the dishes), are tourist traps serving bland food at inflated prices. Thankfully, not all are and it's perfectly possible to eat very well.

★ La Cantinaccia del Popolo
NEAPOLITAN €

(☑ 366 1015497; Vico Terzo Rota; meals €21; ☉ 11am-3pm & 7-11pm Tue-Sun) Its small, rustic interiors festooned with garlic and prosciutto, this down-to-earth favourite proves that top-notch produce and simplicity are the keys to culinary success. A case in point is the *spaghetti al pomodoro*, a basic dish of pasta and tomato that bursts with flavour, vibrancy and balance. Charcuterie options include La Cantinaccia's own cured meats as well as some interesting Campanian cheeses. Outdoor seating available.

★ Acqu' e Sale
NEAPOLITAN €€

(☑ 081 1900 5967; http://acquesale.it; Piazza Marinai D'Italia 2; pizzas from €6, meals around €37) Despite its proximity to the ferry terminal, Acqu' e Sale is popular among fastidious locals. Heading the open kitchen is chef Antonino Esposito, who turns glistening fresh fish into beautiful, thoughtfully presented dishes. The Neapolitan-style pizzas are gorgeous, with a creative choice of bases that include a very local *al limone* (lemon-flavoured). There's an outdoor patio, numerous gluten-free dishes and fine coffee to boot.

★ Soul & Fish
SEAFOOD €€€

(☑ 081 878 21 70; www.soulandfish.com; Marina Grande; meals €30-42; ☉ noon-2.30pm & 7-10.30pm, closed Nov-Easter; 🐾) Soul & Fish is arguably the best of the waterfront eateries at Marina Grande. While we love the beach shack–chic design and complimentary glass of *prosecco*, it's the beautiful, intriguing dishes that seal the deal. If it's on the menu, start with the *caponatina*, a fresh salad of cuttlefish, rocket, orange pistachio and wholemeal bread. Fresh fish aside, the kitchen also cooks impressive risottos.

♟ Drinking & Nightlife

Bollicine
WINE BAR

(☑ 081 878 46 16; Via Accademia 9; ☉ 6.30pm-late) The wine list at this unpretentious bar with a dark, woody interior includes all the big Italian names and a selection of interesting local labels. If you can't decide what to go for, the amiable bar staff will advise you. There's also a small menu of *panini* (sandwiches), bruschettas and one or two pasta dishes.

Cafè Latino
BAR

(☑ 081 877 37 18; http://cafelatinosorrento.it; Vico Fuoro 4a; ☉ 10am-1am Mar-Dec) Think locked-eyes-over-cocktails time. This is the place to impress your date with cocktails (from €7) on the terrace, surrounded by orange and lemon trees. Sip a Mary Pickford (rum, pineapple, *grenadino* and maraschino) or a glass of chilled white wine. If you can't drag yourselves away, you can also eat here (meals around €35).

La Pergola
BAR

(☑ 081 878 10 24; www.bellevue.it; Hotel Bellevue Syrene, Piazza della Vittoria 5) When it's time for romance (or simply time to treat yourself), style up and indulge with a pre-dinner libation at the Hotel Bellevue Syrene's swoon-inducing terrace bar/restaurant. The clifftop view across the Bay of Naples is breathtaking, taking in soaring Mt Vesuvius and, in the distance, Naples. Not cheap but utterly unforgettable.

☆ Entertainment

Teatro Tasso
THEATRE

(☑ 081 807 55 25; www.teatrotasso.it; Piazza Sant'Antonino; incl cocktail €25; ☉ Sorrento Musical 9.30pm Apr-Oct) The southern-Italian equivalent of a London old-time music hall, Teatro Tasso is home to the *Sorrento Musical,* a sentimental 75-minute revue of Neapolitan classics such as 'O Sole Mio' and 'Trona a Sorrent'.

ℹ Information

Post Office (www.poste.it; Corso Italia 210; ☉ 8.20am-7pm Mon-Fri, to 12.30pm Sat) Just north of the train station.

Main Tourist Office (☑ 081 807 40 33; www.sorrentotourism.com; Via Luigi de Maio 35; ☉ 8.30am-7.30pm Mon-Fri Jun-Oct, to 4pm Nov-May) In the Circolo dei Forestieri (Foreigners' Club), lists ferry and train times. Ask for the useful publication *Surrentum*.

ℹ Getting There & Away

BOAT

Sorrento is the main jumping-off point for Capri and also has ferry connections to Naples and Amalfi coastal resorts during the summer months from its **Ferry & Hydrofoil Terminal** (Via Luigi de Maio).

Caremar (☎ 081 807 30 77; www.caremar.it) runs hydrofoils to Capri (€16, 25 minutes, four daily).

Gescab (☎ 081 807 18 12; www.gescab.it) also runs hydrofoils to Capri (€19, 20 minutes, 17 to 19 daily).

Navigazione Libera del Golfo (p85) runs one daily hydrofoil to Naples (€12.90, 20 minutes).

BUS

SITA Sud (www.sitasudtrasporti.it) buses serve Naples, the Amalfi Coast and Sant'Agata, leaving from the **bus station** (Piazza Giovanna Battista de Curtis) across from the entrance to the Circumvesuviana train station. Buy tickets at the station or from shops bearing the blue SITA sign.

TRAIN

Sorrento is the last stop on the **Circumvesuviana** (☎ 800 211 388; www.eavsrl.it) train line from Naples. Train services run every half-hour for Naples (€3.90, 70 minutes), via Pompeii (€2.40, 30 minutes) and Ercolano (€2.90, 50 minutes).

THE AMALFI COAST

Deemed an outstanding example of a Mediterranean landscape by Unesco, the Amalfi Coast is one of Italy's most piercing destinations. Here, mountains plunge into the sea in a nail-biting vertical scene of precipitous crags, cliff-clinging abodes and verdant woodland.

Its string of fabled towns read like a Hollywood cast list. There's jet-set favourite Positano, a pastel-coloured cascade of chic boutiques, *spritz*-sipping pin-ups and sun-kissed sunbathers. Further east, ancient Amalfi lures with its Arabic-Norman cathedral, while mountaintop Ravello stirs hearts with its cultured villas and Wagnerian connection. To the west lies Amalfi Coast gateway Sorrento (p102), a handsome cliff-top resort that has miraculously survived the onslaught of package tourism.

Turquoise seas and postcard-perfect piazzas aside, the region is home to some of Italy's finest hotels and restaurants. It's also one of the country's top spots for hiking, with well-marked trails providing the chance to escape the star-struck coastal crowds.

ℹ Getting There & Away

BOAT

Year-round hydrofoil services run between Naples and Sorrento, as well as between Sorrento and Capri. From around May to October, regular ferry services connect Sorrento to Positano and Amalfi, from where ferries continue to Salerno.

BUS

The Circumvesuviana train has services that run from Naples' Piazza Garibaldi to Sorrento, from where there is a regular and efficient **SITA Sud** (p108) bus service to Positano, Amalfi and Salerno.

TRAIN

The **Circumvesuviana** runs every half-hour between Naples' Garibaldi station (beside Napoli Centrale station) and Sorrento. Trains stop in Ercolano (Herculaneum) and Pompeii en route. **Trenitalia** (p78) runs frequent services between Napoli Centrale station and Salerno.

Amalfi

☎ 089 / POP 5150

It is hard to grasp that pretty little Amalfi, with its sun-filled piazzas and small beach, was once a maritime superpower with a population of more than 70,000. For one thing, it's not a big place – you can easily walk from one end to the other in about 20 minutes. For another, there are very few historical buildings of note. The explanation is chilling: most of the old city, and its populace, simply slid into the sea during an earthquake in 1343.

Despite this, the town exudes a sense of history and culture, most notably in its breathtaking cathedral and fascinating paper museum. And while the permanent population is a fairly modest 5000 or so these days, the numbers swell significantly during summer.

Just around the headland, neighbouring **Atrani** is a picturesque tangle of white-washed alleys and arches centred on a lively, lived-in piazza and popular beach; don't miss it.

10

◉ Sights

★ **Cattedrale di Sant'Andrea** CATHEDRAL
(☑ 089 87 10 59; Piazza del Duomo; ⊙ 7.30am-7.30pm) A melange of architectural styles, Amalfi's cathedral, one of the few relics of the town's past as an 11th-century maritime superpower, makes a striking impression at the top of its sweeping flight of stairs. Between 10am and 5pm entrance is through the adjacent **Chiostro del Paradiso** (☑ 089 87 13 24; Piazza del Duomo; adult/reduced €3/1; ⊙ 9am-7.45pm Jul-Aug, reduced hours rest of year), a 13th-century cloister.

The cathedral dates in part from the early 10th century and its striped facade has been rebuilt twice, most recently at the end of the 19th century. Although the building is a hybrid, the Sicilian Arabic-Norman style predominates, particularly in the two-tone masonry and the 13th-century bell tower. The huge bronze doors also merit a look – the first of their type in Italy, they were commissioned by a local noble and made in Syria before being shipped to Amalfi. While the baroque interior is less impressive, indoor highlights include fine statues at the altar and some interesting 12th- and 13th-century mosaics.

★ **Museo della Carta** MUSEUM
(☑ 089 830 45 61; www.museodellacarta.it; Via delle Cartiere 23; €4; ⊙ 10am-6.30pm daily Mar-Oct, 10am-3.30pm Tue, Wed & Fri-Sun Nov-Feb) Amalfi's paper museum is housed in a rugged, cave-like 13th-century paper mill (the oldest in Europe). It lovingly preserves the original paper presses, which are still in full working order, as you'll see during the 30-minute guided tour (in English), which explains the original cotton-based paper production and the later wood-pulp manufacturing. Afterwards you may well be inspired to pick up some of the stationery sold in the gift shop, alongside calligraphy sets and paper pressed with flowers.

Grotta dello Smeraldo CAVE
(€5; ⊙ 9am-4pm) Four kilometres west of Amalfi, this grotto is named after the eerie emerald colour that emanates from the water. Stalactites hang down from the 24m-high ceiling, while stalagmites grow up to 10m tall. Buses regularly pass the car park above the cave entrance (from where you take a lift or stairs down to the rowing boats). Alternatively, **Coop Sant'Andrea** (☑ 089 87 31 90; www.coopsantandrea.com; Lungomare dei Cavalieri 1) runs boats from Amalfi

(€10 return, plus cave admission). Allow 1½ hours for the return trip.

⚓ Activities

Amalfi Marine BOATING
(☑ 338 3076125; www.amalfiboatrental.com; Spiaggia del Porto, Lungomare dei Cavalieri) Amalfi Marine hires out boats (without a skipper from €150 per day, per boat excluding petrol; maximum six passengers). Private day-long tours with a skipper start from €300.

🛏 Sleeping

★ **Albergo Sant'Andrea** HOTEL €
(☑ 089 87 11 45; www.albergosantandrea.it; Via Costanza d'Avalos 1; s/d €60/100; ⊙ Mar-Dec; ❄ 🛜) Enjoy the atmosphere of busy Piazza del Duomo from the comfort of your own room. This modest two-star has basic rooms with brightly coloured tiles and coordinating fabrics. Double glazing has helped cut down the piazza hubbub, which can reach fever pitch in high season – this is one place to ask for a room with a (cathedral) view.

Residenza del Duca HOTEL €€
(☑ 089 873 63 65; www.residencedelduca.it; Via Duca Mastalo II 3; r €70-175; ⊙ Mar-Oct; ❄ 🛜) This family-run hotel has just six rooms, all of them light, sunny, and prettily furnished with antiques, majolica tiles and the odd chintzy cherub. The Jacuzzi showers are excellent. Call ahead if you are carrying heavy bags, as it's a seriously puff-you-out-climb up some steps to reach here and a luggage service is included in the price.

Hotel Lidomare HOTEL €€
(☑ 089 87 13 32; www.lidomare.it; Largo Duchi Piccolomini 9; s/d €65/145; ❄ 🛜) Family run, this gracious, old-fashioned hotel has no shortage of character. The large, luminous rooms have an air of gentility, with their appealingly haphazard decor, vintage tiles and fine antiques. Some have spa baths, others have sea views and a balcony, some have both. Rather unusually, breakfast is laid out on top of a grand piano.

Hotel Centrale HOTEL €€
(☑ 089 87 26 08; www.amalfihotelcentrale.it; Largo Duchi Piccolomini 1; d €100-120; ⊙ year-round; ❄ 🛜) This is one of the best-value hotels in Amalfi. The entrance is on a tiny little piazza in the *centro storico* (historic centre), but many of the small yet tastefully decorated

rooms overlook Piazza del Duomo. The aquamarine ceramic tiling lends a fresh, summery feel and the views from the rooftop terrace are magnificent.

★ Hotel Luna Convento   HOTEL €€€

(☑089 87 10 02; www.lunahotel.it; Via Pantaleone Comite 33; s €270-370, d €290-390, ste €490-590; ☺Easter-Oct; P❋@☎☷) This former convent was founded by St Francis in 1222 and has been a hotel for some 170 years. Rooms in the original building are in the former monks' cells, but there's nothing poky about the bright tiles, balconies and seamless sea views. The newer wing is equally beguiling, with religious frescoes over the bed. The cloistered courtyard is magnificent.

✕ Eating

La Pansa   CAFE €

(☑089 87 10 65; www.pasticceriapansa.it; Piazza del Duomo 40; cornetti from €1, pastries from €4.50; ☺7.30am-11pm, closed early Jan-early Feb) A marbled and mirrored 1830 cafe on Piazza del Duomo where black-bow-tied waiters serve a great Italian breakfast: freshly made *cornetti* (croissants), full-bodied espresso and deliciously frothy cappuccino. Standout pastries include the crisp, flaky *coda di aragosta con crema di limone*, a lobster tail–shaped concoction filled with a rich yet light lemon custard cream.

Le Arcate   ITALIAN €€

(☑089 87 13 67; www.learcate.net; Largo Orlando Buonocore, Atrani; pizzas from €6, meals €30; ☺12.30-3.30pm & 7.30-11.30pm Tue-Sun Sep-Jun, daily Jul & Aug; ☎) On a sunny day, it's hard to beat Le Arcate's dreamy location: at the far eastern point of the harbour overlooking the beach, with Atrani's ancient rooftops and majolica-tiled domes before you. Huge parasols shade the sprawl of tables, while the dining room is a stone-walled natural cave. The food is fine, if not exceptional, with decent pizzas and pasta dishes, including gluten-free options.

★ Marina Grande   SEAFOOD €€€

(☑089 87 11 29; www.ristorantemarinagrande.com; Viale della Regione 4; tasting menu €70, meals €50; ☺noon-3pm & 6.30-10.30pm Wed-Mon Mar-Oct; ☎) 🐟 Run by the third generation of the same family, this savvy beachfront favourite serves fish so fresh it's almost flapping. It prides itself on the use of locally sourced organic produce, which, in Amalfi, means superlative seafood. Reservations recommended.

❶ Information

Post Office (www.poste.it; Corso delle Repubbliche Marinare 31; ☺8.20am-7pm Mon-Fri, to 12.30pm Sat) Next door to the tourist office.

Tourist Office (☑089 87 11 07; www.amalfitouristoffice.it; Corso delle Repubbliche Marinare 27; ☺8.30am-1pm & 2-6pm Mon-Sat Apr-Oct, 8.30am-1pm Mon-Sat Nov-Mar) Just off the main seafront road.

❶ Getting There & Away

BOAT

Between May and October there are daily sailings from Amalfi's **ferry terminal** east to Salerno and west to Positano, Sorrento and Capri.

BUS

From the **bus station** (Lungomare dei Cavalieri) in Piazza Flavio Gioia, **SITA Sud** (☑344 103 10 70; www.sitasudtrasporti.it; Piazza Flavio Gioia) runs up to 27 buses daily to Ravello (€1.30, 25 minutes).

Eastbound, it runs up to 20 buses daily to Salerno (€2.40, 1¼ hours) via Maiori (20 minutes). Westbound, it runs up to 25 buses daily to Positano (€2, 40 minutes) via Praiano (€1.30, 25 minutes). Many continue to Sorrento (€2.90, 1¾ hours).

You can buy tickets from the *tabacchi* (tobacconist) on the corner of Piazza Flavio Gioia and Via Duca Mansone I (the side street that leads to Piazza del Duomo).

Nocelle

☑089 / POP 140

A tiny, still relatively isolated mountain village, located beyond Montepertuso, Nocelle (450m) commands some of the most spectacular views on the entire coast. A world apart from touristy Positano, it's a silent place where not much ever happens and where the few residents are happy to keep it that way. Hikers tackling the Sentiero degli Dei might want to stop off as they pass through.

▭ Sleeping

Villa della Quercia   B&B €

(☑089 812 34 97; www.villadellaquercia.com; Via Nocelle 5; r €75-85; ☺Apr-Oct; ☎) This simple, delightful B&B is located in a former hilltop monastery with a tranquil garden and spectacular, bird's-eye views of the coast. All six rooms come with a terrace or balcony for blissful, languid lounging. To reach the property, catch a local bus (€1.30) from Amalfi to Nocelle. The B&B is about a 10-minute walk from the bus stop.

Eating

Trattoria
Santa Croce
ITALIAN €€

(☑ 089 81 12 60; www.ristorantesantacrocepositano.com; Via Nocelle 19; meals €22; ⊙ noon-3.30pm & 7-9.30pm Apr-Oct) Service here can be woefully inattentive, but this modest trattoria offers spectacular views over the coast. The menu is short and traditional, with a mix of good (if not memorable) surf and turf dishes like rustic lentil soup, *tagliatelle alla genovese* (pasta with a rich, onion-based Neapolitan sauce) and freshly caught fish with local herbs.

❶ Getting There & Away

From Piazza dei Mulini in Positano, a local bus runs up to Nocelle (€1.30, 30 minutes) via Montepertuso around 14 times daily.

If you're driving, follow the signs from Positano. A taxi from Positano costs an extortionate €35 to €40 – avoid.

Positano

☑ 089 / POP 3960

Positano is the Amalfi Coast's most photogenic (and expensive) town, with vertiginous houses tumbling down to the sea in a cascade of sun-bleached peach, pink and terracotta. No less colourful are its steep streets and steps, flanked by wisteria-draped hotels, smart restaurants and fashionable retailers.

Look beyond the facades and the fashion, however, and you will find reassuring signs of everyday reality: crumbling stucco, streaked paintwork and even, on occasion, a faint whiff of drains. There's still a southern-Italian holiday feel about the place, with sunbathers eating pizza on the beach, kids pestering parents for gelato and chic *signore* from Milan browsing the boutiques. The fashionista history runs deep – *moda Positano* was born here in the '60s and the town was the first in Italy to import bikinis from France.

◉ Sights

Positano's most memorable sight is its pyramidal townscape, with pastel-coloured houses arranged down the slope to **Spiaggia Grande**, the main beach. Although it isn't anyone's dream beach, with greyish sand covered by legions of bright umbrellas, the water's clean and the setting is memorable. Hiring a chair and umbrella in the fenced-off areas costs around €20 per person per day, but the crowded public areas are free.

Getting around town is largely a matter of walking. If your knees can take the slopes, there are dozens of narrow alleys and stairways that make walking relatively easy and joyously traffic-free. The easy option is to take the local bus to the top of the town for the best views, and wind your way down on foot, via steps and slopes, enjoying the memorable vistas en route.

Chiesa di Santa Maria
Assunta
CHURCH

(☑ 089 87 54 80; Piazza Flavio Gioia; ⊙ 8am-noon & 4-9pm) This church, with its colourful majolica-tiled dome, is the most famous and – let's face it – pretty much the only sight in Positano. If you are visiting at a weekend you will probably have the added perk of seeing a wedding; it's one of the most popular churches in the area for exchanging vows.

Step inside to see a delightful classical interior, with pillars topped with gilded Ionic capitals and winged cherubs peeking from above every arch.

🏃 Activities

★ Blue Star
BOATING

(☑ 089 81 18 88; www.bluestarpositano.it; Spiaggia Grande; ⊙ 8.30am-9pm) Operating out of a kiosk on Spiaggia Grande, Blue Star hires out small motorboats (half-day/full day €250/350). Consider heading for the archipelago of Li Galli, the four small islands where, according to Homer, the sirens lived. The company organises popular yacht group excursions to Capri (€75) and along the Amalfi Coast (€65), as well as a private sunset *aperitivo* cruise (from €220).

L'Uomo e il Mare
BOATING

(☑ 089 81 16 13; www.escursioniluomoeilmare.it; ⊙ 9am-8pm Easter-Oct) Offers a range of tours, including Capri and Amalfi day trips (from €60), out of a kiosk near the ferry terminal. They also offer private sunset tours to Li Galli, complete with champagne (from €200 for up to 12 people). Private tours should be organised at least a day in advance.

🛏 Sleeping

Positano is a glorious place to stay, but be aware that prices are, overall, high. Like everywhere on the Amalfi Coast, it gets very busy in summer, so book ahead, particularly on weekends and in July and August. Ask at

Positano

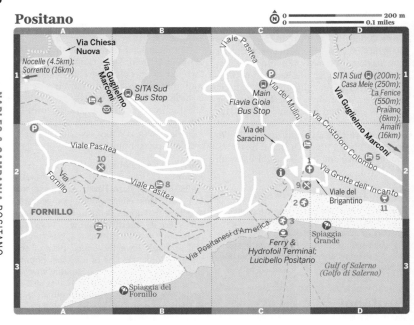

Positano

the tourist office about rooms or apartments in private houses.

★ Villa Nettuno
HOTEL €

(☎089 87 54 01; www.villanettunopositano.it; Viale Pasitea 208; d €80-140; ☺year-round; ❄🛜) Hidden behind a barrage of perfumed foliage, lofty Villa Nettuno is not short on charm. Go for one of the original rooms in the 300-year-old part of the building, decked out in robust rustic decor and graced with a communal terrace. Rooms in the renovated part of the villa lack the same character.

Hostel Brikette
HOSTEL €

(☎089 87 58 57; www.hostel-positano.com; Via Marconi 358; dm €24-50, d €65-145, apt €80-220; ☺mid-Mar–mid-Oct; ❄🛜) The Brikette is a cheerful place with wonderful views and a range of sleeping options, from dorms to doubles and apartments. Some of the dorms have recently been revamped, with handy bunk-side USB sockets and reading lights. Pod-style bunks are expected to replace the tired current bunks in 2018. Breakfast – not included in the price – includes options like pancakes and cold-pressed juices.

Pensione Maria Luisa
PENSION €

(☎089 87 50 23; www.pensionemarialuisa.com; Via Fornillo 42; r €55-160; ☺Mar-Oct; ❄@🛜) The Maria Luisa is a friendly, old-school *pensione*. Rooms are lined with shiny tiles and simple, no-frills decor; those with private balconies are well worth the extra euros for the bay views. If you can't bag a room with a vista, there's a small communal terrace offering the same sensational panorama. Breakfast is an additional €8.

⭐ **La Fenice**   B&B €€
(☎089 87 55 13; www.lafenicepositano.com; Via Guglielmo Marconi 8; d €170; ⊗Easter-Oct; ❋☎☀) With hand-painted Vietri tiles, high ceilings and the odd piece of antique furniture, the rooms at this friendly, family-run place are simple but smart; most have their own balcony or terrace with dreamy views. As with everywhere in Positano, you'll need to be good at stomping up and down steps to stay here.

⭐ **Hotel California**   HOTEL €€
(☎089 87 53 82; www.hotelcaliforniapositano.it; Via Cristoforo Colombo 141; d €160-205; ⊗Easter-Oct; ℙ❋☎) Ignore the incongruous name: this Hotel California is housed in a grand 18th-century palace, its facade washed in soothing pinks and yellows. The rooms in the older part of the house are magnificent, with original ceiling friezes; new rooms are simply decorated though tasteful, spacious and airy.

⭐ **Hotel Palazzo Murat**   HOTEL €€€
(☎089 87 51 77; www.palazzomurat.it; Via dei Mulini 23; d €180-290; ⊗May–mid-Jan; ❋❋☎☀) Hidden behind an ancient wall from the tourists who surge along its pedestrian thoroughfare daily, this magnificent hotel occupies the 18th-century *palazzo* (mansion) that the one-time king of Naples used as his summer residence. Rooms – five (more expensive) in the original part of the building, 25 in the newer section – are decorated with sumptuous antiques, original oil paintings and gleaming marble.

✕ Eating

Take note that, overall, the nearer you get to the seafront, the more expensive everything becomes. Many places close over winter, making a brief reappearance for Christmas and New Year.

⭐ **La Cambusa**   SEAFOOD €€
(☎089 87 54 32; www.lacambusapositano.com; Piazza Vespucci 4; meals €40; ⊗noon-11pm, closed Nov-early Dec; ☎) Sporting summery pastel hues and a seafront terrace, La Cambusa is on the front line, which, given the number of cash-rich tourists in these parts, could equal high prices for less than average food. Happily, that is not the case. Ingredients are top

notch and shine brightly in dishes such as homemade *scialatelli* pasta with seafood or risotto with shrimp and asparagus.

⭐ **Donna Rosa**   ITALIAN €€
(☎089 81 18 06; www.drpositano.com; Via Montepertuso 97-99, Montepertuso; meals from €40; ⊗11am-2pm & 5.30-9.30pm Wed-Mon Apr-Dec, closed lunch Aug) This is one of the coast's top restaurants, located in Montepertuso, above Positano. Once a humble trattoria and now run by Rosa's daughter Raffaella, the lineage is set to continue with Raffaella's daughter Erika, who studied with Jamie Oliver in London. The celebrity chef dined here on his honeymoon and declared it one of his favourite restaurants. Dinner reservations are highly recommended and obligatory at lunch.

⭐ **Casa Mele**   ITALIAN €€€
(☎089 81 13 64; www.casamele.com; Via Guglielmo Marconi 76; tasting menu €60-75; ⊗7pm-midnight Tue-Sun Apr-early Dec) Clever, contemporary Casa Mele celebrates the region's culinary traditions with refreshing innovation. The open kitchen is run by a competent young team, who offer both a traditional and contemporary degustation menu. The latter offers the most thrills, with dishes that might see *triglia* (mullet) caramelised with orange and served with a pesto and almond cream. Traditional and creative pizzas are also offered.

⭐ **Next2**   ITALIAN €€€
(☎089 812 35 16; www.next2.it; Viale Pasitea 242; meals €50; ⊗6.30-11.30pm Apr-Oct) Understated elegance meets subtle culinary twists at this contemporary set-up. Local and organic ingredients are put to impressive use in dishes such as grilled octopus with potato puree and snow peas, or ravioli stuffed with bluefish and fennel seeds. Desserts are wickedly delicious, and the alfresco sea-facing terrace is summer perfection.

🍷 Drinking & Nightlife

Music on the Rocks   CLUB
(☎089 87 58 74; www.musicontherocks.it; Via Grotte dell'Incanto 51; cover €10-30; ⊗10pm-late Easter-Oct; ☎) This is one of the town's few genuine nightspots and one of the best clubs on the coast. The venue is dramatically carved into the tower at the eastern end of Spiaggia Grande. Join a flirty, eye-candy crowd and some of the region's top DJs spinning mainstream house and reliable disco.

ℹ️ Information

Post Office (www.poste.it; Via Marconi 318; ⊙8.20am-1.45pm Mon-Fri, to 12.45pm Sat) On the main highway passing through town.

Tourist Office (📞089 87 50 67; www.azienda turismopositano.it; Via Regina Giovanna 13; ⊙8.30am-8pm Mon-Sat, to 2pm Sun May-Sep, reduced hours rest of year) Provides lots of information, from sightseeing and tours to transport information. Also supplies a free hiking map.

ℹ️ Getting There & Away

BOAT

Positano has excellent ferry service connections to the coastal towns and islands from around May to October from its Ferry & Hydrofoil Terminal.

TraVelMar (📞089 87 29 50; www.travelmar. it) sails to numerous coastal destinations in season, including Amalfi (€8, 25 minutes, around six daily) and Salerno (€12, 70 minutes, around seven daily). Those wanting to reach Minori (€11), Maiori (€11) and Cetara (€11) will need to transfer in Amalfi.

Lucibello Positano (📞089 87 50 32; www. lucibello.it) operates three daily services to Capri (€19.50, 50 minutes).

BUS

Situated about 16km west of Amalfi and 18km from Sorrento, Positano is on the main SS163 coastal road. There are two main bus stops: coming from Sorrento and the west, the first stop you come to is **SITA Sud** (Via Guglielmo Marconi), opposite Bar Internazionale; arriving from Amalfi and the east, the **SITA Sud** (Via Guglielmo Marconi) stop is at the top of Via Cristoforo Colombo. To get into town from the former, follow Viale Pasitea; from the latter (a far shorter route), take Via Cristoforo Colombo. When departing, buy bus tickets at either **Bar Internazionale** (Via Marconi 306; ⊙7am-1am) or (if it's still closed for renovations) the *tabaccheria* (tobacconist) across the road. If headed east, buy your tickets from the **tabaccheria** (📞089 81 21 33; Via Cristoforo Colombo 5; ⊙9.30am-9pm) at the bottom of Via Cristoforo Colombo.

SITA Sud (p108) runs up to 28 daily buses to Sorrento (€2, one hour). It also runs up to 25 daily services to Amalfi (€2, 50 minutes) from where buses continue east to Salerno.

Flavia Gioia (📞089 81 18 95; www.flavio gioia.com) runs local buses following the lower ring road every half-hour. Stops are clearly marked and you can buy your ticket at tobacconists (€1.30) or on board. The **main bus stop** (Via Cristoforo Colombo) in central

Positano is on the corner of Viale Pasitea and Via dei Mulini. Flavia Gioia buses also pass by both SITA Sud bus stops. The company also runs around 14 daily buses up to Montepertuso and Nocelle.

Praiano

📞089 / POP 2050

An ancient fishing village, a low-key summer resort and, increasingly, a popular centre for the arts, Praiano is a delight. With no centre as such, its whitewashed houses pepper the verdant ridge of Monte Sant'Angelo as it slopes towards Capo Sottile. Formerly an important silk-production centre, it was a favourite of the Amalfi doges (dukes), who made it their summer residence.

🏃 Activities

Praiano is 120m above sea level, and exploring involves lots of steps. There are also several trails that start from town, including a scenic walk – particularly stunning at sunset – that leaves from beside the San Gennaro church, descending due west to the **Spiaggia della Gavitelli** beach (via 300 steps), and carrying on to the medieval defensive Torre di Grado. The town is also a starting point for the Sentiero degli Dei.

🛏️ Sleeping

Hotel Onda Verde HOTEL **€€€**

(📞089 87 41 43; www.hotelondaverde.com; Via Terramare 3; d €150-300; ⊙Apr-Oct;) The 'Green Wave' enjoys a stunning cliffside position overlooking picturesque Marina de Praiano. The interior is tunnelled into the stone cliff face, which makes it wonderfully cool in the height of summer. Rooms have lashings of white linen, satin bedheads, Florentine-inspired furniture and majolica-tiled floors. Some spoil guests with terraces and deckchairs for panoramic contemplation. The restaurant comes highly recommended.

🍴 Eating

Fish and seafood dominate the menus in this old fishing town. Its most famous traditional dish is *totani e patate alla praianese*, a soulful combination of soft calamari rings, sliced potato, *datterini* tomatoes, garlic, croutons, *peperoncino* (chilli) and parsley.

DON'T MISS

WALK OF THE GODS

By far the best-known walk on the Amalfi Coast is the three-hour, 12km **Sentiero degli Dei**, which follows the high ridge linking Praiano to Positano. The walk commences in the heart of **Praiano**, where a thigh-challenging 1000-step start takes you up to the path itself. An easier alternative is to opt for the bus to **Bomerano**, near Agerola in the mountains between Sorrento and Amalfi: take the SITA bus to the Agerola turnoff, then another bus to Agerola. Bomerano is located immediately south of Agerola. Do consider the stepped route, though, which winds through well-tended gardens and makes for a charming start.

The route proper is not advised for vertigo sufferers: it's a spectacular, meandering trail along the top of the mountains, with caves and terraces set dramatically in the cliffs and deep valleys framed by the brilliant blue of the sea. It can sometimes be cloudy in the dizzy heights, but that somehow adds to the drama, with the cypresses rising through the mist like dark, shimmering sword blades and shepherds herding their goats through fog-wreathed foliage. Bring a rucksack and plenty of water and wear proper walking shoes, as the going is rough and the descents are steep. You may want to pack swimming gear, too, and end the walk with a refreshing plunge into the sea.

The Praiano tourist office (p114) can provide maps and guidance. Just downhill and on the same side is Alimentari Rispoli (p114), where you can buy *panini*, cheeses, meat, drinks and fruit for the hike (take a penknife for cheese and so on, as they don't make up rolls). The steps out of town begin at Via Degli Ulivi, which leads off the main road almost opposite Hotel Smereldo. Brace yourself for the long climb to come, and be sure to follow the brown arrows placed at regular intervals along the flower-edged paths. After around 45 minutes you'll emerge at **Fontanella**, at Chiesa di Santa Maria a Castro, a lovely whitewashed chapel with a 15th-century fresco of the Madonna. You can also explore the spare chambers of the Convento San Domenico.

Just beyond you'll see a natural rock arch over the path to the right – don't go through it but continue uphill, where after around 20 minutes of steep terrain and craggy rock steps you'll come to the path proper, where you should take the turning to the left, signed 'Positano Nocelle'. It's a long, delightful, gentle descent from here to Nocelle: if there's cloud cover the combination of this and the glimpses of dizzying views is unforgettable. The route is marked by red and white stripes daubed on rocks and trees and is easy to follow.

You eventually emerge at **Nocelle**, where cold drinks and coffee are served at a terraced kiosk with flowers on the tables. Or head a little further through the village to Piazza Santa Croce, where a stall dispenses fantastic freshly squeezed orange and lemon juice.

Continue down through the village and a series of steps will take you through the olive groves and deposit you on the road just east of Positano. A nicer though longer option – especially if you're weary of steps at this point – is to continue on the path that leads west out of Nocelle towards **Montepertuso**. Don't miss the huge hole in the centre of the cliff at Montepertuso, where it looks as though some irate giant has punched through the slab of limestone. From here the route winds its way to the northern fringes of **Positano**. From here you can dip down through town to the beachfront bars and balmy sea.

The CAI (Club Alpino Italiano; Italian Alpine Club) has a website dedicated to the Monti Lattari area (www.caimontilattari.it), with useful information on various trails and downloadable maps. If you prefer a guided hike, there are a number of reliable local guides, including American Frank Carpegna (www.positanofrankcarpegna.com), a longtime resident here, and Zia Lucy (www.zialucy.it).

🍷 Drinking & Nightlife

⭐ **Africana** CLUB
(☑089 81 11 71; www.africanafamousclub.com; Via Terramare 2; €10-35; ☺9pm-3am Sun-Thu, to 5am Fri & Sat May-Sep; 🚌) This club near Marina di Praia makes for a memorable boogie – though beware the pricey drinks.

Africana has been going since the '60s, when Jackie Kennedy was just one of the famous VIP guests. It has an extraordinary cave setting, complete with natural blowholes, a mix of DJs and live music, not to mention a glass dance floor with fish swimming under your feet.

🛍 Shopping

Alimentari Rispoli   FOOD & DRINKS
(☑089 87 40 18; Via Nazionale 82; ⊙8am-1pm & 4-9pm) Sells cheese and cold cuts, as well as fruit and drinks; a useful spot to stock up before embarking on the Sentieri degli Dei hiking trail.

ℹ Information

Tourist Office (☑089 87 45 57; www.praiano. org; Via G Capriglione 116b; ⊙9am-1pm & 4-8pm Mon-Sat) Can provide maps and information for those wanting to hit the area's hiking trails.

ℹ Getting There & Away

SITA Sud (p108) runs up to 27 daily buses to Sorrento (€2.40, 1¼ hours). It also runs up to 25 daily services to Amalfi (€1.30, 25 minutes) from where buses continue east to Salerno. Reduced services on Sunday.

Ravello

☑089 / POP 2490

Sitting high in the hills above Amalfi, Ravello is a refined and polished town almost entirely dedicated to tourism (and increasingly popular as a wedding venue). Boasting impeccable bohemian credentials – Wagner, DH Lawrence and Virginia Woolf all spent time here – it's today known for its ravishing gardens and stupendous views, the best in the world according to former resident Gore Vidal, and certainly the best on the coast.

Most people visit on a day trip from Amalfi – a nerve-tingling 7km drive up the Valle del Dragone – although, to best enjoy its romantic, otherworldly atmosphere, you'll need to stay here overnight. On Tuesday morning there's a lively street market in Piazza Duomo, where you'll find wine, mozzarella and olive oil, as well as discounted designer clothes.

◉ Sights

⭐**Villa Rufolo**   GARDENS
(☑089 85 76 21; www.villarufolo.it; Piazza Duomo; adult/reduced €7/5; ⊙9am-9pm May-Sep, reduced hours rest of year, tower museum 11am-4pm) To the south of Ravello's cathedral, a 14th-century tower marks the entrance to this villa, famed for its beautiful cascading gardens. Created by a Scotsman, Francis Neville Reid, in 1853, they are truly magnificent, commanding

divine panoramic views packed with exotic colours, artistically crumbling towers and luxurious blooms. Note that the gardens are at their best from May till October; they don't merit the entrance fee outside those times.

The villa was built in the 13th century for the wealthy Rufolo dynasty and was home to several popes as well as king Robert of Anjou. Wagner was so inspired by the gardens when he visited in 1880 that he modelled the garden of Klingsor (the setting for the second act of the opera *Parsifal*) on them.

The 13th-century Torre Maggiore (Main Tower) now houses the **Torre-Museo**, an interactive museum that sheds light on the villa's history and characters. Among the latter is Sir Francis Neville Reid, the Scottish botanist who purchased and extensively restored the property in the 19th century. The museum also showcases art, archaeological finds and ceramics linked to the villa. Stairs inside the tower lead up to an outdoor viewing platform, affording knockout views of the villa and Amalfi Coast.

Today Villa Rufolo's gardens stage world-class concerts during the town's classical music festival.

⭐**Villa Cimbrone**   GARDENS
(☑089 85 74 59; www.hotelvillacimbrone.com/ gardens; Via Santa Chiara 26; adult/reduced €7/4; ⊙9am-sunset) Some 600m south of Piazza Duomo, the Villa Cimbrone is worth a wander, if not for the 11th-century villa itself (now an upmarket hotel), then for the shamelessly romantic views from the delightful gardens. They're best admired from the Belvedere of Infinity, an awe-inspiring terrace lined with classical-style statues and busts and overlooking the impossibly blue Tyrrhenian Sea.

Camo   MUSEUM
(☑089 85 74 61; www.museodelcorallo.com; Piazza Duomo 9, Ravello; ⊙10am-noon & 3-5pm Mon-Sat) This very special place is ostensibly a cameo shop – and exquisite they are, too, crafted primarily out of coral and shell – but there's a treasure trove of a museum beyond the showroom. Even more of a treat is if cameo creator and shop founder Giorgio Filocamo is here to explain the background to such pieces as a 16th-century crucifix on a crystal cross, a mid-16th-century Madonna, a 3rd-century-AD Roman amphora, gorgeous

tortoiseshell combs and some exquisite oil paintings.

Festivals & Events

★ Ravello Festival
PERFORMING ARTS

(📞 089 85 84 22; www.ravellofestival.com; ⊘ Jul-Sep) Between early July and September, the Ravello Festival – established in 1953 – turns much of the town centre into a stage. Events range from orchestral concerts and chamber music to ballet performances, film screenings and exhibitions. The festival's most celebrated (and breathtaking) venue is the overhanging terrace in the Villa Rufolo gardens.

🛏 Sleeping

Agriturismo Monte Brusara
AGRITURISMO €

(📞 089 85 74 67; www.montebrusara.com; Via Monte Brusara 32; d €94-100; ⊘ year-round; 🐾) A working farm, this mountainside *agriturismo* (farm stay) is located a tough half-hour walk of about 1.5km from Ravello's centre (call ahead to arrange to be picked up). It is especially suited to families or those who simply want to escape the crowds and drink in the bucolic views.

★ Villa Casale
APARTMENT €€

(📞 089 85 74 12; www.ravelloresidence.it; Via Orso Papice 4; apt €90-186, ste €180-250; ❄🐾🏊) A short, easy walk from Piazza Duomo, Villa Casale consists of two elegant suites and five apartments. Top billing goes to the suites, graced with antiques and occupying the original 14th-century building. All the suites and apartments come with a self-contained kitchen and the property's tranquil terraced gardens include a smart, inviting pool with hypnotic views of the coastline.

★ Belmond Hotel Caruso
HOTEL €€€

(📞 089 85 88 01; www.grandluxuryhotels.com; Piazza San Giovanni del Toro 2; s €605-770, d €748-990; ⊘ Apr-Oct; 🅿❄🐾🏊) There can be no better place to swim than the Caruso's sensational infinity pool. Seemingly set on the edge of a precipice, its blue waters merge with sea and sky to magical effect. Inside, the sublimely restored 11th-century *palazzo* (mansion) is no less impressive, with Moorish arches doubling as window frames, 15th-century vaulted ceilings and high-class ceramics.

✖ Eating

★ Babel
CAFE €

(📞 089 85 86 215; Via Trinità 13; meals €20; ⊘11.30am-3.30pm & 7-11pm Thu-Tue mid-Jun–mid-Sep, closed Jan & Feb; 🐾) A cool little deli-cafe with a compact menu of high-quality, affordable bites, from Campanian *salumi* (charcuterie) and cheeses, to bruschetta, dry polenta and creative salads with combos like lemon and orange with goat's cheese and chestnut honey. There's an excellent range of local wines, smooth jazz on the sound system, plus an assortment of unique, stylish ceramics for sale.

★ Da Salvatore
ITALIAN €€

(📞 089 85 72 27; www.salvatoreravello.com; Via della Republicca 2; meals around €40; ⊘12.30-3pm & 7.30-10pm Tue-Sun Easter-Nov) Located just before the bus stop, Da Salvatore doesn't merely rest on the laurels of its spectacular terrace views. This is one of the coast's best restaurants, serving arresting dishes that showcase local produce with creativity, flair and whimsy; your pre-meal *benvenuto* (welcome) may include an *'aperitivo'* of Negroni encased in a white-chocolate ball. Wines by the glass include knockout super-reds such as Amarone and Barolo.

ℹ Information

Tourist Office (📞 089 85 70 96; www.ravellotime.it; Via Roma 18; ⊘10am-8pm) Provides brochures, maps and directions, and can also assist with accommodation.

ℹ Getting There & Away

From Amalfi's Piazza Flavio Gioia, SITA Sud (p108) runs up to 27 buses daily to Ravello (€1.30, 25 minutes).

SALERNO & THE CILENTO

Salerno

📞 089 / POP 135,300

Salerno may initially seem like a bland big city, but the place has a charming, if gritty, individuality, especially around its vibrant *centro storico* (historic centre), where medieval churches share space with neighbourhood trattorias, trendy wine bars and boutiques. The city has invested in various urban-regeneration programs centred on this historic neighbourhood, which features

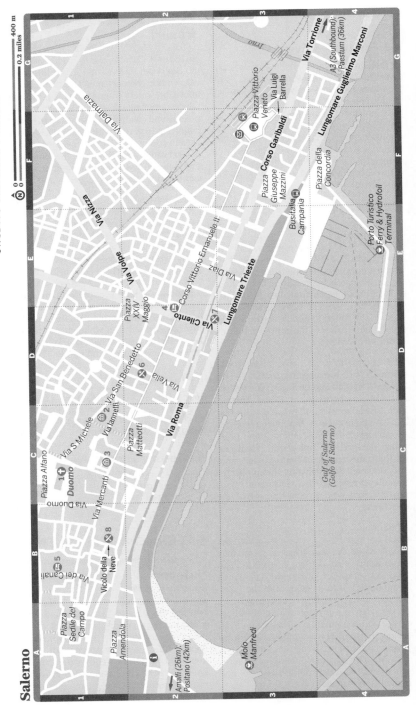

Salerno

Salerno

⊚ Top Sights
1 Duomo C1

⊚ Sights
2 Museo Archeologico Provinciale.........C1
3 Museo Virtuale della Scuola
    Medica Salernitana C1

⊜ Sleeping
4 Hotel Montestella.................................D2
5 Ostello Ave Gratia Plena......................B1

⊗ Eating
6 La Cantina del Feudo D2
7 Pizza Margherita D2
8 Vicolo della Neve B1

a tree-lined seafront promenade widely considered to be one of the most beautiful in Europe.

⊙ Sights

★**Duomo**   CATHEDRAL
(Piazza Alfano; ⊙8.30am-8pm Mon-Sat, 8.30am-1pm & 4-8pm Sun) You can't miss the looming presence of Salerno's impressive cathedral, widely considered to be the most beautiful medieval church in Italy. Built by the Normans in the 11th century and later remodelled in the 18th century, it sustained severe damage in a 1980 earthquake. It is dedicated to San Matteo (St Matthew), whose remains were reputedly brought to the city in 954 and now lie beneath the main altar in the vaulted crypt.

Take special note of the magnificent main entrance, the 12th-century **Porta dei Leoni**, named after the marble lions at the foot of the stairway. It leads through to a beautiful, harmonious courtyard, surrounded by graceful arches and overlooked by a 12th-century bell tower. Carry on through the huge bronze doors (similarly guarded by lions), which were cast in Constantinople in the 11th century. When you come to the three-aisled interior, you will see that it is largely baroque, with only a few traces of the original church. These include parts of the transept and choir floor and the two raised pulpits in front of the choir stalls. Throughout the church you can see extraordinarily detailed and colourful 13th-century mosaic work.

In the right-hand apse, don't miss the **Cappella delle Crociate** (Chapel of the

Crusades), containing stunning frescoes and more wonderful mosaics. It was so named because crusaders' weapons were blessed here. Under the altar stands the tomb of 11th-century pope Gregory VII.

**Museo Archeologico
Provinciale**   MUSEUM
(☑089 23 11 35; www.museoarcheologicosalerno.it; Via San Benedetto 28; adult/reduced €4/2; ⊙9am-7.30pm Tue-Sun) The province's restored and revitalised main archaeological museum is an excellent showcase for a collection of mesmerising grave goods from the surrounding area, dating back to cave dwellers and the colonising Greeks. Seek out the 4th-century-BC bronze candelabra topped with the figures of a warrior and a woman, his arm around her shoulder.

Castello di Arechi   CASTLE
(☑089 296 40 15; www.ilcastellodiarechi.it; Via Benedetto Croce; adult/reduced €4/2; ⊙9am-5pm Tue-Sat, to 3.30pm Sun) Hop on bus 19 from Piazza XXIV Maggio to visit Salerno's most famous landmark, the forbidding Castello di Arechi, dramatically positioned 263m above the city. Originally a Byzantine fort, it was built by the Lombard duke of Benevento, Arechi II, in the 8th century and subsequently modified by the Normans and Aragonese, most recently in the 16th century.

**Museo Virtuale della
Scuola Medica Salernitana**   MUSEUM
(☑089 257 61 26; www.museovirtualescuola medicasalernitana.beniculturali.it; Via Mercanti 74; adult/reduced €3/2; ⊙9.30am-1pm Tue-Wed, 9.30am-1pm & 5-8pm Thu-Sat, 10am-1pm Sun; ⊕) In Salerno's historic centre, this small, slightly forlorn museum deploys videos and touch-screen technology to explore the teachings and wince-inducing procedures of Salerno's once-famous, now-defunct medical institute. Established around the 9th century, the school was the most important centre of medical knowledge in medieval Europe, reaching the height of its prestige in the 11th century. It was closed in the early 19th century.

⊨ Sleeping

**Ostello Ave
Gratia Plena**   HOSTEL **€**
(☑089 23 47 76; www.ostellodisalerno.it; Via dei Canali; dm/s/d €16/45/65; ⊙year-round; @⊚) Housed in a 16th-century convent, Salerno's

excellent HI hostel is right in the heart of the *centro storico*. Inside there's a charming central courtyard and a range of bright rooms, from dorms to great bargain doubles with private bathroom. The 2am curfew is for dorms only.

Hotel Montestella HOTEL €€
(☑089 22 51 22; www.hotelmontestella.it; Corso Vittorio Emanuele II 156; d €80-120, tr €90-150; ❄@🛜) Within walking distance of just about anywhere worth going to, the fresh, modern Montestella is on Salerno's main pedestrian thoroughfare, halfway between the *centro storico* and train station. Although some rooms are quite tight, all are light and contemporary, with firm beds and patterned feature walls. Staff are friendly and helpful, and the breakfast spread is decent.

 Eating

Vicolo della Neve ITALIAN €
(☑089 22 57 05; www.vicolodellaneve.it; Vicolo della Neve 24; meals €20-25; ⏱7.15pm-midnight Mon, Tue & Thu-Sat, 12.30-3.30pm Sun) A city institution on a scruffy street, this is the archetypal *centro storico* trattoria, with brick arches, fake frescoes and walls hung with works by local artists. The menu is unwaveringly authentic, with pizzas and *calzoni, peperoni ripieni* (stuffed peppers) and a top-notch *parmigiana di melanzane* (baked eggplant). It can get incredibly busy: book in advance, especially later in the week.

Pizza Margherita ITALIAN €
(☑089 22 88 80; Corso Garibaldi 201; pizzas/buffet from €3/4, lunch menu €8.50; ⏱12.30-3.30pm & 7.30pm-midnight; 👪) It looks like a bland, modern canteen, but this is, in fact, one of Salerno's most popular lunch spots. Locals regularly queue for the lunchtime buffet that, on any given day, might include buffalo mozzarella, salami, mussels in various guises and a range of salads.

If that selection doesn't appeal, the daily lunch menu (offering pasta, main course and half a litre of bottled water) is chalked up on a blackboard, or there's the regular menu of pizzas, pastas, salads and main courses.

★**La Cantina del Feudo** ITALIAN €€
(☑089 25 46 96; Via Velia 45; meals around €28; ⏱12.30-3.30pm & 7pm-midnight Thu-Tue; 🖊) Frequented by locals in the know, this

restaurant is run by a charming Puglian family. The culinary traditions of their home region are evident on the well-executed menu, which includes *cozze gratinate* (mussels with breadcrumbs) and gorgeous vegetable dishes (try the vegetable antipasto). The interior offers a sophisticated take on the rural trattoria and there's a terrace on the pedestrianised street for al fresco noshing.

ℹ️ Information

Post Office (Piazza Vittorio Veneto 7; ⏱8.20am-1.30pm Mon-Fri, to 12.30pm Sat) Beside the train station.

Tourist Office (☑089 23 14 32; Lungomare Trieste 7; ⏱9am-1pm & 3-7pm Mon-Sat) Has limited information.

ℹ️ Getting There & Away

BOAT

TraVelMar (p112) sails seasonally to Amalfi (€8, 35 minutes, around 12 daily) and Positano (€12, 70 minutes, around seven daily), as well as to Cetara (€5, 15 minutes, around six daily), Maiori (€7, 30 minutes, around six daily) and Minori (€7, 40 minutes, around six daily).

Alicost (☑089 87 14 83; www.alicost.it) runs one daily seasonal ferry service to Capri (€25, 2¼ hours) via Minori (€7), Amalfi (€8) and Positano (€12).

Navigazione Libera del Golfo (p85) runs one daily hydrofoil service to Capri (€25.50) from Easter to mid-October.

TraVelMar services depart from the Porto Turistico, 200m down the pier from Piazza della Concordia. You can buy tickets from the booths by the embarkation point. Alicost and Navigazione Libera del Golfo services depart from Molo Manfredi, 1.8km further west.

BUS

SITA Sud (www.sitasudtrasporti.it) buses for Amalfi depart at least hourly from the **bus station** (Piazza Vittorio Veneto) on Piazza Vittorio Veneto, beside the train station, stopping en route at Vietri sul Mare, Cetara and Maiori. For Pompeii, take **Busitalia Campania** (☑089 48 72 70; www.fsbusitaliacampania. it) bus 4 from nearby Corso Garibaldi (at the corner of Via Luigi Barrella). For the south coast and Paestum, take the hourly bus 34 from Piazza della Concordia near the Porto Turistico ferry terminal.

CAR & MOTORCYCLE

Salerno is on the A3 between Naples and Reggio di Calabria; the A3 is toll-free from Salerno south. Take the Salerno exit and follow signs to the *centro* (city centre). If you want to hire a car, there's a **Europcar** (☑ 089 258 07 75; www.eur opcar.com; Via Clemente Mauro 18; ☺ 8.30am-1pm & 2.30-6.30pm Mon-Fri, 8.30am-1pm Sat) agency not far from the train station.

TRAIN

Salerno is a major stop on southbound routes to Calabria, and the Ionian and Adriatic coasts. From the station in Piazza Vittorio Veneto there are regular trains to Naples (from €4.30, 35 to 45 minutes) and Rome (Intercity from €30.50, three hours).

Cilento Coast

While the Cilento stretch of coastline lacks the sophistication of the Amalfi Coast, it too has its string of craggy, sun-bleached towns, among them popular Agropoli, Palinuro and especially charming Castellabate. The Cilento can even afford to have a slight air of superiority when it comes to its beaches: a combination of secluded coves and long stretches of golden sand with fewer overpriced ice creams and sunbeds. Yet, Campania's southern bookend is more than its waterside appeal. It's here that you'll find the ancient Greek temples of Paestum and the hiking paradise of the Parco Nazionale del Cilento e Vallo di Diano. Together with the monumental Certosa San Lorenzo in Padula, they form one of Italy's Unesco World Heritage sites.

Paestum

Paestum is home to one of Europe's most glorious archaeological zones. Deemed a World Heritage Site by Unesco, the site includes three of the world's best-preserved ancient Greek temples, as well as an engrossing museum crammed with millennia-old frescoes, ceramics and daily artefacts. Among these is the iconic *Tomba del Truffatore* (Tomb of the Diver) funerary fresco.

Paestum, or Poseidonia as the city was originally called (in honour of Poseidon, the Greek god of the sea), was founded in the 6th century BC by Greek settlers and fell under Roman control in 273 BC. Decline later set in following the demise of the Roman Empire. Savage raids by the Saracens and periodic outbreaks of malaria forced the steadily dwindling population to abandon the city altogether.

Today, it offers visitors a vivid, to-scale glimpse of the grandeur and sophistication of the area's past life.

◉ Sights

★ **Paestum's Temples**   ARCHAEOLOGICAL SITE
(Area Archeologica di Paestum; ☑ 0828 81 10 23; www.museopaestum.beniculturali.it; adult/reduced incl museum €9/4.50; ☺ 8.30am-7.30pm, last entry 6.50pm) These temples are among the best-preserved monuments of Magna Graecia, the Greek colony that once covered much of southern Italy. Rediscovered in the late 18th century, the site as a whole wasn't unearthed until the 1950s. Lacking the tourist mobs that can sully better-known archaeological sites, the place has a wonderful serenity. Take sandwiches and prepare to stay at least three hours. In spring the temples are particularly stunning, surrounded by scarlet poppies.

Buy your tickets in the museum, just east of the site, before entering from the main entrance at the northern end. The first structure is the 6th-century-BC **Tempio di Cerere** (Temple of Ceres); originally dedicated to Athena, it served as a Christian church in medieval times.

As you head south, you can pick out the basic outline of the large rectangular forum, the heart of the ancient city. Among the partially standing buildings are the vast domestic housing area and, further south, the amphitheatre; both provide evocative glimpses of daily life here in Roman times. In the former houses you'll see mosaic floors, and a marble *impluvium* that stood in the atrium and collected rainwater.

The **Tempio di Nettuno** (Temple of Neptune), dating from about 450 BC, is the largest and best preserved of the three temples at Paestum; only parts of its inside walls and roof are missing. The two rows of double-storied columns originally divided the outer colonnade from the *cella*, or inner chamber, where a statue of the temple deity would have been displayed. Despite its commonly used name, many scholars believe that temple was actually dedicated to the Greek goddess Hera, sister and wife of Greek god Zeus.

Almost next door, the so-called **basilica** (in fact, a temple to the goddess Hera) is Paestum's oldest surviving monument. Dating from the middle of the 6th century BC, it's a magnificent sight, with nine columns across and 18 along the sides. Ask someone to take your photo next to one of the columns: it's a good way to appreciate the scale.

Save time for the **museum** (☑0828 81 10 23; ⊙8.30am-7.30pm, last entry 6.50pm, closes 1.40pm 1st & 3rd Mon of month), which covers two floors and houses a collection of fascinating, if weathered, metopes (bas-relief friezes). This collection includes original metopes from the Tempio di Argiva Hera (Temple of Argive Hera), situated 9km north of Paestum, of which virtually nothing else remains. The most famous of the museum's numerous frescoes is the 5th-century-BC *Tomba del Tuffatore* (Tomb of the Diver), thought to represent the passage from life to death with its frescoed depiction of a diver in mid-air. The fresco was discovered in 1968 inside the lid of the tomb of a young man, alongside his drinking cup and oil flasks, which he would perhaps have used to oil himself for wrestling matches. Rare for the period in that it shows a human form, the fresco expresses pure delight in physicality, its freshness and grace eternally arresting. Below the diver, a symposium of men repose languidly on low couches and brandish drinking cups.

🛏 Sleeping

⭐ **Casale Giancesare**   B&B €
(☑0828 72 80 61, 333 1897737; www.casale-giancesare.it; Via Giancesare 8; s €50-140, d €60-140, apt per week €600-1300; P❄@🛜🏊) A 19th-century former farmhouse, this elegantly decorated, stone-clad B&B is run by the delightful Voza family, who will happily ply you with their homemade wine, *limoncello* and marmalades (they even make their own olive oil). It's located 2.5km from the glories of Paestum and surrounded by vineyards and olive and mulberry trees; views are stunning, particularly from the swimming pool.

🍴 Eating

Nonna Sceppa   ITALIAN €€
(☑0828 85 10 64; Via Laura 53; meals €35; ⊙12.30-3pm & 7.30-11pm Fri-Wed; 🍴) Seek out the superbly prepared, robust dishes at Nonna Sceppa, a family-friendly restaurant that's gaining a reputation throughout the region for excellence. Dishes are firmly seasonal and, during summer, concentrate on fresh seafood like the refreshingly simple grilled fish with lemon. Other popular choices include risotto with zucchini and artichokes, and spaghetti with lobster.

ℹ Information

Tourist Office (☑0828 81 10 16; www.info paestum.it; Via Magna Grecia 887; ⊙9am-1pm & 3-5pm Apr-Sep, 9am-1pm & 2-4pm Oct-Mar) Across the street from the archaeological site, this helpful tourist office offers a map of the archaeological site, plus information on the greater Cilento region.

ℹ Getting There & Away

Trains run around 16 times daily from Salerno to Paestum (€2.70, 30 minutes).

Busitalia Campania (☑089 48 72 70; www. fsbusitaliacampania.it) Bus 34 goes to Paestum from Piazza della Concordia in Salerno (€2.70, one hour). Buses run roughly every hour to two hours Monday to Saturday and four times on Sunday.

Parco Nazionale del Cilento e Vallo di Diano

Proving the perfect antidote to the holiday mayhem along the coast, the stunning Parco Nazionale del Cilento e Vallo di Diano (Cilento National Park and the Valley of Diano) combines dense woods and flowering meadows with dramatic mountains, streams, rivers and waterfalls. A World Heritage Site, it is the second-largest national park in Italy, covering a staggering 1810 sq km, including 80 towns and villages. To get the best out of the park, you will, unfortunately, need a car. Allow yourself a full day to visit the park's highly regarded grottoes and more if you're intending to hike some of the area's beautiful nature trails.

👁 Sights

⭐ **Grotte di Castelcivita**   CAVE
(☑0828 77 23 97; www.grottedicastelcivita.com; Piazzale N Zonzi, Castelcivita; adult/reduced €10/8; ⊙standard tours 10.30am, noon, 1.30pm & 3pm Mar & Oct, plus 4.30pm & 6pm Apr-Sep; P🚻) The grottoes are fascinating otherworldly caves that date from prehistoric times: excavations have revealed that they were inhabited 42,000 years ago, making them the oldest known settlement in Europe. Don't forget a jacket, and leave the high heels at home, as paths are wet and slippery. Hard hats, and a certain level of fitness and mobility, are required. Located 40km southeast of Salerno, the complex is refreshingly non-commercial.

Although it extends over 4800m, only around half of the complex is open to the public. The one-hour tour winds through a route surrounded by extraordinary stalagmites and stalactites, and a mesmerising play of colours, caused by algae, calcium and iron that tint the naturally sculpted rock shapes.

The tour culminates in a cavernous lunar landscape – think California's Death Valley in miniature – called the Caverna di Bertarelli (Bertarelli Cavern). The caves are still inhabited – by bats – and visitors are instructed not to take flash photos for fear of blinding them.

Certosa di San Lorenzo MONASTERY

(☑ 0975 77 74 45; www.polomusealecampania.be niculturali.it; Viale Certosa, Padula; adult/reduced €4/2; ☺ 9am-7pm Wed-Mon) One of the largest monasteries in southern Europe, the Certosa di San Lorenzo dates from 1306 and covers 250,000 sq metres. Numerologists can swoon at the following: 320 rooms and halls, 2500m of corridors, galleries and hallways, 300 columns, 500 doors, 550 windows, 13 courtyards, 100 fireplaces, 52 stairways and 41 fountains – in other words, it is *huge*.

As it is unlikely you will have time to see everything, be sure to visit the highlights, including the vast central courtyard (a venue for summer classical-music concerts), the magnificent wood-panelled library, frescoed chapels, and the kitchen with its grandiose fireplace and famous tale: apparently this is where the legendary 1000-egg omelette was made in 1534 for Charles V. Unfortunately, the historic frying pan is not on view – just how big was it, one wonders?

Within the monastery you can also peruse the modest collection of ancient artefacts at the Museo Archeologico Provinciale della Lucania Occidentale (☑ 0975 7 71 17; ☺ 9am-6.45pm Wed-Mon; 👪) FREE .

Grotte di Pertosa CAVE

(☑ 0975 39 70 37; www.grottedipertosa-auletta. it; Pertosa; guided visits adult/reduced 100min €20/15, 60min €13/10; ☺ tour times vary, see website; P 👪) (Re)discovered in 1932, the Grotte di Pertosa date back 35 million years. Used by the Greeks and Romans as places of worship, the caves burrow for some 2500m, with long underground passages and lofty grottoes filled with stalagmites and stalactites. The first part of the tour is a boat (or raft) ride on the river; you disembark just before the waterfall (phew!) and continue on foot for around 800m, surrounded by marvellous rock formations and luminous crystal accretions.

Activities

The park has 15 well-marked **nature trails** that vary from relatively easy strolls to serious hikes requiring stamina and good knees. The countryside in the park is stunning and dramatic and, in spring, you'll experience real flower power: delicate narcissi, wild orchids and tulips hold their own among blowsier summer drifts of brilliant yellow ox-eye daisies and scarlet poppies.

Thickets of silver firs, wild chestnuts and beech trees add to the sumptuous landscape, as do the dramatic cliffs, pine-clad mountains and fauna, including wild boars, badgers and wolves and, for bird watchers, the increasingly rare golden eagle.

Even during the busier summer season, the sheer size of the park means that hikers are unlikely to meet others on the trail to swap tales and muesli bars – so getting lost could become a lonely, not to mention dangerous, experience if you haven't done some essential planning before striding out. In theory, the tourist offices should be able to supply you with a guide to the trails. In reality, they frequently seem to have run out of copies. Failing this, you can buy the *Parco Nazionale del Cilento e Vallo di Diano: Carta Turistica e dei Sentieri* (Tourist and Footpath Map; €7) or the excellent *Monte Stella: Walks & Rambles in Ancient Cilento* published by the Comunita' Montana Alento Monte Stella (€3). Most of the *agriturismi* (farm stays) in the park can also organise guided treks.

A popular self-guided hike, where you are rewarded with spectacular views, is a climb of Monte Alburno (1742m). There's a choice of two trails, both of which are clearly marked from the centre of the small town of Sicignano degli Alburni and finish at the mountain's peak. Allow approximately four hours for either route. The less experienced may prefer to opt for a guide.

There are some excellent *agriturismi* here that offer additional activities, including **guided hikes**, **painting courses** and **horse riding**.

🛏 Sleeping

★ Agriturismo i Moresani AGRITURISMO €

(☑ 0974 90 20 86; www.imoresani.com; Località Moresani; d €90-110; ☺ Mar-Oct; ❄ 🛜 🏊) If you are seeking utter tranquillity, head to this *agriturismo* 1.5km west of Casal Velino. The setting is bucolic: rolling hills in every direction, interspersed with grapevines, grazing pastures and olive trees. Family run, the

18-hectare farm produces its own *caprino* goat's cheese, wine, olive oil and preserves. Rooms have cream- and earth-coloured decor and surround a pretty private garden.

Eating

Trattoria degli Ulivi
ITALIAN €

(☑334 2595091; www.tavolacaldadegliulivi.it; Viale Certosa, Padula; set menu €12; ⊙11am-4pm Wed-Mon, also 7pm-midnight Thu-Sun) If you've worked up an appetite walking the endless corridors of the Certoza di San Lorenzo then this restaurant – located just 50m to the west – is the place to come. The decor is canteen-like, but the daily specials are affordable, tasty and generously proportioned. It serves snacks as well as four-course blowout lunches.

Vecchia Pizzeria Margaret
PIZZA €

(☑0975 33 00 00; Via Luigi Curto, Polla; pizza from €3; ⊙7.30pm-midnight Tue-Sun; ☎) Fabulous wheels of pizza, cooked in a wood-fired oven; it also dishes up antipasti and pasta dishes. Service is fast and friendly, and prices are low. You'll find the restaurant just east of the river, near the hospital. It's great for a fill-up after a walk in the national park.

❶ Information

Paestum's **tourist office** (p120) also has some information on the Parco Nazionale del Cilento.

Alpine Rescue (☑118) For emergencies.

Sicignano degli Alburni Pro Loco (☑0828 97 37 55; www.scoprisicignano.it; Piazza Plebiscito 13, Sicignano degli Alburni; ⊙9am-1.30pm & 2.30-5pm Mon-Sat) Tourist information.

Parks.it (www.parks.it/parco.nazionale.cilento/Eindex.html) Useful online information about the national park.

❶ Getting There & Away

Curcio Viaggi (☑800 122012, 0975 39 12 13; www.curcioviaggi.it) operates three to four daily buses each way between Salerno and Polla on weekdays, and one daily service each way on Saturday. **SITA Sud** (p118) runs three daily services between Salerno and Pertosa Monday to Saturday, two of which continue to Polla. It also runs two daily buses from Polla and Pertosa to Salerno Monday to Saturday.

Puglia, Basilicata & Calabria

Best Places to Eat

Best Places to Sleep

Why Go?

The Italian boot's heel (Puglia), instep (Basilicata) and toe (Calabria) are where the 'Mezzogiorno' (southern Italy) shows all its throbbing intensity. Long stereotyped as the poorer, more passionate cousins of Italy's sophisticated northerners, these regions are finally being appreciated for their true richness. You *will* see washing on weather-worn balconies, scooters speeding down medieval alleys and ancient towns crumbling under Mediterranean suns. But look past the pasta-advert stereotypes and you'll find things altogether more complex and wonderful; gritty, unsentimental cities with pedigrees stretching back thousands of years; dramatically broken coastlines that have harboured fisherfolk and pirates for millennia; and above all, proud and generous people, eager to share these delights with you.

Puglia is defined by its coast, the longest in Italy; little Basilicata touches two seas, but is known for forests and mountains; while Calabria, last stop before Sicily, is a hodgepodge of Greek, Latin, African and Norman influences.

When to Go
Bari

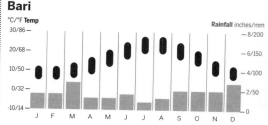

Apr–Jun Spring wildflowers are blooming: perfect for hiking in the Pollino National Park.

Jul & Aug Summer is beach weather and festivals blossom in towns such as Lecce and Matera.

Sep & Oct Crowds have thinned, the weather is mild, and mushrooms are emerging in Sila National Park.

Puglia, Basilicata & Calabria Highlights

1 Matera (p161)
Marvelling at the contrast between miserable caves and soaring cathedrals in this ancient city.

2 Lecce (p147)
Learning to love the flowery excesses of the city's baroque architecture.

3 Valle d'Itria (p140) Eating the best of the Mediterranean diet in the valley's gorgeous hilltowns.

4 Vieste (p132)
Searching for early-morning photo ops around the cream-coloured lanes of this divine coastal town.

5 Maratea (p171)
Driving with the top down and the sea in your nostrils around an impossibly

Isole Tremiti

Croatia

Adriatic Sea

Montenegro

Albania

Greece

100 km
60 miles

MOLISE

Peschici
4 Vieste
Foresta Umbra
Promontorio del Gargano
Parco Nazionale del Gargano
Monte Sant'Angelo
San Giovanni Rotondo

Golfo di Manfredonia

Foggia

A14

A16

CAMPANIA

Monte Cervialto (1808m)

A2

Sele

Golfo di Salerno

Monte Cervati (1900m)

Monte Alburno (1742m)

Parco Nazionale del Cilento e Vallo di Diano

Parco Nazionale del Cilento e Vallo di Diano

S430

Potenza

Castelmezzano

Pietrapertosa

Venosa

S57

BASILICATA

Bradano

Grumentum

Agri

Aliano

Parco Nazionale Dell'Appennino Lucano

S106

Trani

A14

Castel del Monte

Bari

PUGLIA

Polignano a Mare

Grotte di Castellana

Alberobello

Locorotondo

A14

S57

Taranto

Golfo di Taranto

Metaponto

S57

Cisternino

Valle d'Itria

Martina Franca

Ostuni

Oria

S16

S57

Tarantine Murge

Brindisi

2 Lecce

S16

S16

Galatina

SALENTO

8 Otranto

Castro

Gallipoli

1 Matera

3 Valle d'Itria

4 Parco Nazionale del Gargano

5 Maratea

4 Parco Nazionale Dell'Appennino Lucano

N

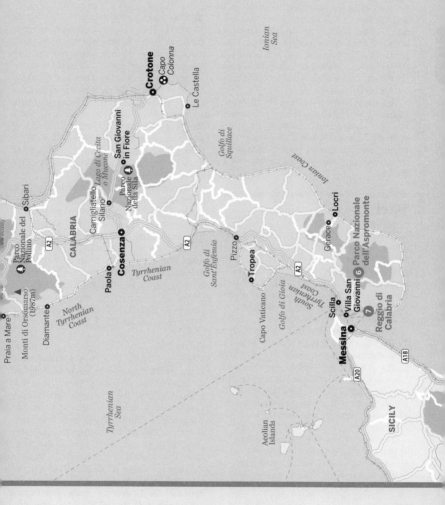

beautiful string of coastal towns.

6 Parco Nazionale dell'Aspromonte
(p178) Rambling in the wild, lonely uplands of this mysterious Calabrian wilderness.

7 Museo Nazionale di Reggio Calabria
(p179) Getting up close and personal with the godlike Riace Bronzes.

8 Otranto Cathedral (p156)
Viewing macabre skulls and magnificent mosaics in this unique Norman basilica.

Praia a Mare

Monti di Orsomarso (1987m)

Parco Nazionale del Pollino

Diamante

North Tyrrhenian Coast

Sibari

Parco Nazionale del Pollino

CALABRIA

A2

Camigliatello Silano

Lago di Cecita o Mucone

San Giovanni in Fiore

Parco Nazionale della Sila

Paola

Cosenza

Tyrrhenian Coast

Tyrrhenian Sea

Le Castella

Capo Colonna

Crotone

Ionian Sea

Golfo di Squillace

A2

Pizzo

Golfo di Sant'Eufemia

Ionian Coast

Tropea

Capo Vaticano

Golfo di Gioia

South Tyrrhenian Coast

A2

Locri

Gerace

Scilla

Villa San Giovanni

Messina

A20

Parco Nazionale dell'Aspromonte 6

Reggio di Calabria 7

A18

SICILY

Aeolian Islands

PUGLIA

Puglia can surely now take its place in the first rank of Italy's famous regions. Clearly, everything the Italophile craves is there in abundance: ancient towns heavy with the tangible past; extravagant churches dreamt up by Europe's finest architects; the footprints of an endless procession of conquerors and cultures, stamped in stone, gold and marble; seas of olives; olive-green seas; and food the equal of any in Italy. Travellers bored or worn down by the crowds of Campania and Tuscany can find still release in the baroque splendour of Lecce, 'Florence of the South', or one of many lesser (but no less beautiful) Puglian towns.

But it's perhaps outside of its cities that Puglia shines brightest. From the ancient Forest of Umbra in the north to the fruitful Valle d'Itria and sun-baked Salento, Puglia's countryside has always been its foundation – the source of its food, its wealth and its culture.

Bari

POP 324,200

If Lecce is the south's Florence, Bari is its Bologna, a historic but forward-looking town with a high percentage of young people and migrants lending it vigour. More urban than Lecce and Brindisi, with grander boulevards and better nightlife, Bari supports a large university, an opera house and municipal buildings that shout confidence.

Most travellers skip Bari on their way to Puglia's big-hitter, Lecce (the towns have a long-standing rivalry, especially over football), but Bari doesn't lack history or culture. The old town contains the bones of St Nicholas (aka Santa Claus) in its Basilica di San Nicola, along with a butch castle and plenty of unfussy trattorias that have the local nosh – *cucina barese* – down to a simple art.

The second-largest town in southern Italy, Bari is a busy port with connections to Greece, Albania and Croatia, and sports an international airport with connections to much of Europe.

❶ Dangers & Annoyances

Once notorious for petty crime, Bari has cleaned up its act of late. Nonetheless, take all of the usual precautions: don't leave anything in your car; don't display money or valuables; and watch out for bag-snatchers on scooters.

⊙ Sights

Most sights are in or near the atmospheric old town, Bari Vecchia, a medieval labyrinth of tight alleyways and graceful piazzas. It fills a small peninsula between the new port to the west and the old port to the southeast, cramming in 40 churches and more than 120 shrines.

★**Basilica di San Nicola**   BASILICA
(☑ 0805 73 71 11; www.basilicasannicola.it; Piazza San Nicola; ⊙ 7am-8.30pm Mon-Sat, to 10pm Sun) Bari's signature basilica was one of the first Norman churches to be built in southern Italy, and is a splendid (if square and solid) example of Puglian-Romanesque architecture. Dating to the 12th century, it was originally constructed to house the relics of St Nicholas (better known as Father Christmas), which were stolen from Turkey in 1087 by local fishing folk. Today, it is an important place of pilgrimage for both Catholics and Orthodox Christians.

St Nicholas' remains, which are said to emanate a miraculous myrrh with special powers, are ensconced in a shrine in the beautiful, vaulted crypt. Above, the interior is huge and simple with a gilded 17th-century wooden ceiling. The magnificent 13th-century *ciborium* over the altar is Puglia's oldest. Other items related to the basilica, including chalices, vestments and crests, are displayed in the **Museo Nicolaiano** (☑ 0805 23 14 29; Largo Papa Urbano II; ⊙ 11am-6pm Thu-Tue) FREE, adjacent.

Cathedral   CATHEDRAL
(☑ 080 521 06 05; www.arcidiocesibaribitonto.it; Piazza dell'Odegitria; ⊙ 8am-7pm Mon-Sat, 8-10am & 11am-7pm Sun) Built over the original Byzantine church, the 12th- to 13th-century Romanesque cathedral, dedicated to San Sabino, is technically Bari's most important church, although its fame pales alongside San Nicola. Inside, the plain walls are punctuated with deep arcades and the eastern window is a tangle of plant and animal motifs. The highlight lies in the subterranean **Museo del Succorpo della Cattedrale** (adult/reduced €3/2; ⊙ 9.30am-4pm Mon, Wed, Sat & Sun, to 12.30pm Tue, Thu & Fri), where recent excavations have revealed remnants left over from an ancient Christian basilica and various Roman ruins.

Bari

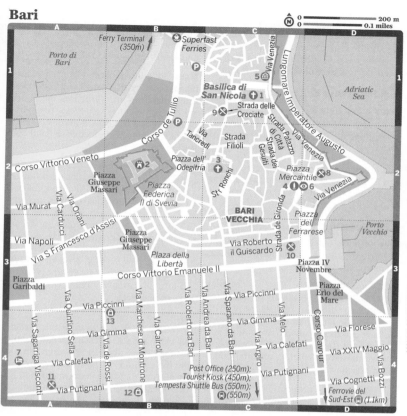

Bari

◎ Top Sights
1 Basilica di San Nicola C1

◎ Sights
2 Castello Svevo B2
3 Cathedral C2
4 Colonna della Giustizia C2
   Museo del Succorpo della
   Cattedrale .... (see 3)
5 Museo Nicolaiano C1
6 Piazza Mercantile D2

⊜ Sleeping
7 B&B Casa Pimpolini A4

⊗ Eating
8 La Locanda di Federico D2
9 Maria delle Sgagliozze C1
10 Paglionico Vini e Cucina C3
11 Terranima A4

⬡ Shopping
12 Enoteca Vinarius de Pasquale B4
13 Il Salumaio B4

Castello Svevo　　　　　　　　　　CASTLE

(Swabian Castle; ☑ 080 521 37 04; Piazza Federico
II di Svevia; adult/reduced/under 18yr €8/4/free;
⊙ 8.30am-7.30pm Thu-Tue) Roger the Norman
originally built this castle, in the 12th century, over the ruins of a Byzantine structure.
Later, Frederick II of Swabia built over the
existing castle, incorporating it into his
design and leaving intact the the two towers
of the Norman structure that still stand. The
bastions, with corner towers overhanging
the moat, were added in the 16th century
during Aragonese rule, when the castle was
a magnificent residence. Excavation is ongoing, uncovering more rich layers of elite
Barese history.

Piazza Mercantile PIAZZA

This beautiful piazza is fronted by the Sedile, the headquarters of Bari's Council of Nobles. In the square's northeast corner is the **Colonna della Giustizia** (Column of Justice), where debtors were once tied and whipped.

Festivals & Events

Festa di San Nicola RELIGIOUS

(⊙7-9 May) The Festival of St Nicholas is Bari's biggest annual shindig, celebrating the 11th-century arrival of St Nicholas' relics from Turkey. On the first evening a procession leaves Castello Svevo for the Basilica di San Nicola. The next day there's a deafening fly-past and a fleet of boats carries the statue of St Nicholas along the coast.

Sleeping

Most of Bari's hotels tend to be bland and overpriced, aimed at business clientele. B&Bs are generally a better option.

B&B Casa Pimpolini B&B €

(📞0805 21 99 38, 333 9580740; www.casapimpo lini.com; Via Calefati 249; s/d €60/80; ❄🅐) This lovely B&B in Bari's new town is within easy walking distance to shops, restaurants and Bari Vecchia (the old town). The two rooms are warm and welcoming, and the homemade breakfast is a treat. Great value.

Villa Romanazzi Carducci HOTEL €

(📞0805 42 74 00; www.villaromanazzi.com; Via Capruzzi 326; s/d from €59/99; 🅿❄🅐🏊) Run by the French Accor group, the Villa Romanazzi shows flair that transcends its workaday (if convenient) location, near the train station. Businesslike rooms are modern and clean-lined, but the real bonuses are in the extras: statue-embellished gardens, picturesque swimming pool (summer only), enormous fitness centre, free bikes, a spa and a decent restaurant with excellent breakfasts.

Eating

One of the best things about Bari is its trattorias, and the simple, delightful seafood and *cucina barese* they serve.

★ Paglionico Vini e Cucina OSTERIA €

(📞338 2120391; Strada Vallisa 23; meals €27; ⊙noon-3pm daily & 7-11pm Mon-Sat) Dishing up what the locals have since 1870, this 100% Barese *osteria* (casual tavern) is an absolute classic. There's no menu, just a chalkboard displaying what's cooking that day. It's all fine salt-of-the-earth Puglian cuisine, with seafood to the fore – the *riso, patate e cozze* (oven-baked rice, potatoes and mussels) is particularly good. The owners/waiters are undemonstrative, and brilliant.

Maria delle Sgagliozze PUGLIAN €

(Strada delle Crociate 13; snacks €1; ⊙from 5pm) Octogenarian Maria dispenses the legendary Barese street food *sgagliozze* (deep-fried polenta cubes) from the front of her house. Sprinkle them with a pinch of salt and Bob's your uncle!

La Locanda di Federico PUGLIAN €€

(📞0805 22 77 05; www.lalocandadifederico.com; Piazza Mercantile 63; meals €35; ⊙noon-3.30pm & 7pm-midnight) With domed ceilings, archways and medieval-style artwork on the walls, this restaurant oozes atmosphere, and a quiet (justified) confidence in its classic Puglian fare. The menu is proudly studded with regional staples such as *orecchiette* ('little ears' of pasta) *con le cime di rape* (with turnip tops) and even *al ragù di cavallo* (with horsemeat sauce).

Terranima PUGLIAN €€

(📞0805 21 97 25; www.terranima.com; Via Putignani 213; meals €32; ⊙noon-3pm daily & 7-11pm Mon-Sat) Peep through the lace curtains into the cool interior of this rustic trattoria, where worn flagstone floors and period furnishings make you feel like you're dining in someone's front room. The menu features fabulous regional offerings such as veal, lemon and caper meatballs, and *sporcamuss,* a sweet flaky pastry.

Shopping

Il Salumaio FOOD & DRINKS

(📞0805 21 93 45; www.ilsalumaio.it; Via Piccinni 168; ⊙8.30am-2pm & 4.30-9pm Mon-Sat) Breathe in the delicious smells of Puglia's best produce at this venerable delicatessen.

Enoteca Vinarius de Pasquale WINE

(📞0805 21 31 92; Via Marchese di Montrone 87; ⊙8am-1.30pm & 4-8.30pm Mon-Sat) Stock up on Puglian drops such as Primitivo di Manduria at this gorgeous old wine shop, founded in 1911.

ℹ Information

From Piazza Aldo Moro, in front of the main train station, streets heading north will take you to Corso Vittorio Emanuele II, which separates the old and new parts of the city.

Tourist Office (☑ 0805 82 14 11; Piazza Aldo Moro 32; ☺ 9am-1pm & 3-7pm Mon-Sat) This kiosk, convenient to Bari's central station, is packed with information on the city and Puglia generally.

Police Station (☑ 0805 29 11 11; Via Murat 4)

Post Office (☑ 0805 25 01 50; Piazza Umberto I 33a; ☺ 8.30am-7pm Mon-Fri, to 12.30pm Sat)

Policlinico di Bari (☑ 800 34 93 49; Piazza Cesare 11) Bari's main hospital has a 24-hour emergency room.

❶ Getting There & Away

AIR

Bari's **Karol Wojtyła Airport** (☑ 0805 80 02 00; www.aeroportidipuglia.it; Viale Ferrari), 10km northwest of the city centre, is served by a host of international and budget airlines, including easyJet, Alitalia and Ryanair.

Pugliairbus (www.aeroportidipuglia.it) connects Bari airport with Foggia and Brindisi airports. It also has services to Matera, Vieste, and Taranto.

BOAT

Ferries run from Bari to Albania, Croatia, Greece and Montenegro. All boat companies have offices at the **ferry terminal**, accessible on bus 20 from the main train station. Fares vary considerably among companies and it's easier to book with a travel agent such as **Morfimare** (☑ 0805 7 98 15; www.morfimare.it; Corso de Tullio 36-40).

The main companies and their routes:

Jadrolinija (☑ 0805 27 54 39; www.jadrolinija. hr; Nuova Stazione Marittima di Bari) For Dubrovnik (Croatia).

Montenegro Lines (☑ 382 30 31 11 64; www. montenegrolines.net; Corso de Tullio 36) For Bar (Montenegro) and Dubrovnik (Croatia).

Superfast (☑ 0805 28 28 28; www.superfast. com; Corso de Tullio 6) For Corfu, Igoumenitsa and Patras (Greece).

Ventouris Ferries (☑ Albania 0808 496685, Greece 0808 761451; www.ventouris.gr; Nuova Stazione Marittima di Bari) For Corfu, Cephalonia and Igoumenitsa (Greece) and Durrës (Albania).

BUS

Intercity buses leave from two main locations. From Via Capruzzi, south of the main train station, **SITA** (☑ 0805 79 01 11; www.sitabus.it) covers local destinations. **Ferrovie Appulo-Lucane** (☑ 0805 72 52 29; http://ferrovie appulolucane.it) buses serving Matera (€4.90, 1¾ hours, six daily) also depart from here, plus **Marozzi** (☑ 0805 79 02 11; www.marozzivt.it) buses for Rome (from €34.50, 4½ to 5½ hours, six daily – note that the overnight bus departs

❶ HEADING EAST

Puglia is the main jumping-off point for onward travel to Greece, Croatia and Albania. The two main ports are Bari and Brindisi, from where you can catch ferries to Vlorë and Durrës in Albania, Bar in Montenegro, and Cephalonia, Corfu, Igoumenitsa and Patras in Greece. Fares from Bari to Greece are generally more expensive than those from Brindisi. Taxes are usually from €9 per person and €12 per car. High season is generally the months of July and August, with reduced services in low season. Tariffs can be up to one-third cheaper in low season.

from Piazza Moro) and other long-distance destinations.

Buses operated by **Ferrovie del Sud-Est** (FSE; ☑ 0805 46 21 11; www.fseonline.it) leave from Largo Ciaia, south of Piazza Aldo Moro and service the following places:

Alberobello (€4.90, 1½ hours, hourly); continues to Locorotondo (€5.60, 1¾ hours) and Martina Franca (€5.60, two hours)

Grotte di Castellana (€2.80, one hour, frequent)

Taranto (€8.40, three hours with change, four per day)

TRAIN

A web of train lines spreads out from Bari. Note that there are fewer services on the weekend.

From the **Bari Centrale Station** (☑ 0805 24 43 86), Trenitalia trains go to Puglia and beyond:

Brindisi (from €8.40, one hour, frequent)

Foggia (from €9.10, one hour, frequent)

Milan (from €59, 6¾ to eight hours, frequent)

Rome (from €40, four hours, four per day)

Ferrovie Appulo-Lucane serves two main destinations:

Matera (€4.90, 1¾ hours, 12 daily)

Potenza (€11, 3¾ hours, four daily)

Ferrovie del Sud-Est trains leave from the southern side of the station where they have their own separate ticket office:

Alberobello (€4.90, 1¾ hours, hourly)

Martina Franca (€5.60, 3¼ hours, five per day)

Taranto (from €8.40, 2½ hours, nine daily)

❶ Getting Around

Central Bari is compact – a 15-minute walk will take you from Piazza Aldo Moro to the old town.

For the ferry terminal, take bus 20 (tickets €1.50) from Piazza Moro.

Street parking is migraine-inducing. There's a large parking area (€1) south of the main port entrance; otherwise, there's a large multi-storey car park between the main train station and the FSE station. Another car park is on Via Zuppetta, opposite Hotel Adria.

TO/FROM THE AIRPORT

For the airport, take the **Tempesta shuttle bus** (www.autoservizitempesta.it) from the main train station (€4, 30 minutes, hourly), with pick-ups at Piazza Garibaldi and the corner of Via Andrea da Bari and Via Calefati. Alternatively, normal city bus 16 covers the same route and a trip is much cheaper (€1), though marginally slower (40 minutes). A taxi trip from the airport to town costs around €25.

Around Bari

The *Terra di Bari* (Land of Bari) surrounding the capital is rich in olive groves and orchards, and the region has an impressive architectural history with some magnificent cathedrals, an extensive network of castles along its coastline, charming seaside towns such as Trani and, inland, the mysterious Castel del Monte.

Trani

POP 56,100

Known as the 'Pearl of Puglia', beautiful Trani has a sophisticated feel, particularly in summer when well-heeled visitors pack the array of marina-side bars. The marina is the place to promenade and watch the white yachts and fishing boats in the harbour, while the historic centre, with its medieval churches, glossy limestone streets, historic Jewish quarter and faded yet charming *palazzi* is an enchanting area to explore. But it's the cathedral, pale against the deep-blue sea, that is the town's most arresting sight.

◉ Sights

Cathedral   CATHEDRAL
(www.cattedraletrani.it; Piazza del Duomo; campanile €5; ⊙ 8.30am-12.30pm & 3.30-7pm Mon-Sat, 9am-12.30pm & 4-9pm Sun Apr-Oct, shorter hours Nov-Mar) This dramatic seafront cathedral is dedicated to St Nicholas the Pilgrim, a Greek Christian who wandered through Puglia crying *'Kyrie eleison'* ('Lord, have mercy'). First thought to be a simpleton, he was posthumously revered after several miracles attrib-

uted to him occurred. Below the church is the **crypt**, a forest of ancient columns that predates the current structure, and where the bones of St Nicholas are kept beneath the altar. You can also visit the **campanile** (bell tower).

Castle   CASTLE
(✆ 080 528 52 49; www.castelloditrani.beniculturali.it; Piazza Manfredi 16; adult/reduced €5/2.50; ⊙ 8.30am-7.30pm) Two hundred metres north of the cathedral is one of Trani's major landmarks, the vast, almost modernist Swabian castle built by Frederick II in 1233. Charles V later strengthened the fortifications and it was used as a prison from 1844 to 1974. While the moat is now dry, the ingenious engineers originally devised a system allowing the level of seawater in it to be precisely controlled.

Scolanova Synagogue   SYNAGOGUE
(✆ 0883 48 17 99; Via Scolanova 23; ⊙ hours vary) This synagogue, one of four once established in Trani's ancient Jewish quarter, has been reborn after over 600 years. Persecutions, forced conversions and confiscations periodically beset the Jews of Trani, culminating in their forced expulsion in 1510. This 13th-century synagogue was converted to a Christian church in an earlier wave of hate, around 1380. Abandoned by the mid-20th century, it has been deconsecrated and returned to life as the Jewish house of worship it originally was.

Ognissanti Church   CHURCH
(http://chiesadiognissanti.it; Via Ognissanti; ⊙ hours vary) Traditionally (but controversially) thought to be built by the Knights Templar in the 12th century, this church became a place of blessing for those setting out on Crusade. Legend has it that it was in this austere and dignified building that the knights of the First Crusade swore allegiance to their leader, Bohemond I of Antioch, before setting off to 'liberate' the Holy Lands. Whatever the truth, it's a treasured example of Puglian-Romanesque architecture of the period.

⌂ Sleeping

B&B Centro Storico Trani   B&B €
(✆ 0883 50 61 76; www.bbtrani.it; Via Leopardi 28; s/d €40/60; ⊛) This simple, old-fashioned B&B inhabits the 14th-century Palazzo Morola in the old Jewish quarter, and is run by a lovely elderly couple. It's basic, but the

FREDERICK II'S TOY CASTLE

You'll see **Castel del Monte** (☑0883 56 99 97; www.casteldelmonte.beniculturali.it; adult/reduced €10/6; ☺10.30am-7.30pm Apr-Sep, 9am-6.30pm Oct-Mar), an inhumanly exact geometric shape on a hilltop, from miles away. Mysterious and perfectly octagonal, it's one of southern Italy's most talked-about landmarks and a Unesco World Heritage Site. No one knows why Frederick II built it – there's no nearby town or strategic crossroads. It was not built to defend anything, as it has no moat or drawbridge, no arrow slits, and no trapdoors for pouring boiling oil on invaders.

Some theories claim that, according to mid-13th-century beliefs in geometric symbolism, the octagon represented the union of the circle and square, of God-perfection (the infinite) and human-perfection (the finite). The castle was therefore nothing less than a celebration of the relationship between humanity and God.

The castle has eight octagonal towers. Its interconnecting rooms have decorative marble columns and fireplaces, and the doorways and windows are framed in corallite stone. Many of the towers have washing rooms with what are thought to be Europe's first flushing loos – Frederick II, like the Arab world he admired, set great store by cleanliness.

To get to the castle without a car, take the Ferrovia Bari-Nord train from Bari to Andria, then bus number 6 from Andria station to the castle (35 minutes, five daily, April to October only). The castle is about 35km from Trani; there's no parking, but a nearby site charges €5 for a car, and €1 for a shuttle up the short, steepish 500m to the castle.

rooms are large and 'Mama' makes a mean *crostata* (jam tart). There's a terrace, laundry and wi-fi in communal areas.

Hotel Regia HOTEL €€
(☑0883 58 44 44; www.hotelregia.it; Piazza Addazi 2; s/d/tr €120/130/170; ❄☎) A lone, lovely building facing the cathedral and the Adriatic, the 18th-century Palazzo Filisio houses this charmingly understated grand hotel. Rooms are sober and stylish, and the location is stupendous. Half- and full-board packages are available, and the in-house restaurant (meals €40) maintains the upmarket vibe with dishes such as risotto with prawns, asparagus and black truffle.

✖ Eating

★ Corteinfiore SEAFOOD €€
(☑0883 50 84 02; www.corteinfiore.it; Via Ognissanti 18; meals €40; ☺1-2.15pm Tue-Sun, 8-10.15pm Tue-Sat) The decking, stiff tablecloths and marquee setting of this famed Trani seafood restaurant set hopes racing, and the food, wine and service deliver in full. Expect lots of seafood, and expect it to be excellent: try the *frutti di mari antipasti*, or the Gallipoli prawns with candied lemon. Also rents delightful rooms (double €120) decked out in pale colours.

La Darsena SEAFOOD €€
(☑0883 48 73 33; Via Statuti Marittimi 96; meals €32; ☺noon-3pm & 8-11.30pm Tue-Sun)

Renowned for its seafood, swish La Darsena is housed in a waterfront *palazzo*. Outside tables overlook the port while inside, photos of old Puglia cover the walls beneath a huge wrought-iron dragon chandelier. Dishes such as *cavatelli* (pasta) with mussels and salted ricotta just sing with unabashed flavour.

ⓘ Information

Tourist Office (☑0883 58 88 30; www.traniweb.it; 1st fl, Palazzo Palmieri, Piazza Trieste 10; ☺10.30am-12.30pm & 5.30-7.30pm Mon-Sat) Located 200m south of the cathedral. Offers free guided walking tours most days at 8pm.

ⓘ Getting There & Away

STP (☑0883 49 18 00; www.stpspa.it) has frequent bus services to Bari. Services depart from **Bar Stazione** (Piazza XX Settembre 23), which also has timetables and tickets.

Trani is on the main train line between Bari (€3.10, 30 to 45 minutes, frequent) and Foggia (€6.30, 40 to 50 minutes, frequent).

Polignano a Mare
POP 18,000

Dip into this positively positioned small town if you can. Located around 34km south of Bari on the S16 coastal road, Polignano a Mare is built on the edge of a craggy ravine pockmarked with caves. The town is thought to be one of the most important ancient settlements in Puglia and was later inhabited by successive invaders ranging from the Huns to the Normans. On Sunday the *logge* (balconies) are crowded with day trippers from Bari who come here to view the crashing waves, visit the caves and crowd out the *cornetterias* (shops specialising in Italian croissants) in the atmospheric *centro storico*.

Activities

Dorino BOATING

(📲329 6465904; www.dorinogb.it; Lungomare Domenico Modugno; adult/child 11-15yr/under 11yr €25/10/free) For excursions into the dramatic sea caves and under the looming coast around Polignano, make a booking with this laid-back operation. Call ahead, as opening hours aren't fixed.

🛏 Sleeping & Eating

B&B Santo Stefano B&B €

(📲0804 24 95 63, 345 1686043; www.santostefano. info; Vico Santo Stefano 9-13; d from €89; 📶) Santo Stefano offers six attractive rooms located in an ancient tower in the old part of Polignano, complete with tufa walls, antique furniture and bright bathrooms. There's a terrace facing the sea, and activities such as biking and trekking can be organised, for a fee.

Antiche Mura PUGLIAN €€

(📲0804 24 24 76; www.ristoranteantichemura. it; Via Roma 11; meals €30; ☺noon-2.30pm & 7.30-11.30pm Wed-Mon) Huddled against the eponymous 'Old Walls' of Polignano, this delightful little restaurant features a vaulted cave-like interior with lanterns and bells adorning the walls. Unsurprisingly, fish is a speciality, with sea bass, octopus and lobster making an appearance in simple yet memorable dishes such as linguine with baby lobster and sea bass from Orbetello (Tuscany) with potatoes and zucchini.

Promontorio del Gargano

The coast surrounding this expansive promontory seems permanently bathed in a pink-hued, pearly light, providing a painterly contrast to the sea, which softens from intense to powder blue as the evening draws in. It's one of Italy's most beautiful corners, encompassing white limestone cliffs, fairy-

tale grottoes, sparkling sea, ancient forests, rare orchids and tangled, fragrant maquis (dense scrub vegetation).

Once connected to what is now Dalmatia (in Croatia), the 'spur' of the Italian boot has more in common with the land mass across the sea than with the rest of Italy. Creeping urbanisation was halted in 1991 by the creation of the **Parco Nazionale del Gargano** (www.parcogargano.gov.it) FREE. Aside from its magnificent national park, the Gargano is home to pilgrimage sites and the lovely seaside towns of Vieste and Peschici.

Vieste

POP 13,950

Clinging to a spectacular headland jutting into the Adriatic, Vieste resembles nothing so much as a cross between Naples and Dubrovnik, with a bit of Puglian magic mixed in. The narrow alleys of the old town, draped with lines of drying clothes and patrolled by slinking cats and the odd friendly dog, are an atmospheric place, day or night, high or off-season. Wedged up against the old town is the equally unpretentious new town, ghostly in winter, but packed with holidaying humanity in summer, especially during the *passeggiata* (evening stroll).

◉ Sights

Cathedral CATHEDRAL

(Via Duomo; ☺7.30am-noon & 4-11pm) Built by the Normans on the ruins of a Vesta temple, this 11th-century 'co-cathedral' (so called because its bishopric is shared with another) is in Puglian-Romanesque style with a fanciful tower that resembles a cardinal's hat. Of note are its beautiful paintings, swirling interior columns and Latin-inscribed altar.

La Salata CEMETERY

(📲0854 70 66 35; Strada Provinciale 52; adult/child €5/free; ☺5.30pm & 6.15pm Mon-Fri Jul & Aug, fewer days Jun & Sep, by appointment Oct-May) This palaeo-Christian graveyard dating from the 4th to 6th centuries AD is 9km out of town. Inside the cave, tier upon tier of narrow tombs are cut into the rock wall; others form shallow niches in the cave floor. Guided tours are mandatory.

Chianca Amara HISTORIC SITE

(Bitter Stone; Via Cimaglia) Vieste's most gruesome sight is this worn and polished stone where thousands were beheaded when Turks sacked Vieste in the 16th century.

🏃 Activities

Superb sandy beaches surround the town: in the south are **Spiagga del Castello**, **Cala San Felice** and **Cala Sanguinaria**; due north, head for the area known as **La Salata**. **Diving** is popular around the promontory's rocky coastline, which is filled with marine grottoes.

From May to September fast boats zoom to the **Isole Tremiti**.

For **hiking** ideas, pick up a *Guida al Trekking sul Gargano* brochure from the tourist office. A section of walk 4 is doable from Vieste. It starts 2.5km south of town off the Lungomare Enrico Mattei, where a track cuts up through olive groves into increasingly wild terrain.

Centro Ormeggi e Sub   BOATING
(☑0884 70 79 83; Scalo Marittimo Sud 18/19) Offers diving courses and rents out sailing boats and motorboats.

👉 Tours

Several companies offer tours of the caves that pock the Gargano coast – a three-hour tour costs around €15.

Motobarca Desirèe   BOATING
(☑360 262386; www.grottemarinegargano.com; Lungomare Vespucci; adult/child €20/10; ☉Apr-Oct) Boat tours of the various caves, arches and *trabucchi* (Puglian fishing structures) that characterise the Gargano coast. Trips are spectacular, though the boats can get crowded. Two departures a day (9am and 2.30pm); buy tickets port-side.

Explora Gargano   CYCLING
(☑0884 70 22 37, 340 7136 864; www.explora gargano.it; Vieste-Peschici km 5.5; tours from €50) To get off the beach for a day or two, take one of the many tours on offer at Explora Gargano. As well as hiking and mountain biking (half-day from €70) in the Foresta Umbra, it offers quad tours and jeep safaris (from €50 per day).

🛏 Sleeping

Campeggio Capo Vieste   CAMPGROUND €
(☑0884 70 63 26; www.capovieste.it; Vieste-Peschici km 8; 2 adults & campsite/1-bedroom cottage €38/164; ☉Mar-Oct; ☎) This tree-shaded campground is right by a sandy beach at La Salata, around 8km from Vieste and accessible by bus. Activities include tennis, a sailing school, beach volleyball and treks in the Gargano.

B&B Rocca sul Mare   B&B €
(☑0884 70 27 19; www.roccasulmare.it; Via Mafrolla 32; per person €45; 🐱) In a former convent in the old quarter, this is a popular, charming and reasonably-priced place, with comfortable high-ceilinged rooms. There's also a rooftop terrace with panoramic views, a suite with a steam bath and simple, tasty meals (€22 for four courses). Bike hire is available and it can arrange fishing trips and cook your catch that evening.

★ Relais Parallelo 41   B&B €€
(☑0884 35 50 09; www.bbparallelo41.it; Via Forno de Angelis 3; r €138; ☉Mar-Oct; ✳🐱) This beautiful small B&B in an updated *palazzo* in the midst of the old town has five renovated rooms, decorated with hand-painted ceilings, luxurious beds and super modern bathrooms. Breakfasts consist of a substantial buffet, and the reception area acts as a mini information centre for local activities. Note that there are minimum stays in July and August.

🍴 Eating

★ Vecchia Vieste   PUGLIAN €
(☑0884 70 70 83; Via Mafrolla 32; meals €25; ☉noon-3pm & 7-11pm) Look beyond the stony, cavernous interior of this modest-seeming restaurant to find what is possibly the best homemade, hand-shaped *orecchiette* in Puglia (and that's saying something). Try it topped with the obligatory *cima di rape* (rapini – a bitter green leafy veg – with anchovies, olive oil, chilli peppers, garlic and *pecorino*).

Osteria Al Duomo   OSTERIA €€
(☑0884 70 82 43; www.osterialduomo.it; Via Alessandro III 23; meals €32; ☉noon-3pm & 7-11pm Mar-Nov) Tucked away in a picturesque narrow alley in the heart of the old town, this welcoming *osteria* has a cosy cave-like interior and outdoor seating under a shady arbour. And it's not relying on its plum position to get diners through the door: real care and innovation goes into experimental-yet-pleasing creations such as *tagliolini* with fish skin, clams and pistachios.

ℹ Information

Post Office (☑0884 70 28 49; Via Vittorio Veneto 7; ☉8.30am-7pm Mon-Sat)

Tourist Office (☑0884 70 88 06; Piazza Kennedy; ☉8am-8pm Mon-Sat) You can weigh yourself down with useful brochures in this office, housed in the old fish market.

Surprises of the South

In the Mezzogiorno, the sun shines on a magical landscape: dramatic cliffs and sandy beaches fringed with turquoise seas; wild rocky mountains and gentle forested slopes; rolling green fields and flat plains. Sprinkled throughout are elegant *palazzi* (mansions), *masserias* (working farms), ancient cave-dwellings and gnome-like stone huts.

Promontorio del Gargano

Along with its charming seaside villages, sandy coves and crystalline blue waters, the Gargano (p132) is also home to the Parco Nazionale del Gargano. It's perfect for hikers, nature trippers and beach fiends alike.

Valle d'Itria

In a landscape of rolling green hills, vineyards, orchards and picture-pretty fields, conical stone huts called *trulli* sprout from the ground en masse in the Disneyesque towns of Alberobello (p141) and Locorotondo (p142).

Salento

In Salento, hot, dry plains covered in wildflowers and olive groves reach toward the gorgeous beaches and waters of the Ionian and Adriatic Seas. It's the unspoilt 'heel' of Italy, with Lecce (p147) as its sophisticated capital.

Matera

The ancient cave city of Matera (p161) has been inhabited since Palaeolithic times. Explore the tangled alleyways, admire frescoes in rock churches, and sleep in millennia-old *sassi* (former cave dwellings).

Parco Nazionale dell'Aspromonte

In this wild park (p178), narrow roads lead to hilltop villages such as spectacularly sited Bova. Waterfalls, wide riverbeds, jagged cliffs and sandstone formations form the backdrop to a landscape made for hiking.

2

UPUNGATO/SHUTTERSTOCK ©

1. Conical *trulli* houses, Alberobello (p141), Valle d'Itria 2. Bova (p178), Parco Nazionale dell'Aspromonte 3. Matera (p161)
4. Grotta Della Poesia, near Lecce (p147), Salento

4

KVIKA/SHUTTERSTOCK ©

ⓘ Getting There & Around

BOAT

Vieste's port is to the north of town, about a five-minute walk from the tourist office. In summer, several companies, including **Linee Marittime Adriatico** (☑ 0884 96 20 23; www.collegamentiisoletremiti.com; Corso Garibaldi 32), head to the Isole Tremiti. Tickets can be bought port-side.

BUS

From Piazzale Manzoni, where intercity buses terminate, a 10-minute walk east along Viale XXIV Maggio, which becomes Corso Fazzini, brings you into the old town and the Marina Piccola's attractive promenade. In summer buses terminate at Via Verdi, a 300m walk from the old town down Via Papa Giovanni XXIII.

SITA (☑ 0881 35 20 11; www.sitabus.it) buses run between Vieste and Foggia via Manfredonia. There are also services to Monte Sant'Angelo (€5) via Macchia Bivio Monte.

From May to September, **Pugliairbus** (☑ 080 580 03 58; http://pugliairbus.aeroportidipuglia.it) runs a service to the Gargano, including Vieste, from Bari airport.

Monte Sant'Angelo

POP 12,550

One of Europe's most important pilgrimage sites, this isolated mountain-top town has an extraordinary atmosphere. Pilgrims have been coming here for centuries – and so have the hustlers, pushing everything from religious kitsch to parking spaces.

The object of devotion is the Santuario di San Michele. Here, in AD 490, St Michael the Archangel is said to have appeared in a grotto to the Bishop of Siponto.

During the Middle Ages, the sanctuary marked the end of the Route of the Angel, which began in Mont St-Michel (in Normandy) and passed through Rome. In 999 the Holy Roman Emperor Otto III made a pilgrimage to the sanctuary to pray that prophecies about the end of the world in the year 1000 would not be fulfilled. His prayers were answered, the world staggered on and the sanctuary's fame grew.

The sanctuary has been a Unesco World Heritage Site since 2011.

THE RICH FLAVOURS OF LA CUCINA POVERA

In Italy's less wealthy 'foot', traditional recipes evolved through economic necessity rather than experimental excess. Local people used whatever ingredients were available to them, plucked directly from the surrounding soil and seas, and kneaded and blended using recipes passed down through generations. The result is called *cucina povera* (literally 'food of the poor'), which, thanks to a recent global obsession with farm-to-table purity, has become increasingly popular.

If there is a mantra for *cucina povera*, it is 'keep it simple'. Pasta is the south's staple starch. Made with just durum wheat and water (and no eggs, unlike some richer northern pastas) it is most commonly sculpted into *orecchiette* ('little ears') and used as the starchy platform on which to serve whatever else might be growing readily and inexpensively. For the same reasons, vegetables feature prominently: eggplants, mushrooms, tomatoes, artichokes, olives and many other staple plants grow prodigiously in these climes and are put to good use in the dishes.

Meat, though present in *cucina povera*, is used more sparingly than in the north. Lamb and horsemeat predominate and are usually heavily seasoned. Unadulterated fish is more common, especially in Puglia, which has a longer coastline than any other mainland Italian region. Popular fish dishes incorporate mussels, clams, octopus (in Salento), swordfish (in northern Calabria), cod and prawns.

A signature Puglian *primi* (first course) is *orecchiette con cima di rape*, a gloriously simple blend of rapini (a bitter green leafy veg with small broccoli-like shoots) mixed with anchovies, olive oil, chilli peppers, garlic and *pecorino*. Another popular *orecchiette* accompaniment is *ragù di carne di cavallo* (horsemeat), sometimes known as *ragù alla barese*. Bari is known for its starch-heavy *riso, patate e cozze*, a surprisingly delicious marriage of rice, potatoes and mussels that is baked in the oven. Another wildly popular vegetable is wild chicory, which, when combined with a fava bean purée, is reborn as *fave e cicorie*.

Standard cheeses of the south include *burrata*, which has a mozzarella-like shell and a gooey centre, and *pecorino di filiano*, a sheep's-milk cheese from Basilicata. There are tons of bread recipes, but the horn-shaped crusty bread from Matera is king.

◉ Sights

The town's serpentine alleys and jumbled houses are perfect for a little aimless ambling. Look out for the different shaped *cappelletti* (chimney stacks) on top of the neat whitewashed houses.

★ Santuario di San Michele   CAVE

(☑ 0884 56 11 50; www.santuariosanmichele.it; Via Reale Basilica; ⊙ 7.30am-7.30pm Jul-Sep, shorter hours rest of year) FREE Over the centuries this sanctuary has expanded to incorporate a large complex of religious buildings that overlay its original shrine. The double-arched entrance vestibule at street level stands next to a distinctive octagonal bell tower built by Carlo I of Naples in 1282. As you descend the staircase inside, look for the 17th-century pilgrims' graffiti. The grotto/shrine where St Michael is said to have left a footprint in stone is located at the bottom of the staircase.

Because of St Michael's footprint, it became customary for pilgrims to carve outlines of their feet and hands into the stone. Etched Byzantine bronze and silver doors, cast in Constantinople in 1076, open into the grotto itself. Inside, a 16th-century statue of the Archangel Michael covers the site of St Michael's footprint. Audio guides cost €3, and it's €5 to get into the museum (or €7 for both together).

Tomba di Rotari   TOMB

(☑ 0884 56 11 50; Largo Tomba di Rotari; €1; ⊙ 9am-noon & 3-7pm Apr-Oct, to 4.30pm Nov-Mar) A short flight of stairs opposite the Santuario di San Michele leads to a 12th-century baptistry with a deep sunken basin for total immersion. You enter the baptistry through the facade of the **Chiesa di San Pietro** with its intricate rose window squirming with serpents – all that remains of the church, destroyed in a 19th-century earthquake. The Romanesque portal of the adjacent 11th-century **Chiesa di Santa Maria Maggiore** has some fine bas-reliefs.

Castle   CASTLE

(☑ 0884 56 54 44; Largo Roberto Giuscardo 2; €2; ⊙ 9am-1pm & 2-6pm) At the highest point of Monte Sant'Angelo is this rugged fastness, first built by Orso I, who later became Doge of Venice, in the 9th century. One 10th-century tower, Torre dei Giganti, survives, but most of what you can see are Norman, Swabian and Aragonese additions. The views alone are worth the admission.

🛏 Sleeping & Eating

Hotel Michael   HOTEL €

(☑ 0884 56 55 19; www.hotelmichael.com; Via Reale Basilica 86; s/d €60/80; 🐾) A small hotel with shuttered windows, located on the main street across from the Santuario di San Michele, this traditional place has spacious rooms, some with with extremely pink bedspreads, and walls spruced up with devotional art. Ask for a room with a view, or just enjoy it as you breakfast on the rooftop terrace.

Casa li Jalantuúmene   TRATTORIA €€

(☑ 0884 56 54 84; www.li-jalantuumene.it; Piazza de Galganis 5; meals €42; ⊙ noon-3pm & 7.30-10.30pm Wed-Mon) This renowned restaurant has a well-known chef, Gegè Mangano, and serves excellent fare. Vegetarians are looked after (try the pasta with wild fennel, cherry tomatoes and ricotta cream), the setting is intimate, there's a select wine list and, in summer, tables spill onto the piazza. There are also four suites on site (from €100), decorated in traditional Puglian style.

ℹ Getting There & Away

SITA (☑ 0881 35 20 11; www.sitasudtrasporti.it) buses run from Foggia (€4.50, 1¾ hours, four daily) and Vieste via Macchia Bivio Monte.

Peschici

POP 4500

Perched above a turquoise sea and tempting beach, Peschici, like Vieste, is another cliff-clinging Amalfi lookalike. Its tight-knit old walled town of Arabesque whitewashed houses acts as a hub to a wider resort area. The small town gets crammed in summer, so book in advance. Boats zip across to the Isole Tremiti in high season.

🛏 Sleeping & Eating

Peschici's ample accommodation stocks can come under stress when it seems half of Puglia heads to Gargano in August.

Baia San Nicola   CAMPGROUND €

(☑ 0884 96 42 31; www.baiasannicola.it; Localita Punta San Nicola; 2 adults & tent/2-person bungalow per week €33/720; ⊙ mid-May–mid-Oct) The best campground in the area, 2km south of Peschici towards Vieste, Baia San Nicola is on a pine-shaded beach, offering camping, bungalows, apartments and myriad amenities.

Locanda al Castello
B&B €€

(☑ 0884 96 40 38; www.peschicialcastello.it; Via Castello 29; s/d €70/120; Ⓟ❄️🛜) Staying here is like entering a large, welcoming family home. It's by the cliffs with fantastic views and it's air-conditioned, should you visit in the height of summer. Enjoy hearty home cooking in the restaurant (meals €23) while the owners' kids run around playing football – indoors!

⭐ Al Trabucco da Mimì
SEAFOOD €€

(☑ 0884 96 25 56; www.altrabucco.it; Localita Punta San Nicola; meals €40; ⊙ 12.30-2pm & 7-11pm Easter-Oct) Mimì sadly passed away in 2016, but his daughter and grandsons keep this delightful place ticking. Sitting on wooden trestles beneath the eponymous *trabucco* (a traditional Puglian wooden fishing platform) you'll eat the freshest seafood, prepared with expertise but no fuss, as you watch the sun sink behind Peschici. The raw seafood antipasti and grilled mullet are stunning. There are three simple rooms for rent, at €50 per person. There's also occasional live music (usually jazz) and *aperitivo* in summer.

⭐ Porta di Basso
ITALIAN €€€

(☑ 0884 35 51 67; www.portadibasso.it; Via Colombo 38; menus €45-60; ⊙ noon-2.30pm & 7-11pm, closed Jan & Feb) 🍴 Superb views of the ocean drop away from the floor-to-ceiling windows beside intimate alcove tables at this adventurous and stylish clifftop restaurant. Choose from one of three degustation menus, and prepare to be delighted by dishes such as smoked bluefish with Jerusalem artichokes, fois gras and honey vinegar.

ℹ Information

Tourist Office (☑ 0884 96 49 66; Via Magenta 3; ⊙ 10am-1pm & 4.30-7.30pm Mon-Sat) Friendly staff give you the lowdown on Peschici and the Gargano.

ℹ Getting There & Away

The bus terminal is beside the sportsground, uphill from the main street, Corso Garibaldi.

From April to September, ferry companies, including **Linee Marittime Adriatico** (p136), serve the Isole Tremiti.

Foresta Umbra

The 'Forest of Shadows' is the Gargano's enchanted interior – thickets of tall, epic trees interspersed with picnic spots bathed in dappled light. It's the last remnant of Puglia's ancient forests: Aleppo pines, oaks, yews and beech trees cloak the hilly terrain. More than 65 different types of orchid have been discovered here, and the wildlife includes roe deer, wild boar, foxes, badgers and the increasingly rare wild cat. Walkers and mountain bikers will find plenty of well-marked trails within the forest's 5790 sq km.

You'll need your own transport to get in and out of the forest.

◉ Sights & Activities

The small visitor centre in the middle of the forest houses a **museum and nature centre** (SP52bis, Foresta Umbra; €1.50; ⊙ 9.30am-6.30pm mid-Apr–mid-Oct, 4-10pm Easter) where you can buy maps, hire bikes and join guided hikes.

There are 15 official trails in the park ranging from 0.5km to 13.5km in length. Several of them start near the visitor centre and the adjacent Laghetto Umbra, including path 9, which can be done as a loop returning on a military road. A park leaflet provides a map and trail descriptions.

🛌 Sleeping

Rifugio Sfilzi
B&B €

(☑ 338 3345544; www.rifugiosfilzi.com; SP528; adult €45, incl half-/full board €85/100, child 4-12 incl full board €50) In the middle of the Foresta Umbra, five kilometres north of the visitor centre on the way to Vico di Gargano, this cosy *rifugio* (mountain hut) offers eight rooms with three- and four-bed configurations, making them ideal for groups or families. It also has a small shop selling locally made products such as jams and oils, and a cafe-restaurant with fantastic homemade cake and coffee.

Isole Tremiti

POP 500

This beautiful archipelago of three islands, 36km offshore, is a picturesque composition of ragged cliffs, sandy coves and thick pine woods, surrounded by the glittering dark-blue sea.

Unfortunately, the islands are no secret, and in July and August some 100,000 holidaymakers head over. If you want to savour the islands in tranquillity, visit during the shoulder season. In the low season most tourist facilities close down and the few permanent residents resume their quiet and isolated lives.

🏃 Driving Tour
Italy's Authentic South

START VIESTE
END MARATEA
LENGTH 650KM TO 700KM; ONE WEEK

Consider a gentle start in lovely, laid-back ❶ **Vieste**, with its white sandy beaches and medieval backstreets, but set aside half a day to hike or bike in the lush green forests of the ❷ **Parco Nazionale del Gargano**. Follow the coastal road past dramatic cliffs, salt lakes and flat farming land to ❸ **Trani**, with its impressive seafront cathedral and picturesque port, before spending a night in ❹ **Bari**, where you'll find boisterous bars and salt-of-the-earth trattorias. The next day head to ❺ **Alberobello**, home to a dense neighbourhood of Puglia's extraordinary cone-shaped stone homes, called *trulli*; consider an overnight *trulli* stay.

Stroll around one of the most picturesque *centro storicos* (historic centres) in southern Italy at ❻ **Locorotondo**. Hit the road and cruise on to lively baroque ❼ **Lecce**, where you can easily chalk up a full day exploring the sights, shops and flamboyantly fronted *palazzi* and churches, including the Basilica di Santa Croce.

Day five will be one to remember. Nothing can prepare you for Basilicata's ❽ **Matera**, where *sassi* (former cave dwellings) are a dramatic reminder of the town's poverty-stricken past. After days of pasta, *fave* beans and *cornetti* (Italian croissants), it's high time for some exercise on the trails of the spectacular ❾ **Parco Nazionale del Pollino**. Finally, wind up the trip with more walking or a day of beach slothing at the spread out coastal town of ❿ **Maratea** with its surrounding seaside resorts, medieval village and cosmopolitan harbour, offset by a thickly forested and mountainous interior.

The islands' main facilities are on San Domino, the largest and lushest island, formerly used to grow crops. It's ringed by alternating sandy beaches and limestone cliffs; inland grows thick maquis flecked with rosemary and foxglove. The centre harbours a nondescript small town with several hotels.

Small San Nicola island is the traditional administrative centre; a castle-like cluster of medieval buildings rises up from its rocks. The third island, Capraia, is uninhabited.

◉ Sights & Activities

San Domino   ISLAND
Head to San Domino for walks, grottoes and coves. It has a pristine, marvellous coastline and the islands' only sandy beach, **Cala delle Arene**. Alongside the beach is the small cove **Grotta dell'Arene**, with calm clear waters for swimming. You can also take a boat trip (around €15 from the port) around the island to explore the grottoes: the largest, Grotta del Bue Marino, is 70m long. A tour of all three islands costs around €20.

Diving in the translucent sea is another option with **Tremiti Diving Center** (☎337 648917; www.tremitidivingcenter.com; Via Federico II, Villaggio San Domino; 1-tank day-/night-dive €40/50). There's an undemanding, but enchanting, walking track around the island, starting at the far end of the village.

San Nicola   ISLAND
Medieval buildings thrust out of San Nicola's rocky shores, the same pale-sand colour as the barren cliffs. In 1010, Benedictine monks founded the **Abbazia e Chiesa di Santa Maria** here; for the next 700 years the islands were ruled by a series of abbots who accumulated great wealth.

Although the church retains a weatherworn Renaissance portal and a fine 11th-century floor mosaic, its other treasures have been stolen or destroyed throughout its troubled history, which has seen various religious orders come and go including the Benedictines, the Cistercians and the Lateran Canons. The only exceptions are a painted wooden Byzantine crucifix brought to the island in AD 747 and a black Madonna, probably transported here from Constantinople in the Middle Ages.

Capraia   ISLAND
The third of the Isole Tremiti, Capraia (named after the wild caper plant) is uninhabited. Bird life is plentiful, with impressive flocks of seagulls. There's no organised transport, but trips can be negotiated with local fishing folk.

🛏 Sleeping & Eating

La Casa di Gino   B&B €€
(☎0882 46 34 10; www.hotel-gabbiano.com; Via dei Forni, San Nicola; s/d from €110/170; ❄) A tranquil accommodation choice on San Nicola, away from the frenzy of San Domino, this B&B run by the Hotel Gabbiano has stylish white-on-white rooms. Great views and quiet space to amble or relax are two of its most delightful aspects.

Hotel Gabbiano   HOTEL €€
(☎0882 46 34 10; www.hotel-gabbiano.com; Via Garibaldi 5, Villaggio San Domino; d from €123; ❄ 🐕 🛜) An established icon on San Nicola and run for decades by the same Neapolitan family, this smart hotel has pastel-coloured rooms with balconies overlooking the town and the sea. It also has a seafood restaurant, spa and gym.

Architiello   SEAFOOD €€
(☎0882 46 30 54; Via Salita delle Mura 5, San Nicola; meals €30; ◷noon-3pm & 7.30-11pm Apr-Oct) A class act with a sea-view terrace, this place specialises in – what else? – fresh fish.

ⓘ Getting There & Away

Boats for the Isole Tremiti depart from several points on the Italian mainland: Manfredonia, Vieste and Peschici in summer, and Termoli in nearby Molise year-round. Most boats arrive at San Domino. Small boats regularly make the brief crossing to San Nicola (€6 return) in high season; from October to March a single boat makes the trip after meeting the boat from the mainland.

Valle d'Itria

Between the Ionian and Adriatic coasts rises the great limestone plateau of the Murgia (473m). It has a strange karst geology: the landscape is riddled with holes and ravines through which small streams and rivers gurgle, creating what is, in effect, a giant sponge. At the heart of the Murgia lies the idyllic Valle d'Itria.

The rolling green valley is criss-crossed by dry-stone walls, vineyards, almond and olive groves, and winding country lanes. This is the part of Puglia most visited by foreign tourists and is the best served by hotels and luxury *masserias* (working farms) or manor farms.

Alberobello

POP 10,750

Unesco World Heritage Site Alberobello resembles an urban sprawl – for gnomes. The *zona dei trulli* on the westernmost of the town's two hills is a dense mass of 1500 beehive-shaped houses, white-tipped as if dusted by snow. These dry-stone buildings are made from local limestone; none are older than the 14th century. Inhabitants do not wear pointy hats, but they do sell anything a visitor might (or might not) want, from miniature *trulli* to woollen shawls.

The town is named after the primitive oak forest Arboris Belli (beautiful trees) that once covered this area. It's an amazing place, but also something of a tourist trap – from May to October busloads of tourists pile into *trullo* homes, drink in *trullo* bars and shop in *trullo* shops.

If you park in Lago Martellotta, follow the steps up to Piazza del Popolo, where the Belvedere Trulli lookout offers fabulous views over the whole higgledy-piggledy picture.

◎ Sights

Rione Monti
AREA

Within the old town quarter of Rione Monti more than 1000 *trulli* cascade down the hillside, many of which are now souvenir shops. The area is surprisingly quiet and atmospheric in the late evening, once the gaudy stalls have been stashed away.

Rione Aia Piccola
AREA

On the eastern side of Via Indipendenza is Rione Aia Piccola. This neighbourhood is much less commercialised than Rione Monti, with 400 *trulli*, many still used as family dwellings. You can climb up for a rooftop view at many shops, although most do have a strategically located basket for donations.

Trullo Sovrano
MUSEUM

(☑ 080 432 60 30; www.trullosovrano.eu; Piazza Sacramento 10; adult/reduced €1.50/1; ☉ 10am-1.30pm & 3.30-7pm Apr-Oct, to 6pm Nov-Mar) Trullo Sovrano dates in parts to the early 17th century, and is Alberobello's only two-floor *trullo*. Built by a wealthy priest's family, it's now a small 'living' museum recreating *trullo* life, with sweet, rounded rooms that include a recreated bakery, bedroom and kitchen. The souvenir shop here has a wealth of literature on the town and surrounding area, plus Alberobello recipe books.

⊨ Sleeping

Casa Albergo Sant'Antonio
HOTEL €

(☑ 080 432 29 13; www.santantonioalbergo.it; Via Isonzo 8a; s/d/tr/q €50/78/95/110; ☎) Excellent value right in the heart of the Rione Monti neighbourhood, this simple hotel is in an old monastery and located next to a unique *trulli*-style church with a conical roof. The tiled rooms are relatively monastic and spartan, but will do the trick for the unfussy.

Camping dei Trulli
CAMPGROUND €

(☑ 080 432 36 99; www.campingdeitrulli.com; Via Castellana Grotte km 1.5; camping 2 people & car €19.50, bungalows per person €20, trulli €40; P @ ☒) This campground 1.5km out of town has some nice tent sites, a restaurant, a market, two swimming pools, tennis courts and bicycle hire. You can also rent *trulli* off the grounds. It has 120 pitches, 30 for campervans, lots of pines for shade and good shower blocks.

Trullidea
RENTAL HOUSE €€

(☑ 080 432 38 60; www.trullidea.it; Via Monte Sabotino 24; trulli from €120; ☎) Trullidea has numerous renovated, quaint, cosy and atmospheric *trulli* in Alberobello's historic centre available on a self-catering, B&B, or half- or full-board basis. Half-board is €25 person, and the buffet breakfast is included in the price.

✕ Eating

Trattoria Amatulli
TRATTORIA €

(☑ 080 432 29 79; Via Garibaldi 13; meals €20; ☉ 12.30-3pm & 7.30-11.30pm Tue-Sun) The cheerily cluttered interior of this excellent trattoria is papered with photos of smiley diners, obviously put in the best mood by dishes like *orecchiette scure con cacioricotta pomodoro e rucola* ('little ears' pasta with cheese, tomato and rucola). Wash it down with the surprisingly drinkable house wine, only €4 a litre. It won't add much to an invariably reasonable bill.

★ Trattoria Terra Madre
VEGETARIAN €€

(☑ 080 432 38 29; www.trattoriaterramadre.it; Piazza Sacramento 17; meals €30; ☉ 12.15-2.45pm & 7.15-9.45pm Tue-Sat, 12.15-2.45pm Sun; ☑) ✿ Vegetables take pride of place in Italian kitchens, especially at this enthusiastic vegetarian-ish (some meat is served) restaurant. The farm-to-table ethos rules – most of what you eat comes from the organic garden outside. Start with the huge vegetable antipasti and save room for *primi* like *capunti* 'Terra Madre' (pasta with eggplant, zucchini and peppers) and the perfect house-baked desserts.

Il Poeta
Contadino   ITALIAN €€€
(☑080 432 19 17; www.ilpoetacontadino.it; Via Indipendenza 23; menu €65; ☺noon-2.30pm & 7-10.30pm Tue-Sun Feb-Dec; ☑) Vegetarians can be pleased here, as vegetables step timidly out of the *contorni* shadow, into the *primi* limelight. Alongside the swordfish, shrimp and clams that predominate, you'll find a flan of cave-aged cheese, celery and potato cream with turnip and ricotta, and other good, imaginative things. The dining room has a medieval feel, with its sumptuous decor and chandeliers.

❶ Information

Tourist Information Office (☑080 432 28 22; www.prolocoalberobello.it; Monte Nero 1; ☺9am-7pm) Local office in the *zona dei trulli*.

❶ Getting There & Away

Alberobello is easily accessible from Bari (€4.90, 1½ hours, hourly) on the FSE Bari–Taranto train line. From the station, walk straight ahead along Via Mazzini, which becomes Via Garibaldi, to reach Piazza del Popolo.

Locorotondo

POP 14,200

Locorotondo is endowed with a whisper-quiet pedestrianised *centro storico,* where everything is shimmering white aside from the blood-red geraniums that tumble from the window boxes. Situated on a hilltop on the Murge Plateau, it's a *borgo più bella d'Italia* (www.borghipiubelliditalia.it) – that is, it's rated as one of the most beautiful towns in Italy. There are few 'sights' as such – rather, the town itself is a sight. The streets are paved with smooth ivory-coloured stones, with the church of **Santa Maria della Graecia** as their sunbaked centrepiece.

From **Villa Comunale**, a public garden, you can enjoy panoramic views of the surrounding valley. You enter the historic quarter directly across from here.

Not only is this deepest *trulli* country, it's also the liquid heart of the Puglian wine region. Sample some of the local *verdeca* at Controra.

🛏 Sleeping

Locorotondo and the surrounding country are blessed when it comes to quality accommodation. If you're going to stay on a *masseria* or in a *trullo* while in Puglia, this is the place to do it.

Truddhi   AGRITURISMO €
(☑080 443 13 26; www.trulliresidence.it; Contrada Trito 161; d/tr per week from €450/624; ☑) This charming cluster of 11 self-catering *trulli* in the hamlet of Trito near Locorotondo is surrounded by olive groves and vineyards. It's a tranquil place and you can take cooking courses (per day €80) with Mino, a lecturer in gastronomy. The *trulli* sleep between two and six people, depending on size.

★Sotto le
Cummerse   APARTMENT €€€
(☑0804 31 32 98; www.sottolecummerse.it; Via Vittorio Veneto 138; apt incl breakfast from €200; ❄🖤) At this *albergo diffuso* (dispersed hotel) you'll stay in one of 13 tastefully furnished apartments scattered throughout Locorotondo's *centro storico*. The apartments are traditional buildings that have been beautifully restored and furnished, and you can book activities such as horse riding, cooking classes and historical tours. A delightful base for exploring the Valle d'Itria.

🍴 Eating & Drinking

★Quanto Basta   PIZZA €
(☑080 431 28 55; Via Morelli 12; pizza €7; ☺7.30-11pm Tue-Sun; 🖤) Craft beer and pizza make an excellent combination, no more so than at Quanto Basta, a quietly stylish old-town restaurant with wooden tables, soft lighting and stone floors. It's hard to stop at *quanto basta* ('just enough') when the pizza, carpaccio, salads and antipasti are so good, to say nothing of the lovely Itrian wines.

La Taverna del Duca   TRATTORIA €€
(☑080 431 30 07; www.tavernadelducascatigna.it; Via Papatodero 3; meals €35; ☺noon-3pm & 7.30pm-midnight Tue-Sat, noon-3pm Sun & Mon) In a narrow side street off Piazza Vittorio Emanuele, this well-regarded trattoria serves robust Itrian fare such as pork cheek in a primitivo reduction and donkey stew. If they sound daunting, there's always Puglia's favourite pasta (*orecchiette* 'little ears' pasta), thick vegetable soup and other more comforting foods.

GROTTE DI CASTELLANA

The spectacular limestone caves of **Grotte di Castellana** (☑080 499 82 21; www.grotte dicastellana.it; Piazzale Anelli; short/full tour €12/16; ⊙9am-6pm Aug, shorter hours other months, by appointment Jan & Feb), 40km southeast of Bari, are Italy's longest natural subterranean network. The interlinked galleries, first discovered in 1938, contain an incredible range of underground landscapes, with extraordinary stalactite and stalagmite formations – look out for the jellyfish, the bacon and the stocking. The highlight is the **Grotta Bianca** (White Grotto), an eerie alabaster cavern hung with stiletto-thin stalactites. 'Speleonights' take small torch-wieding groups into the caves after dark, among the bats, beetles, and crustacea that live there.

There are two tours in English: a 1km, 50-minute tour that doesn't include the Grotta Bianca (€12, on the half-hour); and a 3km, two-hour tour (€16, on the hour) that does include it. The staff like you to assemble in good time before your scheduled tour, and remember that temperatures inside the cave average 18°C, so take a light jacket.

In the same complex, you'll also find a speleology **museum** (☑080 499 82 30; www. grottedicastellana.it; ⊙9.30am-1pm & 3.30-6.30pm mid-Mar–Oct, 10am-1pm Nov–mid-Mar) and an **observatory** (☑080 499 82 13; www.osservatorio.grottedicastellana.it; adult/child 6-14yr €5/3; ⊙tours by appointment Jul & Aug).

Grotte di Castellana can be reached by rail from Bari on the FSE Bari–Taranto train line (€3.20, 1¼ hours, roughly hourly).

Controra WINE BAR
(☑339 6874169; Via Nardelli 67) Treat this laid-back little place either as a sandwich shop or wine bar, sampling *prosit* (sparkling rose), *verdeca* and other niche wines of the Valle d'Itria, all over amazing sandwiches, platters of regional produce and Locorotondo's uniformly stunning views.

ℹ Information

Tourist Office (☑080 431 30 99; www.prolo colocorotondo.it; Piazza Emanuele 27; ⊙9am-1pm & 5-7pm) Offers free internet access and multilingual tourist information.

ℹ Getting There & Away

Locorotondo is easily accessible via frequent trains from Bari (€5.60, 1½ to two hours) on the FSE Bari–Taranto train line.

Cisternino

POP 11,600

An appealing, whitewashed hilltop town, slow-paced Cisternino has a charming *centro storico* beyond its bland modern outskirts; with its kasbah-like knot of streets, it has been designated as one of the country's *borghi più belli* (most beautiful towns). Beside its 13th-century **Chiesa Matrice** and **Torre Civica** there's a pretty communal garden with rural views. If you take Via Basilioni next to the tower you can amble along an elegant route right to the central piazza, Vittorio Emanuele.

✗ Eating

Micro VEGETARIAN €
(☑340 5315463; Via Santa Lucia 53; meals €20; ⊙10am-3pm & 6-11pm Wed-Mon; ✈) This tiny, charismatic little juice bar/lunch spot is the necessary counterbalance to the meaty excesses Cisternino is famous for. Boxloads of fresh vegetables and herbs arrive each morning, whatever's in the market, and are turned into soups, salads, torte, vegetarian sushi and more. There are some choices for carnis, but for once it's they who are the afterthought.

Rosticceria L'Antico Borgo BARBECUE €€
(☑080 444 64 00; www.rosticceria-lanticoborgo. it; Via Tarantini 9; meals €30; ⊙6.30-11pm daily summer, Mon-Sat winter) A classic *fornello pronto* (half butcher's shop, half trattoria), this is the place for a cheerful, no-frills meat fest. The menu is brief, listing a few simple pastas and various meat options (priced per kilo), including Cisternino's celebrated *bombette* (skewered pork wrapped around a piece of cheese). Choose your roast meat and eat it with red wine, chips and salad.

ℹ Getting There & Away

Cisternino is accessible by regular trains from Bari (€5.80, 45 minutes). STP Brindisi runs hourly buses between Cisternino and Ostuni.

MASSERIAS: LUXURY ON THE FARM

Masserias are unique to southern Italy. Modelled on the classical Roman villa, these fortified farmhouses – equipped with oil mills, cellars, chapels, storehouses and accommodation for workers and livestock – were built to function as self-sufficient communities. These days, they still produce the bulk of Italy's olive oil, but many have been converted into luxurious hotels, *agriturismi* (farm-stay accommodation), holiday apartments or restaurants. Staying in a *masseria* is a unique experience, especially when you can dine on home-grown produce.

Il Frantoio (☑ 0831 33 02 76; www.masseriailfrantoio.it; SS16 km 874, Ostuni; d €216; ⓟ✳@☎) Stay at this charming, whitewashed farmhouse, where the owners still live and work producing high-quality organic olive oil (*a frantoio* is an oil-press). Owner Armando takes guests for a tour of the farm each evening in his 1949 Fiat, and local producers are regularly invited to share their produce and the love they have for it.

Masseria Torre Maizza (☑ 080 482 78 38; www.masseriatorremaizza.com; Contrada Coccaro, Fasano; d/ste €568/696; ✳☎✉) Definitely at the high end of the *masseria* experience is this luxurious *agriturismo*. You won't get your hands dirty, but you will destress – playing golf, riding horses, getting a massage, sweating it all out in the hammam or just lolling by the pool, drink in hand. There are two restaurants on site and little expense has been spared in the suites.

Masseria Torre Coccaro (☑ 080 482 93 10; www.masseriatorrecoccaro.com; Contrada Coccaro 8, Fasano; d/ste €453/650; ⓟ✳☎✉) For pure luxury, stay at this super chic yet countrified *masseria*. There's a glorious spa set in a cave, a beach-style swimming pool, cooking courses on offer and a restaurant (meals €90) dishing up home-grown produce. It's around 10km from Locorotondo.

Borgo San Marco (☑ 080 439 57 57; www.borgosanmarco.it; Contrada Sant'Angelo 33, Fasano; ste €210; ⓟ✳☎✉) Once a *borgo* (medieval town), this *masseria* has 16 rooms and a spa in the orchard, and manages to be traditional while also showing a bohemian edge. Nearby are some frescoed rock churches. Note: there's a four-night minimum stay in July, and seven-night minimum in August.

Martina Franca

The old quarter of this town is a picturesque scene of winding alleys, blinding white houses and blood-red geraniums. There are graceful baroque and rococo buildings here too, plus airy piazzas and curlicue ironwork balconies that almost touch above the narrow streets.

This town is the highest in the Murgia, and was founded in the 10th century by refugees fleeing the Arab invasion of Taranto. It only started to flourish in the 14th century when Philip of Anjou granted tax exemptions (*franchigie,* hence Franca); the town became so wealthy that a castle and defensive walls complete with 24 solid bastions were built.

◉ Sights & Activities

The best way to appreciate Martina Franca's beauty is to wander around the *centro storico's* narrow lanes and alleyways.

Passing under the baroque **Arco di Sant'Antonio** at the western end of pedestrianised Piazza XX Settembre, you emerge into Piazza Roma, dominated by the imposing, 17th-century rococo **Palazzo Ducale** (☑ 080 480 57 02; Piazza Roma 28; ⊙ 9am-8pm Mon-Fri, from 10am Sat & Sun mid-Jun–Sep, shorter hours rest of year) FREE, whose upper rooms have semi-restored frescoed walls and host temporary art exhibitions.

From Piazza Roma, follow the fine Corso Vittorio Emanuele, with baroque townhouses, to reach Piazza Plebiscito, the centre's baroque heart. The piazza is overlooked by the 18th-century **Basilica di San Martino**, its centrepiece a statue of city patron, St Martin, swinging a sword and sharing his cloak with a beggar.

Walkers can ask for the free *Carta dei Sentieri del Bosco delle Pianelle* brochure at the tourist office, which maps out 10 walks in the nearby **Bosco delle Pianelle** (around 10km west of town). This lush woodland is part of the larger 1206-hectare **Riserva**

Naturale Regionale Orientata, populated with lofty trees, wild orchids, and a rich and varied bird life, including kestrels, owls, buzzards, hoopoe and sparrow hawks. There's a small museum dedicated to the park in the Palazzo Ducale.

✪ Festivals & Events

Festival della Valle d'Itria   MUSIC
(☏ 080 480 51 00; www.festivaldellavalleditria.it; single-event tickets from €15; ⊙ Jul & Aug) Festival della Valle d'Itria is a summer music festival that takes over Martina Franca's venues from mid-July to early August. Musical theatre, especially opera, tops the bill, but concertos and other recitals also abound. For information, contact the Centro Artistico Musicale Paolo Grassi in the Palazzo Ducale.

⌧ Sleeping

Villaggio In   APARTMENT €
(☏ 080 480 59 11; www.villaggioincasesparse.it; Via Arco Grassi 8; studio/apt/ste €75/90/160; ❋ 🛜) These charming apartments are located in original *centro storico* homes. Arched stone ceilings, large pastel-coloured rooms and antique furniture are common features of the various apartments, which sleep two to six people. There's a self-serve laundry and vouchers for breakfast in a local cafe, but unfortunately the wi-fi only really works near reception.

B&B San Martino   B&B €
(☏ 080 48 56 01; http://xoomer.virgilio.it/bed-and-breakfast-sanmartino; Via Abate Fighera 32; s/d from €50/80; ❋ ▨) A stylish B&B in a historic palace with rooms overlooking gracious Piazza XX Settembre. The rooms have exposed stone walls, shiny parquet floors, wrought-iron beds and small kitchenettes (only one has a working cooker) and there's a pool to take a dip when it's hot.

✗ Eating

Don't miss the chance to try the *capocollo* – cured pork neck – that Martina Franca is famous for.

Gran Caffè   CAFE €
(☏ 080 480 54 91; Via Santoro 7a; snacks €2-3; ⊙ 7.30am-2am) With a broad communal bar, ever-hissing espresso machines and outdoor tables aligned towards busy Piazza XX Settembre, this is the quintessential Italian cafe. Sit. People-watch. Sip coffee. Nibble *cornetto*. Repeat.

Nausikaa   ITALIAN €€
(☏ 080 485 82 75; Vico Arco Fumarola 2; meals €30; ⊙ noon-3pm Tue-Sun, 7.30-11.30pm Tue-Sat) Tucked away down a dogleg alley off Martina Franca's main pedestrian drag is this lovely little modern Italian, run by brothers Francesco and Martino. Tradition is not sacrificed to forward-thinking, and vice versa – a 'caprese' salad, for instance, is stuffed inside a silky pasta bundle, anointed with 'basil pearls'. The Puglia-focused wine list is a joy, too.

Osteria Garibaldi   OSTERIA €€
(☏ 080 430 49 00; Via Garibaldi 17; meals €28; ⊙ noon-3pm & 7.30pm-midnight Thu-Tue) A highly recommended green-shuttered *osteria* in the *centro storico*. Delicious aromas entice you into the cave-like interior and the *cucina tipica* menu of typical Pugliese food doesn't disappoint. Worthy of a long lunch.

❶ Information

Tourist Office (☏ 080 480 57 02; www.agenziapugliapromozione.it; Piazza XX Settembre 3; ⊙ 10.30am-1.30pm & 4.30-7pm Jul & Aug, shorter hours rest of year) The tourist office is to the right of the Arco di Sant'Antonio, just before you enter the old town.

❶ Getting There & Away

The FSE train station is downhill from the historic centre. From the train station, go right along Viale della Stazione, continue along Via Alessandro Fighera to Corso Italia, then continue to the left along Corso Italia to Piazza XX Settembre.

FSE (☏ 080 546 21 11; www.fseonline.it) trains run to/from Bari (€5.60, 2¼ hours, hourly) and Taranto (€2.50, 50 minutes, four per day).

FSE buses run to Alberobello (€1.10, 20 minutes, frequent).

Ostuni

POP 31,150

Chic Ostuni shines like a pearly white tiara, extending across three hills with the magnificent gem of a cathedral as its sparkling centrepiece. It's the end of the *trulli* region and the beginning of the hot, dry Salento. With some excellent restaurants, stylish bars and swish yet intimate places to stay, it's packed in summer.

Ostuni is surrounded by olive groves, so this is the place to buy some of the region's DOC 'Collina di Brindisi' olive oil – either delicate, medium or strong – direct from producers.

⊙ Sights & Activities

The surrounding countryside is perfect for cycling. **Ciclovagando** (www.ciclovagando. com), based in Mesagne, 30km south of Ostuni, organises guided tours. Each tour covers approximately 20km and departs daily from various towns in the district, including Ostuni and Brindisi. For an extra €15, you can sample typical Puglian foods on the tour.

Museo di Civiltà Preclassiche della Murgia   MUSEUM
(☑ 0831 33 63 83; www.ostunimuseo.it; Via Cattedrale 15; adult/reduced €5/3; ☉ 10am-1pm & 6-10pm Jul–mid-Sep, shorter hours rest of year) Located in the Convento delle Monacelle, the museum's most famous exhibit is Delia, a 25,000-year-old expectant mother. Pregnant at the time of her death, her well-preserved skeleton was found in a local cave. Many of the finds here come from the Palaeolithic burial ground, now the **Parco Archeologico e Naturale di Arignano** (☑ 0831 30 39 73; ☉ 9.30am-1pm Sun, or by appointment).

Cathedral   CATHEDRAL
(Piazza Beato Giovanni Paolo II; €1; ☉ 9am-noon & 3.30-7pm) Dedicated to the Assumption of the Virgin Mary, Ostuni's dramatic 15th-century cathedral has an unusual Gothic-Romanesque-Byzantine facade with a frilly rose window and an inverted gable. The 18th-century sacred art covering the ceiling and altars is well worth stepping inside to see.

⁂ Festivals & Events

La Cavalcata   RELIGIOUS
Ostuni's annual feast day is held on 26 August. Processions of horsemen dressed in glittering red-and-white uniforms (resembling Indian grooms on their way to be wed) follow the statue of Sant'Oronzo around town.

🛏 Sleeping

Le Sole Blu   B&B €
(☑ 0831 30 38 56; www.webalice.it/solebluostuni; Corso Vittorio Emanuele II 16; s/d €40/80) Located in the 18th-century (rather than medieval) part of town, Le Sole Blu only has one room available: fully renovated, it's large with a separate entrance, but the bathroom is tiny. However, the two self-catering apartments nearby are excellent value.

★ La Terra   HOTEL €€
(☑ 0831 33 66 51; www.laterrahotel.it; Via Petrarolo 16; d from €170; P ❋ 🕾) This former 13th-century *palazzo* offers atmospheric and stylish accommodation with original niches, dark-wood beams and furniture, and contrasting light stonework and whitewash. There's a colonnaded terrace, wi-fi throughout, a more-than-decent restaurant and a truly cavernous bar – tunnelled out of a cave.

🍴 Eating

Osteria del Tempo Perso   PUGLIAN €€
(☑ 0831 30 33 20; www.osteriadeltempoperso. com; Via Vitale 47; meals €35; ☉ 12.30-3pm & 7.30-11pm Tue-Sun, open Mon Jul & Aug) A wonderful temple of Puglian cuisine in a cavernous former bakery, this laid-back place makes masterful use of the best of the region's produce, from Martina Franca's *capocollo* (cured pork neck) to whatever's been hauled from the nearby sea. If you're in Ostuni for a while, and want to get deeper into Puglia's food, consider the cooking courses the *osteria* offers.

Osteria Piazzetta Cattedrale   OSTERIA €€
(☑ 0831 33 50 26; www.piazzettacattedrale.it; Largo Arcidiacono 7; meals €40; ☉ 12.30-3pm & 7pm-12.30am Wed-Mon; 🖉) This compact *osteria* serves up great food in a setting that manages to keep it classy, despite a kitsch chandelier and muzak soundtrack competing with more tasteful mise-en-scene. While lovers of fish, fowl and flesh won't be disappointed, the menu includes plenty of vegetarian options, making great use of local mushrooms, cheeses and greens.

★ Porta Nova   ITALIAN €€€
(☑ 0831 33 89 83; www.ristoranteportanova.com; Via Petrarolo 38; meals €50; ☉ 1-3.30pm & 7-11pm) Scenically installed in the Aragonese fortifications, this terraced restaurant is a special occasion charmer. Seafood is wonderful here, with a whole section of the menu devoted to *crudo mare* (raw fish). Ease into what will be a splendid hour or so of indulgence with seabass carpaccio, then ramp it up with rosemary-scented Gallipoli prawns on beech-smoked potato.

ⓘ Information

Tourist Office (☑ 0831 33 96 27, 0831 30 12 68; Corso Mazzini 6; ☉ 8am-2pm & 3-8pm) Located off Piazza della Libertà, this helpful office can organise guided visits of the town in summer, and bike rental.

ⓘ Getting There & Away

STP Brindisi (p155) buses run to Brindisi (€3.10, 50 minutes, six daily) and to Martina

14

Franca (€2.10, 45 minutes, three daily), leaving from Piazza Italia in the newer part of Ostuni.

Trains run frequently to Brindisi (€4, 25 minutes) and Bari (€9, 50 minutes). A half-hourly local bus covers the 2.5km between the station and town.

Salento

The Penisola Salentina, better known simply as Salento, is hot, dry and remote, retaining a flavour of its Greek past. It stretches across Italy's heel from Brindisi to Taranto and down to Santa Maria di Leuca. Here the lush greenery of Valle d'Itria gives way to flat, ochre-coloured fields hazy with wildflowers in spring, and endless olive groves.

Lecce

POP 95,000

If Puglia were a movie, Lecce would be cast in the starring role. Bequeathed with a generous stash of baroque buildings by its 17th-century architects, the city has a completeness and homogeneity that other southern Italian metropolises lack. Indeed,

so distinctive is Lecce's architecture that it has acquired its own moniker, *barocco leccese* (Lecce baroque), an expressive and hugely decorative incarnation of the genre replete with gargoyles, asparagus columns and cavorting gremlins. Swooning 18th-century traveller Thomas Ashe thought it 'the most beautiful city in Italy', but the less-impressed Marchese Grimaldi said the facade of Basilica di Santa Croce made him think a lunatic was having a nightmare.

Either way, it's a lively, graceful but relaxed university town with some upmarket boutiques, decent Puglian restaurants, and a strong tradition for papier-mâché making. Both the Adriatic and Ionian Seas are within easy access and it's a great base from which to explore the Salento.

◉ Sights

Lecce has more than 40 churches and at least as many *palazzi*, all built or renovated between the 17th and 18th centuries, giving the city an extraordinary cohesion. Two of the main proponents of *barocco leccese* (the craziest, most lavish decoration imaginable)

LECCE'S NOTABLE CHURCHES

Lecce's unique baroque style is perhaps best seen in its churches; the city harbours dozens of them.

Chiesa dei Santi Nicolò e Cataldo (Via Cimitero; ⊗ 9am-noon & 5-7pm Jun-Aug, shorter hours rest of year) The beautiful church of Saints Nicolò and Cataldo, located in the monumental cemetery outside the city walls, was built by the Normans in 1180. It got caught up in the city's baroque frenzy and was revamped in 1716 by the prolific Giuseppe Cino, who retained the Romanesque rose window and portal. The 16th-century fresco cycles inside tell stories from the saints' lives.

Chiesa di Santa Chiara (Piazzetta Vittorio Emanuele II; ⊗ 9am-1pm & 4.30-6.30pm) A notable 15th-century church given a baroque makeover between 1687 and 1691, Santa Chiara is one of the most important and admired churches in Lecce. Inside, every niche and surface swirls with twisting columns and ornate statuary. The ceiling is 18th-century Leccese *cartapestra* (papier-mâché) masquerading as wood.

Chiesa di Sant'Irene (Corso Vittorio Emanuele II; ⊗ 7.30-11am & 4-6pm) Dedicated to Lecce's former patron saint and modelled on Rome's Basilica di Sant'Andrea della Valle, this church was completed in 1639. Inside you'll find a magnificent pair of mirror-image baroque altarpieces, facing each other across the transept.

Chiesa di San Matteo (Via dei Perroni 29; ⊗ 8.30am-1pm & 5-8pm) Known by the locals as Santa Maria della Luce, this graceful little church bears the fingerprints of Giuseppe Zimbalo, as much of baroque Lecce does. The famed architect completed the building, with its elaborate facade and more restrained interior, when the original architect died before completion.

Chiesa del Rosario (Via Libertini 5; ⊗ 8.30-11.30am & 5-6pm) Also known as the Chiesa di San Giovanni Battista (Church of John the Baptist), this elaborately fronted church was prodigious Leccese architect Giuseppe Zimbalo's last commission. He died before it was completed, and a quick-fix wooden roof was put up, instead of the dome he had intended.

Lecce

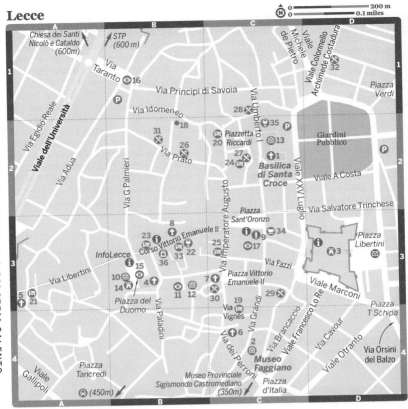

were brothers Antonio and Giuseppe Zimbalo, who both had a hand in the fantastical Basilica di Santa Croce.

★ Basilica di Santa Croce
BASILICA

(☎0832 24 19 57; Via Umberto I; ☺9am-noon & 5-8pm) FREE It seems that hallucinating stonemasons have been at work on the basilica. Sheep, dodos, cherubs and beasties writhe across the facade, a swirling magnificent allegorical feast. Throughout the 16th and 17th centuries, a team of artists under Giuseppe Zimbalo laboured to work the building up to this pitch. The interior is more conventionally baroque, and deserves a look, once you've drained your camera batteries outside. Spare a thought for the expelled Jewish families whose land the basilica was built on.

Zimbalo also left his mark in the former Convento dei Celestini, just north of the basilica, which is now the **Palazzo del Governo** (Via Umberto I), the local government headquarters. Look for his profile on the facade of the basilica.

Piazza del Duomo
PIAZZA

Piazza del Duomo is a baroque feast, the city's focal point and a sudden open space amid the surrounding enclosed lanes. During times of invasion the inhabitants of Lecce would barricade themselves in the square, which has conveniently narrow entrances. Lecce's 12th-century cathedral, episcopal palace and **museum of sacred art** (☎0832 24 47 64; http://museo.diocesilecce. org; Piazza del Duomo 5; €4; ☺9.30am-12.30pm & 4-7pm Mon-Fri) face one another in silent dignity across the square.

Cathedral
CATHEDRAL

(☎0832 30 85 57; Piazza del Duomo; crypt €1; ☺7am-noon & 4-6.30pm) Giuseppe Zimbalo's 1659 reconstruction of Lecce's original 12th-century cathedral is recognised as

Lecce

being among his finest work. Zimbalo, Lecce's famous 17th-century architect, was also responsible for the thrusting, tiered **bell tower**, 72m high. The cathedral is unusual in that it has two facades, one on the western end and the other, more ornate, facing the piazza. It's framed by the 17th-century **Palazzo Vescovile** (Episcopal Palace) and the 18th-century **Seminario**, designed by Giuseppe Cino.

Palazzo Vescovile   PALACE
(Episcopal Palace; Piazza del Duomo) Facing Lecce's cathedral is the arched arcade loggia of the 15th-century Palazzo Vescovile, one-time residence of Neapolitan royalty and one of Lecce's baroque masterpieces.

★**Museo Faggiano**   MUSEUM
(☑0832 30 05 28; www.museofaggiano.it; Via Grandi 56/58; €3; ☺9.30am-8pm) Descend through Lecce's rich historical strata in this fascinating home-turned-museum, where sewerage excavations led to the chance discovery of an archaeological treasure trove. The deepest finds take you all the way back to the Messapii culture of the 5th century BC; you then ascend through Roman crypts, medieval walls, Jewish insigna and Knights Templar symbols in the rooftop tower.

Castello di Carlo V   CASTLE
(☑0832 24 65 17; www.castellocarlov.it; Via XXV Luglio; adult/reduced/child 6-12yr €3/2/1; ☺9am-8.30pm Mon-Fri, from 9.30am Sat & Sun, closes later in summer) While the Normans built the original castle in the 12th century, it became associated with the Spanish Holy Roman Emperor Charles V, who enlarged it extensively in the 16th century. Bound within enormous trapezoidal walls cornered with stout bastions, it is Puglia's largest castle, and has been used as a prison, court, military barracks and now the headquarters of Lecce's cultural authorities. You can wander around inside, catch a recital, and visit the on-site **papier-mâché museum**.

Museo Provinciale Sigismondo Castromediano   MUSEUM
(☑0832 68 35 03; Viale Gallipoli 30; ☺8.30am-7.30pm Mon-Sat, 9am-1pm Sun) **FREE** This museum stylishly covers 10,000 years of history, from Palaeolithic and Neolithic bits and bobs to a handsome display of Greek and Roman jewels, weaponry and ornaments. The stars of the show are the Messapians, whose jaunty Mycenaean-inspired jugs and bowls date back 2500 years. There's also an interesting collection of 15th- to 18th-century paintings.

Roman Amphitheatre AMPHITHEATRE

(Piazza Sant'Oronzo; ☺ tours 10.15am-7.15pm Fri-Wed) Below the ground level of the piazza is this restored 2nd-century-AD amphitheatre, discovered in 1901 by construction workers. It was excavated in the 1930s to reveal a perfect horseshoe with seating for 15,000. A little colonised by weeds, it's nonetheless an impressive centrepiece to Lecce's main communal square. Book tickets for tours (€2, 10.15am, 12.15pm, 5.15pm and 7.15pm) at the neighbouring tourist office (p152).

MUST GALLERY

(Museo Storico Citta di Lecce; ☑ 0832 24 10 67; www.mustlecce.it; Via degli Ammirati 11; adult/reduced €4.50/2.50; ☺ noon-7pm Tue-Sun) The beautifully restored 15th-century Monastery of Santa Chiara houses this civic museum and gallery, and has a great view of the Roman theatre from the back window. Exhibits focus on the history of Lecce, from the Messapians of 2500 years ago to the present day, while the work of modern Leccese artists hangs in the ground-floor gallery.

Colonna di Sant'Oronzo MONUMENT

(Piazza Sant'Oronzo) Two Roman columns once marked the end of the Appian Way in Brindisi. When one of them crumbled in 1582 some of the pieces were rescued and subsequently donated to Lecce (the base and capital remain in Brindisi). The old column was rebuilt in 1666 with a statue of Lecce's patron saint placed on top. Sant'Oronzo is venerated for supposedly saving the city of Brindisi from a 1656 plague.

Museo Teatro Romano MUSEUM

(☑ 0832 27 91 96; Via degli Ammirati 5; adult/reduced €3/2; ☺ 9.30am-1pm Mon-Sat) Exhibiting artefacts revealed excavating the adjacent Roman theatre, this museum also has displays recreating classical Roman life, including a reconstruction of Roman Lupiae (Lecce). The museum is housed in a handsome 17th-century *palazzo*.

Porta Napoli GATE

The main city gate, Porta Napoli, was erected in 1548 in anticipation of a state visit from Charles V. It's a typically bombastic effort by Gian dell'Acaja (builder of Lecce's fortified walls), who modelled it on a Roman triumphal arch and gave it a pointy pediment carved with toy weapons and an enormous Spanish coat of arms.

🍽 Courses

Awaiting Table COOKING

(☑ 334 7676970; www.awaitingtable.com; Via Idomeneo 41; day/week €195/1895) Silvestro Silvestori's splendid culinary- and wine-school provides day- or week-long courses with market shopping, tours, tastings, noteworthy lecturers – and lots of hands-on cooking. Week-long courses are held in Silvestro's home, but you'll need to arrange your own accommodation. Book well in advance as courses fill up rapidly.

🛏 Sleeping

★Palazzo Rollo B&B, APARTMENT €

(☑ 0832 30 71 52; www.palazzorollo.it; Corso Vittorio Emanuele II 14; s/d €75/90; P❄@) This tastefully restored 17th-century *palazzo* – the Rollo family seat for more than 200 years – makes a delightful base from which to explore Lecce. The grand B&B suites (with kitchenettes) have high curved ceilings and chandeliers while, downstairs, the contemporary-chic studios open onto an ivy-hung courtyard. There are also self-catering apartments (€75 per person) and a rooftop garden with wonderful views.

B&B Idomeneo 63 B&B €

(☑ 333 9499838; www.bebidomeneo63.it; Via Idomeneo 63; d/ste €85/120; ☎) You'll be looked after like a VIP at this wonderfully curated B&B in the midst of Lecce's baroque quarter, complete with six colour-coded rooms and a funky entrance lounge. Decked out boutique-hotel style, it manages to seamlessly incorporate older features like stone ceiling arches. The two 'apartments', with kitchenettes, are great value.

Azzurretta B&B B&B €

(☑ 0832 24 22 11; www.hostelecce.com; Via Vignes 2; d/tr/apt €72/87/105; P☎) Tullio runs this arty B&B located in an historic *palazzo*. Of the four rooms, ask for the large double with a balcony, wooden floors and vaulted ceiling. Massage is available in your room or on the roof terrace – also a splendid place to take a sundowner. You get a cafe voucher for breakfast.

B&B Prestige B&B €

(☑ 349 7751290; www.bbprestige-lecce.it; Via Libertini 7; s/d/q €70/100/140; P@☎) On the corner of Via Santa Maria del Paradiso in the historic centre, the rooms at this lovely B&B are light, airy and beautifully finished. The communal sun-trap terrace has views over

15

San Giovanni Battista church. Breakfast is an extra €5 per day.

Centro Storico B&B
B&B €

(☑ 0832 24 27 27, 328 8351294; www.centros toricolecce.it; Via Vignes 2; s/d/ste €60/70/90; ⓟ❄🛜) This friendly and efficient B&B located in the 16th-century Palazzo Astore features big rooms, double-glazed windows and pleasantly old-fashioned decor. The huge rooftop terrace has sun loungers and views. Cafe vouchers are provided for breakfast, and there are also coffee- and tea-making facilities.

Palazzo Belli B&B
B&B €€

(☑ 0832 169 05 05, 348 0946802; Corso Vittorio Emanuele II 33; d €110; ❄🛜) A wonderfully central, elegant and well-priced option located in a handsome *palazzo* near the cathedral. Rooms have marbled floors and wrought-iron beds, and breakfast is served in your room.

Patria Palace Hotel
HOTEL €€

(☑ 0832 24 51 11; http://patriapalace.com; Piazzetta Riccardi 13; d from €114; ⓟ❄@🛜) This sumptuous hotel is traditionally Italian with large mirrors, dark-wood furniture and wistful murals. The location is wonderful, the bar gloriously art deco with a magnificent carved ceiling, and the shady roof terrace has views over the Basilica di Santa Croce. The attached restaurant, **Atenze** (https://patriapalace.com/it/ristorante-atenze; Piazzetta Riccardi; meals €50; ⊙12.30-3pm & 7-11pm), is one of Lecce's finest.

Risorgimento Resort
HOTEL €€€

(☑ 0832 24 63 11; www.risorgimentoresort.it; Via Imperatore Augusto 19; d/ste €220/355; ⓟ❄@🛜) A warm welcome awaits at this stylish five-star hotel in the centre of Lecce. The rooms are spacious and refined with high ceilings, modern furniture and contemporary details reflecting the colours of the Salento. The bathrooms are enormous, too. There's a restaurant, wine bar and rooftop garden.

✖ Eating

★ Baldo Gelato
GELATO

(☑ 328 0710290; Via Idomeneo 78; medium cone or cup €3; ⊙11am-8pm Mon-Thu, to midnight Fri-Sun) The couple behind Baldo Gelato make the best gelato in Lecce, hands down. The dark chocolate may be the most intensely chocolatey thing you've ever put in your mouth.

★ Trattoria Il Rifugio della Buona Stella
PUGLIAN €

(☑ 0832 181 05 11; www.ilrifugiodellabuonastella.it; Via Prato 28; meals €23; ⊙noon-3pm & 7-11.45pm Wed-Mon) A third-generation family restaurant in a gorgeous Leccese building with sandy stone walls and medieval decor, this wonderful trattoria serves utterly delicious Pugliese food at more-than-reasonable prices. Start off with the homemade bread, proceed to pasta with swordfish and rapini (turnip tops), and round off a happy evening's gluttony with the grilled sausages with mushrooms.

★ Trattoria le Zie – Cucina Casareccia
TRATTORIA €€

(☑ 0832 24 51 78; Viale Costadura 19; meals €30; ⊙12.30-2.30pm Tue-Sun & 7.30-10.30pm Tue-Sun) Where better to eat *cucina casareccia* (home cooking) than a place that feels like a private home, with patterned cement floor tiles, paper-strewn desk and a welcoming hostess (Carmela Perrone)? Known locally as simply 'le Zie' (the aunt) it's here you'll taste true *cucina povera*, such as horse meat in *salsa piccante* (spicy sauce). Booking is a must.

La Torre di Merlino
PUGLIAN €€

(☑ 0832 24 20 91; Via Giambattista del Tufo 10; meals €45; ⊙12-2.30pm & 7.30-11.30pm) This sweet courtyard restaurant is dependably one of Lecce's best eating options. There are pizzas, but why would you, when the seafood's so good? Try the *antipasti di crude di mare* (spanking-fresh raw scallops, red Gallipoli prawns, and whatever else that day's market suggested).

Alle due Corti
PUGLIAN €€

(☑ 0832 24 22 23; www.alleduecorti.com; Via Prato 42; meals €30; ⊙12.30-2pm & 7.30-11pm Mon-Sat, closed Jan) Rosalba de Carlo, a noted repository of Salento gustatory wisdom, is the presiding authority in this authentic-as-it gets Puglian kitchen. 'The Two Courts' keeps it strictly seasonal and local, dishing up classics such as *ciceri e tria* (crisply fried pasta with chickpeas) and *turcineddhi* (offal of kid) in a relaxed, traditional restaurant environment.

La Cucina di Mamma Elvira
PUGLIAN €€

(☑ 331 5795127; www.mammaelvira.com; Via Maremonti 33; meals €30; ⊙12.30pm-midnight) An offshoot of the stylish Enoteca Mamma Elvira, 'The Kitchen' makes use of a bigger space than that available to its older sibling to deliver more ambitious and substantial food. There's still the same focus on Puglian wine, simply augmented by a menu that offers seafood antipasti, lovely vegetarian options (try the eggplant fritters), robust Puglian pastas and more.

Drinking & Nightlife

Via Umberto I, just north of the Palazzo del Governo, is now an unbroken stretch of stylish bars, spilling out onto the pavement.

★ Enoteca Mamma Elvira   WINE BAR
(☑ 0832 169 20 11; www.mammaelvira.com; Via Umberto I 19; ☺ 8am-3am; ☎) All you need to know about emerging Salento wine will be imparted by the hip but friendly staff at this cool new joint near the Santa Croce church. Taster glasses are dispatched liberally if you order a few snacks. You'll need to order a few if you're going to properly research the 250+ Puglian wines it stocks.

All'Ombra del Barocco   WINE BAR
(☑ 0832 24 55 24; Corte dei Cicala 1; ☺ 7am-midnight) Open throughout the day, this cool restaurant/cafe/wine bar has most meals covered, offering a range of teas, cocktails and *aperitivi*. It's open for breakfast, hosts musical events and the modern cooking is

---

LECCE'S PAPIER-MÂCHÉ ART

Lecce is famous for its papier-mâché art *(cartapesta)*. Statues and figurines are sculpted out of a mixture of paper and glue before being painted and used to adorn churches and other public buildings. Lecce's *cartapesta* culture originated in the 17th century when glue and paper offered cheap raw materials for religious artists who couldn't afford expensive wood or marble. Legend has it that the first exponents of the art were Leccese barbers who shaped and chiseled their statues in between haircuts.

These days the art is still practiced in Lecce and you'll see a number of traditional workshops such as **Cartapesta Riso** (☑ 0832 24 34 10; www.cartapesta riso.it; Corso Emanuele II 27; ☺ 9.30am-7.30pm) scattered around the old town centre. Also worth perusing are the papier-mâché museum inside the Castello di Carlo V (p149) and the decorative papier-mâché ceiling inside the Chiesa di Santa Chiara (p147).

---

well worth a try. Tables fill the little square outside, an ideal place from which to watch the *passeggiata*.

Caffè Alvino   CAFE
(☑ 0832 24 67 48; Piazza Sant'Oronzo 30; ☺ 7am-2am Wed-Mon; ☎) Treat yourself to great coffee and *pasticciotto* (custard pie) at this iconic chandeliered cafe in Lecce's main square. And try to get past the lavish display of cakes without at least having second thoughts.

ℹ Information

Hospital (Ospedale Vito Fazzi; ☑ 0832 66 11 11; Piazza Filippo) Has a 24-hour emergency room.

InfoLecce (☑ 0832 52 18 77; www.infolecce. it; Piazza del Duomo 2; ☺ 9.30am-1.30pm & 3.30-7.30pm Mon-Fri, 10am-1.30pm & 3.30-7pm Sat & Sun) Independent and helpful tourist information office. Has guided tours and bike rental (per hour/day €3/15).

Police Station (☑ 0832 69 11 11; Viale Otranto 1)

Post Office (Piazza Libertini 5; ☺ 8.30am-7pm Mon-Fri, to 12.30pm Sat)

Puglia Blog (www.thepuglia.com) An informative site run by Fabio Ingrosso with articles on culture, history, food, wine, accommodation and travel in Puglia.

Tourist Office (☑ 0832 68 29 85; Corso Vittorio Emanuele II 16; ☺ 10am-1pm & 4-6pm) One of three main government-run offices. The others are in **Castello di Carlo V** (☑ 0832 24 65 17; ☺ 9am-8.30pm Mon-Fri, 9.30am-8.30pm Sat & Sun, closes later in summer) and **Piazza Sant'Oronzo** (☑ 0832 24 20 99; ☺ 10am-1pm & 4-6pm).

ℹ Getting There & Away

BUS
The city bus terminal is located to the north of Porta Napoli.

Pugliairbus (http://pugliairbus.aeroportidi puglia.it) Connects with Brindisi airport.

STP (☑ 0832 35 91 42; www.stplecce.it) STP runs buses to Brindisi, Gallipoli and Otranto from the **STP bus station** (☑ 800 43 03 46; Viale Porta D'Europa).

TRAIN
The main **train station**, 1km southwest of Lecce's historic centre, runs frequent services.

Bari from €9, 1½ to two hours

Bologna from €59.50, 7½ to 9½ hours

Brindisi from €2.80, 30 minutes

Naples from €53.10, 5½ hours (transfer in Caserta)

Rome from €66, 5½ to nine hours

FSE trains head to Otranto, Gallipoli and Martina Franca; the ticket office is located on platform 1.

Brindisi

POP 87,800

Like all ports, Brindisi has its seamy side, but it's also surprisingly slow paced and balmy, particularly along the palm-lined Corso Garibaldi, which links the port to the train station, and the promenade stretching along the interesting *lungomare* (seafront).

The town was the end of the ancient Roman road Via Appia, down whose length trudged weary legionnaires and pilgrims, crusaders and traders, all heading to Greece and the Near East. These days little has changed except that Brindisi's pilgrims are now sun-seekers rather than soul-seekers.

Sights

Museo Archeologico Provinciale Ribezzo   MUSEUM
(☑0831 56 55 01; Piazza del Duomo 6; adult/reduced €5/3; ⊙9.30am-1.30pm Tue-Sat, plus 3.30-6.30pm Tue) This superb museum covers several floors with well-documented exhibits (in English), including some 3000 bronze sculptures and fragments in Hellenistic Greek style. There are also terracotta figurines from the 7th century, underwater archaeological finds, and Roman statues and heads (not always together).

Roman Column   MONUMENT
(Via Colonne) The gleaming white column above a sweeping set of sun-whitened stairs leading to the waterfront promenade marks the terminus of the Roman Via Appia at Brindisi. Originally there were two columns, but one was presented to the town of Lecce back in 1666 as thanks to Sant'Oronzo for having relieved Brindisi of the plague.

Tempio di San Giovanni al Sepolcro   CHURCH
(☑0831 52 30 72; Piazzetta San Giovanni al Sepolcro) This 12th-century church, a brown hulk of Norman stone conforming to the circular plan the Templars so loved, is a wonderfully evocative structure, austere and bare. You'll see vestigial medieval frescoes on the walls, and glimpses of the crypt below.

Palazzo Granafei-Nervegna   MUSEUM
(Via Duomo 20; ⊙10am-1pm & 5-8pm Tue-Sun) FREE A 16th-century Renaissance-style palace named for the two different families who owned it. The building is of interest because it houses the huge ornate capital that used to sit atop one of the Roman columns that marked the end of the Appian Way (the rest of the column is in Lecce). Also on site are a pleasant cafe, a bookshop, exhibition spaces and the archaeological remains of a Roman *domus* (house).

Cathedral   CATHEDRAL
(Piazza del Duomo; ⊙8am-9pm Mon-Fri & Sun, to noon Sat) This 12th-century cathedral was substantially remodelled after an earthquake in 1743. You can see how the original Romanesque structure may have looked by studying the nearby **Porta dei Cavalieri Templari**, a fanciful portico with pointy arches – all that remains of a medieval Knights Templar's church that once also stood here.

Sleeping

Grande Albergo Internazionale   HISTORIC HOTEL €€
(☑0831 52 34 73; www.albergointernazionale.it; Viale Regina Margherita 23; s/d €100/160; P ✱ 🛜) Built in 1869 for English merchants en route to India, the Internazionale definitely offers grandeur, albeit of the rather faded variety. It has great harbour views, large rooms with grandly draped curtains, and stately common areas. There are mod cons, but gadgetry takes second place to history here (wi-fi is available only in public areas). Check for off-season deals online.

Hotel Orientale   HOTEL €€
(☑0831 56 84 51; www.hotelorientale.it; Corso Garibaldi 40; r €130; P ✱ 🛜) This sleek, modern hotel overlooks the long palm-lined *corso*. Rooms are pleasant, the location is good and it has a small fitness centre, private car park and (rare) cooked breakfast option.

Eating

Il Giardino   PUGLIAN €€
(☑0831 52 49 50; Via Tarantini 14-18; meals €30; ⊙12.30-2.30pm & 8-10.30pm Tue-Sat, 12.30-2.30pm Sun) Established more than 40 years ago in a restored 15th-century *palazzo*, sophisticated Il Giardino serves refined seafood and meat dishes in a delightful garden setting. You won't be disappointed with the pizza, but try something a little different, like the pasta with *bottarga* (dried mullet roe).

PUGLIA, BASILICATA & CALABRIA SALENTO

Brindisi

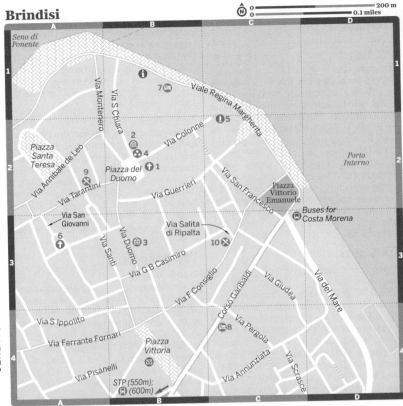

Trattoria Pantagruele TRATTORIA €€

(☑ 0831 56 06 05; Via Salita di Ripalta 1; meals €30; ⊙12.30-2.30pm Mon-Sat, 7.30-10.30pm Mon-Fri) Named after the Rabelaisian giant Pantagruel, this charming trattoria three blocks from the waterfront serves up excellent fish and grilled meats. Expect fresh anchovies in season, and lovely homemade pasta in all seasons.

❶ Information

Antonio Perrino Hospital (☑ 0831 53 71 11; Strada Statale 7 per Mesagne) Has an emergency room. Southwest of the centre; take the SS7 for Mesagne.

Post Office (☑ 0831 22 55 95; Piazza Vittoria 10; ⊙8am-6.30pm Mon-Fri, to 1pm Sat)

Tourist Office (☑ 0831 52 30 72; www.viaggiareinpuglia.it; Viale Regina Margherita 44; ⊙10am-6pm Mon, 8am-8pm Tue-Sun) Has a wealth of information and brochures on the area. If you are interested in pedal power, pick up *Le Vie Verdi* map, which shows eight bicycling routes in the Brindisi area, ranging from 6km to 30km.

❶ Getting There & Away

AIR

From **Salento Airport** (BDS; ☑ 0831 411 74 06; www.aeroportidipuglia.it; Contrada Baroncino), Brindisi's small airport, there are domestic flights to Rome, Naples and Milan. Airlines include Alitalia and easyJet. There are also direct flights from London Stansted with Ryanair.

BOAT

Ferries, all of which take vehicles, leave Brindisi for Greece and Albania.

Ferry companies have offices at Costa Morena (the newer port), which is 4km from the train station. A free minibus connects the two.

Grimaldi Lines (☑ 0831 54 81 16; www.grimaldi-lines.com; Costa Morena Terminal) Frequent

Brindisi

Sights
1 Cathedral B2
2 Museo Archeologico Provinciale
   Ribezzo..B2
3 Palazzo Granafei-Nervegna B3
4 Porta dei Cavalieri Templari................B2
5 Roman Column C2
6 Tempio di San Giovanni al
   Sepolcro..A3

Sleeping
7 Grande Albergo Internazionale..........B1
8 Hotel Orientale C4

Eating
9 Il Giardino...A2
10 Trattoria Pantagruele...........................C3

year-round ferries to Igoumenitsa and Patras in Greece.

Red Star Ferries (☑ 0831 57 52 89; www.directferries.co.uk/red_star_ferries.htm; Costa Morena Terminal) To Vlorë in Albania, once a day.

BUS

Pugliairbus (www.aeroportidipuglia.it) has services to Bari airport and Lecce from Brindisi's airport.

Ferrovie del Sud-Est buses serving local towns leave from Via Bastioni Carlo V, in front of the train station.

Marozzi (☑ 0831 52 16 84; www.marozzivt.it) Runs to Rome's Stazione Tiburtina from Viale Arno.

STP Brindisi (www.stpbrindisi.it) Buses go regularly to Ostuni, Lecce and other towns throughout the Salento. Most leave from Via Bastioni Carlo V, in front of the train station.

TRAIN

Brindisi train station has regular services to the following destinations:

Bari from €8.40, 1¼ hours
Lecce from €2.80, 30 minutes
Milan from €99.50, 8½ to 11 hours
Rome from €70, eight to 12 hours
Taranto from €4.90, one hour

❶ Getting Around

Major and local car-rental firms are represented at the airport. To reach the airport by bus, take the STP-run **Cotrap** (☑ 800 232 042; www.stpbrindisi.it; single ticket €1) bus from Via Bastoni Carlo V.

A free minibus connects the train station and old ferry terminal with Costa Morena. It departs two hours before boat departures. You'll need a valid ferry ticket.

Galatina

POP 27,100

With a charming historic centre, Galatina, 18km south of Lecce, is at the core of the Salentine Peninsula's Greek past. It is almost the only place where the ritual *tarantismi* (Spider Music) is still practised. The tarantella folk dance evolved from this ritual, and each year on the feast day of St Peter and St Paul (29 June), it is performed at the (now deconsecrated) church.

◉ Sights

Basilica di Santa Caterina d'Alessandria
BASILICA

(Piazzetta Orsini; ⏱ 4-6.30pm daily & 8.30am-12.30pm Mon-Sat Apr-Sep, shorter hours rest of year) Most people come to Galatina to see the incredible 14th-century Basilica di Santa Caterina d'Alessandria. Its interior is a kaleidoscope of frescoes and is absolutely beautiful, with a pure-white altarpiece set against the frenzy of frescoes. It was built by the Franciscans, whose patron was Frenchwoman Marie d'Enghien de Brienne.

🛏 Sleeping

Samadhi
AGRITURISMO €€

(☑ 0836 60 02 84; www.agricolasamadhi.com; Via Stazione 116, Zollino; d €130; 🅿🌡🛜🍴) 🍴 Soothe the soul with a stay at Samadhi, located around 7km east of Galatina in tiny Zollino. It's on a 10-hectare organic farm and the owners are multilingual. As well as Ayurvedic treatments, shiatsu and yoga courses, there's a vegan restaurant offering organic meals. Check the website for upcoming retreats and courses.

❶ Getting There & Away

Ferrovie del Sud runs frequent trains between Lecce and Galatina (€2.10, 30 minutes), and Galatina and Zollino (€1, eight minutes).

Otranto

POP 5750

Bloodied and bruised by an infamous Turkish massacre in 1480, Otranto is best appreciated in its amazing cathedral, where the bones of 813 martyrs are displayed in a glass case behind the altar. Less macabre is the cathedral's other jaw-dropper, its medieval mosaic floor, which rivals the famous early

Christian mosaics of Ravenna in its richness and historical significance.

Lying deep in Italy's stiletto, Otranto has back-heeled quite a few invaders over the centuries and been brutally kicked by others – most notably the Turks. Sleuth around its compact old quarter and you can peel the past off in layers – Greek, Roman, Turkish and Napoleonic. These days the town is a generally peaceful place, unless you're fighting for beach space at the height of summer.

◉ Sights

★ Cathedral
CATHEDRAL

(☑0836 80 27 20; Piazza Basilica; ⊗7am-noon & 3-8pm, shorter hours in winter) Mosaics, skulls, crypts and biblical-meets-tropical imagery: Otranto's cathedral is like no other in Italy. It was built by the Normans in the 11th century, incorporating Romanesque, Byzantine and early Christian styles with their own, and has been given a few facelifts since. Covering the entire floor is its pièce de résistance, a vast 12th-century mosaic of a stupendous tree of life balanced on the back of two elephants.

Castello Aragonese Otranto
CASTLE

(☑0836 21 00 94; Piazza Castello; adult/reduced/under 17yr €5/2/free; ⊗10am-7pm summer, shorter hours rest of year) Built in the late 15th century, when Otranto was more populous and important than today, and not long after the calamitous Ottoman raid that resulted in the execution of hundreds for refusing Islam, the castle is a blunt and grim structure, well preserved internally and offering splendid views from the outer walls. It is famous,

---

SCENIC DRIVE: OTRANTO TO CASTRO
....

For a scenic road trip, the drive south from Otranto to Castro takes you along a wild and beautiful coastline. The coast here is rocky and dramatic, with cliffs falling down into the sparkling, azure sea; when the wind is up you can see why it is largely treeless. Many of the towns here started life as Greek settlements, although there are few monuments to be seen. Further south, the resort town of Santa Maria di Leuca is the tip of Italy's stiletto and the dividing line between the Adriatic and Ionian Seas.

---

among other things, from Horace Walpole's *The Castle of Otranto* (1764), recognised as the first Gothic novel. Last tickets are sold an hour before closing.

Chiesa di San Pietro
CHURCH

(Via San Pietro; ⊗10am-noon & 4-8pm Jun-Sep, by request rest of year) The origins of this cross-shaped Byzantine church are uncertain, but some think they may be as remote as the 5th century. The present structure seems to be a product of the 10th century, to which the oldest of the celebrated frescoes decorating its three apses dates.

🏃 Activities

There are some great beaches north of Otranto, especially **Baia dei Turchi**, with its translucent blue water. South of Otranto a spectacular rocky coastline makes for an impressive drive down to Castro. To see what goes on underwater, speak to **Scuba Diving Otranto** (☑0836 80 27 40; www.scubadiving.it; Via del Porto 1; 1-/2-tank dive incl equipment €48/75; ⊗7am-10pm).

🛏 Sleeping

Palazzo de Mori
B&B €€

(☑0836 80 10 88; www.palazzodemori.it; Bastione dei Pelasgi; s/d €105/140; ⊗Apr-Oct; ✳@) 🏊 In Otranto's historic centre, this charming B&B serves fabulous breakfasts on the sun terrace overlooking the port. The rooms are decorated in soothing white on white.

★ Palazzo Papaleo
HOTEL €€€

(☑0836 80 21 08; www.hotelpalazzopapaleo.com; Via Rondachi 1; r from €200; ℗✳@🛜) 🏊 Located next to the cathedral, this sumptuous hotel, the first to earn the EU Eco-label in Puglia, has magnificent rooms with original frescoes, exquisitely carved antique furniture and walls washed in soft greys, ochres and yellows. Soak in the panoramic views while enjoying the rooftop spa, or steam yourself pure in the hammam. The staff are exceptionally friendly.

🍴 Eating

La Bella Idrusa
PIZZA €

(☑0836 80 14 75; Lungomare degli Eroi 1; pizza €7; ⊗7pm-midnight) You can't miss this pizzeria right by the huge Porta Terra as you enter the historic centre. Despite the tourist-trap location, the food doesn't lack authenticity. Pizza's the main event, but there is support: seafood, grilled meat, vegetarian *contorni* (side dishes) and pasta are all there to lend a hand.

★ L'Altro Baffo
SEAFOOD €€

(☑ 0836 80 16 36; www.laltrobaffo.com; Via Cenobio Basiliano 23; meals €40; ⊘ 12-2.30pm & 7.30pm-midnight Tue-Sun) This elegant modern restaurant near the castle stands out in Otranto's competitive dining scene. It stays in touch with basic Pugliese and Italian principles, but ratchets things up several notches: the 'carbonara' made with sea-urchin roe is a daring instant classic. The menu is mainly seafood, but there are a few vegetarian dishes that are anything but afterthoughts.

Information

Tourist Office (☑ 0836 80 14 36; Via del Porto; ⊘ 9am-1pm & 3-6pm) Down in the new port area.

ⓘ Getting There & Away

Otranto can be reached from Lecce by FSE train (€3.50, 1½ hours). It is on a small branch line, which necessitates changing in Maglie and sometimes Zollino too. Services are reduced on Sundays.

Castro
POP 2450

One of Salento's most striking coastal settlements, the walled commune of Castro has a pedigree that predates the Romans, who gave it the name *Castrum Minervae*, or 'Minerva's Castle'. The castle and walls that remain today date to the 16th-century rule of the Aragonese, who built atop foundations laid by the Angevins and Byzantines before them. The charming old town, which also boasts a 12th-century cathedral, the remains of a Byzantine church and a cliff-top piazza with delightful sea views, sits above a marina (which really comes alive in summer) and terraced olive groves leading to a limestone coast riddled with spectacular caves.

⊙ Sights

Grotta Zinzulusa
CAVE

(☑ 0836 94 38 12; Via Zinzulusa; adult/reduced €6/3; ⊘ 9.30am-7pm Jul & Aug, shorter hours rest of year; Ⓟ) An aperture on the Ionian coast below Castro leads into the magnificent stalactite-festooned Cave of Zinzulusa, one of the most significant coastal limestone karst formations in Italy. The portion accessible to the public stretches hundreds of metres back from the cliff face, terminating in a chamber grand enough to justify the sobriquet 'Il Duomo'. Divided into three distinct geomorphological sections, Zinzulusa is home to endemic crustacea and other 'living fossils' known nowhere else on the planet.

Castello Aragonese
CASTLE

(☑ 0836 94 70 05; Via Sant Antonio 1; adult/reduced €2.50/2; ⊘ 10am-1pm & 3-7.30pm) Primarily the work of the Aragonese who ruled southern Italy in the 16th century, this sturdy redoubt retains elements built by the Angevins in previous centuries, on earlier Byzantine foundations. Partly ruinous by the 18th century, it's been thoroughly restored, and now houses the small **Antonio Lazzari Civic Museum**, exhibiting Messapian, Greek and Roman archaeology uncovered in Castro and the surrounding area. Its prize piece is a torso of the goddess Minerva (Athena), buried at the ancient city gates.

ⓘ Getting There & Away

STP Lecce runs a daily bus between Castro and Lecce (€4, 90 minutes).

Gallipoli
POP 20,700

Like Taranto (p158), Gallipoli is a two-part town: the modern hub is based on the mainland, while the older *centro storico* inhabits a small island that juts out into the Ionian Sea. With a raft of serene baroque architecture usurped only by Lecce, it is, arguably, the prettiest of Salento's smaller settlements.

The old town, ringed by the remains of its muscular 14th-century walls, is the best place to linger. It's punctuated by several baroque chapels, a traditional fishing port, a windswept sea drive, and narrow lanes barely wide enough to accommodate a Fiat *cinquecento* (500).

⊙ Sights

Gallipoli has some fine beaches, including the **Baia Verde**, just south of town. Nature enthusiasts will want to take a day trip to **Parco Regionale Porto Selvaggio**, about 20km north – a protected area of wild coastline with walking trails among the trees and diving off the rocky shore.

Cattedrale di Sant'Agata
CATHEDRAL

(www.cattedralegallipoli.it; Via Duomo 1; ⊘ hours vary) On the island, Gallipoli's 17th-century cathedral is a baroque beauty that could compete with anything in Lecce. Not surprisingly, Giuseppe Zimbalo, who helped beautify Lecce's Santa Croce basilica, worked on the facade. Inside, it's lined with paintings by local artists.

Frantoio Ipogeo HISTORIC SITE
(☑ 0833 26 42 42; Via Antonietta de Pace 87; €3; ⊘10am-mindnight Jul & Aug, shorter hours rest of year) This is only one of some 35 olive presses buried in the tufa rock below the town. It was here, between the 16th and early 19th centuries, that local workers pressed Gallipoli's olive oil, which was then stored in one of the 2000 cisterns carved beneath the old town.

🛏 Sleeping

Insula B&B €€
(☑ 329 8070056, 0833 20 14 13; www.bbinsulagallipoli.it; Via Antonietta de Pace 56; s/d €80/150; ⊘Apr-Oct; ✳@) A magnificent 16th-century building houses this memorable B&B. The five rooms are all different but share the same princely atmosphere with exquisite antiques, vaulted high ceilings and cool pastel paintwork. Directly adjacent to the cathedral, it couldn't be any more central.

Hotel Palazzo del Corso HOTEL €€€
(☑ 0833 26 40 40; www.hotelpalazzodelcorso.it; Corso Roma 145; r/ste €239/389; P✳@ 🛜🗎) It's worth forking out a bit extra for this beautiful new town hotel, if you fancy a bit of luxury. The rooms are furnished distinctively enough to avoid looking too corporate, there's a gym and a fantastic terrace (complete with a small swimming pool), and there's also a fine terrace restaurant, La DolceVita, serving lots of seafood (meals €40).

🍴 Eating

Gallipoli is famous for its red prawns and its soothing *spumone* layered ice cream.

Baguetteria de Pace SANDWICHES €
(Via Sant'Angelo 8; baguettes from €5; ⊘11am-2.30pm & 7-11pm) The Italian art of making truly exceptional sandwiches is practised assiduously here. Choose the dense Italian bread (or a baguette if you're feeling fluffy) and have the friendly staff stuff it with top-notch smallgoods, cheeses, vegetables and whatever else takes your fancy. It also sells craft beer and Salento wines.

Caffè Duomo CAFE €
(☑ 0833 26 44 02; Via Antonietta de Pace 72; desserts €9; ⊘7.30am-1am) For good Gallipoli *spumone* (layered ice cream with candied fruit and nuts) and refreshing *granite* (ices made with coffee, fresh fruit or locally grown pistachios and almonds), head to Caffè Duomo. The tables set up in the lee of the cathedral make a good place to people-watch as you refresh yourself.

★ La Puritate SEAFOOD €€€
(☑ 0833 26 42 05; Via Sant'Elia 18; meals €50; ⊘12.30-3pm & 7.30-10.30pm, closed Wed winter) Book ahead to ensure your table at *the* place for fish in this seafood-loving town. Follow the practically obligatory seafood *antipasti* with delicious *primi* (first courses). Anything fishy is good (especially the prawns, swordfish and tuna) and the picture windows allow splendid views of the waters whence it came.

ℹ Information

Tourist Office (☑ 0833 26 25 29; Via Antonietta de Pace 86; ⊘8am-9pm summer, 8am-1pm & 4-9pm Mon-Sat winter) Near the cathedral in the old town.

ℹ Getting There & Away

FSE (www.fseonline.it) buses and trains head direct to Lecce.

Taranto

The once-mighty Greek-Spartan colony of Taras is, today, a city of two distinct parts – a mildewed *centro storico* on a small artificial island protecting a lagoon (the Mar Piccolo), and a swankier new city replete with wide avenues laid out in a formal grid. The contrast between the two is sudden and sharp: the diminutive old town with its muscular Aragonese castle harbours a downtrodden, almost derelict air, while the larger new city is busier, plusher and bustling with commerce.

Not generally considered to be on the tourist circuit, Taranto is rimmed by modern industry, including a massive steelworks, and is home to Italy's second biggest naval base after La Spezia. Thanks to an illustrious Greek and Roman history, it has been bequeathed with one of the finest Magna Graecia museums in Italy. For this reason alone, it's worth a stopover.

Taranto

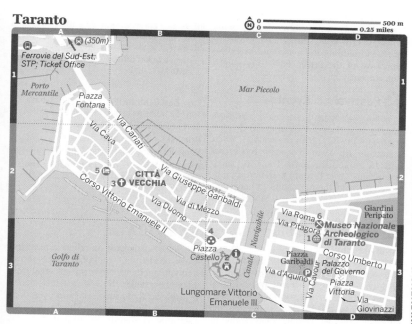

◉ Sights

★**Museo Nazionale
Archeologico di Taranto**   MUSEUM
(☏099 453 21 12; www.museotaranto.org; Via
Cavour 10; adult/reduced €5/2.50; ⊙8.30am-
7.30pm) Sitting unassumingly in a side street
in Taranto's new town is one of Italy's most
important archaeological museums, chief-
ly dedicated to the archaeology of ancient
Taras (Taranto). It houses, among other
artefacts, the largest collection of Greek
terracotta figures in the world. Also on display are fine collections of 1st-century BC
glassware, classic black-and-red Attic vases
and stunning gold and jewellery from Magna Grecia (Italy's ancient Greek cities), such
as a 4th-century BC bronze and terracotta
crown.

Cathedral   CATHEDRAL
(Piazza Duomo; ⊙4.30-7.30pm daily & 7.30am-
noon Sat & Sun) The 11th-century cathedral is
one of Puglia's oldest Romanesque buildings
and an extravagant treat. It's dedicated to
San Cataldo, an Irish monk who lived and
was buried here in the 7th century. Within,
the **Capella di San Cataldo** is a baroque
riot of frescoes and polychrome marble
inlay.

Taranto

◉ Top Sights

◉ Sights

⊜ Sleeping

⊗ Eating

Castello Aragonese   CASTLE
(☏0997 75 34 38; www.castelloaragonesetaranto.
it; Piazza Castello; ⊙9.30am-1.30am summer,
shorter hours rest of year) FREE Guarding the
swing bridge that joins the old and new
parts of town, this impressive 15th-century
structure, built on Norman and Byzantine
predecessors, was once a prison and is currently occupied by the Italian navy, which
has restored it. Multilingual and free guided
tours, mandatory to get inside, are led by naval officers throughout the day. Opposite are
the two remaining columns of the ancient
Temple of Poseidon (Piazza Castello).

PUGLIA, BASILICATA & CALABRIA BASILICATA

Palazzo del Governo
NOTABLE BUILDING

(Via Anfiteatro 4) The gigantic rust-red 1930s Palazzo del Governo, inaugurated by Mussolini, is a forbidding and masculine structure, expressive of the fascist ideas of strength then current.

★ Festivals & Events

Le Feste di Pasqua
RELIGIOUS

Taranto is famous for its Holy Week celebrations – the biggest in the region – when bearers in Ku Klux Klan–style robes carry icons around the town. There are three processions: the Perdoni, celebrating pilgrims; the Addolorata (lasting 12 hours but covering only 4km); and the Misteri (even slower at 14 hours to cover 2km).

🛏 Sleeping & Eating

Hotel Akropolis
HOTEL €€

(☑ 099 470 41 10; www.hotelakropolis.it; Vico Seminario 3; s/d €105/145; ❀@🌐) If Taranto's richly historic yet crumbling old town is ever to be reborn, it will be due to businesses such as this hotel – a converted medieval *palazzo* with a heavy Greek theme. It offers 13 stylish cream-and-white rooms, beautiful majolica-tiled floors, a panoramic rooftop terrace and an atmospheric bar and restaurant, decked out in stone, wood and glass.

Trattoria al Gatto Rosso
TRATTORIA €€

(☑ 340 5337800, 099 452 98 75; www.ristorantegattorosso.com; Via Cavour 2; meals €35; ⏰ noon-3pm & 7.30-11pm Tue-Sun) Unsurprisingly, seafood is the thing at the Red Cat. Relaxed and unpretentious, its heavy tablecloths, deep wine glasses and solid cutlery set the scene for full enjoyment of dishes such as spaghetti with local clams and slow-cooked swordfish with eggplant *caponata* (sweet-and-sour vegetable salad).

ℹ Information

Tourist Office (☑ 334 2844098; Castello Aragonese; ⏰ 9am-8pm summer, shorter hours rest of year)

ℹ Getting There & Away

BUS

Buses heading north and west depart from Porto Mercantile. **FSE** (☑ 080 546 21 11; www.fseonline.it) buses go to Bari; **STP** (☑ 080 975 26 19) buses go to Lecce, with a change at Monteparano.

Marozzi (☑ 080 5799 0211; www.marozzivt.it) has express services serving Rome's Stazione Tiburtina; **Autolinee Miccolis** (☑ 099 470 44 51; www.miccolis-spa.it) serves Naples.

The bus **ticket office** (⏰ 6am-1pm & 2-7pm) is at Porto Mercantile.

TRAIN

From **Bari Centrale** (Piazza Moro), Trenitalia and FSE trains go to the following destinations:

Bari €8.40, 1¼ hours, frequent

Brindisi €4.90, one hour, frequent

Rome from €50.50, six hours, five daily

AMAT (☑ 099 452 67 32; www.amat.taranto.it) buses run between the train station and the new city.

BASILICATA

Much of Basilicata is an otherworldly landscape of mountain ranges, trackless forests and villages that seem to sprout organically from the granite. Not easily penetrated, it is strategically located, and has been dominated by the Lucanians, Greeks, Romans, Germans, Lombards, Byzantines, Saracens, Normans and others. Being the plaything of such powers has not been conducive to a quiet or happy fate.

In the north the landscape is a fertile zone of gentle hills and deep valleys; the interior is dominated by the Lucanian Apennines and the Parco Nazionale del Pollino. The Tyrrhenian coast is a fissured wonderland of rocky coves and precariously sited villages. Here, Maratea is one of Italy's most charming seaside resorts.

But it is inland Matera, where primitive *sassi* (caves) lurk under grand cathedrals, that is Basilicata's most precious gem. The third-oldest continuously inhabited city in the world, it's intriguing, breathtaking and tragic in equal measures.

History

Basilicata spans Italy's 'instep', and is landlocked apart from slivers of Tyrrhenian and Ionian coastline. It was known to the Greeks and Romans as Lucania, after the Lucani tribe who lived here as far back as the 5th century BC. Their name survives in the 'Lucanian Dolomites', 'Lucanian cooking' and elsewhere. The Greeks also prospered in ancient Basilicata, possibly settling along the coastline at Metapontum and Erakleia as far back as the 8th century BC. Roman power came next, and the Punic Wars between that expanding power and Carthage. Hannibal, the ferocious Carthaginian general, rampaged through the region, making the city of Grumentum his base.

In the 10th century, the Byzantine Emperor Basil II (976–1025) bestowed his title, 'Basileus', on the region, overthrew the Saracens in southern Italy and reintroduced Christianity. The pattern of war and overthrow continued throughout the Middle Ages right up until the 19th century, as the Normans, Hohenstaufens, Angevins and Bourbons ceaselessly tussled over this strategic location. As talk of the Italian unification began to gain ground, Bourbon-sponsored loyalists took to Basilicata's mountains to oppose political change. Ultimately, they became the much-feared bandits of local lore who make scary appearances in writings from the late 19th and early 20th centuries. In the 1930s, Basilicata was used as a kind of open prison for political dissidents – most famously the painter, writer and doctor Carlo Levi – sent into exile to remote villages by the fascists.

The rugged region's hardscrabble history is perhaps best expressed in Levi's superb 1945 memoir, *Christ Stopped at Eboli* – a title suggesting Basilicata was beyond the hand of God, a place where pagan magic still existed and thrived.

Matera

POP 60,350

Matera, Basilicata's jewel, may be the third-longest continuously inhabited human settlement in the world. Natural caves in the tufa limestone, exposed as the Gravina cut its gorge, attracted the first inhabitants perhaps 7000 years ago. More elaborate structures were built atop them. Today, looking across the gorge to Matera's huddled *sassi* (cave dwellings) it seems you've been transported back to the ancient Holy Land. Indeed, the 'Città Sotterranea' (Underground City) has often been used for biblical scenes in films and TV.

Old Matera is split into two sections – the Sasso Barisano and the Sasso Caveoso – separated by a ridge upon which sits Matera's gracious *duomo* (cathedral). The *sassi*, many little more than one-room caves, once contained such appalling poverty and

CRIPTA DEL PECCATO ORIGINALE

A fascinating Benedectine site dating to the Lombard period, the **Cripta del Peccato Originale** (Crypt of Original Sin; ☏320 3345323; www.zetema.org; Contrada Pietrapenta; adult/child 7-17yr/child under 7yr €10/8/free; ☉10am-1pm & 4-7.30pm Tue-Sun Apr-Sep, shorter hours rest of year) houses well-preserved 8th-century frescoes – depicting vivid scenes from both Old and New Testaments – that have earned it a reputation as the 'Sistine Chapel' of Matera's cave churches. It's 7km south of Matera: group visits must be booked through the website, then joined at the ticket office (at Azienda Agricola Dragone on Contrada Pietrapenta) 30 minutes prior to the scheduled starting time.

unthinkable living conditions that in the 1950s Matera was denounced as the 'Shame of Italy', and the *sassi*-dwellers were moved on. Only in later decades has the value of this extraordinarily built environment been recognised.

⊙ Sights

The two *sassi* districts – the more restored, northwest-facing **Sasso Barisano** and the more impoverished, northeast-facing **Sasso Caveoso** – are both extraordinary, riddled with serpentine alleyways and staircases, and dotted with frescoed *chiese rupestri* (cave churches) created between the 8th and 13th centuries. Modern Matera still contains some 3000 habitable caves.

The *sassi* are accessible from several points. There's an entrance off Piazza San Francisco, or take Via delle Beccherie to Piazza del Duomo and follow the tourist itinerary signs to enter either Barisano or Caveoso. Sasso Caveoso is also accessible from Via Ridola.

For a great photograph, head out of town for about 3km on the Taranto–Laterza road and follow signs for the *chiese rupestri*. This takes you up on the Murgia Plateau to the **belvedere** (Contrada Murgia Timone), from where you have fantastic views of the plunging ravine and Matera.

Matera

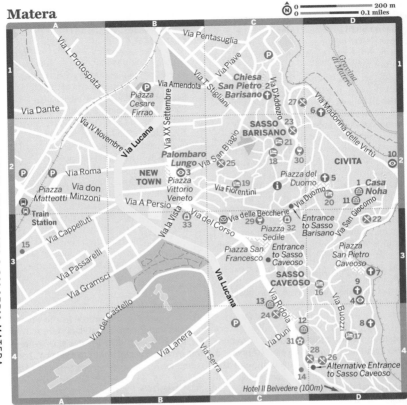

⊙ Sasso Barisano

Chiesa di Madonna delle Virtù &
Chiesa di San Nicola del Greci CHURCH
(☑ 377 4448885; www.caveheritage.it; Via Madonna delle Virtù; ☺ 10am-8pm Jun-Sep, shorter hours rest of year) FREE This monastic complex, one of the most important monuments in Matera, comprises dozens of chambers carved into the tufa limestone over two floors. Chiesa di Madonna delle Virtù was built in the 10th or 11th century and restored in the 17th century. Above it, the simple Chiesa di San Nicola del Greci is rich in frescoes. The complex was used in 1213 by Benedictine monks of Palestinian origin.

★ Chiesa San Pietro Barisano CHURCH
(☑ 342 0319991; www.oltrelartematera.it; Piazza San Pietro Barisano; adult/reduced €3/2, incl Chiesa di Santa Lucia alle Malve & Chiesa di Santa Maria €6/4.50; ☺ 10am-7pm Apr-Oct, to 4pm

Nov-Mar) Dating in its earliest parts to the 12th-century Saint Peter's, the largest of Matera's rupestrian churches, overlays an ancient honeycomb of niches where corpses were placed for draining. At the entrance level can be found 15th- and 16th-century frescoes of the Annunciation and a variety of saints. The empty frame of the altarpiece graphically illustrates the town's troubled recent history: the church was plundered when Matera was partially abandoned in the 1960s and '70s.

⊙ Sasso Caveoso

★ Casa Noha MUSEUM
(☑ 0835 33 54 52; www.visitfai.it/casanoha; Recinto Cavone 9; adult/reduced €5/3; ☺ 9am-7pm Apr-Oct, shorter hours rest of year) Highly recommended as a precursor to visiting the *sassi* themselves, this wonderful 25-minute multimedia exhibit, spread across three rooms of a 16th-century family home donated to the

Matera

PUGLIA, BASILICATA & CALABRIA MATERA

Fondo Ambiente Italiano, relates the astonishing and often painful social history of the town and its *sassi*. Your appreciation of Matera's unique history and renaissance, and the tribulations of the *sassi* dwellers, will be transformed.

Chiesa di San Pietro Caveoso CHURCH
(☎0835 31 15 10; Piazza San Pietro Caveoso 1; ☉mass 7pm Mon-Sat, 11am & 7pm Sun) FREE
The only church in the *sassi* not dug into the tufa rock, Chiesa di San Pietro Caveoso was originally built in 1300 and has a 17th-century Romanesque-baroque facade and frescoed timber ceiling.

Chiesa di Santa Maria di Idris CHURCH
(☎344 2763197; www.oltrelartematera.it; Piazza San Pietro Caveoso; adult/reduced €3/2, incl Chiesa San Pietro Barisano & Chiesa di Santa Lucia alle Malve €6/4.50; ☉10am-7pm Apr-Oct, to 4pm Nov-Mar) Dug into the Idris rock, this church has an unprepossessing facade, but the narrow corridor communicating with the recessed church of San Giovanni in Monterrone is richly decorated with 12th- to 17th-century frescoes.

Chiesa di Santa Lucia alle Malve CHURCH
(☎342 0919624; www.oltrelartematera.it; Rione Malve; adult/reduced €3/2, incl Chiesa San Pietro

Barisano & Chiesa di Santa Maria €6/4.50; ☉10am-7pm Apr-Oct, to 4pm Nov-Mar) Dating to the 8th century, when it was built as the Benedictine Order's first foothold in Matera, this cliff-face church has a number of 13th-century frescoes, including an unusual breastfeeding Madonna. The church originally comprised three aisles, with two later adapted as dwellings.

Casa-Grotta di Vico Solitario HISTORIC SITE
(€3; ☉9.30am-late) For a glimpse of life in old Matera, visit this historic *sasso* off Via Bruno Buozzi. There's a bed in the middle, a loom, a room for manure and a section for a pig and a donkey. You also have access to a couple of neighbouring caves: in one, a black-and-white film depicts gritty pre-restoration Matera.

Museo della Scultura
Contemporanea MUSEUM
(MUSMA; ☎366 9357768; www.musma.it; Via San Giacomo; adult/reduced €5/3.50; ☉10am-2pm & 4-8pm Tue-Sun Apr-Sep, shorter hours rest of year) The setting of this fabulous museum of contemporary sculpture – deeply recessed caves and the frescoed rooms of the 16th-century Palazzo Pomarici – is as extraordinary as the exhibits. Italian sculpture from the

late 19th century to the present day is the principal focus, but you can also see beautiful examples of graphic art, jewellery and ceramics.

◉ New Town

The nucleus of the new town is **Piazza Vittorio Veneto**, an excellent, bustling meeting point for a *passeggiata* (sociable evening stroll). It's surrounded by elegant churches and richly adorned *palazzi* with their backs deliberately turned on the *sassi*: an attempt by the bourgeois to block out the shameful poverty the *sassi* once represented.

★ Palombaro Lungo   HISTORIC SITE
(☑ 339 3638332; Piazza Vittorio Veneto; guided tour €3; ☉ 10am-1pm & 3-6pm) This giant cistern, arguably as magnificent as a subterranean cathedral, is one of Matera's great sights. Lying under the city's main square with arches carved out of the existing rock, it is mind-boggling in its scale and ingenuity, and was still supplying water to Materans within living memory. Book ahead for a 25-minute tour with the multilingual guides, who explain its conception and history (English-language tours generally leave at 10.30am, 12.30pm, 3.30pm and 5.30pm).

Museo Nazionale d'Arte Medievale
e Moderna della Basilicata   MUSEUM
(☑ 0835 25 62 11; Piazzetta Pascoli 1, Palazzo Lanfranchi; adult/18-25yr/child €3/1.50/free; ☉ 9am-8pm Thu-Tue) The Palazzo Lanfranchi, built as a seminary incorporating an earlier church in the 17th century, now houses this intriguing museum of sacred and contemporary art. The stars of the show here are Carlo Levi's paintings, including the panoramic mural *Lucania '61* depicting peasant life in biblical Technicolor. There are also some centuries-old sacred art from the *sassi*.

Cathedral   CATHEDRAL
(☑ 0835 33 29 08; www.matera-irsina.chiesacattolica.it; Piazza del Duomo; ☉ 9am-1pm & 4-7pm) Set high up on a spur between the two natural bowls of the *sassi*, the wan, graceful exterior of the 13th-century Puglian-Romanesque cathedral makes the neobaroque excess within all the more of a surprise. Following 13 years of renovation, it's possible once again to admire the ornate capitals, sumptuous chapels, 17th-century frescoes, 13th-century Byzantine Madonna and two 12th-century frescoed crypts, uncovered in the works. Note the pediments mounted on the cathedral's altars, which come from Greek temples at Metaponto.

Museo Nazionale Ridola   MUSEUM
(☑ 0835 31 00 58; www.beniculturali.it; Via Ridola 24; adult/reduced €2.50/1.25; ☉ 9am-8pm Tue-Sun, 2-8pm Mon) This impressive collection includes local Neolithic finds and some remarkable Greek pottery, such as the *Cratere Mascheroni,* a huge urn more than 1m high.

EXPLORING THE GRAVINA GORGE

In the picturesque landscape of the Murgia Plateau, the **Matera Gravina** cuts a rough gouge in the earth, a 200m-deep canyon pockmarked with abandoned caves and villages and roughly 150 mysterious *chiese rupestri* (cave churches). The area is protected as the **Parco della Murgia Materana**, an 80-sq-km wild park formed in 1990 and, since 2007, included in Matera's Unesco World Heritage site. You can hike from the *sassi* into the gorge; steps lead down from the parking place near the **Monasterio di Santa Lucia** (Via Madonna delle Virtù; ☉ 7.30am-1pm & 5-8.30pm). At the bottom of the gorge you have to ford a river and then climb up to the belvedere (p161) on the other side; this takes roughly two hours.

Cave churches accessible from the belvedere include San Falcione, Sant'Agnese and Madonna delle Tre Porte. The belvedere is connected by road to the **Jazzo Gattini** (☑ 0835 33 22 62; www.ceamatera.it; Contrada Murgia Timone; ☉ 9.30am-2.30pm & 4-6.30pm Apr-Oct, shorter hours rest of year) visitor centre, housed in an old sheepfold. Guided hikes can be organised here, as can walks to the nearby Neolithic village of **Murgia Timone**. For longer forays into the park, including a long day trek to the town of Montescaglioso, consider a guided hike with **Ferula Viaggi** (☑ 0835 33 65 72; www.ferulaviaggi.it; Via Cappelluti 34; ☉ 9am-1.30pm & 3.30-7pm Mon-Sat).

Beware: paths and river crossings in the park can be treacherous during and after bad weather.

☞ Tours

There are plenty of official guides for the *sassi* – find one to suit you at www.sassi web.it.

Altieri Viaggi   TOURS
(☑ 346 6453440, 0835 31 43 59; www.altieri viaggi.it; Via Ridola 61; ☺ 9am-9pm) Runs tours around the *sassi* and rupestrian churches of Matera and the Parco della Murgia, starting from €15 for a 50-minute tour (minimum four people). Altieri also offers plenty of other trips, including hiking and *sassi* tours by *ape calessino* (auto rickshaw). Tours usually end with a tasting of typical local products.

✸ Festivals & Events

Sagra della Madonna della Bruna   RELIGIOUS
(☺ 2 Jul) This week-long celebration of Matera's patron saint has 14th-century roots. The culminating day, 2 July, begins at dawn with the colourful 'Procession of Shepherds', in which an image of the Virgin is carried through Matera's neighbourhoods. The finale is the *assalto al carro*, when the crowd descends on the ornately decorated main float and tears it to pieces.

Gezziamoci   MUSIC
(☑ 331 4711589; www.onyxjazzclub.it; ☺ summer) Run by the Onyx Jazz Club since 1987, the Jazz Festival of Basilicata brings music to diffuse venues around Matera: not only bars, but the cavernous, acoustically rich *sassi* and the surrounding Parco della Murgia Materana.

🛏 Sleeping

Matera's unique appeal has seen accommodation options mushroom, across the *sassi* and the new town. Take your pick: a smartly refurbished *sasso*, a room in a repurposed *palazzo*, or something more modern in the new town. Cheaper options can still be found.

La Dolce Vita B&B   B&B €
(☑ 328 7111121, 0835 31 03 24; www.ladolcevi tamatera.it; Rione Malve 51; r €80; ☎) ⏴ This delightful, ecofriendly B&B in Sasso Caveoso comprises two self-contained apartments with solar panels, rainwater recycling, a scenic terrace and cool, comfortable furnishings. Owners Vincenzo and Carla are passionate about Matera and are mines of information on the *sassi*.

Il Vicinato   B&B €
(☑ 380 1828935; www.ilvicinato.com; Piazzetta San Pietro Caveoso 7; s/d €60/90; ❄☎) Run by Luigi and Teresa, 'The Neighbourhood' is wonderfully located in Sasso Caveoso, in a building dating in parts to around 1600. Rooms are decorated in clean modern lines, with views across to the Murgia Plateau. As well as the standard rooms, there's a room with a balcony and a small apartment, each with an independent entrance.

Locanda di San Martino   HOTEL €€
(☑ 0835 25 66 00; www.locandadisanmartino.it; Via Fiorentini 71; d from €134; ❄☎⛲) The main lure of this Sasso Caveoso hotel is its subterannean *termae romanae* (Roman baths). Cave accommodation, with niches and rustic brick floors, is set around a warren of cobbled paths and courtyards. Featuring a *tepidarium* (warm pool), *caldarium* (steam bath) and other basics of classical Roman baths, the spa is open only to adults, and costs €20.

★ Hotel Il Belvedere   HOTEL €€
(☑ 0835 31 17 02; www.hotelbelvedere.matera. it; Via Casalnuovo 133; d from €134; ☎) This cave boutique looks unremarkable from its street-side perch on the edge of the Sasso Caveoso, but you'll feel your jaw start to drop as you enter its luxurious entrails and spy the spectacle of Old Matera sprawling below a jutting terrace. Cavernous rooms sport mosaics, mood lighting and curtained four-poster beds. Two-night minimums apply in August.

Sassi Hotel   HOTEL €€
(☑ 0835 33 10 09; www.hotelsassi.it; Via San Giovanni Vecchio 89; d/ste from €119/165; ❄☎) Established in 1996 (making it the first hotel in the *sassi*), the Sassi Hotel is set in a rambling edifice dating in parts to the 16th century. Some of the 35 rooms are set into the rock, and some built above it. Singles are smallish but doubles are gracefully furnished and those with balconies have superb views of the cathedral.

L'Hotel in Pietra   BOUTIQUE HOTEL €€
(☑ 0835 34 40 40; www.hotelinpietra.it; Via San Giovanni Vecchio 22; s/d/ste from €70/115/230; ❄☎) The lobby of this hotel in Sasso Barisano makes sensitive use of a former 13th-century chapel complete with soaring arches, while the nine rock-cut rooms combine soft golden stone with the natural cave

THE RESURRECTION OF LA CITTÀ SOTTERRANEA

Named 2019 European City of Culture, Matera has taken huge strides in burying the unpleasant ghosts of its past. In the 1950s and '60s, the town and its ancient cave-houses were ingloriously considered to be the shame of Italy, a giant slum where malaria was rampant and a desperate populace subsisted on or below the breadline. After years of political squabbling, Matera's inhabitants were eventually evacuated (some forcibly) and resettled in a burgeoning new town higher up the gorge. Neglected and uncared for, the old town and its *sassi* (former cave dwellings) fell into a steep decline. By the 1980s old Matera was a virtual ghost town, an unholy mess of unlivable abodes.

Help came with a three-pronged attack of film-making, tourism and Unesco intervention. Italian director, Pier Paolo Pasolini was one of the first to put Matera on the map, making use of the town's biblical landscapes in his 1964 film, *The Gospel According to St Matthew*. The success of the film and its eerie backdrops inspired others, including Hollywood heavyweights such as Mel Gibson, who arrived in Matera in 2004 to film *The Passion of the Christ*.

Celluloid fame led to a trickle of curious tourists and this, in turn, fuelled an increasing desire among Italians to clean up the once-dilapidated *sassi* and showcase their historical value for future generations. In 1993, Unesco gave the town an extra boost when it named Matera's *sassi* and rupestrian churches a World Heritage Site. Progress has been rapid since. Bars and restaurants now inhabit once abandoned cave-houses and meticulous restoration work has saved ancient frescoes from almost certain decay.

Priming itself for 2019, Matera meticulously restored its 13th-century cathedral and opened the interactive museum, Casa Noha, which tells the story of Matera's recent past in blunt, uncensored detail. In 2015, the *sassi* provided a backdrop for the remaking of the movie *Ben Hur*, starring Morgan Freeman and Jack Huston.

interior. Furnishings are Zen-style with low beds, and the bathrooms are super stylish and include vast sunken tubs.

★ **Palazzo Gattini**   HOTEL €€€
(☑ 0835 33 43 58; www.palazzogattini.it; Piazza del Duomo 13; d/ste from €300/480; P🔊📶❄) The Gattini is the Matera's plushest hotel, located in the former palatial home of the city's most noble family. And if the nobility of yesteryear could see the palace's 20 luxuriously refurbished rooms today, with their smooth stone walls, quality furnishings and intricate detailing, they'd surely still feel right at home. Prices drop during the week.

✗ Eating

I Vizi degli Angeli   GELATO €
(☑ 0835 31 06 37; www.ivizidegliangeli.it; Via Ridola 36; medium cone €2.50; ⊙ noon-11pm Thu-Tue) 'The Angels' Vices', an artisinal gelato 'laboratory' on the busy promenade of Via Domenico Ridola, is Matera's best. Alongside classics such as pistachio, you'll find experimental flavours such as grapefruit with pink pepper and thyme and mallow, which taste even better than they read.

★ **Soul Kitchen**   ITALIAN €€
(☑ 0835 31 15 68; www.ristorantesoulkitchen.it; Via Casalnuovo 27; meals €35; ⊙ 12.15-2.45pm & 7.30-11pm Fri-Wed) If you thought Basilicata was somehow lagging behind the rest of Italy in the food stakes, correct your prejudice with pleasure at Soul Kitchen: this cavernous restaurant with sharp colour accents epitomises Matera's ambitious drive to reinvent its image. Grab a pew on the mezzanine and tuck into recognisably Basilicatan dishes that have been given modern twists, and presented with artistic aplomb.

Osteria al Casale   OSTERIA €€
(☑ 329 8021190; www.osterialcasale.it; Via Casale 24; meals €30; ⊙ 1-3pm & 8-11pm Thu-Tue; 🍴) While al Casale's *secondi* are uniformly meaty, this charming *osteria* does offer more vegetarian options than most. *Antipasti* such as *sformatino* (a 'mis-shapen' dumpling) of eggplant with tomato and basil and *primi* such as truffle ravioli with Parmesan and toasted pinenuts provide enough options to piece together an excellent non-carnivorous meal.

Dedalo
ITALIAN €€

(📞 0835 197 30 60; www.dedalomatera.it; Via D'Addozio 136-140; meals €40; ⊘12.30-2.30pm & 7.30-10.30pm Wed-Mon) Dedalo's motto 'sensi sommersi' (submerged senses) will either hint at pretension, or indicate the lengths this classy fine diner goes to to wow its clientele. Surrounded by modern art in a softly lit and impeccably stylish cave, you can expect top-notch service and divine dishes such as eggplant agnolotti with tender *scottona* (yearling beef).

La Grotta nei Sassi
ITALIAN €€

(📞 0835 33 48 91; www.ristorantesassidimatera.com; Via Rosario 73; meals €40; ⊘12.30-3pm & 7.30-11.30pm Tue-Sun) This welcoming little cave restaurant is a great bet for Materan classics and spanking fresh seafood. Try the tuna tagliata, stuffed mussels or *orecchiette* with turnip-tops, but leave room for dessert. In good weather, choose the small terrace overlooking Sasso Barisano over the cosy twin-chambered interior.

L'Abbondanza Lucana
ITALIAN €€

(📞0835 33 45 74; Via Buozzi 11; meals €35; ⊘noon-3pm Tue-Sun, 7-11pm Tue-Sat) The paradoxical bounty of Lucania's *cucina povera* is laid out before you in this stone cellar in Sasso Caveoso. For a fantastic introduction to a range of *prodotti tipici* (typical products) from the region, start with the Lucanian tasting plate, laden with delights such as wild boar, baked ricotta and a soup of chestnuts with Sarconi's famous beans.

Baccanti
ITALIAN €€€

(📞 0835 33 37 04; www.baccantiristorante.com; Via Sant'Angelo 58-61; meals €50; ⊘1-3.30pm & 8-11.30pm Tue-Sat, 1-4pm Sun) Baccanti is as classy as a cave can be. The design is simple glamour against the low arches of the cavern; the dishes – perhaps ash-baked potato with stracciatella cheese and crumbled *taralli* (crackers) or ravioli with *pezzente* (pork sausage) and beans – make refined use of robust local ingredients; and the gorge views are sublime.

Drinking & Entertainment

Options for drinking and socialising have mushroomed, along with Matera's renaissance. You'll find wine bars, pubs and *enotecas* along Via Domenico Ridola, Via Fiorentina, Via San Biagio and Via delle Beccherie, and dotted throughout the *sassi*.

★ Vicolo Cieco
WINE BAR

(📞 338 8550984; Via Fiorentini 74; ⊘6pm-2am Tue-Thu, from noon Fri-Sun) Matera's renaissance and new-found relaxed vitality come to the fore at this wine-bar in a typical cavehouse off Sasso Barisano's main drag. The eccentric decor signals its friendly, upbeat spirit – retro jukeboxes, a wall-mounted Scalextric track, chairs cut in half and glued to the wall in the name of art, and a chandelier of repurposed cutlery.

Birrificio 79
MICROBREWERY

(📞 328 3587369; Via delle Beccherie 54; ⊘noon-3pm & 7pm-1am) This diminutive microbrewery spills out onto the adjoining piazza, providing tables, occasional live music and permanent good cheer to help the Black Lake stout and Little John English ale down. Hearty plates (perhaps lasagna with artichokes, or roast-beef carpaccio) provide ballast for longer sessions.

Area 8
CINEMA, LIVE MUSIC

(📞 333 3369788; http://area8.it; Via Casalnuovo 15; ⊘7.30pm-midnight Thu & Sun, to 3am Fri & Sat) This unusual cafe/bar and 'nano-theatre' is a production agency by day, but comes alive four nights a week to host film screenings, live music, product launches and other events beneath its beautiful creamy arches.

🛍 Shopping

Il Buongustaio
FOOD & DRINKS

(📞0835 33 19 82; www.ilbuongustaiomatera.it; Piazza Veneto 1; ⊘8.30am-1.30pm Mon-Sat & 5-8.30pm Fri, Sat & Mon-Wed) With walls and deli cabinets bursting with preserves, pasta, cheeses, sweetmeats and smallgoods, this is the place to stock up on Matera's *prodotti tipici*.

Geppetto
ARTS & CRAFTS

(📞0835 33 18 57; Piazza Sedile 19; ⊘9.30am-1pm & 3.30-8pm) This craft shop stands out among the tawdrier outlets selling tufa lamps and tiles. Its speciality is the *cuccù*, a brightly painted ceramic whistle in the shape of a cockerel, which was once prized by Matera's children. The whistles were traditionally considered a symbol of good luck and fertility.

ℹ Information

Basilicata Turistica (www.aptbasilicata.it) is the official tourist website with useful information on history, culture, attractions and sights. Sassiweb (www.sassiweb.it) is another informative website on Matera. Quite a few private operators

PUGLIA, BASILICATA & CALABRIA MATERA

also advertise themselves as tourist infomation offices. They're there to sell tours, generally, but can still give good (if not impartial) advice.

The maps *Carta Turistica di Matera* and *Matera: Percorsi Turistici* (€1.50), available from various travel agencies, bookstores and hotels around town, describe a number of itineraries through the *sassi* and the gorge.

Presidio Ospedaliero Madonna delle Grazie (☑ 0835 25 31 11; Contrada Cattedra Ambulante; ☺ 24hr) About 1km southeast of the centre.

Parco Archeologico Storico Naturale delle Chiese Rupestri del Materano (☑ 0835 33 61 66; www.parcomurgia.it; Via Dolori 10; ☺ 9.30am-6.30pm) Materan office of the Parco della Murgia Materana.

Police Station (☑ 0835 37 81 11; Via Gattini 12)

Post Office (☑ 0835 25 70 40; Via del Corso 15; ☺ 8am-1.30pm Mon-Fri, to 12.30pm Sat; 🖥)

❶ Getting There & Away

BUS

The bus station is north of Piazza Matteotti, next to the subterranean train station.

Grassani (☑ 0835 72 14 43; www.grassani.it) For Potenza

Marino (www.marinobus.it) For Naples

Marozzi (☑ 06 225 21 47; www.marozzivt.it) For Rome

Pugliairbus (☑ 080 579 02 11; www.aeroporti dipuglia.it) For Bari airport

SITA (☑ 0835 38 50 07; www.sitabus.it) For Taranto and Metaponto

TRAIN

Ferrovie Appulo-Lucane (FAL; ☑ 800 050500; http://ferrovieappulolucane.it) For Bari.

Metaponto

POP 1050

In stark contrast to the dramatic Tyrrhenian coast, Basilicata's Ionian coast is undistinguished and dotted with large tourist resorts. Metaponto, once a Greek Achaean colony known as Metapontum, is an exception. A sprawling archaeological site, all that remains of a prosperous city of tens of thousands, is twinned with a museum built expressly to house the archaeology the site keeps giving up. Together they bring alive the ancient civilisation of Magna Graecia in southern Italy.

Archaeologists studying the undisturbed ruins have managed to map the entire ancient urban plan. Settled by Greeks in the 8th and 7th centuries BC, Metaponto's most famous resident was Pythagoras (he of the theorem), who founded a school here after being ban-ished from Crotone (in Calabria) in the 6th century BC. After Pythagoras died, his house and school were incorporated into the Temple of Hera (known as the Tavole Palatine), whose elegantly ruined columns remain.

◎ Sights

Museo Archeologico Nazionale   MUSEUM
(☑ 0835 74 53 27; Via Aristea 21; €2.50; ☺ 9am-8pm Tue-Sun, 2-8pm Mon) This small but important museum is a real throwback to the days when precious artefacts of the past sat soberly behind glass, accompanied only by simple interpretative cards. Mirrors, ceramics, votive offerings and other relics of the area's Greek and Roman past are laid out for quiet contemplation. Signage is in Italian.

Parco Archeologico   ARCHAEOLOGICAL SITE
(☑ 0835 74 53 27; ☺ 9am-1hr before sunset) FREE
Not to be confused with the Tavole Palatine, the Parco Archeologico is a larger, if less immediately impressive collection of Metaponto ruins that contains the remains of a Greek theatre and the Doric Tempio di Apollo Licio. The classical coastal Greek colony that once flourished here can be readily imagined, walking through the quiet fields and shin-high remains. It's especially interesting to see where the artefacts displayed in the Museo Archeologico Nazionale, 2km northwest, came from.

Tavole Palatine   ARCHAEOLOGICAL SITE
(Palatine Tables; Strada Statale 106 Jonica; ☺ 9am-1hr before sunset) FREE The remains of the 6th-century Temple of Hera – 15 columns and sections of pavement – are Metaponto's most impressive sight. They're known as the Tavole Palatine (Palatine Tables), since knights, or paladins, are said to have gathered here before heading to the Crusades. The ruins are 3km north of town, just off the highway – to find them, follow the slip road for Taranto onto the SS106.

🛏 Sleeping

Palazzo Margherita   HOTEL €€€
(☑ 0835 54 90 60; www.coppolaresorts.com/palaz zomargherita; Corso Umberto I 64; d/ste from €520/1000; 🖥) Located near the birthplace of director Francis Ford Coppola's grandfather, this 19th-century *palazzo* has been thoughtfully resurrected as a boutique hotel, complete with colourful frescoes and tiles. There are a number of bars scattered about the property and guests can learn from the chefs as they prepare lip-smacking Basilicatan fare.

Potenza

POP 67,200

Basilicata's regional capital, Potenza, has been ravaged by earthquakes (the last in 1980) and, as the highest town in the region, broils in summer and shivers in winter. You may find yourself passing through as it's a major transport hub.

Potenza's few sights are in the old centre, at the top of the hill. To get there, take the elevators from Piazza Vittorio Emanuele II. The ecclesiastical highlight is the cathedral, erected in the 12th century and rebuilt in the 18th. The elegant Via Pretoria, flanked by a boutique or two, makes a pleasant traffic-free stroll, especially during the *passeggiata*.

The town centre straddles a high ridge, east to west. To the south lie the Trenitalia and Ferrovie Appulo-Lucane train stations, connected to the centre by buses 1 and 10.

◉ Sights

Cathedral   CATHEDRAL
(☑0971 2 24 88; Via Scafarelli 6; ☺7.30am-1pm & 5-8pm) Potenza's Cattedrale di San Gerardo is the town's ecclesiastical highlight. Originally erected in the 12th century but rebuilt in the 18th (since then it has survived bombs and earthquakes) it houses the remains of Saint Gerard, Potenza's patron saint.

⌂ Sleeping

B&B Al Convento   B&B €
(☑348 3307693; http://alconventopotenza.it; Vicolo San Michele Arcangelo; s/d €55/80; ❄⛧) In central Potenza, Al Convento is a great accommodation choice. It's in an early 19th century building (funnily enough, once a convent), housing a mix of polished antiques and design classics.

ⓘ Getting There & Away

Grassani (☑0835 72 14 43; www.grassani.it) has buses to Matera (€8, 1¾ hours, five daily). Buses leave from Via Appia 185 and also stop near the Scalo Inferiore Trenitalia train station. **Liscio** (☑0971 5 46 73; www.autolineeliscio. it) buses serve various cities including Rome (€25, 4½ hours).

There are regular train services from Potenza to Foggia (€6, 2¼ hours), Salerno (from €6, 1¾ hours) and Taranto (€8.20, 2¼ hours). For Bari (from €15, four hours, four daily), take the **Ferrovie Appulo-Lucane** (☑800 050500; http://ferrovieappulolucane.it) train at Potenza Superiore station.

Appennino Lucano

The Appennino Lucano (Lucanian Apennines) bite Basilicata in half like a row of jagged teeth. Sharply rearing up south of Potenza, they protect the lush Tyrrhenian coast and leave the Ionian shores gasping in the semi-arid heat. Much of the area is protected by the **Parco Nazionale Dell'Appennino Lucano**, inaugurated in 2007 and the second-youngest of Italy's 25 national parks .

Aside from its gorgeous mountain terrain, the park's most iconic site is the abandoned Roman town of Grumentum (p170), 75km south of Potenza and just outside the town of Grumento Nova. In the granite eyries of Pietrapertosa and Castelmezzano, it can also lay claim to two of Italy's most strikingly situated hill towns.

Castelmezzano & Pietrapertosa

The two mountaintop villages of Castelmezzano (elevation 985m) and Pietrapertosa (elevation 1088m), ringed by the Lucanian Dolomites, are spectacular. Basilicata's highest villages, they're often swathed in cloud, making you wonder why anyone would build here – in territory best suited to goats.

Castelmezzano is surely one of Italy's most theatrical villages: the houses huddle along an impossibly narrow ledge that falls away in gorges to the Rio di Caperrino. Pietrapertosa is possibly even more amazing: the Saracen fortress at its pinnacle is difficult to spot as it is carved out of the mountain. Despite difficulties of access, the towns can be swarmed by Italian tourists on weekends and holidays. Foreign visitors are scarcer.

You can 'fly' between these two dramatic settlements courtesy of Il Volo dell'Angelo, two heart-in-mouth ziplines across the void.

⚹ Activities

★**Il Volo dell'Angelo**   ADVENTURE SPORTS
(Angel's Flight; ☑Castelmezzano 0971 98 60 20, Pietrapertosa 0971 98 31 10; www.volodellangelo. com; singles €35-40, couples €63-72; ☺9.30am-6.30pm May-Oct) The extraordinary situation of Pietrapertosa and Castelmezzano, two steepling Basilican hill towns, is the inspiration behind 'Angel's Flight', two ziplines running over 1400m between the peaks, dropping over 100m and reaching speeds of up to 120kmh. Tandem flights are possible, providing the couple's combined weight

GRUMENTUM

The **Parco Archeologico di Grumentum** (☑ 0975 6 50 74; Contrada Spineta, Grumento Nova; incl museum €2.50; ⊗ 9am-1hr before sunset; P) – sometimes known as Basilicata's 'Little Pompeii' – contains remains of a theatre, an amphitheatre, Roman baths, a forum, two temples and a *domus* (villa) with mosaic floors. Knowing something of its history ratchets up the interest: among its illustrious inhabitants numbers Hannibal, who made it his headquarters in the 3rd century BC. Its swansong came when the Saracen invasions of the 10th century forced its abandonment in favour of Grumento Nova, on a nearby hill.

Many of the artefacts found here are on display at the nearby **Museo Nazionale dell'Alta Val d'Agri** (www.beniculturali.it; incl archaeological site €2.50; ⊗ 9am-8pm Tue-Sun, 2-8pm Mon; P).

doesn't exceed 150kg. It's only open daily in August; check the website for details.

🛏 Sleeping & Eating

La Casa di Penelope e Cirene   B&B €
(☑ 338 3132196; Via Garibaldi 32, Pietrapertosa; d €90) This delightful B&B, the 'House of Penelope and Cirene', offers just two handsomely furnished rooms in the heart of Pietrapertosa. There's a sitting room, kitchenette, and great views over the Lucanian Dolomites.

Al Becco della Civetta   RISTORANTE €€
(☑ 0971 98 62 49; Vico I Maglietta 7, Castelmezzano; meals €35; ⊗ 1-3pm & 8-10pm) Don't miss the authentic Lucano restaurant Al Becco della Civetta in Castelmezzano, which serves excellent regional cuisine based on seasonal local ingredients. It also offers 22 traditionally furnished, simple whitewashed rooms (doubles €90), some with lots of dark wood, others with vivid murals, and many with fabulous views. Booking recommended.

❶ Getting There & Away

SITA SUD (☑ 0971 50 68 11; www.sita sudtrasporti.it) bus 102 runs twice a day between Potenza and Castelmezzano (€5, 80 minutes) but you'll probably want your own wheels to explore properly.

Venosa

POP 11,850

About 70km north of Potenza, unassuming Venosa was once the thriving Roman colony of Venusia, which owed much of its prosperity to its position on the Appian Way. It was also the birthplace of the poet Horace (65 BC). The main reason to come here is to see the remains of Basilicata's largest monastic complex.

Venosa's main square, **Piazza Umberto I**, is dominated by a 15th-century Aragonese castle; within is the small **Museo Archeologico** (☑ 0972 3 60 95; Piazza Umberto I 49; adult/reduced €2.50/1.25; ⊗ 9am-8pm Wed-Mon, from 2pm Tue), while to the northeast of the centre lie Venosa's two other principal attractions, the ruins of the **Roman settlement** (⊗ 9am-1hr before dusk Wed-Mon, from 2pm Tue) and the graceful later ruins of **Abbazia della Santissima Trinità** (☑ 0972 3 42 11).

🛏 Sleeping

Hotel Orazio   HOTEL €
(☑ 0972 3 11 35; www.hotelorazio.it; Vittorio Emanuele II 142; s/d/tr €45/65/85) Named for Venosa's most famous son, the Roman poet Horace, this hotel occupies a 17th-century palace complete with antique majolica tiles, frescoes, marble floors and a terrace with beautiful views. The Lacolla family and their staff do all they can to make your stay comfortable.

❶ Getting There & Away

Venosa can be reached by taking highway S658 north from Potenza and exiting at Barile onto the S93. Buses run Monday to Saturday from Potenza (€3.30, two hours, two daily).

Basilicata's Western Coast

Resembling a mini Amalfi, Basilicata's Tyrrhenian coast is short but sweet. Squeezed between Calabria and Campania's Cilento peninsula, it shares the same beguiling characteristics: hidden coves and pewter sandy beaches backed by majestic coastal cliffs. The SS18 threads a spectacular route along the mountains to the coast's star attraction: the charming seaside settlements of Maratea.

Maratea

POP 5150

A sparkling, sun-drenched contrast to Basilicata's rugged interior, Maratea is a pure delight. In fact a disparate collection of placid coastal villages, rather than a single place, it's the centrepiece of Basilicata's Tyrrhenian coast. Embellished with lush vegetation, riven by rock-walled coves below well-tended hillside villages, Maratea's joys might be compared to those of the Amalfi. Perhaps the biggest, most welcome disparity is the number of tourists – far fewer here, and notably fewer non-Italians. You can climb the steep hill above Maratea to see the ruins of the prior settlement, take boat cruises and fishing trips, poke around venerable hilltop churches (44 of them), or just kick back with a coffee in a perfectly photogenic piazza, watching the sun play on the waters below.

⊙ Sights & Activities

The deep green hillsides that encircle this tumbling conurbation offer excellent walking trails, providing a number of easy day trips to the surrounding hamlets of Acquafredda and Fiumicello, with its small sandy beach. The tourist office (p173) in Maratea Borgo's main square can provide an excellent map.

Maratea Superiore   RUINS

FREE The ruins of the original settlement of Maratea, supposedly founded by the Greeks, are situated at a higher elevation than the current village on a rocky escarpment just below the Christ the Redeemer statue. Abandoned houses with trees growing in their midst, some thought to be over 1000 years old, have long been given over to nature.

Statue of Christ the Redeemer   STATUE

The symbol of Maratea, visible from multiple vantage points along the coast, this 22m-high statue of Christ faces inland towards the Basilica di San Biagio. Slightly smaller than Rio's Christ the Redeemer, it's made of concrete faced with Carrara marble and sits atop 644m-high Monte San Biagio. A dramatic winding asphalt road leads to the top, although it's more fun to walk the steep path (number 1) that starts off Via Cappuccini in Maratea Borgo.

Marvin Escursioni   BOATING

(📞 338 8777899; Porto di Maratea; half-day boat trips €25; ⊗ 9am-1pm & 2.30-6pm) This operator based in the Porto di Maratea offers half-day boat tours that include visits to surrounding grottoes and coves.

🛏 Sleeping

★**Locanda delle Donne Monache**   HOTEL €€

(📞 0973 87 61 39; www.locandamonache.com; Via Mazzei 4, Maratea Borgo; d/ste €175/335; ⊗ Apr-Oct; P ❄ @ 🕾 ≋) Overlooking the medieval *borgo,* this exclusive hotel is in a converted 18th-century convent with a suitably lofty setting. It's a hotch-potch of vaulted corridors, terraces and gardens fringed with bougainvillea and lemon trees. The rooms are elegantly decorated in pastel shades and there's a fitness centre, Jacuzzi and a stunning panoramic outdoor pool.

Hotel Villa Cheta Elite   HOTEL €€€

(📞 0973 87 81 34; www.villacheta.it; Via Canonica 48, Acquafredda; r from €224; ⊗ Apr-Oct; P ❄ 🕾 ≋) Set in an art nouveau villa in Acquafredda, this hotel is like a piece of plush Portofino towed several hundred kilometres south. Enjoy a broad terrace with spectacular views of the Gulf of Policastro, a fabulous restaurant (1pm to 2pm and 8pm to 9.30pm), a pool and large rooms where antiques mix seamlessly with modern

> ### ℹ ORIENTATION
>
> What is usually referred to as Maratea is actually a collection of small settlements split into several parts, some of them walkable if you're relatively fit and the weather cooperates. Maratea's main train station sits roughly in the middle.
>
> The **Porto** is clustered around a small harbour and is about a 10-minute walk below the station (towards the sea). The 'village' of **Fiumicello** is in the same direction, but reached by turning right rather than left once you've passed under the railway bridge. The main historic centre, known as **Maratea Borgo**, is perched in the hills behind. A bus leaves every 30 minutes or so from the station, or you can walk up a series of steps and paths (approximately 5km; the town is always visible). It has plenty of cafes and places to eat. The **Marina di Maratea** is located 5km south along the coast and has its own separate train station. The village of **Acquafredda** is 8km in the other direction, kissing the border of Campania.

amenities. Bright Mediterranean foliage fills sun-dappled terraced gardens.

Eating

Il Sacello   MODERN ITALIAN **€€**
(☑0973 87 61 39; www.locandamonache.com; Via Mazzei 4, Maratea Borgo; meals €35; ☺12.30-2.30pm & 7.30-10pm; ☎) The in-house *risto-rante* of the Locanda delle Donne Monache hotel, Il Sacello serves wonderful Lucanian fare and seafood, overlooking the red rooftops of Maratea Borgo. Try the pasta with local sausage, the beef tartare or delicately wrought desserts such as the buffalo-ricotta souffle. Il Sacello sometimes closes on Monday or Tuesday night in June.

PARCO NAZIONALE DEL POLLINO

The **Pollino National Park** (www.parcopollino.it), Italy's largest, straddles Basilicata and Calabria and covers 1960 sq km. It acts like a rocky curtain separating the region from the rest of Italy and has the richest repository of flora and fauna in the south.

The park's most spectacular areas are **Monte Pollino** (2248m), **Monti di Orsomarso** (1987m) and the canyon of the Gole del Raganello. The mountains, often snowbound, are blanketed by forests of oak, alder, maple, beech, pine and fir. The park is most famous for its ancient *pino loricato* trees, which can only be found here and in the Balkans. The oldest specimens reach 40m in height.

Your own vehicle is needed to explore within Pollino. To get there, however, there's a daily **SLA Bus** (☑0973 2 10 16; www.slasrl.it) between Naples and Rotonda, while **SAM Autolinee** (☑0973 66 38 35; www.samautolinee.com) buses operate around some of Pollino's Basilicatan villages.

Basilicata

In Basilicata the park's main centre is **Rotonda** (elevation 626m), which houses the official park office, **Ente Parco Nazionale del Pollino** (☑0973 66 93 11; Via delle Frecce Tricolori, Rotonda, Complesso Monumentale Santa Maria della Consolazione; ☺9am-1pm & 2-4pm Mon-Fri). Interesting villages to explore include the unique Albanian villages of **San Paolo Albanese** and **San Costantino Albanese**. These isolated and unspoilt communities fiercely maintain their mountain culture and the Greek liturgy is retained in the main churches. For local handicrafts, visit the town of **Terranova di Pollino** for wooden crafts, **Latronico** for alabaster, and **Sant'Arcangelo** for wrought iron.

The chalet-style **Picchio Nero** (☑0973 9 31 70; www.hotelpicchionero.com; Via Mulino 1, Terranova di Pollino; s/d €65/78; ℗) in Terranova di Pollino, with its Austrian-style wooden balconies and recommended restaurant, is a popular hotel for hikers.

Two highly recommended restaurants include **Luna Rossa** (☑0973 9 32 54; www.federicovalicenti.it; Via Marconi 18, Terranova di Pollino; meals €35; ☺noon-3pm & 7-10pm Thu-Tue) in Terranova di Pollino and **Da Peppe** (☑0973 66 12 51; Corso Garibaldi 13, Rotonda; meals €30; ☺noon-3pm & 7.30-11pm Tue-Sun) in Rotonda.

Calabria

Civita was founded by Albanian refugees in 1746. Other towns worth visiting are **Castrovillari**, with its well-preserved 15th-century Aragonese castle, and **Morano Calabro** (look up the beautiful MC Escher woodcut of this town). Naturalists should also check out the wildlife museum **Centro Il Nibbio** (☑0981 3 07 45; www.ilnibbio.it; Vico Il Annunziata 11, Morano Calabro; €4; ☺9am-6pm Jul & Aug, shorter hours rest of year) in Morano, which explains the Pollino ecosystem.

White-water rafting down the spectacular Lao river is popular in the Calabrian Pollino. **Centro Lao Action Raft** (☑0985 9 10 33; www.laoraft.it; Via Lauro 10/12, Scalea) in Scalea can arrange rafting trips as well as canyoning, trekking and mountain-biking. **Ferula Viaggi** (p164) in Matera runs mountain-bike excursions and treks into the Pollino.

The park has a number of *agriturismi*. Tranquil **Agriturismo Colloreto** (☑347 3236914, 0981 3 12 55; www.colloreto.it; Contrada Colloreto, Morano Calabro; half pension per person €56) near Morano Calabro, and **Locanda di Alia** (☑0981 4 63 70, 339 8346881; www.alia.it; Via letticelle 55, Castrovillari; s/d from €76/86; ℗✳☎☎) in Castrovillari are noteworthy.

Lanterna Rossa
SEAFOOD €€

(☑ 0973 87 63 52; Via Arenile, Maratea Porto; meals €40; ☉ 11am-3pm & 7-11.30pm) This terrace restaurant, sitting above the Bar del Porto overlooking the marina, has been knocking out delightful Lucanian seafood for over 20 years. Sit either in the tastefully art-strewn interior or on the terrace to enjoy dishes such as *zuppa di pesce* (fish soup) and octopus with wild beans and fennel. Bookings are advised, especially in July and August.

ℹ Information

Maratea Porto Tourist Office (☑ 371 1446350, 0973 87 71 15; Via Arenile 35, Maratea Porto; ☉ 8am-1pm & 3-7pm Jun-Oct, shorter hours rest of year)
Tourist Office (☑ 0973 03 03 66; Piazza Vitolo 1, Maratea Borgo; ☉ 10am-1pm & 5-10pm Mon-Fri, daily Jul & Aug)

ℹ Getting There & Around

Maratea is easily accessed via the coastal train line. InterCity and regional trains on the Rome–Reggio line stop at Maratea train station. Some slower trains stop at Marina di Maratea.

Local buses (€1.10) connect the coastal towns and Maratea train station with Maratea Borgo, running more frequently in summer. Some hotels offer pick-ups from the station.

CALABRIA

If a Vespa-riding, siesta-loving, unapologetically chaotic Italy still exists, it's in Calabria. Rocked by recurrent earthquakes and lacking a Matera or Lecce to give it high-flying tourist status, this is a corner of Italy less globalised and homogenised. Its wild mountain interior and long history of poverty, Mafia activity and emigration have all contributed to its distinct culture. Calabria is unlikely to be the first place in Italy you'd visit. But if you're intent on seeing a candid and uncensored version of *la dolce vita* that hasn't been dressed up for tourist consumption, look no further, *ragazzi* (guys).

Calabria's gritty cities are of patchy interest. More alluring is its attractive Tyrrhenian coastline, broken by several particularly lovely towns (Tropea and Scilla stand out). The mountainous centre is dominated by three national parks, none of them particularly well-explored. Its museums, collecting the vestiges of rich classical past are probably its greatest treasure.

History

Traces of Neanderthal, Palaeolithic and Neolithic life have been found in Calabria, but the region only became internationally important with the arrival of the Greeks in the 8th century BC. They founded a colony at what is now Reggio di Calabria. Remnants of this colonisation, which spread along the Ionian coast with Sibari and Crotone as the star settlements, are still visible. However, the fun didn't last forever, and in 202 BC the cities of Magna Graecia all came under the control of Rome, the rising power in Italy. The Romans did irreparable environmental damage, destroying the countryside's handsome forests. Navigable rivers became fearsome *fiumare* (torrents) dwindling to wide, dry, drought-stricken riverbeds in high summer.

Post-Rome, Calabria's fortified hilltop communities weathered successive invasions by the Normans, Swabians, Aragonese and Bourbons, and remained largely undeveloped. Although the late 18th-century Napoleonic incursion and the later arrival of Garibaldi and Italian unification inspired hope for change, Calabria remained a disappointed, feudal region and, like the rest of the south, was racked by malaria.

A by-product of this tragic history was the growth of banditry and organised crime. Calabria's Mafia, known as the 'ndrangheta (from the Greek for heroism/virtue), inspires fear in the local community, but tourists are rarely the target of its aggression. For many, the only answer has been to get out and, for at least a century, Calabria has seen its young people emigrate in search of work.

Northern Tyrrhenian Coast

The good, the bad and the ugly all jostle cheek-by-jowl along Calabria's northern Tyrrhenian coast. The *Autostrada del Mediterraneo* (A2), one of Italy's great coastal drives, ties them all together. It twists and turns through mountains, past huge swathes of dark-green forest and flashes of cerulean-blue sea. But the Italian penchant for cheap summer resorts has taken its toll here and certain stretches, particularly in the south, are blighted by shoddy hotels and soulless stacks of flats.

A 30km stretch of wide, pebbly beach runs south from the border with Basilicata, from the popular and not-too-garish resort town of Praia a Mare to Diamante, a fashionable seaside town famed for its chillis and bright murals painted by local and foreign artists. Inland are the precariously perched, otherworldly villages of Aieta and Tortora, reached by a tortuously twisted but rewarding mountain drive. Further south, Paola is worth a stop to see its holy shrine.

◎ Sights

Santuario di San Francesco di Paola   CAVE
(☑ 0984 47 60 32; www.santuariopaola.it; Via San Francesco di Paola, Paola; ⊗ 6am-1pm & 2-6pm Oct-Mar, 6am-1pm & 2-8pm Apr-Sep) FREE Watched over by a crumbling castle, the Santuario di San Francesco di Paola is a curious, empty cave with tremendous significance to the devout. The saint lived and died in Paola in the 15th century and the sanctuary that he and his followers carved out of the bare rock has attracted pilgrims for centuries. The cloister is surrounded by naive wall paintings depicting the saint's truly incredible miracles. The original church contains an ornate reliquary of the saint.

Isola di Dino   ISLAND
Visible from the Praia a Mare seafront is an intriguing rocky chunk off the coast, the Isola di Dino. The tourist office (Tyrrhenian Tourist Consortium; ☑ 0985 77 76 37; Via Amerigo Vespucci 4, Praia a Mare; ⊗ 9am-noon Mon-Fri) has information on the island's sea caves; alternatively, expect to pay around €10 for a guided tour from the old boys who operate from the beach.

❶ Getting There & Away

Paola is the main train hub for Cosenza, about 25km inland. From Praia a Mare, **Autolinee Preite** (☑ 0984 41 30 01; www.autoservizipreite.it) buses go to Cosenza via Diamante and to Aieta and Tortora, (6km and 12km from Praia respectively). **SITA** (☑ 0971 50 68 11; www.sitabus.it) buses run to Maratea and regular trains also pass through for Paola and Reggio di Calabria.

Cosenza

POP 67,600

Cosenza epitomises the unkempt charm of southern Italy. It is a no-nonsense workaday town where tourists are incidental and local life, with all its petty dramas, takes centre stage. The modern city centre is a typically chaotic Italian metro area that serves as a transport hub for Calabria and a gateway to

the nearby mountains of Sila National Park. The old town, stacked atop a steep hill, has a totally different atmosphere. Time-warped and romantically dishevelled, its dark weathered alleys are full of drying clothes on rusty balconies, old curiosity shops and the freshly planted shoots of an arty renaissance.

◎ Sights

In the new town, pedestrianised Corso Mazzini serves as an open-air museum with numerous sculptures lining the corso, including Saint George and the Dragon by Salvador Dalí.

In the old town, head up the winding, charmingly dilapidated Corso Telesio, which has a raw Neapolitan feel to it and is lined with ancient tenements and antiquated shopfronts. At the top is Cosenza's 12th-century cathedral (☑ 0984 7 78 64; www.cattedraledicosenza.it; Piazza del Duomo 1; ⊗ 8am-noon & 3-7.30pm), rebuilt in restrained Baroque style in the 18th century after devastating earthquakes.

Head further along the corso to Piazza XV Marzo, an appealing square fronted by the Palazzo del Governo and the handsome neoclassical Teatro Rendano (☑ 0984 81 32 27; Piazza XV Marzo; adult/reduced €3/2), a leading Calabrian venue for opera and classical music.

From Piazza XV Marzo, follow Via Paradiso, then Via Antonio Siniscalchi for the route to the restored Norman castle (☑ 0984 181 12 34; www.castellocosenza.it; Piazza Frederico II; adult/reduced €4/2; ⊗ 9.30am-6pm Tue-Sat, from 10am Sun).

Cosenza's culture is low-key, but you can see a noteworthy collection of southern-Italian paintings at the Galeria Nazionale (☑ 0984 79 56 39; Via Gravina; ⊗ 10am-6pm Tue-Sun) FREE, or spend an hour in the Museo dei Brettii e degli Enotri (☑ 0984 2 33 03; www.museodeibrettiiedeglienotri.it; Salita Agostino 3; adult/reduced €4/3; ⊗ 9am-1pm & 3.30-6.30pm Tue-Fri, 10am-1pm & 3.30-6.30pm Sat & Sun), which displays finds from the Bronze Age Enotri culture, and the Brettii people who founded Cosenza in the 4th century BC.

🛌 Sleeping

B&B Via dell'Astrologo   B&B €
(☑ 338 9205394; www.viadellastrologo.com; Via Rutilio Benincasa 16; r from €65; 🖾) A gem in the historic centre, this small B&B is tastefully decorated with polished wooden floors, white bedspreads and good-quality artwork. Brothers Mario and Marco, the venue's own-

ers, are a mine of information on Cosenza and Calabria in general.

Royal Hotel
HOTEL €

(☎ 0984 41 21 65; www.hotelroyalcosenza.it; Via delle Medaglie d'Oro 1; s/d/ste from €56/69/75; P ❋ ☎) Probably the best all-round hotel central Cosenza can provide, the four-star Royal is a short stroll from Corso Mazzini right in the heart of town. Rooms are fresh and businesslike, and there's a bar, restaurant and parking on site.

✗ Eating

Il Paesello
CALABRIAN €

(☎ 349 4385786; Via Rivocati 95; meals €25; ⊙ 7-11pm Mon-Sat, noon-3pm Sun) Beloved of the locals, this unpretentious trattoria is one of Cosenza's best. Simple, robust dishes such as *fagioli con cozze* (beans with mussels), tagliatelle with porcini mushrooms and anything plucked from the sea are executed with care and skill.

Gran Caffè Renzelli
CAFE €

(www.renzelli.com; Corso Telesio 46; cakes from €1.20; ⊙ 7am-9pm; ☎) This venerable cafe behind the *duomo* has been run by the same family since 1803 when the founder arrived from Naples and began baking gooey cakes and desserts. Sink your teeth into *torroncino torrefacto* (a confection of sugar, spices and hazelnuts) or *torta telesio* (made from almonds, cherries, apricot jam and lupins).

Ristorante Calabria Bella
CALABRIAN €€

(☎ 0984 79 35 31; www.ristorantecalabriabella.it; Piazza del Duomo 20; meals €28; ⊙ noon-3pm & 7pm-midnight) Traditional Calabrian cuisine, such as *cavatelli con cozze e fagioli* (pasta with mussels and beans) and *grigliata mista di carne* (mixed grilled meats), is dished up with aplomb at this cosy restaurant in the old town.

❶ Orientation

The main drag, Corso Mazzini, runs south from Piazza Bilotti (formerly known as Piazza Fera), near the bus station, and intersects Viale Trieste before meeting Piazza dei Bruzi. Head further south and cross the Busento river to reach the old town.

❶ Getting There & Away

AIR

Lamezia Terme Airport (Sant'Eufemia Lamezia, SUF; ☎ 0968 41 43 85; www.sacal.it; Via Aeroporto 40, Lamezia Terme), 63km south of Cosenza, at the junction of the A3 and SS280

motorways, links the region with major Italian cities. The airport is served by Ryanair, easyJet and charters from northern Europe. A shuttle leaves the airport every 20 minutes for the airport train station, where **Autolinee Romano** (☎ 0962 2 17 09; www.autolineeromano.com) runs two buses a day to Cosenza.

BUS

Cosenza's main **bus station** (☎ 0984 41 31 24) is northeast of Piazza Bilotti. Services leave from here for Catanzaro and towns throughout La Sila. **Autolinee Preite** (☎ 0984 41 30 01; www.autoservizipreite.it) has buses heading daily along the north Tyrrhenian coast; **Autolinee Romano** serves Crotone as well as Rome and Milan.

TRAIN

Stazione Nuova (Via Vaglio Lise) is about 2km northeast of the centre. Regular trains go to Reggio di Calabria (from €14.60, 2¾ hours) and Rome (from €52.40, four to six hours), both usually with a change at Paola, and Naples (from €16.90, three to four hours), as well as most destinations around the Calabrian coast.

Regular buses link the centre and the main train station, although they follow a roundabout route.

Parco Nazionale della Sila

'La Sila' is a big landscape, where wooded hills stretch to endless rolling vistas. Dotted with hamlets, it's cut through with looping roads that make driving a test of your digestion.

The park's 130 sq km are divided into three areas: the Sila Grande, with the highest mountains; the strongly Albanian Sila Greca (to the north); and the Sila Piccola (near Catanzaro), with vast forested hills.

The highest peaks, covered with tall Corsican pines, reach 2000m – high enough to generate enough winter snow to attract skiers. In summer the climate is coolly Alpine; spring sees carpets of wildflowers; and there's mushroom hunting in autumn. Gigantic firs grow in the Bosco di Gallopane (Forest of Gallopane). There are several beautiful lakes, the largest of which is Lago di Cecita o Mucone near Camigliatello Silano. There is plenty of wildlife here, including the light-grey Apennine wolf, a protected species.

◉ Sights & Activities

La Sila's main town, San Giovanni in Fiore (1049m), is named after the founder of its beautiful medieval abbey. Today, the abbey houses a home for the elderly and the **Museo Demologico** (☑ 0984 97 00 59; Abbazia Forense; adult/reduced €1.50/1; ☺ 8.30am-6.30pm Mon-Sat year round & 9.30am-12.30pm Sun mid-Jun–mid-Sep). San Giovanni's handsome old centre is famous for its Armenian-style handloomed carpets and tapestry. See how it's done at the studio and shop of master carpet maker **Domenico Caruso** (☑ 0984 99 27 24; http://carusotessiture.it; Via Gramsci 195; ☺ 8.30am-8pm Mon-Sat).

A popular ski-resort town with 6km of slopes, **Camigliatello Silano** (1272m) looks much better under snow. A few lifts operate on Monte Curcio, about 3km to the south. Around 5.5km of slopes and a 1500m lift can be found near **Lorica** (1370m), on gloriously pretty **Lago Arvo** – the best place to camp in summer.

Scigliano (620m) is a small hilltop town located west of the Sila Piccola section of the park and 75km south of Cosenza.

🎉 Festivals & Events

During August, **Sila in Festa** takes place, featuring traditional music. Autumn is mushroom season, when you'll be able to frequent mushroom festivals, including the **Sagra del Fungo** in Camigliatello Silano.

🛏 Sleeping & Eating

⭐ **B&B Calabria** B&B €
(☑ 349 8781894; www.bedandbreakfastcalabria.it; Via Roma 7, Scigliano; s/d €40/60; ☺ Apr-Nov; ℗) This B&B in the mountains has five clean, comfortable and characterful rooms, all with separate entrances. Owner Raffaele is a great source of information on the region and can recommend places to eat, visit and go hiking. There's a wonderful terrace overlooking endless forested vistas. Mountain bikes are available. and there's wi-fi in public areas. Cash only.

Albergo San Lorenzo HOTEL €
(☑ 0984 57 08 09; www.sanlorenzosialberga.it; Campo San Lorenzo, near Camigliatello Silano; d/tr/q €110/130/160; ℗ ✳ 🛜) Above their famous restaurant, the owners of La Tavernetta have opened the area's most stylish sleep, with 21 large, well-equipped rooms done up in colourful, modernist style.

⭐ **La Tavernetta** CALABRIAN €€€
(☑ 0984 57 90 26; www.sanlorenzosialberga. it; Campo San Lorenzo, near Camigliatello Silano; meals €50; ☺ 12.30-3pm & 7.30-11pm Tue-Sun)

Among Calabria's best eats, La Tavernetta marries rough country charm with citified elegance in warmly colourful dining rooms. The food is first-rate and based on the best local ingredients, from wild anise seed and mushrooms to mountain-raised lamb and kid. Reserve ahead on Sundays and holidays.

🛍 Shopping

⭐ **Antica Salumeria Campanaro** FOOD
(☑ 0984 57 80 15; Piazza Misasi 5, Camigliatello Silano; ☺ 9am-9pm) Even among Italian delicatessens, this long-established *salumeria* is something special. It's a temple to all things fungoid (get your Sila porcini here) as well as an emporium of fine meats, cheeses, pickles, sweetmeats and wines.

ℹ Information

Good-quality information in English is scarce. You can try the national park **visitors centre** at Cupone, 10km from Camigliatello Silano, or the **Pro Loco tourist office** (☑ 0984 57 81 59; www.prolococamigliatello.it; Via Roma, Camigliatello Silano; ☺ 9.30am-6.30pm Tue-Sun) in Camigliatello Silano. A useful internet resource is the official park website (www.parcosila.it). The people who run B&B Calabria in the park are extremely knowledgeable and helpful.

For a map, you can use *La Sila: Carta Turistico-Stradale ed Escurionistica del Parco Nazionale* (€7). *Sila for 4* is a mini-guide in English that outlines a number of walking trails in the park. The map and booklet are available at tourist offices.

Visitors Centre (☑ 0984 53 71 09; www. parcosila.it; Via Nazionale, Lorica)

ℹ Getting There & Away

You can reach the park's two main hubs, Camigliatello Silano and San Giovanni in Fiore, via regular **Ferrovie della Calabria** buses from Cosenza or Crotone.

Ionian Coast

With its flat coastline and wide sandy beaches, the Ionian coast has some fascinating stops from **Sibari** to **Santa Severina**, with some of the best beaches around **Soverato**. However, it has borne the brunt of some ugly development and is mainly a long, uninterrupted string of resorts, thronged in the summer months and mothballed from October to May.

It's worth taking a trip inland to visit Santa Severina, a spectacular mountain-top town, 26km northwest of Crotone. The town is dominated by a **Norman castle** and is home to a beautiful **Byzantine church**. But the true glories of this long stretch of coast are its museums and archaeological sites, preserving what remains of the pre-Roman cities of Magna Graecia (Greater Greece).

Le Castella

This town is named for its impressive 16th-century Aragonese **castle** (☎ 0965 36 21 11; €3; ⊙ 9am-midnight Jul & Aug, shorter hours

FOOTPRINTS OF MAGNA GRAECIA

Long before the Romans colonised Greece, the Greeks were colonising southern Italy. Pushed out of their homelands by demographic, social and political pressures, the nebulous mini-empire they created between the 8th and 3rd centuries BC was often referred to as Magna Graecia by the Romans in the north. Many Greek-founded cities were located along the southern coast of present-day Puglia, Basilicata and Calabria. They included (west to east) Locri Epizephyrii, Kroton, Sybaris, Metapontum and Taras (now known, respectively, as Locri, Crotone, Sibari, Metaponto and Taranto).

Magna Graecia was more a loose collection of independent cities than a coherent state with fixed borders, and many of these cities regularly raged war against each other. The most notable conflict occurred in 510 BC when the athletic Krotons attacked and destroyed the hedonistic city of Sybaris (from which the word 'sybaritic' is derived).

Magna Graecia was the 'door' through which Greek culture entered Italy, influencing its language, architecture, religion and culture. Though the cities were mostly abandoned by the 5th century AD, the Greek legacy lives on in the Griko culture of Calabria and the Salento peninsula, where ethnic Greek communities still speak Griko, a dialect of Greek.

Remnants of Magna Graecia can be seen in numerous museums and architectural sites along Calabria's Ionian coast.

Locri

Museo Nazionale di Locri Epizephyrii (☎ 0964 39 00 23; www.locriantica.it; Contrada Marasà, Locri; adult/reduced €4/2; ⊙ 9am-8pm; P ♿) Situated 3km south of modern-day Locri, the Greek colony of Locri Epizephyrii was founded in 680 BC, later subsumed by Rome and finally abandoned following Saracen raids in the 10th century AD. The archaeological site is sprawling and full of interest, including harbour structures, the *centocamere* (hundred rooms) and the Casino Macri – a Roman bathhouse later repurposed as a farming villa. The attached museum is well curated, and includes artefacts found in the numerous nearby necropoli.

Sibari

Museo Archeologico Nazionale delle Sibaritide (☎ 0981 7 93 91; Località Casa Bianca, Sibari; €3; ⊙ 9am-8pm Tue-Sun) Founded around 730 BC and destroyed by the Krotons in 510 BC, Sybaris was rebuilt twice: once as Thurii by the Greeks in 444 BC, and again in 194 BC by the Romans, who called it Copia. Prehistoric artefacts and evidence of all three cities are displayed at this important (if underpatronised) museum, 5km southeast of the modern beach resort of Sibari. The nearby archaeological park has been affected by flooding in the past: check ahead to ensure it's open.

Crotone

Museo Archeologico Nazionale di Crotone (☎ 0962 2 30 82; Via Risorgimento 14, Crotone; €2; ⊙ 9am-8pm) Founded in 710 BC, the powerful city state of Kroton was known for its sobriety and high-performing Olympic athletes. Crotone's museum is located in the modern town, while the main archaeological site is at Capo Colonna, 11km to the southeast. Votive offerings and other remnants of the famous Hera Lacinia Sanctuary at Cape Colonna are a highlight.

rest of year, closed Mon Oct-Mar), a vast edifice linked to the mainland by a short causeway. Evidence shows it was begun in the 4th century BC, designed to protect Crotone in the wars against Pyrrhus.

Le Castella is situated south of a rare protected area along this coast, Capo Rizzuto, rich not only in nature but also in Greek history. For further information on the park, try www.riservamarinacapo rizzuto.it.

With around 15 campgrounds near Isola di Capo Rizzuto to the north, this is the Ionian coast's prime camping area. Try **La Fattoria** (☑ 0962 79 11 65; Via del Faro, Isola di Capo Rizzuto; camping 2 people, car & tent €25, bungalow €60; ☺ Jun-Sep), 1.5km from the sea. Otherwise, **Da Annibale** (☑ 0962 79 50 04; Via Duomo 35; s/d €50/70; P ✳ @ 🛜) is a pleasant hotel in town with a splendid fish **restaurant** (☑ 0962 79 50 04; Via Duomo 35; meals €40; ☺ noon-3pm & 7.30-11pm).

For expansive sea views dine at bright and airy **Ristorante Micomare** (☑ 0962 79 50 82; Via Vittoria 7; meals €35; ☺ noon-3pm & 7.30-11pm).

Gerace

POP 2650

A spectacular medieval hill town, Gerace is worth a detour for the views alone – it's dramatically sited on a rocky fastness rearing up from the inland plain, culminating in the photogenic ruin of a Norman castle that seems to grow from the stone itself.

Gerace is graced by numerous handsome churches – some dating back to the Byzantine 9th century – and has Calabria's largest Romanesque **cathedral** (Via Duomo 28; ☺ 9.30am-12.30pm & 3-6.30pm). Dating to 1045, later alterations have not robbed it of its majesty.

For a taste of traditional Calabrian cooking, **Ristorante A Squella** (☑ 0964 35 60 86; Via Ferruccio 21; meals €25; ☺ 12.30-2.30pm daily & 7.30-10.30pm Mon-Sat) serves reliably good seafood and Calabrian dishes. Afterwards you can wander down the road and admire the views.

Further inland is **Canolo**, a small village seemingly untouched by the 20th century. Buses connect Gerace with Locri and also Canolo with Siderno, both of which link to the main coastal railway line. To explore these quiet hills properly, you'll need your own transport.

Parco Nazionale dell'Aspromonte

Most Italians think of the Parco Nazionale dell'Aspromonte (www.parcoaspromonte. gov.it) as a hiding place used by Calabrian kidnappers in the 1970s and '80s. It's still rumoured to contain 'ndrangheta strongholds, but as a tourist you're unlikely to encounter any murky business.

The park, Calabria's second-largest, is dramatic, rising sharply inland from Reggio. Its highest peak, **Montalto** (1955m), is dominated by a huge bronze statue of Christ and offers sweeping views across to Sicily.

Subject to frequent mudslides and carved up by torrential rivers, the mountains are nonetheless awesomely beautiful. Underwater rivers keep the peaks covered in coniferous forests and ablaze with flowers in spring. It's wonderful walking country and is crossed by several colour-coded trails.

Extremes of weather and geography have resulted in some extraordinary villages, such as **Pentidàttilo** and **Roghudi**, clinging limpet-like to the craggy, rearing rocks and now all but deserted. It's worth the drive to explore these eagle-nest villages. Another mountain eyrie with a photogenic ruined castle is **Bova**, perched at 900m above sealevel. The drive up the steep, dizzying road to Bova is not for the faint-hearted, but the views are stupendous.

Maps are scarce. Try the **national park office** (☑ 0965 74 30 60; www.parcoaspromonte. gov.it; Via Aurora 1, Gambarie; ☺ 10.30am-12.30pm Mon & Fri & 3-6pm Tue) in **Gambarie**, the Aspromonte's main town and the easiest approach to the park. The roads are good and many activities are organised from here – you can ski and it's also the place to hire a 4WD; ask around in the town.

It's also possible to approach from the south, but the roads aren't as good. The co-operative **Naturaliter** (☑ 347 3046799; www. naturaliterweb.it), based in Condofuri, is an excellent source of information, and can help arrange walking and donkey treks or place you in B&Bs throughout the region. **Co-operativa San Leo** (☑ 347 3046799), based in Bova, also provides guided tours and accommodation. In Reggio di Calabria, you can book treks and tours with **Misafumera** (☑ 347 0804515, 0965 67 70 21; Via Nazionale 306d, Reggio di Calabria Bocale 2; treks €260-480).

Hotel Centrale (☑0965 74 31 33; www.hotelcentrale.net; Piazza Mangeruca 22, Gambarie; s/d €50/100; P ❄ ⑦) in Gambarie is a large, all-encompassing place reminiscent of a ski hotel in the Italian Dolomites. It has a decent restaurant, a comprehensive modern spa, wood-finished rooms and the best cafe in town. It's located right at the bottom of the ski lift.

To reach Gambarie, take ATAM (p181) city bus 319 from Reggio di Calabria (€1, 1½ hours, up to six daily). Most of the roads inland from Reggio eventually hit the SS183 road that runs north to the town.

Reggio di Calabria

POP 182,550

Port, transport nexus and the main arrival and departure point for Sicily, Reggio seems more functional than fascinating. That is up until the point you set foot inside its fabulous national museum, custodian of some of the most precious artefacts of Magna Graecia known.

The city's architectural eclecticism is a result of its tectonic liveliness: in 1908 the last big earthquake triggered a tsunami that killed over 100,000. By Italian standards, little of historical merit remains, although the *lungomare,* with its views across the Messina Strait to smouldering Mt Etna is, arguably, one of the most atmospheric places in Italy for an evening *passeggiata.*

Fortunately, there's no need to doubt the food. Reggio hides some of Calabria's best salt-of-the-earth restaurants. You can work up an appetite for them by hiking in the nearby Parco Nazionale dell'Aspromonte, or exploring the coastline at nearby seaside escapes along the Tyrrhenian and Ionian coasts.

👁 Sights

★ Museo Nazionale di Reggio Calabria   MUSEUM
(☑0965 81 22 55; http://sabap-rc.beniculturali.it; Piazza de Nava 26; adult/reduced €8/5; ⊘9am-8pm Tue-Sun; 🖋) Partly closed during years of renovation from 2009, southern Italy's finest museum is now fully reopened. Over several floors you'll descend through millennia of local history, from Neolithic and palaeolithic times through Hellenistic, Roman and beyond. The undoubted crown jewels are, probably, the world's finest examples of ancient Greek sculpture: the Bronzi di Riace, two extraordinary bronze statues discovered on the seabed near Riace in 1972 by a snorkelling chemist from Rome.

You'll have to stand for three minutes in a decontamination chamber to see the bronzes, but they're more than worth the wait. Larger than life, they depict the Greek obsession with the body; inscrutable, determined and fierce, their perfect form is more godlike than human. The finest of the two has ivory eyes and silver teeth parted in a faint *Mona Lisa* smile. No one knows who they are – whether human or god – and even their provenance is a mystery. They date from around 450 BC, and it's believed they're the work of two artists.

In the same room as the bronzes is the 5th-century-BC bronze *Philosopher's Head,* the oldest-known Greek portrait in existence. Also on display are impressive exhibits from Locri, including statues of Dioscuri falling from his horse.

Castle Ruins   RUINS
(Piazza Castello) Only two towers, restored in 2000, remain of the Aragonese Castle damaged by earthquake and partially demolished in 1922. The site is used for events and performances today.

🛏 Sleeping

Finding a room should be easy, even in summer, since most visitors pass straight through en route to Sicily.

B&B Casa Blanca   B&B €
(☑340 9032992; www.bbcasablanca.it; Via Arcovito 24; s/d/tr €55/75/85; P ❄ ⑦) A little gem in Reggio's heart, this 19th-century *palazzo* has three floors of spacious rooms gracefully furnished with white-on-white decor. There's a self-serve breakfast nook, a small breakfast table in each room and two apartments available. Breakfast is a celebration of fresh pastries.

Hotel Continental   HOTEL €
(☑0965 81 21 81; www.hotelcontinentalrc.it; Via Vincenzo Florio 10; r from €69; P ❄ ⑦) Right next to the port, the Continental does a brisk trade in overnight travellers bound for Sicily. The decor holds no surprises, but the service is exceedingly polite and professional. A breakfast buffet can be procured for €10, and a room with a view to Sicily for another €20.

Reggio di Calabria

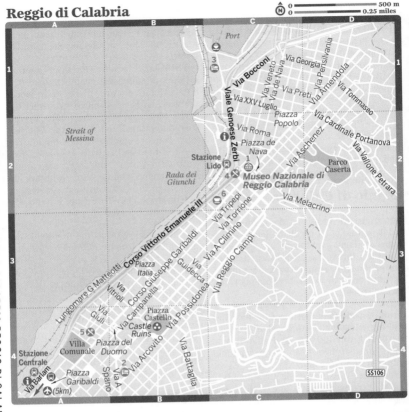

Reggio di Calabria

◉ **Top Sights**
1 Museo Nazionale di Reggio
   Calabria C2

🛏 **Sleeping**
2 B&B Casa Blanca B4
3 Hotel Continental C1

🍴 **Eating**
4 Cèsare C2
   La Cantina del Macellaio .... (see 2)
5 Le Nasse U Bais A4

🍷 **Drinking & Nightlife**
6 Gelateria Matteotti C2

🍴 Eating

Reggio's well stocked with no-nonsense trattorias serving Calabrian classics the way the locals demand they should be. You'll struggle to eat badly here.

Cèsare GELATO €
(Piazza Indipendenza 2; gelato from €2.40; ⊙ 6am-1am) The most popular gelateria in town is in a modest green kiosk at the end of the *lungomare* (seafront promenade). Try the Kinder Egg flavour.

La Cantina del Macellaio TRATTORIA €€
(📞 0965 2 39 32; www.lacantinadelmacellaio.com; Via Arcovito 26/28; meals €30; ⊙ 12.30-3pm & 7.30-11.30pm Wed-Mon) One of the best restaurants in Reggio, serving *fagioli cu l'oghiu bonu* (Sicilian beans), *maccheroni al ragù di maiale* (handmade pasta with pork sauce) and *involtini di vitello* (veal rolls) in an open, tiled dining room with exposed stonework and green flasks on the walls. The mostly Calabrian wines are equally impressive, as is the service.

Le Nasse U Bais SEAFOOD €€
(📞 0965 89 72 66; www.ubais.it; Via Lemos 6; meals €40; ⊙ noon-3pm & 7.30-11pm Tue-Sun)

Offering a long wine list and locally caught seafood such as *pesce spada* (swordfish), this restaurant looks like a sophisticated version of a fisherman's whitewashed shack. The food follows the same theme – quality, fresh ingredients, served up with care and intelligence.

Gelateria Matteotti   CAFE
(☑ 0965 89 11 61; www.caffematteotti.it; Corso Vittorio Emanuele III 39; ☺ 7am-2am Mon-Fri, to 4am Sat & Sun) This gelateria/cafe is one of the prime people-watching spots on Reggio's *lungomare* (seafront). Across from the main premises you'll find a sea-facing terrace furnished with stylish white tables and chairs, perfect for your *aperitivi*.

ⓘ Information

Tourist Information Kiosk (☑ 0965 2 11 71; Via Roma 3; ☺ 9am-noon & 4-7pm) There are also information kiosks at both the airport (☑ 0965 64 32 91; ☺ 9am-5pm) and the Stazione Centrale (☑ 0965 2 71 20; ☺ 9am-5pm).

Police Station (☑ 0965 41 11; Corso Garibaldi 442)

Grande Ospedale Metropolitano Bianchi Melacrino Morelli (☑ 800 19 86 29, emergency 118; www.ospedalerc.it; Via Melacrino; ☺ 24hr) Reggio di Calabria's main hospital has a 24-hour *pronto soccorso* (emergency department).

ⓘ Getting There & Away

AIR

Reggio's **airport** (REG; ☑ 0965 64 05 17; www.aeroportodellostretto.it) is at Ravagnese, about 5km south. It has Alitalia flights to Rome and Milan.

BUS

Most bus services terminate at the **Piazza Garibaldi bus station** (Piazza Garibaldi), situated in front of the Stazione Centrale. Several different bus companies operate services to towns in Calabria and beyond. Regional trains are more convenient than bus services to Scilla and Tropea.

ATAM runs bus 127 to Gambarie in the Aspromonte National Park.

Lirosi (☑ 0966 5 79 01; www.lirosiautoservizi.com) has two daily buses to Rome.

CAR & MOTORCYCLE

The A2 ends at Reggio, via a series of long tunnels. If you are continuing south, the SS106/E90 hugs the coast around the 'toe', then heads north along the Ionian Sea.

TRAIN

Trains stop at **Stazione Centrale** (☑ 0965 32 41 91; Via Barlaam 1), the main train station at the town's southern edge. Of more use to ferry foot passengers and those visiting the Museo Nazionale is the **Stazione Lido** (Viale Zerbi), near the harbour. There are frequent trains to Milan, Rome and Naples. Regional services run along the coast to Scilla and Tropea, and also to Catanzaro and less frequently to Cosenza and Bari.

ⓘ Getting Around

Orange local bus services run by **ATAM** (☑ 800 43 33 10; www.atam-rc.it) cover most of the city area including regular buses that run between the port and Piazza Garibaldi outside Stazione Centrale. The Università–Aeroporto bus, bus 27, runs from Piazza Garibaldi to the airport and vice versa (15 minutes, hourly). Buy your ticket at ATAM offices, tobacconists or news stands.

PUGLIA, BASILICATA & CALABRIA REGGIO DI CALABRIA

ⓘ ONWARD TO SICILY

Reggio is the gateway to Sicily, via the island's main port, Messina. There are also boats to the Aeolian Islands.

Note that there are two main departure ports for Sicily: the **Stazione Marittima** in Reggio di Calabria, and the ferry port in the town of Villa San Giovanni, 14km north of Reggio and easily accessible by train.

There is a ferry from Reggio's Stazione Marittima operated by **Meridiano** (☑ 0965 81 04 14; www.meridianolines.net), which runs a dozen ferries a day on weekdays (three to four on weekends).

The other main ferry company operating is **Liberty Lines** (☑ 0923 87 38 13; http://eng.libertylines.it), which runs passenger-only ferry services to Messina, Stromboli and Vulcano.

The car ferries from Villa San Giovanni are run by **Caronte & Tourist** (☑ 800 62 74 14; www.carontetourist.it). This is also the port used by Trenitalia's train-ferry – carriages are pulled directly onto the ferry.

Southern Tyrrhenian Coast

North of Reggio di Calabria, along the coast-hugging **Autostrada del Mediterraneo (A2)**, the scenery rocks and rolls to become increasingly beautiful and dramatic, if you can ignore the shoddy holiday camps and unattractive developments that sometimes scar the land. Like the northern part of the Tyrrhenian coast, it's mostly quiet in winter and packed in summer.

Scilla

POP 4900

In Scilla, cream-, ochre- and earth-coloured houses cling on for dear life to the jagged promontory, ascending in jumbled ranks to the hill's summit, which is crowned by a castle and, just below, the dazzling white confection of the **Chiesa Arcipretale Maria Immacolata**. Lively in summer and serene in low season, the town is split in two by the tiny port. The fishing district of Scilla Chianalea, to the north, harbours small hotels and restaurants off narrow lanes, lapped by the sea. It can only be visited on foot.

Scilla's high point is a rock at the northern end, said to be the lair of Scylla, the mythical six-headed sea monster who drowned sailors as they tried to navigate the Strait of Messina. Swimming and fishing off the town's glorious white sandy beach is somewhat safer today. Head for **Lido Paradiso** from where you can squint up at the castle while sunbathing on the sand.

◉ Sights

Castello Ruffo   CASTLE

(☑0965 70 42 07; Piazza San Rocco; admission €2; ☺8.30am-7.30pm) An imposing fortress surmounting the headland commanding Scilla, this castle has at times been a lighthouse and a monastery. It houses a *luntre*, the original boat used for swordfishing, and on which the modern-day *passarelle* (a special swordfish-hunting boat equipped with a 30m-high metal tower) is based.

⌂ Sleeping

The old fishing village of Chianalea, on Scilla's eastern flank, holds some delightful sea-facing B&Bs.

Hotel Principe di Scilla   HOTEL €€

(☑0965 70 43 24; www.ubais.it; Via Grotte 2; ste from €150; ☒☎) Get lulled to sleep by the sound of lapping waves in this grand old family residence on Scilla's seafront. Two suits of armour guard the front door while inside six individually themed suites are stuffed with countless antiques. In warm weather throw the windows open onto lovely views of the fishing village of Chianalea and, beyond, the sparkling Tyrrhenian.

Le Piccole Grotte   B&B €€

(☑338 2096727; Via Grotte 10; d €120; ☒☎) In the picturesque Chianalea district, 'The Small Caves' is a sweet B&B housed in a 19th-century fisherman's house beside steps leading to the lapping Tyrrhenian. Rooms have small balconies facing the cobbled alleyway or the sea.

✕ Eating & Drinking

Bleu de Toi   SEAFOOD €€

(☑0965 79 05 85; www.bleudetoi.it; Via Grotte 40; meals €35; ☺noon-3pm & 8pm-midnight Wed-Mon) Soak up the atmosphere at this lovely little restaurant, where blue lampshades, a Blue Note soundtrack and glimpses of the blue Tyrrhenian set the mood. It has a terrace over the water and excellent seafood dishes, made with local ingredients such as Scilla's renowned swordfish, perhaps with fresh pasta and eggplant. Ask for the homemade Amaro (herbal liqueur) to finish.

Dali City Pub   BAR

(☑347 5541586; Via Porto 6; ☺noon-midnight) On the beach in Scilla town, this popular bar has a Beatles tribute corner (appropriately named the Cavern) and has been going strong since 1972.

❶ Getting There & Away

Scilla is on the main coastal train line. Frequent trains run to Reggio di Calabria (€2.40, 30 minutes). The train station is a couple of blocks from the beach.

Tropea

POP 6400

Tropea, a puzzle of lanes and piazzas, is famed for its beauty, dramatic cliff's-edge site and spectacular sunsets. It sits on the Promontorio di Tropea, which stretches from Nicotera in the south to Pizzo in the north. The coast alternates between dramatic cliffs and icing sugar–soft sandy beaches, all edged by translucent sea. Unsurprisingly, hordes of Italian holidaymakers descend here in summer. If you hear English being spoken, it is probably from Americans visiting relatives: enormous numbers left to forge better lives in America in the early 20th century.

Despite the legend that Hercules founded the town, it seems this area has been settled as far back as Neolithic times. Tropea has been occupied by the Arabs, Normans, Swabians, Anjous and Aragonese, as well as being attacked by Turkish pirates. Perhaps they were all after the town's famous red onions, so sweet they can be turned into marmalade?

◉ Sights

Cathedral
CATHEDRAL

(Largo Duomo 12; ⊙7am-noon & 4-8pm) The beautiful Norman cathedral has two undetonated WWII bombs near the door: it's believed they didn't explode due to the protection of the town's patron saint, Our Lady of Romania. A Byzantine icon (1330) of the Madonna hangs above the altar – she is also credited with protecting the town from the earthquakes that have pummeled the region.

Santa Maria dell'Isola
CHURCH

(☑347 2541232; www.santuariosantamariadellisolatropea.it; garden & museum €2; ⊙9am-1pm & 3-7.30pm Apr-Jun, 9am-8.30pm Jul & Aug, shorter hours rest of year) Tropea's number one photo opp is Santa Maria dell'Isola, a medieval monastic church given several facelifts over centuries of wear and tear (mainly attributable to earthquakes). Sitting on what was once its own rocky little island, it's now joined to the mainland by a causeway created by centuries of silt, and is reached via a flight of steps up the cliff-face. Access to the church is free, but the small museum and garden costs €2.

🛏 Sleeping

★ Donnaciccina
B&B €€

(☑0963 6 21 80; www.donnaciccina.com; Via Pelliccia 9; s/d/ste €75/150/240; ❉🛜) Look for the sign of a bounteous hostess bearing fruit and cake to find this delightful B&B, overlooking the main *corso*. The 17th-century *palazzo* retains a tangible sense of history with carefully selected antiques, canopy

beds and terracotta tiled floors. There are nine restful rooms, a nearby suite (itself dating to the 15th century) and a chatty parrot at reception.

Residenza il Barone
B&B €€

(☑0963 60 71 81; www.residenzailbarone.it; Largo Barone; ste from €180; ❉🛜) This graceful *palazzo* has six suites that are decorated in masculine neutrals and tobacco browns, with dramatic modern paintings by the owner's brother adding pizzazz to the walls. There's a computer available in each suite and you can eat breakfast on the small roof terrace with views over the old city and out to sea.

Eating

Al Pinturicchio
ITALIAN €

(☑0963 60 34 52; Via Dardono 2; meals €22; ⊙7.30pm-midnight) Recommended by the locals, this restaurant in a smartly whitewashed cellar in the old town has a romantic ambience, candlelit tables and a solid repertoire of Calabrian dishes.

Osteria del Pescatore
SEAFOOD €€

(☑0963 60 30 18; Via del Monte 7; meals €26; ⊙noon-2.30pm & 8pm-midnight Wed-Mon) Swordfish (*spada*) is a speciality on this part of the coast and it rates highly on the menu at this simple seafood place tucked away in the backstreets. Also arranges fishing trips in good weather.

ℹ Information

Tourist Office (☑0963 6 14 75, 347 5318989; www.prolocotropea.eu; Piazza Ercole; ⊙9am-1pm & 4-8pm) In the old town centre.

WORTH A TRIP

CAPO VATICANO

There are spectacular views from this rocky cape, around 7km south of Tropea, with its beaches, ravines and limestone sea cliffs. Birdwatchers' spirits should soar. There's a lighthouse, built in 1885, which is close to a short footpath from where you can see as far as the Aeolian Islands. Capo Vaticano beach is one of the balmiest along this coast.

ⓘ Getting There & Away

Trains run to Pizzo-Lamezia (€2.40, 30 minutes, 12 daily), Scilla (€4.60, 1¼ hours, frequent) and Reggio (from €6.40, 1¾ hours, frequent). **Ferrovie della Calabria** (☑ 0961 89 62 39; www.ferroviedellacalabria.it) buses connect with other towns on the coast.

Pizzo

POP 9300

Stacked high up on a sea cliff, pretty little Pizzo is the place to go for *tartufo*, a death-by-chocolate ice-cream ball, and to see an extraordinary rock-carved grotto church. It's a popular and cheerful tourist stop. Piazza della Repubblica is the heart, set high above the sea with great views. Settle here at one of the many gelateria terraces for an ice-cream fix.

⊙ Sights

Castello Murat CASTLE
(☑ 0963 53 25 23; www.castellomurat.it; Scesa Castello Murat; adult/reduced €2.50/1.50; ⊙ 9am-11pm Jul & Aug, to 7pm Apr-Jun, Sep & Oct, shorter hours rest of year) This neat little 15th-century castle is named for Joachim Murat, brother-in-law of Napoleon Bonaparte and briefly King of Naples, captured in Pizzo and sentenced to death for treason in 1815. Inside the castle, you can see his cell and the details of his grisly end by firing squad, which is graphically illustrated with waxworks. Although Murat was the architect of enlightened reforms, the locals showed no great concern when he was executed.

Chiesa Matrice di San Giorgio CHURCH
(Via San Giorgio 1; ⊙ hours vary) In town, the 16th-century Chiesa Matrice di San Giorgio, with its splendid Baroque facade and dressed-up Madonnas, houses the tomb of Joachim Murat, the French-born former king of Naples and brother-in-law of Napoleon.

Chiesetta di Piedigrotta CHURCH
(☑ 0963 53 25 23; Via Riviera Prangi; adult/reduced €2.50/1.50; ⊙ 9am-1pm & 3-7.30pm Jul & Aug, shorter hours rest of year) The Chiesetta di Piedigrotta is an underground cave full of carved stone statues. It was carved into the tufa rock by Neapolitan shipwreck survivors in the 17th century. Other sculptors added to it and it was eventually turned into a church. Later statues include the less-godly figures of Fidel Castro and John F Kennedy. It's a bizarre, one-of-a-kind mixture of mysticism, mystery and kitsch, especially transporting when glowing in the setting sun.

🛏 Sleeping

Armonia B&B B&B €
(☑ 0963 53 33 37; www.casaarmonia.com; Vico II Armonia 9; s/d €60/85; @) Run by the charismatic Franco in his 16th-century family home, this B&B has three relaxing rooms and spectacular sea views.

Piccolo Grand Hotel BOUTIQUE HOTEL €€
(☑ 0963 53 32 93; www.piccolograndhotel.com; Via Chiaravalloti 32; s/d €110/158; ❄ 🔊) This pleasant four-star boutique hotel is hidden on an unlikely and rather dingy side street. But its exuberant blue-and-white design, upscale comforts and panoramic rooftop breakfasts make it one of Pizzo's top sleeps. There's also a small fitness area and e-bikes to rent.

🍴 Eating

Bar Gelateria Ercole GELATO €
(☑ 0963 53 11 49; Piazza della Repubblica 18; tartufo €5; ⊙ 8am-midnight) Pizzo enjoys something of a reputation for its gelato, and, on the main square, Ercole is reckoned by many to serve the best in town. The most admired flavours include *tartufo* (chocolate and hazelnut) and *cassata* (egg cream with candied fruit).

Ristorante Don Diego di Pizzo PIZZA €
(☑ 340 8924469; www.dondiegoristorante.com; Via Salomone 243; meals/pizza €25/7; ⊙ noon-3pm & 7pm-midnight Thu-Tue; 🖶) You'll earn your carbs walking uphill from central Pizzo to reach this welcoming restaurant, but be amply recompensed with fantastic views from a panoramic terrace and food to match. Don Diego is particularly known for its pizza.

ⓘ Getting There & Away

Pizzo is just off the major A3 autostrada. There are two train stations. Vibo Valentia-Pizzo is located 4km south of town on the main Rome–Reggio di Calabria line. A bus service connects you to Pizzo. Pizzo-Lamezia is south of the town on the Tropea–Lamezia Terme line. Shuttle buses (€2) connect with trains or you can walk for 20 minutes along the coast road.

Sicily

Best Places to Eat

➜ Accursio (p236)

➜ Il Barcaiolo (p216)

➜ Ristorante Crocifisso (p234)

➜ Osteria La Bettolaccia (p248)

➜ Punta Lena (p213)

Best Places to Stay

➜ Hotel Ravesi (p210)

➜ B&B Crociferi (p221)

➜ Stanze al Genio Residenze (p195)

➜ Villa Quartarella (p235)

➜ Pensione Tranchina (p245)

Why Go?

More of a sugar-spiked espresso than a milky cappuccino, Sicily rewards visitors with an intense, bittersweet experience. Overloaded with art treasures and natural beauty, undersupplied with infrastructure, and continuously struggling against Mafia-driven corruption, Sicily's complexities sometimes seem unfathomable. To really appreciate this place, come with an open mind – and a healthy appetite. Despite the island's perplexing contradictions, one factor remains constant: the uncompromisingly high quality of the cuisine.

After 25 centuries of foreign domination, Sicilians are the heirs to an impressive cultural legacy, from the refined architecture of Magna Graecia to the Byzantine splendour and Arab craftwork of the island's Norman cathedrals and palaces. This cultural richness is matched by a startlingly diverse landscape that includes bucolic farmland, smouldering volcanoes and kilometres of island-studded aquamarine coastline.

When to Go
Palermo

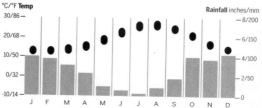

Easter Colourful religious processions and marzipan lambs in every bakery window.

May Wildflowers, dreamy coastal walking and Syracuse's festival of classic drama.

Sep Warm weather and seaside fun without summer prices.

Sicily Highlights

1 Teatro Massimo (p195) Joining the ranks of impeccably dressed opera-goers at this elegant theatre in Palermo.

2 Catania (p218) Bargaining with fish vendors at dawn, climbing Europe's most active volcano in the afternoon, and returning to buzzing nightlife.

3 Segesta (p250) Marvelling at the majesty of the 5th-century ruins, whose Doric temple sits in splendid isolation on a windswept hillside.

4 Taormina (p213) Watching international stars perform against Mt Etna's backdrop at summer festivals.

5 **Aeolian Islands** (p202)
Observing Stromboli's volcanic fireworks and hiking on these stunningly scenic islands.

6 **Syracuse** (p227)
Wandering in Ortygia's atmospheric alleys or stepping back in time at an Ancient Greek theatre performance.

7 **Villa Romana del Casale** (p237) Admiring prancing wild beasts and dancing bikini-clad gymnasts on the mosaic floors.

8 **Cefalù** (p200) Being dazzled by Byzantine mosaics and splendid coastal sunsets.

History

Sicily's most deeply ingrained cultural influences originate from its first inhabitants – the Sicani from North Africa, the Siculi from Latium (Italy) and the Elymni from Greece. The subsequent colonisation of the island by the Carthaginians (also from North Africa) and the Greeks, in the 8th and 6th centuries BC respectively, compounded this cultural divide through decades of war when powerful opposing cities struggled to dominate the island.

Although part of the Roman Empire, Sicily didn't truly come into its own until after the Arab invasions of 831 AD. Trade, farming and mining were all fostered under Arab influence and Sicily soon became an enviable prize for European opportunists. The Normans, desperate for a piece of the pie, invaded in 1061 and made Palermo the centre of their expanding empire and the finest city in the Mediterranean.

Impressed by the cultured Arab lifestyle, Norman king Roger squandered vast sums on ostentatious palaces and churches and encouraged a hedonistic atmosphere in his court. But such prosperity – and decadence (Roger's grandson, William II, even had a harem) – inevitably gave rise to envy and resentment and, after two centuries of pleasure and profit, the Norman line was extinguished. The kingdom passed to the austere German House of Hohenstaufen with little opposition from the seriously eroded and weakened the Norman occupation.

In the centuries that followed, Sicily passed to the Holy Roman Emperors, Angevins (French) and Aragonese (Spanish) in a turmoil of rebellion and revolution that continued until the Spanish Bourbons united Sicily with Naples in 1734 as the Kingdom of the Two Sicilies. Little more than a century later, on 11 May 1860, Giuseppe Garibaldi planned his daring and dramatic unification of Italy from Marsala on Sicily's western coast.

Reeling from this catalogue of colonisers, Sicilians struggled in poverty-stricken conditions. Unified with Italy, but no better off, nearly one million men and women emigrated to the US between 1871 and 1914 before the outbreak of WWI.

Ironically, the Allies (who were seeking Mafia help in America for the re-invasion of Italy) helped in establishing the Mafia's stranglehold on Sicily. In the absence of any suitable administrators, they invited the undesirable *mafioso* (Mafia boss) Don Calógero Vizzini to do the job. When Sicily became a semi-autonomous region in 1948, Mafia control extended right to the heart of politics and the region plunged into a 50-year silent civil war. It only started to emerge from this after the anti-Mafia maxi-trials of the 1980s, in which Sicily's revered magistrates Giovanni Falcone and Paolo Borsellino hauled hundreds of Mafia members into court, leading to important prosecutions.

The assassinations of Falcone and Borsellino in 1992 helped galvanise Sicilian public opposition to the Mafia's inordinate influence, and while organised crime lives on, the thuggery and violence of the 1980s has diminished. A growing number of businesses refuse to pay the extortionate protection money known as the *pizzo*, and important arrests continue, further encouraging those who would speak out against the Mafia.

On the political front, anti-Mafia crusaders currently serve in two of the island's most powerful positions: Palermo mayor Leoluca Orlando and Sicilian governor Rosario Crocetta. Nowadays the hot topics on everyone's mind are the island's continued economic struggles and Sicily's role as the gateway for the flood of immigrants from northern Africa.

ⓘ Getting There & Away

AIR

A number of airlines fly services direct to Palermo airport (PMO) and Catania airport (CTA), Sicily's two main international airports. A few also serve the smaller airports of Trapani (TPS) and Comiso (CIY). **Alitalia** (www.alitalia.com) is the main Italian carrier, while **Ryanair** (www.ryanair.com) is the leading low-cost airline serving Sicily.

BOAT

Regular car and passenger ferries cross the strait between Villa San Giovanni (Calabria) and Messina, while hydrofoils connect Messina with Reggio di Calabria.

Sicily is also accessible by ferry from Naples, Genoa, Civitavecchia, Livorno, Salerno, Cagliari, Malta and Tunis. Prices rise between June and September, when advanced bookings may also be required.

Sicily Ferry & Hydrofoil Crossings

ROUTE	COST PER ADULT FROM (€)	DURATION
Genoa–Palermo	80	20hr
Malta–Pozzallo	70	1¾hr
Naples–Catania	45	11hr
Naples–Palermo	45	10hr
Naples–Trapani	108	7hr
Reggio di Calabria–Messina	3.50	35min
Tunis–Palermo	49	10hr

BUS

SAIS Trasporti (☎ 091 617 11 41; www.sais trasporti.it) runs long-haul services to Sicily from Rome and Naples.

TRAIN

For travellers originating in Rome and points south, InterCity trains cover the distance from mainland Italy to Sicily in the least possible time, without a change of train. If coming from Milan, Bologna or Florence, your fastest option is to take the ultra-high-speed Frecciarossa as far as Naples, then change to an InterCity train for the rest of the journey.

All trains enter Sicily at Messina, after being transported by ferry from Villa San Giovanni at the toe of Italy's boot. At Messina, trains branch west along the Tyrrhenian coast to Palermo, or south along the Ionian coast to Catania.

ⓘ Getting Around

AIR

Mistral Air (www.mistralair.it) offers direct flights to the offshore islands of Pantelleria (from Palermo and Trapani) and Lampedusa (from Palermo and Catania).

BUS

Bus services within Sicily are provided by a variety of companies. Buses are usually the fastest option if your destination involves travel through the island's interior; trains tend to be cheaper (and sometimes faster) on the major coastal routes. In small towns and villages tickets are often sold in bars or on the bus.

CAR & MOTORCYCLE

Having your own vehicle is advantageous in the interior, where public transport is often slow and limited. Autostradas connect the major cities and are generally of good quality, especially the A18 and A20 toll roads, running along the Ionian and Tyrrhenian coasts, respectively. Even so, the island's highways have suffered some high-profile problems in recent years – most notably the landslide-induced collapse of a key

section of the A19 between Catania and Palermo in 2015. Drive defensively; Sicilian drivers are some of Italy's most aggressive, with a penchant for overtaking on blind corners, while holding a mobile phone in one hand and gesticulating wildly with the other!

TRAIN

Sicily's train service is very efficient along the north and east coasts. Services to towns in the interior tend be infrequent and slow, but the routes can be very picturesque. InterCity trains are the fastest and most expensive, while the *regionale* is the slowest.

PALERMO

POP 657,000

Palermo is a city of both decay and splendour, and – provided you can handle its raw energy, deranged driving and chaos – has plenty of appeal. Unlike Florence or Rome, many of the city's treasures are hidden, rather than scrubbed up for endless streams of tourists.

At one time an Arab emirate and the seat of a Norman kingdom, Palermo became Europe's grandest city in the 12th century, then underwent a further round of aesthetic transformations during 500 years of Spanish rule. The resulting treasure trove of palaces, castles and churches has a unique architectural fusion of Byzantine, Arab, Norman, Renaissance and baroque gems.

While some of the crumbling *palazzi* (mansions) bombed in WWII are being restored, others remain dilapidated, turned into shabby apartments, the faded glory of their ornate facades just visible behind strings of brightly coloured washing. The evocative history of the city remains very much part of the daily life of its inhabitants, and the dusty web of backstreet markets in the old quarter has a Middle Eastern feel.

The flip side is the modern city, a mere 15-minute stroll away, parts of which could be neatly jigsawed and slotted into Paris, with a grid system of wide avenues lined by seductive shops and handsome 19th-century apartments.

◉ Sights & Activities

Via Maqueda is the main street, running north from the train station, changing names to Via Ruggero Settimo as it passes the landmark Teatro Massimo, then finally widening into leafy Viale della Libertà north of Piazza Castelnuovo, the beginning of the city's modern district.

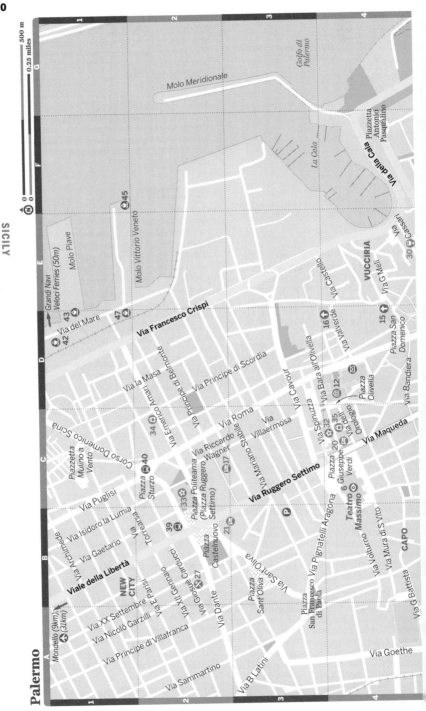

SICILY

Palermo

0 ⌒ N
0   0.25 miles
0   500 m

Golfo di Palermo

Molo Meridionale

La Cala

Piazzetta Antonio Pasqualino

Via della Cala

VUCCIRIA

Via G Meli

Via Cassari

30

15

16

Molo Piave

Grandi Navi Veloci Ferries (50m)

Molo Vittorio Veneto

45

Via del Mare

42 43

47

Via Francesco Crispi

Via la Masa

Via Emerico Amari

Via Principe di Belmonte

Via Principe di Scordia

Via Roma

Via Cavour

Via Castello

Via Valverde

Piazza Olivella

Via dell'Orologio

Via Bara all'Olivella

Via Spinuzza

32 35

12

20

Via Bandiera

Piazza San Domenico

Via Maqueda

Corso Domenico Scina

Piazzetta Mulino a Vento

Via Puglisi

Piazza Sturzo

40

34

Via Riccardo Wagner

Via Mariano Stabile

Via Villaermosa

17

Piazza Politeama (Piazza Ruggero Settimo)

33

Via Ruggero Settimo

Piazza Giuseppe Verdi

6

Teatro Massimo

Via Isidoro la Lumia

Via Archimede

Via Gaetario

Via Torrearsa

39

21

P

Via Pignatelli Aragona

CAPO

Via Mura di S Vito

Via G Battista

Viale della Libertà

NEW CITY

Via E Parisi

Via XII Gennaio

27

Piazza Castelnuovo

Via Sant'Oliva

Via Pignatelli Aragona

Via Volturno

Mondello (9km); (31km)

Via XX Settembre

Via Nicolò Garzilli

Via Giosuè Carducci

Via Dante

Piazza Sant'Oliva

Piazza San Francesco di Paola

Via Goethe

Via Principe di Villafranca

Via Sammartino

Via B Latini

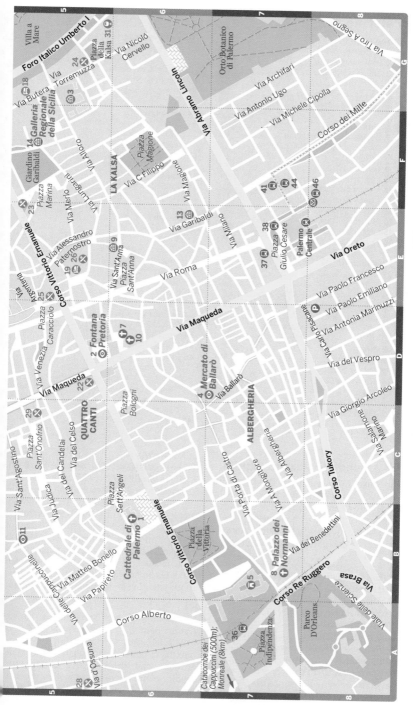

SICILY

Palermo

◎ Around the Quattro Canti

The busy intersection of Corso Vittorio Emanuele and Via Maqueda is known as the Quattro Canti. Forming the civic heart of Palermo, this crossroads neatly divides the historic nucleus into four traditional quarters – Albergheria, Capo, Vucciria and La Kalsa.

★ Fontana Pretoria   SQUARE

(Piazza Pretoria) This huge, ornate fountain, with tiered basins and sculptures rippling in concentric circles, forms the centrepiece of **Piazza Pretoria**, a spacious square just south of the Quattro Canti. The city bought the fountain in 1573; however, the flagrant nudity of the provocative nymphs proved too much for Sicilian churchgoers attending Mass next door, and they prudishly dubbed it the Fountain of Shame.

La Martorana   CHURCH

(Chiesa di Santa Maria dell'Ammiraglio; Piazza Bellini 3; adult/reduced €2/1; ⏲9.30am-1pm & 3.30-5.30pm Mon-Sat, 9-10.30am Sun) On the southern side of Piazza Bellini, this luminously beautiful 12th-century church was endowed by King Roger's Syrian emir, George of Antioch, and was originally planned as a mosque. Delicate Fatimid pillars support a domed cupola depicting Christ enthroned amid his archangels. The interior is best appreciated in the morning, when sunlight illuminates magnificent Byzantine mosaics.

Chiesa Capitolare di San Cataldo   CHURCH

(Piazza Bellini 3; adult/reduced €2.50/1.50; ⏲9.30am-12.30pm & 3-6pm) With its dusky-pink bijou domes, solid square shape, blind arcading and delicate tracery, this 12th-century church perfectly embodies the synthesis of Arab and Norman architectural styles. The interior, while more austere, has a lovely inlaid floor and some fine stone- and brickwork.

⦿ Albergheria

Southwest of the Quattro Canti, Albergheria is a rather shabby, rundown district once inhabited by Norman court officials, now home to a growing number of immigrants who are attempting to revitalise its dusty backstreets. The top tourist draws here are the Palazzo dei Normanni (Norman Palace) and its exquisite chapel, both at the neighbourhood's far western edge.

★ Palazzo dei Normanni   PALACE
(Palazzo Reale; ☑ 091 626 28 33; www.federico secondo.org; Piazza Indipendenza 1; adult/reduced Fri-Mon €12/10, Tue-Thu €10/8; ⊙ 8.15am-5pm Mon-Sat, to 12.15pm Sun) This venerable palace dates to the 9th century but owes its current look (and name) to a major 12th-century Norman makeover, during which spectacular mosaics were added to its **Royal Apartments** and priceless jewel of a chapel, the **Cappella Palatina**. Designed by Roger II in 1130, the chapel glitters with stunning gold mosaics, its aesthetic harmony further enhanced by the inlaid marble floors and wooden *muqarnas* ceiling, a masterpiece of Arab-style honeycomb carving that reflects Norman Sicily's cultural complexity.

The chapel is Palermo's top tourist attraction. Note that queues are likely, and that you'll be refused entry if you're wearing shorts, a short skirt or a low-cut top. The top level of the palace's three-tiered loggia houses Sicily's regional parliament and the Royal Apartments, including the mosaic-lined Sala dei Venti, and Sala di Ruggero II, King Roger's magnificent 12th-century bedroom. These latter attractions are only open to visitors from Friday to Monday.

Chiesa di San Giovanni
degli Eremiti   CHURCH
(☑ 091 651 50 19; Via dei Benedettini 20; adult/reduced €6/3; ⊙ 9am-6.30pm Mon-Sat, to 1pm Sun) Surrounded by a garden of citrus trees, palms, cacti and ruined walls, this remarkable, five-domed remnant of Arab-Norman architecture is hidden away in an otherwise rather squalid neighbourhood. It's built atop a mosque that itself was superimposed on an earlier chapel. The peaceful Norman cloisters outside offer lovely views of the Palazzo dei Normanni.

★ Mercato di Ballarò   MARKET
(⊙ 7.30am-8pm Mon-Sat, to 1pm Sun) Snaking for several city blocks southeast of Palazzo dei Normanni is Palermo's busiest street market, which throbs with activity well into the early evening. It's a fascinating mix of noises, smells and street life, and the cheapest place for everything from Chinese padded bras to fresh produce, fish, meat, olives and cheese – smile nicely for a taste.

⦿ Capo

Northwest of Quattro Canti is the Capo neighbourhood, a densely packed web of interconnected streets and blind alleys.

★ Cattedrale di Palermo   CATHEDRAL
(☑ 091 33 43 73; www.cattedrale.palermo.it; Corso Vittorio Emanuele; cathedral free, tombs €1.50, treasury & crypt €2, roof €5, all-inclusive ticket adult/reduced €7/5; ⊙ cathedral 7am-7pm Mon-Sat, 8am-1pm & 4-7pm Sun, royal tombs, treasury & roof 9am-5.30pm Sat, tombs only 10am-1pm Sun) A feast of geometric patterns, ziggurat crenellations, maiolica cupolas and blind arches, Palermo's cathedral has suffered aesthetically from multiple reworkings over the centuries, but remains a prime example of Sicily's unique Arab-Norman architectural style. The interior, while impressive in scale, is essentially a marble shell whose most interesting features are the **royal Norman tombs** (to the left as you enter) and the **treasury**, home to Constance of Aragon's gem-encrusted 13th-century crown.

Mercato del Capo   MARKET
(Via Sant'Agostino; ⊙ 7am-8pm Mon, Tue, Thu-Sat, to 1pm Wed & Sun) Capo's street market, running the length of Via Sant'Agostino, is a seething mass of colourful activity during the day, with vendors selling fruit, vegetables, meat, fish, cheese and household goods of every description.

Catacombe dei Cappuccini   CATACOMB
(www.catacombepalermo.it; Piazza Cappuccini; adult €3, child under 8yr free; ⊙ 9am-1pm & 3-6pm, closed Sun afternoon Nov-Mar) These catacombs house the mummified bodies and skeletons of some 8000 Palermitans who died between the 17th and 19th centuries. Earthly power, gender, religion and professional status are still rigidly distinguished, with men and women occupying separate corridors, and virgins set aside in a first-class section. From Piazza Indipendenza, it's a 15-minute walk.

SICILY PALERMO

◉ Vucciria

Once a notorious den of Mafia activity, the Vucciria retains a grungy, authentic edge. In the evenings it becomes a destination for bar-hopping and seriously down-to-earth street food. It's also home to some of Palermo's finest baroque artwork.

Museo Archeologico Regionale MUSEUM
(☑091 611 68 07; www.regione.sicilia.it/bbccaa/salinas; Piazza Olivella 24; ⊘9.30am-6.30pm Tue-Sat, to 1.30pm Sun) Situated in a converted Renaissance monastery, this splendid, wheelchair-accessible museum has been undergoing renovations since 2010, and has partially reopened, with attractive new exhibition spaces spread around its gracious courtyard. It houses some of Sicily's most valuable Greek and Roman artefacts, including the museum's crown jewel, a series of original decorative friezes from the temples at Selinunte.

Oratorio di Santa Cita CHAPEL
(www.ilgeniodipalermo.com; Via Valverde; admission €4, incl Oratorio di San Domenico €6; ⊘9am-6pm Mon-Sat) This 17th-century chapel showcases the breathtaking stucco work of Giacomo Serpotta, who famously introduced rococo to Sicilian churches. Note the elaborate *Battle of Lepanto* on the entrance wall. Depicting the Christian victory over the Turks, it's framed by stucco drapes held by hundreds of naughty cherubs modelled on Palermo's street urchins. Serpotta's virtuosity also dominates the side walls, where sculpted white stucco figures hold gilded swords, shields and a lute, and a golden snake (Serpotta's symbol) curls around a picture frame.

Oratorio di San Domenico CHAPEL
(www.ilgeniodipalermo.com; Via dei Bambinai 2; admission €4, incl Oratorio di Santa Cita €6; ⊘9am-6pm Mon-Sat) Dominating this small chapel is Anthony Van Dyck's fantastic blue-and-red altarpiece, *The Virgin of the Rosary with St Dominic and the Patronesses of Palermo*. Van Dyck completed the work in Genoa in 1628, after leaving Palermo in fear of the plague. Also gracing the chapel are Giacomo Serpotta's amazingly elaborate stuccoes (1710–17), vivacious and whirling with figures. Serpotta's name meant 'lizard' or 'small snake', and he often included these signature reptiles in his work; see if you can find one!

◉ La Kalsa

Due to its proximity to the port, La Kalsa was subjected to carpet bombing during WWII, leaving it derelict and run down. Mother Teresa considered it akin to the shanty towns of Calcutta and established a mission here. Certain areas of La Kalsa, especially the part nearest the Quattro Canti, have undergone extensive renovation in recent years – for example, the former stock exchange has been converted into a high-end hotel. However, the neighbourhood still feels scruffy around the edges, with a decaying ambience that some will find intriguing, others off-putting.

★**Galleria Regionale della Sicilia** MUSEUM
(Palazzo Abatellis; ☑091 623 00 11; Via Alloro 4; adult/reduced €8/4; ⊘9am-6.30pm Tue-Fri, to 1pm Sat & Sun) Housed in the stately 15th-century Palazzo Abatellis, this fine museum features works by Sicilian artists from the Middle Ages to the 18th century. Its greatest treasure is *Triunfo della Morte* (Triumph of Death), a magnificent fresco in which Death is represented as a demonic skeleton mounted on a wasted horse, brandishing a wicked-looking scythe while leaping over his hapless victims.

Museo dell'Inquisizione MUSEUM
(Palazzo Chiaramonte-Steri; ☑091 2389 3788; Piazza Marina 61; adult/reduced €8/3; ⊘10am-6pm Tue-Sun) Housed in the lower floors and basements of the 14th-century Palazzo Chiaramonte-Steri, this unique museum offers a chilling but fascinating look at the legacy of the Inquisition in Palermo. Thousands of 'heretics' were detained here between 1601 and 1782; the honeycomb of former cells has been painstakingly restored to reveal multiple layers of their graffiti and artwork (religious and otherwise). Excellent guided visits of the prison and the palace itself are available in English with advance notice.

Galleria d'Arte Moderna MUSEUM
(☑091 843 16 05; www.gampalermo.it; Via Sant'Anna 21; adult/reduced €7/5; ⊘9.30am-6.30pm Tue-Sun) This wheelchair-accessible museum is housed in a sleekly renovated 15th-century *palazzo* and former convent. The wide-ranging collection of 19th- and 20th-century Sicilian art is beautifully displayed on three floors, along with regular modern-art exhibitions. There's an excellent bookshop and gift shop. English-language audio guides cost €4.

◉ New City

North of Piazza Giuseppe Verdi, Palermo elegantly slips into cosmopolitan mode. Here you'll find fabulous neoclassical and art nouveau buildings hailing from the last golden age of Sicilian architecture, along with late 19th-century mansion blocks lining the broad boulevard of Viale della Libertà.

★ Teatro Massimo   THEATRE

(☑ tour reservations 091 605 32 67; www.teatro massimo.it; Piazza Giuseppe Verdi; guided tours adult/reduced €8/5; ⊙ 9.30am-6pm) Palermo's grand neoclassical opera house (built 1875-97) took more than 20 years to complete and has become one of the city's iconic landmarks. The closing scene of *The Godfather: Part III*, with its visually stunning juxtaposition of high culture, crime, drama and death, was filmed here. Guided 25-minute tours are offered throughout the day in English, Spanish, French, German and Italian.

🎎 Festivals & Events

Festino di Santa Rosalia   RELIGIOUS

(U Fistinu; www.festinodisantarosaliapalermo.it; ⊙ 10-15 Jul) Palermo's biggest annual festival celebrates patron saint Santa Rosalia, beloved for having saved the city from a 17th-century plague. The most colourful festivities take place on the evening of 14 July, when the saint's relics are paraded aboard a grand chariot from the Palazzo dei Normanni through the Quattro Canti to the waterfront, where fireworks and general merriment ensue.

🛏 Sleeping

Budget options can be found around Via Maqueda and Via Roma in the vicinity of the train station. Midrange and top-end hotels are concentrated further north. Parking usually costs an extra €10 to €15 per day.

★ Stanze al Genio Residenze   B&B €

(☑ 380 3673773; www.stanzealgeniobnb.it; Via Garibaldi 11; r €75-98; ❄ �🛜) Speckled with Sicilian antiques, this B&B offers four gorgeous bedrooms, three with 19th-century ceiling frescoes. All four are spacious and thoughtfully appointed, with Murano lamps, old wooden wardrobes, the odd balcony railing turned bedhead, and top-quality, orthopaedic beds. That the property features beautiful maiolica tiles is no coincidence; the B&B is affiliated with the wonderful **Museo delle**

Maioliche (Stanze al Genio; ☑ 340 0971561; www.stanzealgenio.it; adult/reduced €7/5; ⊙ by appointment), downstairs.

B&B Amélie   B&B €

(☑ 328 8654824, 091 33 59 20; www.bb-amelie.it; Via Prinicipe di Belmonte 94; s €40-60, d €60-90, tr €90-100; ❄ @ 🛜) On a pedestrianised New City street a stone's throw from Teatro Politeama, the affable, multilingual Angela has converted her grandmother's spacious 6th-floor flat into a cheery B&B. Rooms are colourfully decorated, and the corner triple has a sunny terrace. Angela, a native Palermitan, generously shares her local knowledge and serves a tasty breakfast featuring homemade cakes and jams.

Palazzo Pantaleo   B&B €

(☑ 091 32 54 71; www.palazzopantaleo.it; Via Ruggero Settimo 74h; s/d/ste €80/100/150; 🅿 🛜) Offering unbeatable comfort and a convenient location, Giuseppe Scaccianoce's classy B&B occupies the top floor of an old *palazzo* half a block from Piazza Politeama, hidden from the busy street in a quiet courtyard with free parking. Five rooms and one spacious suite feature high ceilings, marble, tile or wooden floors, soundproof windows and modern bathrooms.

Butera 28   APARTMENT €€

(☑ 333 3165432; www.butera28.it; Via Butera 28; apt per day €70-220, per week €450-1500; ❄ 🛜 🧺) Delightful multilingual owner Nicoletta rents 12 comfortable apartments in the 18th-century Palazzo Lanzi Tomasi, the last home of Giuseppe Tomasi di Lampedusa, author of *The Leopard*. Units range from 30 to 180 sq metres, most sleeping a family of four or more. Four apartments face the sea; most have laundry facilities; and all have well-equipped kitchens.

Massimo Plaza Hotel   HOTEL €€

(☑ 091 32 56 57; www.massimoplazahotel.com; Via Maqueda 437; r €100-250; 🅿 ❄ 🛜) Boasting a prime location along Palermo's pedestrianised Via Maqueda, this older hotel is a Palermo classic. Seven of the 15 rooms boast full-on views of the iconic Teatro Massimo across the street. The included breakfast (continental or American) can be delivered directly to your room at no extra charge, and enclosed parking costs €15 per day.

Grand Hotel Piazza Borsa   HOTEL €€€

(☑ 091 32 00 75; www.piazzaborsa.com; Via dei Cartari 18; s/d/ste from €154/208/454; 🅿 ❄ @ 🛜)

Grandly situated in Palermo's former stock exchange, this four-star hotel encompasses three separate buildings housing 127 rooms. Nicest are the high-ceilinged suites with jacuzzis and windows facing Piazza San Francesco. Parking costs €18 per 24-hour period.

Eating

Restaurants rarely start to fill up before 9pm. Many places close on Sundays, especially in the evening. For cheap eats, wander the tangle of alleys east and south of Teatro Massimo, or snack with locals at the street-food carts in Palermo's markets.

★ Trattoria al Vecchio Club Rosanero
SICILIAN €

(☑ 091 251 12 34; Vicolo Caldomai 18; meals €15; ☺ 1-3.30pm Mon-Sat & 8-11pm Thu-Sat; ☎) A veritable shrine to the city's football team (*rosa nero* refers to the team's colours, pink and black), cavernous Vecchio Club scores goals with its bargain-priced, flavour-packed grub. Fish and seafood are the real fortes here; if it's on the menu, order the *caponata e pesce spada* (sweet-and-sour vegetable salad with swordfish), a culinary victory. Head in early to avoid a wait.

★ Bisso Bistrot
BISTRO €

(☑ 091 33 49 99, 328 1314595; Via Maqueda 172; meals €14-18; ☺ 9am-11.30pm Mon-Sat) Frescoed walls, high ceilings and reasonably priced appetisers, *primi* and *secondi* greet diners at this historic Liberty-style bookstore at the northwest corner of the Quattro Canti, which has been converted into a classy but casual bistro. Lunch and dinner menus range from traditional Sicilian pasta, meat and fish dishes to sardine burgers, with cafe service in the mornings and afternoons.

DON'T MISS

PALERMO'S STREET FOOD

If you were taught that it is bad manners to eat in the street, you can break the rule in good company here. The mystery is how Palermo is not the obesity capital of Europe, given how much eating goes on. Palermitans are at it all the time: when they're shopping, commuting, discussing business, romancing...basically at any time of the day. What they're enjoying is the *buffitieri* – little hot snacks prepared at stalls and meant to be eaten on the spot.

Kick off the morning with *pane e panelle*, Palermo's famous chickpea fritter sandwich – great for vegetarians and a welcome change from a sweet custard-filled croissant. If you like, ask for it with a few *crocchè*, potato croquettes flavoured with fresh mint, also cheekily nicknamed *cazzilli* (little penises). Then again, you might want to go for some *sfincione* (a spongy, oily pizza topped with onions and *caciocavallo* cheese). In summer, locals also enjoy a freshly baked brioche filled with gelato or a *granita* (crushed ice mixed with fresh fruit, almonds, pistachios or coffee).

From 4pm onwards the snacks become decidedly more carnivorous, and you may wish you hadn't read the following translations: how about some barbecued *stigghiola* (goat intestines filled with onions, cheese and parsley), for example? Or a couple of *pani ca meusa* (bread rolls stuffed with sautéed beef spleen)? You'll be asked if you want your roll *schietta* (single) or *maritata* (married). If you choose *schietta*, the roll will only have ricotta in it before being dipped into boiling lard; choose *maritata* and you'll get the beef spleen as well.

You'll find street-food stalls all over town. Classic spots include Piazza Caracciolo in the Vucciria district, **Francu u Vastiddaru** (Corso Vittorio Emanuele 102; sandwiches €1.50-3.50; ☺ 8am-1am) and **Friggitoria Chiluzzo** (Piazza della Kalsa; sandwiches €1.50-2; ☺ 8am-5pm Mon-Sat) in the Kalsa, and the no-name *pane e panelle* cart on Piazza Carmine in Ballarò market.

For expert guidance, check out the low-key tours offered by **Palermo Street Food** (www.palermostreetfood.com; 3hr tours per person €30) and **Streaty** (www.streaty.com; 3/4hr tours per person €30/39). Both offer the chance to wander Palermo's backstreets with a knowledgable local guide, stopping for a taste (or two, or three) at the city's most authentic hang-outs.

Trattoria Ai Cascinari
SICILIAN €

(☑091 651 98 04; Via d'Ossuna 43/45; meals €20-25; ☺12.30-2.30pm Tue-Sun, plus 8-10.30pm Wed-Sat) Yes, it's a bit out of the way, but this friendly neighbourhood trattoria, 1km north of the Cappella Palatina, is a long-standing Palermitan favourite, and deservedly so. It's especially enjoyable on Sunday afternoons, when locals pack the labyrinth of back rooms and waiters perambulate nonstop with plates of scrumptious seasonal antipasti, fresh seafood and desserts.

Pasticceria Cappello
PASTRIES €

(☑091 611 37 69; www.pasticceriacappello.it; Via Nicolo Garzilli 19; desserts from €1.70; ☺7.30am-9.30pm Thu-Tue) One of Palermo's finest bakeries, Cappello is famous for its *setteveli* (seven-layer chocolate-hazelnut cake), invented here and long since copied all over Palermo. Its display case brims with countless other splendid pastries and desserts, including the dreamy *delizia di pistacchio* (a granular pistachio cake topped with creamy icing and a chocolate medallion) and ricotta-filled treats such as *cannoli* and *sfogliatelle*.

Il Maestro del Brodo
TRATTORIA €€

(☑091 32 95 23; Via Pannieri 7; meals €22-31; ☺noon-3pm Tue-Sun, plus 7.30-11pm Fri & Sat) This trattoria in the Vucciria offers delicious soups, an array of ultrafresh seafood and a sensational antipasto buffet (€8) featuring a dozen-plus homemade delicacies: *sarde a beccafico* (stuffed sardines), eggplant *involtini* (roulades), smoked fish, artichokes with parsley, sun-dried tomatoes, olives and more.

Osteria Ballarò
SICILIAN €€

(☑091 32 64 88; www.osteriaballaro.it; Via Calascibetta 25; meals €30-45; ☺noon-3.15pm & 7-11.15pm) This classy restaurant-cum-wine bar marries an atmospheric setting with fantastic island cooking. Bare stone columns, exposed brick walls and vaulted ceilings set the stage for delicious seafood *primi*, local wines and memorable Sicilian *dolci* (sweets). Reservations recommended. For a faster eat, you can snack on street food at the bar or take away from the hole-in-the-wall counter outside.

🍷 Drinking & Nightlife

Palermo's liveliest clusters of bars can be found along Via Chiavettieri in the Vucciria neighbourhood (just northwest of Piazza Marina) and in the Champagneria district east of Teatro Massimo, centred on Piazza Olivella, Via Spinuzza and Via Patania. Higher-end bars and dance venues are concentrated in the newer part of Palermo. In summer, many Palermitans decamp to Mondello by the sea.

Bocum Mixology
COCKTAIL BAR

(☑091 33 20 09; www.bocum.it; Via dei Cassari 6; ☺6pm-1.30am Tue-Sun) All hail Bocum, Palermo's first proper cocktail bar. While the ground-floor cantina is a fine spot for cognoscenti wines and DOP (Denominazzione di Origine Protetta; Protected Designation of Origin) *salumi* (charcuterie), the real magic happens upstairs. Here, on your right, lies the mixology lounge, where skilled hands shake and stir seamless, nuanced libations. Add flickering candlelight and crackling jazz, and you have yourself one rather bohemian Palermo evening.

Kursaal Kalhesa
BAR

(☑340 1573493; www.facebook.com/kursaalkalhesa; Foro Umberto I 21; ☺8pm-12.30am Tue & Wed, to 2am Thu, to 3am Fri-Sun) Restyled Kursaal Kalhesa has long been a noted city nightspot. Touting itself as a restaurant, wine bar and jazz club, it draws a cool, in-the-know crowd who come to hang out over *aperitivi,* dine alfresco or catch a gig under the high vaulted ceilings. It's in a 15th-century *palazzo* on the city's massive sea walls.

☆ Entertainment

The daily paper *Il Giornale di Sicilia* (http://gds.it/articoli/cultura) has a listing of what's on. If you can read some Italian, www.balarm.it is another excellent resource.

★ Teatro Massimo
OPERA

(☑box office 091 605 35 80; www.teatromassimo.it; Piazza Giuseppe Verdi) Ernesto Basile's six-tiered art nouveau masterpiece, with lions flanking its grandiose columned entrance and an interior gleaming in red and gold, is Europe's third-largest opera house and one of Italy's most prestigious, right up there with La Scala in Milan, San Carlo in Naples and La Fenice in Venice. The theatre stages opera, ballet and music concerts from September to June.

Teatro dei Pupi di Mimmo Cuticchio
THEATRE

(☑091 32 34 00; www.figlidartecuticchio.com; Via Bara all'Olivella 95; adult/reduced €10/5) This puppet theatre is a charming low-tech choice for children (and adults), staging

SICILIAN PUPPET THEATRE

Since the 18th century, the Opera dei Pupi (traditional Sicilian puppet theatre) has been enthralling adults and children alike. The shows are a mini theatrical performance, with some puppets standing 1.5m high – a completely different breed from the popular glove puppet. These characters are intricately carved from beech, olive or lemon wood and have realistic-looking features; flexible joints ensure they have no problem swinging their swords or beheading dragons.

Effectively the soap operas of their day, Sicilian puppet shows expounded the deepest sentiments of life – unrequited love, treachery, thirst for justice, and the anger and frustration of the oppressed. The swashbuckling tales centre on the legends of Charlemagne's heroic knights, Orlando and Rinaldo, with an extended cast including the fair Angelica, the treacherous Gano di Magonza and forbidding Saracen warriors. Puppeteers are judged on the dramatic effect they can create – lots of stamping feet and a gripping running commentary – and on their speed and skill in directing the battle scenes.

traditional shows with fabulous handcrafted puppets.

Teatro Politeama Garibaldi
PERFORMING ARTS
(☑ 091 607 25 11; Piazza Ruggero Settimo) This grandiose theatre is a popular venue for opera, ballet and classical music, staging afternoon and evening concerts. It's home to Palermo's symphony orchestra, the Orchestra Sinfonica Siciliana.

Shopping

Via Bara all'Olivella is good for arts and crafts.

Il Laboratorio Teatrale
ARTS & CRAFTS
(☑ 091 32 34 00; Via Bara all'Olivella 40; ⊙10am-1pm & 4-7pm Tue-Sat) A true artists' workshop, this enchanting space is where the Cuticchio family constructs puppets for its famous theatre across the street. High-quality puppets dating from the late 19th century to the present are displayed here, and are available for purchase by serious enthusiasts.

Gusti di Sicilia
FOOD & DRINKS
(www.gustidisicilia.com; Via Emerico Amari 79; ⊙8.30am-11pm) Stock up on beautifully packaged Sicilian edibles, from tins of tuna to jars of *caponata* (sweet-and-sour vegetable salad), capers and marmalade, and bottles of wine and olive oil.

ⓘ Information

EMERGENCY
For an ambulance, call ☑118 or ☑091 666 55 28.
Police (Questura; ☑ 091 21 01 11; Piazza della Vittoria 8) Main police station.

MEDICAL SERVICES
Hospital (Ospedale Civico; ☑ 091 666 11 11; www.arnascivico.it; Piazza Nicola Leotta; ⊙24hr) Emergency facilities.

TOURIST INFORMATION
Municipal Tourist Office (☑ 091 740 80 21; http://turismo.comune.palermo.it; Piazza Bellini; ⊙ 8.30am-6.30pm Mon-Fri, from 9.30am Sat) The most reliable of Palermo's city-run information booths. Others, located at Piazza Castelnuovo, Teatro Massimo, the Port of Palermo and Mondello, keep shorter hours.
Tourist Information – Falcone-Borsellino Airport (☑ 091 59 16 98; www.gesap.it/tourist-information-office; ⊙ 8.30am-7.30pm Mon-Fri, to 6pm Sat) Downstairs in the Arrivals hall.

ⓘ Getting There & Away

AIR
Falcone-Borsellino Airport (☑ 800 541880, 091 702 02 73; www.gesap.it) is at Punta Raisi, 31km west of Palermo.

Alitalia and other major airlines such as Air France, Lufthansa and KLM fly from Palermo to destinations throughout Europe. Several cut-rate carriers also offer flights to/from Palermo, including Ryanair, Volotea, Vueling and easyJet. Falcone-Borsellino is the hub airport for regular domestic flights to the islands of Pantelleria and Lampedusa.

BOAT
The ferry terminal is located just east of the corner of Via Francesco Crispi and Via Emerico Amari.
Grandi Navi Veloci (☑ 010 209 45 91, 091 6072 6162; www.gnv.it; Calata Marinai d'Italia) Runs ferries to Civitavecchia (from €59, 14 hours), Genoa (from €100, 19½ hours), Naples (from €48, 10 hours) and Tunis (from €49, 9½ hours).

Grimaldi Lines (☑ 091 611 36 91, 081 49 64 44; www.grimaldi-lines.com; Via del Mare) Runs ferries twice weekly to Salerno (from €40, 9½ hours) and Tunis (from €56, 11 hours), and thrice weekly to Livorno (from €65, 18 hours).

Liberty Lines (☑ 0923 87 38 13; www.liberty lines.it; Molo Vittorio Veneto) From late June to early September, Liberty operates one daily hydrofoil to Lipari (€57.30, four hours), Stromboli (€75.10, 5½ hours) and other points in the Aeolian Islands.

Tirrenia (☑ 892123; www.tirrenia.it; Calata Marinai d'Italia) Ferries to Cagliari (from €50, 12 hours, once or twice weekly) and Naples (from €45, 10¼ hours, daily).

BUS

Offices for all bus companies are located within a block or two of Palermo Centrale train station. The two main departure points are the **Piazzetta Cairoli bus terminal** (Piazzetta Cairoli), just south of the train station's eastern entrance, and **Via Paolo Balsamo**, due east of the train station.

AST (Azienda Siciliana Trasporti; ☑ 091 680 00 11; www.aziendasicilianatrasporti.it; New Bus Bar, Via Paolo Balsamo 32) Services to southeastern destinations including Ragusa (€13.50, four hours, four daily Monday to Saturday, two on Sunday).

Autoservizi Tarantola (☑ 0924 310 20; www.tarantolabus.it; New Bus Bar, Via Paolo Balsamo 32) Buses to Segesta (one way/return €8/12.70, 80 minutes) run once daily, with two buses returning daily to Palermo.

Cuffaro (☑ 091 616 15 10; www.cuffaro.info; Via Paolo Balsamo 13) Services to Agrigento (€9, two hours, three to seven daily).

SAIS Autolinee (☑ 800 211020, 091 616 60 28; www.saisautolinee.it; Piazzetta Cairoli bus station) To/from Catania (€13.50, 2¾ hours, nine to 13 daily) and Messina (€14, 2¾ hours, four to six daily).

SAIS Trasporti (☑ 091 617 11 41; www.saistrasporti.it; Via Paolo Balsamo 20) Thriceweekly overnight service to Rome (€34, 12 hours).

Salemi (☑ 091 772 03 47; www.autoservizi salemi.it; Piazzetta Cairoli bus station) Several buses daily to Marsala (€11, 2½ hours) and Trapani's Birgi Airport (€11, 1¾ hours).

CAR & MOTORCYCLE

Palermo is accessible on the A20-E90 toll road from Messina and the A19-E932 from Catania via Enna. Trapani and Marsala are also easily accessible from Palermo by motorway (A29), while Agrigento and Palermo are linked by the SS121 and SS189, good state roads through the island's interior.

Most major auto-hire companies are represented at the airport; you'll often save money by booking online before leaving home. Given the city's chaotic traffic and expensive parking, and the excellent public transport from Palermo's airport, it's generally best to postpone rental car pick-up until you're ready to leave the city.

TRAIN

From Palermo Centrale station, just south of the centre at the foot of Via Roma, regular trains leave for the following destinations:

Agrigento €9, 2¼ hours, eight to 10 daily

Catania €13.50, 2¾ hours, three to six daily

Cefalù €5.60, 45 minutes to one hour, hourly

Messina from €12.80, 2¾ hours to 3½ hours, hourly

From Messina, InterCity trains continue to Reggio di Calabria, Naples and Rome.

ℹ Getting Around

TO/FROM THE AIRPORT

Prestia e Comandè (☑ 091 58 63 51; www.prestiaecomande.it; one way/return €6.30/11) runs a half-hourly bus service from the airport to the centre of town, making stops outside Teatro Politeama Garibaldi (35 minutes) and Palermo Centrale train station (50 minutes). Buses are parked to the right as you exit the airport Arrivals hall. Buy tickets at the kiosk adjacent to the bus stop. Return journeys to the airport run with similar frequency, picking up at the same points.

Service on Trenitalia's Trinacria Express train, which normally runs half-hourly between Palermo Centrale and the airport (Punta Raisi station) was indefinitely suspended as of 2017 due to construction. Check www.trenitalia.com for current status.

A taxi from the airport to downtown Palermo costs €40 to €45.

BUS

Palermo's orange, white and blue city buses, operated by **AMAT** (☑ 848 800817, 091 35 01 11; www.amat.pa.it), are frequent but often crowded and slow. The free map handed out at Palermo tourist offices details all the major bus lines; most stop at the train station. Tickets, valid for 90 minutes, cost €1.40 if pre-purchased from *tabaccherie* (tobacconists) or AMAT booths, or €1.80 if purchased on board the bus. A day pass costs €3.50.

Especially useful for visitors is AMAT's Navetta Centro Storico, a free orange shuttle bus that makes a circular loop connecting Palermo's main downtown landmarks, including the train station, the Palazzo dei Normanni, the cathedral and Teatro Massimo.

CAR & MOTORCYCLE

Driving is frenetic in the city and best avoided, if possible. Use one of the staffed car parks around town (from €12 to €20 per day) if your hotel lacks parking.

WORTH A TRIP

AROUND PALERMO

A few kilometres outside Palermo's city limits, the beach town of Mondello and the dazzling cathedral of Monreale are both worthwhile day trips. Just offshore, Ustica makes a great overnight or weekend getaway.

Monreale

In the hills 8km southwest of Palermo, **Cattedrale di Monreale** (☑ 091 640 44 03; Piazza del Duomo; admission to cathedral free, north transept, Roano chapel & terrace €4, cloisters adult/reduced €6/3; ⏰ cathedral 8.30am-12.45pm & 2.30-5pm Mon-Sat, 8-10am & 2.30-5pm Sun, cloisters 9am-6.30pm Mon-Sat, to 1pm Sun) is considered the finest example of Norman architecture in Sicily, incorporating Norman, Arab, Byzantine and classical elements. Inspired by a vision of the Virgin, it was built by William II in an effort to outdo his grandfather, Roger II, who was responsible for the cathedral in Cefalù and the Cappella Palatina in Palermo. The interior, completed in 1184 and executed in shimmering mosaics, depicts 42 Old Testament stories. Outside the cathedral, the **cloister** is a tranquil courtyard with a tangible oriental feel. Surrounding the perimeter, elegant Romanesque arches are supported by an exquisite array of slender columns alternately decorated with mosaics. To reach Monreale, take AMAT bus 389 (€1.40, 35 minutes, every 1¼ hours) from Piazza Indipendenza in Palermo or AST's Monreale bus (one way/return €1.90/3, 40 minutes, hourly Monday to Saturday) from in front of Palermo Centrale train station.

Mondello

Tucked between dramatic headlands 12km north of Palermo, Mondello is home to a long, sandy beach that became fashionable in the 19th century, when people came to the seaside in their carriages, prompting the construction of the huge art nouveau pier that still graces the waterfront. Most of the beaches near the pier are private (two sun loungers and an umbrella cost from €10 to €20); however, there's a wide swath of public beach opposite the centre of town with all the requisite pedalos and jet skis for hire. Given its easygoing seaside feel, Mondello is an excellent base for families. To get here, take bus 806 (€1.40, 30 minutes) from Piazza Sturzo in Palermo.

Ustica

A 90-minute boat trip from downtown, the 8.7-sq-km island of Ustica was declared Italy's first marine reserve in 1986. The surrounding waters are a playground of fish and coral, ideal for snorkelling, diving and underwater photography. To enjoy Ustica's wild coastline and dazzling grottoes without the crowds, try visiting in June or September. There are numerous dive centres, hotels and restaurants on the island, as well as some nice hiking. To get here from Palermo, take the once-daily car ferry (€18.85, three hours) operated by **Siremar** (☑ 090 36 46 01; www.siremar.it) or the faster, more frequent hydrofoils (€27.60, 1½ hours) operated by Liberty Lines (p199). For more details on Ustica, see Lonely Planet's *Sicily* guide.

TYRRHENIAN COAST

The coast between Palermo and Milazzo is studded with popular tourist resorts attracting a steady stream of holidaymakers, particularly between June and September. The best of these is Cefalù, a resort second only to the Ionian coast's Taormina in popularity. Just inland lie the two massive natural parks of the Madonie and Nebrodi mountains.

Cefalù

POP 14,300

This popular holiday resort wedged between a dramatic mountain peak and a sweeping stretch of sand has the lot: a great beach, a truly lovely historic centre with a grandiose cathedral, and winding medieval streets lined with restaurants and boutiques. Avoid the height of summer when prices soar, beaches are jam packed and the charm of the place is tainted by bad-tempered drivers trying to find a car park.

◎ Sights

★ Duomo di Cefalù   CATHEDRAL
(☑ 092 192 20 21; www.cattedraledicefalu.com; Piazza del Duomo; cloisters adult/reduced €3/2; ⊙ duomo 8.30am-6.30pm Apr-Oct, 8.30am-1pm & 3.30-5pm Nov-Mar, cloisters 10am-1pm & 3-6pm daily Apr-Oct, 10am-1pm Mon-Fri & by arrangement Sat Nov-Mar) Cefalù's cathedral is one of the jewels in Sicily's Arab-Norman crown, equalled in magnificence only by the Cattedrale di Monreale (southwest of Palermo) and Palermo's Cappella Palatina. Filling the central apse, a towering figure of Christ All Powerful is the focal point of the elaborate Byzantine mosaics – Sicily's oldest and best preserved, pre-dating those of Monreale by 20 or 30 years.

★ La Rocca   VIEWPOINT
(adult/reduced €4/2; ⊙ 8am-7pm May-Sep, 9am-4pm Oct-Apr) Looming over the town, this imposing rocky crag is the site where the Arabs built their citadel, occupying it until the Norman conquest in 1061 forced them down to the port below. To reach the summit, follow signs for Tempio di Diana from the corner of Corso Ruggero and Vicolo Saraceni. The 30- to 45-minute route climbs the Salita Saraceno, a winding staircase, through three tiers of city walls before emerging onto rock-strewn upland slopes with spectacular coastal views.

🏃 Activities

Cefalù's crescent-shaped beach, just west of the medieval centre, is lovely, but in the summer get here early to find a patch for your umbrella and towel.

You can escape with a boat tour along the coast during the summer months, through agencies along Corso Ruggero, including Visit Sicily Tours (☑ 0921 92 50 36; www.visitsicilytours.com; Corso Ruggero 83; boat tours €30-80; ⊙ Apr-Oct), right next door to the tourist office.

🛌 Sleeping

Bookings are essential in summer.

Dolce Vita   B&B €
(☑ 0921 92 31 51; www.dolcevitabb.it; Via Bordonaro 8; s €35-60, d €50-110) This popular B&B has one of the loveliest terraces in town, complete with deckchairs overlooking the sea and a barbecue for those warm balmy evenings. Rooms are airy and light, with comfy beds, though the staff's lackadaisical attitude can detract from the charm.

Scirocco Bed & Breakfast   B&B €
(☑ 0392 644 41 31; www.sciroccobeb.com; Piazza Garibaldi 8; s €50-70, d €70-110; ❀ 🕾) Convenient location and spectacular views are the two big selling points at this B&B halfway between the train station and the cathedral. Four comfortable and bright upper-floor guest rooms are crowned by a rooftop terrace that's perfect for watching the sun set over the Tyrrhenian Sea, or for monitoring cafe life on Piazza Garibaldi, directly below.

Hotel Kalura   HOTEL €€
(☑ 0921 42 13 54; www.hotelkalura.com; Via Vincenzo Cavallaro 13; s €100-134, d €157-200, 4-person apt €215-259; P❀@🏊🐕) East of town on a rocky outcrop, this German-run, family-oriented hotel has its own pebbly beach, a restaurant and a fabulous pool. Most rooms have sea views, and the hotel staff can arrange loads of activities, including mountain biking, hiking, canoeing, pedalos, diving and dance nights. It's a 20-minute walk into town.

🍴 Eating & Drinking

Ti Vitti   SICILIAN €€
(☑ 0921 92 15 71; www.ristorantetivitti.com; Via Umberto I 34; meals €35-45; ⊙ noon-3pm & 6.30-11pm Wed-Mon) Named after a Sicilian card game, this restaurant serves up fresh-from-the-market fish dishes, locally sourced treats such as *basilisco* mushrooms from nearby Monte Madonie, and scrumptious *cannoli* (pastry shells filled with ricotta or custard) for dessert. For something more casual, head to its affiliated pizzeria, Bottega Ti Vitti (☑ 0921 92 26 42; www.bottegativitti.com; Lungomare Giardina 7; pizza, salads & burgers €5-12; ⊙ 10am-midnight, closed Tue Nov-Apr), whose waterfront setting is perfect for sunset *aperitivi* (pre-dinner drinks).

La Galleria   SICILIAN, CAFE €€
(☑ 0921 42 02 11; www.lagalleriacefalu.it; Via Mandralisca 23; meals €30-40; ⊙ noon-3pm & 7-11pm Wed-Mon) This is about as hip as Cefalù gets. Functioning as a restaurant, cafe and occasional gallery space, La Galleria has an informal vibe, a bright internal courtyard and an innovative menu that mixes standard *primi* and *secondi* with a range of all-in-one dishes (€14 to €16) designed to be meals in themselves.

THE MADONIE MOUNTAINS: CEFALÙ'S BACKYARD GETAWAY

Due south of Cefalù, the 400sq-km **Parco Naturale Regionale delle Madonie** incorporates some of Sicily's highest peaks, including the imposing Pizzo Carbonara (1979m). The park's wild, wooded slopes are home to wolves, wildcats, eagles and the near-extinct ancient Nebrodi fir trees that have survived since the last ice age. Ideal for hiking, cycling and horse trekking, the park is also home to several handsome mountain towns, including **Castelbuono**, **Petralia Soprana** and **Petralia Sottana**.

The region's distinctive rural cuisine includes roasted lamb and goat, cheeses, grilled mushrooms, and aromatic pasta with *sugo* (meat sauce). A great place to sample these specialties is **Nangalarruni** (☑0921 67 12 28; www.hostariananangalarruni.it; Via delle Confraternite 7; fixed menus €28-35; ☺12.30-3pm & 7-10pm, closed Wed Nov-Mar) in Castelbuono.

For information, contact the **park headquarters** (☑0921 68 40 11; www.parcodellemadonie.it; Corso Paolo Agliata 16) in Petralia Sottana or the **branch office** (☑0921 92 33 27; www.parcodellemadonie.it; Corso Ruggero 116; ☺8am-6pm Mon-Sat) in Cefalù.

Bus service to the park's main towns is limited; to fully appreciate the Madonie, you're better off hiring a car for a couple of days.

Locanda del Marinaio   SEAFOOD €€
(☑0921 42 32 95; Via Porpora 5; meals €30-40; ☺noon-2.30pm & 7-11pm Wed-Mon) Fresh seafood rules the chalkboard menu at this eatery along the old town's main waterfront thoroughfare. Depending on the season, you'll find dishes such as red tuna carpaccio with toasted pine nuts, shrimp and zucchini on a bed of velvety ricotta, or grilled octopus served with thyme-scented potatoes, all accompanied by an excellent list of Sicilian wines.

ⓘ Information

Hospital (☑0921 92 01 11; www.fondazionesanraffaelegiglio.it; Contrada Pietrapollastra; ☺24hr) On the main road out of town in the direction of Palermo.

Tourist Office (☑0921 42 10 50; strcefalu@regione.sicilia.it; Corso Ruggero 77; ☺9am-7.30pm Mon-Fri, 8am-2pm Sat) English-speaking staff, lots of leaflets and good maps.

ⓘ Getting There & Away

The best way to get to and from Cefalù is by rail. Hourly trains go to Palermo (€5.60, 50 minutes) and virtually every other town on the coast.

AEOLIAN ISLANDS

The Aeolian Islands are a little piece of paradise. Stunning cobalt sea, splendid beaches, some of Italy's best hiking and an awe-inspiring volcanic landscape are just part of the appeal. The islands also have a fascinating human and mythological history that goes back several millennia: the Aeolians figured prominently in Homer's *Odyssey,* and evidence of the distant past can be seen everywhere, most notably in Lipari's excellent archaeological museum.

The seven islands of Lipari, Vulcano, Salina, Panarea, Stromboli, Alicudi and Filicudi are part of a huge 200km volcanic ridge that runs between the smoking stack of Mt Etna and the threatening mass of Vesuvius above Naples. Collectively, the islands exhibit a unique range of volcanic characteristics, which earned them a place on Unesco's World Heritage List in 2000. The islands are mobbed with visitors in July and August, but out of season things remain delightfully tranquil.

ⓘ Getting There & Away

Liberty Lines (☑0923 87 38 13; www.libertylines.it) runs hydrofoils year-round from Milazzo, the mainland city closest to the islands. Almost all boats stop first at Vulcano and Lipari, then continue to the ports of Santa Marina and Rinella on Salina island. Beyond Salina, boats either branch off east to Panarea and Stromboli, or west to Filicudi and Alicudi. Liberty Lines also operates limited year-round service to Lipari from Messina and summertime service from Reggio Calabria.

Frequency of service on all routes increases in the summer. Note that hydrofoils are sometimes cancelled due to heavy seas.

Both **Siremar** (☑090 36 46 01; www.siremar.it) and **NGI Traghetti** (☑090 928 40 91; www.ngi-spa.it) run year-round car ferries from Milazzo to the islands; these are slightly cheaper but slower and less regular than the hydrofoils. Siremar also runs twice-weekly overnight ferries from Naples to the Aeolians, docking first at Stromboli before continuing to the other islands.

Additional seasonal services include Liberty Lines hydrofoils from Palermo (once daily late June to early September) and **SNAV** (☑ 081 428 55 55; www.snav.it) hydrofoils from Naples (daily July to early September, plus weekends in June).

❶ Getting Around

BOAT

Liberty Lines operates year-round, inter-island hydrofoil services, while Siremar offers inter-island ferries. Ticket offices with posted time-tables can be found close to the docks on all islands.

CAR & SCOOTER

You can take your car to Lipari, Vulcano or Salina by ferry, or garage it at Milazzo or Messina on the mainland from €12 per day. The islands are small, with narrow, winding roads. You'll often save money (and headaches) by hiring a scooter on-site, or better yet, exploring the islands on foot.

Lipari

POP 11,200 / ELEV 602M

Lipari is the Aeolians' thriving hub, both geographically and functionally, with regular ferry and hydrofoil connections to all other islands. Lipari town, the largest urban centre in the archipelago, is home to the islands' only tourist office and most dependable banking services, and has enough restaurants, bars and year-round residents to offer a bit of cosmopolitan buzz. Meanwhile, the island's rugged shoreline offers excellent opportunities for hiking, boating and swimming.

As evidenced by its fine archaeological museum and the multilayered ruins strewn about town, Lipari has been inhabited for some 6000 years. The island was settled in the 4th millennium BC by Sicily's first known inhabitants, the Stentinellians, who developed a flourishing economy based on obsidian, a glassy volcanic rock. Commerce subsequently attracted the Greeks, who used the islands as ports on the east–west trade route, and pirates such as Barbarossa (or Redbeard), who sacked the city in 1544.

Lipari's two harbours, Marina Lunga (where ferries and hydrofoils dock) and Marina Corta (700m south, used by smaller boats) are linked by a bustling main street, Corso Vittorio Emanuele, which is flanked by shops, restaurants and bars. Overlooking the colourful snake of day-trippers is Lipari's clifftop citadel, surrounded by 16th-century walls.

◉ Sights & Activities

★ Museo Archeologico
Regionale Eoliano   MUSEUM

(☑ 090 988 01 74; www.regione.sicilia.it/beniculturali/museolipari; Via Castello 2; adult/reduced €6/3; ☉ 9am-6.30pm Mon-Sat, to 1pm Sun) A must-see for Mediterranean history buffs, Lipari's archaeological museum boasts one of Europe's finest collections of ancient finds. Especially worthwhile are the Sezione Preistorica, devoted to locally discovered artefacts from the neolithic and Bronze Age periods to the Graeco-Roman era, and the Sezione Classica, whose highlights include ancient shipwreck cargoes and the world's largest collection of miniature Greek theatrical masks.

★ Quattrocchi   VIEWPOINT
Lipari's best coastal views are from a celebrated viewpoint known as Quattrocchi (Four Eyes), 3km west of town. Follow the road for Pianoconte and look to your left. Stretching off to the south, great grey cliffs plunge into the sea, while in the distance plumes of sinister smoke rise from neighbouring Vulcano.

SICILY LIPARI

HYDROFOILS TO THE AEOLIAN ISLANDS

FROM	TO	COST (€)	DURATION	FREQUENCY
Messina	Lipari	27.80	1½-2¾hr	4 daily in summer, 1 daily in winter
Milazzo	Alicudi	34.20	3hr	2-3 daily
Milazzo	Filicudi	28.75	2½hr	2-3 daily
Milazzo	Lipari	22.30	1hr	13-17 daily
Milazzo	Panarea	24.30	1½-2½hr	3-7 daily
Milazzo	Salina	22.05	1½hr	12 daily
Milazzo	Stromboli	27.45	1¼-3hr	3-7 daily
Milazzo	Vulcano	21.50	45min	12-16 daily

Lipari Town

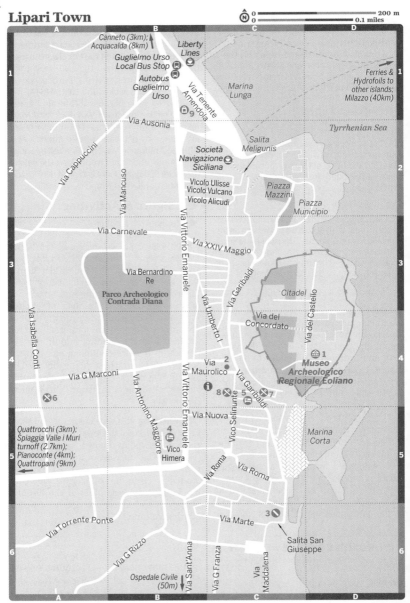

★ **Spiaggia Valle i Muria**   BEACH

Lapped by clean waters and surrounded by sheer cliffs, this dark, pebbly beach on Lipari's southwestern shore is a dramatically beautiful swimming and sunbathing spot. From the signposted turn-off, 3km west of Lipari town towards Pianoconte, it's a steep 15-minute downhill walk; come prepared with water and sunscreen. In good weather, Lipari resident **Barni** (☑ 349 1839555, 339 8221583) sells refreshments from his rustic cave-like beach bar, and provides scenic boat transfers to and from Lipari's Marina Corta (€5/10 one way/return).

Lipari Town

◉ Top Sights
1 Museo Archeologico Regionale
   Eoliano... D4

◉ Activities, Courses & Tours
2 Da Massimo/Dolce Vita...................... C4
3 Diving Center La Gorgonia C6

◉ Sleeping
4 Diana Brown B5
5 Enzo Il Negro C4

◉ Eating
6 E Pulera A4
7 Gilberto e Vera C4
8 Kasbah C4

◉ Shopping
9 La Formagella...................................... B1

Diving Center La Gorgonia   DIVING
(☑090 981 26 16; www.lagorgoniadiving.it; Salita San Giuseppe; per dive with own/rented equipment €35/55, courses €70-750) This outfit offers courses, boat transport, equipment hire and general information about scuba diving and snorkelling around Lipari. See the website for a complete price list.

☞ Tours

Numerous agencies in town, including the dependable **Da Massimo/Dolce Vita** (☑090 981 30 86; www.damassimo.it; Via Maurolico 2), offer boat tours to the surrounding islands. Prices are around €25 for a circuit around Vulcano; €30 for a tour of Salina; €40 to visit Filicudi and Alicudi; €40 for a day trip to Panarea and Stromboli; and €75 to €80 for a late-afternoon trip to Stromboli, including a guided hike up the mountain at sunset and a late-night return to Lipari.

🛏 Sleeping

Lipari is the Aeolians' best-equipped base for island-hopping, with plenty of places to stay, eat and drink. Note that prices soar in summer; avoid August if possible.

★ Diana Brown   B&B €
(☑090 981 25 84, 338 6407572; www.dianabrown. it; Vico Himera 3; s €35-65, d €50-80, tr €65-105; ❄🐾) Tucked down a narrow alley, South African Diana's delightful rooms sport tile floors, abundant hot water and welcome extras such as kettles, fridges, clothes-drying racks and satellite TV. Units downstairs are darker but have built-in kitchenettes. There's a sunny breakfast terrace and a solarium with deckchairs, plus a book exchange and laundry service. Optional breakfast costs €5 extra per person.

Enzo Il Negro   GUESTHOUSE €
(☑090 981 31 63; www.enzoilnegro.com; Via Garibaldi 29; s €40-50, d €60-90; ❄🐾) Family-run for decades, this down-to-earth guesthouse near picturesque Marina Corta offers spacious, tiled, pine-furnished rooms with fridges. Two panoramic terraces overlook the rooftops, the harbour and the castle walls.

★ B&B Al Salvatore di Lipari   B&B €€
(☑335 8343222; www.facebook.com/BBAlSalvatore; Via San Salvatore, Contrada al Salvatore; d €80-100; ☺Apr-Oct; 🐾) It's a trek to reach this hillside oasis 2km south of town, but once here, you'll never want to leave. Artist Paola and physicist Marcello have transformed their Aeolian villa into a green B&B that works at all levels, from dependable wi-fi to a panoramic terrace where guests enjoy one of Sicily's best breakfasts, featuring home-marinated tuna, omelettes and house-made marmalade.

Pre-arrange pick-up at the hydrofoil dock or take the 'Linea Blanca' bus from Marina Lunga to Capistello (€1.30, 10 minutes) and walk 200m steeply uphill.

🍴 Eating & Drinking

Fish abound in the waters of the archipelago and include tuna, mullet, cuttlefish and sole, all of which end up on local menus. Try *pasta all'eoliana,* a simple blend of the island's excellent capers with olives, olive oil, anchovies, tomatoes and basil.

Bars are concentrated along Corso Vittorio Emanuele and down by Marina Corta.

Gilberto e Vera   SANDWICHES €
(☑090 981 27 56; www.gilbertoevera.it; Via Garibaldi 22; half/full sandwich €3.50/5; ☺8am-2.30pm & 4pm-midnight mid-Mar–mid-Nov) This straightforward shop sells two dozen varieties of sandwiches, served with a smile. Sicilian ingredients such as capers, olives, eggplant and tuna all make frequent appearances. Long hours make this the perfect spot to purchase early-morning hiking or beach-hopping provisions, or to sip a mid-afternoon or late-evening glass of wine on the streetside terrace.

WORTH A TRIP

COASTAL HIKES AROUND LIPARI

Lipari's rugged northwestern coastline offers excellent walking opportunities. Most accessible is the pleasant hour-long stroll from Quattropani to Acquacalda along Lipari's north shore, which affords spectacular views of Salina and a distant Stromboli. Take the bus to Quattropani (€2.40, 25 minutes), then simply proceed downhill on the main road 5km to Acquacalda, where you can catch the bus (€1.55) back to Lipari.

More strenuous, but equally rewarding in terms of scenery, is the three- to four-hour hike descending steeply from Pianoconte (€1.90, 15 minutes by bus) down past the old Roman baths of Terme di San Calogero to the western shoreline, then skirting the clifftops along a flat stretch before climbing steeply back to Quattropani.

Kasbah MODERN SICILIAN, PIZZA €€
(☑090 981 10 75; www.kasbahlipari.it; Vico Selinunte 45; pizzas €6-8, meals €33-35; ☺7-11.30pm Apr-Oct) Tucked down a narrow alleyway, with a window where you can watch the chefs at work, this place serves everything from fancy pasta, fish and meat dishes to simple wood-fired pizzas. The stylish dining room with its grey linen tablecloths is complemented by a more casual outdoor terrace.

E Pulera MODERN SICILIAN €€
(☑090 981 11 58; www.pulera.it; Via Isabella Conti; meals €30-45; ☺7pm-midnight late Apr–mid-Oct) With its serene garden setting, low lighting, tile-topped tables and exquisite food – from tuna carpaccio with blood oranges and capers to *cassata* (sponge cake, ricotta, marzipan, chocolate and candied fruit) served with sweet Malvasia wine for dessert – E Pulera makes an upmarket but relaxed choice for a romantic dinner.

🛍 Shopping

La Formagella FOOD & DRINKS
(☑090 988 07 59; Corso Vittorio Emanuele 250; ☺8am-8.30pm Mar-Oct) You simply can't leave the Aeolian Islands without a small pot of capers and a bottle of sweet Malvasia wine.

You can get both, along with meats, cheeses and other delicious goodies, at this gourmet grocery-deli just around the corner from the hydrofoil dock.

ℹ Information

Corso Vittorio Emanuele is lined with ATMs. The other islands have relatively few facilities, so it's best to sort out your finances here before moving on.

Ospedale Civile (☑090 988 51 11; Via Sant'Anna) First-aid and emergency services.

Tourist Office (☑090 988 00 95; infopoint eolie@regione.sicilia.it; Via Maurolico 17; ☺9am-1pm & 4.30-7pm Mon, Wed & Fri, 9am-1pm Tue & Thu) Lipari's sporadically staffed tourist office provides information covering all of the Aeolian Islands.

ℹ Getting There & Around

BOAT

Lipari is the Aeolians' transport hub. The main port is Marina Lunga, where you'll find the hydrofoil jetty to the north and the ferry docks to the south. Timetable information is displayed at the adjacent ticket offices.

Year-round ferries and hydrofoils serve Milazzo and all the other Aeolian Islands; less frequent services include year-round hydrofoils to Messina and ferries to Naples, and summer-only hydrofoil services to Palermo. Websites for **Liberty Lines** (☑090 981 24 48; www.libertylines.it), **Siremar** (☑090 981 10 17; www.siremar.it) and NGI Traghetti (p202) have complete schedules and price details.

BUS

Autobus Guglielmo Urso (☑090 981 10 26; www.ursobus.com/orariursobus.pdf) runs buses around the island roughly hourly from its bus stop adjacent to Marina Lunga. The Linea Urbana follows the eastern shoreline, making stops at Canneto (€1.30) and Acquacalda (€1.55), while the Linea Extraurbana climbs to the splendid Quattrocchi viewpoint (€1.90) and the western highland settlements of Pianoconte (€1.90) and Quattropani (€2.40). Discounts are available for round-trip journeys or multiple rides (six-/10-/20-ride tickets from €7/10.50/20.50).

CAR & MOTORCYCLE

Several places around town rent bicycles (€10 to €15 per day), scooters (€15 to €50) and cars (€30 to €80), including **Da Marcello** (☑090 981 12 34; www.noleggiodamarcello.com; Via Sottomonastero), down by the ferry dock.

Vulcano

POP 720 / ELEV 500M

Vulcano is a memorable place, not least because of the vile smell of sulphurous gases. Once you escape the drab and dated tourist centre, Porto di Levante, the island has a delightfully tranquil, unspoilt quality. Beyond the well-marked trail to the looming Fossa di Vulcano, the landscape gives way to rural simplicity, with vineyards, birdsong and a surprising amount of greenery. The island is worshipped by Italians for its therapeutic mud baths and hot springs, and its black beaches and weird steaming landscape make for an interesting day trip.

Boats dock at Porto di Levante. To the right, as you face the island, are the mud baths and the small Vulcanello peninsula; to the left is the volcano. Straight ahead is Porto di Ponente, 700m west, where you will find the Spiaggia Sabbia Nera (Black Sand Beach).

◉ Sights & Activities

At Porto di Ponente, on the far side of the peninsula from Porto di Levante, the dramatic and only mildly commercialised black-sand beach of **Spiaggia Sabbia Nera** curves around a pretty bay. It is one of the few sandy beaches in the archipelago. A smaller, quieter black-sand beach, **Spiaggia dell'Asino** (Donkey Beach), can be found on the island's southern side near Gelso.

★ Fossa di Vulcano   HIKING

Vulcano's top attraction is the straightforward trek up its 391m volcano (no guide required). Start early if possible and bring a hat, sunscreen and water. Follow the signs south along Strada Provinciale, then turn left onto the zigzag gravel track that leads to the summit. It's about an hour's scramble to the lowest point of the crater's edge (290m).

Laghetto di Fanghi   HOT SPRINGS

(€3, shower/towel €1/2.60; ⊙ 7am-10pm Jul & Aug, 9am-6.30pm late Mar-Jun & Sep-early Nov) Backed by a *faraglione* (rock tower) and stinking of rotten eggs, Vulcano's harbourside pool of thick, coffee-coloured sulphurous gloop isn't exactly a five-star beauty farm. But the warm (28°C) mud is considered an excellent treatment for rheumatic pains and skin diseases, and rolling around in it can be fun if you don't mind smelling funny for a few days. Keep the mud away from your eyes

(and hair), as the sulphur is acidic and can damage your cornea.

Sicily in Kayak   WATER SPORTS

(☎ 329 5381229; www.sicilyinkayak.com) This outfit offers kayaking tours around Vulcano and the other Aeolians, along with sailing and stand-up paddleboarding excursions.

⌨ Sleeping & Eating

Unless you're here for the walking and the mud baths, Vulcano isn't a great place for an extended stay; the town is pretty soulless and the sulphurous fumes really do smell. However, there are some good options for those who choose to stick around.

★ Casa delle Stelle   B&B €

(☎ 334 9804104, 347 3626282; Contrada Gelso; s €30-45, d €50-90; ℗) This lovely hideaway, high in the hills above the island's south shore, is run by former Gelso lighthouse keeper Sauro and his wife, Maria. The two guest rooms share a living room, a fully equipped kitchen, and a panoramic terrace with spectacular views of the Mediterranean and a distant Mt Etna. In summer, local buses will drop you at the gate.

La Forgia Maurizio   SICILIAN €€

(☎ 334 7660069; www.laforgiamaurizio.it; Strada Provinciale 45, Porto di Levante; meals €30-35; ⊙ 12.30-3pm & 7-11pm; ✎) The owner of this devilishly good restaurant spent 20 winters in Goa, India; Eastern influences sneak into the menu of Sicilian specialties, and several items are vegan- and/or vegetarian-friendly. Don't miss the *liquore di kumquat e cardamom,* Maurizio's homemade answer to *limoncello* (lemon liqueur). The multicourse tasting menu is an excellent deal at €30 including wine, water and dessert.

ℹ Getting There & Around

BOAT

Vulcano is an intermediate stop between Milazzo and Lipari; both Liberty Lines and Siremar run multiple vessels in both directions throughout the day. The hydrofoil journey to or from Lipari takes only 10 minutes, making Vulcano an easy and popular day-trip destination.

CAR & MOTORCYCLE

Sprint da Luigi (☎ 347 7600275, 090 985 22 08; www.nolosprintdaluigi.com; Porto di Levante; bicycle/scooter/car rental per day from €7/25/50) Rent some wheels from this well-signposted outfit near the port.

Delightful Desserts

From citrus-scented pastries filled with ricotta, to ice cream served on brioche, to the marzipan fruits piled in every confectioner's window, Sicily celebrates the joys of sugar morning, noon and night.

Multicultural Roots

People from the Arabs to the Aztecs have influenced Sicily's culture of sweets: the former introduced sugar cane; the latter's fiery hot chocolate so impressed the Spaniards that they brought it to Sicily. The land also supplied inspiration, from abundant citrus, almond and pistachio groves to Mt Etna's snowy slopes, legendary source of the first *granita*.

Sweet Sicilian Classics

The all-star list of Sicilian desserts starts with *cannoli,* crunchy pastry tubes filled with sweetened ricotta, garnished with chocolate, crumbled pistachios or a spike of candied citrus. Vying for the title of Sicily's most famous dessert is *cassata,* a coma-inducing concoction of sponge cake, cream, marzipan, chocolate and candied fruit. Feeling more adventurous? How about an *'mpanatigghiu,* a traditional Modican pastry stuffed with minced meat, almonds, chocolate and cinnamon?

A SUGAR-FUELLED ISLAND SPIN

Pasticceria Cappello Renowned for its *setteveli*, a velvety seven-layer chocolate cake. (p197)

Da Alfredo Dreamy *granita* made with almonds and wild strawberries. (p211)

Ti Vitti Divine *cannoli* featuring fresh-from-the-sheep ricotta from the Madonie Mountains. (p201)

Dolceria Bonajuto Aztec-influenced chocolate with vanilla and peppers. (p236)

Gelati DiVini Outlandish ice-cream flavours including Marsala wine, wild fennel and olive oil. (p237)

Maria Grammatico Marzipan fruit, almond pastries and toasted-nut nougat. (p250)

ENKI PHOTO/SHUTTERSTOCK ©

1. Display of marzipan fruit 2. Almond nougat 3. *Cannoli* and *cassata* 4. Strawberry *granita*

GIOVANNI BOSCHERINO/SHUTTERSTOCK ©

Multilingual owners Luigi and Nidra offer tips for exploring the island and also rent out an apartment (€40 to €70) in Vulcano's tranquil interior.

Salina

POP 2200 / ELEV 962M

Ah, green Salina! In stark contrast to sulphur-stained Vulcano and lava-blackened Stromboli, Salina's twin craters of Monte dei Porri and Monte Fossa delle Felci – nicknamed *didyme* (twins) by the ancient Greeks – are lushly wooded and invitingly verdant, a result of the numerous freshwater springs on the island. Wildflowers, thick yellow gorse bushes and serried ranks of grapevines carpet the hillsides in vibrant colours and cool greens, while its high coastal cliffs plunge dramatically towards beaches. The famous Aeolian capers grow plentifully here, as do the grapes used for making Malvasia wine.

⊙ Sights & Activities

There are numerous wineries outside Malfa where you can try the local Malvasia wine. Signposted off the main road 1km east of town is award-winning **Fenech** (☑090 984 40 41; www.fenech.it; Via Fratelli Mirabito 41). About 3km further east, another important Malvasia is produced at the luxurious Capofaro resort on the 13-acre Tasca d'Almerita estate between Malfa and Santa Marina.

Pollara   VILLAGE

Don't miss a trip to sleepy Pollara, sandwiched dramatically between the sea and the steep slopes of an extinct volcanic crater on Salina's western edge. The gorgeous beach here was used as a location in the 1994 film *Il Postino*, although the land access route to the beach has since been closed due to landslide danger.

You can still descend the steep stone steps at the northwest end of town and swim across to the beach, or simply admire the spectacular view, with its backdrop of volcanic cliffs.

★ Monte Fossa delle Felci   HIKING

For jaw-dropping views, climb to the Aeolians' highest point, Monte Fossa delle Felci (962m). The two-hour ascent starts from the **Santuario della Madonna del Terzito**, an imposing 19th-century church at Valdichiesa, in the valley separating the island's two volcanoes. From the top, gorgeous perspectives unfold on the symmetrically arrayed

volcanic cones of Monte dei Porri, Filicudi and a distant Alicudi.

🛌 Sleeping & Eating

The island remains relatively undisturbed by mass tourism, yet offers some of the Aeolians' finest hotels and restaurants. Accommodation can be found in Salina's three main towns: Santa Marina Salina on the east shore, Malfa on the north shore and Rinella on the south shore, as well as in Lingua, a village adjoining ancient salt ponds 2km south of Santa Marina. Note that many hotels have their own excellent restaurants.

★ Hotel Ravesi   HOTEL **€€**

(☑090 984 43 85; www.hotelravesi.it; Via Roma 66, Malfa; d €90-240, ste €160-300; ⊗mid-Apr–mid-Oct; ❋🐾📶❄) Star attractions at this peach of a hotel in a converted family home beside Malfa's town square include the delightful grassy lounge and bar area, the chiming of church bells next door, and the outdoor deck with an infinity pool overlooking Panarea, Stromboli and the sea. Especially nice are the brand-new honeymoon suite with private terrace and the corner room 12 upstairs.

Homemade bar snacks during the sunset *aperitivi* hour, and freshly made jams from the fruit trees in the hotel garden are icing on the cake.

A Cannata   PENSION **€€**

(☑090 984 30 57; www.hotelacannata.it; Via Alfieri 9, Lingua; d €80-180, ste €120-200; 🐾) Remodelled in classic Aeolian style, with peach-coloured stucco, cheerful blue doors and reproduction historic tiles, this family-run *pensione* offers 25 spacious units, many of which (along with the breakfast terrace) overlook Lingua's picturesque salt lagoon. The adjacent **restaurant** (☑090 984 31 61; Via Umberto I 13, Lingua; meals €30-35; ⊗12.30-2.30pm & 7.30-10pm) features menus built around freshly caught seafood and home-grown veggies and herbs. Half board costs €35 extra per person.

Hotel Mamma Santina   BOUTIQUE HOTEL **€€**

(☑090 984 30 54; www.mammasantina.it; Via Sanità 40, Santa Marina Salina; d €140-250; ⊗Apr-Oct; ❋@📶❄) A labour of love for its architect owner, this boutique hotel has inviting rooms decorated with pretty tiles in traditional Aeolian designs. Many of the sea-view terraces come with hammocks, and on warm evenings the attached restaurant (meals from €35 to €40) has outdoor seating overlooking the glowing blue pool and landscaped garden.

★ **Hotel Signum**   BOUTIQUE HOTEL €€€
(☑ 090 984 42 22; www.hotelsignum.it; Via Scalo 15, Malfa; d €250-600, ste €500-750; ❄ 🛜 🌊) Hidden in Malfa's hillside lanes is this alluring labyrinth of antique-clad rooms, peach-coloured stucco walls, tall blue windows and vine-covered terraces with full-on views of Stromboli. The attached wellness centre, **Signum Spa** (Salus Per Aquam; €30, treatments extra; ⊙ 10am-8pm Apr-Sep), a stunning pool and one of the best-regarded restaurants on the island make this the perfect place to unwind for a few days in utter comfort.

Capofaro   BOUTIQUE HOTEL €€€
(☑ 090 984 43 30; www.capofaro.it; Via Faro 3; d €290-570, ste €490-780; ⊙ May-mid-Oct; ❄ @ 🛜 🌊) Immerse yourself in luxury at this five-star boutique resort halfway between Santa Marina and Malfa, surrounded by well-tended Malvasia vineyards and a picturesque lighthouse. The 20 rooms all have sharp white decor and terraces looking straight out to smoking Stromboli. Tennis courts, poolside massages, wine tasting and vineyard visits complete this perfect vision of island chic.

★ **Da Alfredo**   SANDWICHES €
(Piazza Marina Garibaldi, Lingua; granite €2.60, sandwiches €9-13; ⊙ 8am-11pm Jun-Sep, 10am-6pm Oct-May) Salina's most atmospheric option for an affordable snack, Alfredo's place is renowned all over Sicily for its *granite:* ices made with coffee, fresh fruit or locally grown pistachios and almonds. It's also worth a visit for its *pane cunzato* (open-faced sandwiches piled high with tuna, ricotta, eggplant, tomatoes, capers and olives); split one with a friend – they're huge!

❶ Getting There & Around

BOAT
Hydrofoils and ferries serve Santa Marina Salina and Rinella from Lipari and the other islands. You'll find ticket offices in both ports.

BUS
CITIS (☑ 090 984 41 50; www.trasportisalina. it) runs buses every hour or two in low season (more frequently in summer) from Santa Marina Salina to Lingua and Malfa. In Malfa, make connections for Rinella, Pollara, Valdichiesa

and Leni. Fares cost from €1.90 to €2.90 depending on your destination. Timetables are posted online, and at ports and bus stops.

CAR & MOTORCYCLE
Above Santa Marina Salina's port, **Antonio Bongiorno** (☑ 338 3791209; www.rentbongiorno. it; Via Risorgimento 222, Santa Marina Salina) rents bikes (per day from €8), scooters (€25 to €30) and cars (€60 to €70). Several agencies in Rinella offer similar services – look for signs at the ferry dock.

Stromboli
POP 400 / ELEV 924M

Stromboli's perfect triangle of a volcano juts dramatically out of the sea, its permanently active cone attracting a steady stream of visitors like moths to a giant flame. Volcanic activity has scarred and blackened the northwest side of the island, while the eastern side is untamed, ruggedly green and dotted with low-rise whitewashed houses.

The youngest of the Aeolian volcanoes, Stromboli was formed a mere 40,000 years ago and its gases continue to send up an almost constant spray of liquid magma, a process defined by vulcanologists as *attività stromboliana* (Strombolian activity). The volcano's most dramatic recent activity involved major lava flows that burst forth between June and December 2014, creating a new mass of hardened lava rock below the volcano's northeast crater and cancelling tours to the summit for several months. Several other significant eruptions have occurred in recent time; on 27 February 2007, two new craters opened on the volcano's summit; on 5 April 2003, the village of Ginostra was showered with rocks up to 4m wide; and on 30 December 2002, a tsunami caused damage to Stromboli town, injuring six people and closing the island to visitors for a few months.

Boats arrive at Porto Scari, downhill from the main town of Stromboli at the island's northeastern corner. Accommodation is concentrated within a 2km radius of the port, while San Vincenzo church, the meeting point for guided hikes up the volcano, is a short walk up the Scalo Scari to Via Roma.

◉ Sights
★ **Stromboli Crater**   VOLCANO
For nature lovers, climbing Stromboli is one of Sicily's not-to-be-missed experiences. Since 2005 access has been strictly regulated:

you can walk freely to 400m but will need a guide to continue any higher. Organised treks depart daily (between 3.30pm and 6pm, depending on the season), timed to reach the summit (924m) at sunset and to allow 45 minutes to observe the crater's fireworks.

The climb itself takes 2½ to three hours, while the descent back to Piazza San Vincenzo is shorter (1½ to two hours). All told, it's a demanding five- to six-hour trek to the top and back; you'll need to have proper walking shoes, a backpack that allows free movement of both arms, clothing for cold and wet weather, a change of T-shirt, a handkerchief to protect against dust (wear glasses not contact lenses), a torch (flashlight), 1L to 2L of water and some food. If you haven't got any of these, **Totem Trekking** (☑ 090 986 57 52; www.totemtrekkingstromboli.com; Piazza San Vincenzo 4; ⊙ 9.30am-1pm & 3.30-7pm) hires out all the necessary equipment, including backpacks (€5), windbreakers (€5), boots (from €5), hiking poles (from €3) and torches (from €2).

★**Sciara del
Fuoco Viewpoint** VIEWPOINT

(Path of Fire) An alternative to scaling Stromboli's summit is the hour-long climb to this viewpoint (400m, no guide required), which directly overlooks the Sciara del Fuoco (the blackened laval scar running down Stromboli's northern flank) and offers fabulous if more-distant views of the crater's explosions. Bring plenty of water, and a torch if walking at night. The trail (initially a switchbacking road) starts in Piscità, 2km west of Stromboli's port; halfway up, you can stop for pizza at L'Osservatorio.

🏃 Activities

Stromboli's black sandy beaches are among the best in the Aeolian archipelago. The most accessible and popular swimming and sunbathing is at **Ficograde**, a strip of rocks and black volcanic sand about a 10-minute walk northwest of the hydrofoil dock. Furtherflung beaches worth exploring are at **Piscità** to the west and **Forgia Vecchia**, about 300m south of the port.

La Sirenetta Diving DIVING

(☑ 331 2545288; www.lasirenettadiving.it; Via Mons di Mattina 33; ⊙ late May–mid-Sep) This outfit, opposite the beach at La Sirenetta Park Hotel, offers diving courses and accompanied dives.

👉 Tours

Magmatrek (☑ 090 986 57 68; www.magmatrek.it; Via Vittorio Emanuele) has experienced, multilingual vulcanological guides who lead regular treks (maximum group size 20) up to the crater every afternoon (per person €28). It can also put together tailor-made treks for individual groups. Other agencies charging identical prices include **Stromboli Adventures** (☑ 339 5327277; www.strombolliadventures.it; Via Vittorio Emanuele), **Quota 900** (☑ 090 98 62 51; www.quota900stromboli.it; Via Roma) and **Il Vulcano a Piedi** (☑ 090 98 61 44; www.ilvulcanoapiedi.it; Via Pizzillo).

Società Navigazione Pippo (☑ 338 9857883, 090 98 61 35; pipponav.stromboli@libero.it; Porto Scari) is among the numerous boat companies at Porto Scari offering 2½-hour daytime circuits of the island (€25), 1½-hour sunset excursions to watch the Sciara del Fuoco from the sea (€20) and evening trips to Ginostra village on the other side of the island for dinner or *aperitivi* (€25).

🛏 Sleeping & Eating

More than a dozen places offer accommodation, including B&Bs, guesthouses and fully fledged hotels.

★**Casa del Sole** GUESTHOUSE €

(☑ 090 98 63 00; www.casadelsolestromboli.it; Via Cincotta; dm €25-35, s €30-55, d €60-110) This cheerful Aeolian-style guesthouse is only 100m from a sweet black-sand beach in Piscità, the tranquil neighbourhood at the west end of town. Dorms, private doubles and a guest kitchen all surround a sunny patio, overhung with vines, fragrant with lemon blossoms, and decorated with the masks and stone carvings of sculptor-owner Tano Russo. It's a pleasant 25-minute walk or a €10 taxi ride from the port, 2km away.

Pensione Aquilone GUESTHOUSE €

(☑ 090 98 60 80; www.aquiloneresidence.it; Via Vittorio Emanuele 29; d €50-110) A short distance west of Stromboli's hilltop church square, this cheerful place has a sunny central garden patio and views up to the volcano. Three rooms come with cosy cooking nooks; otherwise, friendly owners Adriano and Francesco provide breakfast.

L'Osservatorio PIZZA €

(☑ 090 958 69 91; www.facebook.com/osservatoriostromboli; pizzas €7-12; ⊙ 10.30am-late) Sure, you could eat a pizza in town, but come on

– you're on Stromboli! Make the 45-minute, 2km uphill trek west of town to this pizzeria and you'll be rewarded with exceptional volcano views from an expansive panoramic terrace, best after sundown.

★ **Punta Lena** SICILIAN €€

(☑ 090 98 62 04; Via Marina 8; meals €35-40; ☉ 12.15-2.30pm & 7-10.30pm early May–mid-Oct) For a romantic outing, head to this family-run waterfront restaurant with cheerful blue decor, fresh flowers, lovely sea views and the soothing sound of waves lapping in the background. The food is as good as you'll get anywhere on the island, with signature dishes including fresh seafood and spaghetti *alla stromboliana* (with wild fennel, cherry tomatoes and breadcrumbs).

Pardès SICILIAN €€

(☑ 337 1505194; www.facebook.com/pardes. stromboli; Via Vittorio Emanuele 81; meals €25-35; ☉ noon-2.30pm & 6-10pm Easter-Oct; 🖥) A 10-minute walk west of San Vincenzo church, this wine bar–cafe has pleasant seating both indoors and on an outdoor terrace where you can sip coffee or wine while using the wi-fi (it's one of the few places on the island with reliable internet access).

ℹ Information

Bring enough cash for your stay on Stromboli. Many businesses don't accept credit cards, and the village's lone ATM on Via Roma is sometimes out of service. Internet access is limited and slow.

ℹ Getting There & Away

Liberty Lines (☑ 090 98 60 03; www.liberty lines.it) offers hydrofoil service to/from Lipari (€19.30, 50 minutes to 1¾ hours), Salina (€20.80, one hour) and all the other Aeolian Islands, as well as one direct early-morning hydrofoil from Milazzo (€27.45, 1¼ hours). **Siremar** (☑ 090 98 60 16; www.siremar.it) offers twice-weekly ferry service to Naples (€53.40, 10 hours) and the other Aeolians. Ticket offices for both companies are at Stromboli's port. Another option is to visit Stromboli on an all-inclusive day trip from Lipari.

IONIAN COAST

Magnificent, overdeveloped, crowded – and exquisitely beautiful – the Ionian coast is among Sicily's most popular tourist destinations and home to 20% of the island's

---

WORTH A TRIP

SICILY'S OFFSHORE ISLANDS

Sicily is an island lover's paradise, with more than a dozen offshore islands scattered in the seas surrounding the main island. Beyond the major Aeolian Islands of **Lipari, Vulcano, Stromboli** and **Salina**, you can detour to the smaller Aeolians: **Panarea, Filicudi** and **Alicudi**. Alternatively, cast off from Trapani on Sicily's western coast to the slow-paced **Egadi Islands** or the remote, rugged volcanic island of **Pantelleria**. South of Agrigento, the sand-sprinkled **Pelagic Islands** of Lampedusa, Linosa and Lampione offer some fantastic beaches. **Liberty Lines** (☑ 0923 87 38 13; www.libertylines.it) and Siremar (p200) provide hydrofoil and/or ferry services to all of these islands. For complete information about the Egadi Islands and the lesser Aeolian Islands, including where to sleep and eat, see Lonely Planet's *Sicily* guide.

---

population. Moneyed entrepreneurs have built their villas and hotels up and down the coastline, eager to bag a spot on Sicily's version of the Amalfi Coast. Above it all towers the muscular peak of Mt Etna (3329m), puffs of smoke billowing from its snow-covered cone.

Taormina

POP 11,100 / ELEV 204M

Spectacularly situated on a terrace of Monte Tauro, with views westwards to Mt Etna, Taormina is a beautiful small town, reminiscent of Capri or an Amalfi coastal resort. Over the centuries, Taormina has seduced an exhaustive line of writers and artists, aristocrats and royalty, and these days it's host to a summer arts festival that packs the town with international visitors.

Perched on its eyrie, Taormina is sophisticated, chic and comfortably cushioned by some serious wealth – far removed from the banal economic realities of other Sicilian towns. But the charm is not manufactured. The capital of Byzantine Sicily in the 9th century, Taormina is an almost perfectly preserved medieval town, and, if you can tear yourself away from the shopping and

214

SICILY TAORMINA

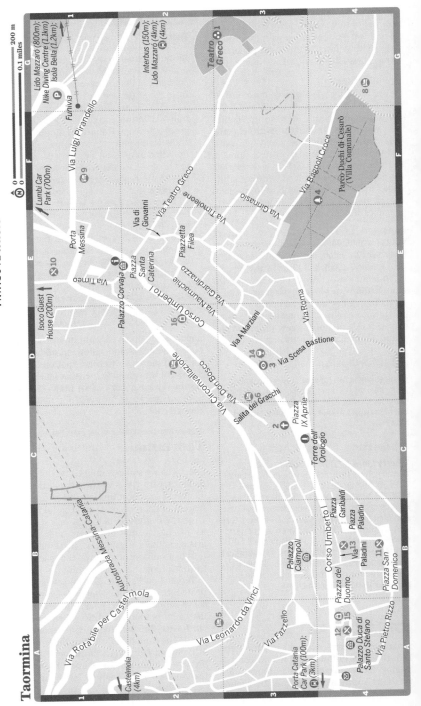

Taormina

Castelmola (4km)

Via Rotabile Per Castelmola

Via Rotabile Messina-Catania Autostrada

Porta Catania Car Park (100m); (3km)

Via Leonardo da Vinci

Via Fazzello

Palazzo Duca di Santo Stefano

Via Pietro Rizzo

Palazzo Ciampoli

Corso Umberto I

Piazza Garibaldi

Piazza del Duomo

Piazza Paladini

Via Paladini

Piazza San Domenico

Torre dell'Orologio

Piazza IX Aprile

Salita dei Gracchi

Via Circonvallazione

Via Don Bosco

Via Scesa Bastione

Via A Marziani

Via Roma

Corso Umberto I

Via Naumachie

Via Giardinazzo

Piazzetta Filea

Piazza Santa Caterina

Palazzo Corvaja

Porta Messina

Via Timeo

Isoco Guest House (200m)

Via di Giovanni

Via Teatro Greco

Via Timoleone

Via Grimasio

Via Bagnoli Croce

Parco Duchi di Cesarò (Villa Comunale)

Lumbi Car Park (700m)

Via Luigi Pirandello

Funivia

Lido Mazzarò (800m); Nike Diving Centre (1.1km); Isola Bella (1.2km);

Interbus (150m); Lido Mazzarò (4km); (4km)

Teatro Greco

200 m
0.1 miles

Taormina

◎ Top Sights
1 Teatro Greco	G3

◎ Sights
2 Chiesa San Giuseppe	C3
3 Corso Umberto I	D3
4 Villa Comunale	F4

⊜ Sleeping
5 Casa Cuseni	A2
6 Casa Turchetti	D3
7 Hostel Taormina	D2
8 Hotel Villa Belvedere	G4
9 Villa Nettuno	F1

⊗ Eating
10 L'Arco dei Cappuccini	E1
11 Osteria Nero D'Avola	B4
12 Osteria RossoDivino	A4
13 Tischi Toschi	B4

◎ Drinking & Nightlife
14 Morgana	D3

⊕ Shopping
15 Dieffe	A4
16 La Torinese	D2

sunbathing, it has a wealth of small but perfect tourist sites. Taormina is also a popular resort with gay men.

Be warned that in July and August the town and its surrounding beaches swarm with visitors.

◉ Sights & Activities

A short walk uphill from the bus station brings you to Corso Umberto I, a pedestrianised thoroughfare that traverses the length of the medieval town and connects its two historic town gates, Porta Messina and Porta Catania.

★ Teatro Greco   RUINS
(☑ 0942 2 32 20; www.parconaxostaormina.it/en; Via Teatro Greco; adult/reduced €10/5; ☺ 9am-1hr before sunset) Taormina's premier sight is this perfect horseshoe-shaped theatre, suspended between sea and sky, with Mt Etna looming on the southern horizon. Built in the 3rd century BC, it's the most dramatically situated Greek theatre in the world and the second largest in Sicily (after Syracuse). In summer, it's used to stage international arts and film festivals.

Corso Umberto I   STREET
Taormina's chief delight is wandering this pedestrian-friendly thoroughfare, lined with stylish boutiques and Renaissance palaces. Midway down, pause to revel in stunning panoramic views of Mt Etna and the coast from **Piazza IX Aprile** and admire the charming rococo **Chiesa San Giuseppe** (Piazza IX Aprile; ☺ usually 8.30am-8pm). Continue west through **Torre dell'Orologio**, the 12th-century clock tower, into **Piazza del Duomo**, home to an ornate baroque fountain (1635) that sports Taormina's symbol,

a two-legged centaur with the bust of an angel.

Villa Comunale   PARK
(Parco Duchi di Cesarò; Via Bagnoli Croce; ☺ 9am-midnight summer, 9am-sunset winter) To escape the crowds, wander down to these stunningly sited public gardens. Created by Englishwoman Florence Trevelyan, they're a lush paradise of tropical plants and delicate flowers. There's also a children's play area.

Castelmola   VILLAGE
For eye-popping views of the coastline and Mt Etna, head for this hilltop village above Taormina, crowned by a ruined castle. Either walk (one hour) or take the hourly Interbus service (one way/return €1.90/3, 15 minutes). While you're up here, stop in for almond wine at **Bar Turrisi** (☑ 0942 2 81 81; www.barturrisi.com; Piazza Duomo; ☺ 9am-2am daily; ☎), a four-level bar with some rather cheeky decor.

Isola Bella   ISLAND
(adult/reduced €4/2) Southwest of Lido Mazzarò is the minuscule Isola Bella, set in a stunning cove with fishing boats. You can walk here in a few minutes but it's more fun to rent a small boat from Mazzarò and paddle round Capo Sant'Andrea.

Lido Mazzarò   BEACH
Many visitors to Taormina come only for the beach scene. To reach Lido Mazzarò, directly beneath Taormina, take the **funivia** (Cable Car; Via Luigi Pirandello; one way/day pass €3/10; ☺ every 15min 9am-1.30am Mon, from 8am Tue-Sun summer, 7.45am-8pm Tue-Sun winter). This beach is well serviced with bars and restaurants; private operators charge a fee for umbrellas and deckchairs (usually about €10 per person per day).

Nike Diving Centre DIVING
(☑ 339 1961559; www.diveniketaormina.com; Spiaggia dell'Isola Bella) Opposite Isola Bella, this dive centre offers a wide range of courses for children and adults.

☆ Festivals & Events

Taormina FilmFest FILM
(www.taorminafilmfest.it; ☉ Jun or Jul) Hollywood big shots arrive for a week of film screenings, premieres and press conferences at Teatro Greco.

Taormina Arte PERFORMING ARTS
(☑ 0942 2 11 42; www.taormina-arte.com; ☉ Jun-Sep) This festival features opera, dance, theatre and music concerts with an impressive list of international names.

🛏 Sleeping

Taormina has plenty of luxurious accommodation, but some less expensive places can be found. Many hotels offer discounted parking (from €10) at Taormina's two public car parks.

Hostel Taormina HOSTEL €
(☑ 0942 62 55 05; www.taorminahostel.net; Via Circonvallazione 13; dm €17-23, r €58-85; ❄ 🛜) Friendly and laid-back, this year-round hostel occupies a house with pretty tiled floors and a roof terrace commanding panoramic sea views. It's a snug, homey set-up with accommodation in three brightly coloured dorms and one private room. Facilities are basic but the owners are helpful and there's a small communal kitchen for DIY catering. Locks are also provided for the lockers.

Villa Nettuno PENSION €
(☑ 0942 2 37 97; www.hotelvillanettuno.it; Via Luigi Pirandello 33; s €38-44, d €60-78, breakfast €4; ❄ 🛜) A throwback to another era, this conveniently located salmon-pink *pensione* has been run by the Sciglio family for seven decades. Its low prices reflect a lack of recent updates, but the pretty gardens, complete with olive trees and potted geraniums, and the sea views from the breakfast terrace, offer a measure of charm you won't find elsewhere at this price. Breakfast costs €4.

Isoco Guest House GUESTHOUSE €€
(☑ 0942 2 36 79; www.isoco.it; Via Salita Branco 2; r €130-220; ☉ Mar-Nov; P ❄ @ 🛜) Each room at this welcoming, LGBT-friendly guesthouse is dedicated to an artist, from Botticelli to Keith Haring. While the older rooms are highly eclectic, the newer suites are chic and subdued, each with a modern kitchenette. Breakfast is served around a large table, and a pair of terraces offer stunning sea views and a hot tub. Multi-night or prepaid stays earn the best rates.

★ Casa Turchetti B&B €€€
(☑ 0942 62 50 13; www.casaturchetti.com; Salita dei Gracchi 18/20; d €220-260, junior ste €360. ste €470; ❄ @ 🛜) Every detail is perfect at this painstakingly restored former music school turned luxurious B&B, on a back alley near Piazza IX Aprile. Vintage furniture and fixtures (including a giant four-poster bed in the suite), handcrafted woodwork and fine homespun sheets exude a quiet elegance. Topping it off is a breathtaking rooftop terrace and the warmth of Sicilian hosts Pino and Francesca.

★ Casa Cuseni B&B €€€
(☑ 0942 2 87 25; www.casacuseni.com; Via Leonardo da Vinci 5; r €175-270; P ❄ 🛜) Pre-booking is essential at this early 20th-century villa once frequented by Tennessee Williams, DH Lawrence, Greta Garbo and Bertrand Russell. Converted to a B&B in 2012, it positively drips with period character and comes surrounded by a seven-tiered garden with views out to the Ionian Sea and Mt Etna. It's only five minutes from Porta Catania but feels a world apart.

Hotel Villa Belvedere HOTEL €€€
(☑ 0942 2 37 91; www.villabelvedere.it; Via Bagnoli Croce 79; s €328-540, d €375-610; ☉ Mar-late-Nov; ❄ @ 🛜 ☷) Built in 1902, the jaw-droppingly pretty Villa Belvedere was one of the original grand hotels, well positioned with fabulous views and luxuriant gardens, which are a particular highlight. There is also a swimming pool with a 100-year-old palm tree rising from a small island in the middle.

🍴 Eating

Eating out in Taormina comes at a cost, and goes hand in hand with posing. Overpriced, touristy places abound.

★ Il Barcaiolo SICILIAN €€
(☑ 0942 62 56 33; www.barcaiolo.altervista.org; Via Castellucci 43, Spiaggia Mazzarò; meals €33-45; ☉ 1-2.30pm & 7-10.45pm May-Sep, to 10pm rest of year) You'll need to book five days ahead come summer, when every *buongustaio* (foodie) and hopeless romantic longs for a table at this fabulous trattoria. Set snugly in a boat-fringed cove at the northern end

of Lido Mazzarò, it's celebrated for its sublimely fresh seafood, from sweet *gamberi rossi marinati agli agrumi* (raw Mazzara shrimps served with citrus fruits) to *sarde a beccaficu* (stuffed sardines). Leave room for the homemade *cassata* or deliciously naughty chocolate-and-orange mousse.

★ **Osteria Nero D'Avola** SICILIAN €€
(☑ 0942 62 88 74; Piazza San Domenico 2b; meals €40; ☉ 12.30-3pm & 7-11pm Tue-Sun Sep-Jun, 7pm-midnight Jul & Aug) Not only does affable owner Turi Siligato fish, hunt and forage for his smart *osteria*, he'll probably greet you at your table, share anecdotes about the day's bounty and play a few tunes on the piano. Here, seasonality, local producers and passion underscore arresting dishes like the signature *cannolo di limone Interdonato* (thinly sliced Interdonato lemon with roe, tuna, tomato and chives).

An impressive wine list showcases local drops, with staff usually happy to open most bottles, even if you're only after a glass.

Tischi Toschi SICILIAN €€
(☑ 339 3642088; www.tischitoschitaormina.com; Via Paladini 3; meals €30-45; ☉ 12.30-2.30pm & 7.30-10.30pm, closed Mon lunch May-Oct, closed Mon Nov-Apr) This family-run, Slow Food–acclaimed trattoria with its charming front patio offers a level of creativity and attention to detail that's generally lacking in touristy Taormina. The limited menu of six *primi* and six *secondi* changes regularly based on what's in season.

L'Arco dei Cappuccini SICILIAN €€
(☑ 0942 2 48 93; Via Cappuccini 5; meals €30-45; ☉ 5-11.30pm mid-Jul–Aug, 12.30-2.30pm & 5-11.30pm rest of year, closed Nov–mid-Dec & early Jan–mid-Mar) If you demand your seafood ridiculously fresh, reserve a table at this superlative local favourite. The *crudo* (raw fish) antipasto makes for a show-stopping prologue, followed by beautifully balanced dishes such as *fettuccine cernia* (pasta with grouper) and an earthy *pasta con le sarde* (spaghetti with sardines, raisins, pine nuts and fennel) in which every ingredient sings. Service is kind and gracious.

Osteria RossoDivino SICILIAN €€€
(☑ 0942 62 86 53; www.osteria-rosso-divino.com; Vico Spuches 8; meals €37-55; ☉ 7pm-2am Jul-Sep, noon-3pm & 7pm-midnight Wed-Mon Oct-Jan & Mar-Jun) With seating in an intimate, candlelit courtyard, this coveted nosh spot (book ahead!) is the passion project of siblings Jacqueline and Sara Ragusa. The day's offerings – written on a blackboard – are dictated by the season, the local fishers' catch, and the siblings' own morning market trawl. Expect anything from heavenly anchovy tempura (the secret: mineral water in the batter) to fragrant seafood couscous.

 ## Drinking & Nightlife

★ **Morgana** COCKTAIL BAR
(☑ 0942 62 00 56; www.morganataormina.it; Scesa Morgana 4; ☉ 7.30pm-late Apr-Oct, closed Tue Nov & Dec) This so-svelte cocktail lounge sports a new look every year, with each concept inspired by Sicilian culture, artisans and landscape. It's the place to be seen, whether on the petite dance floor or among the prickly pears and orange trees in the dreamy, chi-chi courtyard. Fuelling the fun are gorgeous libations, made with local island ingredients, from wild fennel and orange to sage.

 ## Shopping

Taormina is a window-shopper's paradise, especially along Corso Umberto I. The quality in most places is high, but don't expect any bargains.

La Torinese FOOD & DRINKS
(☑ 0942 2 31 43; Corso Umberto I 59; ☉ 9.30am-1pm & 4-8.30pm) Stock up on local olive oil, capers, marmalade, honey and wine. Smashproof bubble wrapping helps to bring everything home in one piece.

Dieffe FASHION & ACCESSORIES
(www.dieffetaormina.com; Corso Umberto I 226; ☉ 10am-10pm summer, 10.30am-8pm rest of year) A bastion of 'Made in Italy', this easy-to-miss boutique offers sharp edits of men's threads, shoes and accessories from unique local and mainland designers. Expect anything from hand-painted leather belts from Sicilian artist Salvatore Montanucci, to handcrafted shoes from Le Marche's Galizio Torresi and beautifully detailed linen shirts from Tuscany's Osvaldo Trucchi. A must for lovers of idiosyncratic Italian style.

ℹ Information

Hospital (Ospedale San Vincenzo; ☑ 0942 57 91; Contrada Sirina) Downhill, 2km from the centre.

Tourist Office (☑ 0942 2 32 43; Palazzo Corvaja, Piazza Santa Caterina; ☉ 8.30am-2.15pm & 3.30-6.45pm Mon-Fri year-round, also 8.30am-2.15pm & 3.30-6.45pm Sat & Sun summer) Has plenty of practical information.

ⓘ Getting There & Around

BUS

Bus is the easiest way to reach Taormina. **Interbus** (www.interbus.it; Via Luigi Pirandello) goes to Messina (€4.30, 50 minutes to 1¾ hours, four daily Monday to Saturday, one on Sunday) and Catania (€5.10, 1¼ hours, hourly), the latter continuing to Catania's Fontanarossa Airport (€8.20, 1½ hours).

CAR & MOTORCYCLE

Taormina is on the A18 autostrada and the SS114 between Messina and Catania. Driving near the historic centre is a complete nightmare and Corso Umberto is closed to traffic. The most convenient places to leave your car are the **Porta Catania car park** (per 24hr €15), at the western end of Corso Umberto, or the **Lumbi car park** (per 24hr €13.50) north of the centre, connected to Porta Messina (at Corso Umberto's eastern end) by a five-minute walk or a free yellow shuttle bus.

TRAIN

There are frequent trains to and from Messina (€4.30, 45 minutes to 1¼ hours) and Catania (€4.30, 35 minutes to one hour), but the awkward location of Taormina's station (a steep 4km below town) is a strong disincentive. If you arrive this way, catch a taxi (€15) or an Interbus coach (€1.90, 20 minutes, half-hourly) up to town.

Catania

POP 296,000

Sicily's second-biggest metropolis, Catania is a city of grit and raw energy, a thriving, entrepreneurial centre with a large university and a cosmopolitan urban culture. Yes, it has its rough edges, but it's hard not to love a city with a smiling elephant gracing its central square and gorgeous snowcapped Mt Etna floating on the horizon. Catania is a true city of the volcano; much of it is constructed from the lava that poured down the mountain and engulfed the city in Etna's massive 1669 eruption. It is also lava-black in colour, as if a fine dusting of soot permanently covers its elegant buildings, most of which are the work of baroque master Giovanni Vaccarini.

In recent years, Catania has made steady moves to pedestrianise its historic centre, which you'll appreciate as you stroll the streets between Via Crociferi, Via Etnea and Piazza del Duomo, where most of the city's attractions are concentrated.

◉ Sights

If you're visiting multiple attractions or travelling frequently by bus and metro, consider picking up a **Catania Pass** (www.cataniapass.it; 1-/3-/5-day pass individual €12.50/16.50/20, family €23/30.50/38), which offers free museum admissions and unlimited use of public transport, including the Alibus service between downtown and Fontanarossa Airport.

Piazza del Duomo   SQUARE
A Unesco World Heritage Site, Catania's central piazza is a set piece of contrasting lava and limestone, surrounded by buildings in the unique local baroque style and crowned by the grand Cattedrale di Sant'Agata . At its centre stands **Fontana dell'Elefante** (Piazza del Duomo), an 18th-century fountain built around a naive, smiling black-lava elephant dating from Roman times, surmounted by an improbable Egyptian obelisk. Another fountain at the piazza's southwest corner, **Fontana dell'Amenano**, marks the entrance to Catania's fish market.

★ La Pescheria   MARKET
(Via Pardo; ⊙7am-2pm Mon-Sat) Catania's raucous fish market, which takes over the streets behind Piazza del Duomo every workday morning, is street theatre at its most thrilling. Tables groan under the weight of decapitated swordfish, ruby-pink prawns and trays full of clams, mussels, sea urchins and all manner of mysterious sea life. Fishmongers gut silvery fish and women in high heels step daintily over pools of blood-stained water. It's absolutely riveting. Surrounding the market are a number of good seafood restaurants.

Parco Archeologico Greco Romano   RUINS
(☑095 715 05 08; Via Vittorio Emanuele II 262; adult/reduced incl Casa Liberti €6/3; ⊙9am-7pm) West of Piazza del Duomo lie Catania's most impressive ancient ruins: the remains of a 2nd-century Roman theatre and its small rehearsal theatre, the Odeon. The ruins are evocatively sited in the thick of a crumbling residential neighbourhood, with vine-covered buildings that appear to have sprouted organically from the half-submerged stage. Adjacent to the main theatre is the **Casa Liberti**, an elegantly restored 19th-century apartment now home to two millennia worth of artefacts discovered during the excavation of the site.

SICILIAN CUISINE

Eating is one of the great joys of any trip to Sicily. In addition to the island's ubiquitous street food, you'll encounter countless uniquely Sicilian specialties that reflect Sicily's multicultural heritage while making abundant use of local ingredients, such as sardines, wild fennel, eggplant (aubergine), ricotta, lemons, almonds and pistachios. Here's a quick primer on the island's most classic dishes:

Busiate con pesto alla trapanese A mainstay of western Sicilian menus, these hollow, corkscrew-shaped pasta tubes come served with a sauce of chopped almonds, garlic and fresh tomatoes.

Caponata The quintessential Sicilian appetiser, made with eggplant, olives, capers and celery marinated in a sweet-and-sour sauce.

Couscous alla trapanese Reflecting the island's Arab roots, this signature dish of western Sicily features couscous with mixed seafood topped with a delicious sauce of tomatoes, garlic and parsley.

Involtini di pesce spada Thinly sliced swordfish fillets, rolled up and filled with bread-crumbs, capers, tomatoes and olives.

Pasta alla Norma A specialty of Catania, Sicily's most famous pasta dish comes topped with fresh ricotta, eggplant, tomatoes and basil.

Pasta con le sarde This Palermitan original features pasta topped with sardines, wild fennel, pine nuts, raisins and toasted breadcrumbs.

Sarde a beccafico A classic Sicilian appetiser or main course of sardines, stuffed with breadcrumbs, pine nuts, raisins, garlic and parsley, then fried or baked to a golden brown colour.

★**Teatro Massimo Bellini** THEATRE
(☑095 730 61 35; www.teatromassimobellini. it; Via Perrotta 12; guided tours adult/reduced €6/4; ☺tours 9am-noon Tue-Thu) A few blocks northeast of the *duomo*, this gorgeous opera house forms the centrepiece of Piazza Bellini. Square and opera house alike were named after composer Vincenzo Bellini, the father of Catania's vibrant modern musical scene.

Cattedrale di Sant'Agata CATHEDRAL
(☑095 32 00 44; Piazza del Duomo; ☺7am-noon & 4-7pm Mon-Sat, 7.30am-12.30pm & 4.30-7pm Sun) Inside the vaulted interior of this cathe-dral, beyond its impressive marble facade sporting two orders of columns taken from the Roman amphitheatre, lie the relics of the city's patron saint. The **Museo Diocesano** (☑095 28 16 35; www.museodiocesanocatania. com; Piazza del Duomo; adult/reduced museum only €7/4, museum & baths €10/6; ☺9am-2pm Mon, Wed & Fri, 9am-2pm & 3-6pm Tue & Thu, 9am-1pm Sat), next door, grants access to the Ro-man baths directly underneath the church and fine views from the roof terrace beneath the cathedral's dome.

Castello Ursino CASTLE
(Piazza Federico II di Svevia) Catania's forbid-ding 13th-century castle once guarded the city from atop a seafront cliff. The 1669 eruption of Mt Etna changed the landscape, however, and the whole area to the south was reclaimed by lava, leaving the castle completely landlocked. The castle now hous-es the **Museo Civico** (☑095 34 58 30; adult/reduced €6/3; ☺9am-7pm Mon-Fri, to 8.30pm Sat & Sun), home to the valuable archaeological collection of the Biscaris, Catania's most im-portant aristocratic family. Exhibits include colossal classical sculpture, Greek vases and some fine mosaics.

Museo Belliniano MUSEUM
(☑095 715 05 35; Piazza San Francesco 3; adult/reduced €5/2; ☺9am-7pm Mon-Sat, to 1pm Sun) One of Italy's great opera composers, Vin-cenzo Bellini (1801–35) was born in Catania. His childhood home, now a museum, boasts an interesting collection of memorabilia, in-cluding original scores, photographs, pianos once played by Bellini, and the maestro's death mask.

Catania

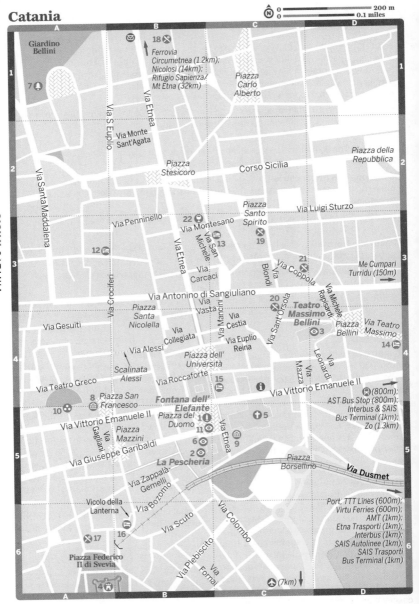

Giardino Bellini PARK

(⊙ 6am-11pm summer, to 10pm spring & autumn, to 9pm winter) Escape the madding crowd and enjoy fine views of Mt Etna from these lovely gardens along Via Etnea.

★ Festivals & Events

If visiting Catania in February or early March, don't miss **Carnevale** (www.carnevale acireale.com) in nearby Acireale, one of Sicily's most colourful festivals.

Catania

Festa di Sant'Agata   RELIGIOUS
(www.festadisantagata.it; ⊙ 3-5 Feb) In what is Catania's biggest religious festival, one million Catanians follow the Fercolo (a silver reliquary bust of St Agatha) along the main street of the city, accompanied by spectacular fireworks.

🛏 Sleeping

Catania is served by a good range of reasonably priced accommodation, making it an excellent base for exploring the Ionian coast and Etna.

★ B&B Crociferi   B&B €
(☑ 095 715 22 66; www.bbcrociferi.it; Via Crociferi 81; d €75-85, tr €100-110, apt €110-170; ❄ 🗜) Perfectly positioned on pedestrianised Via Crociferi, this B&B in a beautifully decorated family home affords easy access to Catania's historic centre. Three palatial rooms (each with private bathroom across the hall) feature high ceilings, antique tiles, frescoes and artistic accoutrements from the owners' travels. The B&B also houses two apartments, the largest (called Leela) with a leafy panoramic terrace. Book ahead.

★ Palazzu Stidda   APARTMENT €
(☑ 095 34 88 26, 338 6505133; www.palazzu-stidda.com; Vicolo della Lanterna 5; d €80-100, q €120-140; ❄ 🗜 🖫) Multilingual hosts Giovanni and Patricia have poured their hearts into creating these three family-friendly apartments (two with kitchens and washing machines) on a peaceful dead-end alley, with all the comforts of home, plus a host of whimsical touches. Each has a flowery mini balcony, and all are decorated with the owners' artwork, handmade furniture, family heirlooms and vintage finds.

B&B Faro   B&B €
(☑ 349 4578856; www.bebfaro.it; Via San Michele 26; s/d/tr €50/80/100, apt €130-150; ❄ @) Polished-wood floors, double-glazed windows, modern bathroom fixtures and antique tiles set a stylish tone at this cosy B&B, owned by artist couple Anna and Antonio. Suites can sometimes be booked for the price of a double during slower periods; free bikes are provided; and there's a studio downstairs at number 30 where visiting artists are invited to come and paint.

Ostello degli Elefanti   HOSTEL €
(☑ 095 226 56 91; www.ostellodeglielefanti.it; Via Etnea 28; dm €19-25, s €40-45, d €60-70; ❄ 🗜) Housed in a 17th-century *palazzo* a stone's throw from the *duomo*, this hostel offers incredible location and value. Three dorms and one private room have frescoed high ceilings and panoramic balconies, and there are reading lights, USB ports and curtains for every bed. The marble-floored former ballroom doubles as a restaurant-lounge, while the rooftop terrace-bar offers incomparable Etna vistas.

★ B&B Habitat   B&B €€
(☑ 095 826 67 55; www.bbhabitatcatania.it; Via Teatro Massimo 29; s €84-117, d €95-140; ❄ 🗜 🖫) Fit for the pages of *Domus* magazine, this 19th-century factory turned B&B is the work of two young architects. Smart, minimalist rooms feature high-quality mattresses and

linen, coffee machines and custom-made furniture in wood and steel. Superior rooms add warmth with wooden floors. The seasonal breakfast buffet is served in a striking communal lounge, lined with floor-to-ceiling jars filled with Sicilian ingredients.

Eating

Popular street snacks in Catania include *arancini* (deep-fried rice balls stuffed with meat, cheese, tomatoes and/or peas) and *seltz* (fizzy water with freshly squeezed lemon juice and natural fruit syrup). Don't leave town without trying *pasta alla Norma* (pasta with basil, eggplant, ricotta and tomato), a Catania original named after Bellini's opera *Norma*.

★ Da Antonio   TRATTORIA €
(☑ 095 218 49 38; www.facebook.com/Trattoria
DaAntonio; Via Castello Ursino 59; meals €20;
⊙ 7.30-11pm daily, plus 12.30-3pm Tue-Sun) Humble yet quietly sophisticated, Da Antonio spoils food lovers with well-priced, beautifully cooked dishes served by knowledgeable waitstaff. Despite having crept onto the tourist radar, it's still the kind of place where well-dressed local families come for Sunday lunch. The antipasti (to sample various offerings ask for an *assaggio*) and *primi* are particularly good, especially those showcasing local seafood.

Trattoria di De Fiore   TRATTORIA €
(☑ 095 31 62 83; Via Coppola 24/26; meals €15-25; ⊙ 7pm-12.30am Mon, 1pm-12.30am Tue-Sun) For more than 50 years, septuagenarian chef Rosanna has been re-creating her great-grandmother's recipes, including the best *pasta alla Norma* you'll taste anywhere in Sicily. Service can be excruciatingly slow, but for patient souls this is a rare chance to experience classic Catanian cooking from a bygone era. Don't miss Rosanna's trademark *zeppoline* (sugar-sprinkled ricotta-lemon fritters) at dessert time.

FUD Bottega Sicula   BURGERS €
(☑ 095 715 35 18; www.fud.it; Via Santa Filomena 35; burgers, panini & pizzas €5-10; ⊙ noon-3pm & 7pm-1am; 🐾) With sharp service and pavement seating on trendy Via Santa Filomena, this hip, back-alley eatery epitomises youthful Catania's embrace of 'Sicilian fast food', all made with high-quality, locally sourced ingredients, from Sicilian cheeses to Nebrodi black pork. With wry humour, every burger and *panino* on the menu is spelled

using Italian phonetics, from the 'cis burgher' (cheeseburger) to the rustic 'cauntri' (country) sandwich.

Millefoglie   VEGETARIAN €
(☑ 331 2505331; Via Sant'Orsola 12; dishes €6-8; ⊙ 12.45-3pm Mon-Sat, closed Sat May-Oct; 🐾 ☑) Delicious, flesh-free grub awaits at little Millefoglie, a shabby-chic, whitewashed eatery with wooden floors, communal tables and an open kitchen. The morning's market produce dictates the menu, which might feature vibrant wholewheat *casarecce* (twisted pasta) with zucchini, fava beans, peas, *pecorino* (sheep's milk cheese), lemon zest and basil, or chocolate mousse with chilli and strawberries. A few vegan dishes usually dot the menu.

★ Mè Cumpari Turiddu   SICILIAN €€
(☑ 095 715 01 42; www.mecumparituriddu.it; Piazza Turri Ferro 36-38; meals €22-30; ⊙ bistro 11am-1am, restaurant noon-12.30am; 🐾) Old chandeliers, recycled furniture and vintage mirrors exude a nostalgic air at this quirky bistro-restaurant–providore, where tradition and modernity meet to impressive effect. Small producers and Slow Food sensibilities underline sophisticated, classically inspired dishes such as ricotta and marjoram ravioli in a pork sauce, soothing Ustica lentil stew or a playful 'deconstructed' *cannolo*. There's a fabulous selection of Sicilian cheeses, lighter bistro fare and cakes.

Le Tre Bocche   TRATTORIA €€€
(☑ 095 53 87 38; Via Mario Sangiorgi 7; meals €35-45; ⊙ two sittings daily, 8.30pm & 10.30pm, plus 1-3pm Sun) A fantastic Slow Food–recommended trattoria that takes pride in the freshest seafood and fish – so much so, it has a stand at La Pescheria market. Short pasta comes with wonderful sauces such as *bottarga* (mullet roe) and artichoke; spaghetti is soaked in sea urchins or squid ink; and risotto is mixed with courgette and king prawns.

Drinking & Nightlife

Not surprisingly for a busy university town, Catania has a reputation for its effervescent nightlife. Areas that bustle with activity after dark include Via Montesano, Via Teatro Massimo, the steps at the western end of Via Alessi, and Via Santa Filomena.

★ Ritz   COCKTAIL BAR
(www.facebook.com/ritzcatania; Via Pantano 54; ⊙ 7.30pm-2am Tue-Sun) Ritz is a svelte, clued-

up spot that takes its libations seriously. Divided into Aperitif, Anytime, Dinner, After Dinner and Long Drink & Muddle, cocktails are made with passion and precision, from the punchy Aviations to a very local Etna Kir (spumante Brut rosé, Etna cherry liqueur and hazelnut crust). There's a small, interesting selection of craft beer and a range of bites, including decent pizzas.

★ **Razmataz** BAR
(☑ 095 31 18 93; Via Montesano 17; ⊗ 9am-late Mon-Sat, 5pm-late Sun; 🛜) Wines by the glass, draught and bottled beer, and an ample cocktail list are offered at this delightful wine bar with tables invitingly spread out across the tree-shaded flagstones of a sweet backstreet square. It doubles as a cafe in the morning, but really gets packed with locals from *aperitivo* time onward.

☆ **Entertainment**

For a current calendar of music, theatre and arts events around Catania, check the website www.lapisnet.it/catania.

Teatro Massimo Bellini THEATRE
(☑ 095 730 61 11; www.teatromassimobellini. it; Via Perrotta 12) Catania's premier theatre is named after the city's most famous son, composer Vincenzo Bellini. Sporting the full red-and-gilt fit-out, it stages a year-round season of opera and an eight-month program of classical music from November to June. Tickets, which are available online, start at around €20 and can rise to more than €100 for a seat in the stalls.

Zo PERFORMING ARTS
(☑ 095 816 89 12; www.zoculture.it; Piazzale Asia 6; 🛜) Housed in Catania's former sulphur works, Zo serves up contemporary art and performance from Italy and beyond. Its eclectic program of events ranges from club nights, concerts and dance performances, to installations, theatre workshops and the occasional film screening. The venue also houses a hip bar serving decent drinks and bites (including vegetarian dishes). Check the website for upcoming events.

ℹ️ **Information**

Hospital (Ospedale Santo Bambino; ☑ 095 743 63 06; www.policlinicovittorioemanuele.it/ ospedale-santo-bambino; Via Tindaro 2) Has a 24-hour emergency doctor.
Tourist Office (☑ 095 742 55 73; www.co mune.catania.it/la-citta/turismo; Via

Vittorio Emanuele 172; ⊗ 8am-7.15pm Mon-Sat, 8.30am-1.30pm Sun) Very helpful city-run tourist office.

ℹ️ **Getting There & Away**

AIR

Catania's airport, **Fontanarossa** (☑ 095 723 91 11; www.aeroporto.catania.it), is 7km southwest of the city centre. Alitalia, Ryanair and two dozen other airlines fly from Catania to destinations throughout Italy and Europe.

BOAT

The ferry terminal is located southwest of the train station along Via VI Aprile.
TTT Lines (☑ 800 627414, 095 34 85 86; www. tttlines.com) Runs nightly ferries from Catania to Naples (from €45, 11 hours).
Virtu Ferries (☑ 095 703 12 11; www.virtu-ferries.com) From May through September, Virtu runs daily ferries from Pozzallo (south of Catania) to Malta (1¾ hours). Fares vary depending on length of stay in Malta (same-day return €88 to €139; open return €116 to €164 depending on season). Coach transfer between Catania and Pozzallo (€12 each way) adds 2½ to three hours to the journey.

BUS

All long-distance buses leave from a terminal 250m north of the train station. Ticket offices for **Interbus** (☑ 095 53 27 16; www.interbus.it; Via d'Amico 187), **SAIS Trasporti** (☑ 090 601 21 36; www.saistrasporti.it; Via d'Amico 181) and **SAIS Autolinee** (☑ 095 53 61 68, 800 211020; www. saisautolinee.it; Via d'Amico 181) are across the street on Via d'Amico.

Interbus services include the following:
Piazza Armerina €9.20, 1¾ hours, two to five daily
Ragusa €8.60, two hours, eight to 13 daily
Syracuse €6.20, 1½ hours, hourly Monday to Friday, fewer on weekends
Taormina €5.10, 1¼ hours, hourly

SAIS Trasporti services go to **Agrigento** (€13.40, three hours, 10 to 14 daily) and **Rome** (€42, 10½ hours overnight). Its sister company SAIS Autolinee has services to **Messina** (€8.40, 1½ hours, hourly) and **Palermo** (€13.50, 2¾ hours, nine to 13 daily).

CAR & MOTORCYCLE

Catania is easily reached from Messina on the A18 autostrada and from Palermo on the A19. From either autostrada, signs for the centre of Catania will bring you to Via Etnea.

TRAIN

Frequent trains run from Catania Centrale station on Piazza Papa Giovanni XXIII.

Messina €7.60, 1½ to two hours, hourly

Palermo €13.50, three hours, six daily, three on Sunday

Syracuse €6.90, 1¼ hours, nine daily, four on Sunday

The private **Ferrovia Circumetnea** train circles Mt Etna, stopping at towns and villages on the volcano's slopes.

ℹ️ Getting Around

TO/FROM THE AIRPORT

Alibus 457, operated by AMT, runs every 25 minutes from 4.40am to midnight from the airport to Catania Centrale train station (€4, 30 minutes). **Etna Transporti/Interbus** (p223) also runs a regular shuttle from the airport to Taormina (€8.20, 1½ hours, hourly 7.15am to 8.45pm). Stops for both buses are to the right as you exit the Arrivals hall.

All the main car-hire companies are represented at the airport.

CAR & MOTORCYCLE

Drivers should note that there are complicated one-way systems around the city, and the centre is increasingly pedestrianised, which means parking is scarce.

PUBLIC TRANSPORT

Several useful **AMT** (📞 095 751 91 11, 800 018696; www.amt.ct.it) city buses terminate in front of Catania Centrale train station, including bus 1-4 (which runs hourly from the station to Via Etnea) and Alibus 457 (running from the station to the airport every 25 minutes from 4.40am to midnight). Also useful is bus D, which runs from Piazza Borsellino (just south of the *duomo*) to the local beaches.

Catania's slowly expanding metro system is currently limited to one line and nine stops, most on the periphery of town. Most useful for visitors are the newly opened Giovanni XXIII and Stesicoro stations, the former located near the train and bus stations, the latter near the heart of town; and the Borgo station, which is a transfer point for the Ferrovia Circumetnea train.

A 90-minute ticket for either bus or metro costs €1. A two-hour combined ticket for both costs €1.20.

TAXI

For a taxi, call **Radio Taxi Catania** (📞 095 33 09 66; www.radiotaxicatania.org).

Mt Etna

ELEV 3329M

Dominating the landscape of eastern Sicily and visible from the moon (if you happen to be there), Mt Etna is Europe's largest volcano and one of the world's most active. Eruptions occur frequently, both from the volcano's four summit craters and from its slopes, which are littered with fissures and old craters. The volcano's most devastating eruptions occurred in 1669, killing 15,000 people and lasting 122 days. Lava poured down Etna's southern slope, engulfing much of Catania and dramatically altering the landscape. The volcano's most destructive recent eruption came in 2002, when lava flows caused an explosion in Sapienza, destroying two buildings and temporarily halting the cable-car service. Less destructive eruptions continue to occur regularly, and locals understandably keep a close eye on the smouldering peak.

Enshrined as a Unesco World Heritage Site in 2013, the volcano is surrounded by the huge **Parco dell'Etna**, the largest unspoilt wilderness remaining in Sicily. The park encompasses a remarkable variety of environments, from the severe, almost surreal, summit to deserts of lava and alpine forests.

🅞 Sights & Activities

The southern approach to Mt Etna presents the easier ascent to the **craters**. The AST bus from Catania drops you off at **Rifugio Sapienza** (1923m) from where the **Funivia dell'Etna** (📞095 91 41 41; www.funiviaetna.com; return €30, incl bus & guide €63; ⊙9am-4.15pm Apr-Nov, to 3.45pm Dec-Mar) cable car runs up the mountain to 2500m. From the upper cable-car station it's a 3½- to four-hour return trip up the winding track to the authorised crater zone (2920m). Make sure you leave enough time to get up *and* down before the last cable car leaves at 4.45pm. You can pay an extra €33 for a guided 4WD tour to take you up from the cable car to the crater zone, but the guides provided by the Funivia tend to be perfunctory at best, and you'll have more freedom to explore if you go it alone.

An alternative ascent is from **Piano Provenzano** (1800m) on Etna's northern flank. This area was severely damaged during the 2002 eruptions, as is still evidenced by the bleached skeletons of the surrounding pine trees. To reach Piano Provenzano you'll need a car, as there's no public transport beyond Linguaglossa, 16km away.

👉 Tours

Several Catania-based companies offer private excursions up the mountain, as do

Gruppo Guide Alpine Etna Sud (☑389 3496086, 095 791 47 55; www.etnaguide.eu) and Gruppo Guide Alpine Etna Nord (☑095 777 45 02; www.guidetnanord.com), official guide agencies based on Etna's slopes.

🛏 Sleeping & Eating

There's plenty of B&B accommodation around Mt Etna, particularly in the small, pretty town of Nicolosi. Contact Nicolosi's **tourist information office** (☑095 791 70 31; Piazza Vittorio Emanuele) for a full list.

Agriturismo San Marco   AGRITURISMO €

(☑389 4237294; www.agriturismosanmarco.com; Rovittello; per person B&B/half board/full board €35/53/68; 🛜🍽🅿) Get back to basics at this delightful *agriturismo* (farm-stay accommodation) near Rovittello, on Etna's northern flank. The bucolic setting, rustic rooms, a swimming pool, a kids' play area and superb country cooking make it a relaxed place to kick back for a couple of days. Call ahead for directions.

Rifugio Sapienza   CHALET €

(☑095 91 53 21; www.rifugiosapienza.com; Piazzale Funivia; s/d €46/70; 🅿🛜) Offering comfortable accommodation with a good restaurant, this place adjacent to the cable car is the closest lodging to Etna's summit.

❶ Information

Catania's downtown tourist office (p223) provides information about Etna, as does the office of **Parco dell'Etna** (☑095 82 11 11; www. parcoetna.ct.it; Via del Convento 45, Nicolosi; 🕘9am-2pm & 4-7.30pm), 1km from the centre of Nicolosi on the mountain's southern flank.

❶ Getting There & Away

BUS

AST (☑095 723 05 11; www.aziendasicil ianatrasporti.it) runs one bus daily from Catania to Rifugio Sapienza (one way/return €4/6.60, two hours), leaving the car park opposite Catania's train station at 8.15am and arriving at Rifugio Sapienza at 10.15am. The return journey leaves Rifugio Sapienza at 4.30pm, arriving in Catania at 6.30pm.

TRAIN

You can circle Etna on the private **Ferrovia Circumetnea** (FCE; ☑095 54 11 11; www. circumetnea.it; Via Caronda 352a, Catania) train line, departing from Catania. From Catania's main train station catch the metro to the FCE station at Via Caronda (metro stop Borgo) or take bus 429 or 432 going up Via Etnea and ask to be let off at the Borgo metro stop.

The train follows a 114km route around the base of the volcano, providing lovely views. It also passes through many of Etna's unique towns, such as Adrano, Bronte and Randazzo. See the website for fares and timetables.

SYRACUSE & THE SOUTHEAST

Home to Sicily's most beautiful baroque towns and Magna Graecia's most magnificent ancient city, the southeast is one of Sicily's most compelling destinations. The classical charms of Syracuse are reason enough to visit, but once you leave the city behind you'll find an evocative checkerboard of river valleys and stone-walled citrus groves dotted with handsome towns.

Shattered by a devastating earthquake in 1693, the towns of Noto, Ragusa and Modica

---

DON'T MISS

NECROPOLI DI PANTALICA

On a huge plateau above the Valle dell'Anapo (Anapo Valley), the **Necropoli di Pantalica** (Via Pantalica) is Sicily's most important Iron and Bronze Age necropolis, with more than 5000 tombs of various shapes and sizes honeycombed along the limestone cliffs. The site is incredibly ancient, dating to between the 13th and 8th centuries BC, and its origins are largely mysterious, although it is thought to be the Siculi capital of Hybla, which gave the Greeks Megara Hyblaea in 664 BC.

Enshrined by Unesco as a World Heritage Site, Pantalica's ruins are surrounded by the beautifully wild and unspoilt landscape of the Valle dell'Anapo, a deep limestone gorge laced with walking trails. Maps posted at the archaeological site's entrance allow you to find your way, but the site is remote, with no services; wear sensible hiking shoes and bring plenty of water. Agencies in Syracuse also offer guided trips.

You'll need your own wheels to get here. From Syracuse, head northwest on the SS124 towards Palazzolo Acreide. After about 36km, turn right towards Ferla; the Necropoli di Pantalica is 11km beyond the town.

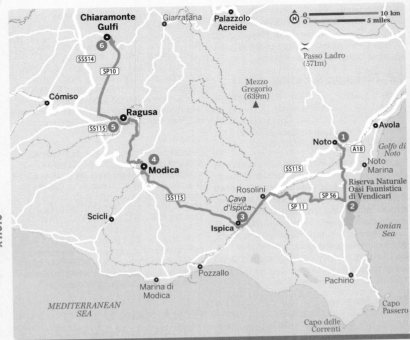

🏃 Driving Tour
Baroque Towns

START NOTO
END CHIARAMONTE GULFI
LENGTH 71KM; TWO DAYS

A land of remote rocky gorges, sweeping views and silent valleys, Sicily's southeastern corner is home to the 'baroque triangle', an area of Unesco-listed hilltop towns famous for their lavish baroque architecture. This tour takes in some of the finest baroque towns in Sicily, all within easy driving distance of each other.

Located just over 35km south of Syracuse, **1 Noto** is home to what is arguably Sicily's most beautiful street – Corso Vittorio Emanuele, a pedestrianised boulevard lined with golden baroque *palazzi* (mansions). From Noto, head 12km south along the SP19 to the **2 Riserva Naturale Oasi Faunistica di Vendicari**, a coastal preserve whose trails, wetlands and beaches are prime territory for walking, birdwatching and swimming. Next, head 23km southwest along the SP56, SP11 and SS115 to **3 Ispica**, a hilltop town

overlooking a huge canyon, the Cava d'Ispica, riddled with prehistoric tombs. Continuing up the SS115 for a further 18km brings you to **4 Modica**, a bustling town set in a deep rocky gorge. There's excellent accommodation here and a wealth of great restaurants, so the town makes a good place to overnight. The best of the baroque sights are up in Modica Alta, the high part of town, but save some energy for the *passeggiata* (evening stroll) on Corso Umberto I in the lower town.

Next morning, a short, winding, up-and-down drive through rock-littered hilltops leads to **5 Ragusa**, one of Sicily's nine provincial capitals. The town is divided in two – it's the lower town, Ragusa Ibla, that you want; it's a claustrophobic warren of grey stone houses and elegant *palazzi* that opens up onto Piazza Duomo, a superb example of 18th-century town planning. Although you can eat well in Ragusa, consider lunching in **6 Chiaramonte Gulfi**, a tranquil hilltop town some 20km to the north along the SP10, famous for its olive oil and delicious pork.

are the superstars here, rebuilt in the ornate and much-lauded Sicilian baroque style that lends the region a cohesive aesthetic appeal. Writer Gesualdo Bufalino described the southeast as an 'island within an island'; indeed, this pocket of Sicily has a remote, genteel air – a legacy of its Greek heritage.

Syracuse

POP 124,000

A dense tapestry of overlapping cultures and civilisations, Syracuse is one of Sicily's most appealing cities. Settled by colonists from Corinth in 734 BC, this was considered to be the most beautiful city of the ancient world, rivalling Athens in power and prestige. Under the demagogue Dionysius the Elder, the city reached its zenith, attracting luminaries such as Livy, Plato, Aeschylus and Archimedes, and cultivating the sophisticated urban culture that was to see the birth of comic Greek theatre.

Arriving in today's drab modern downtown by train or bus, you could be excused for wondering what all the fuss is about. But cross the bridge to the ancient island neighbourhood of Ortygia, and Syracuse's irresistible appeal quickly becomes manifest: in the Ancient Greek temple columns peeking out from the baroque walls of Ortygia's cathedral; the throngs of locals and tourists mingling in the reflected evening glow of Piazza del Duomo's vast marble pavements; the flash of fish swimming amid the papyrus plants in the Fontana Aretusa; and the splash of sunbathers plunging off rocks into the blue Ionian Sea. Adding to the city's magic is Syracuse's annual theatre festival, where classical Greek dramas are staged in one of the Mediterranean's greatest surviving ancient theatres.

Add to this the city's ambitious and enlightened moves towards pedestrian friendliness and environmental sustainability (including the recent launch of a fleet of electric minibuses), and you'll begin to understand why this has become Sicily's number one tourist destination and a city to savour.

◉ Sights

◉ Ortygia

★ **Duomo** CATHEDRAL
(Map p230; Piazza del Duomo; adult/reduced €2/1; ⊙9am-6.30pm Mon-Sat Apr-Oct, to 5.30pm Nov-Mar) Built on the skeleton of a 5th-century

BC Greek temple to Athena (note the Doric columns still visible inside and out), Syracuse's cathedral became a church when the island was evangelised by St Paul. Its most striking feature is the columned baroque facade (1728–53) added by Andrea Palma after the 1693 earthquake. A statue of the Virgin Mary crowns the rooftop, in the same spot where a golden statue of Athena once served as a beacon to homecoming Greek sailors.

Miqwe JEWISH SITE
(Ritual Bath; Map p230; ☑0931 2 22 55; Via Alagona 52; tours in English & Italian €5; ⊙tours 9am-7pm late-Mar–Oct, reduced hours rest of year) Buried 20m beneath the Alla Giudecca hotel in Ortygia's old Jewish ghetto (known as the Giudecca) is an extraordinary ancient Jewish *miqwe* (ritual bath), reputedly Europe's oldest. The baths were once connected to a synagogue, but were blocked by members of the Jewish community when they were expelled from the island in 1492. Regularly scheduled tours are offered in English and Italian.

Fontana Aretusa FOUNTAIN
(Map p230; Largo Aretusa) Stop to relax among papyrus plants and swans at this lovely spring, where fresh water still bubbles up just as it did in ancient times when it was the city's main water supply. Legend has it that the goddess Artemis transformed her beautiful handmaiden Aretusa into the spring to protect her from the unwelcome attention of the river god Alpheus.

Castello Maniace CASTLE
(Map p230; Piazza Federico di Svevia; adult/reduced €4/2; ⊙9am-1.30pm) Guarding the island's southern tip, Ortygia's 13th-century castle is a lovely place to wander, gaze out over the water and contemplate Syracuse's past glories. The castle grounds house two exhibitions, one shedding light on the fortress' evolution through the centuries, the other displaying archaeological finds from the site.

Galleria Regionale di Palazzo Bellomo GALLERY
(Map p230; ☑0931 6 95 11; www.regione.sicilia. it/beniculturali/palazzobellomo; Via Capodieci 16; adult/reduced €8/4; ⊙9am-7pm Tue-Sat, 2-7.30pm Sun) Housed in a 13th-century Catalan-Gothic palace, this art museum's eclectic collection ranges from early Byzantine and Norman stonework to 19th-century Caltagirone ceramics to a beautiful *Annunciation* by Antonello da Messina.

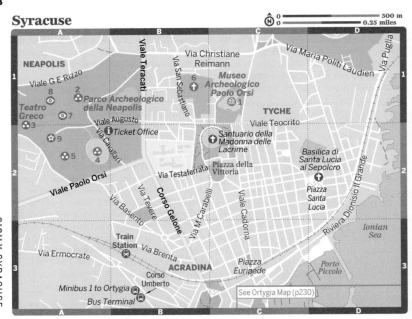

Syracuse

Museo del Papiro　　　　　　　MUSEUM
(Map p230; ☎0931 2 21 00; www.museodelpapiro.
it; Via Nizza 14; adult/reduced €5/2; ⏱10am-7pm
Tue-Sat, to 2pm Sun May-Sep, 9.30am-2pm Tue-Sun
Oct-Apr) This museum exhibits a fine collection of boats, papyrus documents and products, and an English-language film about the
nifty material's history. The papyrus plant
grows in abundance around the nearby Ci-
ane river, and was used to make paper in the
18th century.

◎ Mainland Syracuse

★ Parco Archeologico
della Neapolis　　　　ARCHAEOLOGICAL SITE
(Map p228; ☎0931 6 62 06; Viale Paradiso 14;
adult/reduced €10/5, incl Museo Archeologico
€13.50/7; ⏱9am-1hr before sunset Mon-Sat,
9am-1pm Sun) For the classicist, Syracuse's

real attraction is this archaeological park
and its pearly white 5th-century-BC **Teatro
Greco**. Hewn out of the rocky hillside, this
16,000-capacity amphitheatre staged the
last tragedies of Aeschylus (including *The
Persians*), which were first performed here
in his presence. In late spring it's brought
to life with an annual season of classical
theatre.

Beside the theatre is the mysterious **La-
tomia del Paradiso** (Garden of Paradise),
a deep, precipitous limestone quarry out of
which stone for the ancient city was extract-
ed. Riddled with catacombs and filled with
citrus and magnolia trees, it's also where
7000 survivors of the war between Syracuse
and Athens in 413 BC were imprisoned.
The **Orecchio di Dionisio** (Ear of Dionysius), a 23m-high grotto extending 65m back
into the cliffside, was named by Caravaggio

after the tyrant Dionysius, who is said to have used the almost perfect acoustics of the quarry to eavesdrop on his prisoners.

Back outside this area you'll find the entrance to the 2nd-century **Anfiteatro Romano**, originally used for gladiatorial combat and horse races. The Spaniards, little interested in archaeology, largely destroyed the site in the 16th century, using it as a quarry to build Ortygia's city walls. West of the amphitheatre is the 3rd-century-BC **Ara di Gerone II** (Altar of Hieron II), a monolithic sacrificial altar to Hieron II where up to 450 oxen could be killed at one time.

To reach the park, take Sd'A Trasporti's *linea rossa* minibus ('red' minibus No 2; €1, 15 minutes) from Molo Sant'Antonio, on the west side of the main bridge into Ortygia. Alternatively, walking from Ortygia will take about 30 minutes. If driving, park on Viale Augusto (tickets are available at the nearby souvenir kiosks).

The **ticket office** is located near the corner of Via Cavallari and Viale Augusto, opposite the main site.

★ Museo Archeologico Paolo Orsi

MUSEUM

(Map p228; ☑ 0931 48 95 11; www.regione.sicilia.it/beniculturali/museopaoloorsi; Viale Teocrito 66; adult/reduced €8/4, incl Parco Archeologico €13.50/7; ☉ 9am-6pm Tue-Sat, to 1pm Sun) About 500m east of the archaeological park, this modern museum contains one of Sicily's largest and most interesting archaeological collections. Allow plenty of time to investigate the four sectors charting the area's prehistory, as well as Syracuse's development from foundation to the late Roman period.

Basilica & Catacombe di San Giovanni

CHURCH, CATACOMB

(Map p228; ☑ 0931 6 46 94; www.kairos-web.com; Via San Sebastiano; guided tour adult/reduced €8/5; ☉ 9.30am-12.30pm & 2.30-5.30pm Tue-Sun) Beneath the Basilica di San Giovanni – a pretty, truncated church that served as the city's cathedral in the 17th century – lie these eerie, extensive catacombs, accessible on 30- to 40-minute guided tours (available in English).

🏃 Activities

In midsummer, when Ortygia steams like a cauldron, people flock to the beach south of town at **Lido Arenella**; take bus 23 from Piazza della Posta.

Also a favourite local hang-out for swimming and sunbathing in the summer months is the **platform** (Map p230) along Ortygia's eastern waterfront, surrounded by flat rocks and flanked by the crenellated walls of Forte Vigliena.

⭐ Festivals & Events

Ciclo di Rappresentazioni Classiche

THEATRE

(Festival of Greek Theatre; www.indafondazione.org; ☉ mid-May–Jun) Syracuse boasts the only school of classical Greek drama outside Athens, and in May and June it hosts live performances of Greek plays (in Italian) at the Teatro Greco, attracting Italy's finest performers. Tickets (€26 to €68) are available online, from the **Fondazione Inda ticket office** (Map p230; ☑ office 0931 48 72 00, tickets 800 542644Corso Matteotti 29; ☉ 10am-1pm Mon-Sat) in Ortygia or at the **ticket booth** (☉ 10am-6.30pm) outside the theatre.

Festa di Santa Lucia

RELIGIOUS

(☉ 13 Dec) The enormous silver statue of the city's patron saint wends its way from the cathedral to Piazza Santa Lucia, accompanied by fireworks.

🛏 Sleeping

Stay on Ortygia for atmosphere. Cheaper accommodation is located around the train station.

B&B Aretusa Vacanze

B&B €

(Map p230; ☑ 0931 48 34 84; www.aretusavacanze.com; Vicolo Zuccalà 1; d €59-90, tr €70-120, q €105-147; P ❄ 🛜) This great budget option, elbowed into a tiny pedestrian street in a 17th-century building, has large rooms and apartments with kitchenettes, wi-fi, satellite TV and small balconies from where you can shake hands with your neighbour across the way. Parking costs €7 per day.

★ Hotel Gutkowski

HOTEL €€

(Map p230; ☑ 0931 46 58 61; www.guthotel.it; Lungomare Vittorini 26; d €90-140, tr €140; ❄ @ 🛜) Book well in advance for one of the sea-view rooms at this stylish, eclectic hotel on the Ortygia waterfront, at the edge of the Giudecca neighbourhood. Divided between two buildings, its rooms are simple yet chic, with pretty tiled floors, walls in teals, greys, blues and browns, and a mix of vintage and industrial details.

Ortygia

See Syracuse Map (p228)

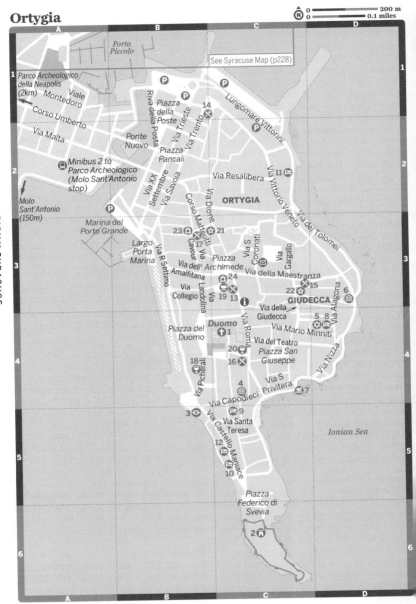

SICILY SYRACUSE

★ **Palazzo Bianco**　　　APARTMENT €€
(Map p230; ☎335 8087841, 0931 2 13 69; www.
casedisicilia.com; Via Castello Maniace; small apt
per night €140-170 (min 3 nights), per week €935-
1124, large apt per night €150-180 (min 3 nights),
per week €945-1134; ❄❢) Two exquisite apart-

ments await in this *palazzo* owned by a Milanese art collector. The larger is decadent,
with luxurious sofas, king-size bed, dining
table, precious artworks and a vaulted stone
ceiling. There's a sea-view terrace and the
bathroom has original stonework and a

Ortygia

SICILY SYRACUSE

hydro-massage shower. The smaller apartment wows with floor-to-ceiling artwork and a romantic four-poster bed. Both have kitchenettes and can accommodate up to four. Minimum three nights.

Alla Giudecca HOTEL €€
(Map p230; ☎0931 2 22 55; www.allagiudecca.it; Via Alagona 52; d €135-220; ❄@🛜) Located in the old Jewish quarter, this charming hotel offers 21 suites with warm terracotta-tiled floors, exposed wood beams and lashings of heavy white linen. The communal areas are a warren of vaulted rooms full of museum-quality antiques and enormous tapestries, and feature cosy sofas gathered around a huge fireplace. A few more expensive rooms have sea views.

Henry's House HOTEL €€€
(Map p230; ☎0931 2 13 61; www.hotelhenryshouse.com; Via del Castello Maniace 68; s €160-200, d €190-230, ste €290-330; ❄🛜) Directly overlooking Ortygia's waterfront, with three communal sun terraces perfect for lounging and soaking up the views, this gorgeous 17th-century *palazzo* was lovingly restored by antique collector Signor Corsaro before opening as a hotel in 2014. If money isn't an issue, book one of the two upstairs suites (one with terrace, both with water views). Complimentary bikes are available to guests.

✖ Eating

Ortygia is the best place to eat. Its narrow lanes are chock-full of trattorias, restaurants, cafes and bars, and while some are obvious tourist traps, there are plenty of quality options in the mix. Most places specialise in seafood.

★ Caseificio Borderi SANDWICHES €
(Map p230; www.caseificioborderi.eu; Via Benedictis 6; sandwiches €5; ⊙7am-4pm Mon-Sat) No visit to Syracuse's market is complete without a stop at this colourful deli near Ortygia's far northern tip. Veteran sandwich-master Andrea Borderi stands out front with a table full of cheeses, olives, greens, herbs, tomatoes and other fixings, and engages in non-stop banter with customers while creating free-form sandwiches big enough to keep you fed all day.

Sicilia in Tavola SICILIAN €
(Map p230; www.siciliaintavolo.eu; ☎392 4610889; Via Cavour 28; meals €20-30; ⊙12.30-2.30pm & 7.30-10.30pm Tue-Sun) One of the longest-established and most popular eateries on Via Cavour, this snug, simple trattoria has built its reputation on delicious homemade pasta and seafood. To savour both at once, tuck into the *fettuccine allo scoglio* (pasta ribbons with mixed seafood) or the equally fine prawn ravioli, paired with sweet cherry tomatoes and chopped mint. Reservations recommended

★ Moon VEGAN €€
(Map p230; ☎0931 44 95 16; www.moonortigia.com; Via Roma 112; meals €18-30; ⊙6-11.30pm; 🛜🍽) If vegan fare usually makes you yawn,

subvert your thinking at boho-chic Moon. A cast of mostly organic and biological ingredients beam in decadent, intriguing dishes that might see a tower of thinly sliced pears interlayered with a rich, soy-based cashew cream cheese, or chickpea and tofu conspiring in a smokey *linguine alla carbonara* as wicked as the original.

Moon also doubles as a performance space, serving up weekly theatre and music performances on its small backstage.

A Putia delle Cose Buone   SICILIAN €€
(Map p230; ☎334 3524585, 0931 44 92 79; www.aputiadellecosebuone.it; Via Roma 8; meals €18-30; ☺12.45-3pm & 7-11pm; ☏) From the whimsical lanterns to the benches draped in colourful pillows, this little bolthole feels welcoming from the word go. Then there's the food: creative, reasonably priced Sicilian dishes that make ample use of local seafood, veggies and extra-virgin olive oil (labelled EVO on the menu). Salads, vegan and vegetarian options also abound. Service is friendly, and there's pavement seating in warm weather.

★ Don Camillo   MODERN SICILIAN €€€
(Map p230; ☎0931 6 71 33; www.ristorantedon camillo.it; Via Maestranza 96; degustation menus €35-70; ☺12.30-2.30pm & 8-10.30pm Mon-Sat; ☏☎) One of Ortygia's most elegant restaurants, Don Camillo specialises in sterling service and innovative Sicilian cuisine. Pique the appetite with mixed shellfish in a thick soup of Noto almonds; swordfish with orange-blossom honey and sweet-and-sour vegetables; or outstanding *tagliata di tonno* (tuna steak) with red-pepper 'marmalade'. A must for Slow Food gourmands.

🍷 Drinking & Nightlife

Syracuse is a vibrant university town, which means plenty of life on the streets after nightfall. Many places are clustered near Piazza del Duomo.

Barcollo   BAR
(Map p230; www.facebook.com/barcollosiracusa; Via Pompeo Picherali 10; ☺7pm-3am; ☎) Hidden away in a flamboyant baroque courtyard, sultry Barcollo lures with its fresh flowers, flickering tealights and chi-chi outdoor deck. *Aperitivo* is served daily between 7pm and 10pm (there's a buffet on Sundays), with DJ sets Fridays and Sundays, and live music Saturdays.

Biblios Cafè   CAFE
(Map p230; www.biblioscafe.it; Via del Consiglio Reginale 11; ☺noon-9pm Wed-Mon Apr-Oct, 10am-2pm & 5-10pm Wed-Mon Nov-Mar) This beloved bookshop-cafe organises a whole range of cultural activities, including wine tasting, literary readings and language courses. It's a great place to drop in any time of day, for coffee or *aperitivi* or just to mingle.

Solaria Vini & Liquori   WINE BAR
(Map p230; ☎0931 46 30 07; www.vini-siciliani.it; Via Roma 86; ☺11.30am-2.30pm & 6pm-1am Mon-Sat; ☎) Thi is a wonderfully old-school *enoteca* (wine bar), with rows of rustic wooden tables and dark bottles lined up on floor-to-ceiling shelves. Stop by for a glass of wine or two, and pair with *vino*-friendly bites including cheese, olives, prosciutto, anchovies, sardines and *crocchè* (potato croquettes). The wine list is extensive and predominantly local, with French vintages and Champagnes thrown in for Gallic flair.

☆ Entertainment

Piccolo Teatro dei Pupi   THEATRE
(Map p230; ☎0931 46 55 40; www.pupari.com; Via della Giudecca 17; ☺6 times weekly Apr-Oct, fewer Nov-Mar) Syracuse's beloved puppet theatre hosts regular performances; see its website for a calendar. You can also buy puppets made at the family's workshop across the street and visit the affiliated puppet museum.

🛍 Shopping

Browsing in Ortygia's quirky boutiques is great fun.

Massimo Izzo   JEWELLERY
(Map p230; ☎0931 2 23 01; www.massimoizzo. com; Piazza Archimede 25; ☺4-8pm Mon, 9am-1pm & 4-8pm Tue-Sat) The flamboyant jewellery of Messina-born Massimo Izzo is not for the faint-hearted. Featuring bold idiosyncratic designs and made with Sciacca coral, gold and precious stones, his handmade pieces are often inspired by themes close to the Sicilian heart: the sea, theatre and classical antiquity.

Fish House Art   ARTS & CRAFTS
(Map p230; ☎339 7771364; www.fishhouseart.it; Via Cavour 29-31; ☺10am-1pm & 4-8pm Mon-Sat) This quirky gallery and shop is swimming with whimsical, beautifully crafted objects inspired by the sea. It's a showcase for both emerging and established Italian artisans, whose wares span richly hued fish made of

hand-blown glass to curious, recycled-metal creatures and wearable art.

ℹ️ Information

Hospital (Ospedale Umberto I; ☎ 0931 72 41 11; Via Testaferrata 1) Hospital between the centre and Parco Archeologico.

Tourist Office (Map p230; ☎ 0931 46 29 46; http://turismo.provsr.it; Via Roma 31; ⏰ 9am-12.30pm Mon-Fri) City maps and lots of good information.

ℹ️ Getting There & Away

Syracuse's train and bus stations are a block apart from each other, halfway between Ortygia and the archaeological park.

BUS

Long-distance buses operate from the bus stop along Corso Umberto, just east of Syracuse's train station.

Interbus (☎ 0931 6 67 10; www.interbus.it) runs buses hourly on weekdays (less frequently on weekends) to Catania (€6.20, 1½ hours) and Catania's Fontanarossa Airport (€6.20, 1¼ hours). Other Interbus destinations include Noto (€3.60, 55 minutes, two to four daily) and Palermo (€13.50, 3¼ hours, two to three daily).

AST (☎ 0931 46 27 11; www.aziendasicil ianatrasporti.it) offers services to Ragusa (€7.50, 3¼ hours, five daily except Sunday), with intermediate stops in Noto (€4, 55 minutes) and Modica (€6.40, 2¾ hours).

CAR & MOTORCYCLE

The modern A18 and SS114 highways connect Syracuse with Catania and points north, while the SS115 runs south to Noto and Modica. Arriving by car, exit onto the eastbound SS124 and follow signs to Syracuse and Ortygia.

Traffic on Ortygia is restricted; you're better off parking and walking once you arrive on the island. Most convenient is the **Talete parking garage** (Parcheggio Talete) at Ortygia's northern tip, which charges a 24-hour maximum of €10 (payable by cash or credit card at the machine when you leave). **Molo Sant'Antonio** on the mainland, just across the bridge from Ortygia, is another option.

TRAIN

From Syracuse's **train station** (Via Francesco Crispi), several trains depart daily for Messina (€10.50, 2½ to 3¼ hours) via Catania (€6.90, 1¼ hours). Some go on to Rome, Turin and Milan as well as other long-distance destinations. For Palermo, the bus is a better option. There are also local trains from Syracuse to Noto (€3.80, 30 minutes, eight daily except Sunday) and Ragusa (€8.30, two to 2½ hours, two daily except Sunday).

ℹ️ Getting Around

Syracuse's most convenient and ecofriendly pubilc transport option is the fleet of electric minibuses operated by **Sd'A Trasporti** (www.siracusadamare.it; one way/day pass/week pass €1/3/10). To reach Ortygia from the bus and train stations, hop aboard the *linea blu* ('blue' minibus No 1), which loops around the island every half-hour or so, making stops at more than a dozen convenient locations. To reach Parco Archeologico della Neapolis, take the *linea rossa* ('red' minibus No 2) from Molo Sant'Antonio, just west of the bridge to Ortygia. For route maps, see Sd'A Trasporti's website.

Noto

POP 23,800 / ELEV 160M

Flattened by the devastating earthquake of 1693, Noto was grandly rebuilt by its nobles into the finest baroque town in Sicily. Now a Unesco World Heritage Site, the town is especially impressive in the early evening, when its golden-hued sandstone buildings seem to glow with a soft inner light, and at night when illuminations accentuate the beauty of its intricately carved facades. The baroque masterpiece is the work of Rosario Gagliardi and his assistant, Vincenzo Sinatra, local architects who also worked in Ragusa and Modica.

◎ Sights

Two piazzas break up the long Corso Vittorio Emanuele: Piazza dell'Immacolata to the east and Piazza XVI Maggio to the west. The latter is overlooked by the beautiful **Chiesa di San Domenico** and the adjacent **Dominican monastery**, both designed by Rosario Gagliardi. On the same square, Noto's elegant 19th-century **Teatro Comunale** is worth a look. For sweeping views of Noto's baroque splendour, climb to the rooftop terrace at **Chiesa di Santa Chiara** (adult/reduced €2/1; ⏰10am-1pm & 3-6.30pm Mar-Jul, Sep & Oct, 9.30am-midnight Aug, 10am-noon Nov-Jan, closed Feb) or the *campanile* (bell tower) of **Chiesa di San Carlo al Corso** (campanile €2; ⏰10am-1pm & 3-6.30pm Mar-Jul, Sep & Oct, 9.30am-midnight Aug, 10am-noon Nov-Jan, closed Feb).

★**Cattedrale di San Nicolò**   CATHEDRAL
(Piazza Municipio; ⏰8am-1pm & 4-8pm) Pride of place in Noto goes to San Nicolò cathedral, a baroque beauty that had to undergo extensive renovation after its dome collapsed during a 1996 thunderstorm. The ensuing decade saw

the cathedral scrubbed of centuries of dust and dirt before reopening in 2007. Today the dome, with its peachy glow, is once again the focal point of Noto's skyline.

Piazza Municipio

PIAZZA

About halfway along Corso Vittorio Emanuele is the graceful Piazza Municipio, flanked by Noto's most dramatic buildings. To the north, sitting in stately pomp at the head of Paolo Labisi's monumental staircase, is the Cattedrale di San Nicolò, surrounded by a series of elegant palaces. To the left (west) is **Palazzo Landolina**, once home to the powerful Sant'Alfano family.

Palazzo Nicolaci di Villadorata

PALACE

(☑338 7427022; www.comune.noto.sr.it/palazzo -nicolaci; Via Corrado Nicolaci; €4; ☉10am-1.30pm & 2.30-7pm) The striking facade of this 18th-century palace features wrought-iron balconies supported by a swirling pantomime of grotesque figures. Inside, the *palazzo*'s richly brocaded walls and frescoed ceilings offer an idea of the sumptuous lifestyle of Sicilian nobles.

🎉 Festivals & Events

Infiorata

CARNIVAL

(www.infioratadinoto.it; ☉mid-May) Noto's big annual jamboree, the Infiorata is celebrated over three days around the third Sunday in May, with parades, historical re-enactments and the decoration of Via Corrado Nicolaci with designs made entirely of flower petals.

🛏 Sleeping & Eating

B&Bs are plentiful in Noto; the tourist office keeps a list.

Locals are serious about their food, so take time to enjoy a meal and follow it up with a visit to one of the town's excellent gelaterie (ice-cream shops).

★ Nòtia Rooms

B&B €€

(☑366 5007350, 0931 83 88 91; www.notiarooms. com; Vico Frumento 6; d €130-150, tr €150-170; 🛜) In Noto's historic workers' quarter, this sophisticated B&B is owned by the gracious Giorgio and Carla, who gave up the stress of northern Italian life to open this three-room beauty. Crisp white interiors are accented with original artworks, Modernist Italian lamps and upcycled vintage finds. Rooms seduce with sublimely comfortable beds and polished modern bathrooms. Gorgeous breakfasts maintain the high standards.

La Corte del Sole

INN €€

(☑0931 82 02 10; www.lacortedelsole.it; Contrada Bucachemi, Eloro, Lido di Noto; d €152-226, q €261-390; 🅿🌀@🛜♿) Overlooking the green fields of Eloro is this stylish hotel housed in a traditional Sicilian *masseria* (farmstead). A delightful place to stay, it also offers a range of activities, including **cooking lessons** (3hr lesson per guest/nonguest €75/90; ☉9.30am-12.30pm Tue-Sat, closed Aug) run by the hotel chef and, in winter, tours to study the 80 or so types of wild orchid found in the area.

★ Caffè Sicilia

GELATO €

(☑0931 83 50 13; Corso Vittorio Emanuele 125; desserts from €2; ☉8am-10pm Tue-Sun) Dating from 1892 and especially renowned for its *granite*, this beloved place vies with its next-door neighbour, Dolceria Corrado Costanzo, for the honours of Noto's best dessert shop. Frozen desserts are made with the freshest seasonal ingredients (wild strawberries in spring, for example), while the delicious *torrone* (nougat) bursts with the flavours of local honey and almonds.

★ Ristorante Crocifisso

SICILIAN €€

(☑0931 57 11 51; www.ristorantecrocifisso.it; Via Principe Umberto 48; meals €30-40; ☉12.30-2.15pm Thu-Tue, plus 7.30-10pm Tue & Thu-Sat) Up in Noto Alta, this Slow Food–acclaimed restaurant with an extensive wine list is widely regarded as Noto's best. Sicilian classics such as *macco di fave* (fava bean purée with wild fennel), garnished with ricotta and toasted breadcrumbs, and *casarecce alla palermitana* (short handmade pasta with sardines and wild fennel) are complemented by juicy roast lamb, Marsala-glazed pork and pistachio- and sesame-crusted tuna.

★ Ristorante Vicari

MODERN SICILIAN €€€

(☑0931 83 93 22; www.ristorantevicari.it; Ronco Bernardo Leanti 9; 5-/7-course degustation menu €50/60; ☉12.30-2pm & 7-10pm Tue-Sun, closed lunch Wed & Sun Jun-Sep) Low-slung lamps spotlight linen-clad tables at Vicari, and rightfully so. In the kitchen is up-and-coming chef Salvatore Vicari, who thrills with his whimsical takes on Sicilian produce: think sea urchin spaghetti with white-bean cream and *selicornia* (sea asparagus), tender rabbit decadently stuffed with liver pâté, or ridiculously succulent octopus barbecued and smoked to perfection. Book ahead.

ℹ Information

Infopoint Noto (☑ 339 4816218; www.notoin
forma.it; Corso Vittorio Emanuele 135; ⊘10am-
10pm Jul & Aug, to 6pm Apr-Jun & Sep, to 5pm
Oct-Mar) A useful tourist office, with maps,
brochures and enthusiastic, multilingual staff
who can also organise excursions.

ℹ Getting There & Away

BUS

From Largo Pantheon on the eastern edge of
Noto's historic centre, **AST** (☑ 840 000323;
www.aziendasiciliatrasporti.it) and **Interbus**
(☑ 0935 2 24 60, 091 34 20 55; www.interbus.
it) serve Catania (€8.40, 1½ hours) and Syracuse (€3.60 to €4, 55 minutes). Service is less
frequent on Sundays.

TRAIN

Trains run to Syracuse (€3.80, 30 minutes, eight
daily except Sunday), but Noto's station is incon-
veniently located 1km downhill from the centre.

Modica

POP 54,700 / ELEV 296M

A powerhouse in Grecian times, Modica remains a superbly atmospheric town, with its
medieval and baroque buildings climbing
steeply up either side of a deep gorge. The
multilayered town is divided into Modica Alta (Upper Modica) and Modica Bassa
(Lower Modica). A devastating flood in 1902
resulted in the wide avenues of Corso Umberto and Via Giarrantana (the river was
dammed and diverted), which remain the
main axes of the town, lined by *palazzi* and
tiled stone houses.

◉ Sights

Aside from simply wandering the streets
and absorbing the atmosphere, make time
to visit Modica's extraordinary churches.
Highlights include **Chiesa di San Giorgio**
(Corso San Giorgio, Modica Alta; ⊘8am-12.30pm
& 3.30-6.30pm), Gagliardi's masterpiece, a
butter-coloured vision of pure rococo splendour perched on a majestic 250-step staircase. Its counterpoint in Modica Bassa is the
Cattedrale di San Pietro (Corso Umberto I,
Modica Bassa; ⊘9am-1pm & 3.30-7.30pm Mon-
Sat, 9.30am-12.30pm & 4-7.30pm Sun), another
impressive church atop a rippling staircase
lined with life-sized statues of the Apostles.
Up the hill in Modica Alta, the big draw is
the **Chiesa di San Giovanni Evangelis-
ta** (off Piazza San Giovanni, Modica Alta; ⊘hours
vary), with its sweeping staircase, elliptical

interior and beautiful, neoclassical stucco work. Nearby, at the end of Via Pizzo, a
viewing balcony offers arresting views over
the old town.

🛏 Sleeping

Modica's quality-to-price ratio is generally
excellent.

⭐**Villa Quartarella** AGRITURISMO €
(☑ 360 654829; www.quartarella.com; Contrada
Quartarella Passo Cane 1; s €40, d €75-80, tr €85-
100, q €90-120; 🅿❊🛜🌊) Spacious rooms,
welcoming hosts and ample breakfasts make
this converted villa in the countryside about
7km south of Modica an appealing choice
for anyone travelling by car. Owners Francesco and Francesca are generous in sharing
their love and encyclopaedic knowledge of
local history, flora and fauna, and can sug-
gest a multitude of driving itineraries in the
surrounding area.

Palazzo Failla HOTEL €
(☑ 0932 94 10 59; www.palazzofailla.it; Via Blan-
dini 5, Modica Alta; s €55-99, d €80-125; ❊@🛜)
Smack in the heart of Modica Alta, this
four-star hotel in an exquisitely restored
18th-century palace has retained much of its
historical splendour, with original frescoed
ceilings, hand-painted Caltagirone floor tiles
and elegant drapes. Start the day with the
generous breakfast buffet and end it at the
well-regarded restaurant down the lane, run
by the hotel's management.

⭐**Casa Gelsomino** APARTMENT €€
(☑ 335 8087841; www.casedisicilia.com; Via Rac-
comandata, Modica Bassa; per night €160-200, per
week €1000-1260; ❊🛜) It's easy to pretend
you're a holidaying celebrity in this stunning
abode, the balconies and private terrace of
which serve up commanding views over
Modica. Incorporating an airy lounge, a fully equipped kitchen, stone-walled bathroom,
laundry room, sitting room and separate
bedroom, the apartment's combination of
vaulted ceilings, antique floor-tiles, original
artworks and plush furnishings take self-
catering to sophisticated highs. Start planning that swank, sunset soirée.

🍴 Eating & Drinking

La Locanda del Colonnello SICILIAN €€
(☑ 0932 75 24 23; www.locandadelcolonnello.it;
Vico Biscari 6, Modica Alta; meals €30-35; ⊘12.30-
2pm & 7.30-10pm Wed-Mon; 🛜) Book ahead for a
table at this Slow Food darling, hidden away

in Modica Alta. Seasonality steers a menu that gives classic Sicilian flavours subtle, elegant twists. Succulent shrimps give earthy *zuppetta di ceci* (chickpea soup) added intrigue, while ricotta and marjoram-stuffed ravioli seduce in a rich pork *sugo* (meat sauce). Finish with a smooth *gelo di limone* (lemon jelly).

★ **Accursio**　　　　　　　MODERN SICILIAN €€€

(☑0932 94 16 89; www.accursioristorante.it; Via Grimaldi 41, Modica Bassa; meals €65, tasting menus €100; ◷12.30-2.30pm Wed-Sat, 7.30-10pm daily) While we love the modernist furniture and vintage Sicilian tiles, the food is the real thrill at this fine-dining maverick, which was honoured in 2016 with its first Michelin star. Head chef Accursio Craparo specialises in boldly creative, nuanced dishes inspired by childhood memories and emblematic of new Sicilian thinking. For a well-rounded adventure, opt for a tasting menu.

Rappa Enoteca　　　　　　　　WINE BAR

(Corso Santa Teresa 97-99, Modica Alta; ◷5pm-midnight Mon-Sat) High ceilings, antique mouldings, tiled floors and chandeliers create a delightful backdrop at this atmospheric *enoteca* in the upper town. Sample a wide range of Sicilian wines, along with cheese and meat platters.

🛍 Shopping

Dolceria Bonajuto　　　　　　　　FOOD

(☑ 0932 94 12 25; www.bonajuto.it; Corso Umberto I 159, Modica Bassa; ◷9am-8.30pm Sep-Jul, to midnight Aug) Sicily's oldest chocolate factory is the perfect place to taste Modica's famous chocolate. Flavoured with cinnamon, vanilla, orange peel and even hot peppers, it's a legacy of the town's Spanish overlords who imported cocoa from their South American colonies. Leave room for Bonajuto's *'mpanatigghi*, sweet local biscuits filled with chocolate, spices...and minced beef!

ℹ Information

Tourist Office (☑ 346 6558227; www.comune. modica.rg.it; Corso Umberto I 141, Modica Bassa; ◷8am-1.30pm & 3.30-7pm Mon-Fri, 9am-1pm & 3.30-7pm Sat) City-run tourist office in Modica Bassa.

ℹ Getting There & Away

BUS

AST (☑ 0932 76 73 01; www.aziendasicil ianatrasporti.it) runs frequent buses from Monday to Saturday, departing Piazzale Falcone-Borsellino at the top of Corso Umberto I, to Syracuse (€6.40, 2¾ hours), Noto (€4, 1¾ hours) and Ragusa (€2.70, 30 minutes). Service is limited on Sundays: two buses each to Noto and Ragusa, none to Syracuse.

TRAIN

From Modica's station, 600m southwest of the centre, five trains daily (except Sunday) head to Syracuse (€7.60, 1¾ hours) and seven to Ragusa (€2.50, 20 to 25 minutes).

Ragusa

POP 72,800 / ELEV 502M

Ragusa is a dignified and well-aged provincial town. Like every other in the region, it collapsed after the 1693 earthquake; a new town called Ragusa Superiore was built on a high plateau above the original settlement. But the old aristocracy was loath to leave their tottering *palazzi*, and so rebuilt Ragusa Ibla on the original site. The two towns were only merged in 1927.

Ragusa Ibla remains the heart and soul of the town, and has all the best restaurants and the majority of sights. A sinuous bus ride or some very steep and scenic steps connect the lower town to its modern sibling up the hill.

◉ Sights

Grand churches and *palazzi* line the twisting, narrow streets of Ragusa Ibla, interspersed with gelaterie and delightful piazzas where the local youth stroll and the elderly gather on benches. Palm-planted Piazza del Duomo, the centre of town, is dominated by 18th-century **Cattedrale di San Giorgio** (Piazza Duomo; ◷10am-12.30pm & 4-7pm Jun-Sep, reduced hours rest of year), which features a magnificent neoclassical dome and stained-glass windows.

At the eastern end of the old town is the **Giardino Ibleo** (☑ 0932 65 23 74; ◷9am-10pm Mon-Thu, to 1am Fri & Sat), a pleasant public garden laid out in the 19th century. It's the perfect spot for a picnic lunch.

🛏 Sleeping & Eating

L'Orto Sul Tetto　　　　　　　　B&B €

(☑ 0932 24 77 85; www.lortosultetto.it; Via Tenente di Stefano 56; s €45-60, d €70-110; ❄🐾) This sweet little B&B behind Ragusa's *duomo* offers an intimate experience, with just three rooms and a lovely roof terrace where breakfast is served.

THE MOSAICS OF VILLA ROMANA DEL CASALE

Near the town of Piazza Armerina in central Sicily is the stunning 3rd-century Roman **Villa Romana del Casale** (☑0935 68 00 36; www.villaromanadelcasale.it; adult/reduced €10/5; ☉9am-6pm Apr-Oct, to 4pm Nov-Mar), a Unesco World Heritage Site and one of the few remaining sites of Roman Sicily. This sumptuous hunting lodge is thought to have belonged to Diocletian's co-emperor Marcus Aurelius Maximianus. Buried under mud in a 12th-century flood, it remained hidden for 700 years before its magnificent floor mosaics were discovered in the 1950s. Visit out of season or early in the day to avoid the hordes of visitors.

The mosaics cover almost the entire floor (3500 sq metres) of the villa and are considered unique for their narrative style, the range of subject matter and variety of colour – many are clearly influenced by African themes. Along the eastern end of the internal courtyard is the wonderful **Corridor of the Great Hunt**, vividly depicting chariots, rhinos, cheetahs, lions and the voluptuously beautiful Queen of Sheba. Across the corridor is a series of apartments, where floor illustrations reproduce scenes from Homer's *Odyssey*. But perhaps the most captivating of the mosaics is the so-called **Room of the Ten Girls in Bikinis**, with depictions of sporty girls in bikinis throwing a discus, using weights and throwing a ball; they would blend in well on a Malibu beach. These most famous of Piazza Armerina's mosaics were fully reopened to the public in 2013 after years of painstaking restoration and are among Sicily's greatest classical treasures.

Travelling by car from Piazza Armerina, follow signs south of town to the SP15, then continue 5km to reach the villa. Getting here by public transport is more challenging. Buses operated by Interbus (p223) run from Catania to Piazza Armerina (€9.20, 1¾ hours); from here catch a local bus (€1, 30 minutes, summer only) or a taxi (€20) for the remaining 5km.

Gelati DiVini
GELATO €

(☑0932 22 89 89; www.gelatidivini.it; Piazza Duomo 20; gelato from €2; ☉10am-late) This exceptional gelateria makes wine-flavoured gelato such as Marsala, *passito* and muscat, plus other unconventional offerings such as pine nut, watermelon, ricotta, and chocolate with spicy peppers.

A Rusticana
SICILIAN €€

(☑0932 22 79 81; www.arusticana-ibla.it; Via Domenico Morelli 4; meals €20-32; ☉12.30-2.30pm & 7.30pm-midnight Wed-Mon) Fans of the *Montalbano* TV series will want to eat here, as it's where scenes set in the fictional Trattoria San Calogero were filmed. In reality, it's a cheerful, boisterous trattoria, where generous portions and a relaxed vine-covered terrace ensure a loyal clientele. The food is defiantly *casareccia* (home-style), so expect no-frills pasta and uncomplicated cuts of grilled meat.

★ Ristorante Duomo
MODERN SICILIAN €€€

(☑0932 65 12 65; www.cicciosultano.it; Via Capitano Bocchieri 31; lunch menus from €60, dinner tasting menus €135-195; ☉12.30-4pm Tue-Sat, plus 7.30-11pm Mon-Sat) Widely regarded as one of Sicily's finest restaurants, behind its stained-glass door Duomo comprises a cluster of small rooms outfitted like private parlours, ensuring a suitably romantic ambience for chef Ciccio Sultano's refined creations. The menu abounds in classic Sicilian ingredients such as pistachios, fennel, almonds and Nero d'Avola wine, combined in imaginative and unconventional ways. Booking is essential.

❶ Information

Tourist Office (☑0932 68 47 80; www.comune.ragusa.gov.it; Piazza San Giovanni; ☉9am-7pm Mon-Fri, plus 9am-2pm Sat & Sun Easter–mid-Oct) Ragusa's main tourist office, with friendly, helpful staff.

❶ Getting There & Around

BUS

Long-distance and municipal buses share a terminal on Via Zama in the upper town. Buy tickets at the Interbus/Etna kiosk in the main lot or at cafes around the corner. **Interbus** (www.interbus.it; Via Zama) runs to Catania (€8.60, two hours, eight to 13 daily). **AST** (☑0932 76 73 01; www.aziendasicilianatrasporti.it; Via Zama) serves Syracuse (€7.20, 2¾ to 3¼ hours, three daily except Sunday) with intermediate stops in Modica (€2.70, 30 minutes) and Noto (€6, 2¼ hours).

Monday through Saturday, AST's city buses 11 and 33 (€1.20) run hourly between the Via Zama bus terminal and Giardino Ibleo in Ragusa Ibla. On Sundays, bus 1 makes a similar circuit.

TRAIN
From the station in the upper town, there are three direct trains daily except Sunday to Syracuse (€8.30, two hours) via Noto (€6.20, 1½ hours).

CENTRAL SICILY & THE MEDITERRANEAN COAST

Central Sicily is a land of vast panoramas, undulating fields, severe mountain ridges and hilltop towns not yet sanitised for tourism. Moving towards the Mediterranean, the perspective changes, as ancient temples jostle for position with modern high-rise apartments outside Agrigento, Sicily's most lauded classical site and also one of its busier modern cities.

Agrigento
POP 59,100 / ELEV 230M

Seen from a distance, modern Agrigento's rows of unsightly apartment blocks loom incongruously on the hillside, distracting attention from the splendid Valley of the Temples below, where the ancient Greeks once built their great city of Akragas. Never fear: once you get down among the ruins, their monumental grace becomes apparent, and it's easy to understand how this remarkable complex of temples became Sicily's preeminent travel destination, first put on the tourist map by Goethe in the 18th century.

Three kilometres uphill from the temples, Agrigento's medieval core is a pleasant place to pass the evening after a day exploring the ruins. The InterCity bus and train stations are both in the upper town, within a few blocks of Via Atenea, the medieval city's main thoroughfare.

◎ Sights

◎ Valley of the Temples

★ **Valley of the Temples**　ARCHAEOLOGICAL SITE
(Valle dei Templi; www.parcovalledeitempli.it; adult/reduced €10/5, incl Museo Archeologico €13.50/7; ⏱8.30am-7pm year-round, plus 7.30-10pm Mon-Fri, 7.30-11pm Sat & Sun mid-Jul–mid-Sep) Sicily's

most enthralling archaeological site encompasses the ruined ancient city of Akragas, highlighted by the well-preserved **Tempio della Concordia** (Temple of Concordia), one of several ridge-top temples that once served as beacons for homecoming sailors. The 13-sq-km park, 3km south of Agrigento, is split into eastern and western zones. Ticket offices with car parks are at the park's southwestern corner (the main Porta V entrance) and at the northeastern corner near the Temple of Hera (eastern entrance).

★ **Museo Archeologico**　MUSEUM
(☑0922 40 15 65; Contrada San Nicola 12; adult/reduced €8/4, incl Valley of the Temples €13.50/7; ⏱9am-7.30pm Tue-Sat, to 1.30pm Sun & Mon) North of the temples, this wheelchair-accessible museum is one of Sicily's finest, with a huge collection of clearly labelled artefacts from the excavated site. Of note are the dazzling displays of Greek painted ceramics and the awe-inspiring reconstructed *telamon*, a colossal statue recovered from the nearby Tempio di Giove.

◎ Medieval Agrigento
Roaming the town's lively, winding streets is relaxing after a day among the temples.

Chiesa di Santa Maria dei Greci　CHURCH
(www.museodiocesanoag.it; Salita Santa Maria dei Greci; ⏱10am-1.30pm & 3.30-7pm Apr-Oct, 10am-1pm Nov-Mar, closed Mon) This small church stands on the site of a 5th-century Doric temple dedicated to Athena. Inside are some badly damaged Byzantine frescoes, the remains of a Norman ceiling and traces of the original Greek columns.

Monastero di Santo Spirito　CONVENT
(☑0922 20664; www.monasterosantospirito.com; Cortile Santo Spirito 9; ⏱9am-7pm) At the top of a set of steps off Via Atenea, this convent was founded by Cistercian nuns around 1290. A handsome Gothic portal leads inside, where nuns are still in residence, praying, meditating and baking heavenly sweets, including *cuscusu* (sweet couscous made with local pistachios), *dolci di mandorla* (almond pastries) and *conchiglie* (shell-shaped sweets filled with pistachio paste). Press the doorbell and say '*Vorrei comprare qualche dolce*' ('I'd like to buy a few sweets').

Agrigento

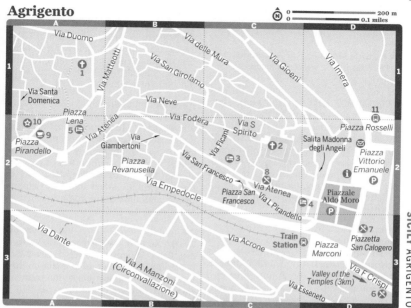

Agrigento

👉 Tours

Associazione Guide Turistiche Agrigento WALKING
(📱 345 8815992; www.agrigentoguide.org) Agrigento's official tour-guide association offers guided visits of the Valley of the Temples, Agrigento and the surrounding area, in English and eight other languages.

Temple Tour Bus BUS
(📱 331 8313720; www.templetourbusagrigento.com; adult/child day ticket €15/8, night ticket €10/6, combo ticket €20/10) This open-roofed bus offers hop-on, hop-off tours both day

and night between Agrigento and the Valley of the Temples.

🛏 Sleeping

⭐ **PortAtenea** B&B €
(📱 349 093 74 92; www.portatenea.com; Via Atenea, cnr Via C Battisti; s €39-50, d €59-75, tr €79-95; ❄🛜) This five-room B&B wins plaudits for its panoramic roof terrace overlooking the Valley of the Temples, and its unbeatable location at the entrance to the old town, just five minutes' walk from the train and bus stations. Best of all is the generous advice about Agrigento offered

by hosts Sandra and Filippo (witness Filippo's amazing Google Earth tour of nearby beaches!).

★Fattoria Mosè AGRITURISMO €

(☎0922 60 61 15; www.fattoriamose.com; Via Mattia Pascal 4a; r per person €50, incl breakfast/half board €60/90, 2-/4-/6-person apt per week €500/800/1100;) If Agrigento's urban jungle's got you down, head for this authentic organic *agriturismo*, 6km east of the Valley of the Temples. Four suites, six self-catering apartments and a pool offer ample space to relax. Guests can opt for reasonably priced dinners (including wine) built around the farm's organic produce, cook for themselves or even enjoy cooking courses (€80) onsite.

Terrazze di Montelusa B&B €

(☎347 7404784, 0922 59 56 90; www.terrazzedimontelusa.it; Piazza Lena 6; s/d/ste €50/75/85;) Occupying a beautifully preserved *palazzo* that's been in the same family since the 1820s, this charming B&B is filled with antique photos, original furniture and period details. As the name implies, it also boasts an inspiring collection of panoramic terraces, the most ample of which is reserved for the upstairs suite (well worth the extra €10).

Camere a Sud B&B €

(☎349 6384424; www.camereasud.it; Via Ficani 6; s €40, d €50-70, tr €70-100, q €90-120;) This lovely B&B situated in the medieval centre has three guest rooms that are decorated with style and taste, where traditional decor and contemporary textiles are matched with bright colours and modern art. Breakfast is served on the terrace in warmer months.

★Villa Athena HISTORIC HOTEL €€€

(☎0922 59 62 88; www.hotelvillaathena.it; Via Passeggiata Archeologica 33; d €423-577, ste €505-1165;) With the Tempio della Concordia lit up in the near distance and palm trees lending an exotic *Arabian Nights* feel, this historic five-star hotel in an aristocratic 18th-century villa offers the ultimate luxury experience. The cavernous Villa Suite, floored in antique tiles with a free-standing jacuzzi and a vast terrace overlooking the temples, might well be Sicily's most dramatic hotel room.

 **Eating & Drinking**

On a hot day, head for **Caffè Concordia** (Piazza Pirandello 36; almond milk €2; ⊙6am-9.30pm Tue-Sat) near Teatro Pirandello for a chilled glass of almond milk made from Agrigento's famous almonds, mixed with sugar, water and a hint of lemon rind.

Trattoria Concordia TRATTORIA €

(☎0922 2 26 68; Via Porcello 8; meals €18-30; ⊙noon-3pm & 7-10.30pm Mon-Fri, 7-11pm Sat) Rough stone walls and wood-beamed ceilings lend a cosy atmosphere to this quintessential family-run trattoria, tucked up a side alley in the old town. Traditional Sicilian starters (frittata, sweet-and-sour eggplant, ricotta and olives) are complemented by tasty grilled fish and meats.

★Aguglia Persa SEAFOOD €€

(☎0922 40 13 37; www.agugliapersa.it; Via Francesco Crispi 34; meals €25-40; ⊙noon-3.30pm & 7-11pm Wed-Mon) Set in a mansion with a leafy courtyard, just below the train station, this place is a welcome addition to Agrigento's fine-dining scene. Opened in 2015 by the owners of Porto Empedocle's renowned Salmoriglio restaurant, it specialises in fresh-caught seafood in dishes such as citrus-scented risotto with shrimp and wild mint, or marinated salmon with sage cream and fresh fruit.

★Kalòs MODERN SICILIAN €€

(☎0922 2 63 89; www.ristorantekalos.it; Piazzetta San Calogero; meals €30-45; ⊙12.30-3pm & 7-11pm Tue-Sun) At this 'smart' restaurant which is situated just outside the historic centre, five cute tables on little balconies offer a pleasant setting to enjoy homemade pasta *all'agrigentina* (with fresh tomatoes, basil and almonds), grilled lamb chops, citrus shrimp or *spada gratinata* (baked swordfish covered in breadcrumbs). Superb desserts, including homemade *cannoli* and almond *semifreddi*, round out the menu.

☆ **Entertainment**

Teatro Pirandello THEATRE

(☎0922 59 02 20; www.teatroluigipirandello.it; Piazza Pirandello; tickets €18-23) This city-run theatre is Sicily's third largest, after Palermo's Teatro Massimo and Catania's Teatro Massimo Bellini. Works by local hero, dramatist and writer Luigi Pirandello (1867–1936), figure prominently. The program runs from November to early May.

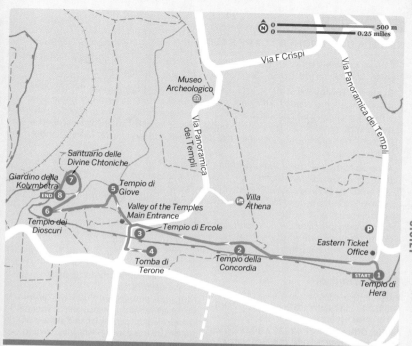

Archaeological Walking Tour
Valley of the Temples

START TEMPIO DI HERA
END GIARDINO DELLA KOLYMBETRA
LENGTH 3KM; THREE HOURS

Begin your exploration in the so-called Eastern Zone, home to Agrigento's best-preserved temples. From the eastern ticket office, a short walk leads to the 5th-century BC **1 Tempio di Hera**, perched on the ridge top. Though partly destroyed by an earthquake, the colonnade remains largely intact, as does a long sacrificial altar. Traces of red are the result of fire damage likely dating to the Carthaginian invasion of 406 BC.

Next, descend past a gnarled 500-year-old olive tree and a series of Byzantine tombs to the **2 Tempio della Concordia**. This remarkable edifice is the model for Unesco's logo. It has survived almost entirely intact since its construction in 430 BC, partly due to its conversion into a Christian basilica in the 6th century, and partly thanks to the shock-absorbing, earthquake-dampening qualities of the soft clay underlying its hard rock foundation.

Further downhill, the **3 Tempio di Ercole** is Agrigento's oldest, dating from the end of the 6th century BC. Down from the main temples, the miniature **4 Tomba di Terone** dates to 75 BC. Cross the pedestrian bridge into the western zone, stopping at the **5 Tempio di Giove**. This would have been the world's largest Doric temple had its construction not been interrupted by the Carthaginian sacking of Akragas. A later earthquake reduced it to the ruin you see today. Lying on his back amid the rubble is an 8m-tall *telamon* (a sculpted figure of a man with arms raised), originally intended to support the temple's weight. It's actually a copy; the original is in Agrigento's archaeological museum.

Take a brief look at the ruined 5th-century BC **6 Tempio dei Dioscuri** and the 6th-century BC complex of altars and small buildings known as the **7 Santuario delle Divine Chtoniche**, before ending your visit in the **8 Giardino della Kolymbetra**, a lush garden in a natural cleft near the sanctuary, with more than 300 (labelled) species of plants and some welcome picnic tables.

WORTH A TRIP

SCALA DEI TURCHI & TORRE SALSA

With your own wheels, you'll find some dreamy beaches and beauty spots west of Agrigento, all within an easy 30- to 45-minute drive of the city via the SS115.

Scala dei Turchi One of the most beautiful sights in the Agrigento area, this blindingly white rock outcrop, shaped like a giant staircase, juts into the sea near Realmonte, 15km west of Agrigento. It's a popular spot with local sun seekers who come to sunbathe on the milky-smooth rock and dive into the indigo sea. To escape the crowds, walk another few hundred metres north along the white rocky shelf, and descend to the long sandy beach below.

Riserva Naturale Torre Salsa (www.wwftorresalsa.it) This stunning 761-hectare natural park, administered by the World Wildlife Fund, is signposted off the SS115. Exit at Siculiana Marina (a small coastal settlement with its own great sandy beach) or continue 10km north to the second Montallegro exit and follow the signs for WWF Riserva Naturale Torre Salsa. There's plenty of scope for walkers here, with well-marked trails and sweeping panoramic views of the surrounding mountains and coast. The long, deserted Torre Salsa beach (reached from the northern entrance) is especially beautiful, although the access road is rough.

ℹ Information

Hospital (Ospedale San Giovanni di Dio; ☑ 0922 44 21 11; Contrada Consolida; ⊙24hr) North of the centre.

Tourist Office (☑ 0922 59 32 27, 800 315555; www.livingagrigento.it; Piazzale Aldo Moro 1; ⊙8am-1pm & 2-7pm Mon-Fri, to 1pm Sat) In the provincial government building.

ℹ Getting There & Away

BUS

The **InterCity bus station** and ticket booths are located on Piazza Rosselli.

Autoservizi Camilleri (☑ 0922 47 18 86; www.camilleriargentoelattuca.it) Runs to Palermo (€9, two hours) four to five times daily Monday to Saturday, once on Sunday.

Cuffaro (☑ 091 616 15 10; www.cuffaro.info) Operates seven buses to Palermo (€9, two hours) Monday to Friday, six on Saturday and three on Sunday.

Lumia (☑ 0922 2 04 14; www.autolineelumia.it) Has departures to Trapani and its Birgi Airport (€11.90, 2½ to 3½ hours) three times daily Monday to Saturday, one on Sunday).

SAIS Trasporti (☑ 0922 2 60 59; www.saistrasporti.it) Runs buses to Catania (€13.40, three hours, 11 to 15 daily).

SAL (Società Autolinee Licata; ☑ 0922 40 13 60; www.autolineesal.it) Offers direct service to Palermo's Falcone-Borsellino Airport (€12.60, 2¾ hours, four daily except Sunday).

CAR & MOTORCYCLE

The SS189 links Agrigento with Palermo, while the SS115 runs along the coast, northwest towards Trapani and southeast towards Ragusa, Modica and Syracuse.

Driving in the medieval town is near impossible due to all of the pedestrianised streets. There's metered parking located at the train station and free parking along Via Esseneto, just below.

TRAIN

From Agrigento Centrale station (Piazza Marconi), direct trains run regularly to Palermo (€9, two hours, six to 10 daily). Service to Catania (from €11.30, 3¼ to six hours) is less frequent and requires a change of trains; for this and most other destinations, you're better off taking the bus.

ℹ Getting Around

City bus 1, operated by **TUA** (Trasporti Urbani Agrigento; ☑ 0922 41 20 24; www.trasportiurbaniagrigento.it), runs half-hourly services from Agrigento's bus and stations to the archaeological museum (15 minutes) and the Porta V entrance to the temples (20 minutes). Bus 2/ (as distinct from bus 2, which has a different route – watch out for the hard-to-spot forward slash) runs services every hour or so to the temples' eastern entrance near the Tempio di Hera (10 to 15 minutes). Tickets cost €1.20 if they are bought in advance from a tobacconist, or €1.70 on board the bus. A day ticket costs €3.40.

The *linea verde* (green line) departs every 50 minutes from the train station, running the length of Via Atenea and looping through the medieval town centre.

WESTERN SICILY

Situated directly across the water from North Africa and still retaining vestiges of the Arab, Phoenician and Greek cultures that once prevailed here, western Sicily has a bit of the Wild West about it. There is plenty to stir the senses, from Trapani's savoury fish couscous to the dazzling views from hilltop Erice and the wild coastal beauty of the Riserva Naturale dello Zingaro.

Marsala & Around

POP 82,300

Best known for its sweet dessert wines, Marsala revolves around a lovely, elegant core of stately baroque buildings within a perfect square of walls. To the east and north lie less attractive modern outskirts that gradually peter out into the surrounding vineyards.

The city was originally founded by Phoenician escapees from the Roman onslaught at nearby Mozia. Not wanting to risk a second attack, they fortified their new home with 7m-thick walls, ensuring that it was the last Punic settlement to fall to the Romans. In 830 AD it was conquered by the Arabs, who gave it its current name, Marsa Allah (Port of God).

It was here in 1860 that Giuseppe Garibaldi, leader of the movement for Italian unification, landed in his rickety old boats with his 1000-strong army – a claim to fame that finds its way into every tourist brochure.

◉ Sights & Activities

For a taste of local life, take a stroll at sunset around pretty **Piazza della Repubblica**, heart of the historic centre.

Whitaker Museum   MUSEUM

(☑ 0923 71 25 98; www.fondazionewhitaker.it; San Pantaleo; adult/reduced €9/5; ☺ 9.30am-6.30pm Apr-Oct, 9am-3pm Nov-Mar) This museum on San Pantaleo island, 10km north of Marsala, houses a unique collection of Phoenician artefacts assembled over decades by amateur archaeologist Joseph Whitaker. Its greatest treasure (returned to Sicily in 2014 after two years at London's British Museum and Los Angeles' Getty) is *Il Giovinetto di Mozia,* a 5th-century-BC Carthaginian-influenced marble statue of a young man.

To get here, drive or cycle to the Mozia dock 10km north of Marsala and catch one of the half-hourly ferries operated by **Mozia Line** (☑ 338 7860474, 0923 98 92 49; www.mozialine.com; round trip adult/reduced €5/2.50; ☺ 9.15am-6.30pm) for the 10-minute crossing.

Museo Archeologico Baglio Anselmi   MUSEUM

(☑ 0923 95 25 35; Lungomare Boeo 30; adult/reduced €4/2; ☺ 9am-6.30pm Wed-Sat, to 1.30pm Tue & Sun) Reopened to the public in 2017 after a multi-year renovation, this museum revolves around the partially reconstructed remains of a Carthaginian *liburna* (warship) sunk off the Egadi Islands during the First Punic War. Displayed alongside objects from its cargo, the ship's bare bones provide the only remaining physical evidence of the Phoenicians' seafaring superiority in the 3rd century BC, offering a glimpse of a civilisation extinguished by the Romans.

WORTH A TRIP

SALINE DI TRAPANI

Along the coast between Trapani and Marsala, the Saline di Trapani present an evocative landscape of *saline* (shallow salt pools) and decommissioned *mulini* (windmills). The salt from these marshes is considered Italy's finest and was big business for centuries; today, only a cottage industry remains, providing for Italy's more discerning dinner tables. The best time to visit is summer, when the sun turns the saltpans rosy pink and makes the salt heaps shimmer. In winter, the heaps – covered with tiles and plastic tarpaulins to keep out the rain – are considerably less picturesque.

The most attractive stretches of coast are protected within two wetland preserves: **Riserva Naturale Saline di Trapani e Paceco** (☑ 0923 86 77 00, 327 5621529; www.salineditrapani.it), to the north near Trapani, and **Riserva Naturale di Stagnone**, to the south near Marsala. The latter encompasses Isola San Pantaleo – home to the noted archaeological site of Mozia – and the larger Isola Lunga, which protects the shallow waters of Stagnone lagoon.

Cantine Florio   WINE

(☑0923 78 13 05; www.duca.it/en/ospitalita/
cellar-tours; Via Vincenzo Florio 1; tours adult/
reduced €13/5; ☉9am-6pm Mon-Fri, to 1pm Sat,
English-language tours 10am & 4pm Mon-Fri, 10am
Sat) These venerable wine cellars just east
of town open their doors to visitors to explain the Marsala-making process and the
fascinating history of local viticulture. Afterwards, visitors can sample the goods in
Florio's spiffy tasting room (tasting of four
wines accompanied by hors d'oeuvres included in tour price). Book in advance for
English-language tours. Take bus 16 from
Piazza del Popolo. Other producers in the
same area include Pellegrino, Donnafugata,
Rallo, Mavis and Intorcia.

🛏 Sleeping & Eating

Marsala has few hotels within the historic
centre.

★ Il Profumo del Sale   B&B €

(☑0923 189 04 72; www.ilprofumodelsale.it; Via
Vaccari 8; s/d €35/60; ☎) Perfectly positioned
in Marsala's historic city centre, this B&B
offers three attractive rooms – including a
palatial front unit with cathedral views from
its small balcony – enhanced by welcoming
touches such as almond cookies, fine soaps
and ample breakfasts featuring homemade
bread and jams. Sophisticated owner Celsa
is full of helpful tips about Marsala and the
surrounding area.

Hotel Carmine   HOTEL €€

(☑0923 71 19 07; www.hotelcarmine.it; Piazza Carmine 16; s €75-105, d €105-125; 🅿❄@☎) This
lovely hotel in a converted 16th-century
monastery has elegant rooms with vintage
touches such as original blue-and-gold
maiolica tiles, stone walls, antique furniture
and lofty beamed ceilings. Enjoy your corn-
flakes in the baronial-style breakfast room
with its historic frescoes and over-the-top
chandelier, or sip your drink by the roaring
fireplace in winter. Modern perks include a
rooftop solarium.

Quimera   SANDWICHES €

(☑349 6783243; www.facebook.com/quimerapub;
Via Sarzana 34-36; sandwiches & salads from €5;
☉noon-3pm & 6.30pm-2am Mon-Sat, 6.30pm-2am
Sun) Smack in the middle of the pedestrianised centre, this is Marsala's hot spot for
artisanal beers, gourmet sandwiches and
meal-sized salads, all served with a smile by
the friendly young owners.

San Lorenzo Osteria   SICILIAN €€

(SLO; ☑0923 71 25 93; www.osteriasanlorenzo.
com; Via Garraffa 60; meals €30-40; ☉7.30-11pm
daily, plus 12.30-2.30pm Sun; ☎) This stylish
eatery is a class act all round – from the ever-
changing menu of fresh seafood scrawled
daily on the blackboard to the interior's
sleek modern lines to the gorgeous presenta-
tion of the food. The wine list, updated regularly, features some local choices you won't
find elsewhere.

❶ Information

Tourist Office (☑0923 71 40 97, 0923 99 33
38; ufficioturistico.proloco@comune.marsala.
tp.it; Via XI Maggio 100; ☉8.30am-1.30pm &
3-8pm Mon-Fri, to 1.30pm Sat) Spacious office
with comfy couches right off the main square;
provides a wide range of maps and brochures.

❶ Getting There & Away

From Marsala, bus operators include **Lumia**
(www.autolineelumia.it), which goes to Agrigento (€10.10, 2½ to three hours, one to three daily),
and **Salemi** (☑0923 98 11 20; www.autoservizi
salemi.it) to Palermo (€11, 2¼ to 2½ hours, at
least 10 daily).

   Train is the best way to get to Trapani (€3.80,
30 minutes, 10 daily Monday to Saturday, four
on Sunday).

Selinunte

The **Ruins of Selinunte** (☑0924 4 62 77;
adult/reduced €6/3; ☉9am-6pm Apr-Oct, to 5pm
Nov-Mar) are the most impressively sited in
Sicily. The huge city was built in 628 BC
on a promontory overlooking the sea, and
over the course of two-and-a-half centuries
became one of the richest and most powerful in the world. It was destroyed by the
Carthaginians in 409 BC and finally fell to
the Romans about 350 BC, at which time
it went into rapid decline and disappeared
from historical accounts.

   The city's past is so remote that the names
of the various temples have been forgotten
and they are now identified by the letters A to
G, M and O. The most impressive, **Temple E**,
has been partially rebuilt, its columns pieced
together from their fragments with part of its
tympanum. Many of the carvings, particularly from **Temple C**, are now in the archaeological museum in Palermo. Their quality is on
par with the Parthenon marbles and clearly
demonstrates the high cultural levels reached
by many Greek colonies in Sicily.

The ticket office and entrance to the ruins is located near the eastern temples. Try to visit in spring when the surroundings are ablaze with wildflowers.

Escape the mediocre restaurants near the ruins by heading for **Lido Zabbara** (📞0924 4 61 94; Via Pigafetta, Marinella di Selinunte; buffet per person €12; ☺noon-3pm Mar-early Nov, plus 7.30-10.30pm Jun-Sep), a beachfront eatery in nearby Marinella di Selinunte that serves good grilled fish and a varied buffet. Alternatively, drive 15km east to **Da Vittorio** (📞0925 7 83 81; www.ristorantevittorio.it; Via Friuli Venezia Giulia, Porto Palo; meals €30-45; ☺12.30-2.30pm & 7-10pm) in Porto Palo, another wonderful spot to enjoy seafood, sunset and the sound of lapping waves.

ℹ Getting There & Away

Selinunte is midway between Agrigento and Trapani, about 10km south of the junction of the A29 and SS115 near Castelvetrano. **Autoservizi Salemi** (📞0924 8 18 26; www.autoservizi salemi.it/tratte/selinunte) runs seven buses daily except Sunday from Selinunte to Castelvetrano (€1.50, 25 to 35 minutes), where you can make onward bus connections with **Lumia** (📞0922 2 04 14; www.autolineelumia.it) to Agri-

gento (€8.60, two hours), or train connections to Marsala (€4.30, 35 to 45 minutes), Trapani (€6.20, one to 1¼ hours) and Palermo (€8.30, three hours).

Trapani

POP 70,600

The lively port city of Trapani makes a convenient base for exploring Sicily's western tip. Its historic centre is filled with atmospheric pedestrian streets and some lovely churches and baroque buildings, although the heavily developed outskirts are rather bleak.

Once situated at the heart of a powerful trading network that stretched from Carthage to Venice, Trapani's sickle-shaped spit of land hugs the precious harbour, nowadays busy with a steady stream of tourist traffic to and from Pantelleria and the nearby Egadi Islands.

◉ Sights

Trapani's pedestrianised historic centre is a Moorish labyrinth; its main thoroughfare, Corso Vittorio Emanuele, is lined with 18th-century baroque gems such as the

---

WORTH A TRIP

SCOPELLO & RISERVA NATURALE DELLO ZINGARO

Saved from development and road projects by local protests, the tranquil **Riserva Naturale dello Zingaro** (📞0924 3 51 08; www.riservazingaro.it; adult/reduced €5/3; ☺7am-7.30pm Apr-Sep, 9am-5pm Oct-Mar) is the star attraction on the Golfo di Castellammare, halfway between Palermo and Trapani. Founded in 1981, this was Sicily's first nature reserve. Zingaro's wild coastline is a haven for the rare Bonelli's eagle, along with 40 other species of bird. Mediterranean flora dusts the hillsides with wild carob and bright yellow euphorbia, and hidden coves, such as Capreria and Marinella Bays, provide tranquil swimming spots. The main entrance to the park is 2km north of the village of Scopello. Several walking trails are detailed on maps available for free at the entrance or downloadable from the park website. The main 7km trail along the coast passes by the visitor centre and five museums that document everything from local flora and fauna to traditional fishing methods.

Once home to tuna fishers, tiny **Scopello** now mainly hosts tourists. Its port, 1km below town and reachable by a walking path, has a picturesque **beach** (www.tonnaradis copello.com; €3; ☺9am-7pm), backed by a rust-red *tonnara* (tuna-processing plant) and dramatic *faraglioni* (rock towers) rising from the water.

Pensione Tranchina (📞0924 54 10 99; www.pensionetranchina.com; Via Diaz 7; B&B per person €36-48, half board per person €55-75; ❄🛜) is the nicest of several accommodation options clustered around the cobblestoned courtyard at Scopello's village centre. Friendly hosts Marisin and Salvatore offer comfortable rooms, a roaring fire on chilly evenings and superb home-cooked meals featuring local fish and home-grown fruit and olive oil. If you're just here on a day trip, the terrace at nearby **Bar Nettuno** (📞0924 54 13 62; Baglio Isonzo 13; meals €30-40; ☺9am-late) makes another brilliant end-of-day destination for seafood and sundowners.

DEAGOSTINI/GETTY IMAGES ©

1. 'Room of the Ten Girls in Bikinis' (p237), Villa Romana del Casale
2. Doric temple (p250), Segesta 3. Duomo (p227), Ortygia,
Syracuse 4. Valley of the Temples (p238), Agrigento

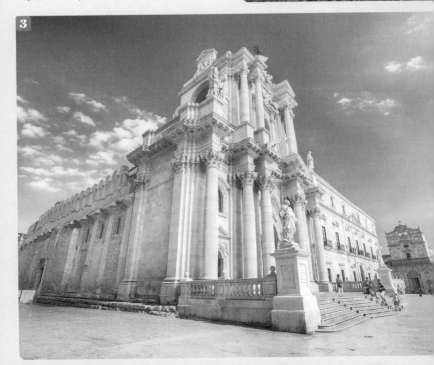

MATEJ KASTELIC/SHUTTERSTOCK ©

A Graeco-Roman Legacy

As the crossroads of the Mediterranean since the dawn of time, Sicily has seen countless civilisations come and go. The island's classical treasure trove includes Greek temples and amphitheatres, Roman mosaics and a host of fine archaeological museums.

Valley of the Temples

Crowning the craggy heights of Agrigento's Valley of the Temples (p238) are five Doric temples – including stunning Tempio della Concordia, one of the best preserved in all of Magna Graecia. Throw in the superb archaeological museum and you've got Sicily's most cohesive and impressive collection of Greek treasures.

Villa Romana del Casale

Bikini-clad gymnasts and wild African beasts prance side by side in remarkable floor decorations in this ancient Roman hunting lodge (p237). Buried under mud for centuries and now gleaming from restoration work completed in 2013, they're the most extensive mosaics in Sicily and a Unesco World Heritage Site.

Segesta

Segesta's perfect Doric temple (p250) perches on a windswept hilltop above a rugged river gorge.

Taormina

With spectacular views of snowcapped Mt Etna and the Ionian Sea, Taormina's Teatro Greco (p215) makes the perfect venue for the town's summer film and arts festivals.

Selinunte

Selinunte's vast ruins (p244) poke out of wildflower-strewn fields beside the sparkling Mediterranean.

Syracuse

Once the most powerful city in the Mediterranean, Syracuse (p227) brims with reminders of its ancient past, from the Greek columns supporting Ortygia's cathedral to the annual festival of classical Greek drama, staged in a 2500-year-old amphitheatre.

Cattedrale di San Lorenzo (Corso Vittorio Emanuele; ⊙8am-4pm) and the **Palazzo Senatorio** (cnr Corso Vittorio Emanuele & Via Torrearsa). The best time to stroll here is in the early evening (around 7pm) when the *passeggiata* is in full swing.

Chiesa del Purgatorio CHURCH
(☑0923 56 28 82; Via San Francesco d'Assisi; voluntary donation requested; ⊙7.30am-noon & 4-7pm Mon-Sat, 10am-noon & 4-7pm Sun) Just off Corso Vittorio Emanuele in the heart of the city, this church houses the impressive 18th-century *Misteri,* 20 life-sized wooden effigies depicting the story of Christ's Passion, which take centre stage during the city's dramatic Easter Week processions each year. Explanatory panels in English, Italian, French and German help visitors understand the story behind each figure.

Museo Nazionale Pepoli MUSEUM
(☑0923 55 32 69; www.comune.trapani.it/turismo/pepoli.htm; Via Conte Pepoli 180; adult/reduced €6/3; ⊙9am-5.30pm Tue-Sat, to 12.30pm Sun) In a former Carmelite monastery, this museum houses the collection of Conte Pepoli (1796–1881), who devoted his life to salvaging Trapani's local arts and crafts – most notably the garish coral carvings that were once all the rage in Europe before Trapani's offshore coral banks were decimated. The museum also has a good collection of Gagini sculptures, silverwork, archaeological artefacts and religious art.

⭐ Festivals & Events

Local culinary treasure couscous is the centrepiece of two annual festivals: Trapani's newer addition **Cuscusu** (www.cuscusu.it; ⊙Jun) and the well-established **Cous Cous Fest** (www.couscousfest.it; ⊙mid-late Sep) in nearby San Vito Lo Capo.

I Misteri RELIGIOUS
(www.processionemisteritp.it) Sicily's most venerated Easter procession is a four-day festival of extraordinary religious fervour. Nightly processions, bearing life-sized wooden effigies, make their way through the old quarter to a specially erected chapel in Piazza Lucatelli. The high point is on Good Friday when the celebrations reach fever pitch.

🛏 Sleeping & Eating

The most convenient and attractive places to stay and eat are in Trapani's pedestrianised historic centre, just north of the port.

Sicily's Arab heritage and Trapani's unique position on the sea route to Tunisia have made couscous (or *'cuscusu'* as it's sometimes spelt around here) a local specialty.

Ai Lumi B&B B&B €
(☑0923 54 09 22; www.ailumi.it; Corso Vittorio Emanuele 71; s €53-70, d €85-106, tr €111-132, q €138-159; 🟦🛜) Housed in an 18th-century *palazzo,* this centrally located B&B offers 13 rooms of varying size. Best are the spacious apartments (numbers 32, 34 and 35), with kitchenettes and balconies overlooking Trapani's most elegant pedestrian street. Upstairs apartment 23 is also lovely, with a private balcony reached by a spiral staircase. Guests get discounts at the hotel's atmospheric restaurant next door.

La Gancia HOTEL €€
(☑0923 43 80 60; www.lagancia.com; Piazza Mercato del Pesce; s €75-85, d €110-164, q €179-280; 🟦🛜) Well positioned on the waterfront at the north end of Trapani's historic centre, this immaculate hotel offers 20 comfortable kitchenette-equipped rooms, ranging from lower-priced interior-facing units to a spacious 4th-floor junior suite with its own sea-view terrace. The breakfast room enjoys pretty views of the water, and the port is just a five-minute walk away.

La Rinascente PASTRIES €
(☑0923 2 37 67; Via Gatti 3; cannoli €2; ⊙9am-1.30pm & 3-7pm Mon, Tue, Thu & Fri, 7.30am-2pm Sat & Sun) When you enter this bakery through the side door, you'll feel like you've barged into someone's kitchen – and you have! Thankfully, owner Giovanni Costadura's broad smile will quickly put you at ease, as will a taste of his homemade *cannoli,* which he'll create for you on the spot.

⭐ Osteria La Bettolaccia SICILIAN €€
(☑0923 2 59 32; www.labettolaccia.it; Via Enrico Fardella 25; meals €35-45; ⊙12.45-3pm Mon-Fri, plus 7.45-11pm Mon-Sat) Unwaveringly authentic, this perennial Slow Food favourite just two blocks from the ferry terminal is the perfect place to try *cous cous con zuppa di mare* (couscous with mixed seafood in a spicy fish sauce, with tomatoes, garlic and parsley). Due to its great popularity, it's wise to book ahead.

Caupona Taverna di Sicilia SEAFOOD €€
(☑0923 54 66 18, 340 3421335; Piazza Purgatorio 32; meals €25-36; ⊙1-2.15pm & 8-11.30pm Wed-

Mon) Fresh fish rules the menu at this fabulous family-run spot two blocks from the port. Chef Rosi cooks and husband Claudio works the tables, serving up superb couscous and colourful seafood classics such as *pesce spada alla pantesca* (swordfish in a sauce of tomatoes, garlic, parsley, olives and capers). Save room for the monster-sized *cannoli* (enough to feed two people easily).

ⓘ Information

Hospital (Ospedale Sant'Antonio Abate; ☑ 0923 80 91 11; www.asptrapani.it; Via Cosenza) Five kilometres east of the centre.

Tourist Office (☑ 0923 54 45 33; sport.turismo.spettacolo@comune.trapani.it; Piazzetta Saturno; ⊙ 9am-9pm Jun-Sep, to 5.30pm Mon & Thu, to 2pm Tue, Wed & Fri Oct-May) Just north of the port, Trapani's tourist office offers city maps and information.

ⓘ Getting There & Around

The ferry and hydrofoil docks straggle along Via Ammiraglio Staiti at the peninsula's southern edge. **Egatour** (☑ 0923 2 17 54; www.egatour viaggi.it; Via Ammiraglio Staiti 13), a travel agency opposite the port, offers one-stop shopping for bus, plane and ferry tickets. The bus and train stations lie about 1km east of the centre.

AIR

Trapani's small **Vincenzo Florio Airport** (Birgi Airport; TPS; ☑ 0923 61 01 11; www.airgest.it) is 17km south of town at Birgi. **Ryanair** (☑ 899 018880; www.ryanair.com) offers direct flights to two dozen Italian and European cities, while Alitalia goes to Rome and Mistral Air flies to the Mediterranean island of Pantelleria. **AST** (Azienda Siciliana Trasporti; ☑ 0923 2 10 21; www.astsicilia.it) operates hourly buses from 5.30am to 12.30am connecting the airport with downtown Trapani (€4.90, 45 minutes).

BOAT

Ferry ticket offices are located inside Trapani's ferry terminal, opposite Piazza Garibaldi. Hydrofoil ticket offices are 350m further east along Via Ammiraglio Staiti.

Liberty Lines (☑ 0923 87 38 13; www.liberty lines.it; Via Ammiraglio Staiti) Operates hydrofoils year-round to the Egadi Islands ports of Favignana (€12.80, 25 to 40 minutes), Levanzo (€11.80, 25 to 40 minutes) and Marettimo (€18.80, 1¼ hours), along with summer-only service to Pantelleria (€47, 2¼ hours), Ustica (€32.50, 2½ hours) and Naples (€108, seven hours). The latter two services run on Saturdays only.

Siremar (☑ 090 36 46 01; www.siremar.it; Ferry Terminal) Offers year-round ferry service to Pantelleria (€36.50, six to seven hours) and the Egadi Islands ports of Favignana (€10.70, one to 1½ hours), Levanzo (€9.70, one to 1½ hours) and Marettimo (€14.60, three hours).

Traghetti delle Isole (☑ 0923 2 24 67; www. traghettidelleisole.it) Runs ferries to Pantelleria (€34.50, six to 7¼ hours) daily in July and August, three to five times weekly rest of year.

BUS

InterCity buses arrive and depart from the terminal 1km east of the centre (just southeast of the train station).

Segesta (☑ 0923 2 84 04, 0923 2 19 56; www. buscenter.it) runs express buses to Palermo (€9.60, two hours, hourly). Board at the bus stop across the street from Egatours or at the bus station. **Lumia** (☑ 0922 2 04 14, 0923 2 17 54; www.autolineelumia.it) serves Agrigento (€11.90, 2¾ to 3¾ hours, one to three daily).

ATM (Azienda Trasporto e Mobilità; ☑ 0923 55 95 75; www.atmtrapani.it) operates two free city buses (Nos 2 and 10), which make circular trips through Trapani, connecting the bus station, the train station and the port. Tickets for ATM's other local buses – valid for 90 minutes – cost €1.20 at *tabacchi* (tobacco shops) or €1.40 if purchased on board the bus.

CAR & MOTORCYLE

To bypass Trapani's vast suburbs and avoid the narrow streets of the city centre, follow signs from the A29 autostrada directly to the port, where you'll find abundant paid parking along the broad waterside avenue Via Ammiraglio Staiti, within walking distance of most attractions.

TRAIN

From Trapani's station on Piazza Umberto I, Trenitalia offers efficient connections to Marsala (€3.80, 30 minutes, 10 daily Monday to Saturday, five on Sunday). For Palermo and most other destinations, the bus is a better option.

Erice

POP 28,800 / ELEV 751M

One of Italy's most spectacular hill towns, Erice combines medieval charm with astounding 360-degree views. It sits on the legendary Mt Eryx (750m); on a clear day, you can see Cape Bon in Tunisia. The town has a seductive history as a centre for the cult of Venus. Settled by the mysterious Elymians, the town followed the peculiar ritual of sacred prostitution, with the prostitutes themselves accommodated in the Temple of Venus. Despite countless invasions, the temple remained intact – no guesses why.

These days, the greatest pleasure here is simply wandering Erice's medieval tangle of streets interspersed with churches, forts and tiny cobbled piazzas. Posted throughout town, you'll find bilingual (Italian–English) informational displays, and town maps providing suggested walking routes.

👁 Sights

The best views can be had from **Giardino del Balio**, which overlooks the turrets and wooded hillsides south to Trapani's saltpans, the Egadi Islands and the sea. Looking north, there are equally staggering views of San Vito Lo Capo's rugged headlands.

Castello di Venere   CASTLE

(☑ 366 6712832; www.fondazioneericearte.org/castellodivenere.php; Via Castello di Venere; adult/reduced €4/2; ⊙ 10am-1hr before sunset daily Apr-Oct, 10am-4pm Sat, Sun & holidays Nov-Mar) The Norman Castello di Venere was built in the 12th and 13th centuries over the Temple of Venus, long a site of worship for the ancient Elymians, Phoenicians, Greeks and Romans. The views from up top, extending to San Vito Lo Capo on one side and the Saline di Trapani on the other, are spectacular. To arrange visits in winter, phone at least 24 hours in advance.

🛏 Sleeping & Eating

Hotels, many with their own restaurants, are scattered along Via Vittorio Emanuele, Erice's main street. After the day-trippers have gone, the town assumes a beguiling medieval air.

Erice has a tradition of *dolci ericini* (Erice sweets) made by local nuns. There are numerous pastry shops in town, the most famous being **Maria Grammatico** (☑ 0923 86 93 90; www.mariagrammatico.it; Via Vittorio Emanuele 14; pastries from €2; ⊙ 9am-10pm May, Jun & Sep, to 1am Jul & Aug, to 7pm Oct-Apr), revered for its *frutta martorana* (marzipan fruit) and almond pastries. If you like what you taste, you can even stick around and take cooking classes from Signora Grammatico herself.

Hotel Elimo   HOTEL **€€**

(☑ 0923 86 93 77; www.hotelelimo.it; Via Vittorio Emanuele 75; s €80-110, d €90-130, ste €150-170; ❉ ❅) Communal spaces at this atmospheric historic house are filled with tiled beams, marble fireplaces, intriguing art, knick-knacks and antiques. The bedrooms are more mainstream, although many (along with the hotel terrace and restaurant) have

breathtaking vistas south and west towards the Saline di Trapani, the Egadi Islands and the shimmering sea.

ℹ Information

Up near the Castello di Venere, **Pro Loco Erice** (☑ 329 0658244; www.prolocoerice.it; Via Castello di Venere; ⊙ 10am-6pm) provides a wealth of tourist information.

ℹ Getting There & Away

AST (p249) runs six buses daily (four on Sunday) between Erice and Trapani's bus terminal (€2.90, 40 minutes). Alternatively, catch the **funicular** (Funivia; ☑ 0923 86 97 20, 0923 56 93 06; www.funiviaerice.it; one way/return €5.50/9; ⊙ 1-8pm Mon, 8.10am-8pm Tue-Fri, 9am-9pm Sat, 10am-8pm Sun) opposite the car park at the foot of Erice's Via Vittorio Emanuele; the 10-minute descent drops you in Trapani near Ospedale Sant'Antonio Abate, where you can catch local bus 21 or 23 (€1.40) into the centre of Trapani.

Segesta

ELEV 304M

Set on the edge of a deep canyon in the midst of wild, desolate mountains, the 5th-century BC **Ruins of Segesta** (☑ 0924 95 23 56; adult/reduced €6/3; ⊙ 9am-7.30pm Apr-Sep, to 6.30pm Mar & Oct, to 5pm Nov-Feb) are a magical site. On windy days the 36 giant columns of its magnificent temple are said to act like an organ, producing mysterious notes.

The city, founded by the ancient Elymians, was in constant conflict with Selinunte in the south, whose destruction it sought with dogged determination and singular success. Time, however, has done to Segesta what violence inflicted on Selinunte; little remains now, save the **theatre** and the never-completed **Doric temple**, the latter dating from around 430 BC and remarkably well preserved. A shuttle bus (€1.50) runs every 30 minutes from the temple entrance 1.5km uphill to the theatre.

Tarantola (☑ 0924 3 10 20; www.tarantolabus.com) buses run to Segesta three times daily (except Sunday) from Trapani (one way/return €4/6.60, 45 minutes) and once daily (except Sunday) from Via Balsamo near Palermo's train station (one way/return €8/12.70, 80 minutes); all buses stop just outside the archaeological site's entrance. If driving, exit the A29dir at Segesta and follow signs 1.5km uphill to the site.

Understand Southern Italy

Southern Italy Today

Despite its arresting beauty and cultural riches, southern Italy remains the country's sore point. Unemployment rates are more than double that of the European Union average, while the region's coastline has become the main stage for Europe's ever-deepening refugee crisis. Thankfully, it's not all deflating news, with corporate investment, urban renewal and the stirrings of a southern cultural revival injecting some much-needed optimism across the Mezzogiorno.

Best on Film

Il Postino (*The Postman*; Michael Radford; 1994) Exiled poet Pablo Neruda brings poetry and passion to a drowsy southern isle and a misfit postman.

Matrimonio all'italiana (*Marriage, Italian-Style*; Vittorio De Sica; 1964) A comedy about a cynical businessman and his shrewd Neapolitan mistress.

Cinema Paradiso (Giuseppe Tornatore; 1988) A bittersweet tale about a director who returns to Sicily and rediscovers his true loves: the girl next door and the movies.

Passione (John Turturro; 2010) A documentary about Naples' rich musical heritage.

Best in Print

The Italians (Luigi Barzini; 1964) A revealing look at Italian culture beyond the well-worn clichés.

Christ Stopped at Eboli (Carlo Levi; 1945) Bittersweet recollections from a writer exiled by fascists to a mountain village in Basilicata.

Midnight in Sicily (Peter Robb; 1996) A disturbing yet fascinating portrait of postwar Sicily.

The Silent Duchess (Dacia Maraini; 1992) A feminist-flavoured historical novel set in 18th-century Palermo.

Cultural Revivals

Both Naples and Matera are also enjoying a boost in tourist numbers. In Naples, better-managed museums – most notably the Museo Archeologico Nazionale and Palazzo Reale di Capodimonte – as well as youth-led cultural initiatives such as street-art tours have injected newfound optimism. Once a symbol of abject poverty, Matera's World Heritage-listed *sassi* (cave dwellings) are finding new life as trendy restaurants, bars and accommodation. According to a 2017 report by the University of Siena, more than a quarter of the city's housing stock is available to rent on Airbnb, more than anywhere else in the country. Matera's growing accommodation stock will come in handy in 2019, when the city wears the mantle of European City of Culture.

Palermo is also basking in the cultural spotlight. The Sicilian capital will play host to the 2018 edition of Manifesta, Europe's top biennial of contemporary art. It's only befitting of a city designated as Italy's Capital of Culture in the same year. Indeed, things are looking up for Palermo. Despite the gunning down of Cosa Nostra boss Giuseppe Dainotti in May 2017, mafia killings have become increasingly rare. Urban renewal projects, among them the pedestrianisation of Via Maqueda, have injected the city centre with a new vibrancy, while cultural initiatives such as annual open-house event Le Vie dei Tesori (Streets of Treasures) are nurturing much-needed civic pride.

Migrant Crisis

While Italy's southern coasts are regularly showcased in travel blogs, magazines and TV shows, they have also become accustomed to less ebullient media coverage in recent years. Images of asylum seekers rescued at sea and processed at southern Italian ports have become a recurring feature in local and international media.

Since the EU and Turkey made a pact in 2016 to block the flow of refugees entering Greece from Turkey, Italy has become the continent's main entry point for refugees. In the first third of 2017 alone, 46,000 refugees reached southern Italy from Africa, an increase of 30% from the previous year. Many of them have fled the turmoil in Syria and Iraq, while a significant number are economic migrants from Africa, the Middle East and Asia.

The journey across the Mediterranean from north Africa to outlying Italian islands like Lampedusa is perilous, and often made in small, unseaworthy boats provided by unscrupulous people smugglers. The United Nations Refugee Agency (UNHCR) reports that over 1070 Italy-bound refugees drowned or went missing between January and April in 2017 alone. Despite the risks, refugees continue to reach Africa's northern coast in the hope of setting sail. According to a classified German government report leaked to Germany's *Bild* newspaper in 2017, the number of refugees currently waiting their turn to sail is over 2.5 million.

To many Italians, this extraordinary influx is seen as merely exacerbating the country's high unemployment and general economic uncertainty. It's an anxiety not lost on some of Italy's political figures. In 2017, the District Attorney of Catania, Carmelo Zuccaro, suggested that the very NGOs rescuing refugees at sea could be receiving funding from organised crime syndicates set on flooding Italy with immigrants to destabilise the economy. The accusations have been vehemently refuted by the NGOs, including the Italian branch of Doctors Without Borders.

Unemployment & Opportunity

The sunshine may be abundant, but jobs remain thin on the ground in the *Sud* (south). In early 2017, unemployment rates hovered at around 23% in Calabria, 22% in Sicily, 20% in Campania and 19% in Puglia, all in sharp contrast to the European Union (EU) average of 8.6%. Employment opportunities are most scant among the young. Almost 60% of persons aged 15 to 24 in Calabria and Sicily are jobless, ranking the regions third and fifth respectively for youth unemployment in the EU. Yet, glimmers of hope are visible. In 2016, US tech giant Apple inaugurated its first iOS Developer Academy in suburban Naples, a training centre designed to nurture app developers and boost local employment and study opportunities. Further southeast in Basilicata, the city of Matera is one of five Italian centres slated for a 5G mobile network, aimed at making the city more attractive to high-tech research and innovation companies wanting to invest in the region.

AREA: **84,339 SQ KM**

POPULATION: **17.5 MILLION (2017)**

NUMBER OF UNESCO WORLD HERITAGE SITES: **15**

ANNUAL COFFEE CONSUMPTION: **5.7KG PER CAPITA**

if Italy were 100 people

33 would live in Campania
30 would live in Sicily
23 would live in Puglia
11 would live in Calabria
3 would live in Basilicata

belief systems
(% of population)

71 Christian

26 Other religions

3 Muslim

population per sq km

NAPLES   LOS ANGELES   ITALY

♟ ≈ 201 people

History

Italy's south is ancient, its history tracing back some 8000 years. Writer Carlo Levi called it 'that other world...which no-one can enter without a magic key'. Magical it may be, but there has been plenty to regret – invasions, feudalism and a centuries-long scourge of malaria that stunted the south's development. Venture here and expect to have your preconceptions of modern Italy challenged.

The Early Years

Southern Italy has been active for a very long time. The first inhabitant we know of is the Altamura Man, currently wedged in the karst cave of Lamalunga, Puglia, and slowly becoming part of the crystal concretions that surround him. He's about 130,000 years old.

Fast forward to around 7000 BC, when the Messapians, an Illyrian-speaking people from the Balkans, were settling down in the Salento and around Foggia. Alongside them, other long-gone tribes such as the Daunii in the Gargano, the Peucetians around Taranto and the Lucanians in Basilicata were starting to develop the first settled towns – by 1700 BC there is evidence that they were beginning to trade with the Mycenaeans from mainland Greece and the Minoans in Crete.

The first evidence of an organised settlement on Sicily belongs to the Stentillenians, who came from the Middle East and settled on the island's eastern shores sometime between 4000 and 3000 BC. But it was the settlers from the middle of the second millennium BC who radically defined the island's character and whose early presence helps us understand Sicily's complexities. Thucydides (c 460–404 BC) records three major tribes: the Sicanians, who originated either in Spain or North Africa and settled in the north and west (giving these areas their Eastern flavour); the Elymians from Greece, who settled in the south; and the Siculians (or Sikels), who came from the Calabrian peninsula and spread out along the Ionian Coast.

Magna Graecia

Following the earlier lead of the Elymians, the Chalcidians landed on Sicily's Ionian Coast in 735 BC and founded a small settlement at Naxos.

Archaeological Treasures

Museo Archeologico Nazionale (p64; Naples)

Museo Archeologico Paolo Orsi (p229; Syracuse)

Museo Archeologico (p238; Agrigento)

Museo Archeologico Regionale (p194; Palermo)

TIMELINE	c 200,000– 9000 BC	3000–1000 BC	750–600 BC
	As long ago as 700,000 BC, Palaeolithic humans like the Altamura Man lived precarious lives in caves. Painted caves like the Grotta dei Cervi bear testimony to this period.	The Bronze Age reaches Italy courtesy of the Mycenaeans of Eastern Europe. The use of copper and bronze marks a leap in sophistication, accompanied by a more complex social organisation.	The Greeks begin establishing cities all over southern Italy and Sicily, including Naxos and Syracuse in Sicily, and Cumae, Sybaris, Croton, Metaponto, Eraklea and Taras in southern Italy.

They were followed a year later by the Corinthians, who built their colony on the southeastern island of Ortygia, calling it Syracoussai (Syracuse). The Chalcidians went further south from their own fort and founded a second town called Katane (Catania) in 729 BC, and the two carried on stitching towns and settlements together until three-quarters of the island was in Hellenic hands.

On the mainland, the Greeks' major city was Taras, which dominated the growing region now known as Magna Graecia (Greater Greece). They exploited its harbour well, trading with Greece, the Near East and the rich colonies in Sicily and so built up a substantial network of commerce. Their lucrative business in luxury goods soon made them rich and powerful; by the 4th century BC, the population had swelled to 300,000 and city life was cultured and civilised.

Although few monuments survive, among them the ambitious temples of Paestum in Campania and Selinunte in Sicily, the Greek era was a golden age for the south. Art and sculpture, poetry, drama, philosophy, mathematics and science were all part of the cultural life of Magna Graecia's cities. Exiled from Crotone (Calabria), Pythagoras spent years in Metapontum and Taras; Empedocles, Zeno and Stesichorus were all home-grown talents.

It is commonly said that there is less Italian blood running through modern Sicilian veins than there is Phoenician, Greek, Arabic, Norman, Spanish or French.

HISTORY MAGNA GRAECIA

FEATURE: IMPERIAL INSANITY

Bribes? *Bunga bunga* parties? Spare a thought for the ancient Romans, who suffered their fair share of eccentric leaders. We salute some of the empire's wackiest, most ruthless and downright kinkiest rulers.

Tiberius (ruled AD 14–37) With a steady governing hand but prone to depression, Tiberius had a difficult relationship with the Senate and withdrew in his later years to Capri, where, they say, he devoted himself to drinking, orgies and fits of paranoia.

Gaius (Caligula; ruled AD 37–41) 'Little Shoes' made grand-uncle Tiberius look tame. Sex – including with his sisters – and gratuitous, cruel violence were high on his agenda. He emptied the state's coffers and suggested making a horse consul before being assassinated.

Nero (ruled AD 54–68) Augustus' last descendant, Nero had his pushy stage mother murdered, his first wife's veins slashed, his second wife kicked to death and his third wife's ex-husband killed. The people accused him of playing the fiddle while Rome burned to the ground in AD 64.

Diocletian (ruled AD 284–305) Dalmatian-born Diocletian had little time for the growing cult of Christianity. He ordered the burning of churches and sacred scriptures, and had Christians thrown to wild beasts in a grisly public spectacle. One of them was Naples' patron saint, San Gennaro, slaughtered at Pozzuoli's Solfatara Crater.

264–146 BC	280 BC– AD 109	AD 79	300–337
The Punic Wars rage between the Romans and the Carthaginians. In 216 BC Hannibal inflicts defeat on the Romans at Cannae, but the Romans go on to ultimately defeat the Carthaginians in 146 BC.	The Romans build the Via Appia and then the Via Appia Traiana. The Via Appia Traiana covered 540km and enabled travellers to journey from Rome to Brindisi in 14 days.	Mt Vesuvius showers molten rock and ash upon Pompeii and Herculaneum. Pliny the Younger later describes the eruption in letters; the towns are only rediscovered in the 18th century.	After a series of false starts, the Roman Empire is divided into an Eastern and Western half just east of Rome. In 330 Constantine moves the imperial capital to Byzantium and refounds it as Constantinople.

But despite their shared Greekness, these city-states' deeply ingrained rivalries and parochial politics undermined their civic achievements, ultimately leading to damaging conflicts like the Peloponnesian War (431–399 BC), fought by the Athenians against the Peloponnesian League (led by Sparta). Although Syracuse fought successfully against the attacking Athenian forces, the rest of Sicily was in a constant state of civil war. In 409 BC this provided the perfect opportunity for the powerful city-state of Carthage (in modern-day Tunisia) to seek revenge for its humiliation in 480 BC, in which Carthaginian mercenaries, commanded by Hamilcar, were defeated by the crafty Greek tyrant Gelon. Led by Hamilcar's bitter but brilliant nephew Hannibal, the Carthaginians wrought havoc in the Sicilian countryside, completely destroying Selinunte, Himera, Agrigento and Gela. The Syracusans were eventually forced to surrender everything to Carthage except the city of Syracuse itself.

During the 4th century, the mainland's Greek colonies came under increasing pressure from other powers with expansionist ambitions. The Etruscans began to move south towards the major port of Cumae in Campania and then the Samnites and Sabines started to capture the highlands of the Appenines in Basilicata. Unable to unite and beat off the growing threat, the Greeks had little choice but to make a Faustian pact with the Romans, long-standing admirers of the Greeks and seemingly the perfect allies. It was a partnership that was to cost them dearly; by 270 BC the whole of southern Italy was under Roman control.

Eastern Influences

Roman control of southern Italy was to set the tone for centuries to come. While they turned the Bay of Naples into a holiday hot spot for Rome's elite and built the Via Appia (280–264 BC) and later the Via Appia Traiana (AD 109) – the first superhighway to the south from Rome – the Romans also stripped the southern landscape of its trees, creating just the right conditions for the malarial scourge that the region would face centuries hence. Then they parcelled up the land into huge *latifondi* (estates) that they distributed among a handful of wealthy Romans, who established a damaging agricultural monoculture of wheat to feed the Roman army. Local peasants, meanwhile, were denied even the most basic rights of citizenship.

Despite the Romans' attempts at Latinising the region, this period actually had the effect of reinforcing Eastern influences on the south. As it was, the Romans admired and emulated Greek culture, the locals in cities like Neapolis (modern-day Naples) continued to speak Greek, and the Via Appia made Puglia the gateway to the East. In AD 245 when Diocletian came to power, he determined that the empire was simply too vast for good governance and split it in two. When Constantine came to power in AD 306, the groundwork was already established for an Eastern (Byz-

Messages could be shot around the Roman Empire in days or weeks. At wayside inns, dispatch riders would have a bite and change mounts. The Romans even devised a type of odometer, a cogwheel that engaged with the wheel of a chariot or other vehicle.

476	827–965	1059	1130
The last western emperor, Romulus Augustulus, is deposed. Goths, Ostrogoths and Byzantines tussle over the spoils of the empire.	A Saracen army lands at Mazaradel Vallo in Sicily in 827. The island is united under Arab rule and Palermo becomes the second-largest city in the world after Constantinople.	Pope Nicholas II and Norman mercenary Robert Guiscard sign a concordat at Melfi, making Robert duke of Apulia and Calabria. Robert agrees to rid southern Italy of Saracens and Byzantines.	Norman invader Roger II is crowned king of Sicily, a century after the Normans landed in southern Italy; a united southern Italian kingdom is created.

antine) Empire and a Western Empire – in AD 324 he officially declared Constantinople the capital of Nova Roma.

With southern Italy's proximity to the Balkans and the Near East, Puglia and Basilicata were exposed to a new wave of Eastern influence, bringing with it a brand-new set of Christian beliefs. This new wave of influence would officially reach Sicily in AD 535, when the Byzantine general Belisarius landed an army on the island's shores. Despite falling to the Visigoths in AD 470 after more than 700 years of Roman occupation, the island's population was still largely Greek, both in language and custom. The Byzantines were eager to use Sicily as a launching pad for the retaking of the lands owned by the combined forces of Arabs, Berbers and Spanish Muslims, collectively known as the Saracens, but their dreams were not to be realised.

In AD 827 the Saracen army landed at Mazara del Vallo, in Sicily. Palermo fell in AD 831, followed by Syracuse in AD 878. Under them, churches were converted to mosques and Arabic was implemented as the common language. At the same time, much-needed land reforms were introduced and trade, agriculture and mining were fostered. New crops were intro duced, including citrus trees, date palms and sugar cane, and a system of water supply and irrigation was developed. Palermo was chosen as the capital of the new emirate and, over the next 200 years, it became one of the most splendid cities in the Arab world.

> Get to grips with the history, peoples and wars of Ancient Greece by logging on to www. ancientgreece. com, which gives potted histories of all the key characters and places. It also has an online bookstore.

Pilgrims & Crusaders

Ever since Puglia and Basilicata's colonisation by the Greeks, multifarious myths had established themselves in the region – many were related to the presence of therapeutic waters and the practice called *incubatio,* a rite whereby one had to sleep close to a holy place to receive revelations from a deity. In its early days, the cult of the Archangel Michael was mainly a cult of healing forces based on the saint's revelations. It started to gain currency in the early 5th century but it wasn't until the arrival of the Lombards in the 7th century that it really began to take off.

Sweeping down from the north, the Lombards found in St Michael a mirror image of their own pagan deity, Wodan. In Michael, they saw similar characteristics: the image of a medieval warrior, a leader of celestial armies. There is little doubt that their devotion to the saint was instrumental in their easy conversion to Catholicism, as they repeatedly restored and enlarged the Monte Sant'Angelo shrine, making it the most important centre of the cult in the western world. Soon the trail of pilgrims along the Via Traiana became so great that the road was nicknamed the Via Sacra Langobardorum (Holy Road of the Lombards), and dozens of churches, hostels and monasteries were built to accommodate the pilgrims along the way.

> **Graeco-Roman Greats**
>
> *Pompeii & Herculaneum (Campania)*
>
> *Paestum (Campania)*
>
> *Selinunte (Sicily)*
>
> *Segesta (Sicily)*
>
> *Valley of the Temples (Sicily)*

Side tab: HISTORY PILGRIMS & CRUSADERS

1215	1224	1270–1500	1516
Frederick II is crowned Holy Roman Emperor in Aachen where he symbolically re-inters Charlemagne's body in a silver and gold reliquary. He takes the cross and vows of a crusader.	The Università degli Studi di Napoli Federico II is founded in Naples. The oldest state university in the world, its alumni include Catholic theologian and philosopher Thomas Aquinas.	The French Angevins and Spanish Aragonese spend the best part of two centuries fighting over southern Italy. Instability, warfare, the Black Death and overtaxation strangle the region's economic development.	Holy Roman Emperor Charles V of Spain inherits southern Italy. The region is strategically important to Spain in its battle with France. Charles invests in defences in cities like Lecce.

Another group of pilgrims in this region were the Normans. Ruling over northern France, they arrived in southern Italy in the 10th century, initially en route from Jerusalem, and later as mercenaries attracted by the money to be made fighting for the rival principalities and against the Muslim Saracens in Sicily. By 1053, after six years of mercenary activity, Robert Guiscard (c 1015–85), the Norman conquistador, had comprehensively defeated the combined forces of the Calabrian Byzantines, the Lombards and the papal forces at the Battle of Civitate. Having established his supremacy, Robert turned his attentions to expanding the territories under his control. To achieve this, he had to negotiate with the Vatican. In return for being invested with the titles of duke of Apulia and Calabria in 1059, Robert agreed to chase the Saracens out of Sicily and restore Christianity to the island. He delegated this task – and promised the island – to his younger brother Roger I (1031–1101), who landed his

BORN TO RUMBLE

In the late 10th century, Norman fighters began to earn a reputation across Europe as fierce and tough mercenaries. As inheritance customs left younger sons disadvantaged, younger brothers were expected to seek their fortunes elsewhere – and seek they did, with remarkable success.

According to one legend, Norman involvement in southern Italy began in 1013 at the shrine of St Michael at Monte Sant'Angelo, when Latin rebel Meles, chaffing under Byzantine authority, invited the Normans to serve him as mercenaries. By 1030 what had begun as an offer of service in return for booty became a series of unusually successful attempts at wresting control from local warlords.

At the forefront of the Italian conquests were the Hauteville brothers: the eldest William 'Bras de Fer' (Iron Arm; c 1009–46), who controlled Puglia, and Robert Guiscard (the Cunning; c 1015–85), who rampaged over Calabria and southern Campania. By 1053, after six years of incessant fighting, Robert had defeated the combined forces of the Calabrian Byzantines, the Lombards and the papal forces at Civitate.

Up to this point the Normans (as mercenaries) had fought both for and against the papacy as their needs had required. But Robert's relationship with the Vatican underwent a radical transformation following the Great Schism of 1054, which resulted in a complete break between the Byzantine and Latin churches. In their turn, the popes saw in the Normans a powerful potential ally, and so in 1059 Pope Nicholas II and Robert signed a concord at Melfi, which invested Robert with the titles of duke of Apulia (including Basilicata) and Calabria. In return, Robert agreed to chase the Byzantines and Saracens out of southern Italy and Sicily and restore the southern kingdom to papal rule.

Little would the pope suspect that Roger would go on to develop a territorial monarchy and become a ruler who saw himself as detached from the higher jurisdiction of both Western and Eastern emperor – or even the pope himself.

1600	1647	1714	1798–99
Naples is Europe's biggest city, boasting a population of over 300,000. Among its growing number of residents is renegade artist Caravaggio, who arrives in 1606.	Gross mismanagement causes the southern Italian economy to collapse. In Naples, the Masaniello Revolt breaks out over heavy taxes. Revolt spreads to the provinces and peasant militias rule the countryside.	The end of the War of the Spanish Succession forces the withdrawal of Spanish forces from Lombardy. The Spanish Bourbon family establishes an independent Kingdom of the Two Sicilies.	Napoleon invades Italy and occupies Rome. Ferdinand I sends an army to evict them, but his troops flee. The French counter-attack and take Naples, establishing the Parthenopean Republic.

troops at Messina in 1061, capturing the port by surprise. In 1064, Roger tried to make good on his promise and take Palermo, but was repulsed by a well-organised Saracen army; it wasn't until Robert arrived in 1072 with substantial reinforcements that the city fell into Norman hands. Impressed by the island's cultured Arab lifestyle, Roger shamelessly borrowed and improved on it, spending vast amounts of money on palaces and churches and encouraging a cosmopolitan atmosphere in his court.

By 1130 most of southern Italy, including Sicily, was in Norman hands and it was only a question of time before the prosperous duchy of Naples gave in to the inevitable. It did so in 1139 – the Kingdom of the Two Sicilies was thus complete.

The Wonder of the World

Frederick II, king of Sicily and Holy Roman Emperor, presided over one of the most glamorous periods of southern history. The fact that he came to wield such power and wear Charlemagne's crown at all is one of those unexpected quirks of history.

He inadvertently inherited the crown of Sicily and the south from his mother Constance (the posthumous daughter of Roger I) in 1208 after William II died childless; the crown to the Holy Roman Empire came to him through his father, Henry VI, the son of Frederick Barbarossa. The union of the two crowns in 1220 meant that Frederick II would rule over lands covering Germany, Austria, the Netherlands, Poland, the Czech Republic, Slovakia, southern France, southern Italy, the rich Kingdom of Sicily and the remnants of the Byzantine world.

It was a union that caused the popes much discomfort. For while they wanted and needed an emperor who would play the role of temporal sword, Frederick's wide-reaching kingdom all but encircled the Papal States and his belief in the absolute power of monarchy gave them grave cause for concern.

Like Charlemagne before him, Frederick controlled a kingdom so vast that he could realistically dream of reviving the fallen Roman Empire – and dream he did. Under his rule, Sicily was transformed into a centralised state playing a key commercial and cultural role in European affairs, and Palermo gained a reputation as the continent's most important city; most of the northern Italian city-states were brought to heel. In 1225 he went on to marry Jolanda of Brienne and gained the title of king of Jerusalem, making him the first Roman emperor to bear that title. In 1228 the Crusade he launched was not only nearly bloodless, but it saw the return of the shrines of Jerusalem, Nazareth and Bethlehem to the Christian fold.

As well as being a talented statesman, he was also a cultured man, and many of his biographers see in him the precursor of the Renaissance prince. Few other medieval monarchs corresponded with the sages of

Arab-Norman Highlights

Cappella Palatina (p193) & Palazzo dei Normanni (p193; Palermo)

Chiesa Capitolare di San Cataldo (p192; Palermo)

Cattedrale (p193; Palermo)

Duomo (p201; Cefalù)

HISTORY THE WONDER OF THE WORLD

The Arabs introduced spaghetti to Sicily; 'strings of pasta' were documented by the Arab geographer Al-Idrissi in Palermo in 1150. They also brought couscous and sugar cane to the island.

Judaism and Islam; he also spoke six languages and was fascinated by science, nature and architecture. He even wrote a scholarly treatise on falconry during one of the long, boring sieges of Faenza, and Dante was right to call him the father of Italian poetry.

Yet despite his brilliance, his vision for an international empire was incompatible with the ambitions of the papacy and he struggled throughout his reign to remain on good terms with increasingly aggressive popes. Finally, in 1243, Pope Innocent IV proclaimed him deposed, characterising him as a 'friend of Babylon's sultan' and a heretic. At the same time the northern Italian provinces were straining against his centralised control and years of war and strategising were finally taking their toll. Only in Puglia, his favourite province throughout this reign, did Frederick remain undisputed master.

In December 1250, after suffering a bout of dysentery, he died suddenly in Castel Fiorentino near Lucera. His heirs, Conrad and Manfred, would not survive him long. Conrad died of malaria four years later in Lavello in Basilicata, and Manfred was defeated at the Battle of Benevento in 1266 by Charles of Anjou, the pope's pretender to the throne. Two years later another battle took the life of Manfred's 15-year-old nephew and heir, Conradin, who was publicly beheaded in Naples.

By 1270 the brilliant Hohenstaufen period was officially over. And while Frederick's rule marked a major stage in the transformation of Europe from a community of Latin Christians under the headship of two competing powers (pope and emperor) to a Europe of nation-states, he had failed to leave any tangible legacies. The following ruling family, the Angevins, did not make the same mistake: Naples' Castel Nuovo (built by Charles of Anjou in 1279) and Castel Sant'Elmo (constructed by Robert of Anjou in the early 14th century) remain two of the city's iconic landmarks.

Kingdom in the Sun by English historian John Julius Norwich offers a wonderful romp through the Norman invasions of the south, which lead to their spectacular takeover of Sicily.

Sicily's Inglorious Slide

For a wide-ranging general site on Italian history, check out www.arcaini.com. It covers everything from prehistory to the postwar period, and includes a brief chronology to the end of the 20th century.

Under the Angevins, who succeeded the German Hohenstaufens, Sicily was weighed down by onerous taxes, religious persecution of the island's Muslim population was the order of the day and Norman fiefdoms were removed and awarded to French aristocrats. On Easter Monday 1282, the city of Palermo exploded in rebellion. Incited by the alleged rape of a local girl by a gang of French troops, peasants lynched every French soldier they could get their hands on. The revolt spread to the countryside and was supported by the Sicilian nobility, who had formed an alliance with Peter of Aragon. Peter had landed at Trapani with a large army and was proclaimed king. For the next 20 years, the Aragonese and the Angevins were engaged in the War of the Sicilian Vespers – a war that was eventually won by the Spanish.

1861	1880–1915	1889	1908
By the end of the Franco-Austrian War (1859–61), Vittorio Emanuele II controls Lombardy, Sardinia, Sicily, southern Italy and parts of central Italy, and is proclaimed king of a newly united Italy.	People vote with their feet; millions of impoverished southerners embark on ships for the New World, causing a massive haemorrhage of the most able-bodied and hardworking southern male youth.	Raffaele Esposito invents 'pizza margherita' in honour of Queen Margherita, who takes her first bite of the Neapolitan staple on a royal visit to the city.	On the morning of 28 December, Messina and Reggio di Calabria are struck by a 7.5-magnitude earthquake and a 13m-high tsunami. More than 80,000 lives are lost

By the end of the 14th century, Sicily had been thoroughly marginalised. The eastern Mediterranean was sealed off by the Ottoman Turks, while the Italian mainland was off limits on account of Sicily's political ties with Spain. As a result, the Renaissance passed the island by, reinforcing the oppressive effects of poverty and ignorance. Even Spain lost interest in its colony, choosing to rule through viceroys. By the end of the 15th century, the viceroy's court was a den of corruption, and the most influential body on the island became the Catholic Church (whose archbishops and bishops were mostly Spaniards). The church exercised draconian powers through a network of Holy Office tribunals, otherwise known as the Inquisition.

Reeling under the weight of state oppression, ordinary Sicilians demanded reform. Unfortunately, their Spanish monarchs were preoccupied by the wars of the Spanish succession and Sicily was subsequently passed around for decades from European power to European power like an unwanted Christmas present. Eventually the Spanish reclaimed the island in 1734, this time under the Bourbon king Charles III of Sicily (r 1734–59).

The Bourbon Paradox

Assessment of Bourbon rule in southern Italy is a controversial topic. Many historians consider it a period of exploitation and stagnation. Others, more recently, have started to re-evaluate the Kingdom of the Two Sicilies, pointing out the raft of positive reforms Charles III implemented. These included abolishing many noble and clerical privileges, curtailing the legal rights of landowners within their fiefs and restricting ecclesiastical jurisdiction at a time when the Church was reputed to own almost a third of the land within the kingdom.

Naples had already begun prospering under the rule of Spanish viceroy Don Pedro de Toledo (1532–53), whose building boom attracted some of Italy's greatest artistic talent. Under Charles, the city became one of the great capital cities of Europe, drawing hundreds of aristocratic travellers. On top of this, Charles was a great patron of architecture and the arts. During his reign Pompeii and Herculaneum (both destroyed in the AD 79 eruption of Mt Vesuvius) were discovered and the Archaeological Museum in Naples was founded. He was responsible for the Teatro San Carlo, the largest opera house in Europe, and he built the huge palaces of Capodimonte and Caserta. Some subsequent Bourbon monarchs also made positive contributions, such as Ferdinand II (1830–59), who laid the foundations for modern industry, developing southern harbours, creating a merchant fleet and building the first Italian railway line and road systems, such as the dramatic Amalfi drive for example.

But where Charles might rightfully claim a place among southern Italy's outstanding rulers, later Bourbon princes were some of the most eccentric and pleasure-seeking monarchs in Europe. Charles' son,

Steven Runciman's *Fall of Constantinople 1453* provides a classic account of this bloody episode in Crusading history. It manages to be academically sound and highly entertaining at the same time.

HISTORY THE BOURBON PARADOX

Between January and August of 1656, the bubonic plague wiped out about half of Naples' 300,000-plus inhabitants and much of the economy. The city would take almost two centuries to reach its pre-plague headcount again.

1915	1919	1922	1927
Italy enters WWI on the side of the Allies to win Italian territories still in Austrian hands after Austria's offer to cede some of the territories is deemed insufficient.	Former socialist journalist Benito Mussolini forms a right-wing militant group, the *Fasci Italiani di Combattimento* (Italian Combat Fasces), precursor to his Fascist Party.	Mussolini and his Fascists stage a march on Rome in October. Doubting the army's loyalty, a fearful King Vittorio Emanuele III entrusts Mussolini with the formation of a government.	A study released by the Italian government puts the number of Italian citizens living abroad at around 9.2 million. Southern Italians make up over 60% of the Italian diaspora.

Ferdinand I (1751–1825), was by contrast venal and poorly educated. He spent his time hunting and fishing, and he delighted in the company of the *lazzaroni*, the Neapolitan underclass. He much preferred to leave the business of government to his wife, the ambitious and treacherous Archduchess Maria Carolina of Austria, whose main aim was to free southern Italy from Spanish influence and secure a rapprochement with Austria and Great Britain. Her chosen administrator was the English expatriate Sir John Acton, who replaced the long-serving Tanucci, a move that was to mire court politics in damaging corruption and espionage.

When the French Revolution broke out in 1789, Maria Carolina was initially sympathetic to the movement, but when her sister Marie Antoinette was beheaded, she became fanatically Francophobe. The following French invasion of Italy in 1799, and the crowning of Napoleon as king in 1800, jolted the south out of its Bourbon slumbers. Although Napoleonic rule was to last only 14 years, this brief flirtation with republicanism to awaken hopes of an independent Italian nation. Returning to his beloved Naples in 1815, Ferdinand, who was once so at ease with his subjects, was now terrified of popular revolution and became determined to exert his absolute authority. Changes that had been made by the Bonapartist regime were reversed, causing widespread discontent. Revolutionary agitators sprang up everywhere, and the countryside, now full of discharged soldiers, became more lawless than ever.

Yet there was no putting the genie back in the bottle. The aggressive tactics of Ferdinand II only exacerbated the situation, and in 1848 Sicily experienced a violent revolt that saw the expulsion of the Bourbons from the island. Although the revolt was crushed, Ferdinand's response was so heavy-handed that he earned himself the nickname 'Re Bomba' (King Bomb) after his army mercilessly shelled Messina. From such a promising beginning, the last decades of Bourbon rule were so oppressive that they were almost universally hated throughout liberal Europe. The seeds had well and truly been sown for the Risorgimento (Resurgence), which would finally see the whole peninsula united into a modern nation-state.

The Kingdom of Death

Although not commonly acknowledged, the widespread presence of malaria in the Italian peninsula during the 19th and 20th centuries is one of the most significant factors in the social and economic development (or lack of it) of the modern country. An endemic as well as an epidemic disease, it was so enmeshed in Italian rural society that it was widely regarded as the Italian national disease. Even the word itself – malaria – comes from the Italian *mal aria* (bad air), as it was originally thought that the disease was caused by a poisoning of the air as wet earth dried out during the heat of summer.

The exodus of southern Italians to North and South America between 1880 and WWI is one of the great mass movements of a population in modern times. By 1927, 20% of the Italian population had emigrated.

Edward Gibbon's 18th-century *History of the Decline and Fall of the Roman Empire* is the acknowledged classic work on the subject of the empire's darker days. Try the abridged single-volume version.

1934	1940	1943	1946
Screen siren Sophia Loren is born, and spends her childhood living in Pozzuoli and Naples. Her break would come in 1951, as an extra in Mervyn LeRoy's film *Quo Vadis*.	Italy enters WWII on Nazi Germany's side and invades Greece in October. Greek forces counter-attack and enter southern Albania. Germany saves Italy in March–April 1941 by overrunning Yugoslavia and Greece.	King Vittorio Emanuele III sacks Mussolini. He is replaced by Marshall Badoglio, who surrenders after Allied landings in southern Italy. German forces free Mussolini.	Italians vote in a national referendum in June to abolish the monarchy (by about 12.7 million votes to 10.7 million) and create a republic. The south is the only region to vote against the republic.

The scale of the problem came to light in the decades following Italian unification in 1861. Out of 69 provinces only two were found to be free of malaria; in a population of 25 million people, at least 11 million were permanently at risk of the disease. Most famously, Giuseppe Garibaldi, one of the founding fathers of modern Italy, lost both his wife, Anita, and a large number of troops to the disease. Thus stricken, Garibaldi urged the newly united nation to place the fight against malaria high on its list of priorities.

In the dawning era of global competition, Italian farming was dangerously backward. As a predominantly grain-producing economy, it was tragically ironic that all of Italy's most fertile land was in precisely the zones – coastal plains and river valleys – where malaria was most intense. To survive, farm workers had to expose themselves to the disease. Unfortunately, disease in turn entailed suffering, days of absence and low productivity.

More significantly, although malaria ravaged the whole peninsula, it was pre-eminently an affliction of the south, as well as the provinces of Rome and Grosseto in the centre. Of all the regions, six were especially afflicted – Abruzzo, Basilicata, Calabria, Lazio, Puglia and Sardinia – earning the south the lugubrious epithet 'the kingdom of death'. Furthermore, Giovanni Battista Grassi (the man who discovered that mosquitoes transmit malaria) estimated that the danger of infection in the south was 10 times greater than in northern Italy.

No issue illustrates the divide between the north and south of the country quite so vividly as the malaria crisis. The World Health Organisation defines malaria in the modern world as a disease of poverty that distorts and slows economic growth. In the case of the Italian south, malaria was a significant factor in the underdevelopment of the region at a critical time in its history. Malarial fever thrives on exploitative working conditions, substandard housing and diet, illiteracy, war and ecological degradation, and Italy's south had certainly had its fair share by the early 20th century. As late as 1918, the Ministry of Agriculture reported that 'malaria is the key to all the economic problems of the South'. Against this background of regional inequality, the fever became an important metaphor deployed by *meridionalisti* (southern spokesmen) such as Giustino Fortunato (1848–1932) and Francesco Nitti (1868–1953) to describe the plight of the south and to demand redress. Nitti attributed the entirety of southern backwardness to this single factor.

Between 1900 and 1907, the Italian parliament passed a series of laws establishing a national campaign – the first of its kind in the world – to eradicate or at least control the disease. But it was to take the best part of half a century to bring malaria under control, as two world wars and the fascist seizure of power in 1922 were to overwhelm domestic policies, causing the program to stall and then collapse entirely amid military defeat and occupation.

History of the Italian People, by Giuliano Procacci, is one of the best general histories of the country in any language. It covers the period from the early Middle Ages until 1948.

The Nazis took Naples in 1943, but were quickly forced out during the *quattro giornate di Napoli* (four days of Naples), a series of popular uprisings between 26 and 30 September. These paved the way for the Allies to enter the city on 1 October.

1950s–60s	1980	1999	2003
Soaring unemployment causes another mass migration of about two million people from the south to the factories of northern Italy, Europe and Australia.	At 7.34pm on 25 November, a 6.8 Richter scale earthquake strikes Campania. The quake kills almost 3000 people and causes widespread damage; the city of Naples also suffers damage.	Brindisi becomes a strategic base for the Office of the UN and the World Food Organisation. The disused military airport's hangars are converted into storage space for humanitarian aid.	Sicilian *mafioso* Salvatore 'Totò' Riina is arrested in Palermo. Nicknamed 'The Beast', the 'boss of bosses' had ordered the bombing death of antimafia magistrates Giovanni Falcone and Paolo Borsellino.

Final victory against the disease was only achieved following the end of WWII, when the government was able to re-establish public-health infrastructures and implement a five-year plan which included the use of a new pesticide, DDT, to eradicate malaria. The designation of 'malarial zone' was only officially lifted from the entire peninsula in 1969.

The Southern Question

The unification of Italy meant sudden and dramatic changes for all the southern provinces. The huge upsurge in *brigantaggio* (banditry) and social unrest throughout the last decades of the 19th century was caused by widespread disillusionment about the unification project. Though remembered as a leading figure in the push towards unification, it was never the intention of 19th-century Italian statesman Camillo Benso, Count of Cavour, to unify the whole country. Even later during his premiership, Cavour favoured an expanded Piedmont rather than a united Italy.

For southerners, it was difficult to see the benefits of being part of this new nation-state. Naples was stripped of its capital-city status; the new government carried away huge cash reserves from the rich southern Italian banks; taxes went up and factories closed as new tariff policies, dictated by northern interests, caused a steep decline in the southern economy. Culturally, southerners were also made to feel inferior; to be southern or 'Bourbon' was to be backward, vulgar and uncivilised.

After WWI the south fared a little better, experiencing slow progress in terms of infrastructure projects like the construction of the Puglian aqueduct, the extension of the railways and the improvement of civic centres like Bari and Taranto. But Mussolini's 'Battle for Wheat' – the drive to make Italy self-sufficient in food – compounded many of the southern problems. It destroyed even more valuable pastureland by turning it over to the monoculture of wheat, while reinforcing the parlous state of the southern peasantry, who remained uneducated, disenfranchised, landless and at high risk of malaria. To escape such a hopeless future, many of them packed their bags and migrated to North America, northern Europe and Australia, starting a trend that was to become one of the main features of post-WWII Italy.

In the 1946 referendum that established the Italian Republic, the south was the only region to vote no. In Naples, 80% voted to keep the monarchy. Still, change moved on apace. After the wreckage of WWII was cleared – especially that caused by Allied air raids in Sicily and Naples – the *Cassa per il Mezzogiorno* reconstruction fund was established to bring the south into the 20th century with massive, cheap housing schemes and big industrial projects like the steel plant in Taranto and the Fiat factory in Basilicata. Yet constant interference by the Mafia in southern Italy's economy did much to nullify the efforts of Rome to reduce the

Between 1944 and 1946 the German Wehrmacht systematically sabotaged the pumping systems that drained Italy's marshes and confiscated quinine from the Department of Health. The ensuing malaria epidemic proved as deadly as any WWI ground offensive.

Denis Mack Smith produced one of the most penetrating works on Il Duce in his biography *Mussolini*. It explores the life and career of the Italian dictator and his influence on Adolf Hitler.

2003	2004–05	2005	2010
The Campania government launches Progetto Vesuvia in an attempt to clear Mt Vesuvius' heavily populated lower slopes. The €30,000 offered to relocate is rejected by most in the danger zone.	Tension between rival Camorra clans explodes on the streets of suburban Naples. In only four months, almost 50 people are gunned down in retribution attacks.	Nichi Vendola, representing the Communist Refoundation Party, is elected president of Puglia. He is the first gay communist to be elected president of a southern Italian region.	Local youths in Rosarno, Calabria, shoot air rifles at African migrants returning from work in January. About 2000 migrants subsequently clash with locals in two days of violent rioting

HISTORY ON SCREEN

*Il **Gattopardo*** (The Leopard; Luchino Visconti; 1963) A Sicilian aristocrat grapples with the political and social changes heralded by the 19th-century Risorgimento (reunification period).

*Le **quattro giornate di Napoli*** (The Four Days of Naples; Nanni Loy; 1962) Neapolitan courage shines through in this film about the famous popular uprisings against the Nazis in September 1943.

*Il **resto di niente*** (The Remains of Nothing; Antonietta De Lillo; 2003) Eleonora Pimental de Fonesca, heroine of the ill-fated Neapolitan revolution of 1799, is the protagonist in this tale.

*Salvatore **Giuliano*** (Francesco Rosi; 1963) A neorealist classic about the murder of Sicily's very own modern Robin Hood.

gap between the prosperous north and the poor south. The disappearance of large amounts of cash eventually led the central government to scrap the *Cassa per il Mezzogiorno* fund in 1992.

Clean Hands, Dirty Politics

Hitting the headlines that same year was the Tangentopoli (Bribesville) scandal, which exposed the breadth and depth of institutionalised kickbacks and bribes in Italy (the country's modus operandi since WWII). Although it was largely focused on the industrial north of Italy, the repercussions of the widespread investigation into graft (known as *Mani pulite*, or Clean Hands) were inevitably felt in southern regions like Sicily and Campania, where politics, business and organised crime were long-time bedfellows.

The scandal eventually brought about the demise of the Democrazia Cristiana (DC; Christian Democrats), a centre-right Catholic party that appealed to southern Italy's traditional conservatism. Allied closely with the Church, the DC promised wide-ranging reforms while at the same time demanding vigilance against godless communism. It was greatly aided in its efforts by the Mafia, which ensured that the local DC mayor would always top the poll. The Mafia's reward was *clientelismo* (political patronage) that ensured it was granted favourable contracts.

In the meantime, things were changing in regard to how many southern Italians viewed the Mafia, thanks in no small part to Sicilian investigating magistrates Paolo Borsellino and Giovanni Falcone. The duo contributed greatly to turning the climate of opinion against the Mafia on both sides of the Atlantic, and made it possible for ordinary citizens to speak about and against the Mafia more freely. When they were tragically murdered in the summer of 1992, it was a great loss for Italy and Sicily, but it was these deaths that finally broke the Mafia's code of *omertà* (silence).

Although much has happened since it was written, Paul Ginsborg's *A History of Contemporary Italy: Society and Politics 1943–1988* remains one of the single most readable and insightful books on postwar Italy.

2011	2013	2015	2016
Thousands of boat people fleeing the revolutionary chaos in northern Africa land on the island of Lampedusa. Italy grants 30,000 refugees temporary visas, creating tension with France.	On 4 March, Naples' much-loved Città della Scienza (City of Science) museum is destroyed in an arson attack. The crime is widely blamed on the Camorra, with the mayor tweeting 'Naples is under attack'.	After lengthy delays, Naples' showcase Municipio metro station opens to the public, featuring unearthed ancient ruins and a specially commissioned video-painting by Israeli artist Michal Rovner.	US tech giant Apple opens its first iOS Developer Academy in suburban Naples. The centre's aim is to train both local and foreign app developers using Apple's iOS mobile operating system.

The Southern Way of Life

The Mezzogiorno, or land of the midday sun, is more than haunting ruins, poetic coast lines and peeling *palazzi* (mansions). Its true protagonists are the *meridionali* (southern Italians), whose character and nuances echo a long, nail-biting history of dizzying highs and testing lows. To understand the southern psyche is to understand the complexities and contradictions that have moulded Italy's most misunderstood half.

Dreams & Diasporas
Emigration to Immigration

Above Ostuni (p145)

Severe economic problems in the south following Italy's unification and after each of the world wars led to massive emigration as people searched for a better life in northern Italy, northern Europe, North and South America and Australia. Between 1880 and 1910, more than 1.5 million Sicilians alone left for the US, and in 1900 the island was the world's main area of emigration. In Campania, 2.7 million people left Italy between 1876 and 1976.

Today, huge numbers of young Italians, often the most educated and ambitious, continue to move abroad. According to official estimates, over 100,000 Italians leave the country annually in search of better opportunities abroad, with almost 70% of departing Italians remaining in Europe. This brain-drain epidemic is fuelled in part by a persistently high national youth unemployment rate – around 35% in mid-2017. Another factor is Italy's entrenched system of patronage and nepotism, which commonly makes landing a job more about who you know than what you know.

For southern Italians, the standard of education available is often another contributing factor. A commonly held belief that southern universities aren't up to scratch sees many parents send their children north or overseas to complete their studies. While some return after completing their master's degree, many become accustomed to the freedom and opportunities found in their host city or country and tend to stay.

And yet, somewhat ironically, southern Italy has itself become a destination for people searching for a better life. Political and economic upheavals in the 1980s brought new arrivals from central and eastern Europe, Latin America and North Africa, including Italy's former colonies in Tunisia, Somalia and Ethiopia. More recently, waves of Chinese, Filipino and Sri Lankan immigrants have given Italian streetscapes an Asian twist.

From a purely economic angle, these new arrivals are vital for the country's economic health. Without immigrant workers to fill the gaps left in the labour market by pickier locals, Italy would be sorely lacking in tomato sauce and shoes. From hotel maids on the Amalfi Coast to fruit pickers on Calabrian farms, it is often immigrants who take the low-paid service jobs that keep Italy's economy afloat. Unfortunately, their vulnerability has sometimes led to exploitation, with several reported cases of farmhands being paid below-minimum wages for back-breaking work.

The North–South Divide

In his film *Ricomincio da tre* (I'm Starting from Three; 1980), acting great Massimo Troisi comically tackles the problems faced by southern Italians forced to head north for work. The reverse scenario is tackled in the comedy *Benvenuti al Sud* (Welcome to the South; 2010), in which a northern Italian postmaster is posted to a small southern Italian town, bullet-proof vest and prejudices in tow. Slapstick aside, both films reveal Italy's enduring north–south divide. While the north is celebrated for its fashion empires and moneyed metropolises, Italy's south is often associated with high unemployment, crumbling infrastructure and organised crime. At a deep semantic level, the word *meridionale* (southern Italian) continues to conjure a string of unflattering stereotypes.

From the Industrial Revolution to the 1960s, millions of southern Italians fled to the industrialised northern cities for factory jobs. As the saying goes, 'Ogni vero Milanese ha un nonno Pugliese' (Every true Milanese has a Pugliese grandparent). For many of these domestic migrants, the welcome north of Rome was anything but warm. Disparagingly nicknamed *terroni* (peasants), many faced discrimination on a daily basis, by everyone from landlords to baristas. While such overt discrimination is now practically nonexistent, historical prejudices linger. Some northerners argue that the rich north is unfairly burdened with subsidising the poor south, a belief that has fuelled a number of right-wing northern politicians, among them Umberto Bossi, founder of the Lega Nord party.

Yet prejudices and stereotypes exist on both sides of Rome. Many southerners view their northern compatriots as *freddi* (cold) and uptight. And it's not uncommon to hear southern Italians living in the north complain of life being isolated and anonymous.

A one-man 'Abbott & Costello', Antonio de Curtis (1898–1967), aka Totò, famously depicted the Neapolitan *furbizia* (cunning). Appearing in more than 100 films, including *Miseria e nobiltà* (Misery & Nobility; 1954), his roles as a hustler living on nothing but quick wits would guarantee him cult status in Naples.

Today, people of Italian origin account for more than 40% of the population in Argentina and Uruguay, more than 10% in Brazil, more than 5% in Switzerland, the US and Venezuela, and more than 4% in Australia and Canada.

The Southern Psyche
Beautiful Family, Beautiful Image

Family is the bedrock of southern Italian life, and loyalty to family and friends is usually non-negotiable. As Luigi Barzini (1908–84), author of *The Italians*, noted, 'A happy private life helps tolerate an appalling public life.' This chasm between the private arena and the public one is a noticeable aspect of the southern mentality, and has evolved over years of intrusive foreign domination. Some locals mightn't think twice about littering their street, but step inside their home and you'll get floors clean enough to eat from. After all, you'd never want someone dropping in and thinking you're a *barbone* (tramp), right?

Maintaining a *bella figura* (beautiful image) is very important to the average southerner, and how you and your family appear to the outside world is a matter of honour, respectability and pride. Many continue to believe that you are better than your neighbour if you own more and better things. This mindset is firmly rooted in the past, when owning many things was necessary for attaining certain social roles and, ultimately, for sustaining one's family. Yet *fare bella figura* (making a good impression) goes beyond a well-kept house; it extends to dressing well, behaving modestly, performing religious and social duties and fulfilling all essential family obligations. In the context of the extended family, where gossip is rife, a good image protects one's privacy.

Any self-respecting Italian bookshelf features one or more Roman rhetoricians. To *fare la bella figura* (make a good impression) among academics, trot out a phrase from Cicero or Horace (Horatio), such as 'Where there is life there is hope' or 'Whatever advice you give, be brief'.

It's Not What You Know...

In Europe's most ancient, entrenched bureaucracy, strong family ties are essential to getting things done. Putting in a good word for your son, niece or grandchild isn't just a nice gesture, but an essential career boost. According to Italy's Ministry of Labour, over 60% of Italian firms rely on personal introductions for recruitment. Indeed, *clientelismo* (nepotism) is as much a part of the Italian lexicon as *caffè* (coffee) and *tasse* (taxes); a fact satirised in Massimiliano Bruno's film *Viva L'Italia* (2012), about a crooked, well-connected senator who secures jobs for his three children, among them a talentless TV actress with a speech impediment.

In 2016, Raffaele Cantone – president of the Autorità Nazionale Anti-corruzione (ANAC) – sparked a national debate after claiming that nepotism in Italian universities was playing a major role in the country's ongoing 'brain drain'. It's a sentiment echoed in a 2011 study conducted by the University of Chicago Medical Center. The study found an unu

---

THE OLD PROVERBIAL

They might be old clichés, but proverbs can be quite the cultural revelation. Here are six of the south's well-worn best:

➡ *Cu si marita, sta cuntentu nu jornu, Cu' ammazza nu porcu, sta cuntentu n'annu* (Sicilian). Whoever gets married remains happy for a day, whoever butchers a pig remains happy for a year.

➡ *Aprili fa li ciuri e li biddizzi, l'onuri l'avi lu misi ri maju* (Sicilian). April makes the flowers and the beauty, but May gets all the credit.

➡ *A chi troppo s'acàla 'o culo se vede* (Neapolitan). He who kowtows too low bares his arse.

➡ *Cu va 'n Palermu e 'un viri Murriali, sinni parti sceccu e tonna armali* (Sicilian). Whoever goes to Palermo and doesn't see Monreale goes there a jackass and returns a fool.

➡ *Quannu la pulice se vitte a la farina, disse ca era capu mulinaru* (Pugliese). When the flea found itself in the flour, it said it was the master miller.

➡ *Lu mericu piatusu fa a chiaja virminusa* (Sicilian). A compassionate doctor makes the wound infected.

Procida (p89)

sually high recurrence of the same surnames amongst academic staff at various Italian universities. As the satirist Beppe Severgnini wryly comments in his book *La Bella Figura: A Field Guide to the Italian Mind,* 'If you want to lose an Italian friend or kill off a conversation, all you have to say is "On the subject of conflicts of interest..." If your interlocutor hasn't disappeared, he or she will smile condescendingly.'

A Woman's Place

As in many places in the Mediterranean, a woman's position in southern Italy has always been a difficult one. In the domestic sphere, a mother and wife commands the utmost respect within the home. She is considered the moral and emotional compass for her family; an omnipresent role model and the nightmare of newly wedded wives. In the public sphere, however, her role has less commonly been that of a protagonist.

But times are changing. Only two generations ago, many southern men and women were virtually segregated. In many cases, women would often only go out on Saturdays, and separate beaches for men and women were common. Dating would often involve a chaperone, whether it be the young woman's brother, aunt or grandmother. These days, more and more unmarried southern women live with their partners, especially in the cities. Improvements in educational opportunities and more liberal attitudes mean that the number of women with degrees and successful careers is growing.

Yet true gender equality remains an unattained goal, both in southern Italy and the country as a whole. The World Economic Forum's 2016 Global Gender Gap Report ranked Italy 50th worldwide in terms of overall gender equality, down from 41st position in 2015. It ranked 117th in female economic participation and opportunity, 56th in educational attainment and 25th in political empowerment.

John Turturro's film *Passione* (2010) is a *Buena Vista Social Club*–style exploration of Naples' rich and eclectic musical traditions. Spanning everything from folk songs to contemporary tunes, it offers a fascinating insight into the city's complex soul.

Duomo (p63), Naples

According to the European Commission's *2017 Report on Equality Between Women and Men in the EU*, only 52% of Italian women are in the workforce, compared to 80% in Sweden, 75% in Denmark and 66% in France. On average, Italian women earn 33% less than their male counterparts. And though successful Italian businesswomen do exist – among them Poste Italiane chairperson Bianca Maria Farina and Eni chairperson Emma Marcegaglia – almost 95% of public company board members in Italy remain male and, of these, approximately 80% of them are older than 55.

Italian women fare no better on the domestic front. OECD figures reveal that Italian men spend 103 minutes per day cooking, cleaning or caring, less than a third as long as Italian women, who spend an average of 315 minutes per day on what the OECD labels unpaid work.

The Sacred & the Profane

While the majority of Italians identify as Catholics, only around 15% of Italy's population regularly attends Sunday Mass. Yet, despite the Vatican's waning influence on modern Italian life, religious festivals and tradition continue to play a significant role in southern Italy. Every town has its own saint's day, celebrated with music, special events, food and wine. Indeed, these religious festivals are one of the best ways into the culture of the Mezzogiorno. Cream of the crop is Easter, with lavish week-long events to mark Holy Week. People pay handsomely for the privilege and prestige of carrying the various back-breaking decorations around the town – the processions are usually solemnly, excruciatingly slow.

Pilgrimages and a belief in miracles remain a central part of the religious experience. You will see representations of Padre Pio – the Gargano saint who was canonised for his role in several miraculous recoveries – in churches, village squares, pizzerias and private homes everywhere. Around eight million pilgrims visit his shrine every year. Three times

Turkish-Italian director Ferzan Özpetek explores the clash of southern tradition and modernity in his film *Mine vaganti* (Loose Cannons; 2010), a sitcom about two gay brothers and their conservative Pugliese family.

year, thousands cram into Naples' Duomo to witness their patron saint San Gennaro's blood miraculously liquefy in the phial that contains it. When the blood liquefies, the city is considered safe from disaster. When it doesn't – as was the case in December 2016 – the faithful see it as an ominous sign. Another one of Naples' holy helpers is Giuseppe Moscati (1880–1927), a doctor who dedicated his life to serving the city's poor. According to the faithful, the medic continues to heal from up above, a dedicated section inside the city's Chiesa del Gesù Nuovo heaving with *ex-voti* (including golden limbs) offered in thanks for miraculous recoveries.

Still, the line between the sacred and the profane remains a fine one in the south. In *Christ Stopped at Eboli,* his book about his stay in rural Basilicata in the 1930s, writer-painter-doctor Carlo Levi wrote: 'The air over this desolate land and among the peasant huts is filled with spirits. Not all of them are mischievous and capricious gnomes or evil demons. There are also good spirits in the guise of guardian angels.'

While the mystical, half-pagan world Levi describes may no longer be recognisable, ancient pagan influences live on in daily southern life. Here, curse-deterring amulets are as plentiful as crucifix pendants, the most famous of which is the iconic, horn-shaped *corno*. Adorning everything from necklines to rear-view mirrors, this lucky charm's evil-busting powers are said to lie in its representation of the bull and its sexual vigour. A rarer, but by no means extinct custom, is that of Naples' 'o Scartellat. Usually an elderly man, he'll occasionally be spotted burning incense through the city's older neighbourhoods, clearing the streets of bad vibes and inviting good fortune. The title itself is Neapolitan for 'hunchback', as the task was once the domain of posture-challenged figures. According to Neapolitan lore, touching a hunchback's hump brings good luck...which beats some of the other options, among them stepping in dog poop and having wine spilt on you accidentally.

Calcio (Football): The Other Religion

Catholicism may be Italy's official faith, but its true religion is *calcio*. On any given weekend from September through to May, you'll find millions of *tifosi* (football fans) at the *stadio* (stadium), glued to the TV, or checking the score on their mobile phone. In Naples' Piazzetta Nilo, you'll even find an altar to Argentine football star Diego Maradona, who elevated the city's Napoli team to its most successful era in the 1980s and early 1990s.

It's no coincidence that in Italian *tifoso* means both 'football fan' and 'typhus patient'. When the ball ricochets off the post and slips fatefully through the goalie's hands, when half the stadium is swearing while the other half is euphorically shouting '*Goooooooooooooooool!*', 'fever pitch' is the term that comes to mind.

Indeed, nothing quite stirs Italian blood like a good (or a bad) game. Nine months after Neapolitan Fabio Cannavaro led Italy to victory in the 2006 World Cup, hospitals in northern Italy reported a baby boom. In February the following year, rioting at a Palermo–Catania match in Catania left one policeman dead and around 100 injured. Blamed on the Ultras (a minority group of hardcore football fans), the violence shocked both Italy and the world, leading to a temporary ban of all matches in Italy, and increased stadium security.

Yet, the same game that divides also unites. You might be a Juventus-loathing Bari supporter on any given day, but when the national team *Azzurri* (the Blues) bag the World Cup, you are nothing but a heart-on-your-sleeve *italiano*. In his book *The 100 Things Everyone Needs to Know About Italy*, Australian journalist David Dale writes that Italy's 1982 World Cup win 'finally united twenty regions which, until then, had barely acknowledged that they were part of the one country'.

Italy's culture of corruption and *calcio* (football) is captured in *The Dark Heart of Italy,* in which English expat author Tobias Jones wryly observes, 'Footballers or referees are forgiven nothing; politicians are forgiven everything'.

THE SOUTHERN WAY OF LIFE THE SOUTHERN PSYCHE

The Mafia

To many outside Italy, the Mafia means Sicily's Cosa Nostra, seared into popular culture thanks to Francis Ford Coppola's classic film *The Godfather*. In reality, Cosa Nostra has three other major partners in crime: Campania's Camorra, Calabria's 'ndrangheta and Puglia's Sacra Corona Unita. Apt at everything from loan sharking to trafficking narcotics, arms and people, these four criminal networks produce a staggering annual profit estimated at around €100 billion.

Origins

The concept of the *mafioso* dates back to the late 15th century, when Sicily's rent-collecting *gabellotti* (bailiffs) employed small gangs of armed peasants to help them solve 'problems'. Soon robbing large estates, the bandits struck fear and admiration into the peasantry, who were happy to support efforts to destabilise the feudal system. They became willing accomplices, protecting the outlaws, and although it was another 400 years before crime became 'organised', the 16th and 17th centuries witnessed a substantial increase in the activities of brigand bands. The peasants' loyalty to their own people resulted in the name Cosa Nostra (Our Thing). The early Mafia's way of protecting itself from prosecution was to become the modern Mafia's most important weapon: the code of silence, or *omertà*.

In the 1860s, a band of Sicilians exiled to Calabria began forming their own organised gangs, planting the seeds for the 'ndrangheta. For almost a century, these gangs remained a local menace, known for extortion, racketeering and rural banditry. But it was the murder of a local godfather in 1975 that sparked a bloody gang war, transforming the organisation and creating a rebellious faction infamous for holding northern Italian businessmen to ransom. With its profits invested in narcotics, the 'ndrangheta would transform itself into Italy's most powerful Mafia entity.

The powerful Camorra reputedly emerged from the criminal gangs operating among the poor in late 18th-century Naples. The organisation had its first big break after the failed revolution of 1848. Desperate to overthrow Ferdinand II, pro-constitutional liberals turned to *camorristi* to help garner the support of the masses – the Camorra's political influence was sealed. Dealt a serious blow by Mussolini, the organisation would get its second wind from the invading Allied forces of 1943, which turned to the flourishing underworld as the best way to get things done. The black market thrived and the Camorra slowly began to spread its roots again.

In turn, the Camorra would give birth to the Sacra Corona Unita (Sacred United Crown), created by Camorra boss Raffaele Cutolo in the 1970s to gain access to Puglia's seaports. Originally named the Nuova Grande Camorra Pugliese, it gained its current name in the early 1980 after its Pugliese members cut ties with Campania and strengthened their bond with Eastern Europe's criminal networks.

Mafia-affiliated loan sharks commonly offer struggling businesses cash with an average interest rate of 10%. An estimated 50% of shops in Naples are run with Camorra money. Mafia profits are often reinvested globally in legitimate real estate, credit markets and businesses in what is known as 'the Invisible Mafia'.

The Value of Vice

The combined annual revenue of Italy's four main mafia organisations is equal to around 10% of Italy's entire GDP. This is a far cry from the days of roguish characters bullying shopkeepers into paying the *pizzo* (protection money). As journalist Roberto Saviano writes in his Camorra exposé *Gomorra:* 'Only beggar Camorra clans inept at business and desperate to survive still practice the kind of monthly extortions seen in Nanni Loy's film *Mi manda Picone*'.

The top money-spinner is narcotics. According to the United Nations Office on Narcotics and Crime, the drug trade makes over €32 billion annually for Italy's mafia clans. King of the scene is the Calabrian mafia, whose strong ties to Latin American crime syndicates has allowed it to control between 60% and 80% of Europe's cocaine market. Indeed, the 'ndrangheta is now also the main supplier of cocaine to Italy's rival mafia groups.

Other sources of revenue include the illegal trading of arms, the disposal of hazardous waste and Italy's ongoing refugee crisis. In May 2017, 68 people were arrested in relation to the mismanagement of a Calabrian migrant centre in the town of Isola Capo Rizzuto. According to Italian prosecutors, a powerful 'ndrangheta clan had infiltrated the centre a decade earlier, taking control of key services and skimming government funding allocated to the running of the complex. It's believed that at least €36 million of the circa €103 million in funding between 2006 and 2015 ended up in mafia coffers. The resulting shortfall impacted on the lives of those accommodated at the centre, with many migrants regularly missing out on meals.

Further north in Campania, illegal waste disposal has been one of the Camorra's biggest profit generators. According to the Italian environmentalist association Legambiente, the Camorra has illegally dumped, buried or burned close to 10 million tons of garbage in Campania since 1991. Alarmingly, this includes highly toxic waste, collected from northern Italian and foreign manufacturers lured by the cut-price rates of Camorra-owned waste-disposal companies. Abnormally high rates of cancer and congenital malformations of the nervous and urinary systems have led medical journal *Lancet Oncology* to nickname an area in Naples' northeast hinterland 'the triangle of death'.

Backlash of the Brave

Despite the Mafia's global reach, the war against it soldiers on, with frequent police crackdowns and arrests. In July 2017, police arrested some 116 alleged members of the 'ndrangheta in the country's largest coordinated operation against the Calabrian mafia to date. A month earlier, fugitive 'ndrangheta boss Vincenzo Macri was arrested at Sao Paulo airport in Brazil. The South American country was also the location for the 2015 capture of Camorra boss Pasquale Scotti, on the run for 30 years and convicted in absentia of over 20 murders.

Police crackdowns aren't the only concern for the 'ndrangheta. In recent years a growing number of women within clan families have broken the sacred code of *omertà* (vow of silence) to collaborate with police. Statistics from Italy's Ministry of Justice reveal that the number of women turning their back on their own criminal relatives has more than doubled since 2005. Indeed, this growing defiance of *omertà* is a serious threat to all Italian mafia organisations, whose success relies on fear, loyalty and non-interference.

The Greater Naples region is home to over 100 Camorra clans, with an estimated 10,000 immediate associates, and an even larger number of clients, dependants and supporters.

The *anti-pizzo* (anti protection money) movement was inspired by the defiance of a Palermitan shopkeeper called Libero Grassi, whose anonymous letter to an extortionist was featured on the front page of a local newspaper in 1991. Grassi was murdered seven months later.

The Southern Table

Blessed with sun, mineral-rich soils and the salty goodness of the Mediterranean, southern Italy was always destined for culinary glory. Waves of migration have flavoured the pot – the Greeks supplied the olives, the Arabs brought the pine nuts, eggplants, almonds, raisins and honey, and the Spanish came with tomatoes. The end result is a larder bursting with buxom vegetables, glistening fish, spicy meats and decadent sweets.

The Simple Things

Above Amalfi (p106)

Picture it: wood-fired bread drizzled in extra virgin olive oil, sprinkled with ripe *pomodori* (tomatoes) and fragrant *basilico* (basil). The flavours explode in your mouth. From the char-grilled crunch of the bread to the sweetness of the tomatoes, it's a perfect symphony of textures and flavours.

In many ways, *pane e pomodoro* (bread and tomatoes) captures the very soul of the southern Italian kitchen. Down here, fresh produce is the secret and simplicity is the key. Order grilled fish and chances are you'll get exactly that. No rich, overbearing sauces...just grilled fish with a wedge of lemon on the side. After all, it's the freshness of the fish you should be savouring, right?

This less-is-more approach is a testament to the south's impoverished past. Pasta made without eggs, bread made from hard durum wheat, wild greens scavenged from the countryside are all delicious, but their consumption was driven by necessity. The tradition of *sopratavola* (raw vegetables such as fennel or chicory eaten after a meal) arose because people could not afford fruit. That of *sottaceti* (vegetables cooked in vinegar and preserved in jars with olive oil) is part of the waste-not, want-not philosophy.

In the end, it was the simple goodness of this *cucina povera* (poor man's cuisine) that would make it the darling of health-conscious foodies.

> Tomatoes were not introduced to Italy until the 16th century, when they were sailed across from the Americas by early European explorers. The word *pomodoro* literally means 'golden apple'.

Regional Focus

In reality, southern Italian cuisine encompasses the culinary traditions of five regions: Campania, Puglia, Basilicata, Calabria and Sicily. They might share similarities, but they are all distinctly unique. So raise your fork to the following appetite-piquing regional fortes.

Campania

Everything seems to taste a little bit better in Campania – the tomatoes are juicier, the mozzarella silkier and the *caffè* richer and stronger. Is it the lush volcanic soil? The Campanian sun? Whatever it is, your taste buds will be too high to care.

Perfect Pizza

It was in Naples that the city's most famous *pizzaiolo* (pizza chef), Raffaele Esposito, invented the classic pizza margherita. Esposito was summoned to fire up a treat for a peckish King Umberto I and his wife Queen Margherita on a royal visit in 1889. Determined to impress the Italian royals, Esposito based his creation of tomato, mozzarella and basil on the red, white and green flag of the newly unified Italy. The resulting topping met with the queen's approval and was subsequently named in her honour.

Pizza purists claim that you really can't top Esposito's classic combo when made by a true Neapolitan *pizzaiolo*. Not everyone is in accordance and Italians are often split between those who favour the thin-crust Roman variant, and those who go for the thicker Neapolitan version. Whatever your choice, the fact remains that the pizza they make in Naples is nothing short of superb. It's also a brilliant cheap feed – these giant discs of bubbling perfection often start from €3 or €4.

> For a comprehensive yet easy-to-use guide to Italian cooking, hunt down Marcella Hazan's award-winning *Essentials of Classic Italian Cooking* (1992), which incorporates two of her cult-status cookbooks.

According to the official, non-profit Associazione Verace Pizza Napoletana (Real Neapolitan Pizza Association), genuine Neapolitan pizza dough must be made using highly refined type 00 wheat flour (a small dash of type 0 is permitted), compressed or natural yeast, salt, and water with a pH level between 6 and 7. While a slow-speed mixer can be used for kneading the dough, only hands are allowed to form the *disco di pasta* (pizza base), which should not be thicker than 3mm. The pizza itself should be cooked at 485°C (905°F) in a double-domed, wood-fired oven using oak, ash, beech or maple timber.

The Cult of Caffè

According to the Neapolitans, it's the local water that makes their coffee stronger and better than any other in Italy. While the magic formula is up for debate, there's no doubting that Naples brews the country's thickest, richest, most unforgettable espresso. Indeed, coffee plays a venerable role in Neapolitan cultural identity. Celebrated Neapolitan folk songs include *'O cafè* (Oh, coffee) and *A tazza 'e cafè* (The cup of coffee), while Italian design company Alessi pays tribute to the city's distinctive, stove-top coffee maker with its own *Caffettiera napoletana* (Neapolitan coffee maker), designed by prolific Neapolitan artist Riccardo Dalisi.

Locals still favour the Arabica and Robusta blends that deliver a dense *crema*, higher caffeine jolt, longer shelf life and, crucially, a price point everyone can afford. Chances are you'll be savouring it on your feet. In Naples, as in the rest of Italy, drinking coffee at a bar is usually a moment to pause, but rarely linger. It's a stand-up swirl and gulp, an exchanged *buongiorno* or *buona sera* with the barista, and a hop back onto the street. But don't be fooled – the speed with which it's consumed does not diminish the importance of its quality.

For an excellent food and travel portal, visit www. deliciousitaly. com. The site features articles and interviews about Italy's culinary traditions, as well as regional recipes. It also lists cooking courses and both food and wine tours.

Magnificent Mozzarella

So you think the cow's milk mozzarella served in Capri's *insalata caprese* (a salad made of mozzarella, tomato, basil and olive oil) is delicious? Taste Campania's porcelain-white *mozzarella di bufala* (buffalo-milk mozzarella) and you'll move onto an entirely different level of deliciousness. Best eaten when freshly made that morning, its sweet flavour and luscious texture is nothing short of a revelation. The cheese is made using the milk of black water buffalos reared on the plains surrounding Caserta and Paestum. According to aficionados, Paestum's version has a more delicate flavour than its rival from Caserta. You'll find either one served in *trattorias* (informal restaurants) and restaurants across the region. Indeed, you'll also find it dished up at dedicated mozzarella eateries, among them Muu Muzzarella Lounge (p75) in Naples.

Bought fresh from *latterie* (dairies), it comes lukewarm in a plastic bag filled with a slightly cloudy liquid, the run-off from the mozzarella making. Fresh mozzarella should have an elastic consistency; a tight, smooth surface; and have no yellowish marks or spots. Sliced, it should appear grainy, layered, and seeping pearls of milky whey.

While its most common form is round and fresh, *mozzarella di bufala* also comes in a twisted, plait form *(treccia)*, as well as smoked *(affumicata)*. Its most decadent variation is *burrata*, a mozzarella filled with a wickedly buttery cream. *Burrata* itself was invented in the neighbouring region of Puglia; the swampy fields around Foggia are famed for their buffalo-milk goodness.

Puglia, Basilicata & Calabria

Italy's Beloved Virgin

Campania and Sicily may produce a few impressive olive oils, but southern Italy's *olio* (oil) heavyweight is Puglia. The region produces around 40% of Italy's olive oil, much of it from the region's north. Indeed, Puglia is home to an estimated 50 to 60 million olive trees, and some of these gnarled, silver-green icons are said to be over 1000 years old.

While Pugliese oil is usually made up of two types of olives – faintly bitter coratina (from Corato) and sweet, fat ogliarola (from around Cima di Bitonto) – there is no shortage of common olive varieties. Among these are cellina di nardò, frantoio, leccino, peranzana, garganica, rotondella, cima di bitonto and cima di mola. The European Union itself formally recognises five Denomination of Origin of Production (DOP) areas in Puglia in order to protect the unique characteristics of each terroir: Collina di Brindisi DOP, Dauno DOP, Terra d'Otranto DOP, Terra di Bari DOP and Terre Tarentine DOP. While sweet fruitiness characterises the oils from Collina di Brindisi, Dauno DOP oils are noted for their aromatic, well-rounded nature. Ancient growing regions define both the Terra di Bari DOP and Terra d'Otranto DOP oils, the former known for their clear colour and almond notes, the latter for their darker green hue and fresh herb aroma. Last but not least are Terre Tarentine DOP oils, known for their greenish-yellow colouring, medium bitterness and light spiciness.

Mercato di Ballarò (p193), Palermo

Whatever the origin, the best oil is made from olives that are picked and rushed to the mill, as olives that are left for too long after harvesting quickly become acidic. Pugliese farmers traditionally harvest the easy way: by letting the olives drop into nets, rather than paying for labour-intensive harvesting by hand. This means the olives are too acidic and the oil has to be refined, often taken north to mix with higher quality, costlier oils. That said, more and more places in the south produce stunning oils at low prices; you can buy it at local farms such as organic Il Frantoio (p144).

The Beauty of Bread

Puglia's celebrated olive oils are a fine match for the region's equally esteemed *pane* (bread). Indeed, eating a meal in Puglia or neighbouring Basilicata without bread is like playing tennis without a racquet – it is essential for wiping up the sauce (a practise fondly called *fare la scarpetta*, 'to make a little shoe'). Puglia's wood-fired variety is the stuff of legend, usually made from hard durum wheat (like pasta), with a russet-brown crust, an eggy-golden interior and a distinctively fine flavour. The best comes from Altamura, where it's thrice-risen, getting even better with time.

Many of Puglia's and Basilicata's recipes call for breadcrumbs, among them summery spaghetti with oven-roasted tomatoes, breadcrumbs and garlic, and fusilli pasta with tomato, breadcrumbs and *crusco* (a dried, sweet pepper unique to Basilicata). Across in Calabria, breadcrumbs and pasta meet in classics like spaghetti with anchovies and chilli. The breadcrumbs themselves are made from stale bread – in Italian, it's *pane rafferme* (firmed-up bread), which is a much more glass-half-full way of looking at it.

Another southwest staple is *friselli,* dried bagel-shaped rolls born out of practicality, ideal for labourers on the move. Douse them in water to soften and then dress with tomatoes, olive oil and oregano. Just leave a little room for bagel-shaped *taralli,* hard little savoury biscuits that make for a

Puglia produces around 80% of Europe's pasta, and per-capita consumption of bread and pasta is at least double that of the USA. It's also said that there are between 50 million and 60 million olive trees in the region alone.

Stigghiola (goat intestines filled with onions, cheese and parsley), Palermo

tasty snack. In Bari they're traditionally plain, in Taranto they're sprinkled with fennel seeds and in Lecce they're sexed-up with a kick of chilli.

Sicily

To Market, To Market

Only Naples' Mercato di Porta Nolana (p68) can rival the sheer theatricality and gut-rumbling brilliance of Sicily's *mercati* (markets). Loud, crowded and exhilarating, these alfresco larders are a Technicolor testament to the importance of fresh produce in daily life. To watch the hard-to-please hagglers bullying vendors into giving them precisely what they want is to understand that quality really matters here. And it's these people, the *nonne* (grandmothers) and *casalinghe* (homemakers), who keep the region's culinary traditions alive.

Two of the most atmospheric markets are Palermo's Mercato di Ballarò (p193) and Catania's La Pescheria (p218), their souk-like laneways crammed with glistening tuna and swordfish, swaying sausages and tubs of olives and pungent cheeses. Look out for pistachios from Bronte, almonds from Noto, and *caciocavallo,* one of southern Italy's most renowned cheeses. Don't panic: despite the name 'horse cheese', it's made from cow's milk. It has a distinctive gourd-shaped, pale-mustard exterior, and the name is thought to have arisen either because it was once made from mare's milk, or because it would be hung from the horse's back when transported. When it's young, it tastes *dolce* (sweet); after two months ageing, it's *piccante* (spicy) or *affumicato* (smoked).

La Dolce Vita

From *gelso di melone* (watermelon jelly) and *buccellati* (little pies filled with minced fruit), to *biscotti regina* (sesame-coated biscuits) and *cassatelle* (pouches of dough stuffed with sweetened ricotta and chocolate), Sicilians

The BBC series *Antonio Carluccio's Southern Italian Feast* (1998) offers a fascinating exploration of the south's traditions and flavours. The associated cookbook *Southern Italian Feast: More Than 100 Recipes Inspired by the Flavour of Southern Italy* will get you busy in the kitchen.

have a way with sugar that verges on the pornographic. Down here, *pasticcerie* (pastry shops) are culinary sex shops, leading taste buds into temptation. Ditch the guilt, you're not alone – Sicilians normally migrate from restaurant tables to the nearest pastry shop for a coffee and cake at the bar.

It was the Saracens who first brought sugarcane to Sicily, a novelty that would help kindle the island's passion for sweets. Sicily's legendary *cassata* (a coma-inducing concoction of sponge cake, ricotta, marzipan, chocolate and candied fruit) comes from the Arabic word *qas'ah* (a reference to the terracotta bowl used to shape the cake), while *cannolo* (a pastry shell with a sweet ricotta filling) originates from *canna* (cane, as in sugar cane).

The Arabs also kickstarted the Sicilian mania for all things icy – *granita* (flavoured crushed ice), *cassata* ice cream, *gelato* (ice cream) and *semifreddo* (literally 'semifrozen'; a cold, creamy dessert). The origins of ice cream lie in the Arab *sarbat* (sherbet), a concoction of sweet fruit syrups chilled with iced water, later developed into *granita* (where crushed ice was mixed with anything from fruit juice to coffee and almond milk) and *cremolata* (fruit syrups chilled with iced milk), the forerunner to gelato.

Homemade gelato (*gelato artiginale*) is sold at cafes and bars across the island, and is truly delicious. *Granite* are sometimes topped with fresh whipped cream, or you could try it like a Sicilian – first thing in the morning in a brioche.

Southern Staples
Pasta: Fuel of the South

In the 1954 cult film *Un americano a Roma* (An American in Rome), a US-obsessed Alberto Sordi snubs a plate of pasta in favour of an unappetising 'American-style' concoction. It only takes a few mouthfuls before Sordi thinks better of it, plunging into the pasta with unbridled passion. It's hard not to follow Sordi's lead.

A standard *primo* (first course) on menus across the south, pasta is not only delicious, it's often a filling meal in itself. Your waiter will understand and there is usually no pressure to order a *secondo* (second course). The south's knack for pasta dishes is hardly surprising given that it was here that *pasta secca* (dry pasta) first hit Italy, introduced to Sicily by Arab merchants in the Middle Ages. It was to be a perfect match. Southern Italy's sunny, windy disposition was just right for producing *pasta secca*, while the foodstuff's affordability and easy storage made it handy in the face of hardship. It's no coincidence that *pasta fresca* (fresh pasta) has, traditionally, been more prevalent in Italy's more affluent north.

Arriving from Sicily, dry pasta took off in a big way in Campania, especially after the 1840 opening of Italy's first pasta plant in Torre Annunziata, a town on the Bay of Naples. Not that Torre Annunziata was Campania's first pasta-making hub. Some 30km southeast of Naples, small-town Gragnano has been making pasta since the 17th century. Gragnano's main street was specifically built along the sun's axis so that the pasta put out to dry by the town's *pastifici* (pasta factories) would reap a full day's sunshine. To this day, *pasta di Gragnano* enjoys an air of exclusivity.

And while *pasta secca* may be the dominant form of pasta on southern plates, the Mezzogiorno is not without its fresh pasta icons. The most famous is arguably Puglia's *orecchiette* (meaning 'little ears'), best savoured in dishes such as *orecchiette con cime di rapa* (with turnip tops) and *orecchiette con pomodori e ricotta forte* (with tomato sauce and strong ricotta).

Eat Your Greens... Purples, Reds & Yellows

Vegetables across the world must loathe their southern Italian counterparts. Not only do they often look more beautiful, they're prepared with a know-how that turns them into culinary protagonists. Take the humble *melanzana* (eggplant or aubergine), glammed up in the punchy

Don't believe the hype about espresso: one diminutive cup packs less of a caffeine wallop than a large cup of French-pressed or American-brewed coffee, and leaves drinkers less jittery.

While it's perfectly normal to order 'a biscotti' or 'a cannoli' back home in Sydney or New York, these are actually plural forms in Italian; use the singular form *'un biscotto'* or *'un cannolo'* when in Italy – unless, of course, you're especially peckish.

melanzane ripiene al forno (baked eggplant stuffed with olives, capers and tomatoes) and decadent *parmigiana melanzane* (batter-fried eggplant layered with parmesan, mozzarella, ham and tomato sauce). Another version, simply named *parmigiana,* does the same for *carciofi* (globe artichokes). Campania's *pomodoro San Marzano* (San Marzano plum tomato) is one of the world's most lauded tomatoes. Grown in the shadow of Mt Vesuvius, its low acidity and intense, sweet flavour makes a perfect *conserva di pomodoro* (tomato concentrate). It's this sauce that adorns so many of Naples' signature pasta dishes, including the colourfully named *spaghetti alla puttanesca* (whore's spaghetti).

Ironically, southern Italy's sophisticated flair with vegetables is firmly rooted in centuries of deprivation and misery. The food of the poor, the so-called *mangiafoglie* (leaf eaters), was largely based on the *verdure* (vegetables) grown under the nourishing southern sun, from artichokes and courgettes (zucchini) to tomatoes and peppers. Hardship and sunshine helped develop celebrated antipasto staples like *zucchine fritte* (pan-fried courgettes) and *peperoni sotto aceto* (marinated pickled peppers), as well as celebrated Sicilian dishes like *peperonata in agridolce* (a stew of red, green and yellow peppers, onions, pine nuts, raisins and capers). Onions feel the love in Puglia's moreish *calzone pugliese* (onion pie), while legumes see the light in the region's broad bean and chicory puree; 'a dish to die for' according to celebrity chef, restaurateur and food writer Antonio Carluccio.

Less is more: most of the recipes in Ada Boni's classic *The Talisman Italian Cookbook* have fewer than 10 ingredients, yet the flavours of her mozzarella and anchovy *crostini* or Sicilian-style *caponatina* are anything but simple.

The Vine Revival

Winemaking in the south dates back to the Phoenicians. The Greeks introduced Campania to its now-famous Greco (Greek) grape, and dubbed the south 'Enotria' (Wineland). Yet, despite this ancient viticulture, oenophiles have often dismissed local *vini* (wines) as little more than 'here for a good time, not a long time' drops. A case in point is wine critic Burton Anderson, who in his *Wine Atlas of Italy* (1990) wrote that Campania's noteworthy winemakers could be 'counted on one's fingers'.

Anderson would need a few more hands these days. In little more than two decades, southern Italy has transformed itself into one of the world's in-the-know wine regions, with renewed pride in native varieties and stricter, more modern winemaking practices.

Campania

Lauded producers such as Feudi di San Gregorio, Mastroberardino, Villa Matilde, Pietracupa and Terredora have returned to their roots, cultivating ancient grape varieties like the red Aglianico (thought to be the oldest cultivated grape in Italy) and the whites Falanghino, Fiano and Greco (all growing long before Mt Vesuvius erupted in AD 79). Keeping them company is a growing list of reputable organic and biodynamic wineries, among them I Cacciagalli and Cautiero.

Taurasi, a full-bodied Aglianico wine, sometimes known as the Barolo of the south, is one of southern Italy's finest labels. One of only four in the region to carry Italy's top quality rating, DOCG (Denominazione di Origine Controllata e Garantita; Controlled and Guaranteed Denomination of Origin), it goes perfectly with barbecued and boiled meats. The other three wines to share this honour are Aglianico del Taburno, a full-bodied red from the Benevento area, as well as Fiano di Avellino and Greco di Tufo, both whites and both from the Avellino area.

Other vino-producing areas include the Campi Flegrei (home to DOC-labelled Piedirosso and Falanghina vines), Ischia (whose wines were the first to receive DOC status) and the Cilento region, home to the DOC Cilento bianco (Cilento white) and to the Aglianico Paestum. Mt Vesuvius' most famous drop is the Lacryma Christi (Tears of Christ), a blend of locally grown Falanghina, Piedirosso and Coda di Volpe grapes.

The annual *Italian Wines,* produced by the Gambero Rosso, is considered to be the bible of Italian vino, offering plenty of information about southern wines and wineries. You can buy it at many Italian bookstores or online at www.gamberorosso.it.

Puglia & Basilicata

The different characteristics of these regions' wines reflect their diverse topography and terroir. In Puglia, there are vast, flat acreages of vineyards, while Basilicata's vineyards tend to be steep and volcanic.

It's the Pugliese reds that gain most plaudits. The main grapes grown are the Primitivo (a clone of the zinfandel grape), Negroamaro, Nero di Troia and Malvasia. The best Primitivi are found around Manduria, while Negroamaro reaches its peak in the Salento, particularly around Salice, Guagnano and Copertino. The two grapes are often blended to derive the best from the sweetness of Primitivo and the slightly bitter, wilder edge of Negroamaro.

Almost all Puglia reds work perfectly with pasta, pizza, meats and cheeses. Puglia whites have less cachet; however, those grown on the Murge, particularly Locorotondo and Martina, are good, clean, fresh-tasting wines, while those from Gravina are a little weightier. They are all excellent with fish.

In Basilicata, the red wine of choice is made from the Aglianico grape, the best being produced in the Vulture region. It is the volcanic terroir that makes these wines so unique and splendid. Basilicata, like Puglia, has seen

The word *melanzane* (eggplant or aubergine) comes from 'mela insane', meaning crazy apple. In Latin it was called *solanum insanum* as it was thought to cause madness.

THE SOUTHERN TABLE THE VINE REVIVAL

FESTIVE FAVOURITES

In southern Italy, culinary indulgence is the epicentre of any celebration and major holidays are defined by their specialities. Lent is heralded by Carnevale (Carnival), a time for *sanguinaccio* (blood pudding made with dark chocolate and cinnamon), *chiacchiere* (fried biscuits sprinkled with icing sugar) and Sicily's *mpagnuccata* (deep-fried dough tossed in soft caramel).

If you're in the south around 19 March (St Joseph's Feast Day), expect to eat *zeppole* (fritters topped with lemon-scented cream, sour cherry and dusting sugar) in Naples and Bari, and *crispelle di riso* (citrus-scented rice fritters dipped in honey) in Sicily.

Lent specialities like Sicilian *quaresimali* (hard, light almond biscuits) give way to Easter bingeing with the obligatory lamb, *colomba* (dove-shaped cake) and *uove di pasqua* (foil-wrapped chocolate eggs with toy surprises inside). The dominant ingredient at this time is egg, also used to make traditional regional specialities like Naples' legendary *pastiera* (shortcrust pastry tart filled with ricotta, cream, candied fruits and cereals flavoured with orange water).

If you're in Palermo around late October, before the festival of Ognissanti (All Souls' Day), you will see plenty of stalls selling the famous *frutti della Martorana*, named after the church that first began producing them. These marzipan biscuits, shaped to resemble fruits (or whatever takes the creator's fancy), are part of a Sicilian tradition that dates back to the Middle Ages.

Come Christmas, it's time for stuffed pasta, seafood dishes and national staples like Milan's *panettone* (yeasty, golden cake studded with raisins and dried fruit), Verona's simpler, raisin-free *pandoro* (yeasty, star-shaped cake dusted with vanilla-flavoured icing sugar) and Siena's *panforte* (chewy, flat cake made with candied fruits, nuts, chocolate, honey and spices). It's at this time that Neapolitans throw caution (and scales) to the wind with *raffioli* (sponge and marzipan biscuits), *struffoli* (tiny fried pastry balls dipped in honey and sprinkled with colourful candied sugar) and *pasta di mandorla* (marzipan), while their Sicilian cousins toast to the season with *cucciddatu* (ring-shaped cake made with dried figs, nuts, honey, vanilla, cloves, cinnamon and citrus fruits). Not that the Sicilians stop there, further expanding waistlines with yuletide *buccellati* (dough rings stuffed with minced figs, raisins, almonds, candied fruit and/or orange peel, especially popular around Christmas).

Of course, it's not all about religion. Some Italian holidays dispense with the spiritual premise and are all about the food. During spring, summer and early autumn, towns across Italy celebrate *sagre*, the festivals of local foods in season. You'll find a *sagra della melanzana* (aubergine) in Campania, *del pomodoro* (tomatoes) in Sicily and *della cipolla* (onion) in Puglia (wouldn't want to be downwind of that one). For a list of *sagre*, check out www.prodottitipici.com/sagre (in Italian).

THE BIG FORK MANIFESTO

The year was 1987. McDonald's had just begun its expansion into Italy, and lunch outside the burger bun seemed to be fading into fond memory. Enter Carlo Petrini and a handful of other journalists from the small Piedmontese town of Bra, in northern Italy. Determined to buck the trend, these *neoforchettoni* ('big forks', or foodies) created a manifesto. Published in the like-minded culinary magazine *Gambero Rosso*, the manifesto declared that a meal should be judged not by its speed, but by the pure pleasure it offers.

The organisation they founded would soon become known worldwide as Slow Food. Its mission: to reconnect artisanal producers with enthusiastic, educated consumers. The movement has taken root, with around 100,000 members in over 160 countries – not to mention Slow Food *agriturismi* (farm stay accommodation), restaurants, farms, wineries, cheesemakers and revitalised farmers' markets across Italy.

While traditions in the south remain stronger than in Italy's north, the Slow Food Movement does its bit to prevent their disappearance and to promote interest in food, taste and the way things are produced. For more information, see www.slowfood.com.

a renaissance in recent years with much inward investment, such as that of oenologist Donato d'Angelo at his eponymous winery at Rionero in Vulture.

Sicily

Sicily is one of the largest wine-producing regions in Italy, yet few Sicilian wines are well known beyond the island.

The most common varietal is Nero d'Avola, a robust red similar to syrah or shiraz. Vintages are produced by numerous Sicilian wineries, including Planeta (www.planeta.it), which has six estates around the island; Donnafugata (www.donnafugata.it) in western Sicily; Azienda Agricola COS (www.cosvittoria.it) and Azienda Agricola Arianna Occhipinti (www.agricolaocchipinti.it) in southeast Sicily; and Azienda Agricola G Milazzo (www.milazzovini.com) near Agrigento. Try Planeta's Plumbago, Donnafugata's Mille e una Notte, COS' Nero di Lupo, and Milazzo's Maria Costanza and Terre della Baronia Rosso.

The Sangiovese-like Nerello Mascalese and Nerello Cappuccio are used in the popular Etna Rosso DOC, a dark-fruited, medium-bodied wine that pairs perfectly with lamb and goat's milk cheeses. Winemaker Frank Cornelissen (frankcornelissen.it) uses Nerello Mascalese to produce his powerful, smoky IGT Magma, made using grapes grown on Mt Etna's northern slope.

There is only one Sicilian DOCG, Cerasuolo di Vittoria, a blend of Nero d'Avola and Frappato grapes. COS makes an especially fine version. Called COS Pithos, it's soft, chalky and aged in concrete and glass tanks for 18 to 24 months. The two grapes varietals also conspire in Arianna Occhipinti's celebrated SP68 Rosso.

While Sicily's *vini rossi* (red wines) are good, the region's real forte are its *bianchi* (whites), including those produced at Abbazia Santa Anastasia near Castelbuono, Tasca d'Almerita and Passopisciaro. Common white varietals include Carricante, chardonnay, Grillo, Inzolia, Cataratto, Inzolia, Cataratto, Grecanico and Corinto. Look out for Tasca d'Almerita's Nozze d'Oro Inzolia blend, Abbazia Santa Anastasia's chardonnay blends, and Passopisciaro's Guardiola Chardonnay.

Equally impressive are Sicily's dessert wines. Top billing goes to Marsala's sweet wine; the best labels are Florio and Pellegrino. Italy's most famous Moscato (muscat) is the Passito di Pantelleria from the island of the same name. Deep-amber in colour, its taste is an extraordinary mélange of apricots and vanilla.

The average Italian adult consumes around 34L of wine per annum – a sobering figure compared with the 100L consumed on average back in the 1950s. Somewhat surprisingly, the world's top consumers of wine live in the Vatican City (54L per person).

28

Art & Architecture

Southern Italy is Western Europe's cultural attic – a dusty repository filled to the rafters with some of its most ancient and formative art and architecture. From sea to summit, its landscapes are punctuated with Hellenic and Roman ruins, proud medieval castles, Byzantine mosaics and glorious baroque frescoes, not to mention the brushstrokes and buildings of the south's modern milieu. It's an overwhelming heap, so why not start with the undisputed highlights?

Art

Classical Splendour

The Greeks had settled many parts of Sicily and southern Italy as early as the 8th century BC, naming it Magna Graecia (Greater Greece) and building great cities such as Syracuse and Taranto. These cities were famous for their magnificent temples, many of which were decorated with sculptures modelled on, or inspired by, masterpieces by Praxiteles, Lysippus and Phidias.

The Greek colonisers were equally deft at ceramics, adorning vases with painted scenes from daily life, mythology and Greek theatre. Some of the most vivid examples are the 4th-century-BC phylax vases, with larger-than-life characters and costumes that depict scenes from phylax plays, a type of ancient southern-Italian farce.

In art, as in so many other realms, the Romans looked to the Greeks for examples of best practice, and sculpture, architecture and painting flourished during their reign. Yet, the art produced in Rome was different in many ways from the Greek art that influenced it. Essentially secular, it focused less on harmony and form and more on accurate representation, mainly through sculptural portraits. Innumerable versions of Pompey, Titus and Augustus all show a similar visage, proving that the artists were seeking verisimilitude in their representations, and not just glorification.

Wealthy Roman citizens also dabbled in the arts, building palatial villas and adorning them with statues looted from the Greek world or copied from Hellenic originals. You'll find many fine examples in Syracuse's Museo Archeologico Paolo Orsi, including the celebrated *Venere Anadiomene,* a 1st-century Roman copy depicting a voluptuous goddess of love. Status-conscious Romans didn't stop there, lavishing floors with mosaics and walls with vivid frescoes. Outstanding mosaics continue to enthrall at Sicily's Villa Romana del Casale, Pompeii, Herculaneum and Naples' Museo Archeologico Nazionale. Pompeii itself claims the world's largest ancient wall fresco, a restored wonder inside the Villa dei Misteri.

First published in 1950, Sir EH Gombrich's seminal work *The Story of Art* gives a wonderful, accessible overview of the history of Italian art.

The Glitter of Byzantine

In 330, Emperor Constantine, a convert to Christianity, made the ancient city of Byzantium his capital and renamed it Constantinople. The city became the great cultural and artistic centre of Christianity and it remained so up to the time of the Renaissance, though its influence on the art of that period was never as fundamental as the art of ancient Rome.

Artistically, the Byzantine period was notable for its extraordinary mosaic work and – to a lesser extent – its painting. Its art was influenced by the decoration of the Roman catacombs and the early Christian churches, as well as by the Oriental Greek style, with its love of rich decoration and luminous colour.

As a major transit point on the route between Constantinople and Rome, Puglia and Basilicata were exposed to Byzantine's Eastern aesthetics. Indeed, the art that most encapsulates these regions are its 10th- and 11th-century Byzantine frescoes, hidden away in locked chapels dotted across their expanse. There is an incredible concentration in Matera, the most fantastic of which include the monastic complex of Chiesa di Madonna delle Virtù and Chiesa di San Nicola del Greci. Impressive examples in Puglia include the lively frescoes inside Otranto's Chiesa di San Pietro.

In Sicily, Byzantine, Norman and Saracen influences fused to create a distinct regional style showcased in the mosaic-encrusted splendour of Palermo's Cappella Palatina inside the Palazzo dei Normanni, not to mention the cathedrals of Monreale and Cefalù.

Giotto & the 'Rebirth' of Italian Art

Italy's Byzantine painters were apt with light and shade, but it would take Florentine painter Giotto di Bondone (c 1266–1337) to break the spell of conservatism and venture into a new world of naturalism. Best known for his frescoes in Padua and Assisi, faded fragments of his work survive in Naples' Castel Nuovo and Basilica di Santa Chiara.

Giotto and the painters of the Sienese School introduced many innovations in art: the exploration of perspective and proportion, a new interest in realistic portraiture and the beginnings of a new tradition of landscape painting. The influx of Eastern scholars fleeing Constantinople in the wake of its fall to the Ottoman Turkish Muslims in 1453 prompted a renewed interest in classical learning and humanist philosophy. Coupled with the increasingly ambitious, competitive nature of northern Italy's city states, these developments would culminate in the Renaissance.

Centred in Florence in the 15th century, and Rome and Venice in the 16th century, the Renaissance was slower to catch on in southern Italy, which was caught up in the power struggles between its French and Spanish rulers. One of the south's few Renaissance masters was Antonello da Messina (1430–79), whose luminous works include the *Virgin Annunciate* (1474–77) in Palermo's Galleria Regionale della Sicilia and *Annunciation* (1474) in Syracuse's Galleria Regionale di Palazzo Bellomo.

Bad Boys & the Baroque

With the advent of the baroque, it was the south's time to shine. Under 17th-century Spanish rule, Naples was transformed into Europe's biggest city. Swelling crowds and counter-Reformation fervour sparked a building boom, with taller-than-ever *palazzi* (mansions) and showcase churches sprouting up across the city. Ready to adorn these new landmarks was a brash, arrogant and fiery league of artists, ditching Renaissance restraint for baroque exuberance.

The main influence on 17th-century Neapolitan art was Milanese-born Caravaggio (1573–1610). A controversial character, he escaped to Naples in 1606 after killing a man in Rome; although he only stayed for a year, his impact on the city was huge. Caravaggio's dramatic depiction of light and shade, his supreme draughtsmanship and his naturalist style had an electrifying effect on the city's younger artists. One look at Caravaggio's *Flagellazione* (Flagellation; 1607–10) in Naples' Museo Nazionale di Capodimonte, his *Le sette opere di Misericordia* (Seven Acts of Mercy; c 1607) in the Pio Monte della Misericordia, or his swan song *Martirio di Sant'Orsola* (Martyrdom of St Ursula) in the city's Galleria di Palazzo Zevallos Stigliano and you'll understand why.

Click on to www.exibart.com (in Italian) for up-to-date listings of art exhibitions across Italy. Exhibitions and events can be searched by region and the site also includes exhibition reviews, articles and interviews.

Italy's dedicated art police, the Comando Carabinieri Tutela Patrimonio Culturale, tackles the looting of Italy's priceless heritage. It's estimated that over 100,000 ancient tombs have been ransacked by *tombaroli* (tomb raiders) alone; the contents are often sold to private and public collectors around the world.

One of Caravaggio's greatest fans was artist Giuseppe (or Jusepe) de Ribera (1591–1652), whose combination of shadow, colour and gloomy naturalism is brilliantly executed in his masterpiece, *Pietà* (1637), which is hanging in Naples' Certosa di San Martino. Merciless to the extreme, Lo Spagnoletto (The Little Spaniard, as Ribera was known) reputedly won a commission for the Cappella del Tesoro in Naples' Duomo by poisoning his rival Domenichino (1581–1641), as well as wounding the assistant of a second competitor, Guido Reni (1575–1642). The Duomo would be adorned with the frescoes of a number of rising stars, among them Giovanni Lanfranco (1582–1647) and Luca Giordano (1632–1705).

A fledgling apprentice to Ribera, Naples-born Giordano found great inspiration in the brushstrokes of Mattia Preti (1613–99). By the second half of the 17th century, Giordano would become the single most important artist in Naples. His finest fresco, the *Triumph of Judith,* decorates the treasury ceiling of the Certosa di San Martino's church.

Best for Baroque

....

Lecce (Puglia)

....

Noto (Sicily)

....

Catania (Sicily)

....

Naples (Campania)

Contemporary Movements

Of the many movements that shaped Italy's 20th-century art scene, few match the radical innovation of Arte Povera (Poor Art). Emerging from the economic and political instability of the 1960s, its artists aimed to blur the boundary between art and life. Using everyday materials and mediums ranging from painting and photography to installations, they created works that put the viewer at the centre, triggering personal memories and associations. The movement would ultimately pave the way for contemporary installation art. Its leading practitioners included Mario Merz (1925–2003), Luciano Fabro (1936–2007) and Giovanni Anselmo (b 1934), the latter's sculptures inspired by the geological forces of Stromboli. Another icon of the scene is the Greek-born Jannis Kounellis (b 1936), whose brooding installations often focus on the disintegration of culture in the

MASTERS OF THE NEAPOLITAN BAROQUE

Michelangelo Merisi da Caravaggio (1573–1610) Bridging Mannerism and the baroque, Caravaggio injected raw emotion and foreboding shadow. His greatest masterpiece is the multiscene *Le Sette Opere di Misericordia* (Seven Acts of Mercy; 1607), appearing in Naples' Pio Monte della Misericordia.

Giuseppe de Ribera (1591–1652) Though Spanish born, most of this bullying painter's finest work was created in southern Italy, including his dramatic *St Jerome* (1626) and *Apollo and Marsyas* (c 1637), both in the Museo Nazionale di Capodimonte.

Cosimo Fanzago (1591–1678) This revered sculptor, decorator and architect cut marble into the most whimsical forms, producing luscious, inlaid spectacles. Naples' Certosa di San Martino aside, his beautiful high altar in Naples' Chiesa di San Domenico Maggiore is not to be missed.

Mattia Preti (1613–99) Dubbed 'Il Cavaliere Calabrese' (The Calabrian Knight), Preti infused thunderous, apocalyptic scenes with a deep, affecting humanity. Seek out his *Feast of Absalom* (c 1670) in the Museo Nazionale di Capodimonte.

Luca Giordano (1632–1705) Affectionately nicknamed Luca fa presto (Luca does it quickly) for his dexterous ways with a brush. Fabulous frescoes aside, his canvassed creations include *Apollo and Marsyas* (c 1660) in the Museo Nazionale di Capodimonte.

Francesco Solimena (1657–1747) Lavish and grandiose compositions define this icon's work. One of his best is the operatic fresco *Expulsion of Eliodoro from the Temple* (1725) in Naples' Chiesa del Gesù Nuovo.

Giuseppe Sanmartino (1720–93) Arguably the finest sculptor of his time, Sanmartino's ability to breathe life into his creations won him a legion of fans, including the bizarre alchemist prince, Raimondo di Sangro.

Casa della Venere in Conchiglia (p100), Pompeii

In *M: The Man Who Became Caravaggio,* Peter Robb gives a passionate personal assessment of the artist's paintings and a colourful account of Caravaggio's life, arguing he was murdered for having sex with the pageboy of a high-ranking Maltese aristocrat.

modern world. Naples' MADRE contains a fine collection of Kounellis' creations, as well as other Arte Povera works. Among the wittiest is Michelangelo Pistoletti's *Venere degli stracci* (Venus of the Rags), in which a Greek goddess contemplates a pile of modern hand-me-downs.

Reacting against Arte Povera's conceptual tendencies was the 'Transavanguardia' movement of the late 1970s and 1980s, which refocussed attention on painting and sculpture in a traditional (primarily figurative) sense. Among its leading artists are Mimmo Paladino (b 1948) and Francesco Clemente (b 1952). Both of these Campanian artists are represented in Naples' Novecento a Napoli, a museum dedicated to 20th-century southern Italian art.

While most of Italy's current crop of internationally renowned artists hail from northern and central Italy, one southern standout is Modica-born Pietro Roccasalva (b 1970). The Sicilian artist is famous for using painting as the orbital centre in works that often also include sculpture, performance and video. Many of these creations focus on Roccasalva's fascination with iconography, motion and simulacrum in painting.

Architecture
Ancient Legacies

One word describes the buildings of ancient southern Italy: monumental. The Greeks invented the architectural orders (Doric, Ionic and Corinthian) and used them to great effect in once-mighty cities like Akragas (modern-day Agrigento), Catania and Syracuse. More than two millennia later, the soaring temples of Segesta, Selinunte, the Valley of the Temples and Paestum confirm not only the ancient Greeks' power, but also their penchant for harmonious proportion. This skill also underscored their sweeping theatres, the finest of which still stand in Syracuse, Taormina and Segesta.

Having learned a few valuable lessons from the Greeks, the Romans refined architecture to such a degree that their building techniques, designs and mastery of harmonious proportion underpin most of the world's architecture and urban design to this day. In Brindisi, a brilliant white column marks one end of the Via Appia – the ancient cross-country road connecting Rome to east-coast Brindisi. In Pozzuoli, they erected the Anfiteatro Flavio, the empire's third-largest arena and the very spot where Roman authorities had planned to feed San Gennaro to hungry bears. (In the end, they opted to behead the Christian at the nearby Solfatara Crater.)

Medieval Fusion

Following on from Byzantine architecture and its mosaic-encrusted churches was Romanesque, a style that found four regional forms in Italy: Lombard, Pisan, Florentine and Sicilian Norman. All displayed an emphasis on width and the horizontal lines of a building rather than height, and featured church groups with *campaniles* (bell towers) and baptisteries that were separate to the church. Surfacing in the 11th century, the Sicilian Norman style encompassed an exotic mix of Norman, Saracen and Byzantine influences, from marble columns to Islamic-inspired pointed arches to glass tesserae detailing. Clearly visible in the two-toned masonry and 13th-century bell tower of Amalfi's Cattedrale di Sant'Andrea, one of the greatest examples of the form is the cathedral of Monreale, just outside Palermo.

With the 12th and 13th centuries came the Gothic aesthetic. The Italians didn't embrace this style as enthusiastically as the French, Germans and Spanish did. Its flying buttresses, grotesque gargoyles and over-the-top decorations were just too far from the classical ideal that was (and still is) bred in the Italian bone. This said, the Gothic style did leave its mark in southern Italy, albeit in the muted version encapsulated by Naples' Chiesa di San Lorenzo Maggiore and Chiesa di San Domenico Maggiore, and Palermo's Palazzo Bellomo. The south's most striking Gothic icon, however, is Puglia's Castel del Monte; its Italianate windows, Islamic floor mosaics and Roman triumphal entrance attests to the south's flair for absorbing foreign influence.

Baroque: the Golden Age

Just as Renaissance restraint redefined Italy's north, the wild theatricality of 17th- and 18th-century baroque revamped the south. Encouraging the makeover was the Catholic Church, for whom baroque's awe-inducing qualities were the perfect weapon against the Reformation and its less-is-more philosophy. Deploying swirls of frescoes, gilt and polychromatic marble, churches like Naples' Chiesa del Gesù Nuovo and Chiesa di San Gregorio Armeno turned Catholicism into a no-holds-barred spectacular.

Inlaid marble would become a dominant special effect, adorning everything from tombs and altars to floors and entire chapel walls. The form's undisputed master was Cosimo Fanzago (1591–1678), an occasionally violent sculptor whose masterpieces would include Naples' Certosa di San Martino's church, a mesmerising kaleidoscope of colour, geometry and arresting precision.

In Puglia's Salento region, *barocco leccese* (Lecce baroque) saw the style reach extraordinary new heights. Local limestone was carved into lavish decorative detail around porticoes, windows, balconies and loggias, themselves crowned with human and zoomorphic figures as well as a riot of gargoyles, flora, fruit, columns and cornices. The leading exponents of the style were Gabriele Riccardi (1524–82) and Francesco Antonio Zimbalo (1567–1631), but it was Francesco's grandson Giuseppe Zimbalo (1620–1710), nicknamed Lo Zingarello (The Little Gypsy), who

One of the few well-known female artists of the Italian Renaissance was Artemisia Gentileschi (1593–1652), whose style is reminiscent of Caravaggio's. One of her most famous paintings, the intensely vengeful *Judith and Holofernes*, hangs inside Naples' Palazzo di Capodimonte.

ARCHITECTURE SPEAK: 101

Do you know your transept from your triclinium? Demystify some common architectural terms with the following bite-size list:

Apse Usually a large recess or niche built on a semicircular or polygonal ground plan and vaulted with a half dome. In a church or temple, it may include an altar.

Baldachin (Baldacchino) A permanent, often elaborately decorated canopy of wood or stone above an altar, throne, pulpit or statue.

Balustrade A stone railing formed of a row of posts (called balusters) topped by a continuous coping, and commonly flanking baroque stairs, balconies and terraces.

Impluvium A small ornamental pool, often used as the centrepiece of atriums in ancient Roman houses.

Latrine A Roman-era public convenience, lined with rows of toilet seats and often adorned with frescoes and marble.

Narthex A portico or lobby at the front of an early Christian church or basilica.

Necropolis Burial ground outside the city walls in antiquity and the early Christian era.

Oratory A small room or chapel in a church reserved for private prayer.

Transept A section of a church running at right angles to the main body of the church.

Triclinium The dining room in a Roman house.

was its most exuberant disciple. Among his greatest designs is the upper facade of Lecce's Basilica di Santa Croce.

It would take an earthquake in 1632 to seal Sicily's baroque legacy. Faced with destruction, ambitious architects set to work rebuilding the towns and cities of the island's southeast, among them Noto, Modica and Ragusa. Grid-patterned streets were laid and spacious piazzas were lined with confident, curvaceous buildings. The result was a highly idiosyncratic *barocco siciliano* (Sicilian baroque), best known for its cheeky stone *putti* (cherubs), wrought-iron balustrades and grand external staircases. Equally idiosyncratic was the use of dramatic, centrally placed church belfries, often shooting straight above the central pediment. Two of the finest examples are Ragusa's Cattedrale di San Giorgio and Modica's Chiesa di San Giorgio, both designed by the prolific Rosario Gagliardi (1698–1762).

Sicily's most celebrated baroque architect, however, would be Giovanni Battista Vaccarini (1702–68). Trained in Rome, Vaccarini would dedicate three decades of his life to rebuilding earthquake-stricken Catania, using the region's volcanic black rock to dramatic effect in Piazza del Duomo. His reputation would see him join forces with Neapolitan starchitect Luigi Vanvitelli (1700–73) in the creation of Italy's gargantuan baroque epilogue, the Reggia di Caserta, 30km north of Naples.

Survival Guide

Directory A-Z

Accommodation

Agriturismi & Masserie

An *agriturismo* (*agriturismi* in the plural) is accommodation on a working farm, where you'll usually be able to sample the produce. Traditionally, families simply rented out rooms in their farmhouses; it's still possible to find this type of lodging, although many *agriturismi* have now evolved into sophisticated accommodation.

Unique to southern Italy, *masserie* are large farms or estates, usually built around a fortified watchtower, with plenty of surrounding accommodation to house workers and livestock. Many have been converted into luxurious hotels, *agriturismi* or holiday apartments. A *masseria* isn't necessarily old: sometimes new buildings built around similar principles are called *masserie*.

To find lists of *agriturismi* and *masserie*, ask at any tourist office or check online at these sites:

Agriturist (www.agriturist.com)

Agriturismo.it (www.agriturismo.it)

Agriturismo.net (www.agriturismo.net)

Agriturismo.com (www.agriturismo.com)

Agriturismo-Italia.net (www.agriturismo-italia.net)

Agriturismo Vero (www.agriturismovero.com)

Charming Puglia (www.charmingpuglia.com)

B&Bs

B&Bs are a burgeoning sector of the southern accommodation market and can be found in both urban and rural settings. Options include everything from restored farmhouses, city *palazzi* (mansions) and seaside bungalows to rooms in family houses. Tariffs for a double room cover a wide range, from about €60 to €140.

Lists of B&Bs across southern Italy are available online.

BBItalia.it (www.bbitalia.it)

Bed-and-Breakfast.it (www.bed-and-breakfast.it)

Camping

Italians go camping with gusto and most camping facilities in Campania, Puglia, Calabria and Sicily (less so in Basilicata, where camping options are few and far between) include swimming pools, restaurants and supermarkets. With hotel prices shooting up in July and August, camping grounds can be a splendid option, especially given that many have enviable seaside locations.

Charges often vary according to the season, peaking in July and August, when accommodation should be booked well in advance. Typical high-season prices range from €10 to €20 per adult, up to €12 for children aged under 12, and from €5 to €25 for a site. Tent campers are expected to bring their own equipment, although a few grounds offer tents for hire. Many also offer the alternative of bungalows or even simple, self-contained (self-catering) flats. In high season, some only offer deals for a week at a time. Note that most camping grounds operate only in high season, which is roughly Apr to October (in many cases June to September only).

Lists of campgrounds are available from local tourist offices or online.

Campeggi.com (www.campeggi.com)

Camping.it (www.camping.it)

Italcamping.it (www.italcamping.it)

BOOK YOUR STAY ONLINE

For more accommodation reviews by Lonely Planet authors, check out https://www.lonelyplanet.com/italy/southern-italy/hotels. You'll find independent reviews, as well as recommendations on the best places to stay. Best of all, you can book online.

PRACTICALITIES

Newspapers Key national dailies include centre-left *La Repubblica* (www.repubblica.it) and right-wing rival *Corriere della Sera* (www.corriere.it). For the Vatican's take on affairs, *L'Osservatore Romano* (www.osservatoreromano.va) is the Holy See's official paper.

Radio As well as the principal RAI channels (Radiouno, Radiodue, Radiotre), there are hundreds of commercial radio stations operating across Italy. Popular Rome-based stations include Radio Capital (www.capital.it) and Radio Città Futura (www.radiocittafutura.it).

TV The main terrestrial channels are RAI 1, 2 and 3 run by Rai (www.rai.it), Italy's state-owned national broadcaster, and Canale 5, Italia 1 and Rete 4 run by Mediaset (www.mediaset.it), the commercial TV company founded and still partly owned by Silvio Berlusconi.

Weights & Measures Italy uses the metric system.

Smoking Banned in enclosed public spaces, including restaurants, bars, shops and public transport. Allowed at outdoor tables.

Tap Water Safe to drink except where a tap is marked 'Acqua non potabile' (Water not suitable for drinking).

Convents & Monasteries

Some Italian convents and monasteries let out cells or rooms as a modest revenue-making exercise and happily take in tourists, while others only take in pilgrims or people who are on a spiritual retreat. Many impose a fairly early curfew, but prices tend to be quite reasonable.

Two useful, if ageing, publications are Eileen Barish's *The Guide to Lodging in Italy's Monasteries* and Charles M Shelton's *Beds and Blessings in Italy: A Guide to Religious Hospitality*.

Online resources that can assist you in your search include:

MonasteryStays.com (www.monasterystays.com) A well-organised online booking centre for monastery and convent stays.

In Italy Online (www.initaly.com/agri/convents.htm) Offers a list of monastery and convent accommodation across the country, as well as a general holiday itinerary planning service.

Hostels

Ostelli per la gioventù (youth hostels) are run by the Associazione Italiana Alberghi per la Gioventù, affiliated with Hostelling International (www.hihostels.com). A valid HI card is required in all associated youth hostels in Italy. You can get this in your home country or directly at many hostels.

A full list of Italian hostels, with details of prices and locations, is available online or from hostels throughout the country. Nightly rates in basic dorms vary from around €15 to €50, which usually includes a buffet breakfast. You can often get lunch or dinner for roughly an extra €10 to €15.

Many hostels also offer singles and doubles. Prices can vary greatly between destinations; for instance, a double in high-season will cost around €80 in Naples and €145 in more exclusive Positano. Some hostels also offer family rooms or self-catering apartments. Keep in mind that some hostels have a curfew of 11pm or midnight.

A growing contingent of independent hostels offers alternatives to HI hostels. Many are barely distinguishable from budget hotels. One of many hostel websites is www.hostelworld.com.

Hotels & Pensioni

While the difference between an *albergo* (hotel) and a *pensione* (guesthouse) is often minimal, the latter will generally be of one- to three-star quality while a hotel can be awarded up to five stars. *Locande* (inns) long fell into much the same category as *pensioni*, but the term has become a trendy one in some parts and reveals little about the quality of a place. *Affittacamere* are rooms for rent in private houses. They are generally simple affairs.

Quality can vary enormously and the official star system gives limited clues. One-star hotels/*pensioni* tend to be basic and usually do not offer private bathrooms. Two-star places are similar but rooms will generally have a private bathroom. Three-star options usually offer reasonable standards. Four- and five-star hotels offer facilities such as room service, laundry and dry-cleaning.

Prices are highest in major tourist destinations. A *camera singola* (single room) costs from around €35. A *camera doppia* (twin beds) or *camera matrimoniale* (double room

SLEEPING PRICE RANGES

The following price ranges refer to a double room with bathroom (breakfast included) in high season.

€ less than €110

€€ €110–200

€€€ more than €200

with a double bed) will cost from around €60.

Tourist offices usually have booklets with local accommodation listings. Many hotels are also signing up with (steadily proliferating) online accommodation-booking services. You could start your search on any of the following:

In Italia (www.initalia.it)

Great Small Hotels (www.greatsmallhotels.com/italy)

Secret Places (www.secretplaces.com/italy/guide)

Discount Cards

Free admission to many galleries and cultural sites is available to youth under 18 and seniors over 65 years old; in addition, visitors aged between 18 and 25 often qualify for a discount. In some cases, these discounts only apply to EU citizens.

If travelling to Naples and Campania, consider buying a Campania Artecard (www.campaniaartecard.it), which offers free public transport and free or reduced admission to many museums and archaeological sites.

Electricity

**Type L
220V/50Hz**

**Type F
230V/50Hz**

Electricity in Italy conforms to the European standard of 220V to 230V, with a frequency of 50Hz. Wall outlets typically accommodate plugs with two or three round pins (the latter grounded, the former not).

Embassies & Consulates

Australian Embassy (☐06 85 27 21, emergencies 800 877790; www.italy.embassy.gov.au; Via Antonio Bosio 5; ⊙9am-5pm Mon-Fri; ☐Via Nomentana)

Canadian Embassy (☐06 8 5444 2911; www.canadainternational.gc.ca/italy-italie; Via Zara 30; ⊙9am-noon Mon-Fri; ☐Via Nomentana)

French Embassy (☐06 68 6011; www.ambafrance-it.org; Piazza Farnese 67)

French Consulate (☐081 598 07 11; https://it.ambafrance.org/-Consulat-de-Naples; Via Francesco Crispi 86, Naples; ⓂAmedeo)

German Embassy (☐06 49 21 31; www.rom.diplo.de; Via San Martino della Battaglia 4, Rome)

German Honorary Consulate (☐081 248 85 11; www.neapel.diplo.de; Via Medina 40, Naples; ⓂMunicipio)

Irish Embassy (☐06 585 23 81; www.ambasciata-irlanda.it; Via Giacomo Medici 1, Villa Spada)

Netherlands Embassy (☐06 3228 6001; www.olanda.it; Via Michele Mercati 8; ⊙9am-noon Mon-Wed & Fri, 10am-noon & 2-4pm Thu; ☐Via Ulisse Aldrovandi)

New Zealand Embassy (☐06 853 75 01; www.mfat.govt.nz/en/countries-and-regions/europe/italy/new-zealand-embassy; Via Clitunno 44; ⊙8.30am-12.30pm & 1.30-5pm Mon-Fri; ☐Corso Trieste)

UK Embassy (☐06 4220 0001; www.ukinitaly.fco.gov.uk; Via XX Settembre 80a, Rome)

US Embassy (☐06 4 67 41; www.italy.usembassy.gov; Via Vittorio Veneto 121, Rome)

US Consulate (☐081 583 81 11; https://it.usembassy.gov/embassy-consulates/naples; Piazza della Repubblica 2, Naples; ⓂMergellina)

LGBT Travellers

Homosexuality is legal (over the age of 16) and attitudes towards LGBT people in southern Italy have generally improved in recent years. That said, the region is notably conservative in its attitudes. Overt displays of affection by LGBT couples can attract a negative response, especially in smaller, less cosmopolitan towns and among older generations.

You'll find gay scenes in Naples, Catania and Taormina (the latter mostly in the summer), and to a lesser extent in Palermo and Bari.

Online resources include the following (mostly Italian-language) websites:

Arcigay (www.arcigay.it) Bologna-based national organisation for the LGBT community.

Circolo Mario Mieli (www.mariomieli.org) Rome-based cultural centre that organises debates, cultural events and social functions, including Gay Pride.

Coordinamento Lesbiche Italiano (CLR.; www.clrbp.it) The national organisation for lesbians, holding regular conferences, literary evenings and other cultural special events.

Gay.it (www.gay.it) Website featuring LGBT news, feature articles and gossip.

GayFriendlyItaly.com (www. gayfriendlyitaly.com) English-language site produced by Gay. it, featuring information on everything from hotels and events, to LGBT rights.

Pride (www.prideonline.it) Culture, politics, travel and health with an LGBT focus.

Health

Italy has a public health system that is legally bound to provide emergency care to everyone. EU nationals are entitled to reduced-cost, sometimes free, medical care with a European Health Insurance Card (EHIC), available from your home health authority; non-EU citizens should take out medical insurance.

If you do need health insurance, make sure you get a policy that covers you for the worst possible scenario, such as an accident requiring an emergency flight home. Find out in advance if your insurance plan will make payments directly to providers or reimburse you later for overseas health expenditures.

It's also worth finding out if there is a reciprocal arrangement between your country and Italy. If so, you may be covered for essential medical treatment and some subsidised medications while in Italy. Australia, for instance, has such an agreement; carry your Medicare card.

Availability & Cost of Health Care

Health care is readily available throughout Italy, but standards can vary significantly. Public hospitals tend to be less impressive the further south you travel. A pharmacist (*farmacista*) can give you valuable advice and sell over-the-counter medication

for minor illnesses. Pharmacies generally keep the same hours as other shops, closing at night and on Sundays. A handful, however, remain open on a rotation basis (*farmacie di turno*) for emergency purposes. These are usually listed in newspapers. Closed pharmacies display a list of the nearest ones open.

Pharmacies can also advise you when more-specialised help is required and point you in the right direction. In major cities you are likely to find English-speaking doctors or a translator service available. You can ask about the doctor's fee when making an appointment. The fee is usually payable at the end of your consultation. Always ask for a receipt as you will need to show this to your travel insurance provider if making a claim for reimbursement. Depending on your travel insurance policy, all or a part of the cost will be reimbursed.

If you need an ambulance anywhere in Italy, call ☑118. For emergency treatment, head straight to the *pronto soccorso* (casualty) section of a public hospital, where you can also get emergency dental treatment.

Environmental Hazards

Italian beaches are occasionally inundated with jellyfish. Their stings are painful, but not dangerous. Dousing them in vinegar will deactivate any stingers that have not fired. Calamine lotion, antihistamines and analgesics may reduce the reaction and relieve pain.

Italy's only dangerous snake, the viper, is found

throughout Puglia and Basilicata. To minimise the possibility of being bitten, always wear boots, socks and long trousers when walking through undergrowth where snakes may be present. Don't put your hands into holes and crevices, and be careful when collecting firewood. Viper bites do not cause instantaneous death and an antivenin is widely available in pharmacies. Keep the victim calm and still, wrap the bitten limb tightly, as you would for a sprained ankle, and attach a splint to immobilise it.

Always check all over your body if you have been walking through a potentially tick-infested area. Ticks can cause skin infections and other more serious complications such as Lyme disease and tick-borne encephalitis. If a tick is found attached, press down around the tick's head with tweezers, grab the head and gently pull upwards. Avoid pulling the rear of the body as this may squeeze the tick's gut contents through the attached mouth into the skin, increasing the risk of infection and disease. Lyme disease begins with the spreading of a bull's-eye rash at the site of the bite, accompanied by fever, headache, extreme fatigue, aching joints and muscles, and severe neck stiffness. If untreated, symptoms usually disappear, but disorders of the nervous system, heart and joints can develop later. Treatment works best early in the illness: medical help should be sought. Symptoms of tick-borne encephalitis include blotches around the bite, which is sometimes pale in the middle, and headaches,

---

EATING PRICE RANGES

The following price ranges refer to a meal of two courses, a glass of house wine and *coperto* (cover charge) for one person.

€ under €25

€€ €25-45

€€€ over €45

stiffness and other flu-like symptoms (as well as extreme tiredness) appearing a week or two after the bite. Again, medical help must be sought.

Leishmaniasis is a group of parasitic diseases transmitted by sandflies and found in coastal parts of Puglia. Cutaneous leishmaniasis affects the skin and causes ulceration and disfigurement; visceral leishmaniasis affects the internal organs. Avoiding sandfly bites by covering up and using repellent is the best precaution.

Insurance

A travel-insurance policy to cover theft, loss and medical problems is a very good idea. It may also cover you for cancellation or delays to your travel arrangements. Paying for your ticket with a credit card can often provide limited travel accident insurance and you may be able to reclaim the payment if the operator doesn't deliver. Ask your credit-card company what it will cover.

Worldwide travel insurance is available at www.lonelyplanet.com/travel-insurance. You can buy, extend and claim online anytime – even if you're already on the road.

Internet Access

➡ Several cities and towns offer public wi-fi hotspots, though to use them you will generally need to register online using a credit card or an Italian mobile number. An easier option (no need for a local mobile number) is to head to a cafe or bar offering free wi-fi.

➡ Most hotels, B&Bs, hostels and agriturismi offer free wi-fi to guests, though signals can vary in quality. There will usually be at least one fixed computer for guest use.

Language Courses

Italian language courses are run by private schools and universities throughout Italy. For a list of language schools around the country, see Saena Iulia (www.saenaiulia.it); click on 'Schools in Italy'.

Italian Foreign Ministry (www.esteri.it) Publishes a list on its website of the 83 worldwide branches of the Istituto Italiano di Cultura (IIC), a government-sponsored organisation promoting Italian culture and language. An excellent resource for studying Italian before you leave or finding out more about language learning opportunities in Italy. Locations include Australia (Melbourne and Sydney), the UK (London and Edinburgh), Ireland (Dublin), Canada (Toronto and Montreal), and the USA (Los Angeles, San Francisco, Chicago, New York and Washington, DC). Click on 'Foreign Policy', then 'Culture Diplomacy' and 'The Network of Italian Cultural Institutes'.

Legal Matters

Southern Italy is relatively safe and the average tourist will only have a brush with the law if robbed by a bag-snatcher or pickpocket.

Drugs & Alcohol

➡ If you're caught with what the police deem to be a dealable quantity of hard or soft drugs, you risk prison sentences of between two and 20 years.

➡ Possession for personal use is punishable by administrative sanctions, although first-time offenders might get away with a warning.

➡ The legal limit for blood-alcohol when driving is 0.05% and random breath tests do occur.

Police

The Italian police is divided into three main bodies: the polizia, who wear navy-blue jackets; the carabinieri, in a black uniform with a red stripe; and the grey-clad guardia di finanza (fiscal police), responsible for fighting tax evasion and drug smuggling. If you run into trouble, you're most likely to end up dealing with the polizia or carabinieri.

To contact the police in an emergency, dial 🔲112 or 🔲113.

Polizia statale (state police)	Thefts, visa extensions and permits
Carabinieri (military police)	General crime, public order and drug enforcement
Vigili urbani (local traffic police)	Parking tickets, towed cars
Guardia di finanza	Tax evasion, drug smuggling
Corpo forestale	Environmental protection

Your Rights

➡ You should be given verbal and written notice of the charges laid against you within 24 hours by arresting officers.

➡ You have no right to a phone call upon arrest, though the police will inform your family with your consent. You may also ask the police to inform your embassy or consulate.

➡ The prosecutor must apply to a magistrate for you to be held in preventive custody awaiting trial (depending on the seriousness of the offence) within 48 hours of arrest.

➡ You also have the right to a lawyer. If you do not know of any local lawyers, the police should ask the local bar council for a state-appointed lawyer (difensore di ufficio) to be appointed.

➡ You have the right not to respond to questions without the presence of a lawyer. If the magistrate orders preventive custody, you have the right to then contest this within the following 10 days.

Maps

The city maps provided by Lonely Planet, combined with the good, free local maps available at most Italian tourist offices, will be sufficient for many travellers. For more specialised maps, browse the good selection at national bookshop chain Feltrinelli (www.lafeltrinelli.it), or consult the websites listed here.

Touring Club Italiano (www. touringclub.com) Italy's largest map publisher offers a comprehensive 1:200,000, 592-page road atlas of Italy (€54.90), as well as 1:400,000 maps of northern, central and southern Italy (€8.50). It also produces 15 regional maps at 1:200,000 (€8.50), as well as a series of walking guides with maps (€14.90).

Stanfords (www.stanfords. co.uk) Excellent UK-based shop that stocks many useful maps, including cycling maps.

Money

Currency

Italy's currency is the euro. The seven euro notes come in denominations of €500, €200, €100, €50, €20, €10 and €5. The eight euro coins are in denominations of €2 and €1, and 50, 20, 10, five, two and one cents.

ATMs

➡ ATMs (known as 'Bancomat' in Italy) are widely available throughout the country and most will accept cards tied into the Visa, MasterCard, Cirrus and Maestro systems.

➡ Beware of transaction fees. Every time you withdraw cash, you'll be hit by charges – typically your home bank will charge a foreign exchange fee (usually around 1%) as well as a transaction fee of around 1% to 3%. Fees can sometimes be reduced by withdrawing cash from banks affiliated with your home banking institution; check with your bank.

➡ If an ATM rejects your card, try another one before assuming the problem is with your card.

➡ If your card is lost, stolen or swallowed by an ATM, you can telephone to have an immediate stop put on its use:

American Express (AMEX) (Amex; ☑06 7290 0347)

Diners Club (☑800 393939)

MasterCard (☑800 870866)

Visa (☑800 819014)

Credit Cards

Major cards such as Visa, MasterCard, Eurocard, Cirrus and Eurocheques are widely accepted. Amex is also recognised, although it's less common than Visa or MasterCard.

Changing Money

➡ You can change money in banks, at post offices or in a *cambio* (exchange office). Post offices and banks tend to offer the best rates; exchange offices keep longer hours, but watch for high commissions and inferior rates.

➡ Take your passport or photo ID when exchanging money.

Taxes & Refunds

A 22% value-added tax known as IVA (Imposta sul Valore Aggiunta) is included in the price of most goods and services. Tax-free shopping is available at some shops.

Non-EU residents who spend more than €155 at one shop at a single time can claim a refund when leaving the EU. The refund only applies to purchases from stores that display a 'Tax Free' sign. When making the purchase, ask for a tax-refund voucher, to be filled in with the date of the purchase and its value. When leaving the EU, get this voucher stamped at customs and take it to the nearest tax-refund counter where you'll get an immediate refund, either in cash or charged to your credit card. For more information, see www.tax refund.it.

Opening Hours

Opening hours vary throughout the year. We've provided high-season opening hours; hours will generally decrease in the shoulder and low seasons. 'Summer' times generally refer to the period from April to September or October, while 'winter' times generally run from October or November to March.

Post

Poste Italiane (☑803 160; www.poste.it), Italy's postal system, is reasonably reliable, though parcels do occasionally go missing. *Francobolli* (stamps) are available at post offices and authorised tobacconists (look for the big white-on-black 'T' sign). Since letters often need to be weighed, what you get at the tobacconist for international airmail will occasionally be an approximation of the proper rate. Tobacconists keep regular shop hours.

Postal Rates & Services

The cost of sending a letter by *aerea* (airmail) depends on its weight, size and where it is being sent. Most people use *posta prioritaria* (priority mail), Italy's most efficient mail service, guaranteed to deliver letters sent to Europe within three working days and to the rest of the world within four to nine working days.

Using *posta prioritaria*, mail up to 50g costs €3.50 within Europe, €4.50 to Africa, Asia and the Americas, and €5.50 to Australia and New Zealand. Mail weighing 51g to 100g costs €4.30 within Europe, €5.20 to Africa, Asia and the Americas, and €7.10 to Australia and New Zealand.

Public Holidays

Most Italians take their annual holiday in August, with the busiest period occurring

GOVERNMENT TRAVEL ADVICE

The following government websites offer up-to-date travel advisories.

Australian Department of Foreign Affairs & Trade (www.smartraveller.gov.au)

British Foreign & Commonwealth Office (www.gov.uk/foreign-travel-advice)

Global Affairs Canada (travel.gc.ca/travelling/health-safety)

New Zealand Ministry of Foreign Affairs & Trade (www.safetravel.govt.nz)

US Department of State (travel.state.gov)

around August 15, known locally as Ferragosto. This means that many businesses and shops close for at least a part of that month. It also means that southern Italy's islands and coastal resorts become incredibly lively (and crowded). Settimana Santa (Easter Holy Week) is another busy holiday period for Italians.

National public holidays:

New Year's Day (Capodanno) 1 January

Epiphany (Epifania) 6 January

Easter Monday (Pasquetta) March/April

Liberation Day (Giorno della Liberazione) 25 April

Labour Day (Festa del Lavoro) 1 May

Republic Day (Festa della Repubblica) 2 June

Feast of the Assumption (Ferragosto) 15 August

All Saints' Day (Ognissanti) 1 November

Feast of the Immaculate Conception (Immaculata Concezione) 8 December

Christmas Day (Natale) 25 December

Boxing Day (Festa di Santo Stefano) 26 December

Safe Travel

Despite mafia notoriety, southern Italy is not a dangerous place and the biggest threat you face is from faceless pickpockets and bag-snatchers. The following tips will help ensure a safe and happy stay:

➡ Leave valuables in your hotel room and never leave them in your car.

➡ If carrying a bag or camera, wear the strap across your body and away from the road – moped thieves can swipe a bag and be gone in seconds.

➡ Be vigilant for pickpockets in crowded areas, including at train stations and ferry terminals, on buses and in markets (especially those in Naples, Palermo and Catania).

➡ Never buy electronics, including mobile phones, from market vendors – one common scam sees the boxes filled with bricks.

➡ Always report thefts to the police within 24 hours, and ask for a statement, otherwise your travel insurance company won't pay out.

Telephone
Directory Enquiries

National and international phone numbers can be requested at ☎1254 (or online at 1254.virgilio.it).

Domestic Calls

➡ Italian telephone area codes all begin with ☎0 and consist of up to four digits. The area code is followed by anything from four to eight digits. Area codes are an integral part of all Italian phone numbers and must be dialled even when calling locally.

➡ Mobile-phone numbers begin with a three-digit prefix starting with a ☎3.

➡ Toll-free (free-phone) numbers are known as numeri verdi and usually start with ☎800.

➡ Nongeographical numbers start with ☎840, ☎841, ☎848, ☎892, ☎899, ☎163, ☎166 or ☎199.

➡ Some six-digit national rate numbers are also in use (such as those for Alitalia and Trenitalia).

International Calls

➡ To call Italy from abroad, call your international access number, then Italy's country code (☎39) and then the area code of the location you want, including the leading ☎0.

➡ Avoid making international calls from a hotel, as rates are high.

➡ The cheapest options are free or low-cost apps such as Skype and Viber, connecting by using the wi-fi at your accommodation or at a cafe or other venue offering free wi-fi.

➡ Another cheap option is to use an international calling card. Note, however, that the number of public payphones are shrinking, so consider a pre-paid card that allows you to call from any phone. Cards are available at newsstands and tobacconists.

➡ To call abroad from Italy dial ☎00, then the country and area codes, followed by the telephone number. To make a reverse-charge (collect) international call from a public telephone, dial ☎170. All phone operators speak English.

Mobile Phones

➡ Italian mobile phones operate on the GSM 900/1800 network, which is compatible with the rest of Europe and Australia but not always with the North American GSM or CDMA systems – check with your service provider.

➡ The cheapest way of using your mobile is to buy a prepaid (*prepagato*) Italian SIM card. TIM (www.tim.it), Wind (www.wind.it), Vodafone (www.vodafone.it) and Tre (www.tre.it) all offer SIM cards and have retail outlets in most Italian cities and towns. All SIM cards must be registered in Italy, so make sure you have a passport or ID card with you when you buy one.

➡ You can easily top up your Italian SIM with a recharge card (*ricarica*), available from most tobacconists, some bars, supermarkets and banks.

Payphones & Phonecards

Although public payphones still exist across southern Italy, their numbers continue to fall. Those that are still available take telephone cards (*schede telefoniche*), available from tobacconists and newsstands.

Time

➡ All of Italy occupies the Central European Time Zone, which is one hour ahead of GMT. When it is noon in London, it is 1pm in Italy.

➡ Daylight-saving time (when clocks move forward one hour) starts on the last Sunday in March and ends on the last Sunday in October.

➡ Italy operates on a 24-hour clock, so 3pm is written as 15:00.

Toilets

Beyond museums, galleries, department stores and train stations, there are few public toilets in southern Italy. If you're caught short, the best thing to do is to nip into a cafe or bar. The polite thing to do is to order something at the bar. You may need to pay to use public toilets at some venues (usually €0.50 to €1).

Tourist Information

The quality of tourist offices varies dramatically. One office might have enthusiastic staff, another might be indifferent. Most offices offer at least a few brochures, maps and leaflets, even if they're uninterested in helping in any other way. Outside major cities and international tourist areas, it's fairly unusual for the staff to speak English.

Four tiers of tourist office exist: local, provincial, regional and national.

Local & Provincial Tourist Offices

Despite their different names, provincial and local offices offer similar services. All deal directly with the public and most will respond to written and telephone requests for information. Staff can usually provide a city map, lists of hotels and information on the major sights. In larger towns and major tourist areas, English is generally spoken.

Main offices are generally open Monday to Friday; some also open on weekends, especially in urban areas or during peak summer season. Affiliated information booths (at train stations and airports, for example) may keep slightly different hours.

Regional Tourist Authorities

Regional offices are generally more concerned with planning, budgeting, marketing and promotion than with offering a public information service. However, they still maintain some useful websites. In some cases you'll need to look for the Tourism or Turismo link within the regional site. There is currently no official tourism website for the Campania region.

Basilicata (www.aptbasilicata.it)

Calabria (www.turiscalabria.it)

Puglia (www.viaggiareinpuglia.it)

Sicily (www.regione.sicilia.it/turismo)

Tourist Offices Abroad

The Italian National Tourist Office (www.enit.it) maintains offices in 22 cities on five continents. Contact information for all offices can be found on its website.

Travellers with Disabilities

Italy is not an easy country for travellers with disabilities and getting around can be a problem for wheelchair users. Even a short journey in a city or town can become a major expedition if cobblestone streets have to be negotiated. Although many buildings have lifts, they are not always wide enough for wheelchairs. Not an awful lot has been done to make life for the hearing/vision impaired easier.

The Italian National Tourist Office in your country may be able to provide advice on Italian associations for travellers with disabilities and information on what help is available.

If travelling by train, ring the national helpline 199 303060 to arrange assistance (6.45am to 9.30pm daily). Airline companies should be able to arrange assistance at airports if you notify them of your needs in advance. Alternatively, contact ADR Assistance (www.adrassistance.it) for assistance at Fiumicino or Ciampino airports. Some taxis are equipped to carry passengers in wheelchairs; ask for a taxi for a *sedia a rotelle* (wheelchair).

Italy's official tourism website (www.italia.it) offers a number of links for travellers with disabilities.

Accessible Italy (www.accessibleitaly.com) A San Marino–based company that specialises in holiday services for people with disabilities. This is the best first port of call.

Sage Traveling (www.sagetraveling.com) A US-based agency offering advice and tailor-made tours to assist mobility-impaired travellers in Europe.

Visas

➡ Italy is a signatory of the Schengen Convention, an agreement whereby participating countries abolished customs checks at common borders. EU citizens do not need a Schengen tourist visa to enter Italy. Nationals of some other countries, including Australia, Canada, Israel, Japan, New Zealand, Switzerland and the USA, do not need a tourist visa for stays of up to 90 days. To check the visa requirements for your country, see www.schengenvisainfo.com/tourist-schengen-visa.

➡ All non-EU and non-Schengen nationals entering Italy for more than 90 days or for any reason other than tourism (such as study or work) may need a specific visa. See vistoperitalia.esteri.it or contact an Italian consulate for details.

➡ Ensure your passport is valid for at least six months beyond your departure date from Italy.

Volunteering

Concordia International Volunteer Projects (www.concordiavolunteers.org.uk) Short-term community-based projects covering the environment, archaeology and the arts.

European Youth Portal (http://europa.eu/youth) Has various links suggesting volunteering options across Europe. Navigate to the Volunteering page.

Legambiente (http://internazional.legambiente.it) Offers numerous environmentally focused volunteering opportunities.

World Wide Opportunities on Organic Farms (www.wwoof.

it) For a membership fee of €35 this organisation provides a list of farms looking for volunteer workers.

Women Travellers

➡ Generally speaking, southern Italy is not a dangerous region for women to travel in. That said, in some parts of the country, solo women travellers may be subjected to a high level of unwanted attention.

➡ Eye-to-eye contact is the norm in Italy's daily flirtatious interplay. Eye contact can become outright staring the further south you travel. If ignoring unwanted male attention doesn't work, politely tell your interlocutor that you're waiting for your *marito* (husband) or *fidanzato* (boyfriend) and, if necessary, walk away.

➡ If you feel yourself being groped on a crowded bus or metro, a loud '*che schifo!*' (how disgusting!) will draw attention to the incident. Otherwise take all the usual precautions you would in any other part of the world; avoid wandering around alone late at night, especially in parks and desolate urban areas.

➡ You can report incidents to the police, who are required to press charges.

Work

Citizens of the European Union (EU), Norway, Iceland, Switzerland and Liechtenstein are legally entitled to work in Italy. Those wanting to stay in the country for more than three months are simply required to register with the local *anagrafe* (Register Office) in their Italian municipality of residence.

Working longer-term in Italy is trickier if you are a non-EU citizen. Firstly, you will need to secure a job offer. Your prospective employer will then need to complete most of the work visa application process on your behalf. If your

application is successful, your employer will be given your work authorisation. Your local Italian embassy or consulate will then be informed and should be able to provide you with an entry visa within 30 days. It's worth noting that Italy operates a visa quota system for most occupations, meaning that you will only be offered a visa if the relevant quota has not been met by the time your application is processed. Non-EU citizens planning to stay in Italy for more than 90 days must also apply for a *permesso di soggiorno* (permit to stay) within eight working days of their entry into Italy. Applications for the permit should be made at their nearest *questura* (police station). General information on the permit is available on the Italian State Police website (www.poliziadistato.it).

Italy does have reciprocal, short-term working-holiday agreements with a handful of countries, including Canada, Australia and New Zealand. These visas are generally limited to young adults aged between 18 and 30 or 35 and allow the visa holder to work a limited number of months over a set period of time. Contact your local Italian embassy (www.esteri.it) for more information.

Popular jobs for those permitted to work in Italy include teaching English, either through a language school or as a private freelancer. While some language schools do take on teachers without professional language qualifications, the more reputable (and better-paying) establishments will require you to have a TEFL (Teaching of English as a Foreign Language) certificate. Useful job-seeker websites for English-language teachers include ESL Employment (www.eslemployment.com) and TEFL (www.tefl.org.uk/tefl-jobs-centre). Au pairing is another popular work option; click onto www.aupairworld.com for more information on work opportunities and tips.

29

Transport

GETTING THERE & AWAY

A plethora of airlines link Italy with the rest of the world, and cut-rate carriers have significantly driven down the cost of flights from other European countries. Excellent rail and bus connections, especially with northern Italy, offer efficient overland transport, while car and passenger ferries operate to ports throughout the Mediterranean.

Flights, tours and rental cars can be booked online at www.lonelyplanet.com/bookings.

Entering Italy

Entering Italy from most other parts of the EU is generally uncomplicated, with no border checkpoints and no customs thanks to the Schengen Agreement. Document and customs checks remain standard if arriving from (or departing to) a non-Schengen country.

Passport

➜ European Union and Swiss citizens can travel to Italy with their national identity card alone. All other nationalities must have a valid passport and may be required to fill out a landing card (at airports).

➜ By law you are supposed to have your passport or ID card with you at all times. You'll need one of these documents for police registration every time you check into a hotel.

Air

Italy's main intercontinental gateways are Rome's **Leonardo da Vinci Airport** (Fiumicino; ☎06 6 59 51; www.adr.it/fiumicino) and Milan's **Aeroporto Malpensa** (MXP; ☎02 23 23 23; www.milanomalpensa-airport.com; ⊠Malpensa Express). Both are served by non-stop flights from around the world. Venice's **Marco Polo Airport** (☎flight information 041 260 92 60; www.veniceairport.it; Via Galileo Gallilei 30/1, Tessera) is also served by a handful of intercontinental flights.

Most direct flights into southern Italy are domestic or intra-European, so you may need to change at Rome, Milan or Venice if arriving from outside Europe.

Handy airports in southern Italy include:

Naples International Airport (Capodichino), Naples (www.aeroportodinapoli.it) Connections include London (Gatwick, Stansted and Luton), Paris (Charles de Gaulle and Orly), Basel, Geneva, Berlin (Schönefeld), Frankfurt, Munich, Brussels, Amsterdam, Madrid, Barcelona, Bucharest, Warsaw (Modlin) and Athens. Seasonal connections include Copenhagen, Helsinki and New York (JFK). Airlines include Alitalia, British Airways, Lufthansa, easyJet, Ryanair and Wizzair.

Karol Wojtyła Airport, Bari (www.aeroportidipuglia.it) Flights include London (Gatwick and Stansted), Liverpool, Berlin (Schönefeld), Cologne, Stuttgart, Munich, Barcelona, Prague, Bucharest, Budapest, Katowice, Riga, Sofia and Istanbul. Seasonal routes include Birmingham, Dublin, Frankfurt, Vienna and Athens. Airlines include Alitalia, British Airways, Turkish Airways, Ryanair, easyJet, Germanwings and Wizzair.

Brindisi-Salento Airport (www.aeroportidipuglia.it) Destinations include London (Stansted), Manchester, Basel, Geneva, Frankfurt and Vienna. Seasonal destinations include London (Heathrow and Gatwick), Paris (Orly), Brussels and Barcelona. Airlines include Alitalia, British Airways, easyJet, Eurowings, Germanwings, Ryanair and Vueling.

Lamezia Terme Airport, Cosenza (www.sacal.it) Destinations include London (Stansted), Hamburg, Bucharest and Budapest, with seasonal routes including Zurich, Munich, Vienna, Brussels, Stockholm, Malmö, Tel Aviv and Toronto. Airlines include Alitalia, Ryanair, Germanwings and Wizzair.

Falcone-Borsellino Airport, Palermo (www.gesap.it) European connections include London (Heathrow, Gatwick and Stansted), Paris (Beauvais), Marseilles, Madrid, Berlin

(Schönefeld), Bucharest, Budapest, Malta and Tunis. Seasonal routes include Paris (Charles de Gaulle and Orly), Vienna, Frankfurt, Amsterdam, Brussels, Stockholm and New York (JFK). Airlines include Alitalia, Ryanair, easyJet, Air Malta, Austrian Airlines and Norwegian Air Shuttle.

Fontanarossa Airport, Catania (www.aeroporto.catania.it) Destinations include London (Gatwick and Luton), Manchester, Paris (Charles de Gaulle and Orly), Basel, Geneva, Zurich, Cologne, Berlin (Schönefeld), Amsterdam, Madrid, Barcelona, Bucharest, Budapest and Istanbul. Seasonal routes include Manchester, Birmingham, Marseilles, Munich, Copenhagen, Oslo, Helsinki and Casablanca. Airlines include Alitalia, Air Berlin, Air Malta, KLM, Lufthansa, easyJet, Germanwings and Turkish Airways.

Vincenzo Florio Airport, Trapani (www.airgest.it) Ryanair operates direct flights to a handful of European destinations, including Paris (Beauvais) and Prague. Seasonal destinations include Eindhoven, Girona, Kraków, Warsaw (Modlin) and Malta.

Tickets & Discounts

The internet is the easiest way of locating and booking reasonably priced seats.

Full-time students and those aged under 26 may qualify for discounted fares at agencies such as STA Travel (www.statravel.com). Many of these fares require a valid International Student Identity Card (ISIC).

Land

Reaching southern Italy overland involves travelling the entire length of Italy, which can either be an enormous drain on your time or, if you have plenty to spare, a wonderful way of seeing the country. Buses are usually the cheapest option, but services are less frequent and considerably less comfortable than the train.

Border Crossings

Aside from the coast roads linking Italy with France and Slovenia, border crossings into Italy mostly involve tunnels through the Alps (open year-round) or mountain passes (seasonally closed or requiring snow chains). The list below outlines the major points of entry.

Austria From Innsbruck to Bolzano via A22/E45 (Brenner Pass); Villach to Tarvisio via A23/E55.

France From Nice to Ventimiglia via A10/E80; Modane to Turin via A32/E70 (Fréjus Tunnel); Chamonix to Courmayeur via A5/E25 (Mont Blanc Tunnel).

Slovenia From Sežana to Trieste via SR58/E70.

Switzerland From Martigny to Aosta via SS27/E27 (Grand St Bernard Tunnel); Lugano to Como via A9/E35.

Bus

Buses are the cheapest overland option to Italy, but services are less frequent, less comfortable and significantly slower than the train. Useful companies include:

Eurolines (☏0861 199 19 00; www.eurolines.it) A consortium of coach companies with offices throughout Europe. Italy-bound buses head to Milan, Venice, Florence and Rome, from where Italian train and bus services continue south.

FlixBus (www.flixbus.com) German-owned company offering both interregional and international routes. Interregional services reach numerous cities and towns in southern Italy, including Naples, Matera, Bari, Brindisi, Alberobello, Potenza and Palermo.

Marozzi (☏080 579 02 11; www.marozzivt.it) Regular connections from Rome to Sorrento and the Amalfi Coast, and from Rome to numerous towns and cities in Puglia, including Bari, Alberobello, Taranto, Gallipoli and Otranto.

Autolinee Miccolis (☏099 470 44 51; www.miccolis-spa.it) Runs daily services from Naples to Bari via Pompeii, Salerno, Potenza and Matera. It also runs from Naples to Taranto, Brindisi and Lecce via Potenza.

Marino (www.marinobus.it) Runs daily services from Naples to Bari, Brindisi, Matera, Lecce and Gallipoli.

Liscio (☏097 15 46 73; www.autolineeliscio.it) Daily connections from Potenza to Rome. Also runs daily between Rome and Matera.

Lirosi (☏0966 5 79 01; www.lirosiautoservizi.com) Daily services between Reggio di Calabria and Rome.

CLIMATE CHANGE & TRAVEL

Every form of transport that relies on carbon-based fuel generates CO_2, the main cause of human-induced climate change. Modern travel is dependent on aeroplanes, which might use less fuel per kilometre per person than most cars but travel much greater distances. The altitude at which aircraft emit gases (including CO_2) and particles also contributes to their climate change impact. Many websites offer 'carbon calculators' that allow people to estimate the carbon emissions generated by their journey and, for those who wish to do so, to offset the impact of the greenhouse gases emitted with contributions to portfolios of climate-friendly initiatives throughout the world. Lonely Planet offsets the carbon footprint of all staff and author travel.

Train Routes

Train Journey Durations:
Naples–Sorrento (1hr 8min)
Naples–Bari (4hr)
Naples–Palermo (9hr 15min)
Bari–Brindisi (1hr)
Bari–Lecce (1hr 30min)
Reggio di Calabria–Catania (4hr)

Principal Train Lines
Local Train Lines
Private Train Lines

SAIS Autolinee (☎800 211020, 0935 52 41 11; www.saisauto linee.it) Operates long-haul services to Sicily from numerous centres, including Rome, Naples and Bari.

Car & Motorcycle
FROM CONTINENTAL EUROPE

➡ Every vehicle travelling across an international border should display a nationality plate of its country of registration. Always carry proof of vehicle ownership and evidence of third-party insurance. If driving an EU-registered vehicle, your home country insurance is sufficient. Ask your insurer for a European Accident Statement (EAS) form, which can simplify

matters in the event of an accident. The form can also be downloaded online at http://cartraveldocs. com/european-accident-statement.

➡ A European breakdown assistance policy is a good investment and can be obtained through the **Automobile Club d'Italia** (ACI; ☎803116, from a foreign mobile 800 116800; www.aci.it).

➡ Italy's scenic roads are tailor-made for motorcycle touring, and motorcyclists swarm into the country every summer. With a motorcycle you rarely have to book ahead for ferries and can enter restricted-traffic areas in cities. Crash helmets and a motorcycle licence are compulsory.

➡ The US-based Beach's Motorcycle Adventures (www.bmca.com) offers a number of two-week tours from April to October, with destinations including Sicily. For campervan and motorhome hire, check IdeaMerge (www.ideamerge. com).

FROM THE UK

You can take your car to Italy, via France, by ferry or via the Eurotunnel Shuttle rail service (www.eurotunnel. com). The latter runs up to four times per hour between Folkestone and Calais (35 minutes) in peak times.

For breakdown assistance, both the AA (www.theaa. com) and the RAC (www.rac. co.uk) offer comprehensive cover in Europe.

Train

Regular trains on two western lines connect Italy with France (one along the coast and the other from Turin into the French Alps). Trains from Milan head north into Switzerland and on towards the Benelux countries. Further east, two main lines head for the main cities in Central and Eastern Europe. Those crossing the Brenner Pass go to Innsbruck, Stuttgart and Munich. Those crossing at Tarvisio proceed to Vienna, Salzburg and Prague. The main international train line to Slovenia crosses near Trieste.

FROM CONTINENTAL EUROPE

➡ The comprehensive European Rail Timetable (UK£16.99, digital version UK£11.99), updated monthly, is available for purchase online at www.europeanrailtimetable.co.uk, as well as at a handful of bookshops in the UK and continental Europe (see the website for details).

➡ Reservations on international trains to/from Italy are always advisable, and sometimes compulsory.

➡ Some international services include transport for private cars. Consider taking long journeys overnight, as the supplemental fare for a sleeper costs substantially less than Italian hotels.

➡ Within Italy, direct trains run from Milan, Florence and Rome to Naples, Reggio di Calabria and Messina (Sicily). Trains to Sicily are transported from the mainland by ferry from Villa San Giovanni, just north of Reggio di Calabria. From Messina, services continue on to Palermo, Catania and other provincial Sicilian capitals.

➡ From both Rome and Milan, high-velocity Freccia trains run to Naples and Salerno. Those travelling from Venice will usually need to change trains in Bologna. Trains to Puglia and Basilicata usually require at least one change along Italy's main north–south route.

FROM THE UK

➡ High-velocity passenger train Eurostar (www.eurostar.com) connects London to Lille and Brussels, as well as to Paris, Lyon, Avignon and Marseille. Alternatively, you can get a train ticket that includes crossing the Channel by ferry.

➡ For the latest fare information on journeys to Italy, contact International Rail (www.internationalrail.com).

Sea

➡ Numerous ferry companies connect southern Italy with countries throughout the Mediterranean.

➡ Many routes only operate in summer, when ticket prices also rise. During this period, all routes are busy and you need to book several weeks in advance.

➡ Fares to Greece are generally more expensive from Bari than those available from Brindisi, although unless you're planning on travelling in the Salento, Bari is the more convenient port of arrival and also has better onward links for bus and train travel.

➡ Prices for vehicles vary according to their size.

➡ The helpful website www.directferries.co.uk allows you to search routes and compare prices between the numerous international ferry companies servicing Italy. Another useful resource for ferries from Italy to Greece is www.ferries.gr.

International Ferry Companies Serving Southern Italy

International ferry companies that serve southern Italy include:

Adria Ferries (☑071 5021 1621; www.adriaferries.com)

INTERNATIONAL FERRY ROUTES FROM SOUTHERN ITALY

DESTINATION COUNTRY	DESTINATION PORT(S)	ITALIAN PORT(S)	COMPANY
Albania	Durrës	Bari	Ventouris Ferries, SNAV, Adria Ferries
Croatia	Dubrovnik	Bari	Jadrolinija
Greece	Igoumenitsa, Patras	Brindisi	Grimaldi Lines
Greece	Corfu, Igoumenitsa, Patras	Bari	Superfast, Anek Lines
Malta	Valletta	Pozzallo	Virtu Ferries
Montenegro	Bar	Bari	Montenegro Lines, Jadrolinija
Tunisia	Tunis	Palermo	GNV
Tunisia	Tunis	Palermo, Salerno	Grimaldi Lines

Anek Lines (☑071 207 23 46; www.anekitalia.com)

Grandi Navi Veloci (GNV) (☑010 209 45 91; www.gnv.it)

Grimaldi Lines (☑081 49 64 44; www.grimaldi-lines.com)

Jadrolinija (☑Ancona 071 20 45 16, Bari 080 521 28 40; www.jadrolinija.hr)

Montenegro Lines (☑Bar 382 3030 3469; www.montenegro lines.net)

SNAV (☑081 428 55 55; www. snav.it)

Superfast (☑Athens 30 210 891 97 00; www.superfast.com)

Ventouris Ferries (☑for Albania 0808 496685, for Greece 0808 761451; www.ventouris. gr; Nuova Stazione Marittima di Bari)

Virtu Ferries (☑Catania 095 703 12 11; www.virtuferries.com)

GETTING AROUND

Air

A number of international airlines compete with the country's national carrier, Alitalia (www.alitalia.com), among them Italy's Meridiana (www. meridiana.it) and cut-rate foreign companies Ryanair (www.ryanair.com) and easy-Jet (www.easyjet.com).

Useful search engines for comparing multiple carriers' fares (including those of cut-price airlines) are www. skyscanner.com and www. kayak.com. Airport taxes are factored into the price of your ticket.

Bicycle

➡ Cycling may be more popular in northern Italy, but it can be just as rewarding south of Rome. Cyclotrekking is particularly popular in the Murgia and the Promontorio del Gargano in Puglia. Cycling is also very popular in the Salentine cities of Lecce, Galatina,

Gallipoli and Otranto, with more challenging itineraries in Basilicata's Parco Nazionale del Pollino and on Sicily's hilly terrain.

➡ Avoid hitting the pedal in large cities like Naples and Palermo, where unruly traffic makes cycling a veritable death wish. Cycling along the Amalfi Coast is another bad idea (think blind corners and sheer drops). Bikes are prohibited on the autostradas.

➡ Bikes can be wheeled onto regional trains displaying the bicycle logo. Simply purchase a separate bicycle ticket (*supplemento bici*), valid for 24 hours (€3.50). Certain international trains, listed on Trenitalia's 'Travelling with Your Bike' page, also allow transport of assembled bicycles for €12, paid on board. Bikes dismantled and stored in a bag can be taken for free, even on night trains. Most ferries also allow free bicycle passage.

➡ Bikes are available for hire in most towns. City bikes start at around €10/60 per day/week; mountain bikes a bit more.

If you fancy seeing the south on a saddle, the following reputable organisations offer advice and/or guided tours:

Cycling UK (www.ctc.org.uk) This UK organisation can help you plan your tour or organise a guided tour. Membership costs £43 for adults, £28.50 for seniors and £21.50 for students and under-18s.

Salento Bici Tour (www.salento bicitour.org) A reputable outfit offering bike rental and both guided and self-guided itineraries in Puglia's Salento region, including an Italian-language-course tour.

Gargano Bike Holidays (www. garganobike.com) Specialises in cultural and scenic mountain bike tours exploring the Gargano on half-day to week-long adventures.

Boat

Craft Domestic *navi* (large ferries) service Campania and Sicily, while *traghetti* (smaller ferries) and *aliscafi* (hydrofoils) service the Bay of Naples islands, the Amalfi Coast, the Isole Tremiti in Puglia and the Aeolian Islands off Sicily's north coast. Most services are pared back between October and Easter, and some are suspended altogether during this period. Most ferries carry vehicles; hydrofoils do not.

Routes Ferries for Sicily leave from Naples, as well as from Villa San Giovanni and Reggio di Calabria. The main points of arrival in Sicily are Palermo, Catania, Trapani and Messina.

Timetables and tickets Comprehensive website Direct Ferries (www.directferries.co.uk) allows you to search routes, compare prices and book tickets for ferry routes in Italy.

Overnight ferries Travellers can book a two- to four-person cabin or a *poltrona*, which is an airline-type armchair. Deck class (which allows you to sit/sleep in lounge areas or on deck) is available only on some ferries.

Bus

Numerous companies provide bus services in southern Italy, from meandering local routes to fast and reliable intercity connections.

➡ Buses are usually priced competitively with the train and are often the only way to get to smaller towns. If your destination is not on a main train line (trains tend to be cheaper on major routes), buses are usually a faster way to get around – this is especially true for the Salento in Puglia, Basilicata and for inland Calabria and Sicily.

➡ Services are provided by a variety of companies. While these can be frequent on weekdays, they are reduced considerably on Sundays and holidays – runs between smaller towns often fall to one or none. Keep this in mind if you depend on buses as it is easy to get stuck in smaller places, especially at the weekends.

➡ It's usually possible to get bus timetables (orari) from local tourist offices and the bus companies' websites. In larger cities, most of the intercity bus companies have ticket offices or sell tickets through agencies. In villages and even some good-size towns, tickets are sold in bars – just ask for biglietti per il pullman – or on the bus itself.

➡ Advance booking, while not generally required, is a good idea in the high season for overnight or long-haul trips.

Car & Motorcycle

Italy has an extensive privatised network of autostrade (motorways), represented

on road signs by a white 'A' followed by a number on a green background. The main north–south link is the Autostrada del Sole (the 'Motorway of the Sun'), which extends from Milan to Reggio di Calabria (called the A1 from Milan to Naples, and the A3 from Naples to Reggio di Calabria). The east–west A16 links Naples to Canosa di Puglia. From here, it becomes the A14, shooting southeast to Bari and continuing south to Taranto. From Bari, the SS16 is the main arterial route to the Salento; in summer this can be heavily trafficked.

There are several additional road categories, listed below in descending order of importance.

Strade statali (state highways) Represented on maps by S or SS. They vary from toll-free, four-lane highways to two-lane main roads. The latter can be extremely slow, especially in mountainous regions.

Strade regionali (regional highways connecting small villages) Coded SR or R.

Strade provinciali (provincial highways) Coded SP or P.

Strade locali (local roads) Often not even paved or mapped.

For information in English about distances, driving times and fuel costs, see en.mappy.com. Additional information, including traffic conditions and toll costs, is available at www.autostrade.it.

Automobile Associations

The **Automobile Club d'Italia** (ACI; ☎803116, from a foreign mobile 800 116800; www.aci.it) is a driver's best resource in Italy. Foreigners do not have to join to get 24-hour roadside emergency service but instead pay a per-incident fee.

Driving Licence

All EU driving licences are recognised in Italy. Travellers from other countries should obtain an International Driving Permit (IDP) through their national automobile association.

Fuel & Spare Parts

Italy's petrol prices vary from one service station (benzinaio, stazione di servizio) to another. At the time of writing, lead-free gasoline (senza piombo; 95 octane) was averaging €1.44 per litre, with diesel (gasolio) costing €1.29 per litre.

Spare parts are available at many garages or via the 24-hour ACI motorist assistance number ☎803 116 (or ☎800 116800 if calling with a non-Italian mobile phone account).

Hire

➡ Pre-booking via the internet often costs less than hiring a car in Italy. Online booking agency Rentalcars.com (www.rentalcars.com) compares the rates of numerous car-rental companies.

TO DRIVE OR NOT TO DRIVE

Unless you're a masochist, avoid driving in larger centres such as Naples, Bari, Lecce, Palermo and Catania, where anarchic traffic and parking restrictions will quickly turn your holiday sour. Beyond these urban centres, however, having your own car is the easiest way to get around Italy's south. Buses and trains will get you to most of the main destinations, but they are run by a plethora of private companies, which makes buying tickets and finding bus stops a bit of a bind. Furthermore, the rail network in Salento is still of the narrow-gauge variety, so trains chug along at a snail's pace.

Your own vehicle will give you the most freedom to stray off the main routes and discover out-of-the-way towns and beaches. This is particularly the case in the Parco Nazionale del Cilento e Vallo di Diano in Campania, the Pollino National Park in Basilicata, the Salento in Puglia and throughout much of rural Sicily.

This said, it's also worth considering the downside of driving. Aside from the negative environmental impact, petrol prices are notoriously high, less-travelled roads are often poorly maintained and popular routes (including Campania's Amalfi Coast, the SS16 connecting Bari and the Salento in Puglia, and Sicily's Ionian and Tyrrhenian coastal routes) can be heavily trafficked during holiday periods and throughout the summer.

➡ Renters must generally be aged 21 or over, with a credit card and home-country driving licence or IDP.

➡ Consider hiring a small car, which will reduce your fuel expenses and help you negotiate narrow city lanes and tight parking spaces.

➡ Check with your credit-card company to see if it offers a Collision Damage Waiver, which covers you for additional damage if you use that card to pay for the car. The following companies have pick-up locations throughout Italy:

Auto Europe (www.auto europe.com)

Avis (www.avis.com)

Budget (www.budget.com)

Europcar (www.europcar.com)

Hertz (www.hertz.it)

Italy by Car (www.italybycar.it)

Maggiore (www.maggiore.it)

Sixt (www.sixt.com)

MOTORCYCLES

➡ Agencies throughout Italy rent motorbikes, ranging from small Vespas to larger touring bikes. Prices start at around €35/150 per day/week for a 50cc scooter, or upwards of €80/400 per day/week for a 650cc motorcycle.

Road Rules

➡ Cars drive on the right side of the road and overtake on the left. Unless otherwise indicated, always give way to cars entering an intersection from a road on your right.

➡ Seatbelt use (front and rear) is required by law; violators are subject to an on-the-spot fine. Helmets are required on all two-wheeled vehicles.

➡ Day and night, it is compulsory to drive with your headlights on outside built-up areas.

➡ It's obligatory to carry a warning triangle and fluorescent waistcoat in case of breakdown.

Recommended accessories include a first-aid kit, spare-bulb kit and fire extinguisher.

➡ A licence is required to ride a scooter – a car licence will do for bikes up to 125cc; for anything over 125cc you'll need a motorcycle licence.

➡ Motorbikes can enter most restricted traffic areas in Italian cities, and traffic police generally turn a blind eye to motorcycles or scooters parked on footpaths.

➡ The blood alcohol limit is 0.05%; it's zero for drivers under 21 and those who have had their licence for less than three years.
Unless otherwise indicated, speed limits are as follows:

➡ 130km/h on autostrade

➡ 110km/h on all main, non-urban roads

➡ 90km/h on secondary, non-urban roads

➡ 50km/h in built-up areas

Local Transport

Bus & Underground Trains

Every city or town of any size has an efficient *urbano* (urban) and *extraurbano* (suburban) system of buses. Services are generally reduced on Sundays and holidays. Naples and Catania also have a metro system.

Purchase bus and metro tickets before boarding. Validate bus tickets on-board and metro tickets at the station turnstile. Tickets can be bought from a *tabaccaio* (tobacconist), newsstands, ticket booths or dispensing machines at bus stations and in underground stations, and usually cost €1 to €2. Some cities offer good-value 24-hour or daily tourist tickets.

Taxi

You can catch a taxi at the ranks outside most train and bus stations, or simply telephone for a radio taxi. Note that radio taxi meters start

running from when you've called rather than when you're picked up.

Charges vary somewhat from one region to another. Most short city journeys cost between €10 and €20. Generally, no more than four people are allowed in one taxi.

Train

Trains in Italy are convenient and relatively cheap compared with other European countries. The better train categories are fast and comfortable.

Trenitalia (☑892021; www.trenitalia.com) is the national train system that runs most services. Its privately owned competitor **Italo** (☑89 20 20; www.italotreno.it) runs high-velocity trains between Turin and Salerno, Venice and Naples, and Brescia and Naples. All three routes stop in Bologna, Florence and Rome. The Turin line also stops in Milan.

Italy operates several types of trains:

Regionale/interregionale Slow and cheap, stopping at all or most stations.

InterCity (IC) Faster services operating between major cities.

Alta Velocità (AV) State-of-the-art, high-velocity trains, including Frecciarossa, Frecciargento, Frecciabianca and Italo trains, with speeds of up to 300km/h and connections to the major cities. Marginally more expensive than some InterCity express trains, but journey times are cut by almost half.

As with the bus services, there are a number of private train lines operating throughout Italy's south, including:

Circumvesuviana (www.eavsrl.it) Links Naples and Sorrento, stopping at Ercolano (Herculaneum) and Pompeii.

Ferrovia Cumana (www.eavsrl.it) Connects Naples to the Campi Flegrei to the west. Stops include Pozzuoli.

Ferrotramviaria (www.ferro vienordbarese.it) Services towns in Puglia's Terra di Bari, including Bitonto, Ruvo di Puglia, Andria and Barletta. Replacement bus service operates Sundays.

Ferrovie Appulo Lucane (www. fal-srl.it) Links Bari province with Basilicata, including stops at Altamura, Matera and Potenza. Replacement buses on Sundays.

Ferrovie del Sud Est (www. fseonline.it) The main network covering Puglia's Murgia towns and the Salento, servicing tourist hot spots like Castellana Grotte, Alberobello, Martina Franca, Lecce, Gallipoli and Otranto. Replacement buses on Sundays.

Ferrovia Circumetnea (www. circumetnea.it) A 114km line connecting the towns around the base of Mt Etna in Sicily. No service on Sundays.

Classes & Costs

➡ Prices vary according to the class of service, time of travel and how far in advance you book. Most Italian trains have 1st- and 2nd-class seating; a 1st-class ticket typically costs from a third to a half more than the 2nd-class ticket.

➡ Travel on Trenitalia's InterCity and Alta Velocità (Frecciarossa, Frecciargento, Frecciabianca) trains means paying a supplement, determined by the distance you are travelling and included in the ticket price. If you have a standard ticket for a slower train and end up hopping on an IC train, you'll have to pay the difference on board. (You can only board an Alta Velocità train if you have a booking, so the problem does not arise in those cases.)

➡ Validate train tickets in the green machines (usually found at the head of rail platforms) just before boarding. Failure to do so usually results in a fine.

Reservations

➡ Reservations are obligatory on Alta Velocità trains. Otherwise they're not required on other train lines and, outside of peak holiday periods, you should be fine without them. Reservations can be made on the Trenitalia and Italo websites, at railway station counters and self-service ticketing machines, or through travel agents.

➡ Both Trenitalia and Italo offer a variety of advance purchase discounts. Basically, the earlier you book, the greater the saving. Discounted tickets are limited, and refunds and changes are highly restricted. For all ticket options and prices, see the **Trenitalia** (☑892021; www. trenitalia.com) and **Italo** (☑89 20 20; www.italotreno.it) websites.

30

Language

Standard Italian is taught and spoken throughout Italy. Regional dialects are an important part of identity in many parts of the country, but you'll have no trouble being understood anywhere if you stick to standard Italian, which we've also used in this chapter.

The sounds used in spoken Italian can all be found in English. If you read our coloured pronunciation guides as if they were English, you'll be understood. The stressed syllables are indicated with italics. Note that ai is pronounced as in 'aisle', ay as in 'say', ow as in 'how', dz as the 'ds' in 'lids', and that r is a strong and rolled sound. Keep in mind that Italian consonants can have a stronger, emphatic pronunciation – if the consonant is written as a double letter, it should be pronounced a little stronger, eg *sonno son*·no (sleep) versus *sono so*·no (I am).

BASICS

Hello.	*Buongiorno.*	bwon·*jor*·no
Goodbye.	*Arrivederci.*	a·ree·ve·*der*·chee
Yes./No.	*Sì./No.*	see/no
Excuse me.	*Mi scusi.* (pol)	mee *skoo*·zee
	Scusami. (inf)	*skoo*·za·mee
Sorry.	*Mi dispiace.*	mee dees·*pya*·che
Please.	*Per favore.*	per fa·*vo*·re
Thank you.	*Grazie.*	*gra*·tsye
You're welcome.	*Prego.*	*pre*·go

How are you?
Come sta/stai? (pol/inf) — *ko*·me sta/stai

Fine. And you?
Bene. E lei/tu? (pol/inf) — *be*·ne e lay/too

What's your name?
Come si chiama? (pol) — *ko*·me see *kya*·ma
Come ti chiami? (inf) — *ko*·me tee *kya*·mee

My name is ...
Mi chiamo ... — mee *kya*·mo ...

Do you speak English?
Parla/Parli inglese? (pol/inf) — *par*·la/*par*·lee een·*gle*·ze

I don't understand.
Non capisco. — non ka·*pee*·sko

ACCOMMODATION

campsite	*campeggio*	kam·*pe*·jo
guesthouse	*pensione*	pen·*syo*·ne
hotel	*albergo*	al·*ber*·go
youth hostel	*ostello della gioventù*	os·*te*·lo de·la jo·ven·*too*
Do you have a ... room?	*Avete una camera ...?*	a·*ve*·te *oo*·na *ka*·me·ra ...
double	*doppia con letto matrimoniale*	*do*·pya kon *le*·to ma·tree·mo·*nya*·le
single	*singola*	*seen*·go·la
How much is it per ...?	*Quanto costa per ...?*	*kwan*·to *kos*·ta per ...
night	*una notte*	*oo*·na *no*·te
person	*persona*	per·*so*·na
air-con	*aria condizionata*	*a*·rya kon·dee·tsyo·*na*·ta
bathroom	*bagno*	*ba*·nyo
window	*finestra*	fee·*nes*·tra

DIRECTIONS

Where's ...?
Dov'è ...?　　　　do·ve ...

What's the address?
Qual'è l'indirizzo?　kwa·le leen·dee·ree·tso

Could you please write it down?
Può scriverlo,　　　pwo skree·ver·lo
per favore?　　　　per fa·vo·re

Can you show me (on the map)?
Può mostrarmi　　　pwo mos·trar·mee
(sulla pianta)?　　　(soo·la pyan·ta)

EATING & DRINKING

What would you recommend?
Cosa mi consiglia?　ko·za mee kon·see·lya

What's the local speciality?
Qual'è la specialità　kwa·le la spe·cha·lee·ta
di questa regione?　dee kwe·sta re·jo·ne

Cheers!
Salute!　　　　　　sa·loo·te

That was delicious!
Era squisito!　　　e·ra skwee·zee·to

Please bring the bill.
Mi porta il conto,　mee por·ta eel kon·to
per favore?　　　　per fa·vo·re

I'd like to reserve a table for ...	*Vorrei prenotare un tavolo per ...*	vo·ray pre·no·ta·re oon ta·vo·lo per ...
(eight) o'clock	*le (otto)*	le (o·to)
(two) people	*(due) persone*	(doo·e) per·so·ne
I don't eat ...	*Non mangio ...*	non man·jo ...
eggs	*uova*	wo·va
fish	*pesce*	pe·she
nuts	*noci*	no·chee

Key Words

bar	*locale*	lo·ka·le
bottle	*bottiglia*	bo·tee·lya
breakfast	*prima colazione*	pree·ma ko·la·tsyo·ne
cafe	*bar*	bar
dinner	*cena*	che·na
drink list	*lista delle bevande*	lee·sta de·le be·van·de
fork	*forchetta*	for·ke·ta
glass	*bicchiere*	bee·kye·re
knife	*coltello*	kol·te·lo

KEY PATTERNS

To get by in Italian, mix and match these simple patterns with words of your choice:

When's (the next flight)?
A che ora è　　　　a ke o·ra e
(il prossimo volo)?　(eel pro·see·mo vo·lo)

Where's (the station)?
Dov'è (la stazione)?　do·ve (la sta·tsyo·ne)

I'm looking for (a hotel).
Sto cercando　　　sto cher·kan·do
(un albergo).　　　(oon al·ber·go)

Do you have (a map)?
Ha (una pianta)?　a (oo·na pyan·ta)

Is there (a toilet)?
C'è (un gabinetto)?　che (oon ga·bee·ne·to)

I'd like (a coffee).
Vorrei (un caffè).　vo·ray (oon ka·fe)

I'd like to (hire a car).
Vorrei (noleggiare　vo·ray (no·le·ja·re
una macchina).　　oo·na ma·kee·na)

Can I (enter)?
Posso (entrare)?　po·so (en·tra·re)

Could you please (help me)?
Può (aiutarmi),　　pwo (a·yoo·tar·mee)
per favore?　　　　per fa·vo·re

Do I have to (book a seat)?
Devo (prenotare　de·vo (pre·no·ta·re
un posto)?　　　　oon po·sto)

lunch	*pranzo*	pran·dzo
market	*mercato*	mer·ka·to
menu	*menù*	me·noo
plate	*piatto*	pya·to
restaurant	*ristorante*	ree·sto·ran·te
spoon	*cucchiaio*	koo·kya·yo
vegetarian	*vegetariano*	ve·je·ta·rya·no

Meat & Fish

beef	*manzo*	man·dzo
chicken	*pollo*	po·lo
herring	*aringa*	a·reen·ga
lamb	*agnello*	a·nye·lo
lobster	*aragosta*	a·ra·gos·ta
mussels	*cozze*	ko·tse
oysters	*ostriche*	o·stree·ke
pork	*maiale*	ma·ya·le
prawn	*gambero*	gam·be·ro
salmon	*salmone*	sal·mo·ne
scallops	*capasante*	ka·pa·san·t
shrimp	*gambero*	gam·be·ro

squid	calamari	ka·la·*ma*·ree
trout	trota	*tro*·ta
tuna	tonno	*to*·no
turkey	tacchino	ta·*kee*·no
veal	vitello	vee·*te*·lo

Fruit & Vegetables

apple	mela	*me*·la
beans	fagioli	fa·*jo*·lee
cabbage	cavolo	*ka*·vo·lo
capsicum	peperone	pe·pe·*ro*·ne
carrot	carota	ka·*ro*·ta
cauliflower	cavolfiore	ka·vol·*fyo*·re
cucumber	cetriolo	che·*tree*·o·lo
grapes	uva	*oo*·va
lemon	limone	lee·*mo*·ne
lentils	lenticchie	len·*tee*·kye
mushroom	funghi	*foon*·gee
nuts	noci	*no*·chee
onions	cipolle	chee·*po*·le
orange	arancia	a·*ran*·cha
peach	pesca	*pe*·ska
peas	piselli	pee·*ze*·lee
pineapple	ananas	*a*·na·nas
plum	prugna	*proo*·nya
potatoes	patate	pa·*ta*·te
spinach	spinaci	spee·*na*·chee
tomatoes	pomodori	po·mo·*do*·ree

Other

bread	pane	*pa*·ne
butter	burro	*boo*·ro
cheese	formaggio	for·*ma*·jo
eggs	uova	*wo*·va
honey	miele	*mye*·le
jam	marmellata	mar·me·*la*·ta

SIGNS

Closed	**Chiuso**
Entrance	**Entrata/Ingresso**
Exit	**Uscita**
Men	**Uomini**
Open	**Aperto**
Prohibited	**Proibito/Vietato**
Toilets	**Gabinetti/Servizi**
Women	**Donne**

noodles	pasta	*pas*·ta
oil	olio	*o*·lyo
pepper	pepe	*pe*·pe
rice	riso	*ree*·zo
salt	sale	*sa*·le
soup	minestra	mee·*nes*·tra
soy sauce	salsa di soia	*sal*·sa dee *so*·ya
sugar	zucchero	*tsoo*·ke·ro
vinegar	aceto	a·*che*·to

Drinks

beer	birra	*bee*·ra
coffee	caffè	ka·*fe*
juice	succo	*soo*·ko
milk	latte	*la*·te
red wine	vino rosso	*vee*·no *ro*·so
tea	tè	te
water	acqua	*a*·kwa
white wine	vino bianco	*vee*·no *byan*·ko

EMERGENCIES

Help!
Aiuto!　　　　a·*yoo*·to

Leave me alone!
Lasciami in pace!　la·sha·mee een *pa*·che

I'm lost.
Mi sono perso/a. (m/f)　mee *so*·no *per*·so/a

Call the police!
Chiami la polizia!　*kya*·mee la po·lee·*tsee*·a

Call a doctor!
Chiami un medico!　*kya*·mee oon *me*·dee·ko

Where are the toilets?
Dove sono i　　*do*·ve *so*·no ee
gabinetti?　　ga·bee·*ne*·tee

I'm sick.
Mi sento male.　mee *sen*·to *ma*·le

SHOPPING & SERVICES

I'd like to buy ...
Vorrei comprare ...　vo·*ray* kom·*pra*·re ...

I'm just looking.
Sto solo guardando.　sto *so*·lo gwar·*dan*·do

Can I look at it?
Posso dare un'occhiata? po·so *da*·re oo·no·*kya*·ta

How much is this?
Quanto costa questo?　*kwan*·to *kos*·ta *kwe*·sto

It's too expensive.
È troppo caro.　　e *tro*·po *ka*·ro

There's a mistake in the bill.
C'è un errore nel conto.　che oo·ne·*ro*·re nel *kon*·to

ATM	Bancomat	ban·ko·mat
post office	ufficio postale	oo·fee·cho pos·ta·le
tourist office	ufficio del turismo	oo·fee·cho del too·reez·mo

TIME & DATES

What time is it?
Che ora è?   ke o·ra e

It's (two) o'clock.
Sono le (due).   so·no le (doo·e)

Half past (one).
(L'una) e mezza.   (loo·na) e me·dza

in the morning	di mattina	dee ma·tee·na
in the afternoon	di pomeriggio	dee po·me·ree jo
in the evening	di sera	dee se·ra
yesterday	ieri	ye·ree
today	oggi	o·jee
tomorrow	domani	do·ma·nee

Monday	lunedì	loo·ne·dee
Tuesday	martedì	mar·te·dee
Wednesday	mercoledì	mer·ko·le·dee
Thursday	giovedì	jo·ve·dee
Friday	venerdì	ve·ner·dee
Saturday	sabato	sa·ba·to
Sunday	domenica	do·me·nee·ka

TRANSPORT

boat	nave	na·ve
bus	autobus	ow·to·boos
ferry	traghetto	tra·ge·to
metro	metropolitana	me·tro·po·lee·ta·na
plane	aereo	a·e·re·o
train	treno	tre·no

bus stop	fermata dell'autobus	fer·ma·ta del ow·to·boos
ticket office	biglietteria	bee·lye·te·ree·a
timetable	orario	o·ra·ryo
train station	stazione ferroviaria	sta·tsyo·ne fe·ro·vyar·ya

... ticket	un biglietto ...	oon bee·lye·to
one way	di sola andata	dee so·la an·da·ta
return	di andata e ritorno	dee an·da·ta e ree·tor·no

NUMBERS

1	uno	oo·no
2	due	doo·e
3	tre	tre
4	quattro	kwa·tro
5	cinque	cheen·kwe
6	sei	say
7	sette	se·te
8	otto	o·to
9	nove	no·ve
10	dieci	dye·chee
20	venti	ven·tee
30	trenta	tren·ta
40	quaranta	kwa·ran·ta
50	cinquanta	cheen·kwan·ta
60	sessanta	se·san·ta
70	settanta	se·tan·ta
80	ottanta	o·tan·ta
90	novanta	no·van·ta
100	cento	chen·to
1000	mille	mee·lel

Does it stop at ...?
Si ferma a ...?   see fer·ma a ...

Please tell me when we get to ...
Mi dica per favore quando arriviamo a ...   mee dee·ka per fa·vo·re kwan·do a·ree·vya·mo a ...

I want to get off here.
Voglio scendere qui.   vo·lyo shen·de·re kwee

I'd like to hire a ...	Vorrei noleggiare una ...	vo·ray no·le·ja·re oo·na ...
bicycle	bicicletta	bee·chee·kle·ta
car	macchina	ma·kee·na
motorbike	moto	mo·to

bicycle pump	pompa della bicicletta	pom·pa de·la bee·chee·kle·ta
child seat	seggiolino	se·jo·lee·no
helmet	casco	kas·ko
mechanic	meccanico	me·ka·nee·ko
petrol	benzina	ben·dzee·na
service station	stazione di servizio	sta·tsyo·ne dee ser·vee·tsyo

Is this the road to ...?
Questa strada porta a ...? kwe·sta stra·da por·ta a ...

Can I park here?
Posso parcheggiare qui? po·so par·ke·ja·re kwee

GLOSSARY

abbazia – abbey
agriturismo – farm-stays
(pizza) al taglio – (pizza) by the slice
albergo – hotel
alimentari – grocery shop
anfiteatro – amphitheatre
aperitivo – pre-dinner drink and snack
APT – Azienda di Promozione Turistica; local town or city tourist office
autostrada – motorway; highway

battistero – baptistry
biblioteca – library
biglietto – ticket
borgo – archaic name for a small town, village or town sector

camera – room
campo – field; also a square in Venice
cappella – chapel
carabinieri – police with military and civil duties
Carnevale – carnival period between Epiphany and Lent
casa – house
castello – castle
cattedrale – cathedral
centro storico – historic centre
certosa – monastery belonging to or founded by Carthusian monks
chiesa – church
chiostro – cloister; covered walkway, usually enclosed by columns, around a quadrangle
cima – summit
città – town; city
città alta – upper town
città bassa – lower town
colonna – column
comune – equivalent to a municipality or county; a town or city council; historically, a self-governing town or city
contrada – district
corso – boulevard
duomo – cathedral

enoteca – wine bar

espresso – short black coffee
ferrovia – railway
festa – feast day; holiday
fontana – fountain
foro – forum
funivia – cable car

gelateria – ice-cream shop
giardino – garden
golfo – gulf
grotta – cave

isola – island

lago – lake
largo – small square
lido – beach
locanda – inn; small hotel
lungomare – seafront road/promenade

mar, mare – sea
masseria – working farm
mausoleo – mausoleum; stately and magnificent tomb
mercato – market
monte – mountain

necropoli – ancient name for cemetery or burial site
nord – north
nuraghe – megalithic stone fortress in Sardinia

osteria – casual tavern or eatery

palazzo – mansion; palace; large building of any type, including an apartment block
palio – contest
parco – park
passeggiata – traditional evening stroll
pasticceria – cake/pastry shop
pensione – guesthouse
piazza – square
piazzale – large open square
pietà – literally 'pity' or 'compassion'; sculpture, drawing or painting of the dead Christ supported by the Madonna
pinacoteca – art gallery
ponte – bridge

porta – gate; door
porto – port

reale – royal
rifugio – mountain hut; accommodation in the Alps
ristorante – restaurant
rocca – fortress

sala – room; hall
salumeria – delicatessen
santuario – sanctuary; 1. the part of a church above the altar; 2. an especially holy place in a temple (antiquity)
sassi – literally 'stones'; stone houses built in two ravines in Matera, Basilicata
scalinata – staircase
scavi – excavations
sestiere – city district in Venice
spiaggia – beach
stazione – station
stazione marittima – ferry terminal
strada – street; road
sud – south
superstrada – expressway; highway with divided lanes

tartufo – truffle
tavola calda – literally 'hot table'; pre-prepared meals, often self-service
teatro – theatre
tempietto – small temple
tempio – temple
terme – thermal baths
tesoro – treasury
torre – tower
trattoria – simple restaurant
Trenitalia – Italian State Railways; also known as Ferrovie dello Stato (FS)
trullo – conical house in Perugia

vaporetto – small passenger ferry in Venice
via – street; road
viale – avenue
vico – alley; alleyway
villa – town house; country house; also the park surrounding the house

Behind the Scenes

SEND US YOUR FEEDBACK

We love to hear from travellers – your comments keep us on our toes and help make our books better. Our well-travelled team reads every word on what you loved or loathed about this book. Although we cannot reply individually to your submissions, we always guarantee that your feedback goes straight to the appropriate authors, in time for the next edition. Each person who sends us information is thanked in the next edition – the most useful submissions are rewarded with a selection of digital PDF chapters.

Visit **lonelyplanet.com/contact** to submit your updates and suggestions or to ask for help. Our award-winning website also features inspirational travel stories, news and discussions.

Note: We may edit, reproduce and incorporate your comments in Lonely Planet products such as guidebooks, websites and digital products, so let us know if you don't want your comments reproduced or your name acknowledged. For a copy of our privacy policy visit lonelyplanet.com/privacy.

OUR READERS

Many thanks to the travellers who used the last edition and wrote to us with helpful hints, useful advice and interesting anecdotes: Cathy Wright, Francesco Nadal De Simone, Kimmo Pohjanpalo, Rachel Holland, Romà Massot, Steve Barron, Thomas Breslin

WRITER THANKS
Cristian Bonetto

Mille grazie to Raffaele e Silvana, Joe Brizzi, Alfonso Sperandeo, Carmine Romano, Sylvain Bellenger, Federica Rispoli, the team at Cooperativa La Paranza, Vincenzo Mattiucci, Marcantonio Colonna and the many other friends and locals who offered invaluable tips and insight. At Lonely Planet, many thanks to Anna Tyler and my ever-diligent Italy writing team.

Gregor Clark

Sincere thanks and hugs to my wife Gaen and daughters Meigan and Chloe, who always make coming home the best part of the trip.

Hugh McNaughtan

Thanks for the patience and support of Tasmin, Anna, my girls, the LP tech team and the kind people I met in Italy, who made the research not just possible, but a pleasure.

ACKNOWLEDGEMENTS

Climate map data adapted from Peel MC, Finlayson BL & McMahon TA (2007) 'Updated World Map of the Köppen-Geiger Climate Classification', Hydrology and Earth System Sciences, 11, 163344.

Illustration pp98-9 by Javier Martinez Zarracina.

Cover photograph: Villa Rufolo, Ravello, Amalfi Coast, Susanne Kremer/4Corners ©

THIS BOOK

This 4th edition of Lonely Planet's *Southern Italy* guidebook was researched and written by Cristian Bonetto, Gregor Clark and Hugh McNaughtan. The previous two editions were written by Cristian Bonetto, Gregor Clark and Brendan

Sainsbury. This guidebook was produced by the following:

Destination Editor Anna Tyler
Product Editor Grace Dobell
Senior Product Editor Anne Mason
Senior Cartographers Corey Hutchison, Anthony Phelan
Book Designer Jessica Rose
Assisting Editors Katie

Connolly, Bruce Evans, Carly Hall, Paul Harding, Simon Williamson

Cover Researcher
Naomi Parker

Thanks to Sasha Drew, Elizabeth Jones, Lauren Keith, Kate Kiely, Clara Monitto, Martine Power, Alison Ridgway, Tony Wheeler

Index

Map Legend

Sights

- Beach
- Bird Sanctuary
- Buddhist
- Castle/Palace
- Christian
- Confucian
- Hindu
- Islamic
- Jain
- Jewish
- Monument
- Museum/Gallery/Historic Building
- Ruin
- Shinto
- Sikh
- Taoist
- Winery/Vineyard
- Zoo/Wildlife Sanctuary
- Other Sight

Activities, Courses & Tours

- Bodysurfing
- Diving
- Canoeing/Kayaking
- Course/Tour
- Sento Hot Baths/Onsen
- Skiing
- Snorkelling
- Surfing
- Swimming/Pool
- Walking
- Windsurfing
- Other Activity

Sleeping

- Sleeping
- Camping
- Hut/Shelter

Eating

- Eating

Drinking & Nightlife

- Drinking & Nightlife
- Cafe

Entertainment

- Entertainment

Shopping

- Shopping

Information

- Bank
- Embassy/Consulate
- Hospital/Medical
- Internet
- Police
- Post Office
- Telephone
- Toilet
- Tourist Information
- Other Information

Geographic

- Beach
- Gate
- Hut/Shelter
- Lighthouse
- Lookout
- Mountain/Volcano
- Oasis
- Park
- Pass
- Picnic Area
- Waterfall

Population

- Capital (National)
- Capital (State/Province)
- City/Large Town
- Town/Village

Transport

- Airport
- Border crossing
- Bus
- Cable car/Funicular
- Cycling
- Ferry
- Metro station
- Monorail
- Parking
- Petrol station
- S-Bahn/Subway station
- Taxi
- T-bane/Tunnelbana station
- Train station/Railway
- Tram
- Tube station
- U-Bahn/Underground station
- Other Transport

Routes

- Tollway
- Freeway
- Primary
- Secondary
- Tertiary
- Lane
- Unsealed road
- Road under construction
- Plaza/Mall
- Steps
- Tunnel
- Pedestrian overpass
- Walking Tour
- Walking Tour detour
- Path/Walking Trail

Boundaries

- International
- State/Province
- Disputed
- Regional/Suburb
- Marine Park
- Cliff
- Wall

Hydrography

- River, Creek
- Intermittent River
- Canal
- Water
- Dry/Salt/Intermittent Lake
- Reef

Areas

- Airport/Runway
- Beach/Desert
- Cemetery (Christian)
- Cemetery (Other)
- Glacier
- Mudflat
- Park/Forest
- Sight (Building)
- Sportsground
- Swamp/Mangrove

Note: Not all symbols displayed above appear on the maps in this book

OUR STORY

A beat-up old car, a few dollars in the pocket and a sense of adventure. In 1972 that's all Tony and Maureen Wheeler needed for the trip of a lifetime – across Europe and Asia overland to Australia. It took several months, and at the end – broke but inspired – they sat at their kitchen table writing and stapling together their first travel guide, *Across Asia on the Cheap*. Within a week they'd sold 1500 copies. Lonely Planet was born.

Today, Lonely Planet has offices in Franklin, London, Melbourne, Oakland, Dublin, Beijing and Delhi, with more than 600 staff and writers. We share Tony's belief that 'a great guidebook should do three things: inform, educate and amuse'.

OUR WRITERS

Cristian Bonetto

Curator, Naples & Campania Cristian has contributed to more than 30 Lonely Planet guides to date, including *New York City, Italy, Venice & the Veneto, Naples & the Amalfi Coast, Denmark, Copenhagen, Sweden* and *Singapore*. Lonely Planet work aside, his musings on travel, food, culture and design appear in numerous publications around the world, including *The Telegraph* (UK) and *Corriere del Mezzogiorno* (Italy). When not on the road, you'll find the reformed playwright and TV scriptwriter slurping espresso in his beloved hometown, Melbourne.

Gregor Clark

Sicily Gregor Clark is a US-based writer whose love of foreign languages and curiosity about what's around the next bend have taken him to dozens of countries on five continents. Since 2000, Gregor has regularly contributed to Lonely Planet guides, with a focus on Europe and the Americas. Titles include *Italy, France, Brazil, Costa Rica, Argentina, Portugal, Switzerland, Mexico, South America on a Shoestring, Montreal & Quebec City, France's Best Trips, New England's Best Trips,* cycling guides to Italy and California, and coffee-table pictorials such as *Food Trails, The USA Book* and *The Lonely Planet Guide to the Middle of Nowhere*. Gregor was born in New York City. He has lived in California, France, Spain and Italy prior to settling with his wife and two daughters in his current home state of Vermont.

Hugh McNaughtan

Puglia, Basilicata & Calabria A former English lecturer, Hugh decided visa applications beat grant applications, and turned his love of travel into a full-time thing. Having also done a bit of restaurant reviewing in his home town (Melbourne, Australia), he's now eaten his way across Europe and North America. He's never happier than when on the road with his two daughters. Except perhaps on the cricket field...

Published by Lonely Planet Global Limited
CRN 554153
4th edition – Mar 2018
ISBN 978 1 78657 367 4
© Lonely Planet 2018   Photographs © as indicated 2018
10 9 8 7 6 5 4 3 2 1
Printed in China